THE INSIDERS' GUIDE TO

Boulder

& Rocky Mountain National Park

THE INSIDERS' GUIDE TO

Boulder
& Rocky Mountain National Park

by
Reed Glenn
&
Claire Walter

The Insiders' Guides Inc.

Co-published and marketed by:
Boulder Publishing Co., Inc.
1048 Pearl St.
Boulder, CO 80302
(303)442-1202

Co-published and distributed by:
The Insiders' Guides Inc.
The Waterfront • Suite 12
P.O. Box 2057
Manteo, NC 27954
(919) 473-6100

•

THIRD EDITION
1st printing

•

Copyright ©1996
by Boulder Publishing Co., Inc.

•

Printed in the United States
of America

•

Publications from The Insiders' Guides®
series are available at special discounts
for bulk purchases for sales promotions,
premiums or fundraisings. Special
editions, including personalized covers,
can be created in large quantities for
special needs. For more information,
please write to The Insiders' Guides Inc.,
P.O. Box 2057, Manteo, NC 27954 or
call (919) 473-6100 x 233.

ISBN 1-57380-011-2

Boulder Publishing Co., Inc.

President and Publisher
Harold Higgins

Project Coordinator
James N. Gaasterland

Editorial Manager
Ronda Haskins

Advertising Manager
Michael Turpin

Account Executive
Scott Cherek

The Insiders' Guides Inc.

Publisher/Editor-in-Chief
Beth P. Storie

President/General Manager
Michael McOwen

Affiliate Sales and Training Director
Rosanne Cheeseman

Partner Services Director
Giles MacMillan

Sales and Marketing Director
Julie Ross

Creative Services Director
Mike Lay

Online Services Director
David Haynes

Managing Editor
Theresa Shea Chavez

Fulfillment Director
Gina Twiford

Project Editor
Dan DeGregory

Project Artist
Mel Dorsey

About the Authors

Reed Glenn

Originally from Philadelphia, Reed Glenn has lived in Boulder since 1976. She first visited Rocky Mountain National Park in the summer of her 27th year, experienced the quintessential "Colorado Rocky Mountain High" and within a year moved to Boulder with her cats and 7-year-old son, Luke — now a graduate of the University of Colorado.

A freelance writer and photographer, she specializes in travel, outdoor recreation and environment, writing a biweekly, nationally distributed column, "Earthright," for Knight-Ridder News and travel stories for such newspapers as The Denver Post, Dallas Morning News, New York Newsday and the Los Angeles Times. She has also been a writer and columnist for the Daily Camera newspaper in Boulder since 1985.

Her writing and photography have also appeared in Outside, Runner's World, Running Times, Triathlete, Rodale's Scuba Diving, Caribbean Travel & Life and other magazines. She is the author or co-author of five books, including Frommer's Mexico '92 on $45 A Day, Puerto Vallarta, Manzanillo & Guadalajara '92-93 and The 10 Best Opportunities for Starting a Home Business Today (1993). She was awarded the 1994 Lente de Plata (Silver Lens Award) by the Mexican Ministry of Tourism for photos and stories on Mexico's people. The 1994 anthology Travelers' Tales Mexico includes one of her non-fiction stories.

She enjoys cross-country skiing, windsurfing, hiking, scuba diving, world travel and exploring Colorado.

Claire Walter

Claire Walter grew up in Connecticut, went to college in Massachusetts, launched her career as an editor and writer in New York and moved to Boulder from the New York metropolitan area. When she decided to move in 1988, she considered 3 B's: Boston, Burlington and Boulder. "I'd never lived west of Hoboken, New Jersey, in my life," she says, "so when it was finally time to pick a place, I figured it might as well be a big move." She traded an 1870s brownstone that didn't quite have a view of the Manhattan skyline for an 1890s Prairie Victorian with a view of Flagstaff Mountain and has never regretted her decision.

She is an award-winning ski writer whose travels had brought her to Colorado year after year, but like all her friends who live in ski towns, she now says, "I moved here for the winter and stayed because of summer." She is a long-time contributing editor to Skiing magazine and writes a travel column for Cross Country Skier. She has also written for Shape, Travel & Leisure, The Denver Post and numerous other in-flight, regional and general-interest magazines. Her recent credits include Skiing on a Budget, Buying Your Vacation Home for Fun & Profit, The Colorado Outdoor Activity Guide and the second edition of Rocky Mountain Skiing. The first edition won the 1994 Harold Hirsch Award as the best ski book of the previous three years, and an earlier book, The Best Ski Resorts in America, received a 1988 Lowell Thomas Award in the guidebook category. She was also named Colorado Freelance Writer of the Year in 1991 by Colorado Ski Country USA. Her books in print can be previewed on her website (http://www.netone.com/~cmwalter/).

In addition to having the best skiing in the world at her doorstep, providing her with unending research opportunities for her books and articles, Claire relishes the mountains in summer. "My Eastern friends find it hard to imagine that Vail is two hours from my door, six other ski areas are closer, and Rocky Mountain National Park and the Indian Peaks Wilderness are less than an hour from home too," she relates. She loves living in a small city that nurtures its somewhat urban environment and rather sophisticated lifestyle while surrounding itself with open space to maintain what it's got. She still doesn't take for granted proximity to great skiing, hiking and other outdoor activities. But she also treasures the cultural opportunities Boulder and metro Denver present, including first-rate theater, music and art. "You don't have to decide between culture and the outdoors," she says. "Boulder has both." She lives in Boulder with her husband, Ral Sandberg, her son, Andrew Cameron-Walter, and her feisty cat, Cinderella, who also migrated west.

Acknowledgments

Reed . . .

Special thanks Phyllis Smith for her comprehensive and well-told history of Boulder in her book *A Look at Boulder: From Settlement to City*. Special thanks also to Charlotte Smokler, the *Daily Camera* newspaper librarian, for her generous help and always-amusing comments.

Thanks to *The Insiders' Guide® to Greater Denver* authors Laura Caruso and Robert Ebisch for help with information. Thanks to Fred Koster for his assistance in Grand Lake and for his outdoors expertise, especially in fishing and hunting. Thanks to Nancy Lee and Joan Knapp for their help with research in Estes Park and Rocky Mountain National Park.

Jean Fisher of the Grand Lake Chamber of Commerce provided invaluable information, as did the Central City/Black Hawk, Estes Park and Boulder chambers of commerce, Boulder Open Space Department, Boulder County Parks and Open Space, the Boulder Bicycle program and Bonnie White of Rocky Mountain National Park.

A special acknowledgment goes to former co-author Shelley Schlender, whose lively, user-friendly prose and thoughtful insights still sprinkle some of these pages — and whose talent, hard work and enthusiasm originally helped bring this book into being.

Claire . . .

To Shelley D. Schlender, who co-authored the original version of *The Insiders' Guide® to Boulder* and left such a firm platform for me to jump from, I owe the greatest thanks. Her knowledge of and research about areas of the life and times of Boulder about which I had little background were particularly invaluable. Her ideas and resources go a long way toward making this book as comprehensive as it is. And as a tribute to her thoroughness, when I called or visited to update material Shelley had written, rarely if ever did anyone say, "Oh, that's wrong." Where I made factual changes, it's because I was told, "That's changed." And I am grateful to my co-author, Reed Glenn, a veteran of the two previous editions, for pointing the way and to Carlisle Lee for helping check and update some of those very crucial facts.

To those who make Boulder such a wonderful place, I owe the deepest debt. Visionary officials and entrepreneurs have made the city what it is. It has taken a generation of dedicated city officials and citizen gadflies and watchdogs who steadily monitor the quality of all of our lives and create the framework in which we live. They deserve all our gratitude. They certainly get mine. Similarly, legions of entrepreneurs fill in the framework to make Boulder so extraordinary and interesting. People have put themselves on the line to create and operate Boulder's exceptional shops, restaurants and inns. It is their imagination, energy and commitment to quality that make Boulder such a wonderful place to live and to visit — and write about. I know some of you personally, while I am an anonymous patron of others' businesses. I treasure, admire and support you all.

More personally, I thank my husband, Ral Sandberg, not only for being an engaging companion on our explorations of Boulder and environs, but also for helping me become computer-literate so that I can do books with as much ease as writing ever permits. My son, Andrew Cameron-Walter, has grown up in Boulder. I've seen the city through his eyes and appreciate what it offers to youngsters of many ages.

The *Daily Camera's* Ronda Haskins and Beth Storie, Dan DeGregory and Theresa Chavez at Insiders' Guides Inc. in North Carolina earn my thanks for their conscientious editing — respectively around the corner and across the country. Without good editors, there wouldn't be many good writers.

How To Use This Guide

This guide is for anyone in the Boulder County or Rocky Mountain National Park area. Whether you're here one afternoon or as a summer tourist, newcomer or native, this book is for you. And that's no small thing. Authors Reed and Claire have lived here for years. Our decisions weren't just darts thrown at a map or a shrug of, "We might as well stay." Like many Boulderites, we chose this place as an anchor to our lives and the helium for our dreams. This book explains why. We hope it's so helpful, you'll use it until the corners are as soft as biodegradable tissue . . . and then buy the new edition!

This guide focuses on Boulder County first (and contains chapters on Daytrips and Weekend Getaways less than two hours away). Chapters on Rocky Mountain National Park, Estes Park and Grand Lake follow.

For information fast, check the table of contents, then zip to the chapter you need. Read the chapter's overview, then skip and scan. Headings and boldfaced tips will help.

Also check the index at the back. Many Boulder features appear several times. We couldn't help ourselves. Describing the Pearl Street Mall was like photographing a movie star — the three-quarters shot didn't capture it all. So we did a profile, then a full view. That's why the Pearl Street Mall shows up in the History, Attractions and Shopping chapters, from different perspectives. You'll also find the University of Colorado and Boulder's marvelous pedestrian paths woven throughout the guide. So, if you read something interesting, check the index, check the index to discover where else it's discussed. We've also integrated numerous cross-references into the text, so keep an eye out for them as additional directors. But if you're a skip-around reader, start at the index and scan from there.

And please tell us what you like and don't like in this guide. We revise it annually, so we're always up-to-date about what's best and brightest. Share your insights by writing Insiders' Guides Inc., P.O. Box 2057, Manteo, North Carolina 27954.

Photo: Daily Camera

Chautauqua Park is the starting point for many trails in Boulder's open space.

Table of Contents

Directory of Maps

Boulder
and Surrounding Area

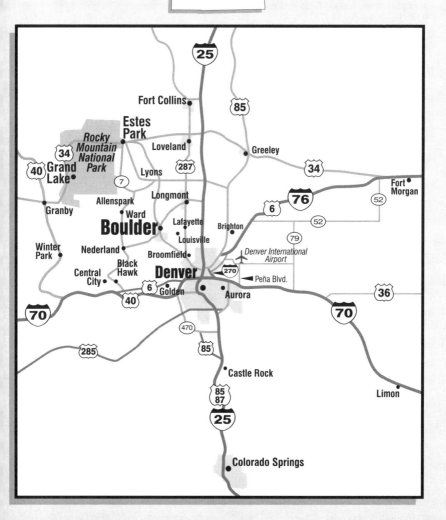

Boulder Area

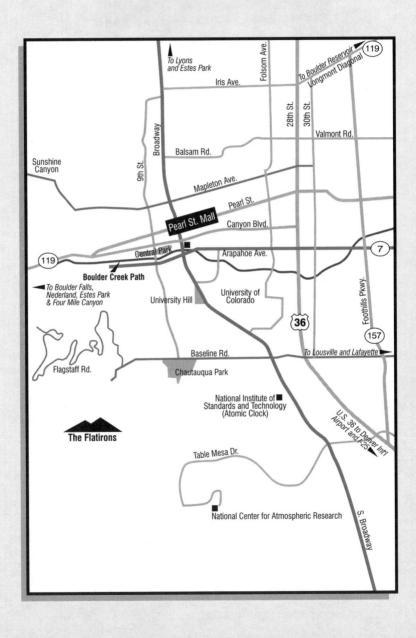

A mere 29 miles from Denver, Boulder is sometimes considered part of the Greater Denver Metropolitan Area for statistical purposes. But Boulder considers itself a world apart — and indeed it is.

Boulder
Overview

Cresting the scenic overlook on U.S. Highway 36 from Denver, first-time visitors gaze down upon Boulder and know they've arrived someplace special. Snuggled serenely against the pine-covered Foothills, punctuated dramatically with the upthrust red Flatirons and crowned with the gleaming white halo of the Continental Divide, Boulder looks like the Promised Land.

That's how it appeared to early settler Capt. Thomas Aikins, who, in 1858, peered at the Boulder Valley through his field glasses and remarked, "The mountains looked right for gold, and the valleys looked rich for grazing." Aikins and his party found gold in the hills above Boulder, and many have driven over the highway hill and found their Shangri-La.

A mere 29 miles from Denver, Boulder is sometimes considered part of the Greater Denver Metropolitan Area for statistical purposes. But Boulder considers itself a world apart — and indeed it is.

This green haven at the foot of the Rocky Mountains is a unique enclave of science, education, research, outdoor enthusiasm, elite athletic training, health food, bicycling, recycling, the arts and New Age culture — a kind of Berkeley of the Rockies, sometimes jokingly dubbed "The People's Republic of Boulder."

Boulder is home to Celestial Seasonings tea company, the Naropa Institute (started by Tibetan Buddhists), the Boulder School of Massage Therapy, the Rolf Institute (international headquarters), Ball Aerospace, the National Center for Atmospheric Research, the National Oceanic and Atmospheric Administration, the National Institute of Standards and Technology (home of the atomic clock, by which all U.S. time is set) and the University of Colorado (referred to throughout this book as CU-Boulder), one of CU's four campuses. The university's student and staff population of almost 28,000 (24,440 students, 3,243 staff) comprise almost one-third of Boulder's total population of 96,076, whose median age is 29. (Boulder County's median age is 31.6.)

The Denver Post once described Boulder as "The little town nestled between the mountains and reality."

Boulder People: A Confluence of Cultures

Boulder is full of old and new refugees from congested East and West Coast cities and Chicago — many of them professionals — seeking a better life. And they find it here, along with compatible company and culture in what many longtime residents feel is near-utopia: low crime, high mountains, plentiful blue skies and sunshine, glacial-melt drinking water, good schools, a lively arts scene, an enlightened city government and a wholesome, healthy outlook. In fact, parents often urge their college-age offspring away from Boulder for an eye-opening dip into "the real world." Escapees from the Midwest find the cultural milieu they were missing — and mountains! Boulder natives do exist, but they're rare creatures. They're usually the ones who don't ski, which almost everyone else in Boulder does.

Though Boulder has a predominately white, upper-middle-class population, there's a cosmopolitan element provided by the staff and students from foreign countries at the many scientific institutions and the university. Thirty-three percent of Boulder adults have four years of college; 26 percent have five or more years of college.

Unfortunately, plentiful well-paying jobs and affordable housing are not among Boulder's amenities. Many local engineers and scientists came to work at IBM or one of the national centers. But most people who live in Boulder have deliberately chosen to do so for the mountains and general ambiance, not necessarily for the job opportunities — and they pay the price in underemployment and a daunting real estate market. Compared to California or Washington, D.C., Boulder's average single-family home price of nearly $270,000 might seem affordable. But for those operating on the local economy, surviving in Boulder can be a real challenge. Students vie for all the low-paying jobs and affordable housing, and many CU-Boulder graduates, originally from other states, stay on.

Traditionally, many people, both young and old, have worked for next to nothing just to live in Boulder. But as rents and housing costs continually escalate, it becomes more difficult. Rock-climbing bums, writers, certified massage therapists (there are hundreds), teachers, psychotherapists and scientists are some of the colorful — often unemployed — clients lingering in local coffeehouses. Some of these same folks may deliver your pizza, drive your cab or sell you skis at a local mountain sports shop. Boulder unemployment is only 3.5 percent, but underemployment is much higher.

Boulderites participate in a number of humanitarian and volunteer efforts including local government, environmental activism, and a strong Sister Cities program. Among Boulder's sister cities are Jalapa, Nicaragua; Lhasa, Tibet; Yamagata, Japan; and Dushanbe, Tajikistan, in the former Soviet Union. The Sister Cities programs include cultural exchange as well as humanitarian aid shipments; environmental projects; and exchange students, doctors and technicians. Boulder families and other organizations host foreign students and sponsor Bosnian refugees and Soviet Jews. In past years many Vietnamese refugees were also brought to Boulder and have succeeded professionally. Habitat for Humanity has a local contingent, and there's a controversial local program to help the trade-embargoed, economically stressed Cubans.

Boulderites do love to travel. Go to a remote island in Fiji, and don't be surprised to bump into someone from Boulder.

Boulder Ethnicity Demographics

Note: Percentages based on 1994 data, the most recent available.

White	89.7%
Hispanic	4.8%
Asian	3.8%
Black	1.2%
Native American	0.4%
Other	0.1%

Open Space, Limited Growth and Enlightened Development

Unlike sprawling Greater Denver and other Colorado communities mushrooming to infinity, Boulder is a sort of fixed island surrounded by the protective reefs of open space. In 1967, Boulder became the first city in the United States to tax itself for funds to be used specifically for the acquisition, management and maintenance of open space — an ongoing program. But even earlier, at the turn of the century, Boulder's city government and citizens established a mountain park system by purchasing portions of the city's dramatic mountain backdrop, often called the Greenbelt, to protect it from development.

Today, Boulder's citizens enjoy more than 25,000 acres of open space in and around the city, 7,000 acres of adjacent city-owned mountain parks, and about 42,000 acres of county open space — some of which is under agricultural lease and is not open to the public. Residents of Greater Denver and nearby communities frequent Boulder's trail-laced open space too, since their land is largely filled with shopping centers, subdivisions and parking lots. The city of Boulder itself encompasses 27.8 square miles.

In 1977 Boulder instituted a limited-growth ordinance called the Danish Plan, the brainchild of city councilman Paul Danish, restricting new building to 2 percent annual growth. In 1985 it was replaced with another growth moratorium, which is still in effect.

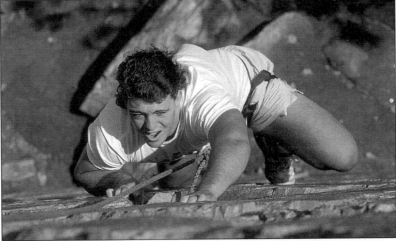

Photo: Daily Camera

The Flatirons and surrounding mountains make the Boulder area a rock-climber's mecca.

There's no getting around the fact that this makes Boulder a more desirable — but more expensive — place to live. Because of limited growth, affordable housing is one of the biggest problems in this small city where the student population occupies most of the lower-priced dwellings. Many people find less-expensive housing in the nearby smaller cities of Louisville and Lafayette, currently bursting at the seams with new development. See our Boulder Neighborhoods and Real Estate chapters for more information.

Because so much natural habitat has been preserved, more than 1,200 deer share the environs with residents. Deer grazing in yards is a common and (to some) pretty sight. But, they also wreak havoc on local gardens. Gardeners have been distressed to find their tomatoes trampled, peas pilfered and tulips nipped off at the bud. Mountain lions and bears occasionally wander into town too. In one case, a concerned citizen fetched his futon to provide a soft landing pad for a treed bear, tranquilized by wildlife officials. Another young bear led police on a merry chase right down the Pearl Street pedestrian mall. Skunks, raccoons and coyotes are regulars in areas near open space. A city-sponsored backyard wildlife program promotes landscaping that will attract and accommodate songbirds, butterflies and bats.

Outdoor-sports Capital

Look in any Boulder garage and you're likely to find several bicycles (mountain, touring and racing), several pairs of skis (downhill and cross-country: racing, touring, skating, telemark and mountaineering), snowshoes, perhaps a windsurfer and/or kayak, crampons, an ice axe and mountaineering gear, rock-climbing ropes and harnesses, backpacks, in-line skates, a fly-fishing rod and a plethora of running shoes. It's no coincidence that *Outside* magazine named Boulder "the sports town."

Residents also engage in more traditional pursuits, such as tennis and golf. Boulder's population of couch potatoes is probably one of the nation's lowest. A 1992 survey by the Centers for Disease Control found that Colorado had fewer fat people per capita and more people who exercise than any other state. Landlocked Colorado ranks second nationally in the number of certified scuba divers (California has the most). Several years ago, *USA Today* ranked Boulder No. 1 in their rating of the top 50 healthiest places to live in the United States. A *Colorado Daily* (local newspaper) poll found that seven out of 10 Boulderites owned bicycles. According to another guidebook, Boulder's bicycle count is 93,000.

Why Boulder? The mountains seem to attract outdoors-oriented people. Perhaps Boulderites felt obliged to lead the way when citizen Frank Shorter became the first American ever to win an Olympic medal in the marathon — gold in 1972 in Munich, silver in 1976 in Montreal. "When Frank won the gold, everybody in America started running," says Neill Woelk, a veteran sports reporter at Boulder's *Daily Camera* newspaper. Shorter, now a Boulder attorney, also sells a line of athletic wear and is a frequent Olympics commentator. Another famous Boulder runner, Arturo Barrios, held the world record for 10 kilometers until 1993.

Boulder is also known nationwide for its huge bicycling population and local celebrities. Boulder cyclist Connie Carpenter won Olympic gold in 1984 for the road race, and her husband, Davis Phinney, was the first American ever to win a Tour de France stage. Alexi Grewal won an Olympic gold medal in 1984 for the road race. With more than 75 miles of bike lanes and off-street bike paths, citizens can cycle almost everywhere, sometimes faster than by car and without the parking hassle.

Elite athletes from all over the world move to Boulder specifically to train in its health-promoting atmosphere and high altitude. The winners of at least 12 of the last 13 Hawaii Ironman world championships — the world's best triathletes — all live or train in Boulder, among them five-time winner Mark Allen, six-time winner Dave Scott, six-time women's champion Paula Newby-Fraser (from Zimbabwe) and two-time winner Erin Baker (New Zealand). Olympic ice skater Debi Thomas trained here. Three-time Boston Marathon women's winner, Uta Pippig, also lives in Boulder. Boulderite Mark Coogan is on the U.S. Olympic team running the marathon. The list goes on and on.

The University of Colorado's football team, the Golden Buffaloes, were the 1990 national champions and are considered to have one of the nation's most successful programs of the last five years. The women's basketball team is also tops. CU-Boulder's Alpine and Nordic ski teams train at nearby Eldora Mountain Resort, only 21 miles away.

For mere mortals there are health clubs galore, the most popular being the great outdoors. Boulder boasts 100 miles of hiking trails in the mountain parks, literally out residents' back doors. The City of Boulder also operates three excellent recreation centers and sponsors an Annual Pedestrian Conference with nationwide attendance. One of the world's largest 10-kilometer footraces, the annual Bolder Boulder through the city's streets attracts more than 30,000 runners. The Flatirons, numerous rock formations and nearby Eldorado Canyon make Boulder a rock-climbing mecca. Get all the scoop on outdoor activities in the chapter on Boulder Participatory Sports.

Time Out

The Atomic Clock — the latest model is called the NIST-7 — has an accuracy of plus or minus one second in 1 million years. As the ancient Aztec Calendar once was in Mexico, NIST-7 at the National Institute of Standards and Technology in Boulder is the official timekeeper of our world — in the United States, anyhow.

The exact time is now set by global agreement. Most major industrialized nations have their own atomic clocks, and about a dozen countries send their official times to Paris, where they are averaged to calculate the universal coordinated time, the world standard. To set your watch by the most correct time on earth — the coordinated universal time from NIST-7 — call 499-7111. Of course, that's also the local time in Greenwich, England; for Boulder Mountain Standard Time, subtract seven hours. If you call, be patient — you might have to wait through a series of beeps and pauses.

Heart and Soul

Boulder's Pearl Street Mall forms the heart and center of the city. Historic buildings, housing shops, galleries, offices and sidewalk cafes line this photogenic, four-block, open-air walkway — formerly part of Pearl Street. Sadly, since the mall was completed in 1976, constant upscaling and rising rents have driven out many of the older businesses, replacing them with a musical-chairs array of new establishments. But Boulder's downtown mall still lures as many locals as visitors — especially on summer evenings when string quartets, bagpipers, Peruvian bands and all manner of performers stake out spots by storefronts. One piano player hauls his instrument in on a wheeled platform; jugglers, fire and sword swallowers, tightrope walkers and even a Rastafarian contortionist complete the circus-like scene. Lively entertainment, people-watching and the piney aroma of the summer breeze make mall strolling a warm-weather favorite.

The Boulder Creek Path, two short blocks from the Pearl Street Mall, meanders along Boulder Creek as a peaceful but sometimes perilous thoroughfare for bicyclists, in-line skaters, joggers and strollers. Seven-and-a-half miles of scenic path follow the creek as it tumbles down from Boulder Canyon and out onto the plains. Bicycling is so highly regarded in Boulder that sometimes the city plows the snow off the bike path before it plows the streets.

During spring runoff and early summer, kayakers and kids of all ages take tumultuous rides down the creek in boats and innertubes. Also along the path, adjacent to Central Park, the Boulder County Farmers Market operates on Saturdays and Wednesdays from spring through fall, offering local, organically grown vegetables, fruits and flowers as well as crafts and baked goods.

No Boulder summer is complete without a concert and meal at Chautauqua. Chautauqua Park, with its 100-year-old dining hall and barn-like concert hall, houses some of the best music and meals anywhere, including the Colorado Music Festival with artists from around the country. Elsewhere in town, summertime offerings include the Colorado Dance Festival, Colorado Shakespeare Festival, Colorado Lyric Opera, Boulder Creek Festival and, less lofty, the Kinetic Sculpture Challenge — a crazy land and water race along and across Boulder Reservoir in wildly imaginative, but not so navigable, conveyances.

Industry and Economics

To dispel any notion of Boulder as a bedroom community to Denver, consider this: 74 percent of Boulder County's population works in the county, 45 percent of the City of Boulder's population works in the city, and 45 percent of the city's work force commutes in from surrounding communities. Boulder industry focuses on education, scientific research and technology at such places as the University of Colorado at Boulder, the National Oceanic and Atmospheric Administration, the National Center for Atmospheric Research and various other government and university scientific institutes.

Celestial Seasonings tea company, the largest U.S. herb-tea manufacturer, makes its home here on Sleepytime Drive. The company revolutionized the tea industry, and founder Mo Siegel picked his way to an herbal tea fortune initially gathering herbs in Boulder's Foothills. He is renowned as the hippie who became a millionaire. A bicycling aficionado, Siegel also brought international bicycle competition to Boulder for more than a decade with the Red Zinger Bicycle Classic race in the mid-1970s, which eventually became the now-extinct Coors Classic.

The University of Colorado, Storage Technology Corp. and the Boulder Valley School District are the top-three employers in Boulder County, with a total of some 11,500 employees. IBM Corp., Ball Aerospace and Neodata Services Inc., a nationwide subscription and mailing service for magazine publishers, are three other major county employers.

The university has in the past housed such scholars as Robert Bakker, a world-renowned paleontologist who transformed the study of dinosaurs with his now widely accepted theory that they were warmblooded and more closely related to birds than reptiles. Movie mogul Steven Spielberg consulted Bakker during the filming of *Jurassic Park*. CU-Boulder is also currently home to Patricia Nelson Limerick, renowned teacher and historian of the American West and a leader among the "new Western historians." Limerick's ground-breaking work on the roles played by women, Native Americans and other ethnic groups in settling the West won her the 1995 MacArthur Fellowship, a "genius grant" of $275,000 with no strings attached over a five-year period. Nobel laureate Thomas Cech of CU-Boulder received the prize for his work proving that the genetic messenger RNA can also function as an enzyme, leading to the speculation that RNA could have played a key role in the origin of life. Cech's current work with therapeutic RNA molecules is expected to lead to medical treatments, from attacking viruses to halting infections and alleviating symptoms of genetic disorders like sickle-cell anemia, muscular dystrophy and cystic fibrosis. Nationally recognized as a leader in the field of educational testing, professor of education Robert Linn received the university's highest honor of distinguished professorship in 1996. He is an advisor to key professional and governmental committees as an expert in evaluating test reliability and validity; test comparison, bias and ethics; and the strength and weakness of the mathematical models that define testing. President Bill Clinton named School of Education assistant professor Nancy Butler Songer one of 30 scientists and engineers nationwide to receive the prestigious Presidential Faculty Fellow awards in 1995. Songer is noted for her work in establishing partnerships among students in grades K through 12 worldwide, using computers and global electronic networks to enrich student learning and communication.

Atmospheric scientist Walter Orr Roberts, who died in 1990, founded the National Center for Atmospheric Research (NCAR — say it en-car) in Boulder, and his work in solar physics established Boulder as a space center, attracting such other scientific facilities as the National Bureau of Standards and Technology (now known as NIST) and Ball Aerospace. He helped found CU-Boulder's Joint Institute for Laboratory Astrophysics and Department of Astrophysical, Planetary and Atmospheric Sciences. Roberts also helped bring Boulder's greatest architectural gem into being: the stunning mesa-top NCAR laboratory, designed by architect I.M. Pei, who also designed the new sections of the Louvre and National Gallery. NCAR also has fame as the futuristic setting of Woody Allen's 1970s comedy film *Sleeper*. See our chapter on Boulder Business for more information.

Climate

It's no wonder that weather and climate are two big topics of study at local scientific institutes: Boulder's climate is marked by unusual extremes. Foot-deep snow and below-zero temperatures can suddenly transform to breezy 60-degree, T-shirt weather by Boulder's capricious Chinook "snow-eater" winds. These warm, dry winds blast down from the eastern slope of the mountains and melt the snow with blinding speed. Boulder's winds have also been known to blow in gusts exceeding 120 miles per hour, removing roofs and toppling telephone poles.

Because of these strong winds, Native Americans chose not to make permanent settlements in the area and mainly visited for summer hunting. The dreaded high winds, Boulder's biggest weather affliction, can come anytime but are the worst in winter and can continue for days. It can be so windy that schools won't let young children leave the building without an adult. Safeway supermarket sometimes puts a note on the door asking that carts be returned to the store so rolling carts don't hit cars in the parking lot. The winds can make people irritable, and there are tales of pioneer women wandering off onto the prairie or committing suicide, driven insane by the gales. Similar winds (in Europe called the foehn or mistral) are common throughout the world near high mountain ranges.

Sometimes it seems like Boulder has only two seasons: summer and winter. Oh, the tulips bloom in spring, and the leaves change in fall for a brief but spectacular show. But these two fickle seasons are often accompanied by a foot of snow, burying the crocuses and lilacs or blackening fall's golden aspen leaves. Halloween is often one of the most miserable nights of the year with the poor trick-or-treaters stumbling about in freezing rain or snow. Then again, Thanksgiving and Christmas can sometimes be T-shirt and outdoor cafe

The Flatirons

Boulder's backdrop and trademark, the spectacular Flatirons, are Pennsylvanian red sandstone and conglomerate that were deposited as alluvial fans and aprons along the edges of the Ancestral Rockies. They were dragged upward at their current angle  by the rebirth of the Rockies about 65 million years ago. The Third Flatiron (third from the north) is one of Colorado's and the nation's premier, classic rock climbs. It towers 1,400 feet high, a couple hundred feet higher than the Empire State Building, and has been climbed by people without using their hands, on roller skates, naked and in 8 minutes (by separate climbers). Parts of the Flatirons are closed to climbers and hikers periodically to allow native raptors to nest in peace.

Photo: Daily Camera

The Flatirons serve as the backdrop for many towns and neighborhoods in the Boulder area.

weather. It rarely rains in Boulder except for summer afternoon thunderstorms and the August monsoon, a week or two of rainy weather.

Boulder's high elevation (5,430 feet) keeps temperatures cool at night even on the hottest summer days. Mountain breezes and low humidity help too. Tornadoes generally stay well to the east, though hailstorms occasionally shred summer flowers and vegetables.

The record low temperature in the area is -33 degrees (1930) and the high is 104 degrees (1954). Boulder has an average of 33 days above 90 degrees and 133 days below 32. January, the coldest month, averages 21 degrees; July, the warmest, averages 88. Average precipitation is 18.24 inches. The most

snow in a season was 142.9 inches; the least, 20.8 inches. Though it may snow or blow, low humidity and a higher-than-California average of sunny days make Boulder's climate one of the most pleasant in the nation.

Area Geography

The Foothills of the Rocky Mountains divide Boulder County from north to south. Eastern Boulder County lies on the western edge of the Great Plains with rolling terrain, small ridges and the Davidson Mesa, which runs northeast from south of Boulder to Louisville. Western Boulder County rises from the Foothills to the Continental Divide, to a breathless

Niwot's Curse

Those who spend any time in Boulder are bound to hear about Niwot's Curse. There are various versions though no evidence that Chief Niwot (meaning Left Hand) of the South Arapaho Indian tribe ever said any of them — or even proclaimed a "curse" — according to sources at Boulder's Carnegie Library for local history.

Nonetheless, the library's official-unofficial version, more comment than curse, is that Niwot said, "The Boulder Valley is so beautiful that people seeing it will want to stay and their staying will be the undoing of the beauty."

Another less-official but more commonly heard version is, "Once you gaze upon the Flatirons, you will never be happy anywhere else."

summit of 14,255 feet atop Longs Peak in Rocky Mountain National Park in the extreme northwestern part of the county.

Boulder Environs

Roughly 20 towns dot the mountains and plains of Boulder County, ranging from rustic, high-country settlements like Eldora and Raymond with only a handful of year-round residents to sizable burgs like Longmont, second-largest city in Boulder County after Boulder. A former sugar beet and canning capital, Longmont — northeast of Boulder — is now home of Longmont Foods Inc., a turkey-breeding and meat-processing company.

Nothing could be further from Longmont in both locale and flavor than lofty, funky Ward, former mining boom-and-bust town, now a home for old and young hippies and other escapees from the system. After Longmont, the small plains cities of Broomfield, Lafayette and Louisville are the next-most populous.

The small towns of Lyons (north of Boulder) and Eldorado Springs (south of Boulder) lie at the mouths of spectacular canyons. Eldorado Springs is also the site of a state park and mineral springs and is a famous rock-climbing area. Hygiene and Allenspark are unincorporated small settlements of a few hundred residents. Jamestown was a former mining boom town with a population of 10,000, now down to less than 300. Its picturesque mercantile cafe is a popular bicycling stop.

Spectacularly sited at the top of Boulder Canyon on Barker Reservoir, Nederland is

Boulder County's largest mountain town and an odd mix of eccentric mountain folk, young families, old hippies, conservative Republicans, environmental activists, self-sufficient rugged individualists and a small contingent of out-of-staters who fall in love with it during the summer, move in, and beat a fast trail out after their first winter.

Needless to say, a lot more can be written and said about each Boulder County town and its unique character and history. See our chapters on Boulder Real Estate and Neighborhoods and Nearby Communities for more information.

Niwot's Curse?

Though Boulder has been utopia for many residents for many years, the city (like the rest of the planet) is currently experiencing an uncomfortable population expansion. Since the late 1970s, the population has increased by about 16 percent, or 16,000 people. The California earthquake a few years ago jettisoned a big wave of West Coasters. "Too many people and too many cars," is the complaint of residents who remember traffic-free streets and the ability to get anywhere in town in 10 minutes. Gone are those days, and in their place are frustrating waits in traffic jams, rude drivers, long lines at supermarkets, restaurants and movies and nowhere to park.

Unfortunately, Boulder is inheriting some of the problems of a bigger city: increased crime, pollution, traffic and overpopulation, and the current challenge is how to deal with them.

Growth-cap initiatives on the ballot and emphasis on bicycling and public transportation versus automobile use continue to be some "driving issues" for the future.

Is Arapaho Chief Niwot's curse, "that people seeing the beauty of the Boulder Valley will want to stay, and their staying will be the undoing of the beauty," beginning to come true?

Boulder, whose name came from the area's plentiful rocks, began as a raw frontier settlement of tents and crude log cabins along Boulder Creek.

Boulder Area
History

Early Boulder bore little resemblance to today's fair city. For one thing, there were no trees — except cottonwoods and willows along the creeks — since the Boulder Valley is part of the Great Plains grasslands.

Visiting the area in 1873, British gentlewoman and world traveler Isabella Bird described Boulder as "a hideous collection of frame houses on the burning plain." Bird authored many bestselling travel books at the time, among them, *A Lady's Life in the Rocky Mountains*. She was also the first woman to be a member of the prestigious Royal Geographical Society. Those who have viewed early photos of Boulder will indeed agree with Miss Bird.

For another thing, today's pub-filled Boulder was "dry" from 1907 until 1967. Some say the teetotaling history was due to strong religious convictions of the townsfolk, while others cite the need for the state's first university town to remain proper and sober.

Pre- and Early History

Trees or not, geology carved out a special setting for Boulder with its most notable landmark, the Flatirons. The name for these unusual vertical rock formations comes from an old-fashioned clothes iron or "flatiron," standing on end — though some historians say they were named for the Flatiron Building in New York. One of New York's oldest and most famous, the Flatiron building at Broadway and Fifth Avenue was completed in 1903 and also has a triangular shape like that of an old-fashioned flatiron.

But Boulder's dramatic red sandstone slabs trace their true lineage back some 300 million years to the Ancestral Rockies. Their sedimentary rock formed by wind and erosion of the mountains, which next spent millions more years submerged beneath swamps and shallow seas. These behemoths were then dragged upward to their current arresting angle when the present-day, "new" Rockies formed around 60 million years ago.

Similar formations are found at Colorado Springs' Garden of the Gods and Denver's Red Rocks Park. In her book, *Roadside Geology: Colorado*, Halka Chronic writes, "the tilting of the sedimentary layers has been so extreme that the layers are upside down. Basement rocks may even be thrust out above them."

First Humans

The first humans passed through Colorado about 10,000 years ago and are believed to have descended from Asians who migrated over the Bering Land Bridge as much as 10,000 years earlier. University of Denver scientists found the bones of animals and the spear points used to kill them in northeastern New Mexico. These "Folsom points" are named for the small town of Folsom, New Mexico, near the Colorado border, where they were found along with the first signs of humanity in North America. The ice-age Folsom man was unearthed in 1924. Such early "Westerners" hunted mastodons, woolly mammoths and giant sloths. Folsom and the nearby Capulin Volcano National Monument make for an interesting trip through some unusual volcanic landscape.

Colorado's first-known settlements were those of the Anasazi in southern Colorado's Four Corners area around 550 A.D. The Anasazi are known for their basketry and distinctive pottery, but most of all for Mesa Verde, the spectacular series of cliff-side dwellings they built and inhabited around 1150 A.D. It's not known why the Anasazi abandoned their cliff dwellings around 1300 and disappeared, but migration south to the Rio Grande valley because of over-farming is suspected. Today's Acoma, Sandia, Taos, Zuni and other Pueblo peoples are believed to be descendants of the Anasazi.

During the 16th and 17th centuries, Colorado was home to several tribes descended from the Shoshone and Algonquins. The Utes were Shoshonean mountain-dwellers. Plains tribes included the Cheyenne, Comanche, Arapaho and Kiowa. Other tribes in the area were the Pawnee, Sioux, Navajo, Blackfoot and Crow.

Native Americans throughout the Southwest visited Colorado for such things as clay for their pottery, fossil seashells for their medicine men's magic and turquoise for adornment. Bands of Cheyenne and Arapaho visited the Boulder Valley regularly to collect flint for arrowheads and colorful clays for war paint.

By the mid-19th century, the Comanche and Kiowa had been driven out of the Boulder Valley by the Cheyenne and Arapaho, who came originally from the Minnesota-Great Lakes area, where they, in turn, had been driven west by the Sioux. The Arapaho wintered here because the game was plentiful and the winters mild. They also enjoyed and venerated the warm thermal waters at Eldorado Springs. The Utes, enemies of the Cheyenne and Arapaho, still dwelled in the mountains above the Boulder Valley and ranged west to the Salt Lake Basin (thus the name, Utah).

First Europeans and Pioneers

Gold brought the first European explorers to the area. Perhaps the first to venture into Colorado was Vásquez de Coronado, who arrived in New Mexico in 1541 searching for the mythical Seven Gold Cities of Cibola.

During the 17th and 18th centuries, both the French and Spanish alternately claimed the territory that included all present states on the Mississippi River plus Montana, Wyoming, the Dakotas and part of Colorado. For a while the Territory was called Louisiana after King Louis XIV of France, then New Spain when the Spanish defeated the French in the French

and Indian War in 1762. In 1800 Napoleon swapped an Italian kingdom for it with the Spanish, reclaiming it again for France.

American adventurer James Purcell of Kentucky explored the area in the early 1800s before it was U.S. territory and found gold along the Platte River. Then, in 1803, President Thomas Jefferson paid $15 million to France in the famous Louisiana Purchase of some 830,000 square miles — doubling the size of the United States. At the time, Jefferson was maligned for squandering money on questionable, unexplored land.

U.S. Army Lt. Zebulon Pike and Maj. Stephen Long were commissioned to explore the territory, and, later, John Fremont came looking for a route across the Rockies. One of Fremont's men, William Gilpin — later to become the first governor of the Colorado Territory — reported that gold could probably be found in the area, stirring some initial interest in what was then considered "the Great American Desert . . . totally unfit for cultivation and, of course, uninhabitable by a people depending upon agriculture for their subsistence," according to Pike.

The Gold Rush

Colorado's and Boulder's first permanent white (and a few black) settlers came in 1858 after gold was discovered in the river sands of the South Platte River near present-day Denver. Prospectors worked their way north, panning Cherry Creek (Denver), Clear Creek (Golden), Boulder Creek and others. As these lower "placer deposits" of gold were eventually mined out, prospectors and miners followed the creeks up into the mountains, sometimes finding the "mother lode" in such places as Central City and Black Hawk, then higher to Breckenridge, Gold Hill (above Boulder), Empire, Aspen, Leadville and Cripple Creek. Along with gold, they would also find silver, iron, tungsten, molybdenum and, on the plains, oil and coal.

First Boulder Settlement

Also in 1858, Capt. Thomas Aikins, a Missouri farmer, led a gold-prospecting group of farmers and merchants to the area. From Fort

Photo: Daily Camera

Re-enacting the way it was during Chautauqua's early years, camping out in tents.

St. Vrain to the northeast, he peered at the Boulder Valley through his telescope and saw "bands of Indian Ponies and bands of deer and antelope grazing close up to the high foothills; . . . and could see that [it] was the loveliest of all the valleys . . . a landscape exceedingly beautiful, those mountains are so high and steep. . . ." In October or November, Aikins and party camped near the mouth of Boulder Canyon beneath the jagged vertical red rocks — an area now designated as Settlers Park. (There's some debate about what Aikins actually viewed through his telescope; the Boulder Valley cannot be seen from Fort St. Vrain because of the topography. There's also "first settler" John Rothrock, about whom less is known.)

According to Aikins, before they had bedded down for the night, Chief Niwot of the Arapaho paid a visit saying, "Go away; you come to kill our game, to burn our wood and to destroy our grass." But the miners fed and flattered the tall, handsome Niwot (whose name means Left Hand), who eventually agreed to coexist in peace.

Shortly thereafter, in January of 1859, the Aikins party found gold in a small creek bed between Sunshine and Four Mile canyons. Word got out and within a month there were 2,000 men and 17 women in the Boulder area.

Town Development

Winter closed in, making mining difficult, so in February, Aikins called a meeting to form a "Town Company." Later that month, A.A. Brookfield became the first president of the Boulder City Town Company, and 56 shareholders divided up 1,280 acres along Boulder Creek into 4,044 lots. Each shareholder received 18 lots; a few lots were given for free to those who promised to provide such services as sawmills. The remaining lots were for sale at $1,000 each. Other homesteading lands at the time cost $1.25 an acre, so the Boulder lots weren't hot sellers, and further settlement was quite slow. Other camps and settlements in the area grew much faster.

Boulder, whose name came from the area's plentiful rocks, began as a raw frontier settlement of tents and crude log cabins along the creek. Roofs and doors were made of split pine, and the floors were dirt.

Originally part of the Nebraska and Kansas territories, Boulder became part of Colorado when the U.S. Congress established the Colorado Territory in 1861. South of present-day Baseline Road was the Kansas Territory; north was Nebraska Territory. In 1867, Boulder became the county seat, and the town was incorporated in 1871. Unlike the region's boom-and-bust mining towns, Boulder's economy remained stable because the city functioned mainly as a supply and transportation center for the miners and prospectors — and, later, as a hub for plains farmers. Boulder's population from 1860 to 1870 remained at about 350.

Boulder's first newspaper, the *Boulder Valley News*, began publication in April 1867.

Land Grabs and The Sand Creek Massacre

The technicalities of stealing the land from the Native Americans came from the Pre-emption Law of 1841, stating that a person had prior right to purchase a piece of land if he occupied it and improved it. And next, the Kansas-Nebraska Act of 1853, which referred to preemption of "the public lands to which the Indian title had been at the time of such settlement extinguished." In 1866 the U.S. Congress validated various settlers' claims to these lands.

Land "ownership" and "improvement" were not understood in the Native American culture as they were by Europeans. If anything, the Native Americans believed the land owned and provided for them and didn't need any "improving." This could be the classic clash of cultures, East vs. West — living in harmony with nature vs. controlling it. After all, the Native Americans were originally from Asia.

But, for the most part, the miners and Native Americans coexisted peacefully in the Boulder Valley until the summer of 1864, when there were reports of Indians attacking some wagon trains and express wagons. The then-anti-Indian (and anti-black) *Rocky Mountain News* helped stir up more fear and negativity. That year, the "100 Day Volunteers" were commissioned under Capt. David Nichols with other citizens. Boulder's friends of Chief Left Hand (Niwot) refused to take part in this brigade, which found and attacked peaceful In-

dian families camped at Sand Creek in eastern Colorado in accordance with treaties. Thinking it was a mistake, the besieged Indians raised the American flag, but were ruthlessly massacred. Women and children were scalped, and gentle Chief Niwot who met with the first settlers was killed.

Bold Miners, Blizzards, Boom and Bust

The original Gold Run deposit that fueled Boulder's early economy was depleted after about a year. Next, silver from mines in Caribou stimulated Boulder's growth, and some said that Caribou taxes built the Boulder County Courthouse. A wagon road from Boulder to Caribou was completed in 1871, and a stagecoach ride cost $3.50. Mail was delivered by sleigh to Caribou from Nederland in winter.

Four miles from the Continental Divide at 10,500 feet, life was cold and tough at Caribou, but in the early 1870s the lure of silver had drawn nearly 500 residents, who built two-story houses so they could find them in the 25-foot-high snow drifts after storms. The second story also allowed citizens to come and go through their bedroom windows in the deep snow. A rope ran from the mine to the town's center so miners could feel their way home in blizzards. When asked about Caribou's winters, one miner remarked that he did not know how long winter lasted, because he had only been there three years. Caribou was eventually destroyed by fire, diphtheria, scarlet fever and the mining bust.

Mines popped up all over the area: Sunshine, Salina and Magnolia — today, the names of a local canyon, town site and road. Many booming mountain mining towns, such as Ward, soon went bust when the gold ran out. A smelter built at Black Hawk in 1868 renewed interest in deeper mining in the area because ores containing gold could be processed. A few years later a gold-silver ore was found at Gold Hill, and during 1892, the peak year, more than $1 million in gold and silver was produced.

In 1900, ferberite, an ore of tungsten, was identified in Nederland, starting a new rush to the area. (Nederland, meaning "low lands," was named earlier by the Dutchmen who bought the higher Caribou mine.) By 1918, Boulder County had become the main producer of tungsten in the United States, with a total production of 24,000 tons of tungsten trioxide worth $23 million.

By 1910, $20 million of silver had come from Caribou, but it finally ran out. "Caribou, like the reindeer it was named after, pawed its food — silver — from beneath the frozen snow. The lifeblood of its silver veins pinched out, and the town stumbled to a stop, and died," wrote historian John Buchanan.

Trains and Transport

Trains were the lifeblood of the mining industry and early settlement of the area. The first railroad line to Boulder came through in 1879, and narrow-gauge railroad lines were built into the mountains, making it easier to supply mining camps. By 1883 Union Pacific Railroad had 14 miles of narrow-gauge track to Four Mile, Salina, Wallstreet, Sunset and, later, Ward. By 1904 the line went all the way to Eldora and was known as The Switzerland Trail. It became a popular tourist attraction that provided an additional source of revenue to the railroads. But the route had financial problems by 1909, and then-owners Colorado and Northwestern folded. The line continued to operate by the reorganized Denver, Boulder and Northwestern Railroad, which spent the next 10 years debating whether to close The Switzerland Trail line. In 1919 a cloudburst washed out 2,500 feet of track, and the line was never rebuilt.

Colorado's First School and The University

Boulder's identity as a center of education had its beginnings in 1860 with the opening of the state's first schoolhouse. Next, citizens lobbied fiercely to have the city chosen for the territorial (later, state) university. Boulder's citizens donated land and money to match the $15,000 appropriated by the state legislature for construction of the university on a hill south of town where the Arapaho had hunted.

In 1876, Colorado became a state, at which time the University of Colorado was under construction. Completed in 1877, Old Main, the university's first building, housed the entire university — a few classrooms along with living quarters for the president, janitor and their families. With much ceremony the university opened its doors in September 1877 to 44 students, a president and one instructor.

When Mary Rippon of Detroit was invited to be CU's third faculty member, the wife of first CU president Joseph A. Sewell predicted that Rippon "would not stay two days in this lonely place." Rippon decided to come West and give it a try after reading about Colorado's wildflowers in the *Atlantic Monthly* and hearing that banker Charles Buckingham had donated $2,000 for a university library. She stayed 57 years as a French and German professor and was the first woman in the United States to teach at a state university. She helped open Boulder's first public library, and CU's lovely outdoor theater, where the Colorado Shakespeare Festival is held, is named for her.

To beautify CU's barren, windswept campus, Mrs. Sewell ordered 50 wagon loads of soil for her landscaping plans. The dirt promptly blew away with the first high wind, but she ordered another 50 wagon loads, and by 1881 had grown 2 acres of lawn with trees and flowers.

Saloons, Red-lights, Religion and Law

Meanwhile, Boulder began to take on the features of a permanent settlement. By 1872, various churches had been built: Presbyterian, Baptist and a Methodist-Episcopalian church. Some citizens became concerned that the town's young men spent too much time in saloons and opened a reading room, where the young men could come and peruse the newspapers while inspecting the genteel young ladies occasionally invited as an inducement.

By the 1870s, Boulder men had acquired money and real estate and needed a government and laws to protect their assets. Loose dogs were a big issue in town. In 1871 a dog-control program was initiated along with a tree-planting program. Liquor licenses of $100 per saloon were established to raise some revenue for the fledgling town.

In 1871, Capt. Aikin's son, Lafayette, was appointed town marshal and paid a salary of $72 a year. The only previous law enforcement was the mining district's "club rules," whereby a wrongdoer would have the hair shaved off half his face and head (opposite sides) and be expelled from town.

By 1875, Republican, Democratic and Prohibition parties had formed. Well-educated and feisty, Boulder's women started lobbying for the vote that year. By 1893 Colorado became the second state after Wyoming (as a territory) to grant women the vote.

Less-liberated women (or, perhaps, more — depending upon one's perspective) occupied a red-light district, which stretched from the north side of Boulder Creek at Canyon Boulevard (formerly Water Street) to the present-day library. These "soiled doves" also did business in other parts of town. Prostitution and gambling were declared illegal in 1873, but then the law was reversed in 1878. Some houses of "ill repute" closed down temporarily and others not at all, and the "brides of the multitude" continued their business.

The increasing number of buildings and fear of fire — a great danger with the high winds — finally brought about the construction of a waterworks in 1874, then the first hook-and-ladder company in 1875. Bucket brigades were the first means of firefighting. The first volunteer firemen were the cream of Boulder society and popular at firemen's balls, parades and firefighting tournaments. So important and highly regarded were the firemen, election of the firemen's officers drew more attention than city elections.

By the late 1870s, increased mining activity was bringing in more crime, and Boulder needed a jail. Prisoners had been kept everywhere from the basement of the fire department to the sheriff's hotel room.

Water also became an issue by the late 1870s, as the population increased and Boulder Creek became polluted with mine tailings. People who didn't have wells had to use the creek water. A reservoir had been built in 1874 at the base of Boulder Canyon but had become increasingly polluted. In 1884, dead horses were found in the creek, and the reservoir was shut down. To avoid the mine-tailing runoff, a new reservoir was built at the mouth of Sunshine Canyon. The Boulder City Improvement Society formed in 1881. By 1882, Boulder's population had reached 3,000. Water had its revenge in the terrifying 100-year flood in 1894 (see this chapter's related Close-up).

Coal, Oil, Newspapers and an International Population

By the late 1860s, there were 77 buildings in town. Local businesses included sawmills, a brickyard, several blacksmiths and general stores, stables and liveries. Downtown Boulder had a wobbly boardwalk that rose and fell to a different height in front of each different shop — ripping ladies' skirts and gouging shoppers with loose nails.

The business of mining was expanding to other minerals. Coal was discovered east of Boulder on David Kerr's farm. Coal prospector Louis Nawatny bought nearby land, registered a town plat in 1878 and named it Louisville after himself. Two years later 500 people had settled there. In 1887 a coal mine was dug in Lafayette (named for Lafayette Miller), and by 1892 there were five mines and 200 homes. Polish, Italian, Greek and French immigrants joined the Welsh, Scots and English miners who had been here since the 1860s. By the 1920s the coal industry would be Boulder County's largest employer with 1,000 men.

Oil was discovered in 1901 near Boulder, and for a while Boulder had its own oil stock exchange and a specialized newspaper, *Oil News*. Wells sprang up all over east of Boulder, and it was predicted that the oil field would stretch to Wyoming. By March of 1902 there were 92 oil companies operating near today's Longmont Diagonal. Natural gas was also discovered along with the oil, but it was considered a nuisance. Ultimately, 183 holes were drilled in Boulder County, but only 81 were functioning. Of these, 76 produced oil; five produced gas.

The weekly *Camera* became the *Daily Camera* in 1891.

Tuberculars, Tourists and Trolleys

Boulder was beginning to draw visitors and newcomers other than miners. From its earliest days Boulder, like other places in the Southwest, drew people with tuberculosis who hoped the pure air, dry climate and vigorous life would restore their health. In 1895 the Seventh-Day Adventists built the sanatorium (later to become Boulder Memorial Hospital) for tuberculars. Many eminent CU professors were recovered tuberculars.

Along with the tuberculars came a group of Texas professors in 1897 looking for an airy summer camp and retreat to escape the Texas heat. To the delight of Boulder citizens, the Texans chose Boulder as a site for their proposed Chautauqua — a respected national movement at the time — and the city bought its first park land and named it Texado Park for the Texans.

The dining hall and auditorium were completed for the grand opening on the Fourth of July in 1898, and the first Chautauquans camped in tents — later replaced by cottages. A 1903 brochure described it as "retirement without loneliness," "not a casino" but "quiet without ennui."

Well-known Boulder photographer Joseph Bevier Sturtevant ("Rocky Mountain Joe") — who produced many memorable photographs of the city's early years — was the official

The 100-year Flood

The winter of 1894 was long, cold and snowy. The heavy snow pack still plastered the Front Range at the end of May. Easterly winds brought a warm spring rain that lasted for 60 hours and melted the snow too quickly. The creeks began to rise in the early morning hours of May 31, soon unleashing an awesome display of nature's power.

 "One seething mass of black water, bowlders [sic] and crushed buildings. Nearly every tree has been torn out by the roots and the road bed is entirely destroyed," read the *Daily Camera*, describing the scene at Left Hand Creek near Glendale.

All the mountain roads, bridges, rooming houses and even mines broke apart on Four Mile Creek, Boulder Creek, Jim Creek, Left Hand Creek and the St. Vrain. Buildings washed away at Sunset, Jamestown, Crisman and Ballarat. Jamestown's church floated downstream with its bell ringing. The 2-year-old boom town of Copper Rock was washed off the map. The raging waters destroyed the road at Estes Park and a section of Lyons.

The flood roared down Boulder Creek into town, first wiping out the railroad bridge at Fourth Street then the bridges on Sixth, Ninth, 12th and 17th streets — each piling up on the other in a maelstrom of boulders, buildings, railroad tracks and trees. Witnesses recalled the terrifying sound of the rock- and wreckage-filled water.

"From the Boulder Hotel to University Hill was one vast lake with here and there a small patch of an island," read the *Camera*. After the waters calmed, one resident caught a 7-inch trout on Water Street (now Canyon Boulevard).

For five days, Boulder was cut off from the outside world, and residents on one side of the creek couldn't get to the other side. CU commencement was postponed, and the first mail arrived after five days with news of flooding all over the Front Range. Afterward, miners were out of work because of flooded mines. Amazingly, no one was killed in the flood, and no crimes were committed except the ransacking of someone's trunk. Boulder cleaned up and rebuilt.

Chautauqua photographer. Chautauqua had a full and varied program, from music and art to political and ethical discussion groups and well-known speakers and performers such as William Jennings Bryan and John Philip Sousa. Operas, magic shows, military tactics, lace making, baby shows, food booths, fish hatchery exhibits, photo contests, children's races and gypsy camps were but a few of the offerings. Physical health and exercise were emphasized from the start, and the Chautauqua Climbers Club made annual hikes to local landmarks and the higher mountains. Boulder druggist Eben Fine, one of Chautauqua's regular climbers, literally stumbled upon the discovery of Arapaho Glacier in 1900 when he nearly fell into one of its crevasses.

The Switzerland Trail railroad was a popular excursion for Chautauquans, who would ride into the mountains for a picnic and snowball fight. The more adventurous rented handcars and pumped their own way up for a day's outing.

Transportation to and from Chautauqua was difficult, so for the camp's second season, 1899, the city inaugurated its first electric streetcar, which for a nickel "sped" visitors from downtown to Chautauqua gate at 15 miles per hour. A few years later a line was put in to the sanatorium, and others followed.

The railroad train brought more tourists to Eldorado Springs, south of Boulder, where a popular resort developed around the area's thermal springs. It attracted such rich or famous — or those soon to be — as young Dwight and Mamie Eisenhower (who honeymooned there), young musician Glenn Miller (a CU student), actress Mary Pickford and her husband, actor Douglas Fairbanks Sr. (a Jamestown native), writer Damon Runyon, fighter Jack Dempsey and gossip columnist Walter Winchell. From 1907 to 1948, Ivy Baldwin performed his famous high-wire walk 600 feet across the canyon on a steel cable averaging 582 feet high. He made his last trip at age 82.

More Parks and City Planning

Chautauqua began Boulder's golden age of land and park acquisition. The day after Chautauqua opened, the city bought the eastern slope of Flagstaff Mountain from the U.S. Government. Shortly after, the city purchased another 1,800 acres of Flagstaff Mountain west to Four Mile Creek and from Sunshine Canyon south to South Boulder Creek.

The Boulder Women's Club planted trees in town, and in 1907 a parks board became an official city department. Next, the city slowly acquired the land along Boulder Creek from the Colorado and Southern Railway. At the time, the parks board wanted to have a park along Boulder Creek stretching from the mouth of Boulder Canyon to the eastern edge of town. Central Park land was acquired in 1906 and, steadily, more lots and parcels from the railroad.

Citizens gave gifts of land. Dr. and Mrs. William J. Baird donated 160 acres of their Gregory Canyon holdings in 1911. Hanna Barker and other citizens gave parcels of land. Boulder bought Arapaho Glacier after a battle with U.S. Park Service, which wanted to add it to Rocky Mountain National Park.

A City Vision

By 1908, Boulder's population was 10,000, and the Boulder City Improvement Association hired Frederick Law Olmsted Jr., Harvard-educated like his father in the new field of landscape architecture. Olmsted Sr. had designed New York City's Central Park. The city asked Olmsted how he thought the city could be improved "to help make it increasingly convenient, agreeable and generally satisfactory as a place in which to live and work?"

Olmsted said Boulder should not arrange itself for the benefit of the tourists, "who hastily pass through . . . and often conducting themselves so as to interfere seriously with the com-

Welcome

Boulder is a beautiful foothills community of about 95,000 people and is the largest city in Boulder County, at approximately 28 square miles in size. Boulder has over 31,000 acres of land dedicated exclusively as open space. The city offers outstanding libraries, parks, recreation centers, hiking trails, cultural events and human services. Boulder is also the proud home of the University of Colorado's flagship campus of nearly 25,000 students.

The secret ingredient to Boulder's majesty is its people. The citizens of Boulder are committed to a high quality of life that celebrates our environment, our distinctiveness, and our history.

NJOY BOULDER ❀ PRESERVE BOULDER

B•O•U•L•D•E•R FYI

Free 24-Hour Information About City Of Boulder Programs And Services

4•4•1•4•0•6•0

Your One Call To City Hall!

Look for **Boulder FYI** directories at Recreation Centers, Senior Centers and City of Boulder offices, and also in the Boulder US West Phone Book.

CITY OF BOULDER NEIGHBORHOOD LIAISON

The Neighborhood liaison Office works with groups of neighbors to create a community atmoshere in Boulder's neighborhoods and helps people build good relationships on their blocks.

The Neighborhood Liason Office prints newsletters and fliers; helps with meeting scheduling and space; provides leadership an communication training; produces The Boulder Neighborhood Handbook and a regular newsletter Supports the Conference of Neighborhoods and regular community dialogues and coming in 1997 Neighborhood Minigrants and the Boulder Blocks Fund.

For more information, please call
MOLLY DESSONVILLE • P.O. BOX 719 • BOULDER, CO 80306 • 303/441-30

DOWNTOWN *Boulder*

Traditionally when you think of a mall, you think of shopping. Although the Downtown Boulder Mall offers some of the best shopping in Colorado, people head downtown for a variety of activities. Satisfy your palate while dining at one of the many fine restaurants or have a hot dog from one of the Mall vending carts. Stop and watch street performers or just grab a spot on a bench and watch the people go by. When you come, bring the kids. There's lots for them, too.

SHOPPING
DINING
ENTERTAINMENT
AND FUN FOR
EVERYONE

Downtown Boulder is home to Boulder's best special events–

Creek Festival in May,
ArtFair in July,
Fall Festival in September,
Lights of December Parade in December,
plus a host of others.

UNIVERSITY HILL

Boulder's University Hill offers an ecclectic mix of businesses and residences, set in one of Boulder's most historic areas. Conveniently located adjacent to the University of Colorado campus, visitors to the Hill are only a short walk or bus ride away from many of the city's premier events, attractions, and activity areas. Whether for shopping, dining, or just visiting, make the history and fun of University Hill part of your day.

BOULDER ·1906-19

BOULDER PARKS AND RECREATION

Three recreation centers • Mountain parks with 50 miles of hiking trails
A reservoir for swimming, boating, and fishing
Two outdoor and three indoor pools • Eighteen hole golf course
Recreational activities for all ages and abilities • 48 urban parks.

For more information call 413-7200
or visit our WEB site at BCN.Boulder.CO.US/Boulder/P-R.

HEALTHY FUN

CITY OF BOULDER
ENVIRONMENTAL AFFAIRS

THE CITY OF BOULDER HAS A LONG HISTORY OF WORKING TO PROTECT THE NATURAL ENVIRONMENT…

…through highly successful recycling and composting programs, a household hazardous waste collection center, energy conservation programs for your home, air quality protection programs, and pollution prevention for your business…

441-3090

ENJOY BOULDER

PRESERVE BOULDER

THE BOULDER PUBLIC LIBRARY... IT'S MORE THAN BOOKS!

Top: Buck Buckner and Gary McCrumb, Bou
Banjo Festival; Priscilla Cohan, Program Assist
Middle: Vicky Anderson and John Caw
Story Gleaner; Story Gleaner performar
Moyo Arts Ensem
Bottom: Boulder Banjo Festi

LIBRARY SPONSORED PROGRAMS ARE FREE

PROTECTING BOULDER'S RESOURCES

XERISCAPE ON CD-ROM

Plan your water-wise garden now using the new
Xeriscape CD-ROM, available on-line at the Main
Library and, for FREE check out at these video
stores: Video Station
            North Village Video
            Basemar Village Video

Call today for a FREE landscape consultation or a
Rebate Application.

**Water
Conservation**
City of Boulder
441-4081

Be a Part of the Water Pollution Solution!

STORM
WATER
QUALITY
City of Boulder

- Storm drains connect to creeks!
  Materials dumped in gutters or storm drains don't
  magically disappear - contaminants such as motor
  oil and paints will end up in the creek nearest your
  home! Please don't pollute!

- Recycle used motor oil, antifreeze, gas, paint,
  varnish and battereies at the Household Hazardous
  Waste drop off center. Call 441-4800.

Photo: Daily Camera

The Boulder Museum of History houses a turn-of-the-century kitchen.

fort and welfare . . . of the permanent residents." Olmsted was suspicious of developers, saying they were usually from out of town. He said that dirty industry only denigrates a community, and to keep it out of Boulder.

On parks, he said, "As with the food we eat and the air we breathe, so the sights habitually before our eyes play an immense part of determining whether we feel cheerful, efficient and fit for life, or the contrary." He was concerned with the "mental and nervous condition of the people." Order was the goal, but "We aim at Order and hope for Beauty," he said.

He envisioned Boulder as a city of homes surrounded by small farms and gardens and advised preserving that feeling of "coziness and quiet attractiveness." He recommended underground wiring and making the Boulder Creek floodplain into a park — "the cheapest way of handling the flood problem." He said the sign of civilized society was the effectiveness of "police" powers to ensure good land use, and he recommended the city manager form of government. Boulderites liked what Olmsted said and, to a large extent, followed his advice.

Slow Growth, Sobering Legislation, War and Depression

Apparently taking Olmsted's advice to heart, Boulder became notable for its lack of industry except for the necessities: sawmills, lumberyards, blacksmith shops, brickyards, flour mills, a brewing company and a foundry. Before World War I, Boulder's biggest industry was Western Cutlery and Manufacturing Company. The CU student population had grown to 6,000, and small businesses began opening in the area around the university known as "The Hill."

By 1908, Boulder's population was 10,000, including enough teetotalers to outlaw liquor 13 years before Prohibition. Boulder remained "dry" from 1907 until 1967. During that period "liquor islands" grew up outside the city limits, where people could purchase package goods. (Not until 1969 did it become legal to serve liquor in a public establishment; the Catacombs Bar in the Hotel Boulderado was the first to do so.)

Then came World War I in 1917 and, on its heels, the Great Depression in 1929, with not much momentum in Boulder or elsewhere. During the 1930s the Civilian Conservation Corps built and improved trails, made fire lanes in mountain parks, pulled out diseased trees and rebuilt Flagstaff Road. They built the Sunrise Amphitheater on Flagstaff, a lodge on Green Mountain and a rock garden at Chautauqua.

The Works Progress Administration built the Mary Rippon Outdoor Theater at the university, a golf course at Flatirons Country Club and other buildings around town.

Small-town America and the Fabulous '50s

To try to raise Depression-weary spirits, the Boulder Pow Wow was begun on August 1, 1934, to celebrate Colorado's statehood day with a rodeo and various contests, including pie-eating and greased-pole climbing. Ladies had rolling-pin and slipper-throwing contests and needle-threading relays. Men tested their strength and skills at hay-pitching, hog-calling and hard-rock drilling.

In 1937 Boulder High was dedicated, and its "modern" nude sculptures entitled "Strength and Wisdom" caused a brief but heated controversy. The stunted, muscular figures were called everything from "powerful and effective" to "wads of chewing gum," but were finally accepted as harmless and have since been nicknamed Minnie and Jake.

By 1945, Boulder was beginning to wake up after the Depression and War. During World War II, 4,077 Boulderites had gone to war and 77 were killed. In 1946, 340 parking meters were installed downtown, and a group of young CU graduates founded Arapahoe Chemicals (bought by Syntex in 1965). Chicago-based Esquire magazine moved its subscription operations to Boulder in 1949, the first Eastern business to do so. In 1950 the National Bureau of Standards chose Boulder

as its main base after considering 26 cities. Boulder's citizens voted to buy 217 acres of land for the bureau and gave it to the United States. Fifteen years later, NBS was a major employer, contributing 10 percent to Boulder's income. Initially at an isolated site south of town, NBS was soon surrounded by small ranch houses in a regular suburbia.

The Boulder-Denver Turnpike (U.S. Highway 36) opened in 1952 and was the nation's first toll road to pay for itself — 13 years ahead of schedule in 1967.

CU's enrollment increased after World War II as returning military personnel took advantage of the GI Bill. In 1947, someone named "Joe" autographed the First Flatiron and began a series of Flatiron-painting pranks, usually by university students painting a giant "C" or "CU" on the First and Third Flatirons. (Look closely at the Third Flatiron and you can still see a faint, slightly orange CU.)

In 1948, an 850-foot ski tow ran up Chautauqua but operated only a few seasons due to poor snow.

The Atomic Energy Commission chose an area south of Boulder to install its secret weapons plant, Rocky Flats, in 1951 — despite many misgivings of area residents.

In 1955, "Tommy" Thompson of Thompson Engineering Co. — builder of the short-lived Chautauqua ski lift — began building respirators for polio victims. Soon after, Automation Industries moved to town. That same year, Beech Aircraft bought 1,500 acres north of town and started its Aerospace Division there.

The chamber of commerce bought 18 acres east of town for Boulder Industrial Park, and Ball Brothers Research Corp. became the major tenant starting in 1957. The Muncie, Indiana, canning-jar company expanded into aerospace technology in Boulder.

With all the new enterprise, Boulder's population shot up in the 1950s, and water became a concern. The population in 1950 was 19,999; by 1960 it was 66,870. In 1959 the Blue Line was established as the first project of the newly formed PLAN-Boulder, an early group of environmentally concerned citizens who wanted to preserve Boulder's unique natural assets. An imaginary boundary line was drawn along the mountain backdrop at an average of 5,750 feet, above which no city water service would be supplied.

The Early 1960s

Young solar physicist Walter Orr Roberts began manning the Harvard-run High Altitude Observatory in Climax, Colorado, (near Leadville) in 1940. In 1960 Roberts was offered the directorship of a new National Center for Atmospheric Research (NCAR), and he recommended Boulder as the site. The state donated 530 acres of mesa land south of town for the new laboratory, which was designed by noted architect I.M. Pei. Though controversial — an exception was made to the new Blue Line ruling to give NCAR water — NCAR was to become a jewel in Boulder's crown.

The U.S. Department of Commerce established its Environmental Sciences Service Administration (ESSA) in Boulder in 1966. ESSA became part of the National Oceanic and Atmospheric Administration (NOAA) in 1970.

Shopping centers began springing up around town, and the Crossroads Shopping Center was begun in 1963 outside the city limits with Texas money.

Boulder's water supplies were increased in 1964 and spurred a controlled-growth plan along several "spokes" radiating outward from the city, one east on Arapahoe, one northeast along the Diagonal Highway and one south. In 1969, there was a big controversy over fluoridation of water, a bond issue for a new library and an amendment for liquor-by-the-drink. All three passed. Though citizens rejected a $500,000 parks bond that same year, two years later they passed a $1 million bond to build the north and south recreation centers.

Historically, all sides agreed on greenbelt acquisition — both liberals and conservatives — and wanted to continue to buy land in the mountains and plains to "belt" the city with undeveloped land. To stop the building of a luxury hotel atop Enchanted Mesa, citizens approved the purchase of 155 acres of that land for $105,000. In 1967 a 1 percent sales tax was passed; 60 percent of revenue to go for street improvements, 40 percent for future purchase of greenbelt lands.

The Turbulent Late '60s and Early '70s

The late '60s brought the hippies, the "transient problem" and general turmoil. The first gentle flower children camped out in Central Park, which had to be closed because it became a health hazard. Later came the more militant anarchists, whose bombs exploded in the Hall of Justice Building, United Bank and Flatirons Elementary School. The Board of Education's auditorium was firebombed. Fortunately, no one was killed in these incidents. An anti-Vietnam War riot in 1971 on University Hill left stores looted and windows broken. Police teargassed the mob and arrested 40 people. In 1972, 3,000 peaceful anti-war demonstrators barricaded the Boulder Turnpike at the Baseline interchange to protest President Nixon's blockade of North Vietnam and the mining of Haiphong Harbor. In 1974, six activists in the Chicano movement were killed in two separate bomb explosions in cars. The explosions were believed by police to be accidental and meant for some other target.

More quietly, the first gay human rights ordinance law was passed by city council in 1973, but when it had its second reading some citizens objected vociferously. New county clerk and recorder Clela Rorex attained notoriety after issuing licenses for several same-sex marriages. To express his opinion, one citizen appeared with his horse, Dolly, saying, "If a boy can marry a boy, and a girl can marry a girl, why can't a lonesome old cowboy get hitched to his favorite saddle mare?" He was refused because the horse was under age. Ultimately, same-sex marriage licenses were declared illegal in 1975 by the state attorney general.

PLAN-Boulder helped write part of Boulder's first Comprehensive Plan in 1970. In 1971 a height-limit ordinance was passed so, in the wave of new construction, residents could keep their mountain views. New buildings could not exceed a height of 55 feet — the height of most mature trees. Voters that year also chose a growth-control study plan to prevent the kind of rapid growth that had occurred in the 1950s.

The "New Wave" Plus Growth and Limitations in the '70s and '80s

The late '70s saw calmer times but also a huge influx of newcomers, particularly from the Northeast, as many young adults tired of life in the drab, polluted, politically corrupt and overcrowded big cities. Most were well-educated and hopeful of finding jobs in one of Boulder's clean industries. Many had visited the area during vacations and were delighted (or requested) to be transferred here by IBM, Ball Brothers or Storage Technology. Many were single parents starting new lives and seeking gold of another sort: good schools and neighborhoods for their children and a happy life.

By word-of-mouth and the "underground" communications network, Boulder had also become known nationwide to former hippies, neo-Buddhists, bicyclists, runners, the urban disenchanted, spiritual seekers, health food converts and just about every New Age religion and movement participant as a great place to live. And it's no wonder. Boulderite Frank Shorter became the first American ever to win Olympic gold and silver in the marathon (1972 and 1976); Celestial Seasonings founder Mo Siegel began the international Red Zinger Bicycle Classic; Tibetan Buddhist leader Chögyam Trungpa Rinpoche founded the Naropa Institute in 1974; and the Boulder School of Massage Therapy opened its doors in 1976.

Meanwhile . . . fearful of urban sprawl and uncontrolled shopping center construction, PLAN-Boulder campaigned in the late '70s for preservation of open space throughout the county. In 1976, almost $2 million was spent to complete Boulder's downtown pedestrian mall on Pearl Street to draw people back into the city's center. In 1977, the Danish Plan — originated by city councilman Paul Danish — was approved to limit residential growth to 2 percent. To discourage the building of a megamall in Louisville (which Danish described as an "environmental pig"), City Council approved a controversial expansion of Crossroads Shopping Mall (now in the Boulder city limits) in 1979.

When a California-based computer software company, System Development Corporation,

---

The Midnight Ride of Capt. David Nichols

A little-known episode in the founding of the University of Colorado became one that sealed Boulder's fate as the chosen site. In 1874 various cities and communities in Colorado were vying for the university, and the situation developed into a bitter rivalry with political intrigues. But the state Territorial House had not yet even passed an appropriation bill for the university, much less decided where it would be.

An 1872 bill for an act appropriating money for a university in Colorado had been defeated. Mountain mining districts opposed the bill saying that Colorado had no use for a university. Republican members of the legislature had agreed in caucus to vote against any but the most necessary appropriations.

Capt. David Nichols of Boulder had been elected Speaker of the Territorial House and put a bill for the university before the legislature again. He got the assembly to approve a bill that said the territory would give $15,000 toward a university on the condition that Boulder contribute an equal amount. In those days $15,000 was a lot of money, and the legislature probably thought that Boulder would be hard put to come up with it. If the bill were tabled again, there would be no telling what would happen to the university.

Nichols jumped on his horse at 6 PM that rainy late-January night and rode from Denver to Boulder, arriving around 11 PM. He banged on the door until he woke up Capt. Frank Tyler, a prominent Boulder citizen, who promised Nichols he would personally take responsibility for raising the funds. Nichols then visited other prominent citizens discussing the situation. Nichols stopped only long enough to change horses, then rode the five hours back to Denver. At 10 AM the next morning he addressed the legislature and announced that he had visited Boulder and obtained promises for the funds.

With a stronger assurance of monetary backing than the other cities, Boulder got the go-ahead for the university with the passage of the new appropriation bill.

Photo: L.P. Bass

Capt. David Nichols secured Boulder as the site of the state university. Also shown is a promissory note from a prominent Boulder citizen as backing for the proposed University of Colorado.

announced its plans in 1980 to locate on county land designated as open space by the Boulder Valley Comprehensive Plan, city officials nixed it. The company then approached other towns in Boulder County, further infuriating some council members. City Council ultimately decided to buy the land to put the issue on hold until Boulder residents could vote on it. In the meantime, discouraged by the strong anti-development sentiment, SDC packed up their plans and left Boulder County.

A furious public art debate broke out in 1983 when a New York sculptor, Andrea Blum, was chosen to design an outdoor sculpture at Ninth Street and Canyon Boulevard. Blum's stark, urban-styled white concrete design reminded many citizens of a subway station or public restroom, and it was ultimately rejected as being inappropriate for Boulder's site.

During the 1980s some of Boulder County's plentiful high-tech industries began to falter. Louisville-based Storage Technology Corporation laid off 1,300 people in October 1984, the largest single-day cutback in county history. By the end of the year it had laid off another 1,290 employees and filed for reorganization under federal bankruptcy law.

The Boulder Creek Path, which runs from Eben Fine Park to 55th Street, was completed in 1987.

After bitter debate in 1988, Boulder voters approved expansion of Boulder's public library at its current site.

Federal agents raided Rocky Flats nuclear weapons plant (8 miles south of Boulder) in 1989 and brought health and safety questions about the plant to local and national attention.

The largest fire ever in the county burned 2,300 acres and destroyed 44 homes in July 1989 on Sugarloaf Mountain.

Shutdowns, The 1990s

By 1991, the beginning of the end had come for Rocky Flats. The U.S. Energy Secretary shut down 1,000 jobs at the plant in non-radioactive work and revealed plans to move the whole operation to Kansas City. Neighbors of the National Institute of Standards and Technology (NIST, formerly called the Bureau of Standards) were upset with the government facility's plans to expand on 205 acres of open land.

In 1992, a Colorado Springs-based group, Colorado for Family Values, promoted a constitutional amendment that would prohibit state or local governments from passing laws or policies that would allow a claim of discrimination based on homosexual orientation. Colorado voters passed the amendment, which was overwhelmingly defeated in Boulder. Within days of the election, Boulder, Denver, Aspen,

Good Books on Colorado Geology, History and Reference

Geology:
Prairie Peak and Plateau by John and Halka Chronic;
Roadside Geology of Colorado by Halka Chronic.

History and Good Reading:
A Look at Boulder: From Settlement to City by Phyllis Smith;
Stampede to Timberline by Muriel Sibell Wolle (stories and legends of Colorado's gold camps);
A Lady's Life in the Rocky Mountains by Isabella Bird.

Other References:
The Coloradans by Robert Athern;
Glory Colorado! by William Davis (University of Colorado history, 1853-1963);
Our Own Generation by Ron James (CU-Boulder history, 1963-1976);
Colorado Handbook by Stephen Metzger;
The Colorado Guide by Bruce Caughey and Dean Winstanley;
Colorado: Off the Beaten Path by Curtis Casewit.

the Boulder Valley School District and individuals including tennis star Martina Navratilova filed a lawsuit challenging the constitutionality of the amendment. Passage of Amendment 2 initiated a nationwide boycott of Colorado. CU-Boulder's football coach Bill McCartney created a statewide furor when he called homosexuality an "abomination of almighty God." McCartney served on the advisory board of Colorado for Family Values and was censured by CU-Boulder's president, Judith Albino, for using his position as coach for espousing negative views of homosexuality. McCartney left his coaching position at the end of the 1994 football season. Albino stepped down herself a year later.

Rocky Flats operators pleaded guilty to 10 environmental crimes after more than two years' investigation by a grand jury, and the site's official work was finished in mid-1992. The building and site are being decontaminated, and officials are still trying to figure out what to do with it all — plus 14.2 tons of plutonium.

Another building moratorium stunned developers in February 1993 when the Boulder City Council decided it needed time to develop the Integrated Planning Project to determine "what's best for what's left" of developable land in Boulder. County commissioners also initiated a moratorium on mountain building. In September of that year the City Council put a hold on developing large parcels — the so-called last 10 percent of developable land — establishing a population growth cap of 2 percent a year by imposing a limit on the number of building permits issued.

Celestial Seasonings stock sold like hot cakes when 2.1 million shares went on the block in July 1994. Local investors complained that all the shares were snatched up by large investors before locals had a chance.

Boulder County voters in the November 1993 election passed a 0.25 percent sales and use tax to buy open space, which could amount to as much as $90 million in the next 16 years. The county purchased 5,000 acres in the Foothills between Left Hand Canyon and Lyons — known as the Heil Ranch.

In mid-December 1993, a Denver district judge ruled the controversial Amendment 2 unconstitutional, and in 1996 the Supreme Court did the same.

The expansion of NIST was finally approved after three years of controversy and debate.

Schwinn Cycling and Fitness moved to Boulder hoping "to update its stodgy image with a Boulder address and new attitude," according to the *Daily Camera*. Warren Miller Entertainment, a California ski- and sports-movie maker, also put down roots in Boulder — the company already shoots most of its ski footage in Colorado. Two new subsidiaries of the IBM Corp. set up shop. Neodata, the world's largest magazine subscription fulfillment service (located in Boulder since 1963), moved its corporate headquarters from Dallas to Louisville (Boulder County) in 1993. Other newcomers are listed in this book's chapter on Boulder Business.

In late 1995, Boulder voters passed an anti-smoking ordinance, making national headlines and creating a local uproar. Voters chose their health over private property rights in the new law, which bans smoking in all indoor public places except dwellings, sites of private social functions and tobacco stores. Some bars and restaurants have built fully enclosed, separately ventilated rooms for smokers. The Boulder Dinner Theatre had to get special dispensation so an actor could light up on stage, as called for in a play. The same year, scientists at the University of Colorado and National Institute of Standards and Technology created a form of matter never before seen but predicted by Albert Einstein

70 years ago. Called a superatom, the matter was created by cooling rubidium atoms to within a fraction of a degree above absolute zero, where theoretically all atomic motion ceases. The scientists created the coldest temperature on earth — and possibly the universe — for the experiment. Practical applications are not yet clear.

Its destiny dictated by geology — gold, silver and other minerals — Boulder still attracts contemporary settlers because of its spectacular mountain setting. Though settled by miners, farmers and fortune seekers, Boulder somehow identified the importance of education, environmental preservation and quality of life from its earliest days. Holding onto these values, the city has nurtured a major university, internationally known research centers, clean industries and an interesting assortment of citizens who have come from around the country and world.

Boulder has seen many changes from its rustic and humble beginnings, but then again, the more things change, the more they remain the same.

Boulder leaders today continue to deal with the same issues as the town's founders: dog control, water, the price of land and housing, what to do with all those newcomers "looking for gold." But now the gold has become Boulder's special quality of life.

Among 14 comparable cities, Boulder ranks No. 1 in people who walk to work, work at home and drive with more than one person in the car.

Boulder
Getting Around

Before you think about where you're going, it's good to know where you are. Boulder is about 25 miles northwest of Denver, via **I-25** and **U.S. 36**. The No. 1 rule of thumb to help newcomers orient themselves in Boulder is: The mountains are to the west. The core of the city is laid out in a traditional, logical grid. Most of the north/south streets are numbered, starting with Third Street on the west side of town then going beyond 75th Street as you head east. **Broadway** is a major north-south thoroughfare on a slight diagonal, and **Folsom Street** is a significant north-south street from the University of Colorado campus to North Boulder. In addition to the city streets and U.S. 36, which becomes 28th Street through Boulder, **Foothills Parkway** is a divided roadway, but with some traffic lights at major intersections, connecting U.S. 36 and the Longmont Diagonal (Colo. Highway 119). It is a way to bypass Boulder, though we wonder why anyone would wish to bypass our wonderful city.

Baseline Road is a significant east-west route, not just to Boulderites, but also to cartographers, for it marks the 40th parallel on maps of the earth. If you made a beeline down this road, after a few hundred miles you'd hit the boundary between Kansas and Nebraska. The major east-west cross-streets are **Table Mesa Road-South Boulder Road** and Baseline Road in the southern part of the city; **Arapahoe Avenue** in central Boulder — and, to an extent, **Canyon Boulevard**, a short but important major street; and the **Alpine Street-Valmont Road** routing and **Iris Avenue** in the northern part of the city.

North Boulder's alphabetical "tree streets" — Alpine, Balsam, Cedar and so on — are easy to find and remember. Making your way through cul-de-sac-filled subdivisions, however, requires good directions. Broadway and

28th Street converge in North Boulder, again becoming U.S. 36 toward Lyons.

You'll find basic orientation maps in the front of this book, and more detailed street maps are in local phone books. A variety of easier-to-tote maps is available from **GO Boulder**, 441-4260, at 11th and Spruce streets in the parking garage on floor 2R, including free pocket-size maps for streets, bus and bicycle routes. And, remember, it never hurts to ask for directions.

More than most cities, Boulder offers and encourages use of alternative modes of transportation to the car and has a city agency, GO Boulder, to promote, set and achieve such goals. Pay close attention to alternative modes. In 1992, nearly 26 percent of work-related trips within Boulder were made by busing, biking or walking. Among 14 comparable cities, Boulder ranks No. 1 in people who walk to work, work at home and drive with more than one person in the car. It ranks second among those who bike. (GO Boulder says Davis, California, probably ranks first, with Boulder a very close second.) Alternative modes can become one of your favorite things about Boulder.

Transportation Issues in Boulder

If you just arrived from a congested metropolitan area on either coast, Boulder might not seem to have much traffic, but if you've been in town a while, you'll sure notice the change in just a few years. As you were inching toward the third cycle of the stoplight at 28th Street and Arapahoe Avenue, you probably were aware of Boulder's traffic. Two hundred thousand cars flow through the city itself, and daily, people drive 2.2 million miles in this little valley. That's loads of cars, especially at a higher altitude prone to air pollution. It's also unsettling to people who don't like the way roads and parking lots eat up land and create canyons clogged with vehicles and the din and exhaust fumes they create.

Boulder has given itself a mandate to reduce the car and traffic problem while enhancing our ability to get around. In a classic example of Boulder's foresight and compulsive worrying about quality-of-life issues before they become crises, the city developed its first Transportation Master Plan in 1989, when — believe it or not — the city was still suffering under a regional recession and few people were worrying about too many commuters, too many jobs or too many homes. GO Boulder tracks traffic patterns, keeps statistics, creates charts and, most important, tries to use these figures to solve the congestion conundrum. Periodic studies confirm that what most people like about downtown Boulder is its atmosphere and pedestrian orientation, and what most people don't like about Boulder is the parking dilemma. The latest version of the Transportation Master Plan, designed to take Boulder through the year 2020, includes a whopping $1 billion worth of projects (including more than $250 million for improved bus service and $30 million for better bike paths), proving that Boulder does take its traffic and growth issues seriously and is willing to back it up with big bucks.

Individuals do their bit too. Some people dream about or design supercars, which would be quieter and safer than current cars and get more than 150 miles to the gallon. Others want better mass transit, including light rail and improved bus service. A few of them serve on the city's Transportation Advisory Board, which studies the issues in depth and makes informed proposals to the city. Planners strive for small-scale neighborhood centers so people don't have to drive as far to reach nec-

FYI

Unless otherwise noted, the area code for all phone numbers in this guide is 303.

essary services. And many people take public transportation whenever possible or get around town on bicycles or on foot whenever they can. A few even put their commitment into action by living carless.

Driving To Boulder

To drive to Boulder from Denver, take I-25 north to U.S. Highway 36 west. The last hill is Davidson Mesa, where you'll get a view or town and you'll find a visitors center kiosk.

If you ask for directions and someone says "Foothills," clarify whether they mean **Foothills Highway** (U.S. Highway 36), which starts as 28th Street and leads to Estes Park, or **Foothills Parkway** (Colo. Highway 157), which links U.S. 36 with Colo. Highway 119 and leads to Longmont.

If you are driving to Boulder from the ski areas on I-70, you have two options. The first is to take the Morrison/Golden exit (Exit 259) to U.S. Highway 40. Go north toward U.S. Highway 6, left on U.S. 6 then head north on Colo. Highway 93 to Boulder. The second, and to us preferable, option is the Central City/Golden exit (Exit 244). Follow U.S. 6 east for about 15 miles through beautiful Clear Creek Canyon. At the second traffic light, just on the outskirts of Golden, turn left (north) on Colo. Highway 93, which becomes Broadway in Boulder.

Car Rentals

The overwhelming majority of fly-in visitors to Boulder rent cars at Denver International Airport or from agencies near the old Stapleton Airport and drive to Boulder, but rental cars are also available in town. Locals whose own vehicles are undergoing major repairs, business travelers in the area for several days but only requiring a car for part of the time, CU-Boulder students (25 and older

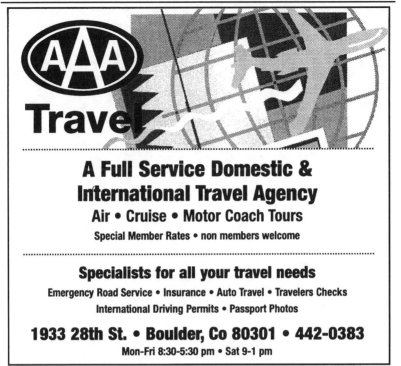
to rent) or visiting academicians and others might wish to rent a car only for the time when they really need one.

The Yellow Pages list local and out-of-town agencies under Automobile Renting. Choices include such national firms as **Hertz**, 443-3520; **Avis**, 499-1136; **National**, 442-5110; and **Budget**, 341-2277. Smaller regional and local companies abound too.

Getting Around Boulder by Car

Plans and dreams aside, the majority of Boulder residents still are dependent on their cars, even if they secretly wish there were a better way. Don't feel guilty if your car's packed with visiting sightseers or your kids' soccer teammates; you're being a carpool! But if you're all alone, at least try to consolidate your errands so you drive less often.

Boulder has many designated bike lanes, but where there is none, bicyclists may oc-

cupy a lane of traffic, just like cars. Pedestrians at crosswalks have the right-of-way, which means you are supposed to stop when you see someone waiting to cross the street; stop so they can.

Except where posted or where there is a red-arrow traffic light, right turns on red are permitted. Wherever the streets are wide enough to make it feasible, which means most arterials, left-turn lanes have been designated at many intersections. As anyplace else when you're turning left at a green light, pull into the intersection and wait for a gap. Once you are in the intersection, it is still legal to turn on yellow. If you try zip into an intersection after the light turns red, however, you are asking for a stiff ticket, to say nothing of perhaps causing a crash.

Rush Hour

Most cities get only two rush periods. Boulder has three. Morning rush spans 7 to 9 AM. Because many of the new commercial and business parks are lacking in restaurants, workers often drive somewhere for lunch, creating a noon mini-rush that starts around 11 AM and lasts until 2 PM. Traffic really swells between 4 and 7 PM. A fourth rush sometimes happens later, depending on how many people are out on the town for any CU-Boulder home football game, which jams streets around campus when cars arrive and when they try to leave. If you hate traffic, make your trips outside these most popular times, or (hint-hint) consider alternative modes (see this chapter's subsequent "Alternative Modes of Transportation" section).

Weather Hazards

Boulder's normally benign climate often lulls us into thinking that the driving, like the living, is easy. But meteorological aberrations can be hazardous. Summer hailstorms can pock windshields, pare visibility and temporarily cause slippery road surfaces. Snowstorms often start with drizzling rain that freezes before the snow falls, and that snow often undergoes several days of melt-to-slush, freeze-to-ice cycles before melting and evaporating completely. Hilly streets and intersections are generally sanded rather than treated with chemicals. Highways and arterials are plowed, but snow on most residential streets is left for nature to take care of. Several years ago, a child walking to an elementary school was killed by a car that had stopped at a red light but was hit from behind by a driver who skidded on the ice. Good snow tires are a must for Colorado winters.

If you drive a camper, a sport-utility vehicle or are moving your belongings into town in a rental truck, you'll want to pay attention to high-wind warnings. Colo. Highway 93 between Boulder and Golden is especially vulnerable to wicked crosswinds and is occasionally closed because of them. Mountain driving can be pleasurable or terrifying, depending on individual drivers' skill and confidence. Shifting into a lower gear helps save wear and tear on the engine while ascending and on the brakes while going downhill.

Accidents

As elsewhere, serious accidents demand a 911 call to dispatch emergency police, ambulance and even fire units. The Boulder Police's accident investigation unit deals with non-injury-producing accidents. For information, call the department's general information line, 441-3300. Vehicle insurance is mandatory in the state of Colorado, with current minimum required coverage of $25,000 for bodily injury, $50,000 per accident and $15,000 property damage. Motorists who leave the scene of an accident without exchanging license, registration and insurance information may have their driver's licenses suspended. (There are other offenses that can result in loss of license too, including driving while intoxicated, reckless driving and possession of certain firearms.)

Emergency Services

You only need to use AAA once to make it pay off. **AAA Colorado**, 442-0383, is best known for its emergency road services, such as changing a flat tire, refueling an empty gas tank, pulling vehicles out of snow drifts or mud or towing a broken-down vehicle to a repair center. Because of the distances involved, anyone who plays in the mountains is probably wise to sign up for AAA Plus, offering towing services from as far as 250 miles from home. In addition to road services, AAA maintains a walk-in center at 1933 28th Street (upstairs from Blockbuster Video), with a travel agency, traveler's check sales, discount luggage, book sales and routing assistance. Many of the services are available for nonmembers as well as members. In addition, AAA sells insurance and provides a locator service for good deals on new cars, bail bonds (not than any Insider would need that!) and other services.

INSIDERS' TIP

Boulder County is at the threshold of 200,000 registered vehicles. In 1995, 198,416 were registered, up from 187,465 a decade earlier.

Parking

If Boulder accommodated every single driver who wanted a quick trip to a perfect parking space, we would need so many roads and parking spaces that little would remain for buildings, sidewalks, trees or flowers. On the other hand, for retail and restaurant businesses to remain viable, there must be reasonably convenient customer parking. Periodic studies confirm that what most people like about downtown Boulder is its atmosphere and pedestrian orientation; and what most people don't like about Boulder is the parking dilemma. Four downtown blocks of Pearl Street are pedestrians-only, so there's obviously no parking there, and meters limit parking on adjacent commercial streets. Some surrounding residential neighborhoods have or will soon have permit parking systems in place to discourage day-long parkers. Two-hour nonresident parking is permitted.

Boulder maintains several staffed parking garages and metered surface lots, which are in great demand. If you get a downtown job, you can get on a waiting list for reserved, long-term parking by checking with the city's Parking Services, 441-3202.

In addition to downtown, another problematic parking area is The Hill. The Hill's main retail and commercial streets are also metered, and a Uni-Hill residential parking permit system is also in place. CU-Boulder has its own Parking Services, 492-7384, for students, faculty and staff.

Pathways

Boulder has been ranked among America's most walkable cities by no less an authority than *Walking* magazine. It's also a wonderful city for runners, bikers, in-line skaters and wheelchair users. The most pleasing "roads" are the pedestrian and bicycle paths. They follow by streams. They go by parks where you can hear birds sing, and they pass pretty homes with kids playing or adults gardening. Many people along the way smile. The major non-motorized-vehicle thoroughfare is the **Boulder Creek Path** (see the Boulder Attractions and Boulder Parks and Recreation Centers chapters), which is primarily an east-west route.

Walking some of these pathways often is faster than driving. Try it with a friend. Eat at some lovely spot on the Pearl Street Mall, then plan to meet on the CU-Boulder campus. You start walking while your friend gets the car. As you head up Broadway look for a little sidewalk just up the hill from Arapahoe Avenue. You'll probably have time to stop at Andrews Arboretum, an area once occupied by train tracks. You can take this pleasant pathway to the university and enjoy the sights on your stroll. You'll get lung-filling exercise and might even have time to read a chapter in your book before your friend gets the car, drives up to the university, parks again and finally joins you.

The city is also home of the International Pedestrian Conference, whose topics include such cosmic issues as urban planning and design, congestion pricing, inter-modal advancements and air quality, and the annual GO Boulder Pedestrian Conference with sessions on such issues with a specific regional and local focus.

Bicycling

Boulder is one of America's best cycling cities. At this writing, the city boasts 85 miles of off-street bike paths, bike lanes on city streets and bike routes. The newest, which debuted in late 1996, is a Pine Street to Balsam Street extension of the 13th Street bike corridor. With the opening of two new underpasses in October, Boulder completed the last segments of a 10-mile loop, suitable for recreational cycling and commuting. Savvy locals know that errands-by-bike sometimes

---

INSIDERS' TIP

For an easy-to-carry, free pocket map of streets and pedestrian/bicycle paths, stop by the GO Boulder offices at 2018 11th Street, just off the Pearl Street Mall in the city's prettiest parking garage. Take the elevator up to 2R.

Photo: Daily Camera

If it's too snowy to drive or bike, some Boulder residents take to their skis.

go faster than errands-by-car. We're not talking about world-class bicyclists racing against clunker cars, either. In the annual "errand race," bicyclists include moms towing kids in bike trailers pedaling against trained delivery van drivers. Points are given for having a good, leisurely time. And the pedalers often arrive faster! The whole idea of the bicycle as transportation is promoted heavily by GO Boulder, especially during the annual Boulder Bike Week in late June.

Bike Week is a statewide program, but Boulder launches into it with more enthusiastic support and programs — and better results — than most communities muster. This major undertaking is designed both as an incentive and to showcase the benefits of the bicycle as transportation. In 1996, about 30 restaurants and bakeries — mostly in Boulder but also one each in Longmont, Louisville, Lafayette and Niwot — offered bicycle commuters free continental breakfasts from 6:30 or 7 to 9 AM. Volunteer mechanics from local bike shops were on hand at six stations around town for minor repairs and bike safety checks. At least one event was held each day, including Bike to Work Day, Bike to Ice Cream Day, Boulder Bikeways Tour, Bike to the Movies Day, Bike to Market Day, Bike to Books Day, Bike to Downtown Day, Ride & Work Your Trails Day, Senior Cyclists' Senior Ride, Bike to the Boulder Banjo Festival and Bike to Worship Weekend. Clinics from a Bike Safety for Kids to "Zen and the Art of Bicycle Maintenance" were offered. And of course, there were free gifts and prize drawings to launch the peak summer cycling season. Expect a bigger, better reprise every year. GO Boulder estimates that more than 4,000 Boulderites commute by bike.

Spokes for Folks is one great intention that has gone somewhat awry. In 1996, a fleet of more than 120 loaner bikes (up from 50 the year before) was launched to provide people with easy pedal power for errands around town. The donated bikes are fixed up by high-school students and painted a rather terrible shade of bright green so they can't possibly be mistaken for anything else. Under Spokes for Folks, people are supposed to pick up a bike, ride it and leave it for the next person. Within a few weeks of launch, some bikes were missing, some were found far out of town, some were trashed and some had even been appropriated by individuals for permanent use. A few beaters were left for their original intention. The long-term future of this idealistic program is questionable, but we still think the concept is great.

Alternative Modes of Transportation

For information about alternative modes of transportation, including pedestrian, bicycle and carpool options, call **GO Boulder**, 441-4260, a city agency whose name stands for "Great Options in Transportation." It offers easy-to-read maps of bus routes, bike paths and open-space trails. The pocket-size maps are free, and the larger full-scale ones are a good value at $2. Call GO Boulder or stop by its offices at 2018 11th Street, a block from the Pearl Street Mall in the city's prettiest parking garage. Take the elevator up to 2R — or use the stairs. GO Boulder's **Ride**

Arrangers, 447-2120, can also help you set up carpools and vanpools. Pool drivers can get special training and the option of using city vans.

To encourage bus use, participating businesses and the **Downtown Management Commission**, 441-4000, provide **ECO-Passes** so their employees can ride the bus free. So far more than 10,000 residents have ECO-Passes. One of the great perks is the guaranteed ride program, which can take people directly to their door at night. See the subsequent section for more details on bus service.

Buses, Limos and Taxis

The **Regional Transportation District**, also known as RTD, is the greater Denver metropolitan area's public transportation agency. RTD recorded-information lines are 299-6000, (800) 366-RIDE or 299-6034 (TDD).

RTD buses are promoted as "The Ride." The main bus station in Boulder, currently the hub of RTD's hub-and-spoke system, is at 14th and Walnut streets. Rides within Boulder cost 60¢ (exact change only), 15¢ for seniors 65 and older (off-peak hours) and 25¢ for disabled individuals with an RTD card; a 10-ride ticket book costs $4.75. Various monthly passes are also available at the bus station and at King Soopers and Safeway markets. Many Boulder businesses and even some neighborhoods provide ECO-Passes for unlimited RTD use. Boulder students can buy reduced-rate bus passes, and CU-Boulder students get RTD passes as part of the student activity fee. Seniors are eligible for discount passes too.

RTD buses on Boulder city routes operate every half-hour. Schedules and prices vary for intercity service to Broomfield, Denver, Golden, Lafayette, Longmont, Louisville, Nederland and Westminster. RTD also offers rush-hour express buses to the Denver Tech Center, hourly express buses to Denver International Airport, and special buses to the Eldora ski

area via Nederland. Buses for Colorado Rockies and Denver Broncos games depart from the main Boulder terminal and various Park-n-Ride lots for $4 round trip.

Many buses are equipped with wheelchair ramps, and many allow some bicycles on board. Call one of the RTD numbers for details on these amenities or how to reach your destination by bus. Tell the RTD operator where you need to be, when and from where you're starting. To use a bus regularly, pick up a schedule on a bus or downtown at the main Boulder terminal. If buses are new to you, you can even borrow an eight-minute video, *How to Ride the Bus*; call 447-2120.

The Hop, 441-4260, is a fantastic idea for unclogging travel without greatly inconveniencing people. It uses midsize buses operating frequently instead of infrequent runs by often-empty behemoths. The Hop's circuit route has 40 stops including Crossroads Mall, the University Hill shopping area near CU-Boulder and the Pearl Street Mall. Buses drive both clockwise and counterclockwise on the circuit. The Hop runs every 10 minutes Monday through Friday, 7 AM to 7 PM, and every 15 minutes Thursday and Friday, 7 to 10 PM, and Saturday, 9 AM to 7 PM. An additional CU-Pearl Street Mall Hop operates on a tighter loop Thursday through Saturday from 10:30 PM to 2:30 AM. The University of Colorado Student Union also sponsors **Night Hop**, which runs a CU-Pearl Street Mall loop Thursday through Saturday from 10:30 PM to 2:30 AM — free to CU students with ID and ECO-pass holders. Look for a purple and cream sign, with a logo rabbit, to hop on The Hop; a frog designates a Night Hop stop. The fare is 25¢, 15¢ for seniors or free for folks with a CU ID or any RTD pass. Some merchants also give out Hop tokens to their customers, good for a complimentary ride.

With the success of The Hop, a similar service to be called **The Skip** is slated for introduction in August 1997. The plan is for 22-passenger buses to operate every 10 minutes and every six minutes during the rush hour, running north-south on Broadway.

INSIDERS' TIP

Two-hundred thousand cars come and go from Boulder daily.

Other transportation companies go beyond the RTD network. **Charles Tour & Travel**, (970) 586-5151, runs year-round shuttle service between the Regal Harvest House, 1345 28th Street, and any Estes Park location. The ride lasts 45 minutes and costs $16 one-way and $30 round trip. Charles runs four shuttles a day and more frequently in summer and also serves Denver International Airport. Call ahead for a schedule and reservations.

The best way to the resorts is via **SkiXPress**, new weekend service to five ski areas within two hours of metro Denver. The service is being underwritten by the Colorado Department of Transportation and the ski areas. This leaves passengers with a tab of just $15 for round-trip transportation from Boulder (or Denver) to Copper Mountain, Loveland, Keystone, Vail and Winter Park on luxurious buses with reclining seats and restrooms — plus the ability to buy discounted lift tickets on board.

Boulder Yellow Cab, 442-2277, can pick up in Lafayette and Louisville as well as Boulder. Drivers charge around $1.20 per mile. There are no taxi stands, so call for service. **Cadillac Cabs**, 776-0496, serves Longmont, Niwot and Lyons. Rates are around $1.50 per mile.

For people with disabilities, life would be all the more challenging without wheelchair-lift-equipped, door-to-door, on-demand transportation service. More than 2,000 use **Boulder's Special Transit**, 447-2848, which offers low-cost rides to people with disabilities. Call well in advance for reservations and prices. **The LIFT**, 665-9085, is a Lafayette-based volunteer program for people who have trouble getting around. Call 24 hours ahead.

High-flying Airports

If you have a private plane, you can fly into one of the region's smaller general-aviation airports. Some also have air taxi services that you can book to fly you quickly to a town not on a regular commercial air route.

Boulder Municipal Airport, just east of town, is — like most airports in Colorado — uncontrolled, meaning it has no control tower. Private propeller planes and a few smaller turbojets land there. To reach the airport, take Valmont Road east to Airport Road. **Flatirons Aviation**, 440-6522, 3300 Airport Road, offers flight instruction ranging from recreational to commercial and is a contact for renting hangars or getting airport information. **Dakota Ridge Aviation**, 444-1017, is another flight school based at Boulder Municipal. Nearby, the **Cloud Base**, 530-2208, 5117 Independence Road, offers glider flights and lessons.

Tri-County Airport/Crosswind Aviation is in east Boulder County, 661-9146, 395 Airport Drive, Erie. This too is an uncontrolled airport whose runway is big enough for small jets, but most of its air traffic is single- and twin-engine propeller planes. A full range of flight instruction is available. Experimental and unique home-built airplanes occupy many hangars. And the jet-set . . . that is, the propeller-set . . . has settled nearby. More than a dozen houses adjacent to the airport sport private hangars with taxi lanes connecting to the runway.

Longmont Airport is yet another uncontrolled landing field with full services for business and pleasure aircraft. **Air West Flight Center Inc.**, 776-6266, 10383 N. 85th Street, is the main contact. **Twin Peaks Aviation**, 776-8467, offers flying lessons.

Jefferson County Airport, 466-2314, 11755 Airport Way, Broomfield, is just outside Boulder County, but it's used by many Boulderites. Also known as Jeffco, it's the third-largest airport in the Denver area and can handle corporate jets and aircraft up to 70,000 pounds. No scheduled commercial passenger flights leave Jeffco, but it has plenty of general aviation. The tower is staffed by 10 controllers and has the best navigational landing aids near Boulder.

Denver International Airport (DIA)
8400 Peña Blvd., Denver • 342-2200, (800) 247-2336

Nineteen carriers service this 2-year-old airport — the biggest in the nation and one of the biggest in the world. United Airlines dominates, with some 70 percent of the lift out of DIA, but American, American West, Continental, Delta, Frontier, Northwest, Reno Air, TWA and Vanguard also serve there. DIA is posh — polished granite floors, $7.5 million of artwork and an expansive main lobby roofed with 34

Photo: Daily Camera/David P. Gilkey

After a year's delay, Denver International Airport opened February 28, 1995.

translucent, Teflon-coated fiberglass tent canopies designed to invoke snow-covered peaks and cast light like stylized, billowy clouds. Those canopies were canted in different directions for structural efficiency in the wind and heavy weather. Despite its monumental 5 million-square-foot inside, walks are short. The ticket counters are a short way from passenger drop-offs on both sides of the main terminal. Common carriers (i.e., buses and vans) use a separate level, off-limits to private cars. There are three concourses. You have the option of walking to Concourse A via an air bridge over a taxiway, but a swift subway whisks you to all concourses. Stand near the front windows if you want to see the little propellers along the walls whirl as the train passes.

DIA has excellent shops, including some not usually found in airports, including Images of Nature, a national wildlife photographer's store; Benjamin Books, a well-stocked bookstore; and Susan Vale Sweaters, offering handmade sweaters from $200 on up. You can also find a travel agency and a chiropractor at DIA. Fast food includes McDonald's, TCBY and specialty pizza, croissant and espresso shops, all by contract required to sell their goods at prices no more than 10 percent higher than they would sell in a regular mall. Most of these are open daily from 7 AM until 11 PM.

If you need information on Denver International Airport's ground transportation, parking or lost and found, call 342-2301.

Buses, Limos and Taxi

Two van services offer scheduled airport shuttle service from Boulder. The **Boulder Airporter**, 444-0808, picks up at Boulder's major hotels, CU-Boulder and your own front door. The hourly service departs the Boulder Broker between 4:30 AM and 9 PM (if you order door-to-door, they'll schedule your pick up to coincide with a departure from the Broker) and from the airport between 8 AM and 11 PM. Door-to-door service is $16 one-way; hotel service is $14 one-way. **Rocky Moun-**

INSIDERS' TIP

If you are a pedestrian, cyclist, in-line skater, skateboarder or motorist and have too close a brush with another pedestrian, cyclist, in-line skater, skateboarder or motorist who is unmindful of rules of the road, you can report it to the Close Call Hotline, 441-4272. This is a message line, not to be used to report an accident or emergency.

tain **Supercoach**, 499-1951 or (800) 499-1051, offers door-to-door airport shuttle service, running from Boulder every hour between 5 AM and 10 PM and from the airport hourly from 6:30 AM to 11:30 PM. The fare is $19 per person one-way and $34 round-trip, with discounts for additional people, children and seniors.

RTD, 299-6000, also operates hourly buses between DIA and Boulder and takes about 90 minutes to reach the Boulder bus terminal, with intermediate stops including the Louisville-Superior and Table Mesa Park-n-Ride lots. The fare is $8 one way ($5 for CU-Boulder students), and you can grab advance $13 round-trip tickets at King Soopers or Safeway.

In late 1996, RTD launched a new family plan, allowing up to three children 15 and younger to ride free with an adult. Children even get a free set of plastic airline-style wings with each ride.

Boulder Yellow Cab, 442-2277, charges around $50 for one to five people and also picks up in Lafayette and Louisville. If you are feeling flush you can call an on-demand limo service. **Airport Luxury Express**, 938-1234 or (800) 708-1160, is a new limo service featuring four-wheel-drive Chevrolet Suburbans equipped with cellular phone, television, beverage service and ski and luggage racks. It operates as an on-demand airport charter, particularly for business travelers and groups. By-the-hour rates are $72 during the day and evening and $84 between 10:30 PM and 6 AM between Boulder, Denver, Louisville or Lafayette and DIA. Prices are higher to Centennial Airport and from Eldorado Springs, Gold Hill, Gold Lake, Lake Valley, Longmont, Pine Brook Hills, Walker Ranch and Ward. Airport Luxury Express also will take you to or pick you up from Colorado Springs, general-aviation airports and mountain towns. Other limo services include **Elegante Limousine**, 443-7723; **Foothills Limousine**, 530-0781, or **Prestige Transportation Services**, 678-8471 or (800) 215-8471.

Car Routes

It's easier to reach the airport with someone else at the wheel, but if you need to drive, here are four options. To choose a route, tune in to KOA radio (850 AM), which has the most frequent traffic-condition reports. The distances listed are based on a *Daily Camera* reporter's story when the airport opened in 1995.

We've found the U.S. 36/I-25/I-76/I-270/I-70/Peña Boulevard (Option B) to be the fastest from central, North or south Boulder. Once you're on U.S. 36, you won't encounter a single traffic light, and the high-occupancy-vehicle

S-turn out east on the Boulder Creek Path.

(HOV) lane from Westminster practically to the I-25 interchange speeds things along even during rush hour. At peak times, you are most likely to encounter congestion on the I-270 leg, and if KOA tells you that route is jammed, your best alternative is Option A. Of course, reverse this to drive from DIA to Boulder.

Option A (38.5 miles): Take U.S. Highway 36 to Sheridan Boulevard. Exit at 104th Avenue/Church Ranch Boulevard and follow 104th Avenue east all the way to Tower Road. Until you get well east of I-25, which is still rural, tremendous growth is happening along this route, which has about two dozen traffic lights. At Tower Road, along the airport's western edge, turn right and take it south to Peña Boulevard, turn left and go east into the airport.

Option B (45 miles): Take U.S. Highway 36 to Denver. Go south briefly on I-25, then I-76 for about a mile to I-270, heading southeast. It merges into I-70 east. Exit at Peña Boulevard and go east into the airport.

Option C (45 miles): This option is best for East Boulder residents. Take Baseline Road (Colo. Highway 7) east to U.S. Highway 85. Take U.S. 85 south to Henderson Road. Go east on Henderson to Tower Road. Take Tower south to Peña Boulevard and go east into the airport.

Option D (42.5 miles): Take U.S. Highway 36 to Broomfield. At Broomfield, take 120th Avenue east to Quebec Street. Jog north on Quebec to Henderson Road. Take Henderson east to Tower Road, turn south to Peña Boulevard and then east on Peña into the airport.

You could enjoy a different Boulder eatery every day and not repeat for weeks.

Boulder
Restaurants

Boulder has earned a nationwide reputation for fine dining. In fact, many of the "best restaurants of Denver" lists include a fair number of Boulder restaurants. Good spots abound in the Pearl Street Mall area, but stupendous possibilities also exist in other shopping areas, the mountains and plains. This chapter is organized by type of restaurant rather than by geographic region, since they're all within an easy drive of Boulder.

You could enjoy a different Boulder eatery every day and not repeat for weeks. Boulder has a stunning variety from rollicking party places to quiet and intimate restaurants for conversation or romance. Basic food, served fast, suits some people, especially families. Others prefer meals custom prepared, and some folks like to linger over a gourmet meal.

In addition to your taste buds, you need to consider your budget. Our price-code key (see subsequent gray box) uses dollar signs to indicate the average cost of dinner for two, including wine and dessert. You can economize by skipping the wine and ordering just entrees, but if it's a special occasion or if the pocketbook's healthy, reward yourself with an unforgettable occasion!

Price-code Key	
Less than $20	$
$21 to $40	$$
$41 to $60	$$$
$61 to $100	$$$$
$101 and more	$$$$$

If you live in Boulder, you've become accustomed to totally smoke-free dining. If you're new or visiting, Boulder's rigid no-smoking regulations might come as a shock. While all restaurants in the City of Boulder must provide nonsmoking areas, none accommodates smokers except in a separate (and separately ventilated) room.

Handicap accessibility is common but worth checking.

If a restaurant sounds elegant, eclectic or spicy, you can bet your booster chairs that your kids will get a fidget attack unless the restaurant caters to children — or unless your children are used to finer dining than the usual pizza and burger joints that parents often choose in the name of family dining. Many places have special children's menus and other entertainment tricks for the kids, so ask about them.

Unless otherwise noted, these restaurants do take Visa and MasterCard. Some also take American Express, Diner's Club and Discover.

By the way, if you love detail, call the Boulder Chamber of Commerce and ask for their free *Boulder County Guide*, which lists menus from many fine establishments and specifics about handicap accessibility, credit cards, kids' menus and so on. For more on take-out or informal food service, or lively nightspots, check our respective Shopping and Nightlife chapters. Our Estes Park and Grand Lake chapters include details on dining over there and might provide your first excuse to explore those mountain towns.

Oh, one final note. Boulder restaurateurs have been playing musical tables and chairs, and if you've been out of town for a few months, have just awoken from a long nap or just haven't been paying attention, you're in for a bunch of surprises. La Estrellita has moved to the old First Wok site, and its vacated space is, at this writing, being readied for a New Orleans-style brew pub. First Wok is no more, and Pearl's is also gone, with a pizza-and-beer place slated for its site on the Pearl Street Mall. Piccolo's appears to have closed forever, and Rio Grande has renovated the building Piccolo's occupied. With Rio Grande out of its location, that space has been developed into the new Pasta Jay's, which had been homeless since its former building was moved to Erie where that town plans to make it into a children's library. Narayan's is now where Bobo China Restaurant used to be. Trios is where Two Bitts was, and Two Bitts, whose first location is now Al Fresco, is replacing Pablo's which, alas, appears gone forever — as is Viet-Hoa, whose off-the-Mall storefront is, at this writing, still vacant.

American

Traditional/Casual

Annie's Cafe
$ • 20 Big Springs Dr., Nederland • 258-3600

Perched atop the Nederland Shopping Center, directly across from the now-shuttered Chalet Suisse, Annie's is a popular local hangout that serves eggs, pancakes, omelettes, sandwiches, salads and homemade soups. It is open for breakfast and lunch daily except Monday.

Bart's Restaurant
$ • 585 South Boulder Rd., Louisville • 665-2060

Sandwiches, steaks and seafood get served here under pictures of WW II airplanes. This spot is especially appealing to families or anyone who loves aviation. The restaurant, which is inexpensive to begin with, offers early-bird specials, whose hours vary according to the days of the week. Bart's is open for lunch Monday through Thursday, for dinner nightly and for breakfast (morning through late night) in summer Friday, Saturday and Sunday.

Boulder Broker Inn
$$$ • 555 30th St., Boulder • 449-1752

The English atmosphere, with dark wood and stained glass, is a perfect complement to entrees such as Filet Wellington, prime rib or Alaskan king salmon. The restaurant also serves HealthMark-style entrees, which means low-fat. A complimentary bowl of in-the-shell Gulf shrimp on ice accompanies each meal, as do a choice of soup or salad plus dessert,

often a French pastry or other tempting treat, varying daily. The Sunday brunch is considered one of Boulder's best and, according to *Westword* magazine, one of Denver's best too, quite naturally because there are also two Brokers in Denver. Boulder's sets up its buffet in two rooms. The happy hour is terrific, with a taco bar on Friday. The inn is open for breakfast, lunch and dinner daily.

Boulder Cork
$$$ • 3295 30th St., Boulder • 443-9505

The Cork is a fortuitous melding of traditional American favorites and contemporary tastes in ambiance and food. The Southwestern decor, excellent wine list and strong presentation of all the meals make it as popular for a business lunch as for a special dinner. With excellent prime rib and steaks, it's as close as Boulder gets to a steakhouse, but chicken and a half-dozen fresh fish are on the menu every evening. You can get a burger here, but, oh, what a burger — thick and perfectly cooked to your specifications. The lunch crab cakes with jicama cole slaw get high ratings. The Cork is known for mud pie, which has earned it a Best of Boulder award by *Daily Camera* readers. You can stop for a sip and a light bite at the bar, or really scarf up serious protein in the attractive restaurant. About one Sunday a month, the Cork produces an "Adventure Series" special dinner. Call to find out what and when. The Cork is open for dinner daily and for lunch on weekdays. It's new smokers' dining room is one of the few in Boulder.

Chautauqua Dining Hall
$$ • 900 Baseline Rd., Boulder • 440-3776

This historic 1898 dining hall has been serving summer visitors for nearly 100 years in beautiful Chautauqua Park. The most popular place to eat is out on the big, wide porches. The dining hall does not take reservations, so if you want to sit on the porch, come early and be prepared to wait, or come on a weekday. After the restaurant closed following its 1996 summer season, longtime leaseholder Steve LeBlang announced he was not renewing, and at this writing, no new operator had been an-

FYI

Unless otherwise noted, the area code for all phone numbers in this guide is 303.

World-famous chef Paul Bocuse (wearing hat) was honored at Boulder Flagstaff House with a five-course dinner prepared by five of America's best chefs, including the Flagstaff's Mark Monette (next to Bocuse).

nounced. So we can't recommend specific dishes or even be assured that it will continue to serve "American" fare. (If the listed phone number is not working, the Chautauqua Association, 442-3282, will surely know the new one.)

ChriSar's Grill & Pasta
$$ • 543 Terry St., Longmont • 651-2772

ChriSar's is mostly American, but with a definite Italian overlay. Hence such dishes as "Sea of Hearts" — shrimp, scallops and artichoke hearts tossed with linguine — is one of many fine seafood, chicken or pasta meals made from scratch in this quaint and casual 1910 Victorian house with several small dining rooms and a patio full of flowers that is open in summer.

This restaurant is open for breakfast and dinner daily except Monday, for lunch weekdays except Monday and for champagne brunch Saturday and Sunday.

Gold Hill Inn
$$$, no credit cards • Gold Hill • 443-6461

This family-owned restaurant has served six-course dinners in an old-style log inn since 1962. The menu depends on what chef Chris Finn deems good and fresh. One June day, the offerings included hot and sour duck soup or a cold banana bisque, a salmon soufflé appetizer, venison with blackberry sauce and a choice of chocolate torte or apricot strawberry pie.

The inn opens in May, when the mountain snow flurries abate, and it closes at the end of October, when the snow starts again. During summertime, it's open for dinner all week except on Tuesday. Reservations are recommended. It's a 20-minute drive up the mountains from Boulder, straight up Sunshine Canyon, and about an hour from Estes Park.

Karen's Country Kitchen
$$ • 700 Main St., Louisville • 666-8020

A historic building with tin walls, cozy rooms and decorative gift items sets the tone for Karen's homestyle cooking. Sandwiches, Southwest Chicken (Karen calls it her adult-style fajita) and pot roasts are popular. Patrons love the liver and onions so much it has stayed on the menu for 20 years. There's also a salad bar and full-line bakery, including turtle cream chocolate/caramel pie and fresh blueberry pie. That's dinner. Breakfast can include thick-sliced bacon, charbroiled local sausage, hash browns, pancakes and Belgian waffles with fresh fruit. "Scramlets" are all the ingredients you want folded into eggs.

Karen's is open for breakfast daily. It's also open for lunch and dinner every day except Sunday.

Karen's in the Country
$$$ • 1900 Plaza Dr., Louisville • 666-8503

The country is more elegant than the kitchen, for Karen's second restaurant is in a three-story Victorian house. It offers many of the same baked goods as Karen's Country Kitchen but adds more continental inspirations, including pasta and chicken dishes. It's open for breakfast, lunch and dinner daily.

Lick Skillet Bakery
$ • 5340 Arapahoe Ave., Boulder • 449-7775

A big old range is center stage for eat-in and carry-out. The fare demonstrates how innovative chefs can elevate basic ingredients. A descendant of a popular spot in Gold Hill that has since closed, this rendition of the Lick Skillet is an informal cafe. The fresh-baked goods are an excellent way to start the day, washed down with strong coffee or good tea. The muffins and omelets are delicious, as is the chocolate mousse cake — for later, of course. Good lunch choices include jasmine rice, well-endowed sandwiches and the vegetarian blackened tofu stir-fry given a *Daily Camera* Best of Boulder award for vegetarian food. Lick Skillet is open for breakfast and lunch daily.

Mustard's Last Stand
$, no credit cards • 1719 Broadway, Boulder • 444-5841

Grease junkies who fear withdrawal symptoms around Boulder's health food can whoop it up at Mustard's Last Stand, where health food is as rare as romaine lettuce at a baseball game. Polish hot dogs, German bratwurst, hamburgers and thick homestyle fries are served in this Boulder institution, and the place provides a funky view of Broadway. OK, they've bowed to popular demand and added veggiedogs and tempeh burgers, but you don't *have* to eat them if you don't want to. *Westword* calls Mustard's the Denver area's best hot dog. Mustard's is open for lunch and dinner daily.

Pioneer Inn
$ • 15 First St., Nederland • 258-7733

The building has been here a long time and has been a favorite Nederland landmark. Funky and fun, the rustic inn is known for tra-

ditional filling breakfasts, all-American and Mexican-accented favorites, great charcoal-grilled burgers, homemade green chile and varieties of beer, but a true indication that Boulderfication has begun is the addition of a veggie burger. The chocolate silk pie is the specialty dessert.

When you come to the Pioneer, you get to hang out at the big bar with gritty local mountaineers as well as skiers and hikers who stop in to be part of the fun. It's open daily for breakfast, lunch and dinner. The bar's open until 2 AM every night (see our Nightlife chapter for after-hours information).

Pressto Sandwiches
$ • 3960 Broadway, Boulder • 444-0780
$ • 1035 Walnut Ave., Boulder • 444-6786

These two sprightly eateries prepare Boulder's favorite sandwiches. The Pressto concept comes from Tom Kramis, who ate grilled sandwiches in Italy, took the idea to Boulder, reduced the grease by cooking on all nonstick grills and added more interesting and adventurous ingredients. Grilled sandwiches come in 12 varieties and can be mated with salads and desserts. The Sausalito has smoked turkey, sun-dried tomatoes, artichoke hearts, four kinds of cheese and pesto, grilled hot on traditional focaccia bread. The Presstos are open weekdays from 8 AM to 7 PM and Saturday from 9 AM to 6 PM.

Red Robin Spirits Emporium
$ • 2580 Arapahoe Ave., Boulder • 442-0320

Enter one of Boulder's major family and teen hangouts. It's a place with high energy, fueled by a variety of burgers, sandwiches and fries. There's a bar up front and a video game room off to the side. It's open for lunch and dinner daily.

Rev. Taylor's Country Restaurant
$$ • 121 Second Ave., Niwot • 652-2020

Rev. Taylor's looks like a big country store that happens to serve food instead of ingredients to make your own. The restaurant is known for its big filling breakfasts and its good soups, salads and sandwiches for lunch. Dinner gets a little fancier — but not much. Steak,

salmon, stew, meat loaf and a few vegetarian offerings comprise the dinner menu. Old-fashioned fountain treats make for traditional American desserts.

Rev. Taylor's booths are so comfortable you could stay put and chat for hours. The place packs with happy families during Sunday brunch. It's open for breakfast, lunch and dinner Monday through Saturday and breakfast and lunch on Sunday.

The Sink
$ • 1165 13th St., Boulder • 444-7465

This college hangout has been gathering character since the 1930s. But without that college grunge, it just wouldn't be authentic. Self-described "Ugly Crust Pizzas" with various toppings, a huge selection of munchies including nachos and pizza bread sticks, Sink-Burgers, soups and salads fill the menu. There's live music, great beers, happy-hour and an unsurpassed youthful exuberance. After all, many of the patrons have recently reached legal drinking age. Organized graffiti

comprises the decor. Robert Redford was once the janitor before he scuttled art at CU-Boulder and went on to make a few major motion pictures. The Sink is open for lunch and dinner daily.

Teddy Roosevelt American Grille
$$ • In the Hotel Boulderado • 2115 13th St., Boulder • 442-4560

Rough riders stampede in . . . actually, Teddy Roosevelt draws business people and tourists ambling off the mall for a pleasant meal at the Hotel Boulderado. Rooseveltiana decorates the room, which feels clubby and traditional. Popular American fare includes eggs Benedict for breakfast, soups, salads and grilled items for lunch, and prime rib, big steaks and fresh seafood for dinner. Sometimes, old favorites get a new twist, such as the chorizo-stuffed pork chops or the pistachio-crusted salmon. Desserts are filling and excellent, and the atmosphere is simply neat. The coffee bar, milk shakes, wine and microbrew lists and full drink bar are bully.

Tom's Tavern
$ • 1047 Pearl St., Boulder • 442-3893

Tom's has a reputation for the juiciest burger in town, though they're a little on the thin side and are more in the manner of a diner than a pub. Still, this friendly neighborhood tavern has been around since 1959, started by Tom Eldridge, a somewhat eccentric sometime-City Council candidate who says he opened the tavern as a young dreamer of 21 and never got out of it. Tom's is so well-known, some people give directions by using it as a landmark. In addition to its well-known burgers, Tom's dishes up steaks, pork tenderloin, ribs and chicken. It's open for lunch and dinner daily.

Contemporary Cuisine

Alice's Restaurant
$$$ • 3371 Gold Lake Rd., Ward • 459-3544

This is a romantic, honeymoon kind of place about 35 minutes up the mountain and over a country road. The 100-year-old lodge is charming and rustic, yet it is big enough to hold a private party for 350 people for special occasions such as wedding receptions. Generally, it's a more intimate crowd, with about half the people staying at the Gold Lake Mountain Resort and the other half coming up from Boulder.

The cuisine is innovative American with Pacific Rim overtones, such as Thai crab cakes with lemongrass. Fare includes gourmet vegetarian, seafood, wild game and juicy steaks. The wines are reasonably priced, and the meal is well worth the trip. You have a cocktail before dinner at Karel's Bar or retire there for an after-dinner drink, but the best treat is to retire to your own quaint cabin for the night instead of driving back to town.

Alice's is open Wednesday through Sunday for dinner all summer, with somewhat shortened winter hours. Reservations are highly recommended.

Dandelion
$$$ • 1011 Walnut St., Boulder • 443-6700

This rather expensive, very stylish and exceptionally wonderful new restaurant has ratcheted Boulder up another notch on the culinary scale. In a light and airy high-ceilinged room, it draws its stylistic influence from Manhattan's best and most sparkling SoHo restaurants but with a definite Rocky Mountain pedigree. Its owner was previously with Denver's vaunted (and considerably more formal) Cliff Young's.

Dandelion serves up splendid contemporary American cuisine that can be summarized in such cliché words and phrases as creativity, innovation, fresh ingredients, fine preparation. But the clichés have real meaning in this restaurant, where ordinary ingredients are extraordinarily fresh and given a little twist to elevate the finished product.

Start your meal with fried calamari and a contrasting lemon caper remoulade and spiced tomatoes. Or a soup. Or a salad so fresh that it tastes just-picked. Herb-crusted roast chicken is one entree. Scallops and rock shrimp with angel hair pasta in a fire-roasted pepper sauce is another. Beautiful presentation, sometimes towering, are hallmarks of this excellent restaurant. The menu changes with seasons, ingredients and chef's choice, and there are also daily specials. The wine list is excellent, and the desserts will make you rethink the concept of "sinful." Reservations are recommended for busy times. Dandelion serves lunch and dinner Monday through Saturday and dinner only on Sunday.

Fourteenth Street Bar and Grill
$$ • 1400 Pearl St., Boulder • 444-5854

See and be seen in this bustling, sunny restaurant with gourmet pizza baked in a wood-burning oven, fine salads and rotisserie chicken. Salmon might have a cantaloupe salsa during the summer. The turkey sandwich is like a Thanksgiving meal. The vanilla bean cheesecake is but one of the knockout desserts. Overall, everything is consistently good, fresh and innovatively prepared. The patio seating lets you be part of the mall scene. It's open for lunch and dinner daily except Sunday, when it's dinner only.

Jax Fish House
$$ • 928 Pearl St., Boulder • 444-1811

Owner/executive chef David Query's restaurant resides on trendy Pearl Street, just west of the Pearl Street Mall. This New England fish house crossed with a New Orleans oyster bar gets raves for fresh seafood, microbrews and good wines and champagnes by the glass. The martinis are also among Boulder's best, so the place predictably gets a good happy-hour crowd. The raw oysters and clams are exceptional. You can doodle on your crisp butcher-paper "tablecloth" while you wait for your spicy gumbo, clam chowder, soft-shelled crab linguine, steamed mussels and vegetarian specials. Save room for the Key lime pie. Jax is open daily for dinner only.

Nancy's Restaurant
$$ • 825 Walnut St., Boulder • 449-8402

If your favorite sister opened a restaurant, it might look like Nancy's — a pretty Victorian bungalow with a frothy rose hedge and cheery dining in small rooms. We call this "American" for lack of a better category, because it has drawn some of the best from various cuisines and tweaked them to reflect a kind of all-American eclectic. Popular offerings include eggs Benedict, which *Travel and Leisure* cited as among America's best. For lunch, there are Senegalese vegetables, and for dinner, chicken Valenciana. The buttermilk biscuits are light as puffy clouds brought down to earth and served with butter.

Nancy's, a popular spot for wedding brunches, is open for breakfast and lunch daily, and for dinner Tuesday through Saturday. Sunday's brunch is excellent, and an afternoon tea, Tuesday through Saturday, includes properly brewed tea along with small sandwiches and desserts.

Q's Restaurant
$$$-$$$$ • In the Hotel Boulderado
• 2115 13th St., Boulder • 442-4880

Travel Holiday magazine called Q's the "hottest new restaurant in Colorado." *Zagat* referred to it one of Colorado's top 20. Started by Boulder star chef David Query, it is now run by John Platt, who has continued the tradition of exceptional contemporary American cuisine, creatively prepared, beautifully presented and well served. This is a small, upstairs restaurant that feels light-years removed from the Boulderado's bustle. It is a special-occasion or expense-account place that is as pleasing to linger in as to dine at.

The menu changes monthly but always features everyday dishes with a stunning, surprising, satisfying contemporary twist and presentation. Nachos might be of lobster. Hash might be chorizo potato with avocado and black bean sauce. Ravioli can be pocketed with sweet potato and served with crawfish. The entrees that follow will be equally interesting, perhaps adobe grilled pork loin with peach salsa, jack cheddar grits and roast zucchini, presented like a 3-D food sculpture. Organically grown green salads accompany all dinners. The wine list is excellent, and the desserts are, well, to die for.

Q's is open for dinner daily. Reservations are recommended.

Trios Grille and Wine Bar
$$$ • 1155 Canyon Blvd., Boulder
• 442-8400

This new restaurant is oh-so-sleek and oh-so-delicious. Stylish and contemporary, it enchants both in the way it looks and what it serves. Outstanding appetizers, notably the salmon carpaccio, and opulent desserts bracket innovative meats, seafood, pasta and vegetarian entrees and, of course, upscale, gourmet pizzas. A jazz trio might perform, and the sommelier certainly will have some excellent selections from the wine bar to offer, considering the restaurant serves some 170 wines.

Trios has its own private parking lot, a special bonus for a large and lively downtown restaurant. It's open for lunch Monday through Saturday and dinner Monday through Thursday and Saturday. Bar hours are later. Trios serves Sunday brunch as well.

Two Bitts Bistro
$$$ • 865 Baseline Rd., Boulder
• 442-8400

By the time you read this, Two Bitts should be up and running in the space vacated by

---

INSIDERS' TIP

If the kids are part of your dinner plans, order take-out food and head to a park.

Pablo's. This is the third location for the restaurant run by the energetic Bittners. We can guess that some popular favorites will be reprised, but no matter what the new rendition will be, it should be good. The former Two Bitts was voted the Best Lunch in Boulder by *Daily Camera* readers and Best Desserts by Denver newspapers. *Zagat* called it one of Colorado's top 20 restaurants; and it has also won the Chocolate Lover's Fling for sheer artistry and taste. In previous incarnations, Two Bitts served healthy and delicious entrees and salads, artfully created and presented. The desserts have been rich and sensational.

Zolo Grill
$$ • 2525 Arapahoe Ave., Boulder • 449-0444

David Query, a key player in many contemporary restaurants including Q's and Jax Fish House in Boulder and Cliff Young's in Denver, sails Zolo Grill, his flagship, into the trendy waters of creative, Southwestern decor and cuisine. Zolo's decor is eclectic electric, from the copper wires crossing the ceiling to the huge abstract murals on the walls, all with a hip Santa Fe underpinning. The menu is comparable and features flamboyant salads, red-chile barbecued duck tacos and grilled banana creme pie. The food is spicy and visually exciting, with lots of zigzag saucy accents, sort of like Zorro marks . . . really, we mean Zolo marks. Start with a Zolorita, the

bartender's special Margarita version, and finish up with a dessert from a list that has earned a Best of Denver award from *Westword*. Zolo is open for lunch and dinner Monday through Saturday and brunch and dinner on Sunday.

Asian

Bangkok Cuisine
$$ • 2017 13th St., Boulder • 440-4830

This pleasant restaurant off the Pearl Street Mall features fresh food of Thai and Vietnamese origins. Vietnamese spring rolls, vegetarian curries, spicy Dungeness crab, chicken sautéed with lemongrass and an excellent noodle dish called pad Thai are among the best dishes. There's also an interesting Southeast Asian version of stuffed grape leaves. Prices are moderate. There is full bar service, including a new back bar where smoking is permitted — which is newsworthy in Boulder. Bangkok Cuisine is open daily for lunch and dinner.

Chez Thuy
$$ • 2655 28th St., Boulder • 442-1700

This pretty restaurant, with deep green, brocade booths and a big, carved dragon-and-peacock motif mural, dishes up elegant Vietnamese food. Specialties include quail stuffed with seafood served with vegetables and noodles, pork sautéed in a clay hot pot,

Dine Out While You Stay In

If you're house-bound or hotel-bound, you'll love Waiters on Wheels, which delivers restaurant meals to your door for just $3 more than the total meal price (the delivery person also appreciates a tip). Forty restaurants subscribe to this service, ranging from sushi palaces to hot dog joints. The restaurants include many Boulder favorites, such as Old Chicago, Creative Cafe, Al Fresco and MijBani. Meals arrive from 20 minutes to

an hour after you call — it's quickest if you order when the restaurant isn't as busy.

Here's how you use this handy service: Grab a Waiters on Wheels restaurant/menu list at your hotel; ask at the front desk if you don't have one in your room. And if you're at home without a menu, call 440-7750 so Waiters on Wheels can deliver one to you. Find the meal you want in the menu listing, and call the number to order for just yourself or for a crowd. It's that simple.

JOHN'S

CLASSIC & CONTEMPORARY DISHES OF
AMERICA ❦ FRANCE ❦ ITALY ❦ SPAIN

1996
"AMERICA'S TOP RESTAURANTS"
ZAGAT SURVEY

❦

"Consistently great European & American Cuisine made with attention to detail" D.C.

❦

"Needless to say, a dinner at John's takes us on a tantalizing excursion into delicate flavors & aromatic pleasures" Daily Camera

❦

"John Bizzarro is serious about his cooking and it shows...the menu is a wonderfully eclectic read, reflecting Bizzarro's diverse experiences...he's skilled in many different cooking styles, and is able to blend them creatively into new compositions" Rocky Mountain News

Reservations 444-5232
2328 Pearl Street Open 5:30

curried chicken and vegetarian specials, all cooked by owner/chef Thuy Twee. The portions are generous, and you can dine in or take out. It's open for dinner daily and for lunch Monday through Saturday.

Chinese Dumpling House
$ • WaterStreet Center • Canyon Blvd. and Folsom St., Boulder • 413-1089

This new, whistle-clean establishment has a limited menu and fast service. Order at the counter, and your food will be brought to your table. The family-owned casual eating spot serves just four varieties of steamed Chinese dumplings, including beef, pork, chicken and vegetarian, plus soups, noodles and salads. There are a few tables inside and a couple more outdoors. You can eat in, take out or fax, 413-1128, and have your order waiting for quick pickup. Chinese Dumpling House is open daily, except Sunday, for lunch and dinner.

Lee Yuan Chinese Cuisine
$ • 4800 Baseline Rd., Boulder • 494-4210

Boulder has a tremendous selection of good, small, family-owned restaurants. Lee Yuan's is one of them. Two decades ago, this was Lee Yuan's Burger Hut, serving both burgers and carry-out Chinese food. Now the restaurant, in the Meadows shopping center, is a morning-glory-decorated, sit-down establishment that is popular for its less-than-$5 lunch specials as well as its dinner selections. It's very friendly for families. Wine and beer are available. It's open for lunch weekdays and for dinner daily.

Orchid Pavilion Chinese Restaurant & Lounge
$$ • 1050 Walnut St., Boulder • 449-4353

Voted Best Chinese restaurant in the *Daily Camera's* reader's poll eight years in a row, the Orchid Pavilion is staffed by New York-style Chinatown chefs, who cook sesame chicken in huge chunks, crispy whole fish, champagne beef and eggplant in garlic sauce. There is also gourmet seafood and Szechuan vegetables. MSG is never used. You don't even need to ask. The soothing, peach-color interior includes a huge, genuine Chinese silkscreen and fine reproductions of Tang Dynasty horses. Children are welcome. The restaurant's early-bird specials take the most popular menu items and add a choice of soups, chicken wings, egg roll and fried wonton as well as a choice of steamed or fried rice for one price. Orchid Pavilion is open for lunch and dinner daily.

Sawaddee
$$ • 1401 Pearl St., Boulder • 447-3321

Garlic pepper shrimp and Thai iced tea, made with spices and sweetened milk, will tempt you. Lemongrass and curried vegetables add to many dishes, characterized by the light flavor of Thai food. It's mildly spicy, and you can ask for hotter or not spicy at all. The chefs will add more vegetables when requested, which is one reason the spot earns high points from Boulder's many health enthusiasts. Sawaddee is open for dinner daily except Monday and for lunch daily except Sunday and Monday.

Siamese Plate & Sumida's Sushi Bar
$$ • 1575 Folsom St., Boulder • 447-9718

Voted Best Thai restaurant in Boulder and Denver since 1986 by *Daily Camera* readers, the Siamese Plate gives diners a choice of Western seating or benches with bright cushions. Try the spicy green curry with vegetables and coconut milk, the green-lipped mussels with spicy garlic sauce or the exceptional red curry with chicken, and get an appetizer from Sumida's Sushi Bar one level below, which also offers happy-hour sushi specials and two-for-one sake midday on weekdays, in the early evening and all evening on Sunday and Monday. If you sit down at Sumida's, you can also order from the Thai menu. Both the Plate and the Sushi Bar are open for lunch Monday through Saturday and for dinner daily.

Silver Palace
$$$ • 3100 Arapahoe Rd., Boulder • 447-3828

The Silver Palace is a fine-dining Chinese restaurant, yet it is related to Silver Palaces in, of all places, Vermont and Florida. Boulder's is a lovely and tranquil spot that includes a secluded, romantic patio and service with fine china and silverware on crisp white tablecloths. Signature dishes include Hunan Popcorn, which is very light tempura-style fried calamari with jalapeño peppers and onion; Crispy Pork with Grand Marnier sauce; and Chicken Gwin Jin, pan-seared with a smoky teriyaki flavor. Silver Palace is open for lunch weekdays and dinner daily.

Sushi Tora
$$ • 2014 10th St., Boulder • 444-2280

This is Boulder's most authentic Japanese sushi restaurant, from the low cloth curtains you walk through to enter during good weather to the excellent raw fish, beautifully presented. This quiet restaurant offers the option of tempura, soups and appetizers. It's open weekdays for lunch and daily for dinner.

Sushi Zanmai
$$ • 1221 Spruce St., Boulder • 440-0733

There is nothing quiet or low-key about this brassy sushi bar and Japanese restaurant. The sushi is first-rate, the owner chef Nao-San is a shameless extrovert, and the restaurant is rarely without a line out the door. This most popular Japanese restaurant was voted by *Daily Camera* readers as the best place for karaoke singing in the metro area. One part of the bustling restaurant features the sushi bar and wood-top tables. At the bar, you can watch the flamboyant Japanese chefs prepare miniature boatloads of artistic sushi. Another part of the restaurant features tatami rooms and Benihani-style grill steak tables where the chef performs cooking magic.

Sing-along karaoke nights starting at 10 PM on Saturdays make a noisy place noisier — and that much more fun. Lunch and happy-hour specials bring down the cost of good Japanese food and great Japanese-accented fun. This restaurant is open for lunch weekdays and dinner nightly.

Tulien's Restaurant
$$ • 808 Main St., Louisville • 665-6868

On the menus at Tulien's are two Chinese characters, "Ta Tung," which stand for family and togetherness. Sure enough, many local families enjoy Tulien's low-key, sea-green interior with lazy Asian contemporary music playing in the background. Tulien's features standard and chef's special dishes on both the Chinese and Vietnamese menus. Some of the best of the Chinese chef's specials are from the sea, including Seafood Delight in Bird's Nest, a sizzling spectacle called Seafood Volcano Platter and Seafood in Clay Pot. Vietnamese chef's specials include an unusual shrimp paste in sugar cane called Chao Tom and shrimp wrapped in thin slices of marinated beef and served with noodles and lettuce under the name Bo Quan Tom. The restaurant has a full bar. Tulien's is open for lunch and dinner Monday through Saturday and for dinner only on Sundays.

Barbecue

Daddy Bruce's Bar-B-Que and Catering
$, no credit cards • 2000 Arapahoe Ave., Boulder • 449-8890

This place is usually packed with folks, so it's fun to carry out after sniffing the maple-stoked stove, where ribs get slathered with sauce that's tangy — not sweet. Not exactly health food, but, oh, what a decadent treat. The beef sandwiches are popular with a side of potato salad. Eat a slab of pork ribs and you'll sweat for two hours . . . with a smile on your face. This place is run by Bruce Randolph Jr., an associate minister of Boulder's Second Baptist Church and son of the late and greatly missed Denver philanthropist "Daddy" Bruce Randolph. Daddy Bruce's is open for lunch ever day except Sunday.

KT's Barbecue Outback
$, no credit cards • 2675 13th St., Boulder • 442-3717

Barbecue comes to North Boulder, specifically to one of the new shops on the "backside" of Community Plaza. KT's serves filling hickory-smoked pork and chicken and all the fixin's. It's open for lunch and dinner daily except Sunday.

KT's Hic'ry Pit BBQ
$, no credit cards • 6254 Arapahoe Rd., Boulder • 786-7608

Hickory-smoked barbecue (fat trimmed) gets served with sweet to spicy sauces rated like ski runs — easy way down, more difficult and double diamond for experts only. Eat in the modest old farmhouse or out on the picnic benches. This KT's is open for lunch and dinner Monday through Saturday.

Kaddy Shack
$$ • 1000 S. Boulder Rd., Louisville • 661-9896

The Gabby Gourmet, a popular metro area restaurant critic, calls this one of Colorado's top barbecues. A Memphis family has operated Kaddy Shack for more than 15 years in a 100-year-old trio of railroad cars that includes a caboose. Owner Woody Woodard has signed portraits of stars including Elvis and Jay Leno — all people who have eaten his barbecue.

Kaddy Shack's is Southern, hickory-wood barbecue, with a sweet sauce on the baby back loin ribs, served with baked beans, potato salad . . . the works. It's open for lunch and dinner weekdays and dinner only on Saturday; closed Sundays.

FYI
Unless otherwise noted, the area code for all phone numbers in this guide is 303.

Breakfast and Lunch

Dot's Diner
$, no credit cards • 799 Pearl St., Boulder • 449-1323

This converted gas station was rated one of America's top 100 "something for everyone" breakfast places by *Travel and Leisure* magazine. We're not surprised. It has some of the best buttermilk biscuits in town, along with huevos rancheros and cinnamon rolls. Vegetarian fare includes tofu and tempeh. And the funky, laid-back '60s-style ambiance counts for plenty. If you choose the shady summer patio above the former gas station, look for all the junk-art sculptures hidden in the trees. Dot's is open for breakfast and lunch daily.

Lucile's
$ • 2124 14th St., Boulder • 442-4743

Sashay up the porch steps of a side-street Victorian house, open the door, and you're in Cajun country. It's just that easy. Faded calico napkins, tables in every nook and a casual, bustling atmosphere are perfect for the red beans and grits. Try eggs sardou or a lunch of crawfish ettouffé. Rice pudding porridge with currants and raspberry sauce is comfort food, Lucile-style. It's open for breakfast and lunch daily.

Marie's Cafe
$, no credit cards • 2660 Broadway, Boulder • 447-0320

Marie's is open through lunch (a hearty Middle European one at that), but it is at breakfast that this cafe really shines. Pancakes, eggs and huge pastries abound. None of the regulars, who include medical professionals from the nearby Boulder Community Hospital and assorted medical groups and support services, seems shy about slathering on the butter or piling on the jam. Maybe they know where to get help if they need it! The atmosphere is luncheonette-basic, with bright lights for perusing the morning paper and suitably efficient service. Marie's is open daily for breakfast and lunch.

Rocky Mountain Joe's Cafe
$ • 1410 Pearl St., Boulder • 442-3969

Breakfast, lunch and Boulder's first espresso bar are here in this upstairs cafe with high ceilings, exposed brick walls and, if you're at a window table, a bird's-eye view of the Pearl Street Mall. Home-fries, breakfast burritos with chorizo, huevos and a half-dozen salads are on the menu, along with pancakes. Breakfast dishes are available at lunchtime, as are soups, sandwiches, daytime burritos and salads. There is also a children's menu. The restaurant was named to honor one of Boulder's first natural scenery photographers, and historic photos line the walls. It's open for breakfast and lunch daily.

Central and Eastern European

Andrea's Fine Food and Spirits
$$ • 216 E. Main St., Lyons • 823-5000

The favorites include a luscious pot roast braised with onion, called *Zwiebel Rostbraten*, and homemade spaetzle. You can also choose pasta, fresh seafood and vegetarian specials. Bavarian native Andrea Liermann is one of the bubbliest, most beloved hostesses in the area. Weekends, accordion and bell musicians play, and dancers perform the "Lederhosen Slapptanz." Open for breakfast, lunch and dinner daily except Wednesday.

Black Bear Inn
$$$ • 42 E. Main St., Lyons • 823-6812

Classic European cuisine with a French touch appears on the menu, which changes seasonally. Wiener schnitzel is especially popular. In the wintertime, patrons with a sweet tooth prefer the chocolate taco. In the summer, they go for homemade ice cream. Open for dinner daily and for lunch Tuesday through Saturday.

Copperdale Inn
$$$ • 10 miles up Coal Creek Canyon from Colo. Hwy. 93, Boulder • 642-3180

Sauerbraten, beef Stroganoff, wiener schnitzel and venison medallions are all real central European dishes, cooked by chefs who love Austrian and German cooking. It's a cozy inn, with red booths and fringed lamps, antler motifs and a family feel. Open for dinner Wednesday through Saturday and lunch and dinner Sunday.

The Little Russian Cafe
$$$ • 1430 Pearl St., Boulder • 449-7696

Red walls, voluptuous paintings and a weekend mandolin player set the mood for 18 flavors of ice-cold vodka — or is it vice versa? This the place for such hard-to-find Russian classics as hot borscht, beef Stroganoff, stuffed cabbage rolls, shish kebab, salmon steaks, potato cakes, lamb stew and chicken Kiev. This is no place to go for a light bite, but on a chilly winter's evening, when the snow is falling on the bricks and branches outside, you can't find a better match of food, weather and a romantic atmosphere that just makes you want to cuddle up. All that's missing is a troika

trotting down the Pearl Street Mall. Open for lunch and dinner daily except Tuesday.

Old Prague Inn
$$$ • 7521 Ute Hwy. (Colo. Hwy. 66), Longmont • 772-6374

Bohemian plates and hand-stenciled walls give this pre-1900 schoolhouse an elegant, homey ambiance. Entrees include roast duck or pork, Czech-style, served with dumplings and sweet-and-sour cabbage. Reservations are recommended. Open for dinner daily except Tuesday.

Continental

European Cafe
$$$$ • 2460 Arapahoe Ave., Boulder • 938-8250

Epicures and critics usually call this one of the top four restaurants in town — and the only stratospheric one that's in a strip shopping mall. What it lacks in exterior charm is compensated for inside, where the decor is delightful and the food is outstanding. *Zagat* pegs it as Colorado's best restaurant. Radek Cerny, owner/executive chef, trained with French legend Paul Bocuse, and he does Paul proud.

What's on the menu depends on what's fresh and in season. Appetizers might include smoked salmon roll with crab meat and angel hair pasta. Diners snap up John Dory, a tender New Zealand white fish. Imagine this — roasted tenderloin with shallots in a sweet soy sauce and lobster meat garnish, served with a honey-ginger vinaigrette. A popular dessert is the light, cool and refreshing crème brûlée. Beautiful plates and presentation are part of the event, down to the homemade mashed potato wreaths that frame many entrees. The waiters dote on customers. Even if dinner at the European Cafe is beyond the normal budget, you can get a darned good, dinner-caliber lunch here for about $10 or even less. Try the fish stew. European Cafe is open weekdays for lunch and daily for dinner.

INSIDERS' TIP

Even Boulder's finest restaurants often have room for drop-ins. Call ahead, or if it's a weekday, try your luck and just stop by.

Fawn Brook Inn

$$$$$ • Colo. Hwy. 7 Bus., Allenspark • 747-2556

This tiny mountain hamlet isn't where you'd expect fine continental dining, but Chef Hermann Groicher and his wife, Mieke, who come from Austria and Holland, respectively, have provided it for years. The 1996 season was their 18th at the Fawn Brook. Secret ingredients include the crisp mountain air and beautiful flower garden, but even if the surroundings weren't so inviting, the Fawn Brook's exquisite homemade fare, from beef vegetable soup through dessert, would be memorable. All that attention to homey mountain detail just makes it better. Venison served with wild berries and mushrooms, and roast duckling are favorite meals. Dinners start around $25, including soup, salad and entree.

Hours vary by the season. During summer, it's open Tuesday through Sunday for dinner. During fall and winter, it's open weekends, depending on the weather. Reservations are recommended. Call ahead for directions. It's about 45 minutes from Boulder and a half-hour from Estes Park.

Flagstaff House

$$$$$ • 1138 Flagstaff Rd., Boulder • 442-4640

When the Emperor and Empress of Japan came to America in 1994, they dined at only one freestanding restaurant on their entire national itinerary: Boulder's Flagstaff House. Chef Mark Monette offered their entourage pan-smoked salmon salad with caviar, tossed with local greens in wasabi vinaigrette along with lobster consommé with spring vegetables and black truffles. Entrees were Boulder trout from the Cline Trout Farm and rack of Colorado lamb with Provencale vegetables, goat cheese and Japanese eggplant chips. Desserts included Golden Egg Surprise, a cocoa sorbet wrapped with 24-carat gold leaf to make it look like a gold egg.

When legendary French chef Paul Bocuse set up a cooking event with great American chefs from both coasts, he chose the Flagstaff House. *Zagat* calls it one of Colorado's top 20 restaurants an it makes every "best" list that covers the Rocky Mountain dining scene. You get the idea?

The Flagstaff House, perched high on Flagstaff Mountain, has the most romantic, panoramic view of Boulder around. The Monette family has owned it for more than 25 years, and chef Mark Monette has trained in Paris at the Taillevent, the Trogois Brothers in Roanne and La Poularde in southern France, and also trained in Singapore, Tokyo, Thailand and Hong Kong. He has applied a rich blend of culinary knowledge, which has brought the restaurant increasing fame. More than 40 entrees grace the menu, which changes daily, but always includes a commendable selection of meat, seafood and game, and all other courses are comparable. The food is extraordinarily well prepared and artfully presented, and service is excellent too. The wine list is nationally renowned, and the sommeliers are knowledgeable and helpful. The tasting menu and paired wines is a fine way to tap into the best and freshest that have inspired the chef's creativity that very evening.

The Flagstaff is by and large an expense-account restaurant, where a full-course dinner for two will easily run into the three figures (the sommelier will gladly fill your request for the recommendation of a bottle of "mid-priced wine," which alone can easily be $50 or more) but is definitely worth a once-in-a-blue-moon, all-out grand dinner. Wise locals drive up at sunset or after the lights start twinkling in the valley below, order appetizers and wine or dessert and wine or coffee — not as grand as a full-course meal, but easier on the pocketbook. The Flagstaff House has also started serving afternoon tea. It's open daily for dinner. Reservations are highly recommended, although drop-ins often can be accommodated.

The Greenbriar Inn

$$$$ • U.S. Hwy. 36, Boulder • 440-7979

Picture an English earl strolling home with his spaniel and stopping at The Greenbriar, and you're close to the ambiance of this country inn. It has stained glass, dark wood decor and the vote from one Denver newspaper as the most romantic restaurant in the area. Michael Comstedt, member of the Cordon Bleu Ribbon Escoffier Society, is the award-winning chef. This is lordly traditional fare, great for special occasions. Game is well prepared, but rack of lamb is the signature plate. Among the

Photo: Daily Camera/David P. Gilkey

This Starbucks Coffee shop is in a remodeled gas station on University Hill.

seafood entrees, the shrimp and scallops ambrosia is divine. Follow with white chocolate cheesecake, or make your own combination for a memorable meal.

The Greenbriar is in the country but only 6.5 miles north of Boulder and about 45 minutes from Estes Park. It's open for dinner Tuesday through Saturday and for Sunday brunch. Reservations are recommended.

John's Restaurant
$$$ • 2328 Pearl St., Boulder • 444-5232

John's ambiance is as quaint and charming as its cuisine is excellent. For more than 20 years, chef/owner John Bizarro has garnered Best Chef awards from *Daily Camera* readers. John's has been featured in novels, and national restaurant critics consistently give it top reviews. Take the *Zagat* national restaurant survey, which calls John's "a small, romantically rustic place that's like eating in the chef's living room, always creative, well-prepared New American fare, wonderful service and sophisticated ambiance." *Rocky Mountain News* considers John's "as warm and pleasing as finding your way home." The French, Italian, Spanish and contemporary American cuisine is innovative yet classic. The Daily Camera calls it "a tranquil eye in the trendy hurricane of food fashions." To quote all the great reviews about John's would fill

more than a chapter. John's, in short, is a Boulder institution.

This gem is just a stroll east of the Pearl Street Mall. It is a small house with herbs and flowers grown in back and flowers out in front. The atmosphere is elegant but understated. The plates are a simple white, as are the tablecloths. The chairs are comfortable, and the lighting is subdued. All this background spotlights the food. We have never dined there without being delighted with each dish, both in service and superb cooking.

Classic French, Italian and Spanish influences are strong, and so is contemporary American cuisine, which is establishing a culinary tradition of its own. Basque-style seafood stew, with perfectly cooked clams, salmon and shrimp comes in a deliciously sea-flavored broth. If you're feeling more decadent, the creamier and meatier entrees are succulent. The filet mignon is fork-tender and rich, while the wild mushroom ravioli with rosemary porcini is a tender melding of pasta, several species of mushrooms and sun-dried tomatoes under a sprinkling of fresh Parmesan. And from sorbet through cheesecake and the dark chocolate desserts, the final tastes are melt-in-the-mouth good. The wine list is on a par with the cuisine, which is beautifully presented and gracefully served. The menu includes light but exquisite menu choices for waist-watchers, but perhaps an evening at John's is an invitation to stop watching for few hours.

John's is a place to go if you love good cooking and a civilized ambiance that invites good conversation. There's a magic about John's that can make your spirits glow. Parties range from friends wanting food that up-lifts their conversation to a solo business traveler reflecting on a day's work over a great meal to couples falling deeper in love. And the exceptional food is not expensive for what you get. Locals learned long ago that John's adds to special occasions. Many engagement rings have first twinkled in the candlelight at John's. Thanks to the attentive staff, engagement rings

Cafes

Great coffee is everywhere, and Boulder has become a great cafe town. Even food and gourmet stores serve eye-opening, high-caffeine espressos right next to the fresh vegetable juices. There's even an espresso bar in the Boulder Public Library. Boulder's coffee craze is most apparent in the abundance of its coffeehouses. Even Starbucks, the Seattle purveyor that launched the craze, has two locations in Boulder, and Peaberry has three. Beans of Boulder, The BookEnd Cafe, The Brewing Market, Buchanan's, Java Junction and Sidney's Cappuccino Bar all have their loyal fans, but the loyalest loyalists of all hang at Penny Lane and the Trident, two vener-

able coffeehouses that preceded the cafe craze.

Some open early enough to provide a 6 AM wake-up jolt (7 AM is the more common opening hour for most coffeehouses). All stay open until around 9 PM. Many manage to keep their eyes open until midnight, and a few, such as Caffe Mars, make it even later on weekends.

Choose mellow, filtered brews or thick, intense espressos with a shot of foamy steamed milk and a crumble of fresh cinnamon. In summer, iced coffee refreshes. Many coffeehouses also cater to the health advocates who find herb teas stimulating enough, thank you. Hot chocolate is for the young at heart.

The Foundry, 447-9591, 1107 Walnut Street, is known for honey-vanilla latte, poppy-seed cookies, sandwiches and cakes. Formerly Beans of Boulder, it now offers even more baked goods and light lunch entrees. **The BookEnd Cafe**, 440-6699, 1115 Pearl Street, is connected to the Boulder Bookstore. It's a see-and-be-seen place for the cellular-phone set, especially those who want a little lunch with their coffee. The scones, spelt muffins and coffee cake start the day off sweetly, and there's a good selection of mostly salads and light fare for lunch and supper. **The Brewing Market**, 444-4858, 2525 Arapahoe Avenue, has been around 20 years. An in-house master roaster roasts the beans. The atmosphere's simple, but it opens at 6 AM, and the crowds line up because they love the coffee as well as excellent chai, which is black tea, sweetened milk and spices. Don't be mislead by the Arapahoe address; The Brewing Market is actually a half-block off Arapahoe, next to McGuckin's on the southwest corner facing Folsom. **Caffe Mars**, 938-1750, in the alley at 1425 Pearl Street, is a big but cozy coffeehouse, serving espressos and cheesecakes for patrons who relax on red velvet couches and other antique furniture, arranged drawing room-style. The live music ranges from national recording artists to local jazz. At **Trident Booksellers and Cafe**, 443-3133, 940 Pearl Street, endangered bohemians love to converse over coffee. The **Peaberry Coffee, Ltd.** stores, 449-4111, at 2721 Arapahoe Avenue, 947 Pearl Street and 2400 Baseline Road, are among the metro area's growing Peaberry's sites. The owners are from Boulder, but they started their stores in Denver, then expanded to Boulder when it became clear Boulderites love gourmet coffee too. **Starbuck's** has settled into two locations, at 3033 Arapahoe Avenue, 440-5090, and near the CU-Boulder campus, at 1402 Broadway, 442-9199. Also near CU-Boulder are **Buchanan's**, 1301 Pennsylvania Avenue, 440-0222, a more yuppie hangout, and **Espresso Roma**, 1103 13th Street, 442-5011, the Hill's version of Cheers — with caffeine. **Penny Lane**, a historic Boulder hippie and teen hangout, relocated several years ago to 18th and Pearl streets, 443-9516, but it still offers local music and poetry, just like in the old days.

Surrounding towns have their cafes too. Nederland's **Acoustic Coffee**, 95 E. First Street, 258-3209, is in a red brick house with a summer patio and decorated rocking chairs on the porch. Inside are tables printed with chess boards where customers can play chess, a sitting area with a tattered Victorian couch and an old wooden ironing board holding the milk and sugar. Used books and new magazines are for sale, and the artwork is both original and daring. In addition to coffee, you can buy herb tea, fresh scones and specials such as mango-apple pie and Italian potato vegetable soup. Locals come here for poetry readings and for music or to read and relax, as they do at the **Javastop**, 301 Main Street, Longmont, 772-1731, in the Old Imperial Hotel.

have even popped up in desserts. That's what happened to Betsy, now wife of *Daily Camera* Food Editor John Lehndorff. The dessert was one of the chocolate ones, of course. But this place can elevate any encounter.

Walk-ins can often be seated promptly. John's is open for dinner daily.

Red Lion Inn
$$$ • 38470 Boulder Canyon Rd., Boulder • 442-9368

This Old World inn is just 4 miles up Boulder Canyon. This rambling country inn is popular for family gatherings, business dinners, banquets and weddings. A specialty is wild game, such as venison or pheasant. Much of the menu has become popularized American cuisine, but there are such decided Austro-German influences as red cabbage and spaetzle noodles, a good accompaniment with entrees, followed by a tasty dessert tray. The restaurant offers early-bird specials. It's open for dinner daily.

French

Bistro St. Tropez
$$ • 7960 Niwot Rd., Niwot • 652-0747

This new restaurant is Mediterranean — the French coast of the Mediterranean. Suffused with informal yet sophisticated charm, it serves French country specialties with a modern flair. Seafood abounds, of course, but the menu also features excellent chicken, lamb, beef and pasta. Reservations are accepted but are not necessary. Bistro St. Tropez is open for lunch weekdays and dinner nightly except Sunday.

Le Français
$ • 2570 Baseline Rd., Boulder • 499-7429

Real French chefs bake their authentic breads and pastries in stone ovens. The breezy, close-to-CU cafe offers an assortment of croissant sandwiches, French bread and onion soup, spinach salads and those wonderfully decadent French desserts. The ambiance is cafe-casual (after all, the pastry counter is right there), but lunches and especially dinners are restaurant-fine. You can order with beer or wine. Do you like Grand Marnier cake with butter cream frosting? How about a thick, rich chocolate mousse shaped like a mouse? This restaurant is open for breakfast, lunch and dinner Monday through Saturday and breakfast and lunch Sunday.

Pour La France Cafe & Bistro
$$ • 1001 Pearl St., Boulder • 449-3929

Every table in this popular corner cafe is often filled, except the spot waiting for you. This sprightly cafe with a South of France accent can be called sophisticated yet casual.

Pour La France's coffee has earned a Best of Boulder award from *Daily Camera* readers, and recently, the cafe also earned Best Desserts awards. The croissant sandwiches, home-made soups and bistro-style dinners are terrific and well-priced too. Many tables are close enough to watch the West Pearl scene through white lace half-curtains, and in the warm months, the outdoor tables are as jammed as the indoor ones. This cafe and bistro is open for breakfast, lunch and dinner daily, through midnight on Friday, Saturday and Sunday and until 10:30 PM weeknights.

Indian

Delhi Darbar
$$ • 826 Pearl St., Boulder • 443-3929

This dimly lit downstairs restaurant, a branch of a popular Denver establishment, serves aromatic and exquisite Indian specialties, including outstanding tandoori offerings from a special clay oven. Chicken, lamb and vegetarian items grace the huge menu. The inexpensive, all-you-can-eat lunch buffet is a winner with the bottomless-pit crowd. In summer, there is also a pleasant brick patio. Delhi Darbar is open daily for lunch and dinner.

Himalayas Restaurant
$$ • 2010 14th St., Boulder • 442-3230

Authentic Indian, Nepalese and Tibetan cuisine includes tandoori breads and *thali*, a vegetarian sampler. You can order the chicken and lamb curries milder or hotter. Live Indian music on Sundays includes sitar — sort of mandolin music without that bluegrassy sound. This restaurant is open for lunch and dinner daily except on Sunday, when it's dinner only. Reservations are recommended on weekends.

MijBani
$-$$ • 2005 18th St., Boulder • 442-7000

Well-known Boulder cooking teacher Jessica Shah made a great leap by opening a small side-street restaurant that bears her personal stamp of unusual vegetarian fare from southern India. She still teaches occasionally, and MijBani also serves special-occasion dinners. You won't get regular chicken curry in this interesting restaurant, which offers both conventional and futon seating and live or recorded Indian music that simply adds to the ambiance. Jessica has devised a distinctive menu of low-fat, authentic, homestyle cuisine.

The menu is divided into themes. You can order from a selection of *thali* combination plates, entrees that come paired with suitable side dishes. Other plates are centered around *idlis*, which are steamed rice cakes, or crepe-like rice breads, served with coconut chutneys and dal soup. Samosas — pastries stuffed with spiced potatoes, onions and peas — are outstanding starters. Exotic varieties of ice cream finish the meal in equal style. Beer and wine are served, but many diners opt for the excellent chai tea, just about Boulder's best. In addition to reasonably complete and à la carte dinners, MijBani also an sets out an inexpensive all-you-can-eat buffet lunch. MijBani is open for lunch and dinner daily except Monday.

Narayan's Nepal Restaurant
$ • 1130 Pearl St., Boulder • 447-2816

Recently relocated to a sizable downstairs restaurant on the Pearl Street Mall, Narayan's is back with the distinctive mountain fare that has captivated the many Boulderites who have trekked or climbed in Nepal. Vegetable-stuffed roti (flatbread) comes with lentil or garbanzo soup and is especially good, but the vegetable sampler remains the No. 1 request from the

---

INSIDERS' TIP

For larger parties or for special places, dinner reservations are recommended. Reservations matter more during summer, especially during weekends or events such as CU-Boulder graduation in May. In winter, Valentine's Day and other special evenings book up fast. That doesn't mean you generally need reservations weeks in advance. Even at the finest places, a call just before you leave can mean a table waiting for you when you arrive.

menu. Locals like the bargain prices. Narayan's is open for lunch and dinner daily.

Royal Peacock
$$ • 5290 Arapahoe Ave., Boulder • 447-1409

Each year, the owners, who are Bombay natives, add yet another peacock motif to their beautiful restaurant. The chai tea with spices and sweetened milk is delicious. Hot curried Indian dishes are served, along with vegetarian choices in rich cream sauces, good basmati rice (order lots for anyone who prefers mild food) and yogurt/cucumber salads. Service is impeccably polite. The staff love kids, although the leisurely pace of the meal can be a bit long for the youngest tykes. Royal Peacock is open for lunch weekdays and daily for dinner.

The Taj
$$ • 2360 Baseline Rd., Boulder • 494-2516

The sights, sounds, smells and tastes of Boulder's best new Indian restaurant are so genuinely Indian that you have trouble putting it in context with the Basemar shopping center's acres of asphalt just outside the windows. This large space is divided into a rambling procession of dining areas brought to intimate scale by the personal service and excellent food. Note that we said "personal," not "speedy" or "efficient," for The Taj is a place for dining and lingering. Everything is custom-prepared at dinner. The opulent, inexpensive lunch buffet provides a sampling if you hurry when you eat. There is a full bar. Open for lunch and dinner.

Italian

Al Fresco
$$ • 2690 Baseline Rd., Boulder • 543-9090

This relaxed version of the European Cafe, owned by the same group, specializes in northern Italian cuisine. Al Fresco gives generous portions, so come with your appetite cocked. Especially popular is ziti al fresco, a signature dish of big tubular pasta bathed in sun-dried tomato, basil cream sauce with spicy sausage.

The tender grilled lamb chops are sauced with balsamic vinegar and Barolo wine, one of the finest wines of northern Italy. The lamb also comes with whole roasted garlic cloves. Try the exquisite tiramisu and *melazenzero*, an apple-ginger cake served with caramel ice cream. Open for lunch daily except Sunday and for dinner daily.

Antica Roma
$$ • 1308 Pearl St., Boulder • 442-0378

This is one of the Pearl Street Mall's most atmospheric restaurants, a stylish trattoria painted and decorated to look like a piazza in a residential quarter of Rome. There's even a fountain in the middle of the room. It's been a steady winner of Best of Boulder honors from the *Daily Camera* as well as in *Westword's* and the *Rocky Mountain News'* ratings; and with good food, a nice selection of matching wines and knockout atmosphere, it's no wonder.

Rich Italian dishes, many from the southern portion of the country, dominate the menu. Popular dishes include *rotolo al sugo rosso*, a lasagna pasta rolled with spinach and ricotta filling and baked casserole-style in a tomato, basil and garlic sauce, and an excellent *salmone alla Miditerranea*, which is a salmon filet marinated in white wine and broiled with aromatic herbs and chopped tomatoes. The lunch and dinner menus both feature an assortment of pastas and other satisfying offerings, but the lunch menu is slightly smaller and lighter. If you sit on the patio in summer, you can watch the Pearl Street scene to your heart's desire. Open from 11:30 AM to 11 PM daily.

Attusso's of Brooklyn Italian Cafe
$$ • 1739 Pearl St., Boulder • 442-2262

This little Italian place just east of the Pearl Street Mall serves traditional manicotti and other dishes whose recipes Italian immigrants brought to New York. "Tradition" is a key word here. This is the place to go for red-sauce Italian favorites, including the aforementioned manicotti, lasagna and various pastas with assorted toppings. Scaloppini saltimbocca is derived from a phrase that means "to jump in the mouth," and Attuso's version is so good that description is apt. People can sit and relax inside or on the porch. Open for dinner daily.

Blue Parrot

$$ • 640 Main St., Louisville • 666-0677

Long before "ethnic" food became trendy, this family-run restaurant was providing locals with informal, inexpensive Italian food. The restaurant opened in 1919, when Louisville's coal mines brought many Italian families into the area. For decades, a special evening in Boulder often would end with a trip to the Blue Parrot for a homestyle Italian meal. Today, the noodles are still homemade, down to the gnocchi, made of mashed potatoes.

You can buy Blue Parrot pasta sauce at grocery stores these days, and it's served by the Boulder Valley Public School system — perhaps that's the telling detail. Lots of kids don't like seasonings, and the food here is certainly not spicy. The atmosphere here has stayed unpretentious, so it's a good choice for casual family dining, especially for finicky young eaters who prefer bland to zesty. Open for breakfast, lunch and dinner daily.

Diva

$$$ • 1965 15th St., Boulder • 442-4222

Veteran caterer Marietta Sisca is now the owner/chef of this stylish new northern Italian trattoria around the corner from the Pearl Street Mall. The antipasti are excellent, as are the seafood entrees and Sisca's renditions of pasta and risotto. Desserts are homemade and delicious. Diva's lunch has been uneven, and at this writing it is still struggling to find a niche. Live jazz, mellow enough for conversation, starts at 8 PM on certain slow evenings. The best dishes are the peer of any in town, and a growing lunch and dinner crowd is coming to recognize Diva's strengths. Open for lunch weekdays and dinner nightly except Sunday.

D'Napoli Ristorante

$$ • 835 Walnut St., Boulder • 444-8434

Filling Italian fare, mostly of the traditional southern Italian variety, is served in this amiable, casual restaurant. Spaghetti, ziti and fettuccine, the most popular pasta shapes, dominate the menu and are available with an assortment of sauces. Perennial favorites including eggplant parmigiana, lasagna with or without meat and shrimp fra diavolo are also served. Some seafood, some poultry, some meat and pizza too are options. Open for dinner 4 to 10 PM nightly except Monday.

Full Moon Grill

$$$ • 2525 Arapahoe Ave., Boulder • 938-8800

This small, cheerful dining room has great food. Northern Italian specialties include seafood and risottos, such as a caper-crusted sea bass fillet with oven-roasted asparagus and citrus emulsion sauce. Great decorative touches are more than merely Italian and include wooden Balinese pigs that decorate the room as visual garnishes to chef Bradford Heap's newest creations. Heap trained in top French and Italian restaurants and at the Culinary Institute of America before settling into Boulder, and his artistry shows. Open for dinner daily and for lunch weekdays.

Laudisio Ristorante Italiano

$$$$ • 2785 Iris Ave., Boulder • 442-1300

The Denver Post calls this the best Italian restaurant in the area. *Zagat* calls it the best Italian restaurant in Colorado. It has received Best of Boulder awards from the *Daily Camera* too. It's one of the most flamboyant dining spots. And why not? The whole Laudisio family is flamboyant, and their namesake restaurant is a metaphor for their passions. They focus on fresh, local ingredients, exquisitely prepared and generously served. The bustling open kitchen puts forth outstanding food as well as a real sense of family celebration. Look for the photograph of Raimondo Laudisio, reclining in his chef's cap, draping spaghetti into his mouth as rapturously as a Greek god dallying with grapes. The wine list is extensive, comprehensive and served with knowledge and grace. There's no grace but a lot of potency to the fiery Italian liqueurs called grappas, which seem to come from vials of an ancient laboratory. Yes, the pasta is superb, and so is the risotto, the perfectly cooked seafood and the chicken. And of course, the desserts — tiramisu, champagne zablagioni and innovative glacés. Ask for patio seating under the grapevines or in the quiet dining room with antique Tiffany-style lamps. Open for lunch weekdays and for dinner daily.

Millsite Inn

$ • 44365 Peak to Peak Hwy., Ward
• 459-3308

They make the dough for their calzones and pizzas fresh here, with a good sauce and anything in them. They have homemade pies and good desserts. Friends give high ratings to their chicken Marsala and other full dinners. The food tends toward Italian-American with a little Mexican, pizza and burgers thrown in. Add to that a comfortably rustic, log-cabin atmosphere. The locals hang out here, meaning residents of the nearby funky town called Ward, skiers and hikers. The guys in the bar have an amiable grubbiness to them and usually pay close attention to the TV broadcasting a game. Open for lunch and dinner daily, with the bar open until 2 AM when someone's still thirsty.

Neapolitan's

$$, no credit cards • 1 W. First St., Nederland • 258-7313

This little place is absolutely mobbed on the weekends, when you might wait up to an hour for a table. People are standing in line for the friendly, busy atmosphere and basic Italian food. During the week, it's not as busy. The stuffed shells are delicious, as is the chicken Marsala. Homemade garlic rolls are always a nice accompaniment. The Gorgonzola salad dressing is a nice touch. For the indecisive, the veggie combo of meatless lasagna, a stuffed shell, ziti and eggplant is a good option. In addition to an array of Italian entrees, Neo's serves an outstanding white pizza in addition to red — both available with a variety of toppings. Reservations are taken and carry-out is available. Open for dinner Monday through Thursday; for lunch and dinner Friday, Saturday and Sunday.

Pasta Jay's

$$ • 1701 Pearl St., Boulder • 444-5800

When Pasta Jay's was located near Ninth and Pearl, it was the busiest of Boulder restaurants and even spawned branches in Breckenridge and Moab. But real estate redevelopment sledgehammered this beloved Boulder institution, and it closed on April 26, 1996, a day that will live in infamy for fans of this popular restaurant. A few months of being

closed and a shift to the other side of the Pearl Street Mall did nothing to dim Pasta Jay's luster. In fact, if anything, loyal patrons seemed to make up for lost time, lining up for the new place as they had for the old.

The high-ceilinged dining room, red-and-white-checkered tablecloths and memorabilia tacked to the exposed brick walls combine to create a pleasant and lively scene. The large roof-top terrace offers dining under the stars, and although longtime regulars might rue the loss of the streetside patio of the old place, it is actually nice to have a view of something other than automobile bumpers. The menu is constructed on a solid foundation of the most popular Italian dishes: manicotti, spaghetti and various tubular pastas with several flavorful sauces and pizza too. Fans love Pasta Jay's mixed salad, drenched in a flavorful dressing, and warm herb and garlic bread. A decent selection of robust domestic and imported wines is available. Pasta Jay's serves continuously from 11 AM until 10:30 PM daily.

Salvaggio's Italian Deli

$, no credit cards • 2609 Pearl St., Boulder • 938-1981

This place has great sandwiches, and they're busy all the time. Salvaggio's serves special Italian sausages and Boar's Head-brand meats — among the highest quality domestic cold cuts you can buy. Prime rib sandwiches are slow-roasted in the rotisserie oven and, when it comes to popularity, they blow everything else away, hands down. The Cajun roast beef and Mortadella ham are knockouts. Roasted red bell peppers and fresh mozzarella can be added too. The sandwich bread is homemade. It's even better for take-out than for eating in. Open for lunch and dinner daily.

Mediterranean/African

Falafel Man

$, no credit cards • Crossroads Mall Food Court • Crossroads Mall, Boulder
• 442-2888

This casual eatery serves falafel sandwiches, along with lamb gyros and baklava, an almond-honey-filo dough dessert — all popular foods from the Mediterranean area.

Falafels are spicy chick-pea balls — deep-fried, then served in pita pockets along with lots of lettuce and a zesty tahini sauce. Spanakopita is a yummy spinach and feta cheese pastry. It's among the more interesting food that you can grab for mall strolling. Falafel Man is open for lunch and dinner daily.

Mataam Fez Moroccan Restaurant
$$$ • 2226 Pearl St., Boulder • 440-4167

This richly decorated, exotic restaurant is as much about entertainment as fine dining. While sitting on plump pillows under tented ceilings and listening to Moroccan drums, you will eat with your fingers, but you won't be eating what we think of as finger food.

Dine sumptuously on five-course meals such as couscous with vegetables, lamb with artichokes and delicious Moroccan tea and pastries. There is a selection of meat and vegetarian dishes.

But best of all, belly dancers entertain Thursday through Sunday. Belly dancing originated to encourage women through childbirth — hence the focus on strong abdominal movements, which perhaps is why we can say, "Belly dancing and children welcome." But, hey, this is Boulder, so it's not Las Vegas belly dancing for heaven's sake! This restaurant serves dinner daily.

The Mediterranean
$$-$$$ • 1002 Walnut St., Boulder • 444-5335

From the bright-red trim to the beautiful iron gate and the avant-garde wood-burning brick oven, this place is stylish and lively. The Mediterranean is another grand restaurant operated by the large Laudisio family. It has been voted best Mediterranean restaurant in the Denver area by *Westword* magazine and Best Appetizers by *Daily Camera* readers. It's what you want it to be: a romantic spot, a congenial gathering place with a good bar and summer patio but also a family spot — kids get kind treatment here.

Spanish tapas, which are small plates of interesting appetizers, include *croquetas de gambase y pollo* (shrimp and chicken) and lovely mini-pizzas. These are served at the bar or at the table. Light dishes include well-prepared calzones and perfectly dressed salads.

Spaghettini di Mare is especially popular. The chefs know how to cook chicken and fish without leaving the heat on a moment too long. Spanish friends say the saffron-gold paella is pretty close to authentic. The Mediterranean is open for dinner daily and for lunch on weekdays.

Ras Kassa's Ethiopian Restaurant
$$ • S. Broadway and Eldorado Springs Dr., Boulder • 494-2919

Meat and vegetarian dishes are served with a big slab of *injera*, a crepe-like Ethiopian sourdough bread, which you use to scoop up the rest of the food. Use the bread like a spoon to capture every drop of the hot, red sauces or the milder ginger and garlic sauces. Entrees include chicken or lamb, sweet potato stew and butternut squash. Eat in the Ethiopian-decorated interior, with authentic basket-woven tables, or out on the patio with its great mountain view.

This is a place to hit early, for it's tiny and personalized, so the tables fill up fast and diners linger as long as they can tolerate the backless stools. It's open for dinner daily.

Shishkabob
$, no credit cards • Crossroads Mall Food Court • Crossroads Mall, Boulder • 443-8844

Nabil Karkamaz could open a bigger restaurant, but he likes the great deal he offers in the serve-it-up style of the Crossroads Food Court. For $6 you can get a full meal and drink. Basmati rice (always fresh and fragrant), cucumber and yogurt salads, vegetarian spinach casseroles and lamb dishes are here. Also some of the best lemonade in town, with rose water adding a special bouquet to the sweet tangy drink. Shishkabob is open for lunch and dinner daily.

Mexican

Casa Alvarez
$$ • 3161 Walnut St., Boulder • 546-0630

No sooner did Casa Alvarez open in a corner of the Walnut Garden shopping center than people started raving about its chili — and the honors started pouring in, including winning the Boulder Chile Ole Contest right out of the blocks. The red and green chili are each just about the best of their type around, but the restaurant has a way with other Mexican specialties too. There are the usual offerings from the "corn kitchen," including tostadas, tacos and taquitos — all well done — plus beef, pork, chicken and seafood specialties; the latter come with a choice of soup or salad. The *caldo de camaron*, a shrimp and vegetable soup, is particularly good. When it's mild out, the patio is a pleasant place to enjoy your meal. Casa Alvarez makes good Margaritas and sells them two-for-one during happy hour, from 4 to 6 PM every evening. There are also beer and well drink specials. ("Well drink" is the western expression for a cocktail made with house-brand spirits.) Takeout is available too. Open for lunch and dinner daily.

Efrain's
$$ • 101 E. Cleveland St., Lafayette • 666-7544

Efrain's is in an old farmhouse, where the dining area is relaxed and homey. The great tamales, green chiles and sizzling tostadas make Efrain's one of Boulder County's favorite Mexican restaurants. There are also costillas, which are Mexican ribs in chile verde sauce. Open for lunch and dinner daily.

Gustavo's
$ • 357 Main St., Longmont • 678-8814

Those in the know say that Gustavo Saenz is just a doll, and the fresh-cooked food's a bargain. Gustavo's has homemade guacamole and delicious enchiladas. You can get a tostada for less than $3. The green chile that smothers burritos and tamales is mild and freshly made. Open for lunch and dinner Tuesday through Saturday.

La Estrellita
$ • 1718 Broadway, Boulder • 939-8822

National Hispanic Magazine chose La Estrellita as one of the top 50 Hispanic restaurants in the United States. This "little star" recently relocated from a dark cave of a place to the large, airy space vacated by First Wok, with indoor dining and the loveliest creekside patio around. The beers and Margaritas are still good. La Estrellita's best seller is a combi-

nation plate with smothered burrito, relleno and enchilada. A farmer in Brighton, Colorado, grows the Anaheim and green chiles for this family-owned restaurant. On Thursday afternoons during the school year, the restaurant sets aside a table where Spanish speakers meet. Open daily for lunch and dinner.

Masa Grill Mexican Taqueria
$, no credit cards • 1265 Alpine Ave., Boulder • 440-9511

Step up to the counter and order yourself to the Burrito Grande, an aptly named, humongous fresh-made burrito in various combinations, which can be tailored to your liking. Tostadas, fajitas and tacos are also on the menu, and there are daily specials as well. The Taqueria's distinctive cilantro rice is an interesting variation on a common theme. There are also decent fresh lime Margaritas, served at bargain prices during the daily happy hour, plus good beers and soft drinks. This good-size restaurant is inexpensive and family-friendly, combining the best elements of fast preparation and service with really good, filling food. *Ole!* Open for lunch and dinner daily.

Rio Grande Mexican Restaurant
$ • 1101 Walnut St., Boulder • 444-3690

The old Piccolo's has undergone a huge renovation to become the new Rio Grande, a popular Margarita dispensary and Mexican restaurant. Colorful Tex-Mex burritos, enchiladas and fajitas with loads of cheddar cheese, black beans and Spanish rice are featured. The restaurant also offers tortilla chips and *pico de gallo*, a spicy vegetable relish. The restaurant is open for lunch and dinner daily.

Tia Bennie
$$ • 450 Main St., Lyons • 823-5014

James Arroyo, a Lyons native, named this casual, family restaurant after his Aunt Bennie. It occupies a 125-year-old flagstone, ranch-style building on the west end of Lyons' main thoroughfare. The cook's combination — cheese enchilada, chile relleno, beans and rice — and the burritos supreme are especially popular. Open daily for lunch and dinner in summer (closing at 6 PM Sunday), but closed on Sunday during the off-season.

Natural

Boulder Harvest Restaurant
$ • 1738 Pearl St., Boulder • 449-6223

This was one of Boulder's first natural-food restaurants, and it's still popular today. It offers scrambled tofu, chicken-cashew salad sandwiches and homemade soups plus smoothies, such as the orange juice, ice, fructose and banana combination (you can add ice cream if you want.) A large table allows singles to join others, and though this was designed to promote mingling, it seems people tend to seat themselves with at least one space between themselves and their neighbors and surround themselves with a barricade of newspapers.

The Harvest serves as much food grown, raised and made in Colorado as possible — natural and preservative-free — but it's not a vegetarian restaurant. Sunday through Thursday, after 5 PM, two children eat free for every adult entree purchase of $6 or more. Open for breakfast daily and until 9:30 PM Sunday through Thursday, with somewhat longer hours on weekends and a long weekend brunch.

Boulder Salad Company
$ • 2595 Canyon Blvd., Boulder • 447-8272

All-you-can-eat salads, soups and pasta, potatoes, baked goods and fruits are strung along this very popular, very healthy grazing bar. You get in line and choose your items cafeteria-style. It's a super choice for groups who can't agree on what to eat. For all the good eating, you can be rewarded with a big, fresh chocolate chip cookie. Or be super-healthy, and say, "No thanks." The Salad Company issues a card entitling you to a free meal after a dozen paid ones. Open for lunch and dinner daily.

Creative Vegetarian Cafe
$ • 1837 Pearl St., Boulder • 449-1952

Old hippiedom meets New Age in this funky dining spot, which is known for excellent and very pure vegetarian meals. The preparation is careful, and the ingredients couldn't be fresher. Tofu, tempeh, natural grains, beans, rice and vegetables, vegetables and more vegetables dominate the menu, but you'll find wonderful desserts too. A small patio is open in summer, and sometimes there's mellow live entertainment during weekend brunch hours. Open for breakfast and lunch weekdays, brunch Saturday and Sunday and dinner nightly except Sunday.

Healthy Habits Restaurant
$ • 4760 Baseline Rd., Boulder • 494-9177

Rocky Mountain News gives this restaurant its Reader's Choice Award. Like the Boulder Salad Company, Healthy Habits is another wholesome restaurant where the grazing is easy. The salad bar is huge, and there are various pastas and soups too. Kids like a slice of pizza, and adults appreciate the cooked vegetables and potatoes at night. It's also great for people attending to their health, for the array of fresh vegetables and low-fat choices is grand. Keep in mind, the chocolate brownie at the dessert counter is still a chocolate brownie, and just because it's called Healthy Habits doesn't mean you can't manufacture an unhealthy meal for yourself by skipping the vegetables and loading up on the buttered bread, cookies and higher-fat items from the salad bar. Open for lunch and dinner daily.

Rudi's Restaurant
$$$ • 4720 Table Mesa Dr., Boulder • 494-5858

This is a natural-food restaurant that looks and feels like a "normal" place, not like a granola-and-tofu dispensary. Still, the fine din-

INSIDERS' TIP

Local two-for-one dining discount cards are good for various deals at more than three dozen restaurants and other services including ski or bike rentals, oil changes, hair care, dry cleaning and more. Some restrictions apply (often weekend dinners are excepted), but then, some are good for multiple offers. Call 604-3169 for details and prices, which vary according to when you order your card.

Photo: Daily Camera

Chautauqua Dining Hall is very popular during summer.

ing is based on a variety of influences from all over the world, but with natural and organic ingredients. Samosas, a type of Indian snack food made with mildly spiced vegetables, is a fine starter. Thai vegetable curry and crab-stuffed trout are typical entrees and are served with homemade soup or salad and brown or basmati rice. The tenderloin filet is organically grown. If you come for brunch, try the ginger-bread pancakes with whipped cream. Home-made desserts include coffee toffee and Key lime pie. Vegans and people on special diets can get made-to-order food here. Open for lunch and dinner daily except Monday and also for weekend brunch.

Turley's
$$ • 2350 Arapahoe Ave., Boulder • 442-2800

This friendly and unpretentious restaurant is the keeper of the flame of a particular kind of Boulder eating place. Paul Turley created the Golden Buff Restaurant and Pablo's, both now gone but similar to this place in ambiance, style and price. Turley's is decorated with photos of food markets from around the world. Entrees include lots of vegetables, served with a choice of quinoa or brown rice, plus grilled tuna, chicken black bean burrito, scrambled tofu and other Boulderish offer-ings that eschew red meat or anything re-sembling gravy. Turley's offers comfort food too, including chicken pot pie and buffalo

meat loaf served with knockout mashed po-tatoes. All entrees come with a choice of soup or salad and a roll or the muffin of the day. There's a good selection of microbrews and wines as well as full bar service, and the res-taurant does fine with smoothies and des-serts as well. If you've hiked your way to a big appetite, try the Granny Smith's sour cream apple pie. Open for breakfast, lunch and dinner daily.

Pizza

Lefty's
$, no credit cards • 364 Second Ave., Niwot • 652-3100

The favorite pizzas at this down-home lo-cal pizza parlor are the California Veggie (arti-chokes, broccoli, sun-dried tomatoes, spinach, mozzarella, garlic and olive oil) and Craig's Cardiac Arrest (pepperoni, ham, sausage and bacon). But you can also get pineapple, jalapeños and black olives. Best of all, the pizzeria delivers in Niwot and the surrounding 80 square miles, ranging from Longmont to north Lafayette. A percentage of all proceeds goes to Niwot's youth team sports. This little pizza parlor is open for lunch and dinner daily.

Mountain Mike's Pizza
$ • 1630 30th St., Boulder • 442-4443

Oh my, good pie! In addition to the usual

list of flavors and combinations, Mountain Mike puts together Louisiana hot links and green chili pizza and mountain veggie-more pizza. Only whole pies are offered for eat-in, take-out or delivery within a limited area, which is different during the day and in the evening. Open for lunch and dinner Monday through Saturday.

Nick-N-Willy's Take-N-Bake Pizza
$ • 801 Pearl St., Boulder • 444-9898
$ • 4800 Baseline Rd., Boulder • 499-9898
Rich in fine cheeses and gourmet touches, Nick-N-Willy's is the pizza version of Alfalfa's and has steadily been voted Best Pizza of Boulder by *Daily Camera* readers. You can buy pizza by the slice and eat it in the store, or call ahead and, 20 minutes later, pick up a whole pizza to take home and bake in your oven. It all started when a friend of Keith McQuillen and Terry Jones opened a great pizza store in California. Keith and Terry found the take-and-bake pizza so delicious, they brought the idea to Boulder. Over the years, they've added different pizzas and toppings, improved their establishments' interiors and have expanded into a dozen different Colorado locations. The Aegean vegetarian pizza is one of the most popular, with olive oil, feta, mozzarella, garlic, spinach, sun-dried tomatoes and oregano. There's a big cooler with soft drinks and pre-made salads if you need something to complement your pie. Open daily for lunch and dinner.

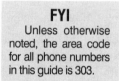

FYI
Unless otherwise noted, the area code for all phone numbers in this guide is 303.

Pubs and Brew Pubs

Bullfrog's
$$ • 1709 Pearl St., Boulder • 442-2542
The owners of The Hungry Toad took their English pub concept and sort of cloned it on Pearl Street, east of the Mall. The food is similar, the atmosphere is sprightlier (there's even a little outdoor seating area) and the feeling more youthful. In addition to English pub fare, there's live entertainment on Wednesday evenings. The best part, for some downtown workers, is the lunches for $5 or less. Open for lunch (from 10 AM on weekends) and dinner daily.

The Hungry Toad
$$ • 2543 Broadway, Boulder • 442-5012
This is Boulder's original English pub. Four English beers are on tap, and eight are available by the bottle. Fish and chips, shepherd's pie, salads and burgers are popular. The food's not arty, my lad, but it's hearty, accompanied by comfortable chatter and a pint at your elbow. Open for lunch and dinner daily.

The James
$$ • 1922 13th St., Boulder • 449-1922
This popular downtown pub, which fronts on a side street and bores deep into the center of the block, is remarkable for its longevity. Happy hour is notable for cheap well drinks (cocktails), beer specials and for bargain burgers and fries — and for its duration, from 4 to 7 PM and again from 10 PM until last call nightly except Sunday. The James dishes up great appetizers, including such ever-green faves as cheese and artichoke dip, tri-color nachos, potato skins and wings. Sandwiches dominate the lunch menu, and grilled entrees are featured at dinner. Of course, there's also something stir-fried, something else baked and another something served over pasta to choose from. Garlic bread comes with everything but the stir-fries, but your server will bring you some regardless if you ask nicely. Open daily for lunch and dinner.

Mountain Sun Pub and Brewery
$, no credit cards • 1535 Pearl St., Boulder • 546-0886
This bustling place is Boulder's New Age brew pub, with seven made-on-the-premises fresh brews that sprang onto the microbrew scene by winning awards. The food is a winner too. Most of it is vegetarian, including meatless salads, chili, soup, garden burgers, burritos and pizzas, so you might call it a health-food brew pub. There are shelves of books patrons can peruse while listening to live folk music on Sundays. Open for lunch and dinner daily.

Oasis Brewery
$$ • 1095 Canyon Blvd., Boulder • 449-0363

About six fresh-brewed beers are generally on tap, including Scarab Red (the name is in keeping with the brewery's Egyptian barge decor), a roasted barley, dry-finished amber ale that has won gold and silver medals at tastings around the country. Excellent munchies plus commendable ribs, seafood and pasta go with the beer. There's patio seating, free parking and a pool parlor upstairs. Open for lunch and dinner through 2 AM daily every night except Sunday, when it closes at midnight.

Old Chicago
$ • 1102 Pearl St., Boulder • 443-5031

It's hard to decide whether to describe this spot on the west end of the Pearl Street Mall as a pub that serves popular Chicago-style pizzas or a pizzeria with a whopping beer selection. More than 110 beers are available from the bar, and the deep-dish pizza is buttery crusted and delicious; whole wheat crust is also available. The main part of the restaurant truly has a pub feel, while the seatings in the back are more generously spaced. There's also a small patio in the rear. Old Chicago's stout mud pie has layers of coffee and chocolate ice cream, flavored with Australian Sheaf Stout beer. Open for lunch and dinner through midnight on weekdays and 1 AM on weekends; unlike many brew pubs, the kitchen stays open till Old Chicago's closes.

Rockies Brewing Company
$ • 2880 Wilderness Pl., Boulder • 444-8448

Eight different fresh ales are made on the premises, including the namesake brew, concocted for the Colorado Rockies baseball team. Three are gold-medal winners, pronounced the best beer in the country at the Great American Beer Festival. Sandwiches and salad go with the fresh beer, and if you arrive around 2 PM, you can tour the establishment, see the whole beer-making process and sample the current brews. This was formerly the Boulder Brewery, the first microbrewery in the city. Open for lunch and dinner daily except Sundays.

Walnut Brewery
$$ • 1123 Walnut St., Boulder • 447-1345

This was Boulder's first true brew pub, and it's still the best. The brewing process is on display here, and you can watch while you drink and dine. The brewmaster concocts six original and seasonal ales, including Buffalo Gold, brewed in small batches to provide a malty, floral happiness . . . we mean, hoppiness. The Walnut Brewery pioneered the practice of donating leftovers from the brewing process to feed happy livestock and to enrich soil in flower beds on the downtown mall. Sometimes, walking the mall is a truly heady experience.

Salads, tenderloin, seafood, pastas and vegetarian entrees help draw the crowds to this distinctive, tall-ceilinged, lively space. Live music on Friday and Saturday can be anything from calypso and reggae to rhythm and blues (see the listing in our Nightlife chapter for details). Open from lunch through 1:15 AM every night except Sunday, when it closes at midnight.

West End Tavern
$ • 926 Pearl St., Boulder • 444-3535

This is more a bar than a pub, for it is really basic and ungentrified — just the way fans like it. It serves good basic salads, soups and plenty of burgers along with 20 different beers and concoctions from the full bar. There's live music or comedy five nights a week and sometimes seven. The rooftop, with the view of the Flatirons, is the most popular summer spot at this friendly neighborhood tavern. Open for lunch and dinner daily; the West End closes at 2 AM.

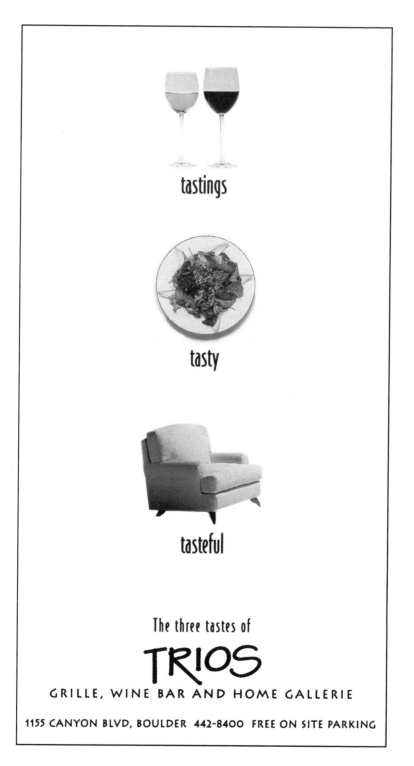

Boulder
Nightlife

Boulder isn't particularly known for its wild nightlife — other than the occasional neighborhood bear or mountain lion — though there's plenty to do and plenty of places to go after dark. The college crowd has its hangouts, as do the single professionals and families. Most residents and visitors looking for a night out go to a restaurant, concert or movie or to one of the many spots listed subsequently.

Because our state is so beautiful and the weather so fine, Boulderites and Coloradans thrive on the out-of-doors. Therefore, many cafes and concert halls are al fresco. On warm evenings from spring through fall one of the most popular activities that's unrivaled in entertainment value (and free) is strolling on the Pearl Street Mall. During summer weekends, especially, this four-block, outdoor pedestrian mall is transformed into a six-ring circus on every block with jugglers, musicians, magicians, bagpipers, Peruvian bands, the amazing "zip code person" (who tells strangers where they live after they tell him their zip code — even naming sections of cities and local restaurants) and all types of sidewalk talent. Some of the mall performers have gone on to fame and fortune. One balance and juggling act appeared on the *Tonight Show* with Johnny Carson. Though the mall entertainment is theoretically free, performers usually have a donation "hat" and appreciate financial support (they have to pay for permits to perform on the mall).

Another uniquely Boulder form of entertainment is *E-Town*, a locally produced weekly public radio show that focuses on the environment and is recorded live with audience participation at the historic Boulder Theater. It's our own homegrown, eco-version of Garrison Keillor's *A Prairie Home Companion*. *E-Town* is aired weekly by National Public Radio on various stations across the country and has had such top celebrities as James Taylor, Dan Fogelberg, Dave Barry, Emmylou Harris, Rickie Lee Jones and The Persuasions. It's quite inexpensive and fun for the audience to play a part in a nationally broadcast radio show.

Those regularly in search of the really bright lights and big names will usually have to travel to Denver to Red Rocks, Fiddler's Green, the Paramount and Ogden theaters and other venues larger than what Boulder has to offer. For a complete Denver listing see *The Insiders' Guide® to Greater Denver*, but some top Denver hot spots regularly frequented by Boulderites are listed subsequently among the Boulder nightspots. Don't forget that the legal drinking age in Colorado is 21.

Accoustic Coffee House
95 E. First Street, Nederland • 258-3209

Folks drive all the way from Denver up to the mountain town of Nederland — even on weeknights . . . in winter — to enjoy various performers at this pleasantly funky little coffeehouse. Performing here are such nationally known musicians as Chuck Pyle, Tim O'Brien, Peter Rowan, Cheryl Wheeler and Catie Curtis. Tickets prices range from $5 to $15, but local performers often play for tips. Microbrews and wine are served in the evenings. The Accoustic is open until 10:30 PM Wednesday through Saturday for various performances, with an open-mike night on Wednesdays at 7:30 PM and a bluegrass jam Thursdays at 8 PM. Other performances generally start around 8 PM. It's also a great stop during the day for fancy coffees, baked goods and tasty sandwiches; open weekdays at 7 AM and weekends at 8 AM. Try a breakfast bagel or one of the delicious scones or brownies. For lunch there's grilled panini sandwiches (focaccia-bread combos grilled in a press).

Though the food is a bit Boulder, the atmosphere is definitely Nederland.

Bentley's Nightclub
The Broker Inn • 555 30th St., Boulder • 449-1752

Bentley's Nightclub at the Broker is a favorite spot for dancing and meeting interesting people. It attracts an older, more professional baby boomer crowd (versus college kids). Underpaid local professionals, such as writers and teachers, like to frequent the quiet and more sedate "Cabaret" bar to enjoy conversation, discounted Margaritas and free hors d'oeuvres weeknights. The Broker has these happy-hour specials Monday through Friday from 4 to 7 PM. Dancing is popular Wednesday and weekends. Comedy shows are featured on Tuesday at 8:30 PM. The bar menu is available every night until 11 PM, and the bar stays open until 2 AM.

The Catacombs
Hotel Boulderado • 2115 13th St., Boulder • 443-0486

The Catacombs was the first bar in Boulder to legally serve liquor in 1969. It has had several reincarnations, including one as an inexpensive Italian restaurant and another as an expensive continental restaurant, but has now resumed its original identity as an easygoing local bar catering to a mixed-age crowd (average age 35). There's live music every night, with an open blues jam on Monday, an open acoustic jam on Tuesday, jazz on Sunday and a blues bar the rest of the week. Live music continues from 9 PM to 1:15 AM — no cover charge. Happy hour is daily from 4:30 to 8 PM, and snacks and appetizers are served until midnight. There are also pool tables. Tuesday is burger night, featuring $2 burgers. There are happy-hour food specials, and a smoking section is available.

Comedy Works
1226 15th St., Denver • 595-3637

"See tomorrow's stars today," is the slogan of this downtown Denver club where Roseanne got her start. Comedy Works regularly runs headliner shows. Tuesday is improv and new-talent night; Wednesday through Sunday are for established performers. Non-smoking performances are Wednesdays and Fridays at 8 PM and Saturdays at 6:45 PM. Other Saturday shows are at 8:45 and 10:45 PM. Reservations are recommended (only ages 21 and older are admitted).

Corner Bar
Hotel Boulderado • 13th and Spruce Sts., Boulder • 442-4344

An extensive wine list by the glass, specialty drinks and eight microbrewery draft beers (seven made in Colorado) are available in this historic bar decorated in dark wood. A beautiful, antique grand piano serves as one of the tables. Upstairs from the Catacombs (see previous entry), the Corner Bar has a casually elegant atmosphere. Food is served until midnight.

El Chapultepec
1962 Market St., Denver • 295-9126

This popular Denver bar near Coors Field is for lovers of jazz, blues and Mexican food. There's live music every night with a mix of local performers and occasional big names. There's no cover charge — the manager doesn't believe in them — and the bar is open until 1 AM daily. Reservations aren't required.

E-Town
E-Town Productions, Boulder Theater • 2032 14th St., Boulder • 443-8696, 784-5765 (24-hour concert info line), 786-7030 (Boulder Theater Box Office, noon to 6 PM weekdays; noon to 5 PM weekends)

"Live from the historic Boulder Theater in the foothills of the Rocky Mountains, it's E-Town," broadcast nationally every week. E-Town is a unique Boulder phenomenon. A radio show that focuses on entertainment and environmental issues — a sometimes difficult twosome — E-Town celebrated its fifth anniversary in 1996. The show is taped live to be run by National Public Radio and commercial stations. The audience is part of the show, clapping and cheering on cue — sometimes for several takes. It's interesting to see how a radio show works.

E-Town records about 35 shows a year. It features musicians, environmentalists, politicians, authors and others. Recent performers and celebrities include James Taylor, Los Lobos, Bruce Hornsby, Dan Fogelberg, Richard Thompson, Sarah McLachlan, Allen Ginsberg, Baxter Black, former U.S. Senators Gary Hart and Tim Wirth, Earth Day founder Denis Hayes, Colorado Governor Roy Romer, Biosphere II botanist Linda Leigh, Amory Lovins, Dennis Weaver, Joan Baez, Bruce Cockburn, Arlo Guthrie, Bare Naked Ladies, Sonia Dada, David Wilcox and Leftover Salmon.

Drinks and snacks are available, so the audience can sip their favorite beverage while they watch the show. Part of the theater has cafe tables and chairs. The Boulder Theater is one of Boulder's two landmark art-deco buildings (the other is the County Courthouse).

Run on a shoestring and volunteer efforts, E-Town is the brainchild of Boulder husband-and-wife co-producers Nick and Helen Forster. Nick was formerly principal bassist, guitarist and vocalist for the bluegrass group Hot Rize (which still has reunion concerts). Tickets cost $7.35 in advance or around $9 at the door. Tickets are available at various locations around town. Call for information. Shows are usually Sunday evenings.

Fiddler's Green
6350 Greenwood Plaza Blvd., Englewood • 220-7000

About a 1½-hour drive from Boulder, Fiddler's Green, southeast of Denver, offers all types of top nationally known groups, including rock, classical and oldies, that aren't likely to visit Boulder. Enjoy these summer outdoor events either with reserved seats or a picnic on the lawn (all types of food and drinks are sold in the amphitheater; big picnic spreads from home are not allowed — but backpacks and blankets are). Concerts happen mid-May through mid-September. For tickets call the box office at 770-2222 or call TicketMaster 830-8497.

Flagstaff House
Flagstaff Rd. (west end of Baseline Rd., partway up the mountain), Boulder • 442-4640

Even those who can't afford dinner at the Flagstaff House — one of Boulder's most elegant and expensive restaurants, perched high on Flagstaff Mountain — can still enjoy the great view and wonderful, outdoor terraced bar for the price of a drink. If you're lucky, you might catch a fantastic summer lightning show out on the plains. For a really romantic drink with someone special, choose this beautiful spot. Open Sunday through Friday from 6 to 10 PM, Saturday from 5 to 10:30 PM.

Fox Theatre and Cafe
1135 13th St., Boulder • 447-0095

Nominated for club of the year by *Performance Magazine* and several others, the Fox has become one of the top clubs for live music in North America. This cafe/concert hall on University Hill holds more than 600 people and has three full bars and nightly live music by local, national and international performers. People of all ages attend the shows. The cafe is open daily from 9 AM until 2 AM serving casual, gourmet Southwestern fare.

The Grizzly Rose Saloon & Dance Emporium
5450 N. Valley Hwy. (I-25), Denver • 295-2353, 295-1330 (for concert information)

Voted the nation's No. 1 country music dance hall by the Country Music Association, Grizzly Rose has a 5,000-square-foot dance floor and gets such top names as Merle Haggard and Wynonna. There are free introductory dance lessons and $1 longnecks Monday through Friday, except on concert nights, from 7 to 8 PM, with various contests and specials other nights (call 42-DANCE for contest information). Concert tickets are available through TicketMaster, 830-8497, or at the door; advanced ticketing is necessary for national acts. The Grizzly Rose is open from 11 AM (serving lunch) to 11 PM Monday through Thursday, from 5 PM until 1:30 AM Friday and Saturday and from 3 until 11 PM Sunday.

The James Pub and Grille
1922 13th St., Boulder • 449-1922

In one of Boulder's older red brick buildings, this bar has Boulder's most authentic

Photo: Daily Camera

The environment-music public radio show *E-town* is produced in Boulder.
That's co-producer Nick Forster at right.

pub atmosphere and 12 of the best tap beers in town, including some of Boulder's locally made beers, and Laughing Lab, Sawtooth, Guinness, Fat Tire and Buffalo Gold. The James was always the place to listen to Irish music until, ironically, it burned down in 1993 on St. Patrick's Day — the bar's biggest night of the year. Happily, it's all rebuilt and has a newly remodeled dart room, but the Irish music is no more. Now there are pool tables. The menu features burgers, sandwiches, pastas and daily specials. There are two happy hours nightly from 4 to 7 PM and 10 PM to 1 AM, with a different menu and drink specials: $1 well drinks and $1.75 for selected drafts. Food is served until midnight. The James is open from 11:30 AM to 1 AM.

J.J. McCabe's Bar
945 Walnut St., Boulder • 449-4131

This Boulder landmark has changed with the times, from fern bar to sports bar, and now has 14 TV screens, two satellite dishes and four pool tables. The food is tasty and served until midnight. Burgers and fresh steaks are popular items. Watch your favorite sports in this comfortable bar, open daily until 2 AM. Happy hours are daily from 4 to 7 PM and from 11 PM until closing.

Mercury Cafe
2199 California St., Denver • 294-9281, 294-9258 (dinner reservations/information)

You name it, the Mercury Cafe has it: Russian rock 'n' roll groups, folk, jazz, pseudo-pagan events, rockabilly and hard rock — to name just a few. Recent popular performers there include Eddie Vedder, Mike Watt, Mojo Nixon, Elastica and Monkey Siren. New this year is live theater and the Mercury's own microbrewed beer, including Vertigo Lager, Amnesia Blue Ribbon and Bitches Brew Black Bitter Stout. On the last Sunday of each month, there's Big Band dancing. Open poetry night is every Friday at 10 PM; open stage is held on Wednesday nights.

The concert hall is separate from the cafe, which serves a continental menu from 5:30 to 11 PM, including vegetarian specials, pasta, Mexican food, seafood, steaks and burgers. All the soups, breads and desserts are homemade. The average dinner price is a remarkably low $5 to $12. Concerts cost $5 and up at this fun, eclectic cafe/concert hall, with an equally eclectic crowd. There are all-age rock shows every Tuesday and some Thursdays. Call for more information.

The Mezzanine
Hotel Boulderado • 13th and Spruce Sts., Boulder • 442-4344

This elegant upstairs area of the Boulderado is furnished with Victorian antique chairs and tables beneath the beautiful stained-glass ceiling window. Locals lament that this former favorite spot is now open to the public only on Friday nights from 6 PM 'til midnight. Live jazz starts at 8 PM and there's no cover charge. Drinks and light meals are served.

Jose Muldoon's
1600 38th St., Boulder • 449-4543

This popular Mexican restaurant also has a sports bar and claims to serve the "biggest Margarita in town" in numerous versions (due, perhaps, to having Boulder's largest selection of tequila). There's an all-you-can-eat tostada bar in the restaurant during the day. The restaurant is open daily until midnight, serving meals until 10 PM.

Oasis Brewery
1095 Canyon Blvd., Boulder • 449-0363

Now brewing five of its own beers plus specialties, this large, attractive microbrewery bar and restaurant has Egyptian decor, complete with gently waving papyrus fans over the bar. The Oasis has daily happy hour from 4 to 7 PM offering discounted beer, wine and mixed drinks made from house liquors. There's free pool during early happy hour every day but Friday in the full game room that includes Foosball, darts, pool and video games. The restaurant serves all types of dishes and has a late-night menu. The Oasis is open until 2 AM Monday through Saturday and until midnight on Sunday. Month-to-month specialty beers are served, such as Belgian Strong Ale and Doppelbock. There are late night happy hours Sunday through Thursday from 10 PM to midnight.

Ogden Theatre
935 E. Colfax Ave. (nine blocks east of the State Capitol), Denver • 830-2525 (box office and recording of upcoming shows)

Big names and performers appear at the Ogden, among them George Clinton, Los Lobos, Great White and The Proclaimers. Call for information on tickets and upcoming shows. Most shows at the Ogden are general admission with no reserved seating necessary. The Ogden box office is open from 9:30 AM to 5:30 PM daily. Ogden tickets are also available in Boulder at Albums-on-The-Hill ticket counter, 443-3399, 1128 13th Street, and through Rocky Mountain Teleseat at the number above.

Old Chicago
11th and Pearl Sts., Boulder • 443-5031

Known far and wide for its World Beer Tour and Hall of Foam, Old Chicago has more than 110 international and microbrewed beers, with 24 on draft. It's also known for its deep-dish, Chicago-style pizza, its pleasant patio and "the big cookie" (a delicious, deep-dish, fresh-baked chocolate-chip cookie served hot). Open daily until 1:30 AM, the restaurant serves food until 1 AM on Friday and Saturday and until midnight all other days.

Paramount Theatre
1631 Glenarm Pl., Denver • 534-8336 (tickets/information)

Built in the 1930s by Temple Hoyne Buell, a renowned Colorado architect, this beautiful art deco theater has one of only two Mighty Wurlitzer organs in the country (the other is in New York's Radio City Music Hall). The theater presents comedy, pop music, rock concerts, children's programming, ballet and noted speakers.

Pioneer Inn
First St., Nederland • 258-7733

For some entertainment with great mountain atmosphere, stop at the rustic "P.I." where you can dance to live music Friday nights. An open blues jam is on Tuesdays. The Pioneer also serves great burgers and Mexican food and has pool tables. The bar closes at 1:30 AM and the kitchen closes at 10 PM.

Potter's
1207 Pearl St., Boulder • 444-3100

One of Boulder's oldest bars, Potter's was there before the Pearl Street Mall was built, and it continues to be a popular stop. There's a daily happy hour from 4 to 8 PM, and a happy-hour menu available from 4 PM to midnight. The bar closes at 2 AM. Potter's has a

Photo: Daily Camera

The art deco-style Boulder Theater now houses the *E-town* public radio show.

full dinner menu, and the kitchen is open until 10 PM (midnight for wings and pizza).

Red Rocks
Off I-70 W. (north of Denver), Morrison • 830-8497 (ticket information)

This spectacular natural-rock amphitheater is the venue for many top performers who come to Denver. Red Rocks information and tickets are available through TicketMaster (call the listed number). Check local newspapers for performers appearing at Red Rocks.

'Round Midnight
1005 Pearl St., Boulder • 442-2176

This dark, downstairs, nicely urban-feeling nightclub/bar features live music, dancing, pool and good local performers nightly from 4 PM to 2 AM. Another feature is more than 50 different varieties of single-malt Scotch. Only drinks (no food) are served, and there are happy-hour specials from 4 to 8 PM daily

with $1.50 well drinks, $1.25 domestic beers and 50¢ off everything else. It's one of the few remaining places in Boulder to dance.

Sundown Saloon
1136 Pearl St., Boulder • 449-4987

A little off the beaten path in atmosphere but right on the Pearl Street Mall, the Sundown is for those who are sick of the typical Boulder scene. It's a bit more blue collar but has an unlikely mix of clientele. College students might find themselves having a beer with a hard-core Harley Davidson biker in black leather or a lawyer in pinstripes. Despite these "endearing qualities," the bartender assures that the bar is safe and quiet. Fans of *The Simpsons* can watch their favorite TV family every Sunday night. There are six pool tables and a big-screen TV, and the bar is open until 2 AM daily (no food, drinks only).

Sushi Zanmai
1221 Spruce St., Boulder • 440-0733

Great authentic Japanese decor and atmosphere, with chefs chopping only inches away, make Sushi Zanmai entertaining unto itself. But those not prepared for the karaoke sing-along party on Saturdays from 10 PM to midnight are in for a treat. Lights flash, a mirror ball spins and the chefs lay down their knives and begin singing, strumming guitars and inviting the diners to do the same. There are daily sushi happy hours from 11:30 AM to 2 PM and from 5 to 6:30 PM, and all evening on Sunday. It's open daily until 10 PM.

Tom's Tavern
1047 Pearl St., Boulder • 443-3893

Ask most longtime Boulderites where to find the best burger, and they'll usually say Tom's. This unpretentious corner tavern has been a favorite spot for more than 30 years. Besides great burgers, there are great beers on tap including Fat Tire, Raspberry Wheat,

Sam Adams, Miller Genuine, Watneys and Coors Light. A full menu is available daily until midnight (Sundays until 9:30 PM). There's a jukebox back by the kitchen.

Walnut Brewery
1123 Walnut St., Boulder • 447-1345

This very popular microbrewery is in a tastefully redecorated old warehouse and makes its own six fresh, delicious beers. Order a sampler and try them all. On Friday and Saturday, there's live music at 10 PM. The complete dinner menu is served until 11 PM Monday through Thursday and until midnight on weekends (see our Restaurants chapter for details). The Walnut Brewery is open until 2 AM Monday through Saturday and until midnight on Sunday. Go early on weekends (before 6 PM) if you don't want to wait in a line that often goes out the door and down the block. The Walnut Brewery also provides beer to go and catering services.

Walrus
11th and Walnut Sts., Boulder • 443-9902

The Walrus has been around for many years, undergoing various changes of personality and clientele from a fancy restaurant to a neighborhood bar. Currently, the latter is its main identity, with pizza, burgers and appetizers as the favorite fare, along with a full bar, beer and wine. There are six pool tables, air hockey and foosball. Last call every night is 1:15 AM.

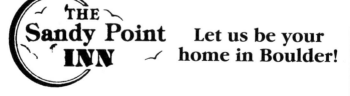

Boulder
Accommodations

Boulder offers more than two dozen places to stay, with around 1,900 rooms ranging from bargain-rate facilities to luxury hotels and romantic bed and breakfast inns. The choices expand when you head for the hills, where country cabins, great adventure ranches and mountain retreats beckon. Many of the accommodations are popular way-stations for travelers planning to continue on to Rocky Mountain National Park/Estes Park. In fact, Boulder itself is only 35 miles from Estes Park, which means roughly an hour's drive up, down and around the mountains. Many country places are even closer, so for these, we've listed the approximate driving time to reach Boulder and Estes Park.

More accommodations are being built, including a new mid-rise motor inn under construction at the time of this writing between Folsom and 28th, Canyon and Walnut, tucked into what had been a parking lot behind McGuckin's Hardware. The long-vacant lot at Ninth and Canyon, on the southwestern edge of downtown, has sporadically been proposed as a hotel site; however, every development proposal thus far has been defeated, often by requirements changed mid-scheme. Don't be surprised ultimately to see a hotel in this convenient spot; then again, don't be surprised if you never do.

Get Your Reservation Early

Where Boulder accommodations are concerned, it pays to start working on your reservation early. From May through October, it's wise to reserve a month in advance. Dates that sell out even sooner include CU-Boulder fall football weekends (especially when CU plays Nebraska), graduation in mid-May and the Bolder Boulder Memorial Day weekend, which all pack the town. Major gatherings in Denver, such as the Promise Keepers gathering, which brings up to 50,000 people the last weekend in July, sell out all the Front Range communities from Colorado Springs to Fort Collins. Since it's not a ski destination, Boulder's slowest season is November through February. Rates are usually lower then too.

Whether you need a room two years from now or right away, the Boulder Chamber of Commerce, 442-2911 or (800) 444-0887, can send you an updated packet of information about Boulder plus the latest hotel/motel rate sheet. The Chamber does not operate a central reservations service. On impact weekends, the Chamber calls around to see if anyone has canceled, making a room available. So if you're desperate, they sometimes can help.

A Word About Smoking

Boulder policy-makers figured out early the harmful consequences of America's legal drug — tobacco — and established many smoke-free zones. In 1995, smoking was banned in all public places. Many accommodations prohibit or restrict smoking too. Most bed and breakfast inns, for instance, don't allow any smoking. While most hotels provide some smoking rooms, there are fewer and fewer all the time; so, if you want the freedom to smoke, be sure to ask for a smoking room

Price Information

Our price-code key, shown in dollar signs ($), is based on average daily summer (peak) rates for a standard room for two adults. Prices may vary throughout the year, dropping in late fall and winter. Some places offer rooms at various price levels. Some properties also offer discounted business rates for extended stays or discounts for AAA members, senior citizens or others. The accommodation you're seeking can provide more details.

Price-code Key	
Less than $55	$
$56 to $75	$$
$76 to $100	$$$
$101 to $125	$$$$
$126 and more	$$$$$

Unless indicated otherwise, assume that the property accepts cash, traveler's checks, personal and company checks (both in-state and out-of-state) and major credit cards.

Country Inns and Bed and Breakfasts

If you've never stayed at a bed and breakfast or a country inn (though often a distinction is not made between the two, in this area, the difference is that a country inn is considered bigger), try one in Boulder. Each room is individually decorated with special treasures, antique furnishings and paintings. Most rooms have private baths, often lavishly appointed. Many are in former mansions or mountain lodges. No, most Boulderites don't live this way, but plenty of us would like to, for these are so peaceful and romantic, you may wish you could linger for years. Extra details of decor and service can add immeasurably to the richness of your stay. No wonder these are popular for honeymoons and anniversaries. Keep to yourself or relax in the living room and strike up a conversation with the staff and other travelers. Most bed and breakfasts offer what they now tend to call "continental-plus breakfast," with homemade breads or rolls, a choice of beverage, fresh fruit and perhaps cereal. Some prepare a full breakfast each morning with a hot entree and cereal available too.

Bed and breakfasts rarely permit smoking or pets, and most inns don't allow children younger than 12. If you book your family somewhere that does permit children, make sure they're well-behaved — and brace them for the absence of standard hotel offerings such

as televisions or indoor heated pools. If you might be arriving during one of Boulder's infrequent hot spells, ask about air-conditioning. Some rooms have it, some don't need it, and others do.

Several of Boulder's best bed and breakfasts belong to an association called the Distinctive Inns of Colorado, (800) 866-0621, which can send you a directory including evocative photographs.

City of Boulder

Many Boulder bed and breakfasts are near the center of the city, often in a mostly residential area. In a way, they make you an instant resident, for they give you a lovely, distinctive place to call your own during your stay. A central location means fun just outside your door. It can also mean traffic noise. Mention a desire for total quiet to the staff if you want a room where you won't notice traffic at all.

The Boulder Victoria Historic Inn
$$$$$ • 1305 Pine St., Boulder • 938-1300

The Dwight-Nicholson House, one of Boulder's earliest mansions, was renovated in 1889 and turned into a gorgeous bed and breakfast more than a century later. Seven distinctive rooms have queen-size brass beds with down comforters, private baths (three with steam showers) and televisions. This wonderful inn is just a block from the Pearl Street Mall. Here you'll find charming Victorian hospitality and plush comfort. The innkeeper serves continental breakfast with homemade fruit breads and muffins, afternoon tea and evening port. In summer, the beautiful front garden is ablaze with flowers.

Briar Rose
$$$$ • 2151 Arapahoe Ave., Boulder • 442-3007

This was Boulder's first bed and breakfast, established in 1981, and it remains one of the coziest. This English-style inn has a landscaped courtyard and garden complete with lovely little pond and waterfall. Each of the nine guest rooms has Boulder-made featherbed comforters. Two of the rooms have woodburning fireplaces. Tea is served in the afternoon, and a homemade breakfast — delicious baked goods, granola and fresh fruit — greets the morning. The inn is within walking distance of Crossroads Mall, CU-Boulder and downtown.

The Earl House Historic Inn
$$$$$ • 2429 Broadway, Boulder
• 938-1400

The landmark Greene-Earl House is a spectacular 1882 Gothic-style stone mansion. It is also Boulder's newest bed and breakfast, opened in November 1995 with a trellised, wrought-iron fence. Original woodwork and tiles hand-painted by the original owner's wife make the interior a treasure too. One room has a double bed, and the rest have queens. All the bathrooms have hand-painted tiles and either steam shower or jetted tub. The parlor and dining room seem a million miles from the bustle of Broadway. Under the same ownership as the Boulder Victoria, the Earl House has adopted the practice of serving continental breakfast, afternoon tea and evening port. Two carriage houses on the property each

have three bedrooms, two bathrooms, a fully equipped kitchen and living room with TV/VCR, stereo and washer/dryer. Each can accommodate up to six people; there is a two-night minimum stay. Carriage house guests are welcome at afternoon tea, but they're on their own for breakfast and evening port.

The Inn on Mapleton Hill
$$$$ • 1001 Spruce St., Boulder
• 449-6528, (800) 276-6528

Five rooms with private baths and two rooms sharing a bath comprise this 1899 home in the Mapleton Hill historic neighborhood. It's just a minute's walk down tree-lined streets to the Pearl Street Mall. The Inn on Mapleton Hill, formerly called The Magpie, sits up on a hill, with views of both the Flatirons and the downtown area. The Cottonwood Room is romantic with a four-poster bed draped in elegant white lace and a sun room opening to a south-facing balcony. The comfortable back parlor has a fireplace and television for all guests to enjoy.

Pearl Street Inn

$$$$ • **1820 Pearl St., Boulder** • **444-5584, (800)232-5949**

Each of the seven Victorian-style rooms here has a wood-burning fireplace. The location is superb, just three blocks east of the Pearl Street Mall, but the inn is tucked behind a high fence and feels private and secluded. There's a lovely garden courtyard for guests to enjoy. Full breakfast, including excellent baked goods and an exceptional oatmeal, is served. The innkeeper also puts out afternoon refreshments, which could be hot spiked apple cider, wine and cheese or tea. The Pearl Street Inn's rates are the same year round. The inn, which once had a restaurant, still has wedding, reception and meeting facilities for up to 125 people.

Bed & Breakfast at Sunset House

$$$ • **1740 Sunset Blvd., Boulder** • **444-0801**

This is a homestay bed and breakfast, meaning you have your choice of one or two rooms in a private home just north of downtown Boulder. Sunset House is a 1950s ranch, not fancy, but beautifully landscaped, homey and secluded. You'll have your own private entrance to rooms that include a fireplace and television and open to a lovely back patio with views of the city and mountains. To complete the homey picture, owners Phyllis and Roger Olson have a small friendly dog. When the Sunset House is full, Phyllis is happy to refer you to other homestays in the area.

The generous, civic-minded Olsons took out a mortgage on their home to enable Historic Boulder to buy the garden next to the Arnett-Fullen House, the organization's headquarters (see our Attractions chapter). When you stay at Sunset House, you'll indirectly be helping Historic Boulder, and the Olsons might even hand you an application in case you want to join.

The Mountains

The peace and quiet of a mountain lodge can be incredible. Some of these places are just a short drive from Boulder. Others are way, way up where the spring flowers bloom in August. Some locations are even secrets... the owners will give you directions when you inquire. Many are open all year, but check in advance, for some close during winter.

Above Boulder Wildlife Safari Lodge

$$$, no credit cards • **Sugarloaf Mountain, Boulder** • **258-7777**

Three rooms are in this very secluded, European-style, big mountain hunting lodge with handmade aspen-log beds, three fireplaces, designer decorations and 300 full-mounted trophies, including grizzly bears, African lions and other wildlife. The owner describes himself as a big-game hunter, professional outdoorsman and environmentalist. Breakfast is continental-plus and often includes wild game sausage. There is a kennel for pets, and children are welcome. It's a five-minute drive from Nederland, 25 minutes from Boulder and 50 minutes from Estes Park.

Allenspark Lodge

$$ • **184 Main St., Allenspark** • **747-2552**

Six rooms with private baths, six rooms with shared baths and three cabins with private baths and full kitchens make up this authentic 1933 log lodge. Construction is of ponderosa pine on the first two levels inside and out, with knotty pine inside on the top floor. Many of the furnishings are the same vintage as the buildings. There are hot tubs, a gift shop, a wine and beer bar and a TV in the great room near the flagstone fireplace. Views from this mountain lodge are tremendous, and Wild Basin and its wonderful hiking trails are nearby. Children younger than 14 are welcome in the cabins, and older kids may stay in the lodge too. It's about a 45-minute drive from Boulder and a 25-minute drive to Estes Park. The lodge includes continental-plus breakfast in its lodge rates.

Alps Boulder Canyon Inn

$$$$$ • **38619 Boulder Canyon Dr., Boulder** • **444-5445, (800) 414-2577**

When you look at this beautiful inn today, it's hard to image that it was the rundown old lodge that housed the fraternal order of the Moose. You enter via a log cabin that was originally a stagecoach stop and bordello during the late 1870s, wander into the lounge that was the old Moose Lodge bar, then head to your room. The inn's 12 enchanting guest rooms are done up with heirloom furnishings. All the rooms different, as are their private bathrooms: six with jetted tubs, two with claw-foot tubs, one with a soaking tub for two and the others just with showers. Each room also has a fireplace, and some feature stained-glass doors. Several rooms are honeymoon-perfect, such as "Wallstreet," which includes that vintage-style tub for two. The inn services a gourmet breakfast, and cheesecake is available in the evening. You can always help yourself to tea and coffee, and hot cider is added in winter. The TV room has a satellite system and VCR with dozens of videos available, and the lounge features a huge stone fireplace, big card table and popular games. There are also fireplaces in the breakfast room and the lobby. The large, rustic dining room has a capacity of 100 people for weddings, receptions and meetings. Children older than 12 are welcome. Hiking and biking trails are close by this inn, which is also close to Boulder Creek. The inn is just a five-minute drive from Boulder and less than an hour from Estes Park.

FYI

Unless otherwise noted, the area code for all phone numbers in this guide is 303.

family retreat. Seventeen charming and distinctive cabins are tucked amid the pine trees. Most have new gas stoves, wood floors, antique furnishings and library areas. Bathrooms are being converted into sybaritic playrooms with plumbing. Popular "Victoria's House" features a velvet fainting couch, and others are . . . well, that Victoria is really something. If Victorian froufrou is too-too for you-you, you might prefer a cabin done in a Southwestern, cowboy or Native American style. The resort's spa offers massages and facials, and you can book a spa package. The 35-acre lake is beautiful for catamaran sailing, canoeing, kayaking and fly fishing in summer, and ice skating in winter. The lakeside hot tubs are a dreamy treat. Summer brings opportunities for horseback riding on mounts you can rent by the hour or day, great mountain biking on challenging trails, volleyball and hiking. Children are more than welcome. Guests and visitors can dine in the excellent and stylish restaurant called Alice's (see our Restaurants chapter), or enjoy cocktails at Karel's Tavern. Gold Lake Mountain Resort is a 45- to 60-minute drive from either Boulder or Estes Park.

Boulder Mountain Lodge and Campground
$$ • 91 Fourmile Canyon Dr., Boulder • 444-0882, (800) 458-0882

Twenty-two rooms, many with kitchenettes or full kitchens, are available at this rustic motel with homey touches. The campground has 25 first-come, first-served sites with electricity and access to water for 25-foot-maximum RVs or for tent campers. The lodge is in the mountains, and the office is in an old narrow-gauge train depot. There's a private fishing pond for kids, a heated outdoor pool (open seasonally) and hot tubs. Smoking is allowed in some rooms, and pets are welcome with a deposit. The lodge is less than 10 minutes from Boulder and about an hour from Estes Park.

Gold Lake Mountain Resort
$$$$$ • 3371 Gold Lake Rd., Ward • 459-3544, (800) 450-3544

This mountain hideaway is evolving into a wonderful escape for honeymooners (or second honeymooners) or for a pleasant close-by

Goldminer Hotel
$$ • 601 Klondike Ave., Eldora • 258-7770, (800) 422-4629

Two rooms with private baths and three with shared baths are in this historic log hotel from Eldora's mining days. The rooms reflect their original character, with antiques and homemade quilts. There is also one cabin with a kitchenette. This is an away-from-it-all place in a quaint old mining town surrounded by mountains. You can enjoy beautiful views from the hot tub. Pets are only permitted in the cabin; children are accepted. A full breakfast is part of the deal. It's about 30 minutes from Boulder, about an hour from Estes Park and a short drive from the Eldora ski area.

Inn at Rock N River Bed and Breakfast & Trout Pond Fishing
$$$-$$$$ • 16868 N. St. Vrain Dr., northwest of Lyons • 443-4611, (800) 448-4611

This delightful riverside complex has seven

rooms near the pond, a loft suite and The Carriage House, which is a two-story cabin accommodating up to four with a large bedroom, a Jacuzzi tub for two and a fireplace. All units include kitchens. Though it's near U.S. Highway 36, the inn is quiet and pretty, with great views of the trout ponds and the St. Vrain River. Full breakfast is included. People stay overnight for the nature and the trout fishing. (You're guaranteed a fish!) Children are welcome. The inn is usually full from May through mid-October, but you can always hope for a cancellation or come in the off-season. It is 3 miles northwest of Lyons (take U.S. 36), 25 minutes from either Boulder or Estes Park.

Lodge at Nederland
$$$ • 55 Lakeview Dr., Nederland
• 258-9463, (800) 279-9463

This oversize log lodge, in the heart of Nederland, is a convenient mountain retreat. Accommodations include rooms with king-size beds for couples and rooms with two queen-size beds or a queen and a set of bunk beds for families. The romantic honeymoon-type Wolftongue Suite is the largest of the suites. All rooms are equipped with hair dryers, coffee makers and small refrigerators; suites also have fireplaces. The spacious lobby has a fireplace, and there's an outdoor hot tub on the deck. There is no restaurant, but Nederland's most popular eating places are within a short walk. In winter, the Lodge at Nederland offers reasonably priced ski packages in cooperation with nearby Eldora Mountain Resort. It is also a great jumping-off place for snowshoeing, backcountry skiing or summer hikes. The activities desk can arrange guided hikes, horseback trail rides and other diversions.

Nederhaus Motel
$$ • 686 Colo. Hwy. 119 S., Nederland
• 444-4705, (800) 422-4629

Twelve rooms are in this lodging, each furnished in antiques. This little hotel with a Swiss-looking facade is within an easy walk of downtown Nederland and is also a short drive to hiking spots and Eldora skiing. Some rooms allow smoking. Pets and children are welcome. The property is about 25 minutes from Boulder and about an hour from Estes Park.

Peaceful Valley Lodge and Guest Ranch
$$$$$ • 475 Peaceful Valley Rd., Lyons
• 747-2881

This family-owned, family-run guest ranch, on the site of an old homestead, is a "got everything" facility with 13 cabins, rooms in the main lodge and various other guest buildings as well as stable and indoor riding arena and other facilities. It has a Bavarian accent to its decor, but its programs are all-American guest ranch. Altogether, Peaceful Valley can house more than 100 people, and conference facilities are available. Staying overnight is dandy, but longer stays are what most seek at Peaceful Valley. Half-week stays are around $725 per person, and full-week packages begin at $1,200 per person during the summer, including all meals, use of ranch facilities and most recreational programs.

The chef cooks ranch-style meals such as prime rib and lemon-flavored catfish. The children's program is extensive. There's an indoor hot tub, indoor swimming pool, sauna, tennis courts and children's petting farm as well as activities that include horseback riding, jeep tours, llama treks and square dancing. The mountainside chapel, with view of the Indian Peaks behind the altar, is a gorgeous wedding site. In winter, Peaceful Valley stocks cross-country skis and maintains a small track on the property. The trailhead for extensive marked but ungroomed trails around Camp Dick are just across the highway. This outstanding resort is just a bit more than an hour from Boulder and about 40 minutes south of Estes Park. Some smoking is allowed, but pets aren't.

The Eastern Plains

These motels, bed and breakfasts and country inns are open all year and offer good variety and reasonable prices.

Briarwood Inn
$ • 1228 N. Main St., Longmont • 776-6622

Seventeen rooms are in this motel, and 10 include kitchenettes. The owner calls his the best back yard in town, with a quiet patio area, a fish pond and a gazebo. Smoking is allowed. Children are welcome. It's a half-hour drive to Boulder and about 45 minutes to Estes Park.

Ellen's Bed & Breakfast in a Victorian House
$$, no credit cards • 700 Kimbark St., Longmont • 776-1676

Two rooms, each with a private bath, are in this beautifully shaded, quiet, 1910 Victorian-style house, with eclectic furnishings including art deco pieces collected by the well-traveled owners. Full breakfast is included, smoking is allowed, and children older than 5 are welcome. It's a half-hour drive from Boulder and 45 minutes to Estes Park.

Sandy Point Inn
$$ • 6485 Twin Lakes Rd., Gunbarrel/Boulder • 530-2939, (800) 322-2939

With 29 air-conditioned studio suites, each with mini-kitchen and cable TV, this is a great place for people relocating or traveling with families. There's one common kitchen with house-style range, oven and utensils for preparing full-scale meals. A membership at Rally Sport, a full-service sports club, is complimentary for guests. A complimentary cold breakfast buffet is served in the common kitchen from 7:30 to 10 AM daily. It's a five-minute drive to Boulder and about an hour from Estes Park. The inn owners also rent one- and two-bedroom condominiums, normally on a monthly basis.

The Victoria Inn
$$ • 20400 W. 17th Ave., Longmont • 772-4667

Each of this inn's 28 executive suites includes a full kitchen, full bath and a sitting room. These are three-story, blue Victorian-style buildings with contemporary furnishings. There's a heated outdoor pool. Smoking is allowed. Cats are considered with a deposit. Children are welcome. It's a half-hour from Boulder and 45 minutes to Estes Park.

Hotels and Motels

Boulder hotels and motels all include non-smoking rooms (ask if you need a smoking room). Most have pools; but if it's cold, check when you call to see whether it's a heated indoor pool. The places we've listed have the usual hotel/motel amenities such as televisions and air-conditioning. Some are simple and sweet, others are lavish. Most don't allow pets. Unless noted, all take major credit cards.

Best Western Boulder Inn
$$ • 770 28th St., Boulder • 449-3800, (800) 233-8469

Around 100 rooms are in this motel, right across the street from the south end of the CU-Boulder campus. Room options include two queen-size beds, one queen-size bed and upgraded kings with bar area. Admission to the nearby Pulse health club is included during the stay, along with a continental breakfast daily. The motor inn has a hot tub, sauna and outdoor pool (open seasonally). Fanatics sports bar is on site.

Best Western Golden Buff Lodge
$$$ • 1725 28th St., Boulder • 442-7450, (800) 999-BUFF

This comfortable, well-located business and family motel has 112 guest rooms with king- or queen-size beds, some suites and conference/banquet space accommodating up to 50 people. On site is The Buff Restaurant, which is open for breakfast and lunch daily. There is a seasonal outdoor pool and an indoor hot tub. The motel is near Crossroads Mall.

Boulder International Youth Hostel
$, no credit cards • 1107 12th St., Boulder • 442-0522

Visitors from all over the world have stayed at this hostel, which is a member of the American Association of International Hostels. Accommodations are scattered among several buildings on University Hill. The hostel has separate dormitories for men and women, at only $12 a night, as well private rooms for couples and families that go for $30 for two people, and apartments for those wanting longer-term facilities. There are no TVs or phones, but cable television hookups are provided if you bring your own apparatus. Kitchens are available.

The Broker Inn
$$$$ • 555 30th St., Boulder • 444-3330, (800) 338-5407

This ornately decorated contemporary hotel has 116 guest rooms and four suites. Rooms feature brass beds, leather recliners and cable TVs with free HBO and Showtime. Services include valet, room service and bell staffs. The acclaimed Broker Restaurant and Bentley's nightclub are on site. Amenities include a hot tub, and the hotel is equipped with conference rooms. Full breakfast is included in room rates. Free passes to the nearby Pulse fitness center are part of your stay. Just south of the campus, The Broker Inn is a short walk or a CU-Boulder shuttle bus (take your pick) away from the University. It is also normally the location where passengers leaving and arriving via the Boulder Airporter transportation service switch from smaller city vans to the larger vehicles that run hourly between Denver International Airport and Boulder.

FYI

Unless otherwise noted, the area code for all phone numbers in this guide is 303.

Coburn Hotel
$$$$$ • 2040 16th St., Boulder • 545-5200

There are 12 rooms in this new boutique-size hotel. Wrought-iron and leather furnishings give it a turn-of-the-century elegance. Guest rooms offer fireplaces, Jacuzzis, private balconies, televisions and phones. Full breakfast is included in all room rates. The hotel speaks with a Western accent. Saddle seats are the stools in the bar. Stained-glass windows, old City of Boulder renderings, authentic oil paintings and Western prints make the interior a visual delight. The widow's watch on the roof gives you a bird's-eye view of downtown and the Flatirons. The Coburn also has three large banquet rooms and business facilities, including a fax machine, meeting rooms that can seat up to 75, and a large catering kitchen. It's great for business or romance.

Colorado Chautauqua Cabins
$ • Ninth St. and Baseline Rd., Boulder • 442-3282

More than two dozen lodge rooms and about 60 cottages are available for rent, with a

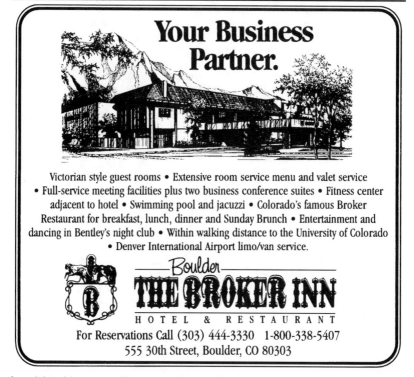
four-night minimum stay. The one- to three-bedroom cottages offer full kitchens but no air-conditioning, TVs or swimming pools. What you get here is a great deal on lodgings, one of the most beautiful locations in town, hiking and superb cultural events right outside your door, and a wonderfully nostalgic step back in time. Bookings start in November for the following summer. Ask about pets. For more information about Chautauqua Park, see our Attractions chapter.

Comfort Inn
$$$ • 1196 Dillon Rd., Louisville
• 604-0181, (800) 228-5150 (nationwide reservations)

The new 68-room Comfort Inn is next to the Mann 12-plex movie theater, just off U.S. 36. Rooms have one or two queen-size beds, and there is also one luxury room with an in-room Jacuzzi and queen-size bed. Continental breakfast, included in all room rates, is served in the breakfast room. This motor inn also has a meeting room and an exercise fa-cility; for those who want a more aggressive workout, the Louisville Recreation Center is a short drive away.

Courtyard by Marriott
$$$$ • 4710 Pearl E. Cir., Boulder
• 440-4700, (800) 321-2211

This business hotel has 12 suites and 137 rooms with either a king-size bed or two doubles, work desks in every room and separate seating areas in the suites. The hotel offers conference rooms, the in-house Court-yard Cafe and Lounge, an indoor pool, whirlpool and workout room. It's right next to the Boulder Creek Path in a quiet location just east of Foothills Parkway (Colo. Highway 157) on Pearl Street.

Days Inn
$$$ • 5397 South Boulder Rd., Boulder
• 499-4422, (800) 329-7466

This good basic motel is on a main thoroughfare, just off U.S. 36 and near the Table Mesa Park-n-Ride. It is just about the most convenient lodging to NCAR and NIST. Some of its 76 rooms have mountain views. Free local phone calls, TV with HBO and complimentary continental breakfast are included.

Econo-Lodge
$$ • 2020 Arapahoe Ave., Boulder • 449-7550, (800) 449-7550

Fifty-one rooms comprise this tidy and pleasant family-owned motel. All rooms have queen-size beds, cable TVs and full baths. Within walking distance of downtown and the University, it features an indoor pool, hot tub and sauna. Coffee and donuts are served in the lobby each morning.

Foot-of-the-Mountain Motel
$$ • 200 Arapahoe Ave., Boulder • 442-5688

Each of this motel's 18 rooms is in a red-trimmed log cabin, making this place a quaint and rustic charmer. All have refrigerators and televisions with free HBO. The mountain against whose foot this motel nestles (hence the name) is Flagstaff. On a quiet street near the pretty Eben Fine Park and the Boulder Creek Path, it is also just nine blocks west of CU-Boulder and the downtown Pearl Street Mall. Pets are welcome.

Hampton Inn
$$$ • 912 W. Dillon Rd., Louisville • 666-7700, (800) HAMPTON (nationwide reservations)

The new Hampton Inn is suited for multi-day business or leisure stays. Each of its 80 well-equipped, traditionally furnished rooms has a king-size bed or two queens, a refrigerator, microwave, coffee maker, hair dryer, two-line speaker phone and television with Nintendo. In addition, there is one hospitality suite for small meetings, an indoor swimming pool, hot tub and exercise facility. Continental breakfast is included in all rates.

Holiday Inn
$$$ • 800 28th St., Boulder • 443-3322, (800) HOLIDAY

This well-maintained Holiday Inn features 165 sizable rooms. The major amenity is the Holidome, which features a large indoor pool, hot tub, sauna and exercise room. The motor

inn also has a game room and Oliver's casual restaurant and pub. Like all hotels along this strip of 28th Street, it's very close to CU-Boulder.

Holiday Inn Express
$$$ • 4777 N. Broadway, Boulder • 442-6600, (800) HOLIDAY

This new North Boulder motor inn has 62 rooms (some with microwaves and refrigerators), two suites, a seasonal outdoor pool, exercise room, guest laundry and complimentary continental breakfast. Free local phone calls also are included. It is close to the intersection of U.S. 36 (28th Street) and Broadway.

Homewood Suites
$$$$$ • 4950 Baseline Rd., Boulder • 499-9922, (800) 225-5466

The 110 apartment-style suites each include a full kitchen and separate living and sleeping areas. There's an outdoor pool, complimentary continental breakfast and a free social hour Monday through Thursday nights, including food and drinks. We know one couple who liked the lifestyle so much, they went back home, sold their big house and moved into a place about the size of a Homewood Suite! Pets are allowed, and children are welcome. The bottom line here is good, basic living for extended-stay guests and mostly business travelers.

Hotel Boulderado
$$$$$ • 2115 13th St., Boulder • 442-4344, (800) 433-4344

Built in 1909, this hotel is a local landmark as well as one of the city's top accommodations. It offers old-style grandeur and is famous for the stained-glass canopy in its huge mezzanine. Theodore Roosevelt, Robert Frost and Louis Armstrong are among its past guests. Its 160 lavishly decorated, Victorian-style rooms are divided between the historic older section of the hotel and the new wing. The VIP suites are the largest and fanciest lodgings. Each has a wrought-iron or four-poster bed, its own stereo and a separate living room furnished with Victorian-style desks and sofas. The fanciest, biggest one goes for more than $200 a night, and it's booked al-

Boulder...

A pretty mountain town with sidewalk cafes, sword swallowers, street musicians and amazing people. While in Colorado call 442-2911 for up-to-date info or directions! Before arriving in Colorado call 1-800-444-0447 and ask for the Boulder "INSIDERS" packet.

Boulder Convention & Visitors Bureau

Photo: Daily Camera

The Hotel Boulderado has been elegantly restored.

most constantly. The hotel has two of Boulder's best restaurants (see our Restaurants chapter), three bars, an espresso shop, a mezzanine entertainment area, lots of conference space, a gift shop and a sensational location just a block from the Pearl Street Mall.

Raintree Plaza Hotel
$$$ • 1900 Ken Pratt Blvd., Longmont • 776-2000, (800) 843-8240

This is Longmont's only full-service hotel. It housed the Emperor of Japan's entourage during the summer of 1994. The following year, the hotel added 65 rooms, for a total of 211, and in early 1997, it was slated to expand by an additional 86 extended-stay rooms, each with a full kitchen, fireplace and living room. The hotel also has a 42,000-square-foot conference center, a restaurant and a heated outdoor swimming pool. Guests get free breakfast and evening cocktails. The hotel is popular with business travelers, families and conventions. It's a 15-minute drive to Boulder and an hour to Estes Park.

Regal Harvest House
$$$$$ • 1345 28th St., Boulder • 443-3850, (800) 545-6285

This is Boulder's biggest hotel, with more than 269 high-quality rooms and great business facilities on 16 acres right next to the Boulder Creek Path. It's an easy walk from CU-Boulder and the Pearl Street Mall. It has resort-type recreation facilities, including indoor and outdoor swimming pools, 15 indoor and outdoor tennis courts, two sand volleyball courts, mountain bike rentals and a workout room. The beautifully landscaped inner courtyard is a lively hangout after a Buffs game. Champs lounge and sports bar and The Fancy Moose restaurant are on site.

Residence Inn by Marriott
$$$$ • 3030 Center Green Dr., Boulder • 449-5545, (800) 331-3131

This village-like complex has 128 studio suites, all with fully equipped kitchens and fireplaces, designed for extended stays or for families who want a comfortable, relaxing refuge.

INSIDERS' TIP

Some Boulder-area motels allow pets in rooms if you check ahead and meet certain requirements: Boulder Mountain Lodge, Broker Inn, Foot-of-the-Mountain Motel, Homewood Suites. If you're traveling elsewhere in the United States, check out *Pets Are Permitted*, a book listing hotel/motel, kennel and pet-sitting services nationwide.

The Pearl Street Inn is a popular bed and breakfast and site for weddings.

The Residence Inn provides a complimentary continental breakfast buffet daily and has an outdoor whirlpool. It's easy-access to central Boulder, close to many of the high-tech and other companies there.

Super 8 Motel
$$ • 970 28th St., Boulder • 443-7800, (800) 525-2149

Seventy-two rooms are in this clean, pleasant motel close to CU-Boulder. Some people have stayed as long as three months in the motel's 12 apartment units, at reduced monthly rates. These relocation units have fully equipped kitchens and sitting rooms. Pets are welcome in some rooms, and children 12 and younger stay free in their parents' room.

University Inn
$$$ • 1632 Broadway, Boulder • 442-3830

This neat little inn at the corner of Broadway and Arapahoe Avenue has 39 rooms with refrigerators, cable TV with free HBO and guest laundry. It's within easy walking of both downtown and the University — and right across the street from Alfalfa's Market (see our Shopping chapter). Although close to a busy intersection, with doors and windows shut, the rooms are fairly quiet. A free continental breakfast is provided.

RV Hookups and Campgrounds

If you're planning to stay in your RV or tent in Boulder, check our Participatory, Spectator and Professional Sports chapter (see the "Camping" section of Participatory Sports). Another place to check is the **Boulder Mountain Lodge and Campground**, 444-0882 (see previous listing).

The **Boulder County Fairgrounds**, 678-1525, 9595 Nelson Road in Longmont, has 20 to 30 campsites and can handle nearly 100 RVs. A site for an RV with no hookups or for one tent costs $10 a night. A site with electricity is $12; one with water and electrical hookups is $14. The maximum stay is two weeks.

The **Denver North Campground**, 452-4120, 20 minutes east of Boulder on Colo. Highway 7, has space for 104 RVs, with 80 full hookups at $23.50 a night for two people, 24 tents at $17 a night, a meeting area and hot showers. Call them for reservations.

The **Colorado Campground and Cabin Resort Association**, 499-9343, has a free directory of camping, cabin and lodge information.

Meeting Spaces

A huge family reunion, a big convention or a bonanza of a business meeting should start with a phone call to the **Boulder Chamber of Commerce**, 442-2911. Be sure to check on available space as soon as possible. For instance, CU-Boulder's **Glenn Miller Ballroom** is regularly booked a year in advance. It has room for 1,200 seated theater-style, 800 seated banquet-style with rectangular tables or 450 seated at round tables. Broomfield's **Interlocken Conference Resort**, which opened in 1996, has room for 1,000. The **Regal Harvest House** currently can seat 400. The **Raintree Plaza Hotel and Conference Center** in Longmont seats 300. The **Boulder Broker Inn** holds 400, and the **Hotel Boulderado** can handle up to 350.

A Place for Your Pet

Most accommodations do not allow pets. Never just leave them in your car. Even with the windows cracked, even on a balmy day, Colorado's strong sun can zoom the temperature to a fatal high within minutes. Check the Yellow Pages under "Kennels" for a complete list of accommodations for your traveling pet. **Cottonwood Kennels**, 442-2602, is one of the biggest, boarding both dogs and cats. But, even it fills quickly. Generally, if you're traveling during the time when the kids are out of school, call six months in advance for kennel reservations. During non-holidays in the winter, give two weeks' notice. When Cottonwood fills, they offer other suggestions.

Pearl Street Mall is lined with historic buildings that house numerous shops, galleries, microbreweries, offices and sidewalk cafes as well as newer buildings of a style and scale that harmonize with the old.

Boulder
Shopping

Visitors and residents alike find one of Boulder's delights to be shopping. As in dining, Boulder is not yet totally overrun with tedious national chains that substitute themes for individuality and imagination. Except at Crossroads, the big indoor mall, which has its share of clones, very distinctive retail stores dominate the Boulder retail scene. You'll find yourself returning time and time again to browse or buy at your favorites, and it isn't unusual to discover a new shop every time you prowl. Note that many of the shops we mention under the information given for the malls are featured later on in the "Specialty Shops" section.

Shopping Areas

Pearl Street Mall
Downtown Boulder

Boulder's Pearl Street Mall, the city's original downtown, is the heart and soul of the city. This photogenic, four-block, open-air walkway has been converted for pedestrians only. It is lined with historic buildings that house numerous shops, galleries, microbreweries, offices and sidewalk cafes as well as newer buildings of a style and scale that harmonize with the old. During the warm months, street entertainers abound, including the Zip Code Man, who can identify towns and sometimes even describe building styles in your neighborhood, based on your ZIP code; Sword Swallower Johnny Fox; and Bongo the Balloon Man. In addition to the buskers who play for the hat, an "out-to-lunch" weekly summer performance series brings live entertainment to the mall. Some of Boulder's most popular shoe and clothing shops, cafes, galleries, bookstores and card and gift shops occupy prime spots along the mall and on adjacent blocks.

Since the mall was completed in 1976, constant upscaling and rising rents have, unfortunately, driven out many of the older landmark businesses, replacing them with a musical-chairs array of new establishments. Pearl Street, both east and west of the mall, is an increasingly eclectic mix of service and retail business plus offices and restaurants. But, the mall and its surrounding streets are still alluring and frequented as much by locals as visitors.

The best parking for the downtown area is in the structures at 14th and Walnut, 11th and Spruce and 11th and Walnut streets. When you park in any of these, ask for validation stickers as you pay at downtown stores. Every sticker is good for a half-hour of parking, so you can shop your way to reduced or free parking.

Crossroads Mall
Between 28th and 30th Sts. and Arapahoe Ave. and Walnut St. • 444-0722

More than 150 stores make this one of Boulder County's biggest enclosed shopping centers. Anchors include Foley's, Sears, Montgomery Ward, JCPenney and Mervyn's, and an array of smaller local and chain establishments.

Kids would love a video arcade called Aladdin's Castle, a candy shop called Scoops, Boulder Baseball Cards, which is popular with the card-trading crowd, and Rocky Mountain Rubber Stamps, which is self-explanatory. It's Your Move has games. Style-seekers head to The Limited Express and a host of other trendy shops. Sexy undergarments are at Victoria's Secret and Frederick's of Hollywood. Computer nerds need the Electronics Boutique and Software Etc. In Good Taste has cookware. The Mole Hole and Paper Doll are two locally owned gift shops which, interestingly, have expanded from the indoor mall and now have branches along Pearl Street. Eddie Bauer, American Eagle and Miller Stockman Western wear are here. There's also a huge Waldenbooks and Waldenkids.

If mall-crawling makes you hungry or just makes your feet hurt, you'll probably end up at the food court with 20 or so fast food stands. Cinnamonster's rolls are as enormous as their name suggests. You might feel as if you could gain 10 pounds just breathing the air outside Mrs. Fields Cookies, Caramel Corn or Abo's pizza. Here you have your basic pizzas and weenies, plus the Falafel Man, Shishkabob, Weebee's Hero's and Ichiban Teriyaki.

Arapahoe Village/The Village/ WaterStreet
Between 28th and Folsom Sts., both sides of Arapahoe Ave. and Canyon Blvd.

This excellent shopping area has so many terraced flower beds that some people tell their landscapers, "I want my yard to look like that." In addition to myriad and varied retail shops, this complex of somewhat upsacle strip malls has developed into a general entertainment center too, with Boulder's greatest concentration of movie houses and some surprisingly good restaurants. The United Artists Village 4 Theatres and Mann's Arapahoe Village Theatres across the street offer a total of eight screens. Memorable restaurants include the Full Moon Grill, Zolo Grill and the European Cafe. More casual eateries in the area include the Boulder Salad Company, Le Peep and several yogurt, soup, breakfast and burger spots. Goodies from Great Harvest Bread, Mountain Man Fruit & Nut Co. and The Brewing Market can help keep body and soul together.

This bustling retail area is where you'll find McGuckin Hardware, Elfriede's Fine Fabrics and Studio Bernina, Rocky Mountain Records and Tapes, Video Station, Ead's News and Smoke Shop and Canterbury Oak and Brass furniture. Children's shops clustered near a pleasant child's pocket park include GrandRabbits, Pour Moi, Kids & Company, Feet First and Rocky Mountain Kids, and nearby is a great kid-clothing store called Zippety Doo-Da. The WaterStreet shopping complex, on the north side of Canyon Boulevard between Folsom and 27th, features some of Boulder's most upscale shops. Christina's Lingerie carries expensive underwear, while The Regiment Shops sell quality men's and women's outerwear. Emerson Green is a new men's store that prides itself on its "exceptional men's clothing," while J.J. Wells carries equally distinctive women's fashions and accessories. Walters & Hogsett and Meyers Jewelers (see the subsequent "Jewelers" section) offer elegant jewelry.

J.J. Wells is an upscale women's shop, as is Talbot's, which once had a Pearl Street Mall location and reopened recently in Arapahoe Village. For upscale, casual men's clothing be sure to browse in Emerson Greene. The little shops are great discoveries. From their names alone, you can guess what fun you'll have at the Colorado Rockies Club, Egghead Software, Aspen Eyewear, Presents Past and the Wild Bird Center. Chains include Safeway, Gart Sports, Eastern Mountain Sports and Pier I Imports.

FYI
Unless otherwise noted, the area code for all phone numbers in this guide is 303.

You can reach this area by many transportation modes, for the Boulder Creek Path is on the south edge (making walking and biking easy), the parking lots are spacious (though they fill up when hit movies are showing) and it's on major bus routes, including the superconvenient Hop.

28th Street and 30th Street
Between Walnut St. and Iris Ave.

These two major north-south streets bracket Crossroads Mall, and a series of strip malls and freestanding stores stretch northward along these two arteries. Because most of them are fronted by parking lots, it's not easy to wander among them. But if you take the trouble, you can find most of Boulder's discount chains such as Target, Kmart, Marshall's and Walgreen's, all strung along 28th Street, and interesting specialty shops.

Along 28th, Colorado Pet & Feed, Tebo's Coin Shop and Sew Good Alterations, a friendly store that can customize anything from blue jeans to wedding gowns, can be found in the Marshall Plaza Shopping Center. You'll also find

Shopping is a heady experience at The Ritz, and the store always stocks plenty of Halloween costumes in adult sizes.

local outposts of nationally known chains such as Barnes & Noble, Toys R Us, Radio Shack and Blockbuster Video. Thirtieth Street merchants include Swalley's Music Studio, Cloth Constructions for designer fabrics and wallpaper and Schwinn Cycling and Fitness.

Basemar Shopping Center
Baseline Rd. and Broadway

Wild Oats, the centerpiece of this L-shape strip mall just north of the CU campus, is the second-biggest health-food market in town and, for some, less showy and "more authentic" than Alfalfa's, even though they are now the same company. Le Français, one of Boulder's most cosmopolitan cafes, and the Basemar Cinema, which shows $1.75 second-run movies, are also located here. This center offers a nice mix of little shops and services, including Buffalo Lock and Key, which is quick at matching keys and getting into locked cars. Herb's Quality Meats has variety and does a good business in a town sometimes nicknamed the Tofu Capital of Colorado. There's a pleasant discount bookstore, a florist and a pharmacy.

The Meadows Shopping Center
Foothills Pkwy. and Baseline Rd.

As Boulder has grown eastward, this strip mall has become busier and busier. More than 50 businesses are now part of this large neighborhood service center, located near several retirement and senior-living facilities. It includes the biggest Safeway in town, along with the Photo Finish, Art Cleaners, Runner's Choice and three quick and easy eateries — Nick-N-Willy's Take-N-Bake Pizza, Lee Yuan and Healthy Habits. Michael's Craft Store and Tuesday Morning, a deep-discount store, are two of the anchors. The Pet Ranch has a very helpful owner. Kid-oriented stores cluster in one corner, including fLearn, which stands for "a fun place to learn." It sells educational toys and software. It is also a center with qualified teachers who can help kids learn how to type, do Kumon math and program in Lego logic. The Meadows Library is on the south side of the shopping center.

North Broadway and Community Plaza
Broadway and Alpine Ave., across from Community Hospital

Metropolitan Home magazine praised the Boulder design group, Communication Arts, for bringing the zip back to these 1960s-era shopping malls sheltered beneath zigzag and loopy roofs. Behind these homey, funky facades, pleasant little shops offer flowers, prescription drugs, haircuts, gifts and more. Ideal is one of Boulder's favorite health-food groceries. Other great shops include the Boulder Wine Merchant, Ava Kids and Moe's Broadway Bagels.

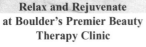

North Village Mart
Broadway and Quince St.

This is the low-key, small-scale shopping area that any neighborhood might want. You won't find choices galore here, but you'll notice just how lovely and cozy a small neighborhood shopping center can be. The area fits its neighborhood well. Kids arrive from the bike trails to pick up videos, wander into the pet store and stop for ice cream. Families and friends winding down after work fill the three respectable restaurants, serving Chinese and Italian food and sandwiches. The sandwich store, Pressto, has a Best of Boulder award from *Daily Camera* readers. The Nomad Players, a well-regarded community theater group, are nearby. North Boulder Mart, which anchors this little shopping center, is a good basic grocery store, with one of the better meat departments in town.

Table Mesa Shopping Center
Broadway and Table Mesa Dr.

In addition to a King Soopers and the usual complement of restaurants and various stores, this South Boulder Shopping Center has many excellent outdoor stores, including The North Face, Neptune Mountaineering, Play It Again Sports, Doc's Ski & Sports, Active Imprints and Weaver's Dive Center. Weaver's is for divers, but weavers go to Shuttles, Spindles and Skeins. The Cooking School of the Rockies holds classes and has a small retail section with gourmet cookware, and Laser Storm is an entertainment center with rousing music and black lights that make white socks and shiny decals on your clothes glow so you become an easy target for your gun-toting opponents. Note the political correctness here . . . you "tag" your opponent. You don't "shoot." Whatever you call it, in the dark, you can act like a banshee and nobody has to know.

University Hill
Broadway, north and south of College Ave.

Just west of campus and affectionately and officially called "The Hill," this area's businesses cater mainly to the university crowd. Named for its location on the side of University Hill, The Hill developed in 1906 as a streetcar stop between the Boulder Depot downtown and Chautauqua Park. In 1928, it received Boulder's first business growth restriction from homeowners who feared their neighbors would eventually sell out to stores, which is the reason that The Hill's retail zone remains so compact. It also explains why many stores look so homey — they actually were homes once.

An eclectic mix of shoppers frequents this college zone, which ranges from the elegant and ultra-tweedy men's shop called Kinsley's to such grunge-generation services as a tattoo and piercing parlor. Gift shops, record stores, bookstores, clothing and jewelry stores and food-and-drink purveyors of all sorts make this a worthwhile area to browse, shop and fit in if you're young and feel young — or perhaps old if you're not. Cafes and/or inexpensive, casual restaurants that make it easy to grab a bite while you stroll include Brillig Works, Bruegger's Bagels, Teresa's Pizzas, The Sink and the Deli Zone. Josh and John's scoops out creamy, locally made ice cream. The coffee is hot at Buchanan's, a more yuppie spot, and Espresso Roma, The Hill's version of Cheers. If you linger past twilight, the '50s-vintage Flatirons Theatre shows avant-garde movies, and *Pollstar* magazine rates the Fox Theatre and Cafe the nation's fourth-best venue among less-than-800 capacity theaters. The Fox's Disco Inferno is a European-style, '70s music night featured several times a month. Stars on their way to the top have done gigs at the Fox, including Sheryl Crowe, Hootie and the Blowfish, 311 and Sarah McLachlan.

Parking is at a premium on The Hill, but its convenient location on the Hop and RTD routes make it easy to reach from Pearl Street and Crossroads malls, as well as from North and south Boulder. Otherwise, it's best to walk or bicycle to this shopping area. Still, some stores, such as Art Hardware, The Boulder Mountaineer and the Colorado Bookstore, have a few free parking lots for their customers, and you can sometimes find metered spaces on campus, a short walk away via a beautiful pedestrian underpass at Broadway and College Avenue. If your interests run deeper, you can pick up a free booklet outlining a self-guided walking tour of The Hill at the Hill Annex, a small "city hall" for students and visitors at 1107 13th Street.

Boulder

It's easy to find everything you need...

right where you need it!

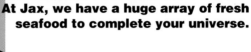

Specializing in magnificent Boulder homes and properties

From the mountains, to the foothills, to the plains we can find the perfect property for you.

WALNUT REALTY

442-3180

1911 11th St., Suite 107
Boulder, CO 80302

East County
Shopping Areas

Twin Peaks Mall
Hover Rd. and Colo. Hwy. 119, Longmont
• 651-6454

More than 130,000 people each week shop at the 80 stores in this regional, enclosed shopping center, which at this writing is being renovated, face-lifted and expanded. The big draws presently include Joslin's, JCPenney (Penney got his start in Longmont), Sears and Fashion Bar. By the spring of 1997, it will mushroom to include a 94,000-square-foot Dillard's and a United Artists 10-screen movie complex.

Local ladies say Stewart's has good women's apparel, and everyone who visits Wicks 'N Lather, which sells bathroom items, knows the store smells wonderful when you walk in. Woodleys Fine Furniture features locally made items, and Colorful Images is an overstock store full of furniture and novelty items. In addition to such sit-down restaurants as the gut-busting Country Buffet and Chelsey London Pub and Grill, there's a food court with flipping burgers, baking pizza and stir-frying Chinese food, plus Renzio's dishing up Greek food.

Lafayette
East on Arapahoe Rd., Baseline Rd. or South Boulder Rd.

Lafayette's main shopping areas are around the intersection of South Boulder Road and Public Road, which is also U.S. 287. Antiques hunters gravitate to West's Antiques, which is a full block long, and nearby Rayburn Antiques and Matthew's Gifts. Lafayette Florists offers the most bedding plants in the county, and the Lafayette Flea Market is the county's best-known. Country General is still a real country general store, selling farm equipment, dog food, tools and horse halters amid the rapid suburbanization of town. You can get a good bite of Mexican food at Efrain's, which serves the hottest green chili around, or La Familia, which is Spanish for "the family," a good name for this homey eatery.

Louisville
East on South Boulder Rd. or Louisville Exit off U.S. 36

Louisville is booming, and its quaint and sleepy downtown is becoming eclipsed by the bright lights of the retail strip along McCaslin Boulevard. While the City of Boulder frets about excessive growth, Louisville welcomes all comers. New big-box retail outlets, fast-food outlets, chain restaurants, a 12-plex theater and hotels have sprung up along what was until recently a relatively sparse roadway. As of this writing, the town has three shopping centers in addition to the traditional downtown. The Village Safeway Shopping Center is at South Boulder Road and Centennial. Louisville Plaza has King Soopers and Kmart at South Boulder Road off of Colo. Highway 42. The Centennial Center, at McCaslin Boulevard and Cherry Street, is near the movie complex and the hotels. In historic downtown, along Main Street, you'll find an Ace Hardware store, The Locker Room for personalized sportswear, Wildwood Music and casual, families-welcome eating places including the Marketplace Bakery, The Blue Parrot and Colacci's restaurants, the Louisville Mine Steak House and Joe's Market for sausage and Italian food. Close by, the Old Louisville Inn features an antique bar and lots of character. A small retail center along South Boulder Road features real train cars that house Kaddy Shack Barbecue, Trails West bookstore and Louisville Cyclery.

INSIDERS' TIP

The best parking for the downtown area is in the structures located at 14th and Walnut, 11th and Spruce and 11th and Walnut streets. When you park in any of these, ask for validation stickers as you pay at downtown stores. Every sticker is good for a half-hour of parking, so you can shop your way to reduced or free parking.

Specialty Shops

Antiques

Boulder has fewer antiques shops than some of the smaller nearby communities. Two of the best are located, respectively, east and west of the Pearl Street Mall. **Bargain Antiques**, 1949 Pearl Street, houses some real treasures and prides itself on high turnover and excellent values. The store spreads through two buildings, a storefront on Pearl Street and an old house around the corner on 19th Street. The "better" goods are in the main store. The annex contains mostly furniture verging on secondhand. **Antiques**, 740 Pearl Street, is actually a consortium of individual dealers, kind of an antiques mini-mall rambling through two commercial buildings. Beautiful old stained-glass windows, lots of furniture and small household objects abound. The city's finest-quality antiques are the specialty of **Sage Gallery**, recently relocated to 5360 Arapahoe Avenue. Quality silver flatware, porcelain, fine Victoriana and Oriental antiques are among their specialties.

Off Her Rocker Antiques in Nederland, 4 E. First Street, is a funky corner shop that feels like a rustic mountain museum. Old wash basins, oak furniture and nifty used clothes go for bargain prices. On nice days, old rockers bedeck the boardwalk out front, rocking gently in the mountain breeze. The shop is known by watch collectors for its interesting collection of old pocket watches in working condition. Local artisans supply such whimsical items to the shop as tinkling wind chimes made from flattened antique spoons and forks.

Longmont's antiques and secondhand stores are strung along Main Street. You could spend an afternoon hunting for golden goodies in Longmont. **Country Road Antiques**, at 463 Main Street, is a branch of the South Broadway dealer on Denver's major antiques row. They offer a good selection of American oak furniture. **Paul's Antiques**, at 923 Main Street, has antiques and junk filling four buildings with dust and treasures. **Cowboy Classics**, 364 Main Street, is just what the name says. The **Little Dickens Antique Shop**, 136 S. Main Street, fills an 1872 Victorian brick house built by the original owner of the Dickens Opera House. **Front Range Flea Market**, 1420 Florida Avenue, has around 50 vendors selling merchandise including household items, furniture, jewelry and sports cards.

Both Lyons and Niwot, respectively north and northeast of Boulder, have become true antique centers, worth a special trip if you're in the market for something specific or just browsing. In Niwot the **Village Collective & Whynot Cafe**, 210 Franklin Avenue, offers antiques, furniture, jewelry, pottery, decorative items, Victorian whatnots and cowboy and Native American knickknacks, along with home cooking at the cafe. The **Niwot Antique Emporium**, at 136 Second Avenue, is the town's giant, a cooperative of more than 40 dealers, many with particular specialties that appeal to collectors. One dealer's booth is a riot of brightly colored Fiestaware, another glistens with Depression glass, still another has a good assortment of oak furniture and so on. If you are restoring an old home or want to give a newer one the patina of age, you can find antique mantelpieces, millwork, doors, architectural accessories and large pieces of furniture at **Wise Buys**, at 190 Second Avenue.

Little Lyons is becoming an antiques mecca too. **Lyons Antique Center**, at the intersection of Colo. Highway 66 and U.S. Highway 36, is a barn-like place with a little bit of everything, including furniture, china, glassware, pottery, jewelry and memorabilia, handled by about a dozen dealers. **Left-Hand's Antique & Western Gallery**, with locations at 401 Main Street and 228 E. Main Street, sells some of lots of things but with a special westward tilt. **Ralston Brothers Antiques**, at 426 High Street, one block north of Main, is in a historic stone building and specializes in vintage radios, phonographs, restored light fixtures and restored antiques, as well as antique toys and choice furniture. The **White Lion**, 418 High Street, Lyons, has antiques, paintings, Huichol Indian art from Mexico, pottery and painted chairs. Owner George Carter creates furniture from old barn wood and local sandstone. The store is one block north of Main Street. It is in a 1898 flagstone livery building between the Old Congregational Church and the post office.

Good Housekeeping calls **Lafayette Flea**

Market, at 130 E. Spaulding Street in Lafayette, one of the nation's best flea markets. Its 500,000 items include clothes, glassware, pots and pans, dishes and antiques. It's open all year, in a clean, well-organized store with friendly salesclerks.

Art Galleries

ArtCycle, on 15th Street just north of the Pearl Street Mall, is such a good idea that's it's gratifying to put it first — alphabetical order being a lucky coincidence. The store is a fine-art consignment shop, where you'll find an ever-changing selection of paintings and quality graphic arts, already framed. It's a great way to change your own style if you're redecorating because you know that someone else will buy and love a painting that's been an old friend of yours.

Art Source International, 1237 Pearl Street, specializes in antique maps and prints. Many are already framed, some are ready for your choice of frame — all are fascinating. In addition to a great selection of 18th- and 19th-century maps, the gallery displays prints from the same era. The storefront was recently refurbished and now is a classy addition to the Pearl Street Mall streetscape.

Art Mart, 1222 Pearl Street, is kind of a crafts supermarket, which bills itself as an "artist outlet store." It overflows with Southwestern objects, including jewelry, pottery, weavings, dream catchers and all the other popular items. The large store carries clothing, candles, wood inlays and a myriad of other crafts. In addition, the outlet has an outlet, Art Mart's Rocky Mountain Factory Outlet at I-25 and U.S. Highway 34 outside of Loveland.

Artist's Proof, 5360 Arapahoe Avenue, couples fine custom framing, hand-carved matting and dry mounting with unusual art dealership. It specializes in interesting sports memorabilia (especially baseball) and original signed black-and-white photographs and other graphic media.

Boulder Arts & Crafts Cooperative, 1421 Pearl Street, is the biggest and most diverse of the city's several crafts co-ops. It shows works of more than 70 participating members and consignees from Colorado and surrounding mountain states displaying high-quality crafts in all media. Pottery, puppets, jewelry, photographs, weavings, stained glass, woodwork, hand-weaving and other items make great gifts or home decor. The co-op will also ship purchases anywhere in the continental United States. The co-op's best sale is generally in early October.

Busch Gallery, 1926 14th Street, is one of Boulder's newer art showcases, and it specializes in newer art, including contemporary paintings, ceramics, jewelry and bronze sculptures beautifully displayed on two levels. David Grosjean, Paulette Broder and Arlene LaDell Lyons are among the contemporary artists who show here.

Mackin-Katz Gallery, 2041 Broadway, showcases Andy Katz's fine photography, including the California wine country, Poland, Israel and Vietnam, as well as other artists' works. Andy started showing locally in a basement gallery of his own under Pour La France and behind a billiards parlor, but this new daylight-filled space is much more conducive to viewing his detailed and delicate works.

MacLaren Markowitz Gallery, 1011 Pearl Street, is a bright, beguiling gallery showing painting, sculpture, jewelry and imports. Perhaps their best-known artist is Doug West, whose acrylics and serigraphs of Western landscapes have become extremely popular. The gallery sometimes puts on Collectors Evenings, including an opportunity to meet personally with artists. Poster signings, art talks and other special events are occasionally on the agenda too.

INSIDERS' TIP

The Hop buses run between three of the area's biggest shopping centers — Pearl Street Mall, University Hill and Crossroads Mall. It costs only 25¢, and it comes by quicker than every 10 minutes. What a speedy, convenient way to explore Boulder's stores. And when you use the Hop, you're helping the environment!

Mary Williams Fine Arts, 2116 Pearl Street, demonstrates how far eastward the spirit of the Pearl Street Mall has spread. This new gallery shows old and new American works, including some with a strong Western and Native American orientation. Fine prints and graphics on such themes as botanicals, natural history, architecture abound. If you want a John James Audubon, a Currier & Ives or an Edward S. Curtis on your walls, here's where you'll find one

Marisol Imports, 915 Pearl Street, offers a stunning display of Zapotec and other Mexican rugs, plus Southwestern furniture, Navajo rugs and crafts. The beautiful but expensive rugs become more affordable at Marisol's annual after-Christmas sale. Pottery, woodcarvings and wrought iron are also stocked.

The Middle Fish, 1728 Pearl Street, honors the childhood nickname of store owner Malinda Fishman. Located next to the Harvest Restaurant, The Middle Fish sells hand-crafted items, including ceramic indoor fountains, garden art, handmade dolls, furniture, lighting, jewelry and Judaica. Contemporary rather than classical pieces dominate.

White Horse Gallery, 1218 Pearl Street, is Boulder's leading gallery for Native American and Southwestern art of the highest quality. Exquisite pueblo pottery, Navajo rugs and weavings, Hopi kachinas, Zuni fetishes, Pacific Northwest baskets and carvings, antique art and contemporary works by nationally known artists are beautifully showcased. White Horse's best-known artist is a Colorado silversmith named Ben Nighthorse, who also is in the center of the political stage as U.S. Senator Ben Nighthorse Campbell. The gallery is open daily and many evenings, making it a satisfying combination with a good downtown dinner.

Arts and Crafts Supplies

Art Hardware, 1135 Broadway, is Boulder's top professional (and amateur) artists' supply center with a full line of art and drafting supplies. The shop also does blue printing, large-format copying for architects and engineers and custom framing. The store boasts free covered parking for customers, a real rarity on The Hill. The store is closed on Sundays.

Le Promenade Bead Shop, 1970 13th Street, just off the Pearl Street Mall, is a small shop with a huge selection of baubles, bangles and bright shiny beads. Glass beads in a stunning variety of hues and sizes, antique beads, African trade beads, sequins, rhinestones, sew-ons, studs, jeweler's string, ear wires, posts, clasps and all the other makings of unique, do-it-yourself jewelry are crammed into Boulder's best beadery. The shop also offers jewelry appraisal by a certified gemologist and professional pearl stringing.

The Dove's Eye, 2425 Canyon Boulevard, is a needleworker's paradise, selling fabrics, yarns, needles and stitching accessories. Custom stitching, classes and unique gifts complete the picture in this special business.

FYI

Unless otherwise noted, the area code for all phone numbers in this guide is 303.

Michael's Arts and Crafts, 4800 Baseline Road, is a bustling warehouse store packed with easy craft items, from dried and plastic flowers to the right kind of muslin and paint sets for creating doll faces. Beads, Styrofoam, jewelry findings and all sorts of kits appeal to crafters of all ages and skills. It's a big, reasonably priced place where kids and adults like to wander and take classes. There's a framing shop in the back.

Shuttles, Spindles and Skeins, 633 S. Broadway, is for anyone who loves a good yarn. The walls and walls of yarn come in a fantastic array of colors for knitting and weaving, and you can find a few handmade items for sale that are masterpieces. Uncarded wool, silk, flax and camel hair are all perfect for making doll hair as well as for spinning. This small, charming store has a cozy atmosphere that just says "welcome." The staff is very knowledgeable, and the shop has a wall of craft books for inspiration and classes to show you how to put the inspiration into action.

Bakeries

Many better groceries stock locally produced breads, or you can go straight to the

Buffalo Exchange, which pioneered the concept of buying, selling, and trading merchandise, offers eclectic atmosphere and diverse clothing.

bakeries so you can swim through bread aromas as soon as you open the door. Most have some sort of frequent-buyer program, giving you a free loaf after a dozen or so purchases.

Daily Bread, 1738 Pearl Street, bakes wondrous crusty, full-bodied, hand-shaped organic loaves in a French *bongard* oven. To picture that oven, imagine four decks made of refractory concrete, surrounded by tubes that carry mineral oil, constantly circulating to heat the huge, heavy oven. Country and city baguettes, a real European-style rye, a sensational Sicilian olive bread and a flat, lacy *foucasse* are among the specialties. You can watch the breads turn golden brown through a big glass window. Daily Bread has earned Best of Boulder awards from *Daily Camera* readers for these delicious items. The bakery also bakes delicious scones, cookies and pastries. A small cafe is part of the bakery.

If Daily Bread has any competition at all, it's **Breadworks**, 2644 Broadway, which bakes 24 different round loaves and baguettes on a rotating weekly schedule. Focaccia, brownies, cookies, muffins and scones also come out of the huge brick and tile oven. Monday is half-price day for breads left over from the weekend. Breadworks unlocks the door at 7 AM daily. **The Great Harvest Bread Company**, 2525 Arapahoe Avenue, is part of a tightly controlled franchise operation that makes rich, chewy healthy feeling breads and

rolls. While other bakeries just put out sample bites, if anything, Great Harvest cuts whole slabs and invites you to slather your "taste" with butter.

Le Français, in the Basemar Center at Broadway and Baseline Road, offers almost real French baguettes (French friends say "real" requires French air wafting through the brick ovens), plus decadent French pastries — both savory and sweet. In addition to takeout baked goods, you can eat in at breakfast, lunch or dinner. Le Français, which is owned by a French baker and comes by its authenticity by right, makes the most gorgeous special-occasion cakes. You might want to get married just to have an excuse to order a wedding cake from this wonderful bakery. **The Creative Bakery** at 1837 Pearl Street is an all-organic bakery that's part of the Creative Cafe.

A Piece of Cake, on the west side of the Table Mesa Shopping Center at Broadway and Table Mesa Drive, makes wedding cakes and other sweets. One of their specialties is color portraits "spray-painted" onto a cake's surface with edible icings. Just bring in a photo, and they do the rest. **Spruce Confections**, 2560 Pearl Street, specializes in scones, cakes, cookies and brownies. **The Lick Skillet Bakery**, at 5340 Arapahoe Avenue, is popular for raspberry-mousse cake, stuffed focaccia bread and wheat-free fruit muffins. For delicious dunkers, try **Donut Factory**, 1480 Midway

Boulevard, across from the new Target in Broomfield. Longmont's **Bavarian Bakery**, at 613 Frontage Road, creates fresh, chewy salt sticks and pungent rye bread at this family-owned store.

Bagels have gone big-time in Boulder. **Moe's Broadway Bagels**, at 2650 Broadway and 3075 Arapahoe Avenue, started the bagel craze with extraordinary fresh bagels, spreads, toppings, sandwiches, good coffee and more. They've created the "Moezone," a delicious combination of a Jewish bagel and an Italian calzone. Talk about multiculturalism! Moe's does great bagel sandwiches, good ice creams and terrific T-shirts too. Check out the bags of half-price day-olds, which still taste fresh. Moe's has won the Best of Boulder Bagel award from the *Daily Camera* for several years. and its lead comes from the extraordinary freshness of its bagels, plus ditzy decor and a noisy, New Yorky ambiance. The competition comes from **Bruegger's** (formerly Bolo), 1116 13th Street on the Hill, and **Beatnik's Bagels**, 2775 Pearl Street. We love the name **Ryes & Shine**, a bagel and bake shop at 1 First Street in Nederland.

Bookstores

Aion Bookshop, 1235 Pennsylvania Avenue, is a used bookstore with a real antiquarian feeling. The shop rambles through a series of small rooms, which are filled, but not crammed, with a fascinating selection of previously owned and previously loved books. The street level features hardbacks, including many of a serious and scholarly nature, as you might expect from a store near campus. Downstairs are more popular books, including paperbacks, sci-fi, mysteries, cookbooks, self-help, sports and such. The selection of science, arts, humanities and great literature is impressive, as is the knowledge of the folks working there.

Barnes & Noble, 1741 28th Street, may be a big chain store, but it's working to offer a more personal touch that's gaining local respect. The store specializes in popular fiction and nonfiction but has a large sampling of more obscure works too. People linger in the in-store coffee shop, and the store is the site of regular meetings of locals who are reading

the popular creative-discovery workbook, *The Artist's Way*, and others interested in both the creative and reading aspects of literature.

If you want to turn the calendar back a few decades, check out the quirky **Beat Book Shop**, 1713 Pearl Street, which specializes in literature, poetry, biography, film, sociology and subculture, with a distinct retro flair. It offers a commendable selection of first editions. The shop also stocks rare records and tapes, some fine art and used CDs.

The **Boulder Bookstore**, 1107 Pearl Street, is a local showpiece, operating since 1973 in the historic Buckingham Building. Bookstore owner David Bolduc and architect Dennis Bloemker received the 1993 award of merit from Historic Boulder for "historic preservation and restoration of the second-floor ballroom." The lovely high-ceilinged room with its antique stained-glass windows is the stage for visiting authors. They have included such famous writers as Barbara Kingsolver, Thomas Moore, William Styron, Amy Tan, Gary Hart, Roger Ebert, Peter Matthiessen, Whitely Strieber, Douglas Coupland and Isabel Allende. The 20,000-square-foot, three-story bookstore offers more than 100,000 titles and also has a large selection of magazines, journals and various book-related items, plus art displays by local artists. The store recently began stocking a small selection of used books too.

The adjacent, but separately owned, **Bookend Cafe**, is connected by an open door and makes a nice stop after browsing through the books. Free parking is available (via validation stickers) for City of Boulder lots and structures.

The **Colorado Bookstore**, at the corner of College Avenue and Broadway next to the big outdoor clock and the pedestrian underpass, is a classic college bookstore. It sells new textbooks and plenty of used books (they buy and sell) and has a mezzanine devoted to general books. You also can buy CU-Boulder sweatshirts, souvenirs and school supplies. There's a small post office substation, copiers, fax machines, prepaid phone cards, photo processing and other services. The store opens at 8:30 AM on weekdays (10 AM on Saturday; closed Sundays).

Ead's News & Smoke Shop, at Canyon

and 28th streets, under the outdoor clock, is actually a mega-newsstand, with Boulder's best selection of magazines and out-of-town newspapers. It also carries an assortment of travel books, popular paperbacks and adult-only books and magazines.

Lighthouse Bookstore, 1201 Pearl Street, located under Ben & Jerry's, is New Age kind of place and a real find for anyone seeking books dealing with spirituality, self-help, religions from around the world and exploring the inner self. It's very well-stocked, and with light filtering in from the streetside windows and the calming music, the atmosphere is conducive to browsing. The staff is especially helpful here too.

The Printed Page, on the Pearl Street Mall, is mostly a stationery and gift store with a small selection of books, mostly local interest and children's books. Their Gunbarrel store called **Page Two**, 6565 Gunpark Drive, not only carries a similar inventory but houses a pleasant cafe as well.

Red Letter Second Hand Books, 1737 Pearl Street, is jammed and crammed with a selection of used books, including classics, travel, biography and all sorts of fiction. It offers classics as well as modern works and is open until 9 PM nightly except Sunday for buying, selling, trading or simply browsing.

Rue Morgue Mystery Bookshop, 946 Pearl, is a mystery lover's paradise for both new and rare used mysteries. This is the oldest, and one of the three biggest, mystery stores in the nation. Sisters in Crime, a group of women mystery writers, meets here, and author book-signings are frequent.

Time Warp Science Fiction and Comics, at 1631 28th Street, is a word-of-mouth favorite among kids and has been nominated as one of the nation's best comic stores. Regionally, it has garnered Best of Boulder and Best of Denver awards from the *Daily Camera* and *Westword*. Time Warp is known for both mainstream and underground comics. If you're a grownup with a secret love of comics, just say you're looking for something for your nephew or niece.

Stage House II, 1039 Pearl Street, is Boulder's king of used books. This massive attic of a store is brimful of 100,000 used and rare items, including a huge selection of paperbacks and hardcovers. Fiction is shelved alphabetically by author and nonfiction by subject, but the stock is so huge that each shelf has overflows stacked on the floor below. Stage House is trying to carve a niche for itself in Boulder's gallery scene, specializing in graphic art, exotic jewelry, African sculptures, original paintings, posters and an extensive collection of Edward S. Curtis and W.H. Jackson photographs. Underneath the affable exteriors of owner Dick Schwartz and staff are brains with the storage capacity of mainframe computers. Ask for an obscure book. They'll wander into the stacks and find it, usually in 5 minutes or less.

Trident Booksellers & Cafe, 940 Pearl Street, has been voted the Best of Boulder coffee shop by *Daily Camera* readers. It looks and feels quite European, in the best and most traditional sense, with interesting-looking people huddled over tables, apparently be engaged in the most existential of conversations. The adjacent bookstore has a potpourri of used books, new remainders, cards and calendars. The sale table just inside the front door always displays interesting books on history, gardening, cooking, travel, spiritual topics and more.

Other specialty and niche booksellers are scattered about the county. **The Lyons Tale**, 228 Main Street in Lyons, is a delightful bookstore, bakery and cafe right on the town's antique row. **Books for the Whole Child**, 311 Terry Street in Longmont, specializes in children's books. It is well-known for the staff's knowledge of children's literature and annual American Girl tea parties.

Clothing and Accessories

For Children

Ava Baby and Ava Kids, in the Community Plaza shopping center at 2628 Broadway, charges outlet prices for brightly colored and charming clothes. **Applause**, at 1123 Pearl Street, is outrageously stylish, offering endearing baby and toddler duds and enchanting ballerina and princess get-ups for little girls who like to dress up. **Zippety Doo-Da**, at 2425 Canyon Boulevard, is a recently expanded kidswear store with more than a hundred lines

of infant and children's clothing. **Pour Moi**, in the Village Shopping Center, also has classy women's and junior clothing. Nearby **Feet First** has a huge selection of children's shoes in a mind-boggling array of sizes from "baby's first" to almost-adult. This store claims to be Colorado's largest Stride Rite dealer, and it also carry such name brands as Nike, Keds, Reebok, LA Gear and Skechers.

With Boulder being as sporty as it is, it was just a matter of time before someone invented **Rocky Mountain Kids**, 1136 Spruce Street, which sells fleece and other outdoorsy, performance clothing even in sizes for infants who can't perform too much yet, as well as kids' packs, baby joggers and carriers for sale or rent. **Pockets**, 2862 Bluff Street, and **Childish Things**, 2081 30th Street, sell consignment clothes and other items for babies on up.

And while you're out, buy a copy of *Baby Bargains*, a nationally sold book by Boulder authors who have thoroughly researched how to find good deals for baby things all across America, including Boulder. Also read the chapter on Boulder Kidstuff for more ideas on where kids love to shop for toys and other amusing items.

Among the chain stores, **Gap Kids**, 2043 Broadway, has high fashion clothes with famous names. **Mervyn's** in the Crossroads Mall has a good selection and moderate prices,

making it popular with pragmatic parents. **Marshall's**, 1875 28th Street, is a discounter with a less predictable but less expensive selection. This week, with-it teens want their clothes from **JCPenney**, also at Crossroads, but who knows what the style will be next week.

For Adults

To dress up in Boulder, lots of people dress down with style, and the city abounds with quality casual and functional clothing that has become a style all its own around here. **Holiday & Co.**, 2015 Broadway, is a neat little women's shop tucked behind Tom's Tavern, with upwardly casual clothes, something between J. Crew and Banana Republic. **Starr's**, at 1712 Pearl Street, has reasonably pricey, rather sporty attire for men, women and children with private parking adjacent. **Barbed Wire Cowboy**, 1955 Broadway, is an upscale cowboy Western place, just south of the Pearl Street Mall's Häagen Dazs, featuring sterling jewelry belt buckle sets, Western-cut clothing, suedes and leathers, fringed vests and selected home furnishings. Go to Broomfield for brand-name casual clothing at outlet prices from the **Woolrich Factory Outlet Store**, at 6900 W. 117th Avenue.

Those whose lifestyle, or at least style, include lots of traveling love **Timbuktu Station**, just west of the Pearl Street Mall at 1035 Pearl Street, which features fun, casual and professional travel clothes. **Banana Republic**, 1147 Pearl Street, also sells durable shorts, skirts, pants, blouses and other gear you can wear outdoors and to work, depending on how neatly you tuck things in. **C.P. Shades**, 2035 Broadway near the corner of Spruce Street, sells clothing that won't wrinkle, or some say that is pre-wrinkled and designed to be so, that packs like a dream. The annual New Year's sale is worth waiting for. On the first of the year, many garments were marked down to $19.97, which next year will inflate to $19.98.

Understated elegant career clothes can be found at **Solo**, 1110 Pearl Street, a locally owned store with contemporary designer women's clothes and accessories that have made Solo a welcome part of the mall since 1978. **Knit Wit**, 2021 Broadway, offers elegant New York and L.A. styles. **Ann Taylor**, 2070 Broadway, is one of Boulder's best career clothes centers, with a good sense of what's casual but elegant, from the blouse to the pumps. **Talbot's** is back, with a large new freestanding store in Arapahoe Village. **The Studio**, 2425 Canyon Boulevard, is a Boulder-inspired idea where you come in, try on the mix-and-match sports and party clothes, then order your favorite in exactly the color and size you want.

Offbeat clothing abounds too. **The Pipefitter**, 1352 College Avenue, has hippie kinds of batik clothes, Guatemalan vests, jewelry and Grateful Dead paraphernalia. **Fresh Produce Sportswear** is locally manufactured, easy-to-wear knits, with a retail store on the Pearl Street Mall at 1136 Pearl Street. **College Corner**, on the upper level at 1310 College Avenue, has CU-Boulder sweatshirts, T-shirts, hats and other memorabilia. Champion reverse weave sweatshirts and CU-Boulder baseball caps are especially popular in a dozen cap sizes ranging from kids to huge. **Applause**, 1123 Pearl Street, is in a class by itself, with cutting-edge sportswear and dresses. Applause sometimes sells fabulous suits, other times fabulous pants and shirts. This ahead-of-the-crowd store went through the pleated cowgirl skirt craze years ago. The constant theme is high-quality, moderate-to-expensive clothes to die for, eye-catching shoes and jewelry and sensational kids' clothes that are almost too adorable to get dirty.

Go to University Hill's **Jacque Michelle Apparel and Home Decor**, 1118 13th Street, a little "everything shop," selling items from T-shirts to locally made hats, cards and arty things. A second branch called **Jacque Michelle II** opened at Community Plaza, 2670 Broadway. **Serendipity Boutique**, 1140 13th Street, has women's clothes, including easy-care Bali imports and 1940s Swiss tuxedo jackets for around only $40. Sweaters, leggings, jeans and funky stuff are also affordable, plus everything from body lotion to rugs and tapestries.

Occasionally, even Boulder guys need new suits. **Kinsley & Co.**, 1155 13th Street on The Hill, is Boulder's prime men's clothier. Currently, it carries Armani and Hugo Boss suits and locally made Carrot & Gibbs bow ties and Ferrell Reed regular neckties, items which unfortunately aren't available directly from the factories. **The Regiment Shops**, at 2425 Canyon Boulevard, have updated, tailored business clothes such as Perry Ellis for men and blazer/skirt combinations for women. **Robert Schmidt Clothier**, at 1050 Walnut Street, also offers good suits. And for well-dressed men who want casual wear, **Weekends**, 1101 Pearl Street, has stylish shirts, sweaters, vests and slacks.

Jila Designs, 2035 Broadway, sells original-design women's clothing, in gorgeous silks and rayons. Another Boulder original, Jila is now offering clothes in some national department stores, such as Nordstrom's. **Webb Weaving and Design**, 189 Spring Lane, offers custom hand-woven outerwear; make sure you schedule an appointment before visiting. Hand-woven or dyed clothes also can be found at local arts and crafts stores.

For fancy, fancy affairs, the **Bride's Gallery**, at 4740 Table Mesa Drive, has tuxes and formal gowns to buy or rent. But when you want to fling it all to passion, consider **Christina's Lingerie**, at 2425 Canyon Boulevard, which offers exquisite lingerie and also well-fitting swimsuits plus a staff that is truly helpful at telling you what styles flatter your figure. Another late, late, under-the-covers place is **Gioia**, at 1215 Pearl Street. Sure, you can find seductive stuff in these stores, but also flannel nightgowns with little roses on them, proper enough for your great-grand-aunt.

Whether you make your own clothing or struggle with hemming napkins, you'll enjoy **Elfriede's Fine Fabrics Studio Bernina**, at 2460 Canyon Boulevard, which stocks Liberty of London cottons and Loro Piana woolens. At the same location is **Studio Bernina**, a full-fledged sewing school that sells Bernina machines. Other stops for fabri-holics include **Hancock Fabrics**, at 649 Broadway in the Table Mesa Shopping Center, and **So-Fro Fabrics** at 2440 Arapahoe Avenue in Arapahoe Village.

To dress down and out . . . outdoors, that is, buy layers for Boulder's changeable weather. The closest description we've heard of the "Boulder look" is "always ready for a hike." You could wear out the bottoms of your Vibram-sole boots trekking between all the Boulder stores that have great outdoor gear. See the section on "Sporting Goods Shops" later in this chapter for more information.

If your feet start hurting from all that shopping, head to the **Pedestrian Shops** for comfortable shoes. There's one on the Pearl Street Mall and another near McGuckin Hardware, facing Folsom Street.

The greatest concentration of clothing shops is, not surprisingly, at Crossroads Mall. **Foley's** is a full-service department store with women's, junior and petite clothing, plus shoes, earrings and everything in between. The store offers a wide selection of casual and elegant clothing. Moderately priced and very stylish casual fashions are at **Express**. It features foreign cuts with the store's Express label.

Consignment and Resale Shops

No Place Like Home, 3550 Arapahoe Avenue, is one of the cleanliest used-furniture stores you'll ever see, with a nice selection of nearly new items. Those with a sharp eye can find some real bargains, but some of the furniture is surprisingly high-priced considering that it's secondhand. Turnover is rapid, so if you're on the lookout for something in particular, it's best to check fairly frequently. The best stuff borders on the antique; less-inspired offerings are simply used. The store also carries some

tableware, framed pictures and other small objects. If you consign to them, they'll pick up. If you buy, they'll deliver.

The area east of the Mall has become a real mecca for vintage clothing enthusiasts. **Clothes Encounters of the Second Kind** gets the prize for the best name for a used-clothing consignment store. At 1622 Pearl Street, the shop specializes in men's and women's apparel from the '70s into the '90s, which is certainly not vintage. They have recently added some new clothing, including black vinyl, which was hot as this book was being prepared. Clothes Encounters spawned a second store nearby that now specializes in true vintage clothing. **Counter Evolution**, 1628 Pearl Street, carries clothing for both men and women mostly from the '20s through the '50s with shoes and accessories to match. The longest-running resale emporium in this area is **Twice Nice**, 1646 Pearl Street, a resale shop for women's and children's clothing. Scoot around the corner to **The Buffalo Exchange**, 1717 Walnut Street, which specializes in current and retro vintage clothing. If you've got stuff to sell, this place has liberal policies. They buy during all business hours. And rather than taking items on consignment, they buy outright for 40 percent cash or 55 percent credit toward a store trade.

The Ritz, around the corner from the Pearl Street Mall, 959 Walnut Street, inventories a fabulous selection of classic '40s fashions, flouncy prom gowns from the '50s, elegant cocktail attire from various decades and other unusual and vintage clothing. The store also sells and rents great costumes (Halloween and otherwise), including gorilla suits, creepy creatures from horror films and masks of current politicians' faces.

People trek far into North Boulder to **Candy's Vintage Clothing**, 4483 Broadway. The selection is large, and the variety astonishing. You might be lucky enough to find a nice Harris tweed jacket or Pendleton shirt. For used maternity and baby clothes, plus toys, games, books and other baby equipment, check **Pockets**, at 3103 28th Street. Once the baby has arrived, you can get clothing, furnishings and toys suitable for infants to preteens at **Childish Things**, 2081 30th Street. **Second Hand Rose**, 630 Front Street in Louisville, offers bargains on new and near-new clothing for all ages, plus furniture and small appliances.

Farmers Markets and Food Co-ops

As much of a happening and social event as a shopping opportunity, the **Boulder County Farmers Market**, on 13th Street between Arapahoe Avenue and Canyon Boulevard, operates 8 AM to 2 PM on Saturdays and 11 AM to 4 PM on Wednesdays from spring through fall. There's a mouthwatering selection of organically grown vegetables and fruits, baked goods, herbs, bedding plants, fresh flowers, crafts and baked goods. (See the Attractions chapter for more details.) Niwot has its own farmers market too, open 9 AM to 1 PM on Saturdays, across from Rev. Taylor's restaurant on Second Street. Louisville's is from 8 AM to 2 PM on Saturdays, at the corner of Spruce and Front streets.

Mountain Peoples Co-op, a humble Nederland food store at 925 E. First Street, is a blast from the past. It is a cooperative, and members pay slightly lower prices. Behind its eye-popping paint job, the co-op harkens back to the old-time, small-town neighborhood grocery but with a New Age twist. They carry a good selection of some of the tastiest organic and locally grown fruits and vegetables. There are also coffee beans, grains, good breads and other wholesome items — no junk food — and most necessities from toilet paper and cat food to Ben & Jerry's Ice Cream.

Market on the Hill, on College Avenue between Broadway and 13th streets, sells its wares 11 AM to 5 PM on Sundays.

Gadgets

The Better Back Store, at 3034 Walnut Street in the Walnut Gardens shopping center, is hardly a frivolity to those in discomfort or pain. You'll find back-strengthening exercise equipment, ergonomic office furniture, home furniture such as Ekornes Stressless Chairs from Norway, and Backsaver recliners, cervical pillows, Tempur Pedic pillows and mattresses, back cushions, lumbar belts and rolls, seat supports, massage equipment and creams, inversion units and boots, Backsaver snow shovels and other tools, and video and cassette tapes. All these gadgets aim to help you save your back or just to relax, feel good and even prevent back problems.

Changes in Latitude, 2416 Arapahoe Avenue, Arapahoe Village Shopping Center, is a nifty shop with everything for the traveler. High-quality travel luggage and accessories and packs, water purifiers, security gadgets and a snazzy assortment of Ex Officio and Royal Robbins casual wear for men and women will set you off in safety and style. The shop also features a large assortment of books and maps. They'll do passport photos and also have a travel agency. The online computer travel information center contains State Department reports and files on every country, which they'll print out for you if you need the latest information on necessary inoculations for different countries. The store puts on a series of interesting slide presentations, normally on Thursday evenings, which will inspire all but the most home-bound to hit the road, and there are occasional tourist language courses too.

The slogan of **McGuckin Hardware**, 2525 Arapahoe Avenue, is, "If we don't have it, you don't need it." It's just about true. This gigantic hardware superstore carries a do-it-yourselfer's dream of hand- and power-tools and stuff to do with them. McGuckin's is everything but a lumber yard or plumbing supply house, so you won't find plywood, 4-by-6s or miles of piping, but you will find wood trim, door and window hardware, lighting fixtures and accessories, electrical and plumbing supplies and the biggest selection of screws, nuts, bolts, clamps, washers, springs, gaskets and every other gizmo and widget you can imagine. High-end bathroom fixtures and cabinet hardware take up a separate store. Nearby is The special-order desk can get items that aren't in stock. In addition, there are good-quality paint and housewares departments. One department makes keys and sells locks, another has video and audio tapes. Christmas decorations abound in winter, and patio furniture moves in with warm weather. Gardening tools and supplies, as well as seeds, annual and perennial plants, herald summer. Pet supplies,

mail boxes, gas-log fireplaces, fencing materials and more pack into this huge space. McGuckin's also sells sporting equipment, including fishing and hunting supplies, backpacks and camping equipment and some outdoor books.

The spring and fall tent sales are three-day extravaganzas that include closeout and special-purchase merchandise at tremendous savings, as well as a blanket 10 percent off everything in the store. What sets McGuckin's apart from every other hardware store around, especially the big-box chains, is personal service. A veritable army of green-vested salespeople are there to help, advise, guide and point the way to the department you're looking for.

The Peppercorn, at 1235 Pearl Street, is the queen of Boulder's kitchen stores — and one of the very best in the country. They now have a mail-order catalog, but it's more far more fun to visit this very pretty, full-to-bursting kitchen store with fine cookware, kitchen gadgets, table linens, a huge assortment of cookbooks and gourmet foods. Need a mushroom brush? A butter mold? A Madeleine pan? A replacement blade for your coffee mill? A spoon rest with a clever design? A set of Calphalon pots? A food processor in Mama Bear, Papa Bear or Baby Bear sizes? Peppercorn has them all — and, oh, so much more. Celebrity author-chefs sometimes do book signings and occasionally put on cooking demonstrations too. Fine china, porcelain, flatware and crystal from the world's best-known makers are what make The Peppercorn a popular spot for bridal registries. Across the alley, fronting Spruce Street, is **Peppercorn Collection**, a high-end bed and bath shop with gorgeous linens and accessories.

The West End Gardener, 805 W. Pearl Street, is a delightful new shop selling top-quality gardening tools, books, fountains, garden signs, wreaths, annuals and bulbs in season, gifts and goodies for plant-lovers. It makes a putterer want to garden seriously, and a serious gardener strive to make the garden more perfect.

Gift and Specialty-food Shops

With so many great Boulder restaurants, you might wonder who bothers to cook. After checking the equally great food shops, you might conclude that many Boulderites dine out just to get ideas for creating memorable meals at home. You can find ingredients from ordinary to exotic all over the city. Ethnic food stores so authentic that they transport you to distant lands are tucked into surprising little corners of the city and surrounding communities. Big supermarkets carry a variety of interesting foodstuffs to remain somewhat competitive even for these exotic niches.

Boulder has several first-rate, no-frills ethnic food stores, where the fragrance can inspire you to whip up a meal from a faraway land, and some also offer excellent take-out fare. **The Oriental Food Market**, 1750 30th Street, No. 84, carries all the ingredients you'll need for all manner of Asian cuisine. Need some dried bonito flakes, pickled daikon radishes, lemongrass or divine curries? The Oriental Food Market has them all. **The Asian Deli**, at 2829 28th Street, includes Asian produce and freshly made Vietnamese spring rolls — cilantro and shrimp enclosed in a delicate rice wrapper. The **Morocco International Food Market**, 2690 28th Street, owned by a Libyan family, carries Middle Eastern and North African specialties.

INSIDERS' TIP

You'll find frazzled and deadline-driven Boulderites at two 24-hour Kinko's copy and computer centers, including a huge new superstore at 28th and Pearl streets. Other useful services are franchises of Mail Boxes Etc., The Mail Station and Pak Mail, which handle packing, shipping and other chores that normally take a couple of stops. And as a bonus, there rarely are lines. Federal Express has a drop-off at Walnut and 14th streets, while UPS is off E. Pearl Street.

Photo: Daily Camera

It takes two weeks to make your own special brew at The Beer Store.

House of Fire, 1108 Pearl Street, offers more than 1,000 hot mustards, spices, salsas and other hot foods from all over the world. If you grew up in the East, Longmont's **El Mercado**, in the old train station at 137 Main Street, will seem exotic for its real Mexican food ingredients plus tamales-to-go and menudo-to-go. If you are a Westerner, you expect to be able to buy authentic Mexican foodstuffs. If you grew up in the West, **Salvaggio's Italian Deli**, 2809 Pearl Street, and **Da Nonna Italian Market**, 1664 30th Street, might seem exotic; if you're a former Easterner, they can satisfy your craving for good Italian fare. Salvaggio's is best for Italian cold cuts and cheeses, including fresh, water-packed mozzarella, while Da Nonna has excellent fresh pastas and sauces.

The **Cheese Importer's Warehouse – Willow River Company**, 33 S. Pratt Parkway in Longmont, has bargains on wheels of foreign and domestic cheeses and bags of perfect, meltable dark chocolate, all set on industrial-strength shelving in a huge, refrigerated room. A small shop also carries other gourmet foods, coffee, tea and cookware. **Herb's Meats & Specialty Foods**, in the Basemar Shopping Center, is just what the name says. **Scoops**, at Crossroads Mall, has more than 500 kinds of candy, including chocolate-covered gummy bears, gummy spiders and so many rows of colorful, sweet-filled bins, it's

like landing in Candyland. **Mountain Man Fruit & Nut Co.** is a locally owned store at 2525 Arapahoe Avenue, just north of the Village Theatre, that carries gourmet candy such as double-dipped malted-milk balls, all kinds of nuts and dried fruits, trail mixes, peach salsa and dried soups from corn chowder to Circle R Ranch jalapeño black bean, plus teas, coffees, mustards and jellies. They do gift baskets too. If you are ambitious and want to decorate your own cakes, you can get supplies from **Colorado Craft and Cake Supply**, 1750 30th Street, Suite 12. They sell powdered meringue for frosting and incredible cake decorations.

Boulder's natural food stores aren't just for the granola and tofu crowd. Many have great delis and gourmet sections, which can mean delicious bonbons and butter-drenched pastries (but without chemicals or preservations). Carry-out food includes grape-leaved Greek dolmades, Mexican burritos, interesting salads and sandwiches and everything you'd need to throw together a multi-course dinner. But even the decadent stuff is natural, for heaven's sake! And if you want something totally nutritious, stick to the organic produce sections, the natural meat/fish departments and the bins of whole grains. Or go to the juice bars, which are like regular bars, but instead of choosing from scotch and bourbon, you choose from freshly made vegetable or fruit juice . . . usually next to a good espresso machine. Check out **Wild Oats** markets at either the Basemar Shopping Center or at 1825 Pearl Street; **Alfalfa's Market**, at Broadway and Arapahoe Avenue; **Arapahoe Fresh**, at 5320 Arapahoe Avenue; and **Ideal Market**, at 1275 Alpine Avenue. All feature natural and organic foods. Arapahoe Fresh is a large produce stand, and the others are small supermarkets.

Boulder has big supermarkets too.

King Soopers offers five full-service, 24-hour supermarkets in Boulder County, each with a grocery, pharmacy, floral department and cheap video rentals. If you don't have time to shop, are ill or are caring for someone who is, you can phone your grocery order in to **Teleshopper** delivery, 778-KING, and your groceries will be delivered to your door. The service costs $10. King Soopers also sells Rockies tickets, discount ski lift tickets, discount RTD bus passes and often tickets to such seasonal events as the Colorado Renaissance Festival, the Parade of Homes and the National Western Stock Show in Denver. The recycling center takes glass, plastic, cans, Styrofoam, cardboard and newspapers, with a payback for cans. Travel agents who can snap up bargain airline tickets are stationed at King Soopers during normal business hours. Western Union and UPS delivery/pickup are available too. You can rent or buy pagers and cellular phones. There's a drop-off for shoe repair, and, in many stores, a FirstBank as well as ATMs. Take home free lettuce scraps for your pets. The list goes on. King Soopers stores are at 1650 30th Street near Arapahoe Avenue, 3600 Table Mesa Drive and 6550 Lookout Road, all in Boulder, 2255 N. Main in Longmont, and at 1375 S. Boulder Road in Louisville.

Safeway has two supermarkets in Boulder (and many more in the county) with full delis, bakeries, pharmacies, seafood shops and so on. Video rental, Western Union, fax service and photo-finishing are here. It's a typical all-around grocery, generally smaller than King Soopers. In addition, they sell RTD bus tickets and discount ski passes. Boulder stores are at 4800 E. Baseline Road, near Foothills Parkway, and 2798 Arapahoe Avenue.

In addition, **Albertson's** has stores in the Diagonal Plaza at the intersection of 30th Street and the Longmont Diagonal, in Boulder, and

in the county. **Leever's**, the newest market in the Boulder firmament, is at 1850 30th Street. In addition to the customary profusion of goods and services, it has its own smokehouse for meat, poultry and fish.

High Spirits

The Boulder Wine Merchant, at 2690 Broadway in the Community Plaza, is owned by two of the world's great wine experts, Wayne Belding and Sally Mohr. Both Master Sommeliers, with unerring noses for fine wine, can wax poetic about the alkaline soil on a hidden Portuguese mountain and why, after a thunder shower on an afternoon three decades ago, it gave a grape overtones of chocolate and black currants. Fewer than 30 Master Sommeliers are active in the United States, and another few dozen have earned the title worldwide. With such expertise, it's no wonder that they team up with the Cooking School of the Rockies to present wonderfully informative wine-tasting classes. The whole staff loves to help customers find a match to palate and pocketbook. Undiscovered wines at great bargains abound — some for less than $5. The Boulder Wine Merchant is also the place to go for unique bottles worth $500.

The Liquor Mart, at the corner of 15th Street and Canyon Boulevard, is a supermarket-size liquor store, one of the largest in the United States. The variety is staggering, including hard liquor, beer, ale, wine, champagne, mixers and soft drinks. If you want something exotic, you're as likely to find it here as anywhere in the state. The helpful staff is known for offering informed advice. The store's policy is to grant a 15 percent discount on any unopened case of liquor or wine and 10 percent off a mixed case. If you fax your order to 938-WINE, it'll be ready for you to pick when you get to the store.

For a huge general selection store, The Liquor Mart's wine selection is surprising both in its depth and its breadth. Dick Fetter, formerly the *Daily Camera* wine columnist, is on hand occasionally as a consultant. He has written extensively about wines and food, and he imports fine wines for a number of Boulder's excellent spirit shops. He and the other wine managers conduct wine-tasting classes, and if you ever can go to one, do. You're in for a treat of fine wines and homey lore about the personalities of great vineyard families. If your taste goes more toward the basic grain, wheel your grocery cart into the refrigerated room full of the world's — and Colorado's — great beers. Sometimes, they also stock locally produced mead, a drink made from fermented honey. Or how about a Krug Clos de Mesnil? At less than $250, it's a deal. Single malt scotches include a 25-year-old MacAllan. If you feel like slumming, there's even MD 20/20 and wines flavored with orange and pineapple. On a CU football weekend, the young crowd lines up for cases and kegs.

The Beer Store, 637 South Broadway, is a place where you can enjoy the fun side of brewing your own fresh beer, but a crew handles all the cleanup. If you haven't got your own formula, the store offers dozens of beer recipes and all the equipment and ingredients you need to create your own, personal, absolutely fresh brew. Among the favorites are Beaverstooth Ale, deep amber-colored and hoppy, and Wildfire Red, a robust, slightly sweet red ale. Brewing takes two weeks — just right for the start and end of a nice vacation.

The Beer Emporium, 4700 Table Mesa Drive, is to beer what **The Boulder Wine Merchant** is to wine — simply staggering in its variety. English, German, Belgian, Dutch, French, Asian, Latin American, Australian and, of course, domestic beers and ales are inventoried. From Amstel Light (Holland) to Zyweig (Poland), the Beer Emporium's got it.

Home-brewing supplies are available at **What's Brewing**, 2886 Bluff Street in Boulder and 1011 Main Street in Longmont. Brewlovers also should know Boulder is headquarters for the **American Home Brewer's Association**, 734 Pearl Street, founded by local entrepreneur Charlie Papazian, who bursts with heady ideas. Thanks to his initiative, Denver now hosts the annual Great American Beer Festival. Papazian is also the founder of the American Pie Council, which celebrates pies locally during the Victorian Fair at the Harbeck House. What do beer and pie have in common? All-American, we suppose. But to keep things eclectic, Charlie also is an expert in brewing mead.

Home Furnishings

It's a toss-up as to whether clients come to **Bartlett Interiors**, 2020 Pearl Street, more for the stylish decorating advice or for the elegant and unusual upholstered and wood furniture, lamps, wallpaper and window treatments. The inventory is eclectic, with many unusual and dramatic pieces to create a distinctive look.

Rustic furniture, such as peeled log beds, is the specialty at **Boulder Creek Furniture**, 3216 Arapahoe Avenue, which sells living room, dining room and bedroom furniture. Materials sound like a forest — aspen, lodgepole, pine and cedar — and the look is attractive and distinctive. It also carries outdoor furniture, entertainment or "home theater" centers as well as furnishings for the home office. Upholstery services are available. Boulder Creek's harmonious "condo packages," comprised of living room, dining area and bedroom pieces, are excellent choices for the start-up furniture buyer.

Country West Furniture, 2525 Arapahoe Avenue, in the Village Shopping Center next to McGuckin Hardware, has been making country, Southwestern, wrought-iron and mountain log furniture for more than a decade. In addition to thoughtful designs, this store takes pride in its quality items, boasting of dovetail drawers and hand-rubbed oil finishes. Country West can also make custom pieces. Armoires, bedroom pieces, dining room sets, entertainment centers, storage units of oak, pine, cherry and maple, and a variety of accessories are available.

The Boulder outpost of **Front Range Futons**, 2125 Pearl Street, carries futons of various sizes plus futon frames, futon-sofas and some accessories. It is, of course, a popular style of furniture in a college town.

Innerspace/Techline, 1600 Pearl Street, a purveyor of contemporary furniture, is known for its inventory of attractive and functional office and home-business pieces. The showroom also offers professional planning and design consultation.

The sprightly showroom at **Marisol Imports**, 915 Pearl Street, features wonderful wood pieces from Mexico, including tables, chairs and hutches plus wrought-iron chairs, tables, bar stools and étagères that mesh ideally with either a country or Southwestern look. Zapotec rugs, pottery, large clay jugs, weavings, pillows and all manner of harmonious accessories also are stocked.

Attractive and well-priced Euro-rustic armoires, hutches, tables, chairs and bedroom pieces are the specialties at **Madeiras**, 30th and Walnut streets, in the Walnut Gardens shopping center. The style is heavy in the Mediterranean influences of Spain, but with a lighter, more contemporary look than traditional Mediterranean.

Mother Goose Down, 1401 Pearl Street, on Pearl Street Mall, has some gift items and some antique jewelry, but it's really best known for its terminally snuggly, authentic down comforters, pillows and quilts in a broad selection of sizes, thicknesses and colors. Mother Goose also sells fine bed and bath linens.

Jewelers

In addition to dedicated jewelry stores, you'll find jewelry in the Boulder Arts & Crafts Cooperative and other crafts stores as well as in many of Boulder's art galleries.

Family-owned **Hurdle's**, 1402 Pearl Street, is a very traditional jeweler. And well it should be, for it was established back in 1947. There's even a little repair booth right in the window, armed with loupes, velvet cushions and the teeny instruments necessary to perform surgery on delicate watches and jewelry. Hurdle's carries estate and new jewelry of all sorts as well as fine watches, including TAGHeuer from Switzerland.

The Little Jewel, 1225 Pearl Street, on Pearl Street Mall, crams in a lot of pieces in a

---

INSIDERS' TIP

Artwalk is a self-guided tour of a dozen or so galleries on and near Pearl Street that open on the first Friday of every month from 6 to 9 PM. Often, artists are on-hand, and some of the galleries also serve complimentary refreshments.

lot of styles. There's some Southwestern turquoise and silver. There's some Italian gold. There are chains, earrings, bracelets and wedding sets. And often, there are special sales.

Founded in 1960, **Meyers Jewelers**, 1595 Canyon Boulevard, is known for diamond pieces and wedding sets in contemporary and traditional styles. Among its distinctive, exclusive designs are pendants and earrings depicting the Flatirons and, for CU fans, rings and bracelets of nose-to-tail buffaloes marching along in bands of gold of silver. Meyers Jewelers remains a family business, with talented veterans handling on-site jewelry repair and remounts.

Gold, silver and gemstones make **Walters & Hogsett**, 2425 Canyon Boulevard, a highly regarded jeweler. It stocks fine domestic and imported jewelry, watches, crystal and silver. In addition to repairs, Walters & Hogsett floats an annual fall special on replating silver flatware and hollow ware.

Miscellany

The sounds that pluck Boulder's heart strings range from gentle fluty folk stuff to something heavier than grunge metal. **Boulder Early Music Shop**, at 2010 14th Street, has folk instruments such as recorders and hand drums, small, dear items you could pack back home in a suitcase. Hard-to-get sheet music, CDs of early music and learned musicological journals and books are all in stock. The store is a good place to get tickets for local music performances, including those by the excellent Rocky Mountain Chorale as well as events in the Swallow Hill concert series. New Age music is the specialty at **Mysterium**, 1833 Pearl Street, which features more than a thousand titles. **Robb's Music**, at 1580 Canyon Boulevard, has digital pianos and other gizmo machines. **Wildwood Music**, at 804 Main Street in Louisville, specializes in guitars. **Swalley's**, at 2095 30th Street, sells lots of pianos and sheet music. Isn't Chris Finger a simply grand name for the owner of a piano store? The **Chris Finger's** store at 101 Second Street in Niwot also sells grandfather clocks, and fingers grow on hands, so that seems OK too.

Soundtrack Audio/Video, 1685 28th Street, sells stereos, computers and car audio systems. This Colorado-based company has Boulder's largest selection of electronic entertainment equipment, including huge TVs and audio-surround systems.

Within many a stylish Boulder professional beats the proud heart of a geek. Technoweenies head for **Office Max**, 1880 30th Street, a cavernous store that offers more than a dozen different mouse styles for your computer. They have great printer displays, and they don't seem to mind if you push the buttons. Your favorite mechanical pencil will cost much less here, as will all the papers, filing supplies, pens, pencils, calculators, paper clips, staplers and other office supplies you might need. **Business Express**, at 19th and Pearl streets, is a purple palace that is also a good office, copy and self-service computer store. Real computer nerds, of course, buy through mail-order catalogs. But if you're only posing as a nerd and secretly can't tell a CD-ROM from a VDT, the staff of **Connecting Point**, at 2333 30th Street, is friendly, and the store offers both Macintosh and IBM systems.

The Ph.D. crowd told us that this guide wouldn't be complete without **Allen Scientific Glass Blowers**, at 1752 55th Street. Ray Allen is called the "God of Scientific Glass." He can make anything out of glass and glass/metal transitions. You know . . . all those things you always wanted for your lab but couldn't find at a really good price.

Nature Stores

Crystal Galleries Ltd., 1302 Pearl Street, features a fine collection of minerals, crystal, fossils and jewelry made from semiprecious gemstones. **Nature's Own Imagination**, 1133 Pearl Street, and **Nature's Own** in Nederland, at 5 E. First Street, keep shoppers entertained for hours with their unusual items, including minerals, garden items, nature games, gifts and home decor. **Indian Peaks Trading Co.**, 98 W. First Street in Nederland, has similar merchandise and is worth a visit. Rockhound and photographer Cliff Whitney is the spirit behind **Ancient Image**, 505 W. Main Street in Lyons. It's a rock shop that also has jewelry and photography.

The **Wild Bird Center**, 1641 28th Street, Buffalo Village Shopping Center, has everything you need to attract avian creatures, such as birdhouses, kits, seed, books, hummingbird feeders and lots of inside information on local birds from bird-watching owner Steve Frye.

Photographic Equipment

Like the Boulder Bookstore, **Mike's Camera**, 2500 Pearl Street, is a local landmark that recently expanded to dazzling proportions. It's Boulder's only complete camera shop dedicated exclusively to photographic equipment, related items and services. Mike's services include camera and video repairs, rentals (full spectrum), used cameras sales, digital imaging and photo and video industrial equipment.

Jones Drug & Camera Center, 1370 College Avenue, has a very good line of fine cameras, lenses, film and photo accessories, including filters, bags, books, albums and frames. In addition to processing film, Jones has a full selection of darkroom supplies and one of the best selections of black-and-white enlarging paper in the state. The store also sells high-quality used equipment and has a very knowledgeable and helpful staff.

In Boulder, you can get quick film processing with better quality than those one-hour photo kiosks provide. **Photo Finish**, with branches in the Meadows and Community Plaza shopping centers, is mainly geared to amateur snap-shooters. The pros are divided as to whether **Photo Craft**, in a recently expanded lab at 4335 Arapahoe Road, or **Amaranth**, 2540 Frontier Avenue, does the best work.

Sporting-goods Shops

From one end of town to the other, Boulder is speckled with sporting goods shops, including a number of exceptional mountaineering and climbing stores. You don't have to leave Boulder to find such high-country gear as hiking boots, parkas, Alpine and Nordic skis, snowboards, snowshoes, in-line skates, rock-climbing, camping and backpacking equipment, clothing and accessories for any terrain or activity. Most stores rent as well as sell clothing, and some of the best deals are end-of-season closeouts of rental equipment. Many world-class mountaineers live in or frequent Boulder, so if you're preparing for a Himalayan assault or an Antarctic expedition, you've come to the right place. Or just a day hike in Rocky Mountain National Park; you can find what you need right in town. Most of these mountaineering/climbing/ski shops are locally owned and are institutions of a sort. In addition to high-quality equipment and apparel, they offer slide programs, talks and clinics by local experts and, in some cases, classes. But there are also places to buy tennis rackets, golf clubs, basketballs, soccer balls and fishing rods.

The Boulder Mountaineer, 1355 Broadway, offers a great selection of the latest styles of high-tech fabrics in outerwear, hats, gloves, sleeping bags, backpacks, long underwear, all manner of climbing hardware and lots of other outdoor equipment for backcountry skiing and hiking. The store can arrange private guiding and classes in rock and ice climbing.

The first among equals for hard-core climbers and mountaineers is **Neptune Mountaineering**, 633 S. Broadway in Table Mesa Shopping Center. This huge store is owned by Gary Neptune, a prominent U.S. mountaineer who has reached the summit of Mount Everest and other high peaks. Besides ice axes, ropes, climbing shoes and boots, the store has a good selection of Nordic ski equipment and outdoor clothing. Its book department is one of the best around. Gary's private collection of mountaineering memorabilia, including rarities of immense historic value, are displayed throughout this large store.

Mountain Sports, 821 Pearl Street, as the name implies, focuses on a variety of activities, including climbing, camping, hiking, snowshoeing and Nordic skiing. It offers a fine selection of top-quality equipment and apparel, with friendly, very helpful service. The store sponsors periodic slide shows, lectures and courses. A log book close to the front door

> **FYI**
> Unless otherwise noted, the area code for all phone numbers in this guide is 303.

enables customers to comment on recent hikes or ski tours they've taken and conditions they've encountered.

The North Face, 629-K S. Broadway, Table Mesa Center, is a national wholesaler/manufacturer that has established one of its handful of retail stores in Boulder. The Berkeley, California-based company sells its tents, packs, sleeping bags, ski jackets and other products to 800 shops across the country. The Boulder North Face store also has a large selection of camping equipment, plus maps, books and other outdoor gadgets. **Eastern Mountain Sports**, 2550 Arapahoe Avenue, is a national chain of East Coast origin that also sells North Face equipment and other top brands, as well as a large number of private-label EMS items. Clothing and equipment are available. It's a great place for fleece items, boots, skis and good service. For all types of daypacks, backpacks and smaller packs, visit the **Madden Factory Store**, 2400 Central Avenue. For some reason, Madden's packs are more popular in Europe among the outdoor set than in the United States, but this local company makes high-quality, sturdy packs of every description that will last for years, and it's for sale at factory outlet prices.

The **Hind Outlet**, 1412 Pearl Street, carries its own brand of running tights, swimsuits, shorts, windbreakers and other lightweight gear, with special emphasis on products and has some real deals on irregulars and seconds. All of the above, plus a great selection of combat fatigues and casual fashions, is available at the **Boulder Army Store**, 1545 Pearl Street. True to its name, the store also features a full array of such army surplus items as ammo cases, camouflage clothing, combat boots and canteens. It's a good place to shop for backpacks, nylon climbing rope, hiking boots, sunglasses, hats and gloves of every description.

Rocky Mountain Racquet Specialists, 2425 Canyon Boulevard, is where Boulder's major tennis, squash and racquetball enthusiasts go for the gear and duds. Racquets and balls, of course, are available, but so is name-brand clothing, footwear and accessories such as eyewear and gloves. This store offers 24-hour racquet stringing and can also make custom grips.

Sequel Outdoor Clothing, 1416 Pearl Street, is a Colorado-owned company that manufactures its products in Durango. This store has a storm-test chamber in the front window that simulates rain, wind, hail, lightning and thunder. Enter this chamber and you can experience how the clothes you're planning to buy work in heavy weather. Yes, the water is real. Nearby **Terrasystems**, 1122 Pearl Street, is a very with-it retailer, carrying active-sports footwear and clothing, gardening supplies, New Age music tapes, skin-care products and various other goods dedicated to purveying "best-in-kind products for home, sport, work and the outdoors in a mix that serves the spirit, sensibilities and lifestyles of the 21st-century pioneers." The store is bright and upbeat.

Gart Sports, 2525 Arapahoe Avenue, and 3320 28th Street, offers a wide assortment of sporting goods from tennis and golf to skiing, fishing and hunting supplies. Gart's is a Colorado-owned company with other stores in Denver and elsewhere in the West. It is ideal for gear for team sports, exercise paraphernalia, logo clothing, athletic shoes and low- to mid-priced sporting goods for skiers and other recreational athletes. Gart's annual fall "Sniagrab" ("bargains" spelled backward) is a gigantic ski equipment sale that starts in the Denver Sportscastle on Labor Day and eventually spills over to a long-vacant supermarket space in the Table Mesa Shopping Center.

Fly fishers will find everything they need at **Front Range Anglers Inc.**, 629-B S. Broadway, Table Mesa Center, including tackle, rods, reels, waders, classic wool shirts and other gear and garments. The shop conducts beginner and advanced fly-tying and rod-building classes. If you and all that gear have piscatorial wanderlust, you can sign on for a guided trip in United States or to a foreign country. Books, videos, gifts and fish art are also for sale.

Boulder Ski Deals, 2404 Pearl Street, sells equipment and clothing for Alpine and Nordic skiing and snowboarding. There's a full-service boot and ski repair shop and custom boot fitting. Mostly new but also some traded-in used equipment is available. The store also sells such accessories as hats, gloves, long johns, socks, sunglasses, goggles and sun-

Photo: Daily Camera

A unicyclist on Boulder's Pearl Street Mall.

screen. In summer, the shop partially switches over to in-line skating and watersports, including snowboards and kayaking. Similar ski and snowboard inventory is carried at **Doc's Ski & Sports** in the Table Mesa Shopping Center. Doc's switches over to bicycles in the summer.

Soccer is a big deal in Boulder. Apparel and equipment such as shin guards, balls and cleats are available from **Rocky Mountain Soccer**, 2767 Iris Avenue. It's a real mecca for soccer-holics and has meeting space available for groups who want to plan events centered around this round-ball sport.

Play It Again Sports, 653 S. Broadway in Table Mesa Shopping Center, and **Boulder Sports Recycler**, 1717 15th Street, are great places to pick up used and close-out skis, in-line skates and equipment for racquetball, hockey, baseball, golf, camping, football, watersports, biking, tennis, soccer, fishing and weight-lifting. The stores also sell used sports clothing.

Runners Choice, with locations at 4800 Baseline Road in the Meadows Shopping Center and at 2460 Canyon Boulevard near McGuckin's, and **Runners Roost**, 1129 Pearl Street, have full lines of running shoes and accessories, plus books, tapes and magazines. Both stores offer free consultations with podiatrists who can analyze runners' gaits and answer questions about foot or knee problems, etc. Check at the stores for the doctor's schedule. Runners Choice Meadows store manager Hal Kyles leads weekly group fun runs for runners of all abilities. Meet at the Baseline store at 7 PM on Mondays. Running stores also take Bolder Boulder entry forms. Runners Roost is owned by Boulder resident celebrity and two-time Olympian, Frank Shorter, who won a gold medal in the marathon in 1972 and a silver four years later.

Rocky Mountain Diving Center, 1737 15th Street; **Scuba Joe**, 3156 28th Street; and **Weaver's Dive & Travel Center**, in the Table Mesa Shopping Center at 637 S. Broadway, sell dive gear, wetsuits and swimwear. If you don't know how to dive, they'll teach you and help you get certified. If you dive, you can book a group or individual dive trip to some of the world's top underwater destinations. Weaver's has a full-service travel agency on site. The stores also rent and repair diving equipment. Rocky Mountain Diving trip veterans participate in an informal dive club with slide shows and periodic potluck dinners. The **Boulder Outdoor Center**, 2510 47th Street, and the **Paddle Shop**, 786-8799, concentrate on kayaking equipment for sale or rent but also rent and sell canoes and rafts. The shops carry wet suits and all other related accessories. Kayak instruction and raft trips are available throughout the shop. In winter, the Outdoor Center rents snowshoes and avalanche beacons.

You can buy or rent mountain, road, street and tandem bikes from **Morgul-Bismark**, 1221 Pennsylvania Avenue; **University Bicycles**, Ninth and Pearl streets; **Louisville Cyclery**, 1032 S. Boulder Road in Louisville, and **Bike-n-Hike**, 1136 Main Street in Longmont. You can go to any of these stores for helmets, other accessories, cyclewear, bike repairs, customizing and other related goods and services. Morgul-Bismark is owned by ex-racers Davis Phinney and Connie Carpenter-Phinney. Davis was the first American to win a Tour de France stage, and Connie brought home a gold medal from the 1984 Olympics. The **Peleton**, on the backside of the Community Plaza shopping center on 13th Street, is a new high-end shop that specializes in serious road and racing bikes and everything you need to embark on really serious cycling.

INSIDERS' TIP

If you love the idea of handmade items crafted by someone's grandmother or grandfather, even if not your own, plan to stop at the Boulder Senior Services annual Arts & Crafts Fair, normally on a Friday and Saturday early in November. In 1996, the fair introduced a children's room, with entertainment and a table of $1 to $2 gifts, where children 12 and younger could do their holiday shopping.

The Corral, 1711 15th Street, is an excellent equestrian shop, carrying everything the persnickety rider needs except the horse. Here in the informal Stetson-and-cowboy-boot ambiance of the American West, this specialty shop represents a corner of English gentility. It carries fine English riding saddles and tack and such apparel for dressage and hunting as helmets, top hats and breeches for adults and children. A master saddler handles saddle and tack repairs and fitting. There is also an impressive assortment of books, videos and gift items played in the key of horse.

Other Good Junk

Blake's Small Car Salvage, on 2559 Weld County Road, No. 5, in Erie, was featured on the *CBS Evening News* because the junkyard is so darned pretty. Car parts, from 1959 Anglias to a 1993 Geo Storm, are arranged by country. A Japanese flag flies near the Hondas; a German flag marks the BMWs. Little parts are stored picturesquely in yellow school buses and Chevy vans. The Colorado New Music Association came out here one fall and made, along with other instruments, drums from the hubcaps. What a concert! Talk about heavy metal!

Construction Recycling, 3220 Weld County Road, No. 8, Erie, is the place to go to save money and do a good deed. At this reinventive company, building scraps become fiberboard, tree branches turn into mulch, and concrete and asphalt get reshaped as road base and landfill. This "recycling" yard charges much less than a regular landfill, and 85 percent of what comes through the door gets recycled.

Yard Sales

Lastly, perhaps some of the best shopping in town is at Boulder's yard and garage sales. Check the classified sections of the *Daily Camera* and *Colorado Daily*, or just drive around town on weekends and keep an eye out for homemade signs on trees and utility poles. Many sales start on Fridays, but Saturdays are the big days — and a few dribble over into Sunday too.

In south Boulder, the bridge across Bear Creek at Table Mesa Drive and the King Soopers entrance is always plastered with yard sale signs around the weekend. Downtown, the corner of Arapahoe Avenue and Ninth Street is often festooned with garage sale signs. With its transient population of students and upwardly mobile adults, Boulder's yard sales offer everything from skis, bicycles, snowboards and windsurfing equipment to violins, art and antiques.

It's xeriscape (ZER-rih-scape). Not zero-scape.

It's xeriscape. Not zero-scape. It's beautiful plants that thrive in our dry, windy climate. It's not rocked-over yards or lawns addicted to herbicides, pesticides and fertilizers. Boulder is a center for xeriscaping. At least a half-dozen books have been published by Boulder-area experts on waterwise gardening. And why not? Water use

is critical in a climate that gets less than 17 inches of rain a year. What's more, after wandering Boulder's beautiful open space trails, many gardeners grow a liking for this vanishing natural style. By comparison, the traditional green lawn is, well, boring.

Great garden stores, filled with bedding plants, perennials and ornamentals include **Lafayette Florists**; **The Flower Bin** in Longmont; **Sturtz and Copeland**; and **Fruehauf's**. **McGuckin Hardware** has been voted by readers of Boulder's *Daily Camera* as the best place for garden supplies. It's also a good spot for finding plants if you like the flowers you see around the Village shopping center. (For more on marvelous McGuckin's, read this chapter's "Gadgets" section.) Boulder County has its own plant kingdoms. Most are on the way to Longmont, including the

GreenSpot Nursery; **The Tree Farm**; and **TreeHouse Nursery**. Mikl and Linda Brawner's **Harlequin's Market** is little but unique, down to the beautiful display of native and/or xeriscape plants in the Brawners' front yard next door. Wander their display garden and point to whatever gorgeous, thriving plant you like. Then ask Mikl or Linda to guide you to the potted version of the plant — small and inexpensive. For more plant stores, check the Yellow Pages under "Nurseries."

If you're shopping for garden space, consider this: 480-square-foot garden plots are available behind the North Boulder Recreation Center. The fee is $25, including water. (Gardeners must provide their own hoses.) Call 441-3400. Or how about a free tree? If you move into a Boulder home with a bare front yard, you can apply to have the city plant a city-owned tree close to the street for you. For information, contact Boulder's forestry division at 441-4406.

Now, about those garden books. Here are gems about Boulder area plants and gardens. *Pieces of Light* by Susan Tweit; *The Xeriscape Flower Gardener: A Waterwise Guide for the Rocky Mountain Region* by Jim Knopf; *Gardening in the Mountain West* by *Daily Camera* columnist Barbara Hyde; *Grow Native: Landscaping With Native and Apt Plants of the Rocky Mountains* by Sam Huddleston and Michael Hussey; *The Shortgrass Prairie* by Ruth Carol Cushman and Stephen R. Jones; *Personal Landscapes* by Jerome Malitz; and *The Undaunted Garden* by Lauren Springer.

For the price of a good dinner, eat all the chocolate you want and benefit a good cause too on the Friday or Saturday before Valentine's Day at the Chocolate Lover's Fling.

Boulder
Festivals and
Annual Events

Special events make an evening or weekend sparkle. Where possible, listings include dates, times and prices. Other events bloom with serendipity, so planners can't say exactly when and how much until the event draws near. The chapter ends with "Events Central," mentioning groups that track happenings. You can find even more possibilities by checking our Boulder Attractions and Boulder Arts chapters. Keep in mind, volunteers run many of these festivals, and you're welcome to lend your hand.

Winter

January

Polar Bear Club Ice Plunge
Boulder Reservoir • 51st St., Boulder • 441-3461

Pay around $15 to brave ice-crusted water, dance a jig, screech, then hurry to shore (or stay in as long as you wish). Rescue workers stand by in case anyone gets hypothermia. Plungers say, "It's intensely painful, in a pleasurable sort of way." For spectators, admission to this New Year's Day event is free.

Colorado Mahlerfest
Macky Auditorium (on the CU-Boulder campus) and Boulder Public Library (11th St. and Arapahoe Ave.), Boulder • 494-1632

Mahler-freaks rave about this one-of-a-kind concertfest during the second week in January. It began in 1988, when enthusiasts played Mahler's Symphony No 1. Each year, they have played the Bohemian composer's next symphony in line, which means the 1997 event features Symphony No. 10, and in 1998 — Symphony No. 11. Because Mahler "only" wrote 11 symphonies, organizers will then decide whether to proceed to his song cycles, start over with No. 1, or whatever. Ticket prices vary but generally are $10 and $15, with public recitals at the Boulder Public Library free.

Boulder Bach Festival
P.O. Box 1896, Boulder 80306 • 494-3159

Only a handful of American festivals play nothing but J.S. Bach. This is one. Local professional musicians and well-known guest artists keep the music lively, playing those hummable tunes you might have thought were modern. Concerts take place on an irregular schedule from September through May (this one in late January) at locations that include the Abbey of St. Walburga, the University of Colorado's Grusin Music Hall, the Boulder Public Library Auditorium and Denver's St. John's Cathedral. Ticket prices vary.

February

Chocolate Lover's Fling
CU-Boulder Ballroom (on CU-Boulder campus), Boulder • 449-8623 (SafeHouse)

For the price of a good dinner ($20 to $25), eat all the chocolate you want and benefit a good cause too on the Friday or Saturday before Valentine's Day at the Chocolate Lover's

Fling. Feast your eyes on chocolate TV dinners, armadillos, cabbages and castles. Boulder's best professional chefs vie with talented amateurs in categories ranging from "Sheer Artistry" to yummy. Enter your creation, or just eat the entries. Profits go to the Boulder County SafeHouse, which helps battered families.

March

4-H Carnival
Boulder County Fairgrounds • 9595 Nelson Rd., Longmont • 776-4865

This all-day family event on the second Saturday in March has homemade pies and kid-decorated variety booths. Throw shaving-cream pies and walk through a maze of bright-colored calico walls. You might win a T-shirt by putting a stuffed toy lamb on a plywood catapult then launching it into a cute little pen. Admission is free.

St. Patrick's Day Parade
Ninth and Canyon Sts., Boulder • 449-4130

It began when patrons of J.J. McCabe's marched to a now-closed bar with an Irish name practically next door. Since 1978, the "world's shortest" St. Patrick's Day parade has grown to a whopping 1,200 feet and includes the likes of Clancy Sheehy, Boulder's own leprechaun; a cow-bell percussion group; bagpipers; Jose Muldoon's Lawn Chair Drill Team and a double-decker bus. The parade starts at 1 PM on the Saturday closest to St. Paddy's Day and proceeds two blocks north to 11th Street, where everyone turns around and heads back. Do check before you go. An event as serendipitous as this is hard to predict. You know, Blarney stones and all that.

Denver's parade is a little bigger — one of the nation's largest. But, hey, doesn't Boulder get points for enthusiasm and style? For information on the Denver parade, call 399-9226.

Boulder Bach Festival — Kids for Bach
Boulder Public Library • 11th St. and Arapahoe Ave., Boulder • 494-3159

Children audition by tape to perform in this charming, hour-long program. Musicians range from 6 to 17 years old, playing pianos, violins and harps. Admission is free to this mid-March event.

Photo: Daily Cmaera

Actress Joan Van Ark, a Boulder native, attended a recent
Boulder Creek Festival Parade.

Spring

April

Conference on World Affairs
CU-Boulder campus, Boulder • 492-2525

International flags festoon the campus during this week-long series of forums held the week after CU-Boulder's spring semester resumes following spring break. More than 100 speakers jet to Boulder at their own expense to participate. Call ahead for session topics, or just wander into the University Memorial Center to pick up a schedule and slip into one of the many discussions. Admission is free.

Alferd Packer Day
UMC Terrace (CU-Boulder campus), Boulder • 492-6284 (UMC Food Services)

Alferd (yes, that's Alferd) Packer was a gold-mining-era, hungry kind of guy and the only American ever convicted of cannibalism. Judge Melville Gerry sentenced Packer, complaining that he had eaten five of the seven Democrats in Colorado's Hinsdale County. This pre-finals party at the university packs in the rib-eating contest, regular food, obstacle races and live music. It's student excess with a weird historical twist at this event on the third or fourth Friday in April.

Taste of the Nation
CU-Boulder's Glenn Miller Ballroom, Boulder • 443-0623 (Community Food Share)

More than 40 of Boulder's finest chefs prepare nibble-sized samples, which evening guests quaff with everything from wine and local brew pub beer to mineral water. This late April event is one of Boulder's best food festivals. Profits go to Community Food Share. In 1996, tickets were $45 in advance and $55 at the door.

Loyalty Parade
Downtown Lafayette • 665-9993

Get ready for fifes, drums, flags and equestrian teams. VFW Post 1771 sponsors this state parade, which was founded to counter communism's May Day celebrations. The "Evil Empire" is no more, but Lafayette's parade remains. It starts at 10 AM on the Saturday closest to May 1, heading south from Public Road to Waneka Parkway.

Kinetic Conveyance Parade
Pearl Street Mall, Boulder • 444-KBCO

On the last Saturday in April, more than 50 teams each year enter wild, wacky and wonderful kinetic conveyances — that is, non-motorized contraptions designed to race across water and land. Always imaginative and sometimes even functional during the later challenge portion of the two-pronged competition, kinetic conveyances make a colorful parade. Panache earns points, so the Floating Elvises in a pink "cadillac," the deliciously tasteless and terminally politically incorrect Hooters Guys and the Mud Sharks have been favorites. The parade morning starts with "vehicles" on display at 10 AM, followed by a 1 PM parade. At the judging booth, contestants attempt undue influence through skits and bribes . . . the more outrageous, the better. Entrance deadline is mid-April and costs around $15 per craft and $7 for each team member. Watching the parade is, of course, free.

May

Kinetic Conveyance Challenge
Boulder Reservoir • 51st St., Boulder • 444-KBCO

Around 30,000 people attend this race, which begins at 11 AM on the first Saturday in May; but some spectators arrive as early as 6:30 AM to get the best spots and enjoy the balloon festival and pancake breakfast. Some conveyances barely make it more than a few yards from shore before sinking. Especially in the early minutes of the race, rescue craft are busy towing the wrecks back to shore. The race consists of a water leg, an overland stretch and a return across the water. Due to negative impact on wetlands, the popular mud portion was scrapped in 1996. The swiftest contestants finish in 45 minutes, and the lumbering laggards end four hours later. The winners usually have a combination canoe/bicycle thing powered by good-looking legs and shoulders. Fees are roughly $20 for beach parking, $10 for outlying parking and $2 per pedestrian or cyclist.

Cinco de Mayo
Pearl St. Mall, Boulder • 441-3975

In the past, this free event has been held the second Saturday in May, with Mariachi bands from Mexico, South American bands, children's festival dancing, professional folk dancing and food stands. At press time, the organizing committee had decided to cancel the 1997 festival, perhaps replacing it with a dance, for which there would be an admission fee. Call in advance to confirm the committee's plans for '97.

Boulder Creek Festival and Rubber-duckie Race
Boulder Creek, Boulder • 441-4420

This popular rite of spring has been rated the Best Annual Children's Event by *Daily Camera* readers. The Friday opener includes a parade, a carnival and a dance. Saturday highlights are a kayak race and a fishing derby. All Memorial Day weekend long, craft booths, music and dance, carnival rides and food stands entertain the throngs who edge their way through the tightly packed venue all the way from Sixth to 13th streets and between Canyon Boulevard and Arapahoe Avenue. The Spring Children's Fair, held on Saturday and Sunday in conjunction with the Boulder Creek Festival, includes "kidstuff" booths, with an emphasis on local artists and community services, demonstrations of trained rescue dogs and endangered raptors plus a zillion other things.

On Sunday, more than 4,000 yellow rubber duckies bobble from the Ninth Street and Canyon Boulevard bridge to the Peace Garden at 11th Street and Arapahoe Avenue — all in the name of fun and charity, benefiting the Boulder Parks and Recreation Department and helping expand the therapeutic program for children and adults with disabilities. It costs $5 to enter a duck, and prizes range from the trivial to major vacations. The success of this popular festival depends on volunteers, and

festival organizers are always looking for extra hands, from general area cleanup the Saturday before the festival until the last event winds down at 10 PM on Sunday.

Bolder Boulder 10K Race
From 30th and Iris Sts. to Folsom Field, Boulder • 444-RACE

This Memorial Day race is rated one of the top road races in the nation and Boulder's Best Annual Event by *Daily Camera* readers. It's amazing how much fun it can be to run or walk more than 6 miles. More than 30,000 participants, from the most fleet-footed elite amateur runners in the A wave to first-time walkers in the ZZ, make this one of the nation's largest citizen races. An international field of celebrity runners and top wheelchair athletes make this an important race on the national 10K calendar too. The Bolder Boulder's nonstop party atmosphere is exhilarating. In addition to aid and water stations, entertainment is provided along the route. It's a neat feeling to be part of this throng of happy, energetic people. All runners finish at CU-Boulder's Folsom Field, where thousands of spectators watch world-class professional racers compete after the amateur races are through.

FYI
Unless otherwise noted, the area code for all phone numbers in this guide is 303.

The 1996 race fee was $21, including a commemorative T-shirt and lunch, or $15 without the shirt. Every runner is timed, so you will get your time and ranking calculated in a variety of ways after the race. You can register at local running stores or at race headquarters at 3103 Iris Street, Suite 150, just north of the Bank of Boulder. Try to get your application in by early April. (If the race doesn't fill up, you can register on race morning too, but the price is $10 higher.)

Nearly 35,000 runners make a quite pack, but the race never feels so crowded, for organizers stagger the starting times in successive waves to give everyone room. Along the way, you'll see belly dancers, including the lady with the sword on her head, and high-stepping grandmas, decked out in fringed cowgirl skirts. You'll hear everything from live jazz bands to bagpipers playing rock 'n' roll. Don't fear wimping out. In the ZZ wave, the pace is a

Photo: Daily Camera

The Bolder Boulder 10k Memorial Day Race has been voted Boulder's Best Annual Event.

pleasant amble, and the cheers from the crowd are just as enthusiastic.

The citizens' race starts at 7:45 AM at 30th and Iris. The elite professionals, among the fastest in the world, start at 11:25 AM so that citizen racers can watch the pros' final laps in Folsom Field. If you decide to watch, pick a spot anywhere along the course or at Folsom Field. Runners have included wedding parties and guys who leapfrog the whole way. Marines usually sign up in the "M" and run in formation; but, then again, so do youngsters from Mapleton Elementary School. Blind runners and wheelchair racers inspire us all, as do the fleet-footed gazelle types and seniors running with their grandchildren.

Summer

Summer is the high season in Boulder — so long, sunny, pleasant and grand that several festivals stretch through all three summer months. These include the Colorado Music Festival, the Colorado Dance Festival and the Colorado Shakespeare Festival. Check for these and other longer seasonal events in our Boulder Attractions and Arts chapters.

June

Artwalk
Pearl St. Mall, Boulder • 444-9116 (Linton-Haslam Gallery)

The Artwalk is an evening open house featuring downtown galleries. Some serve refreshments, and many give you the opportunity to meet with the artists and artisans whose works they show. Schedules and maps are available at galleries along the Pearl Street Mall. Artwalk takes place the first weekend in June.

Promise Keepers National Men's Conference
Mile High Stadium, Denver • 433-7466 (ticket office)

More than 50,000 men come to this annual mid-June conference on Christian men's issues founded by former CU-Boulder football coach Bill McCartney. Fathering, marriage and family are the main topics. The two-day event began in Boulder's Folsom Field, outgrew it and moved to Denver, but many attendees still stay here during the convocation. The admission fee had not been set at press time.

Summer Solstice Festival
Generally second or third weekend in June
Pearl Street Mall, Boulder • 530-3917

This Native American festival features storytellers, dance and drum presentations. Foods include blue corn and amaranth breads plus Lakota salads with watercress and maple syrup dressing. Arts and crafts by Ute, Arapaho, Cheyenne and Shoshone create visual appeal. Admission to this mid-June weekend event is free.

Chipeta Powwow
Chipeta Park, Nederland • 258-0532

Local and international dancers join the fun at this event, which features Native American dancing and costumes along with plenty of food, arts and crafts. This mid-June festival is presented by the Nederland Arts and Humanities Council. Admission had not been set at press time, although the fee for past events has been around $1.

Boulder County Garden Tour
Various gardens throughout Boulder
• 666-4435

Local gardeners weed and plant like mad for this late June tour, which benefits the Boulder County Mental Health Foundation and features beautiful gardens at private homes. There are also speakers on gardening topics, a plant sale and door prizes. Maps and details are available from local garden centers. Tickets are around $12.

Taste of Louisville
Louisville's shopping districts • 666-5747

Less-than-a-dollar samples from many Louisville eateries are part of this mid-June celebration, which includes 80 participating businesses. The weekend often includes country dancing lessons, face-painting and shuttle buses, which take revelers between this growing city's shopping areas.

July

Colorado Freedom Festival
Central Park and other locations in Boulder • 665-2733

Boulder makes much of multiculturalism throughout the year, but this event, which takes place in Central Park, on the library lawn and in the library auditorium, is where this commitment is put on display. This festival is essentially one big party, celebrating the arts and cultural diversity. Dance, art exhibits, a children's talent show, a health expo, ethnic food and more offer variety. The festival, often held the weekend preceding the Fourth of July, generally starts early Friday afternoon, runs all day on Saturday and winds down on Sunday.

Fourth of July

An overture of real thunder often ends just before the planned fireworks begin. The public gatherings are grand, but so is a quiet, Foothills nook. From a high roost, you can see those giant, bright-colored dandelion puffs all the way to Denver. Once the sun sets, it can get cold. Bring a heavy sweater or blanket. Many other Boulder County communities, such as Longmont, Louisville and Broomfield, have their own fireworks, often with community picnics and concerts.

Boulder Concert in the Park
Chautauqua Park • Ninth St. and Baseline Rd., Boulder • 442-3282

This Fourth of July outdoor concert by the Colorado Music Festival's nationally recognized summer orchestra features pop and sing-along music. Insiders bring picnic baskets and blankets then linger here to watch distant fireworks. The concert starts at 5 PM, and admission is free.

Boulder Fireworks
Folsom Field (on CU-Boulder campus), Boulder • 444-KBCO

Even without great fireworks, which are launched at dark, this evening extravaganza would be a kick, for the live entertainment is good, and the sing-alongs include popular rock and hokey camp songs. Up With People and other well-known groups have performed in the past. Admission is free, but it's best to get there reasonably early, because the place begins to fill up long before the sun sets.

Louisville Fourth of July Picnic and Fireworks
Downtown Louisville and Coal Creek Golf Course • 666-6565

Enjoy a community picnic, art festival, children's games and a band in Memory Square Park, then "Fireworks on the Links," with the couples on the temporary dance floor swinging.

Nederland Fourth of July Parade and Fireworks
Downtown Nederland and Barker Reservoir • 258-3936

A small-town parade and fireworks put a real old-fashioned spin on this most traditional holiday.

Boulder Folk and Bluegrass Festival
Chautauqua Auditorium • Ninth St. and Baseline Rd., Boulder • No current phone contact

Local and international performers who have appeared at this popular mid-July event include stars such as Doc Watson. Since ticket prices vary, it's best to call for complete information.

Chili Ole Chili Contest
Regal Harvest House • 1345 28th St., Boulder • 713-1523

Summer wouldn't be summer without a chili cook-off, and Boulder's great restaurants make the variety and offerings memorable at this mid-July event. (Note: Organizers indicated at press time that the 1997 event likely will take place in mid-September.) It might be a Maalox moment, but it's worth every twinge because of the great tastes. Admission the day of the event ranges from $8 to $12 per person; advance tickets usually are available at discounted rates, so contact Krista Agramonte at the listed number for details.

Ol' Timers and Miners Days
Throughout Nederland • 258-3936

Head up the canyon to enjoy a pancake breakfast, a barbecue or the festival's Sow-Bellie Lunch. Or join in such contests as the Women's Spike Driving and Men's Hand Mucking competitions. The whole festival harkens back to Nederland's mining history. Admission to this late July event is free.

August

Boulder County Fair
Boulder County Fairgrounds • 9595 Nelson Rd., Longmont • 772-7170

Kids of all ages love the goats and rabbits at this down-home country fair, which draws more than 100,000 spectators. Sheep yell "Ma-a!" as 4-H dads do the final, pre-show shearing. The harness horses prance, their braided manes decorated with flowers. At the old-timers' rodeo on the last Friday, see bucking broncos and fancy riding. Admission to the fairgrounds is free, but call ahead to check fees for such events as the rodeo. The fair runs from the first through the second weekend in August.

Rocky Grass Festival
Rocky Grass Hollow, Lyons • 449-6007

In a pretty creekside field, internationally known bluegrass fiddlers and banjo pickers entertain campers and picnickers. Bluegrass workshops, late-night campfires and dips in the St. Vrain River add to the old-time ambiance. In 1996, a three-day pass was $60 ($80 including camping). Tickets are also available by the day for this weekend event in early August. The producer also presents the famous Telluride Bluegrass Festival in south-western Colorado.

Boulder Victorian Fair
1206 Euclid Ave., Boulder • 449-3464

Sponsored by the Boulder Museum of History, this festive day, held at adjacent Beach Park in early August, includes military drill re-enactments, carriage rides, blacksmithing and craft demonstrations, children's games and entertainment. Colorado foods, quilts and vintage cars abound. And how about a pie bake-off? It's a perfect event for Boulder, home of the American Pie Council. There's also a beauty contest for teddy bears and dolls.

Fall

September

Louisville Fall Festival and Labor Day Parade
Louisville Downtown • 666-6565

Louisville's Labor Day parades, one of Colorado's largest, attracts more than 25,000 people. The Saturday and Sunday of Labor Day weekend feature an art fair, carnival, music and pancake breakfast. The Monday parade includes pets, the King Soopers Shopping Cart Drill Team, marching bands and antique cars. The parade down Main Street starts at 10 AM.

"New Renaissance" Festival
Central Park • Between Canyon Blvd. and Arapahoe Ave. (east of Broadway), Boulder • 939-8463 (Solstice Institute)

Not Renaissance as in Michelangelo and Italy, but a new Renaissance. This is 21st century stuff, a future-vision complete with solar- and electric-powered vehicles. Even the stages are solar-powered. The children's

mural painting area is popular, as are arts and food booths. Health booths start with "A" for acupuncture and go at least to "P" for physicians who specialize in preventive medicine. This event takes place during Labor Day weekend.

Boulder Blues Festival
Generally second weekend in Sept.
Boulder Courthouse lawn • 14th and Pearl Sts., Boulder • No current phone contact

Approximately 8,000 people come to hear local and international players at this mid-September event. Saturday's courthouse lawn shows are free. Tickets are required for Friday and Saturday evenings at the Boulder Theater, 786-7030.

Golden Aspen Trees
Sometime in Sept. or Oct.,
Peak to Peak Hwy. (Colo. Hwy. 72) north of Nederland and other locations
• 555-MOTHER NATURE (Just kidding)

The greatest fall festival is the natural one — the annual gilding of the aspen. Mother Nature never calls ahead to reserve a day for the best sight of leaves, so watch local papers for reports of favorable turnings. The *Daily Camera* runs stories and maps. The aspen east of the Continental Divide generally turn gold, but sometimes pinkish foliage peeks out among the yellow. Often, a whole grove changes at once, for aspen are large, cloned families, connected by their roots. Because "quakies" have loose leaf stems, the shiny leaves really shimmer. The biggest aspen fields are along the Peak to Peak Highway outside of Nederland. Driving is fun. But even better, park at a trailhead and take a stroll. Rocky Mountain National Park boasts several astonishing stands of aspen. The park rangers can direct you to the best. Wherever you hike, the filtered golden light, the tannin scent of fall and the sound of fluttering aspen leaves are unforgettable.

INSIDERS' TIP

The Bolder Boulder 10K is a 30,000-plus moving party with some of the world's most fleet runners, thousands of amateur runners, a whole bunch of walkers and live entertainment to cheer people along the way.

Walker Ranch Living History
Walker Ranch • Flagstaff Rd. (west of Chautauqua Park), Boulder • 441-3950

In late September and into early October, blacksmiths pound a ringing "whang" on red-hot iron while the billows release a throaty sigh. Sunbonnet-clad women prepare victuals at a potbellied stove. They're volunteers, trained by Boulder County Parks and Open Space to live the old-fashioned way for a few days. The ranch is open 10 AM to 3 PM and has free everything, from watching the horses plow and to sampling the homemade bread and hand-churned butter. This gorgeous area frequently has brilliant mountain bluebirds. The ranch is on the left, 7.5 miles west of Chautauqua Park, up Flagstaff Road.

Celebrate Lafayette
Old Town Lafayette • 665-5588

Lafayette loves a parade, and this one in late September features the Recycled Seniors Umbrella Team, a wild-animal float with real lions and bears and other highlights. The daylong festival also includes a free pancake breakfast, entertainers, bargain hot-air balloon rides, fun booths and a bed race.

Boulder Fall Festival
Pearl Street Mall, Boulder • 449-3774

Loosely styled after a European Oktoberfest, this celebration in late September has become a primo showcase for local and visiting craftsmen. It still includes flowing beer — though now more microbrews than German brews — plus bands, carnival rides and a petting zoo for the kids and lots of food. It runs 11 AM to 10 PM on Friday and Saturday and 11 AM to 6 PM on Sunday.

October

Museum in the Dark
University of Colorado Museum • Broadway and 15th St., Boulder • 492-6892

Bring your flashlight, for tonight the lights are off at the dinosaur museum so that kids discover the real triceratops head and flying pterodactyl with their own, modern torches.

This is an educational (rather than a scary) night, and science volunteers bring exhibits such as bats and live snakes. The idea is to take the spooky out of Halloween but keep the delicious sense of discovery. It's also a great chance to get familiar with this excellent, family-oriented museum that always has special exhibits. Call ahead to reserve tickets, which usually sell out by party night. Tickets are $4. Museum in the Dark usually happens the Friday before Halloween.

Kids' Halloween Parade
Last Sun. in Oct.
Boulder Courthouse lawn • 14th and Pearl Sts., Boulder • 449-3774

On the last Sunday in October, approximately 2,000 costumed kids traipse through downtown with their parents plus Bongo, his Blue Balloon Band and other performers. The parade runs from 1 to 3 PM.

November

Nutcracker Ballet
Macky Auditorium (on CU-Boulder campus), Boulder • 449-1343

The Boulder Philharmonic teams up with the Boulder Ballet for four packed performances of this favorite family ballet during Thanksgiving weekend. Everything's magic when local children play the mice, and rising local stars portray Clara and her Prince. During intermission, kids can peek in the orchestra pit, where friendly musicians demonstrate instruments that include the celeste, which makes those little tinkly bell sounds for the Sugar Plum Fairy. Tickets for the 1996 event ranged from $8 to $27.

Hmong New Year
Lafayette Elementary School • 101 N. Bermont Ave., Lafayette • 665-5046

During this four-day event in late November, coinciding with Thanksgiving weekend, the 700 Hmong who live in Boulder County invite others in Colorado's Laotian refugee (and non-refugee) community to join this celebration, which includes traditional clothing and food. The needlework is stunning. This event is free.

Photo: Daily Camera/Crissy Pascual

Members of the Hmong communities host a New Year's celebration in November.

December

Lights of Downtown Parade
Pearl St. Mall, Boulder • 449-3774

This eclectic parade on the first Friday in December launches Boulder's holiday season. Like many parades throughout the year, the route circumnavigates the pedestrian center.

The parade is both sweet and hokey. You'll see everything from Boulder's Girl Scout troops with battery-operated Christmas lights in their hair to the local Polar Bear Club members prancing about the cold streets barefoot and bathing-suited, hopping into a hot tub on wheels whenever they need to warm up again. Eco-elves prance by in curled-toe green slippers, passing out information about recycling;

local marching bands play; and gleaming antique cars and fire trucks get festooned with ornaments. The parade starts around 7 PM.

Louisville Parade of Lights
Downtown Louisville • 665-7137

Garlands swing from Main Street lamps, and choral groups perform by City Hall. There are open houses and hay rides. More than 20 floats join the parade, which starts at 7 PM on the first Friday in December.

Artwalk
Pearl Street Mall, Boulder • 444-9116 (Linton-Haslam Gallery)

On the first weekend in December, grab a gallery guide at any local gallery, then enjoy this tour of Boulder's gorgeous arts and crafts purveyors. This self-guided tour of open galleries is free.

Historic Boulder Historic Homes for the Holidays
Various Boulder homes • 444-5192

Grand homes deck their halls for the holidays, and everyone is invited to have a look during the first weekend in December. Mapleton Hill Victorians and Romanesque Uni-Hill homes are among those that have been on tour in recent years. The decorating by the owners and professionals is spectacular. This fund-raiser for Historic Boulder also includes a gift shop and drawings for door prizes. Ticket prices vary; in 1996, they were $15 for non-

members of Historic Boulder and $13.50 for seniors 60 and older.

Messiah Sing-along
St. John's Episcopal Church • 14th and Pine Sts., Boulder • 442-5346

Professionals fly in to sing the solos, and the choir practices for weeks to lead a rousing rendition of Handel's *Messiah*. But the passion comes from friends, families and people who just like to sing. Some singers filling the pews are practically pros, while others have never sung before, but they all join in for the rousing "Hallelujah Chorus" which must be audible all the way to the heavens. There are two evening performances and one matinee the weekend before Christmas Eve. Tickets are around $10.

Events Central

Many festivals occur throughout the year. The *Daily Camera's* "Friday Magazine" is loaded with entertainment information for the upcoming weekend. The chambers of commerce also have information on specific local events, and remember to sample the choices listed in our Boulder Attractions chapter. If you're casting about for something to do, call any (or all) of the following organizations: **Boulder Chamber of Commerce**, 442-1044; **Boulder County Fairgrounds**, 678-6235; **CU-Boulder Cultural Events/Concert Line**, 492-3228; or **Chautauqua Association**, 442-3282.

The Wall Street Journal has called the Pearl Street Mall one of the nation's most successful pedestrian malls, and it has won national design awards.

Boulder
Attractions

Boulder's top five, must-see attractions detailed here are followed by a smorgasbord of other treats if time and taste permit. Also see chapters on Boulder Festivals and Annual Events, Kidstuff, Participatory, Spectator and Professional Sports and Neighborhoods and Nearby Communities.

The Top Five

Pearl Street Mall
Pearl St. from 11th to 15th Sts., Boulder

Business people in the 1970s bit their nails as Boulder plunked more than a million dollars into a pedestrian mall. How on earth would people shop, some wondered, if they couldn't park in front of a store?

Since then, *The Wall Street Journal* has called the Pearl Street Mall one of the nation's most successful pedestrian malls, and it has won national design awards. It's Boulder's people-watching spot, from kids climbing the bronze frog to college-age lovers buying gauzy new clothes to business people grabbing a savory pie at the Empañadas window. Street musicians embroider the air with a saxophone's blue tones, steel-drum calypso, folk guitar and more. Breathe deeply. The aroma of fresh pretzels might draw you to a kiosk in front of the Courthouse; fresh popcorn or stir-fried something might bring you to a pushcart vendor; or a thick, dark river of perfume might sweep you into the Rocky Mountain Chocolate Factory.

In addition to matchless people-watching, the Pearl Street Mall offers abundant free entertainment — though, of course, the jugglers, clowns and magicians appreciate tips. In the warm months, you can sit to have your portrait painted, your fortune told or get a neck and shoulder message; or you might pick a ringside seat in one of the many excellent restaurants with patio tables. Thanks to Boulder's clear skies and mild days, people-watchers often sit out even in winter. Some of Boulder's finest restaurants, galleries and shops are found on the Mall. Discover them as you wander, or check our chapters on Boulder Shopping, Arts and Restaurants.

Pearl Street's history does not always reflect such a stylish past. It started Wild West style, with drunks horse-racing down the dirt lane that was the main street. And no proper lady walked a white poodle, for these dogs were popular among the "soiled doves" whose creekside homes advertised, "Men Taken In and Done For." To civilize the street, storekeepers built plank walks, but they didn't match sidewalk height between stores, so shoppers bobbed up and down along the way.

By the 1970s, Pearl Street was drearily, Midwesterny respectable. Aluminum facades hid brick storefronts, cars jammed streets, and "for lease" signs proliferated like mushrooms growing in decay. To halt decline, planners suggested everything from a covered shopping mall to high-rises. It seemed so risky to restore the original buildings, tweak the Old West character and create strolling space with sculptures, trees and flowers. Now that it's done and has a two-decade track record of success, please exult: "What a great idea!"

If you're a history buff, stop by the **Hotel Boulderado**, 442-4344, at 2115 13th Street, just north of the mall. This red-brick hotel, named after Boulder and Colorado, was built in 1909, the city's pride, with Italianate porch corners, a cherry cantilevered staircase and an Italian stained-glass ceiling. Theodore Roosevelt, Robert Frost and Louis Armstrong were among the guests. But the Boulderado suffered decline too. The glass ceiling crashed in a 1960s snowstorm; kitchen cooks hung bait over vats to drown rats; and vagrants slept in empty rooms. In the 1980s, Boulderado Concept Ltd. restored the grand old hotel. Wander inside. The Catacombs Bar in the basement has live blues, reggae and jazz most nights of the week, and the there's live music on the mezzanine on Friday evenings; it's reserved for private parties other times.

Another historic area is the **Boulder Courthouse Square**, Pearl Street between 13th and 14th streets. The location started as the town's baseball diamond and then was the site of Boulder County's grand Victorian courthouse, which burned down in the 1930s. Local architect Glenn Huntington designed the light-colored stone, art deco courthouse you see today. The lawn, which was extensively redesigned in 1996, is a popular festival spot.

Just east, at 2032 14th Street, is the **Boulder Theater**, 786-7030, a turn-of-the-century opera house renovated in the 1930s as the gaudy little sister of the plain blond courthouse. The art deco facade is as lavish as a peacock's tail, and the restored interior has gorgeous, hand-painted, flowery murals. Find an excuse to enter, such as the locally produced E-Town live music/talk performances, which National Public Radio broadcasts to more than 150 cities.

From the Pearl Street Mall, it's an easy walk to **Central Park**, between Canyon and Arapahoe streets east of Broadway. An art deco band shell currently being reconstructed, a steam locomotive and frequent festivals can be found in Central Park.

On Saturday mornings from spring through early fall and on Wednesday afternoons in summer, the **Boulder Farmers Market**, 494-4997, takes place along 13th Street (see the subsequent Boulder Creek Path entry for details about this market). On the east of the street is the **Boulder Museum of Contemporary Art** (see subsequent entry), and the Boulder Creek Path, the next must-see attraction, runs along the south side of the park.

Boulder Creek Path
Throughout Boulder

Boulder's most popular "architecture" is 12 feet wide, 6 miles long and flat on the ground. This 1980s project lets non-car commuters travel the prettiest possible way. The Creek Path dips under 10 major intersections, transforming traffic's roar into a whispered "whoosh." More than a half-dozen wooden pedestrian bridges crisscross the stream, clattering merrily as bicyclists and in-line skaters pass. The bridges are to snap to the side and reduce debris if a big flood hits. The whole path was designed built with a rising creek in mind. Major flooding is rare, but every few years, some overflow happens.

Each year, nearly 2 million bicyclists, in-line skaters, walkers, runners — you name it — use the Boulder Creek Path. Other non-motor-vehicle routes connect from all over the city, so people can really get around without cars. Be alert, however. Some fierce bicyclists and in-line skaters ignore speed signs and can scare the daylights out of walkers. Especially in busy areas near downtown, keep an eye on kids, your dogs and your own tendency to stray. Choose your chariot — bicycle, feet, in-line skates or wheelchair — and head to the path.

The **Boulder Public Library's** main branch, 441-3100, at 10th Street and Arapahoe Avenue is a good place to start, and in fact, a stop to admire this gleaming facility is worthwhile too. About 3,000 folks use it daily. Look for the dramatic glass entry on the Arapahoe Avenue side. Outside are a Pooh-garden, scent garden and flowers. Inside, the library has approximately 250,000 circulating books, an artists' register showing slides of local artwork and a computerized media/browsing system. Books can be brought to the home-bound who can't get to the library, and another service transcribes text into Braille. Kid-pleasing attractions include a beautiful rocking horse, a trout habitat and storytelling hours. The library auditorium on the Canyon Boulevard side is the site of a free year-round film and concert series. The Learning to Read program provides free, confidential tutoring for everyone from children to adults. The library is open 9 AM to 9 PM Monday through Thursday, 9 AM to 6 PM Friday and Saturday and noon to 6 PM Sunday.

Just west of the library is the **West Boulder Senior Center** at Ninth Street and Arapa-

---

FYI

Unless otherwise noted, the area code for all phone numbers in this guide is 303.

hoe Avenue. After passing under Ninth Street, be sure to notice the sculpture of Chief Niwot (Niwot means "left hand") on the left. Continue westward to Sixth Street and Canyon Boulevard, where you'll find the **Children's Fishing Pond**, marked by an abstract metal sculpture that looks like leaping fish. On your right is the **Boulder County Justice Center**, with courts for dreary things from speeding tickets to criminal cases, but also where civil marriage ceremonies are performed. Just beyond, west along the Creek Path, the **Xeriscape Demonstration Garden** displays native plants that make environmentally wise gardening choices for Colorado's arid climate, an herb garden and a "wheel" of lawns comparing bluegrass, two buffalo grasses, fescue and blends.

Continuing westward, the path opens out to **Eben Fine Park** at Fourth Street, a favorite shady picnic and Frisbee-throwing area, with playgrounds and a congenial family atmosphere. At the park, you'll see a tunnel to the north, or right, under Canyon Boulevard. It leads to **Red Rocks/Settlers Park**, site of the 1858 campsite along Boulder Creek by the gold seekers who became Boulder's first citizens. Historical plaques explain some of Boulder's early history. Near more picnic tables, you'll see a steep trail up to the nearly vertical red rocks, naturally called Red Rocks, and a fine hilltop view of the whole area. Take care should you decide to scramble up the rocks for an even better vista.

Back along the creek path and just west of the park is **Boulder's kayak course**. Even if you're not into whitewater yourself, it's thrilling to watch kayakers and canoeists test their skills in the rapids during spring and early summer. Innertube riders crawl into their black doughnut-shaped vessels here too for a bracing ride down to Broadway. Two historic markers along the path tell about The Switzerland Trail railroad line and Farmers' Ditch, two early landmarks in the development of Boulder County.

For a lovely walk into **Boulder Canyon**, keep going up the hill and to the west along the Creek Path (watch out for speeding downhill cyclists). After a while, the pavement ends, the path dips under the canyon road and deposits you at the base of the **Elephant But-**

tresses and the **Dome**, two of Boulder's most popular rock-climbing spots. In one vista, you'll see an old water flume and Lycra-clad rock climbers, a perfect combination on the Boulder firmament. Farther along the path, wild roses and purple asters bloom in summer beside the frothy creek, and wild plums and grapes ripen in the fall. The gravel path continues up along the creekside under the rustling cottonwoods and glinting ponderosa pines to **Four Mile Canyon** about 1.5 miles away. The total distance from Eben Fine Park — the lower bridge at the east end of the park with a boulder marked 0 miles — to the end of the trail is 2.25 miles.

If instead you head east from the Boulder Public Library, you'll soon get to **Central Park** at Broadway. There are small waterfalls, historic railroad cars, a band shell (currently under reconstruction) and sometimes an outdoor sculpture exhibit. The **Boulder Museum of Contemporary Art** (see subsequent entry) is across the street, east of the park.

On Saturday mornings from spring through fall and Wednesday afternoons during the summer, the **Boulder County Farmers Market**, 494-4997, stretches on both sides of 13th Street between Arapahoe Avenue and Canyon Boulevard. This assembly features a colorful parade of produce, flowers, homegrown and homemade goodies and weekly cooking demonstrations by local chefs. This beguiling attraction features a changing cornucopia of produce and related wares and has become Colorado's most successful open-air market. Regulars use it as an opportunity to shop, stroll, nibble and socialize. The location is perfect, close to the Pearl Street Mall and right next to Central Park. During the market's early weeks, vendors specialize in seedlings that you can take home and plant. At summer's peak, the street packs with local fresh tomatoes, Western Slope peaches, Rocky Ford cantaloupe and honeydew melons, green beans, lettuce, fresh herbs and more. Tamales, pirogen and focaccia give the market a true international ambiance. Fresh and dried flowers, lavender water, hot corn on the cob, honey and delicacies from goat cheese to smoked trout tempt from many stands. Don't forget sweet ices, lemonade and fresh-baked pastries, all in a big colorful crowd. The market opens in mid-

April and runs through the end of October. Saturday hours are 8 AM to 2 PM. After June 1, a smaller version is also open Wednesday from 11 AM to 4 PM until the weather turns cold in the fall. Downtown workers appreciate the lunchtime menu introduced at the Wednesday market in 1996.

The farmers market currently spills over onto the paved lot just north of the Boulder Museum of Contemporary Art, but eventually, an elaborate teahouse from Tajikistan is supposed to be erected on this parcel. In 1986, the residents of Boulder's sister city of Dashanbe crated and shipped this elegant tile teahouse to Colorado. In typical Boulder fashion, since there was no unanimity on where it should be built, the crates have remained warehoused. Now, officials have indicated the 13th Street site is the place, but no one is giving odds until construction actually begins.

Return to the Creek Path and continue east, past **Boulder High School** and its athletic fields, to a sunny, stone-bench alcove just west of the 17th Street bridge. It's a few steps down, under dappled shade, to the creek babbling below where you'll find the **Fish Observatory** at the **Regal Harvest House**, 443-3850, south of Arapahoe Avenue on 28th Street. The hotel donated the land, and the city, local businesses and Trout Unlimited helped fund it. The observatory's portholes get scum-covered, and fish are, in truth, rarely seen, but kids still like gazing underwater.

Just beyond is **Scott Carpenter Park**, 441-3427, south of Arapahoe Avenue on 30th Street. Carpenter, a Boulder native who became one of the early astronauts, named his spaceship the *Aurora 7* after a local school. The playground has a spacecraft theme, and the park also has an outdoor swimming pool and a popular skateboard facility. The sledding hill is one of Boulder's enduring winter meccas. It was the city's landfill years ago.

Farther east, just before Foothills Parkway, you'll pass the **CU-Boulder Research Park**. Landscape designers decided the standard lawn would take too much care, guzzle water and look boring. So, they planted something much better — low-maintenance, drought-tolerant meadows that attract butterflies and birds. The result is so lovely, it's almost too popular.

At the intersection of Arapahoe Avenue and Foothills Parkway is a **prairie dog town**. Prairie dogs get a bad rap as vermin spreaders, but health officials say it's undeserved, and they are appropriate prey for raptors nesting nearby. Still, don't feed them; they are wild animals and should stay that way. Kids love how they stand like little soldiers, then yip before diving underground. Prairie dogs are a remnant of the shortgrass prairie ecosystem and are food for swooping hawks.

You can take the Creek Path northeast from here, to the tent-roofed stands of the **Stazio Ballfields**, 441-3454, at 2445 Stazio Drive, which are well-lighted and busy well into evening all summer long. Notice that the path veers away from the oldest cottonwood trees. Playing by the creek is fun, but human activity has caused creekside wildlife to decline. By keeping people farther away, critters, such as the red-eyed vireo and yellow warbler, have a better chance. If you ever hear a warbler sing, you'll thank creek planners for giving those birds privacy. As the creek path spreads its tentacles, you can take offshoots either to the north and south through residential as well as industrial areas, one reason that it is so popular for commuting.

Chautauqua Park
Ninth St. and Baseline Rd., Boulder
• 442-3282

At the turn of the century, sites across the nation became gathering spots for summer cultural and educational institutes, all named "Chautauqua" after Chautauqua Lake in upstate New York, where the first such gathering was held. Dozens of Chautauquas once existed, but few remain. Boulder's was one of the rare Western locations. The **Chautauqua**

INSIDERS' TIP

Get your sinuses cleared in a millisecond by the 5,000 bales of mint in Celestial Seasonings' peppermint isolation room. This free tour includes a taste test of new teas.

Photo: Daily Camera/Nico Toutenhoofd

Boulder Falls is a favorite spot for photographs and recreation.

Auditorium and Dining Hall, 440-3776, built in 1898, and a charming nearby colony of wooden cottages comprise the last original site west of the Mississippi. A fascinating display of historic photographs is at the **Chautauqua Association's Archive and History Room**. It is normally open 8:30 AM to noon and 2 to 5 PM on weekdays, but before you make a special trip, call 442-3282 to confirm hours. Chautauqua's main buildings, decked out in crisp gray, would still be a perfect setting for banjo-strumming gallants in flat-brimmed hats, but summer offerings now draw modern crowds with contemporary interests. There's a nod to the past with July's silent films, accompanied by live piano. The **Colorado Chautauqua Association Forum** is a lecture series dating from 1898, but today's speakers address topics such as health issues, transportation and world affairs.

The **Colorado Music Festival**, 449-1397, has a full orchestra of musicians invited here for the summer and features internationally renowned guest artists as well as rising stars with promising futures. The vast majority of classical performances are instrumental, for the wooden Auditorium tends to swallow voices. An orchestra or a powerful soloist can make the wonderful barn resonate with great sound. For ticket events, call the Box Office, 440-7666, between May and September. To rent a cottage for the summer or to learn about the summer programs, call the **Chautauqua Association**, 442-3282. The **Chautauqua Gift Cottage**, 443-5839, is open daily in the summer.

Children like the **Chautauqua Park** playground, especially after they discover low-branched trees for playing hide-and-seek. (Only kids can scamper through. Moms and dads have to hunch.) The **Chautauqua Ranger Cottage**, 441-3408, near the big meadow on the west side of the park, is generally open 8 AM to 4 PM daily. Its small garden displays native plants, and the rangers dispense plenty of hiking information. The rangers can answer questions, and they're trained to handle emergencies. They also lead free interpretive hikes that depart from the Ranger Cottage at 8 AM Saturday mornings in summer.

Trails lead everywhere. The Boulder Mountain Parks trail system includes everything from short, nearly flat strolls to steep hikes. One of the easiest, and shadiest, is the **McClintock Trail**, starting southeast of the Chautauqua Auditorium. You can head west on the **Chautauqua Trail**, cross the big meadow and watch rock climbers. Or head west and south to the **Mesa Trail**. It's 3 up-and-down miles to the next major attraction, **NCAR** (see subsequent entry) and twice that far to the Mesa Trail's southern terminus just off the Eldorado Canyon Road.

National Center for Atmospheric Research

West end of Table Mesa Dr., Boulder
• 497-1000

Anyone who has ever gazed at the sky can find something of interest at NCAR (pronounced "en-car"), founded in 1960 to study world climate. Scientists from all over the globe study our wonderful blanket of air, and interesting displays present the fundamentals of their fields of expertise. Sky-watchers can learn about clouds, air currents, lightning, hail, tornadoes and other weather phenomena, including global warming. I.M. Pei designed this mesa-top complex, which helped establish his reputation as a world-class architect. "The mountains," said Pei, "gave us scale trouble from the beginning. We had to return to elemental forms. The Rockies humbled us." Local red limestone was mixed into the concrete so it would blend with the Flatirons. The building's angular forms mimic keyhole doors at the Mesa Verde cliff dwellings. This building is considered one of the nation's finest public structures. Two galleries feature community art. The computers in the basement are some of the world's fastest and largest.

Self-guided tours, with brochures from the lobby, are always available. Guided walking tours take place at noon Mondays and Wednesdays all year, and weekdays during the summer. No reservations are needed for the guided tours, but for information, call 497-1174. If you want to bring a school, scout or any other group, tours must be arranged in advance by calling 497-1173.

NCAR is open 8 AM to 5 PM Monday through Friday and 9 AM to 3 PM weekends and holidays. Admission is free. The cafeteria is open to the public, weekdays, for lunch.

In addition, short nature trails near NCAR are spectacular. The **Walter Orr Roberts Nature Trail**, 0.3 mile long, just west of the laboratory is not paved but is wheelchair-accessible.

University of Colorado at Boulder

Intersections of Baseline and Broadway/ Folsom and Colorado/Broadway and College, Boulder • 492-1411

CU-Boulder's 600-acre campus is considered one of the nation's most beautiful. The buildings are a visual symphony of red tile roofs and warm native stone walls that make the entire campus harmonize, and the landscaping is splendid. **Norlin Quadrangle** is the three-block-long, tree-lined lawn next to Broadway. Nearby are the oldest buildings on campus, including Macky Auditorium, Old Main, Hale Science Building and the Koenig Alumni Center. **Kittredge Pond**, near Fleming Law School, and **Varsity Pond**, just off the intersection of Broadway and College, are "water features" created decades before such amenities got a trendy name. The big old trees, quacking mallards and basking turtles help time stand still — even among the achingly with-it students all around.

For many, the campus's main draw is the sports teams, and rabid fans might never get past **Folsom Field** or the **Coors Events Center**. Call 492-8337 for information about Big 12 conference games, or see the Boulder Participatory, Spectator and Professional Sports chapter for more information. For other folks, the campus is fun for exploring. Maps located throughout the campus pinpoint spots of interest, or call 492-6301 for information about campus visits and tours. A hour-long information briefing followed by a one-hour tour is given at 9:30 AM and 1:30 PM Monday through Friday and at 10:30 AM Saturdays from the University Memorial Center in front of Room 235.

The **University Memorial Center**, known on campus as "the UMC," is at Euclid, just east of Broadway. The **Glenn Miller Lounge**

INSIDERS' TIP

Some of Boulder's most popular stores have become attractions in their own right. Boulderites often take out-of-towners to Alfalfa's Natural Food Market, McGuckin Hardware, The Peppercorn and other distinctive retail establishments just for the fun of it. (See our Boulder Shopping chapter for more information.)

and Ballroom are named after the CU jazz trombone player who popularized Big Band swing and was a CU student. A short walk to the northeast is **Norlin Library**, 492-8705, with more than 10 million books, periodicals, manuscripts, government publications and more — the biggest such collection library in the state. The CU-Boulder's public art gallery is in the **Sibell-Wolle Fine Arts Building**, 492-8300. The **Colorado Centennial Foucault Pendulum**, 492-6952, is at Duane Physical Laboratory, inside Gamow Tower, just south of Gate 2 of Folsom Field. It might seem that the 40-meter pendulum changes direction during the day, but it actually stays steady while the earth rotates underneath it. (At the equator, it would swing the same direction all the time.)

The domed **Fiske Planetarium** on Regent Drive is a campus landmark housing a great theater for star shows and featuring one of the finest star-gazing machines in the world. Scientists use it to turn the celestial skies back so that they can compare ancient ruins to an ancient sky. Often, they discover important building features align with star patterns that occurred long ago. Regular visitors can enjoy laser light shows and talks — fun in those leaned-back chairs that coddle your neck while you're staring upward. Star shows are normally scheduled on Friday evenings and Saturday afternoons. Adult admission is $3.50, and children and seniors pay $2 for evening shows, including admission to the adjacent **Sommers-Bausch Observatory** afterwards, weather permitting. Matinees are $3 for adults and $1.50 for children and seniors. You can get recorded information on the current week's shows by calling 492-5001. For more detailed information, call 492-5002. At the observatory, the real sky, not a planetarium show, is occasionally open for public viewing. Astronomy students man the telescopes during a special heavenly show, like a spectacular comet, meteor shower or eclipse; but in recent years, clouds have obscured the most heralded events. Still, you can arrange to visit the observatory if you call ahead, 492-5002.

The **Herbarium**, 492-3216, houses nearly a half-million dried plant specimens from Colorado and around the world. While not a browsing library, it is open to students of botany who call for reservations.

The Heritage Center, a CU-Boulder museum, 492-6329, is in Old Main, which housed the whole university from 1876 through 1884. This authentic Victorian landmark has been renovated, and the beautiful Chapel is an especially cozy area for small performances. The Heritage Center on the top floor is noteworthy for its "Space Room" honoring CU-Boulder's 13 astronauts and for the sensational collection of sports memorabilia. The distinguished alumni gallery in the Center includes retired Supreme Court Justice Byron White, Miss America 1958 Marilyn Van Derber-Atler, Robert Redford, *M*A*S*H* actor Larry Linville and the 1989 Nobel Prize won by CU-Boulder chemist Tom Cech. An architectural gallery shows the original models for CU, including its rural Italian design. Hours are 10 AM to 4 PM Tuesday through Friday. Special tours can be arranged, and it's open before and after home football games. Admission is free.

University of Colorado Museum, 492-6892, at Broadway and 15th Street in the Henderson Building, displays dinosaur fossils that include a triceratops head and a pterodactyl, taxidermy specimens and touchable items for kids, including a sea turtle shell you can try on for size. Established in 1902, the museum has grown to include a diversity of displays, notably in paleontology, anthropology and botany. Seasonal programs include a "Museum in the Dark" show for kids just before Halloween, and traveling exhibits are booked into the museum too. It is open 9 AM to 5 PM weekdays, 9 AM to 4 PM Saturdays and 10 AM to 4 PM Sundays. Admission is free.

For academic information about CU-Boulder, check the chapter on Boulder Child Care and Education.

More Museums, Historic Buildings and Special Places

The Arnett-Fullen House
646 Pearl St., Boulder • 444-5192

This fanciful Victorian landmark is a few blocks west of the Pearl Street Mall. Historic Boulder, a nonprofit group based here, sells a walking-tour guidebook and conducts regular walking summer tours. These inexpensive tours include Pearl Street, the Chautauqua Park area, University Hill and the Whittier and Mapleton Hill neighborhoods. (See our Neighborhoods and Nearby Communities chapter for schedules and rates.) You may also request custom tours, including CU's Norlin Quadrangle. This group also organizes a Christmas house tour and a spring tour of fine local homes in various neighborhoods.

The Arnett-Fullen House is one of the most extreme forms of Gothic gingerbread around, its flamboyance befitting its original owner. Will Arnett was a true 19th-century character. He used $10 gold coins for buttons, built his dream house for twice the $2,000 cost of an average home in those days and died in 1900 while prospecting for gold in Alaska. No wonder his 1877 turreted Pearl Street home is ornate. Arnett also loved his cast-iron fence, which he had shipped from Pittsburgh for $2,000, a fortune back then. Historic Boulder bought the home in 1993 for $329,000. The first floor of the house, including the gift shop, is open for viewing from 9 AM to 4 PM weekdays. If you drop in, be sure to notice the walnut-inlaid spiral staircase.

After much wrangling, Historic Boulder bought the garden just west of the Arnett-Fullen House in 1996. Volunteers will restore it to reflect its true Victorian period. It looks beautiful now, but it will be positively glorious in spring and summer as the "new old" plantings mature.

Boulder County Fairgrounds
9595 Nelson Rd., Longmont • 441-3927

Anytime you visit, something's happening at the fair. This big, big fairground hosts antique and craft shows, barrel racing (for non-cowboys, that means racing horses in hairpin turns around barrels), national dog shows, bridge tournaments, circuses, motorcycle shows . . . the list goes on. Some events attract more than 100,000, and some are small.

To reach the fairgrounds, head north to Longmont on Colo. Highway 119. Turn left at Hover Road, whose intersection is marked with big stoplights. Go north on Hover past the Twin Peaks shopping mall to Nelson Road. The fairground's on your right. Call for an event schedule.

Boulder Museum of Contemporary Art
1750 13th St., Boulder • 443-2122

This not-for-profit museum has three exhibition spaces for rotating shows as well as performing arts and mixed-media space. Local, national and international artists and photographers have shown at BMoCA. The small museum is open Tuesday through Friday from 11 AM to 5 PM, Saturday from 8 AM to 5 PM and Sunday from noon to 5 PM. Admission is $2.

Boulder Museum of History
1206 Euclid Ave., Boulder • 449-3464

The three-story, blond brick Harbeck-Bergheim house, home of the Boulder Museum of History, was built by a New York merchant in 1899 as a summer home. Its most renowned feature is a spectacular 9-foot-tall Tiffany stained-glass window. The museum is an eclectic grandma's attic-type showcase of Boulder County history. Artifacts show how mining, ranching and everyday life affected Boulder. A costume gallery, one of the largest collections in the state, is on the second floor. The museum and gift shop are open noon to 4 PM Tuesday through Saturday. Admission is $2 for adults and $1 for children, seniors and students.

Callahan House
312 Terry St., Longmont • 776-1870

In the early 1900s, a Longmont businessman named T.M. Callahan hired an unemployed Longmont butcher who had gone bankrupt because he refused to pay off the hotel chef with a weekly bottle of bourbon. That

INSIDERS' TIP

No summer is complete without a stop at Boulder's Farmers Market. It's on 13th Street, between Arapahoe and Canyon streets, on Saturdays and Wednesday afternoons.

butcher, J.C. Penney, went to work for Callahan's chain of "Golden Rule" notion stores, and the Wyoming Golden Rule he and Callahan started became the first store in the Penney chain.

The Callahan home was presented to the city of Longmont in 1938. Each year, it is used for meetings, weddings, showers, receptions, dinners and other social events. The interior is opulently Victorian, with pink tones, ornately carved wood, swirly plaster moldings and exquisite light fixtures.

Callahan House is home to the St. Vrain Historical Society, the Longmont equivalent to Historic Boulder. The society provides brochures for self-guided tours. These are available at the Longmont Museum or the carriage house behind the Callahan House. Group guided tours can be arranged by appointment. Call ahead for reservations and fees. Terry Street, by the way, is just west of Longmont's Old Main downtown.

Collage Children's Museum
2065 30th St., Boulder • 440-9894

The museum's philosophy is: "I hear, I forget; I see, I remember; I touch, I understand." Therefore, dancing with shadows, art and play are major parts of this nonprofit hands-on museum that features changing exhibits and also sponsors community events for children. Past exhibits include "Good Vibrations," about sound; "Energize," about how to conserve energy; and "Animation." The museum is open Wednesdays from 2 to 5 PM, Thursday through Saturday 10 AM to 5 PM and Sunday 1 to 5 PM with extended summer hours. Story hour is 3:30 to 4:30 PM on Wednesdays. Admission is $2.50 per person; $8 per family; and free for members and children younger than 2.

The Leanin' Tree Museum of Western Art
6055 Longbow Dr., Boulder • 530-1442

Landscapes, bronze sculptures and other original art comprise one of the nation's largest privately owned Western art collections. The artworks, primarily post-Russell and Remington, include paintings and sculpture and are available as a result of Leanin' Tree founder Ed Trumble's 40-year friendship with Western artists. The growing collection keeps expanding into the Leanin' Tree greeting card company's workspace.

Since opening in 1974, the museum has welcomed well more than a quarter-million visitors. The gift shop sells greeting cards, framed art and T-shirts produced at Leanin' Tree. To reach the museum, take the Diagonal Highway (Colo. Highway 119) north to 63rd Street. Turn right to Longbow Drive. The company and museum are the third building on the right.

Photo: Daily Camera

Fourth of July picnic at Chautauqua.

The museum is open 8 AM to 4:30 PM Monday through Friday and 10 AM to 4 PM Saturday. Admission is free.

Carnegie Branch Library for Local History
1125 Pine St., Boulder • 441-3110

This small, stately marble-columned building was Boulder's original library. Its original interior has been restored and contains local historic materials including books, diaries, oral histories, tapes, genealogical papers, 200,000 photographs, 700,000 documents and various materials donated by the Boulder Historical Society. If you are researching your house or property, this is the best place to start. Hours are 1 to 9 PM Monday; 11 AM to 5 PM Tuesday through Saturday, with hours extended from 9 AM to 5 PM on Wednesday. Admission is free.

Dougherty Antique Museum
8306 N. 107th St., Longmont • 776-2520

The late Ray Dougherty didn't realize he was collecting when, as a teenager, he bought a reed organ. His wife, Dorothy Dougherty, says the hobby of collecting antique cars, farm equipment and musical instruments just grew and grew (there's also a stagecoach). The antique autos have starred in many parades. That doesn't happen much anymore, because few have the knack for driving them. After all, you don't just turn the key when a car has a steam engine or needs a handcrank.

A mile south of Longmont on U.S. Highway 287 at the family farm, this exhibit is open from 10 AM to 4 PM Saturdays and Sundays. Admission is $3 for adults, $2 for ages 6 to 12, and free for kids 5 and younger. Large groups are welcome if they call ahead.

Flagstaff Nature Center
Flagstaff Mountain Summit, Boulder • 441-3408

The small log cabin atop Flagstaff Mountain that contained the most basic interpretive exhibits on Front Range ecology received some $40,000 in grants during 1996 and will triple in size by the time it opens for the 1997 summer season. Its rustic log appearance remains, but the new environmentally sensitive building will have room for more displays and

an increased staff. Call the Chautauqua Ranger Cottage at the listed phone number for details on new hours and expanded facilities. Nearby is the landmark Flagstaff Amphitheater, built by the Civilian Conservation Corps, and still the site of evening ranger presentations and, often, weddings. The area affords excellent views of the Boulder Valley and beyond.

To reach the center, follow Baseline Road to Flagstaff Road. The road leading to the large parking lot is well-marked and to the right.

Lafayette Miner's Museum
108 E. Simpson St., Lafayette • 666-6686, 665-7030

This refurbished 1890s coal miner's home was moved into town during the 1910 coal strike. The six-room house, maintained by the Louisville Historical Society, displays clothing, tools and other mining equipment and household items of the time. Hours are 2 to 4 PM Thursday and Saturday and by appointment. Admission is free.

Longmont Museum
375 Kimbark St., Longmont • 651-8374

This permanent exhibit has earned a national historic award for its Native American beaded buckskin dresses and flint arrows. The museum also displays equipment similar to that used by Maj. Stephen Long and his party, who explored the area in the 1820s for the Army; Longs Peak and Longmont are named for him. Farming history and large-scale reproductions of early buildings are here. Kidspace includes dress-up, arts and sciences and bubble-blowing. The museum is open 9 AM to 5 PM Monday through Friday; 10 AM to 4 PM Saturdays. There are extended summer hours. Admission is free.

Louisville Historical Museum
1001 Main St., Louisville • 665-9048

Coal mining gave birth to Louisville, and artifacts from the town's early days plus household and personal items fill this small museum. Hours are 1 to 3 PM Thursday or by appointment. Admission is free.

Lyons Redstone Museum
340 High St., Lyons • 823-5271

Take a scenic drive from Boulder north to

Lyons the town whose sandstone quarries have yielded so much of the building material you see at the University of Colorado and elsewhere in Boulder County. This restored 1881 schoolhouse features displays on the town's history. Hours are 9:30 AM to 4:30 PM Monday through Saturday; 12:30 to 4:30 PM Sunday. Admission is free, but donations are welcomed.

Old Mill Park
237 Pratt St., Longmont • 776-1870

The oldest log cabin in Boulder County is situated in a privately owned, tree-lined park. A real mill wheel turns at the pond. The park can be reserved through the St. Vrain Historical Society for weddings and meetings. Old Mill Park is open daily to the public for free between 8 AM and dusk, except during private events. Call ahead if you want a tour of the furnished interiors.

Tower of Compassion
Missouri St. and S. Pratt Pkwy., Longmont • No phone

This 60-foot-tall pagoda was donated to the city in 1972 by the Kanemoto family, who settled in Longmont in the early 1900s to work in sugar-beet fields. Their family farm later was developed as residences and this city park. The tower was inspired by a visit to Japan and the Kanemoto's gratitude to the people of Longmont. Its five levels represent love, empathy, understanding, gratitude and giving selflessly of oneself — all elements of true compassion.

Business and Science Attractions

Celestial Seasonings Tour
4600 Sleepytime Dr., Boulder • 530-5300

Your sinuses will clear as soon as you take a whiff of the 5,000 bales of mint in Celestial Seasoning's peppermint isolation room. Each year, 50,000 people enjoy a 45-minute tour of the nation's largest manufacturer of specialty and herb teas. The tour includes an assembly line where tea gets packed in those pretty little boxes, and there are taste-testing opportunities. Children of employees create safety posters, and the walls are festooned with sayings from the tea boxes. This is a New Age business to its very bones, now with a sleek all-business overlay that belies its counterculture origins is Boulder's haute hippie era.

Tours run every hour from 10 AM to 3 PM Monday through Saturday and 11 AM to 3 PM Sunday. Arrive early to get tickets. Children must be 5 or older to go on the factory portion of the tour. Groups of eight or more must make reservations. You can also visit the Tea Shop and Emporium, the herb garden and lunchtime cafe whether or not you take the tour. Shop hours are 9 AM to 6 PM Monday through Friday, 9 AM to 5 PM Saturday and 11 AM to 5 PM Sunday. To reach the plant, take the Longmont Diagonal Highway (Colo. Highway 119) to Jay Road. Turn right (east), go a mile to Spine Road, turn left and continue a half-mile to Sleepytime Drive and Celestial Seasonings. Admission is free.

Eco-Cycle
5030 Pearl St., Boulder • 444-6634

It would be unromantic as well as technically incorrect to describe this as a "trip to the dump," but that's virtually what it is. It is enlightening to see what happens to your recyclables after they leave the curb. Kids love this big, noisy, impressive operation with a magnetic separator, which draws out the steel and leaves aluminum and other nonferrous materials behind. Eco-Cycle is one of the nation's oldest, and still largest, nonprofit recycling companies. Its many honors include a national Excellence Award from the National Recycling Coalition for leadership and environmental protection. Tours can be scheduled for six or more people (smaller groups can piggyback along); call ahead. Admission is free.

INSIDERS' TIP

Historic Walking Tours of Boulder, 444-5192, sells a walking-tour guidebook and conducts regular summer tours.

Federal Aviation Administration Tours

2211 17th Ave., Longmont • 651-4315

More than 90 air-traffic controllers watch approximately 40 radarscopes that show the weather and planes moving across nine states. These folks can tell any plane in their area to change routes, altitude and speed because of traffic-on-high or weather. Tours of the FAA facility are available by appointment, and aviators are the most likely to get in the control room. Admission is free.

Long's Iris Gardens

3240 Broadway, Boulder • 442-2353

For nearly a century, the Long family has chugged an old tractor out to tend their iris fields. The 2,000 varieties range from pretty mongrels to prize-winning queens. You can go to the big yellow farmhouse in early May to mid-June, depending on the year's weather, or pick your own plants. (The Longs will provide supplies so you can dig your own iris clumps.) The delicate scents and the rows of colorful, fluttering petals can make any day better. Digging-season hours are generally 10 AM to 6 PM daily. An iris clump costs less than $5. The farm is close to town, on Broadway, just south of Iris Avenue (guess how *that* street got its name). Catalogs come out in April.

National Institute of Standards and Technology

325 Broadway, Boulder • 497-3244

Bring your wristwatch. A self-guided tour takes visitors to the nation's timekeeper, the atomic clock. The leap second gets added here at this very clock. The Solar Forecasting Center is where visitors can watch researchers study the sun. This is the nation's warning system for solar flares. The 90-minute guided tour includes a demonstration in cryogenics, the study of how extremely low temperatures (-320 F) affect various materials. Guided tours are offered Thursdays at 1:30 PM. Summers include an additional tour on Tuesdays at 10:30 AM.

This is a period building, by the way. Built in the 1950s, it has a crew-cut look, from the sparkling pink travertine walls to the shiny terrazzo floors. The building is open 8 AM to 6 PM Monday through Friday. Admission is free.

National Oceanic and Atmospheric Administration

3100 Marine St., Boulder • 497-6286

Boulder is nowhere near the beach, but it's a center for incredibly sophisticated weather forecasting and oceanic research, thanks to high-powered scientists and their computers that study world weather. Call a few days in advance if you'd like a free tour.

Seasonal Events

Summer is Boulder's high season. The weather is wonderful, and everything's beautiful. Cultural activities shift into high gear too. (See our Arts chapter for more information about the following events.)

The **Colorado Music Festival**, 449-1397 or 449-2413 to subscribe, features a first-rate, full orchestra that plays great music at the Chautauqua Auditorium throughout the summer. The CMF season starts with a special children's performance and includes a free Fourth of July outdoor concert. You can get a subscription or single tickets to CMF concerts. Insiders often bring a picnic and blanket for a pre-concert dinner on the grassy lawn, and many cluster behind the auditorium and listen to the sounds of brass and strings that waft through the wooden walls. Another popular pre-concert option is eating at the historic Chautauqua Dining Hall, especially for the lucky parties that get seating on the porch.

The **Colorado Shakespeare Festival**, 492-0554, calls CU-Boulder's Mary Rippon Outdoor Theatre home. This festival started in 1958 and has presented all the Shakespeare plays, and is now the fifth-largest Shakespeare company in the United States, according to the Shakespeare Theatre Association. The lushly costumed, lavishly acted plays are produced from mid-June through mid-August. The season includes four plays, three by Shakespeare and one by another playwright. In 1996, the plays were *A Midsummer Night's Dream*, *The Merchant of Venice*, *Othello* and Molière's *The Miser*.

A four-play subscription also includes a backstage tour and one catered box dinner. Before the play starts, an actor costumed as the Bard of Avon strolls around the lawn outside the theater and engages in provide interpretive, interactive conversations with members of the audience, and directors, costume designers and other back-of-the-house specialists hold scheduled pre-performance discussion sessions. Insiders take a soft blanket to picnic on the lawn.

The Shakespearean plays are performed under the stars in the Mary Rippon Theatre. Because the Rippon's amphitheater-style benches are made of stone, the wise theatergoer brings or rents a soft cushion or a stadium chair. After the sun goes down, the evening can turn cool, so bringing a sweater, jacket and even rain gear is smart too. The non-Shakespearean play is performed indoors in the University Theatre.

Broadway comes to Boulder during the short season of performances put on by CU's **Lyric Theatre Festival**, 492-8008. In recent years, it has presented musical theater such as *Fiddler on the Roof* and *Man of La Mancha* during July. It's lighter entertainment than Shakespeare.

Some groups do everything at once. **Naropa Summer Institute Performing Arts Series**, 444-0202, brings dancers, musicians, writers and lecturers from all over the nation. Artists and scholars have included Allen Ginsberg, Anne Waldman, Phillip Glass, Cecil Taylor, Meredith Monk and the Gardzienice Theater Group from Poland. Performances run from June through August.

Boulder is also a dancing mecca, so the choices are enormous. The **Colorado Dance Festival**, 442-7666, is an independent group that presents classes, workshops and performances at the university and other spaces throughout Boulder in July. Three hundred students join them during the summer, with more than 35 performing and teaching artists.

**After a winter storm,
Scott Carpenter Park is
Snow Sled Central.**

Boulder
Kidstuff

Fun Things To Do With Kids

"I'm b-o-r-r-e-e-d!!!"

If you have kids, it's an all-too-familiar refrain. But what to do?

Here are ideas for when you get a little bored with your children's boredom. (Also check the chapters on Boulder Festivals and Annual Events, Attractions and Daytrips.)

Pick a Park

The top kid parks and play areas are Scott Carpenter Park (rated Boulder's Best Park by *Daily Camera* readers); Chautauqua Park; the children's play areas along the Pearl Street Mall; Cave Park, east of Eisenhower School on Eisenhower Drive; and the new additions to the East Boulder Community Center. **Scott Carpenter Park**, named after a local astronaut, features a climbing apparatus resembling a rocket ship. In winter, the park is Boulder's most popular sledding area. **Chautauqua Park** boasts a great expanse of lawn, away from traffic, as well as some playground equipment. The gravel-lined pits and small climb-upon boulders (just west of the Courthouse) make the **Pearl Street Mall** as popular a playground for children as for adults. **Cave Park** offers the best and most creative array of playground equipment around. You'll find that neighborhood elementary schools have pretty good playground stuff too. The **East Boulder Community Center** features a new sand area and nearby nature trails.

Find Water: Liquid or Frozen

Swimming

Thank your lucky splashers that so many Boulder area recreation centers have indoor swimming pools, kiddie pools, water slides and Lazy River pools, which residents and out-of-towners can use for a small fee. All schedule open and family swims as well as swimming lessons for children and adults. Call for hours and details on facility features: **East Boulder**, 441-4400; **North Boulder**, 441-3444; **South Boulder**, 441-3448; **Broomfield**, 469-5351; **Louisville**, 666-7400; and **Lafayette**, 665-0469. In the warm months, youngsters also enjoy outdoor pools, including Boulder's Spruce and Scott Carpenter pools.

Boulder Reservoir beach is also a magnet for families (see our Parks and Recreation Centers chapter).

Sailing and Paddling

Viele Lake at the South Boulder Recreation Center, 441-3448, has canoes, paddleboats and lots of Canada geese. **Boulder Reservoir**, 441-3456, has a sand beach and rents such non-power watercraft as canoes, rowboats, paddleboats and Sunfish. Lafayette's **Waneka Lake**, 665-0469, has a

INSIDERS' TIP

Grab some wheels and head to the Boulder Creek Path. Don't have wheels? Rent in-line skates or bikes at many bike shops.

great deal on canoe rentals and a pretty area where the herons hang out.

Sledding and Ice Skating

After a winter storm, **Scott Carpenter Park** is Snow Sled Central. The sledding hill is small enough to be manageable but big enough to be exciting. West Boulder youngsters often take their sleds to the hill on the north side of **Casey Middle School**. During the winter, the **Aspen Lodge** near Estes Park, 440-3371, offers free outdoor ice skating during daylight hours and rents skates in adults' and children's sizes. **CU-Boulder's indoor ice-skating rink**, 492-7255, is free to students and members, otherwise the cost is less than $4 plus a small fee for skates. You must be a the guest of a student or member guest to use that facility, so isn't it time you made friends with some students?

Skiing

Eldora Mountain Resort, 440-8700, is tailor-made for family skiing with easy and challenging downhill trails plus lots of ski and snowboarding instructors. The Eldorables Children's Center provides day care for ages 3 months to 6 years. Children's lessons are available for kids 4 and older. In conjunction with the Mom's Monday, a series of women-only classes on Monday afternoons, Little MAC (an acronym for Monday Afternoon Club) provides two-hour lessons and rental equipment for 4- to 6-year-olds. The Nordic Center is adjacent to the downhill ski areas. In addition to beautiful, wind-sheltered Nordic trails, cross-country instructors set up the lessons so everything's a game, and because there's so much movement, kids tend to stay warmer than they do during downhill skiing.

Get Wheels

The **Boulder Creek Path** and its tributaries are perfect for in-line skating or bicycling. Many places rent in-line skates and adult bikes. In the summer, the **Boulder Bikesmith**, 443-1132, 2432 Arapahoe Avenue, and **University Bicycles**, 444-4196, 839 Pearl Street, rent kids' bikes, bike trailers, tandem bikes and trail-a-bikes, a new style of hybrid tandem with an adult-size bike in front and a kid-size one in the rear . . . all good for family wheels.

If your child lacks a bike, isn't it time to buy one? "Pl-e-a-s-e? Pretty please?" The bike trails in Boulder are so wonderful, wheels can be the highlight of a child's vacation or life in Boulder. But make sure children wear helmets. In fact, set a good example and wear one yourself, and ride with them until you're sure they understand trail safety and bicycling rules. Although most riders are polite and considerate of children, paths can get crowded, and a few rude racers are ruthless.

Take a Hike

Hardcore mountaineers wouldn't call the **Boulder Creek Path** (see our Boulder Attractions chapter) a "hike," but for small fry, it can be a real adventure. A stroll along the path — keeping mindful of fast-moving cyclists and in-line skaters, please — can take on exploratory aspects with small detours down the creek along the way, to the murky but well-intentioned trout-viewing windows near the Regal Harvest House bridge or to the duck-pond overlook between Ninth Street and the Justice Center. Freelance musicians might be playing in the park between Broadway and 13th Street. Be sure to read the interpretive signs along the way.

Short-legged, short-burst-of-energy little hikers often do best with modest walks along relatively flat trails. After the paved Creek Path, a logical next step might be some of the area's easiest unpaved trails. From the **Bobolink** trailhead at Baseline and Cherryvale roads, it's just a little more than .75-mile to the East Boulder Community Center and about 1.3 miles to South Boulder Road. The **Baseline-EBCC** section features a series of interpretive signs on grasslands, wetlands and river ecology. The **Teller Farm Trail** runs 2.2 miles through a picturesque rural area between Arapahoe (the signed trailhead is off a dirt road between 75th and 95th streets) and Valmont Road (the trailhead is near 95th Street). Partway along the trail is a small lake

FYI

Unless otherwise noted, the area code for all phone numbers in this guide is 303.

(fishing permitted). The nearby **White Rocks Trail**, whose trailhead is also near Valmont Road and 95th Street, is about 4 miles long, and its first stretch is really flat. For information on these trails, call the **City of Boulder Open Space**, 441-4142.

Walden Ponds is a beguiling 113-acre complex of ponds reclaimed from old gravel pits — now an example that demonstrates nature's ability to heal a scarred landscape. The ponds, their aquatic vegetation and fish have become an attractive habitat and breeding area for waterfowl, painted turtles, muskrats and other fauna. Two miles of ultra-gentle trails, picnic areas and fishing areas make Walden Ponds a fine family destination.

With older children who have more stamina, the options multiply. **Red Rocks** is a good starter. This short, steep trail, accessible from a well-marked trailhead at the mouth of Boulder Canyon, makes a suitable first challenge with some optional rock scrambling on top. Trails in the **Boulder Mountain Parks**, **Walker Ranch** way up Flagstaff Road, the new **Rabbit Mountain** open space near Lyons, **Brainard Lake** and the **Indian Peaks Wilderness** west of Ward and Rocky Mountain National Park are among the abundant nearby hikes for various levels of stamina and interest. (See our Parks and Recreation chapter and our Rocky Mountain National Park Overview.) If it's windy, a trail right against the Foothills can provide some shelter from big gusts. If it's snowy, choose a flat one. If it's hot, find a creek with shade, or drive up to the mountains. Remember to watch little ones closely near any creeks with fast-moving waters.

Go to the Library

Most Boulder area libraries offer abundant reading nooks, computers and storytelling times. Boulder's **Main Library**, 441-3100, at 1000 Canyon Boulevard at Ninth Street between Canyon and Arapahoe, is an eye-popper with an outstanding selection of books, publications, videos and other materials. But the branch libraries are treats too. The **George Reynolds Branch**, 441-3120, 3595 Table Mesa Drive, and the **Meadows Branch**, 441-4390, 4800 Baseline Road at Foothills Parkway, both have children's sections. The librar-

ies in **Lafayette**, 665-5200, 1290 Public Road, and **Longmont**, 651-8470, 409 Fourth Avenue, also have good children's sections. The videotape libraries are extensive, and audio tapes are a lifesaver if you're car-bound. There's nothing like happy kids in the back seat, listening to good yarns on their Walkmans.

Visit a Children's Museum

The motto of **Boulder Collage Children's Museum**, 440-9894, 2065 30th Street, is "I hear, I forget; I see, I remember; I touch, I understand." Past displays include an interactive computer, dancing with colored shadows and the "Dragons of the Dump" with "recycled" dragons created by kids. **KIDSPACE** at the Longmont Museum, 651-8374, 375 Kimbark Street, is a children's gallery specializing in self-structured hands-on science, historical and art activities, such as a puppet area, pioneer dress-up theater, reading area and rotating activities including a water table, an electronic board and "Tub-O'Bubbles," where kids can create giant soap bubbles with wands. Both museums charge a nominal admission fee and accept donations too.

The **University of Colorado Museum**, 492-6892, Broadway and 15th Street, has a kids' corner and numerous kids' activities and special events. This place is definitely one of Boulder's best-kept secrets. Find the real Triceratops head, and try on the sea-turtle shell.

If you're up for a drive or heading that direction anyway, the biggest, most comprehensive children's museum around is the **Denver Children's Museum**, 433-7433, 2121 Children's Museum Drive (just off Interstate 25), which features a stunning variety of laboratories, interactive displays, a miniature grocery store where youngsters can shop or act as cashiers and a terrific toddler area.

Be a Sport

Team sports are a great way for youngsters to learn cooperation and team spirit and for newcomers to town to make friends. **Boulder Junior Soccer**, 443-1618, 602 Maxwell Avenue, is the biggest program around, with spring and fall seasons for children as young as kindergartners ranging through Boulder Barrage for strong older players. The **YMCA**, 442-2778, 2850 Mapleton Avenue, has baseball programs in spring and summer; basketball in winter and spring; and soccer, volleyball, flag football and in-line hockey in fall. **Little League** baseball, **Lake Eldora Ski Racing Team**, 447-8104, and the **Poseidon Swim Team**, 465-9198, are other options.

Spectator sports are good diversions too. Very young children often get a charge out of watching older ones play soccer, Little League baseball and other team sports. High school and college sports abound in Boulder, and pro teams are no farther away than Denver. See our Boulder Participatory, Spectator and Professional Sports chapter for further information.

Take a Class

Local recreation centers offer children's classes in everything from arts and crafts to yoga. They include one-day workshops, multiweek sessions and options in between. Gymnastics, dancing and swimming are popular. To give your toddler a head start in the cybernetic age, **Computertots** is designed to introduce preschoolers to computers, using the latest educational software. Children's and child/parent pottery classes are given at the city's **Pottery Lab**, 1010 Aurora Street, 441-3446.

The **Boulder Rock Club**, 447-2804, 2952 Baseline Road, has an indoor rock-climbing wall and a variety of children's programs. They start with RockKids — 1½ hours of climbing time for children ages 5 to 9 (available individually or for four lessons). Youth Rock (ages 9 to 12), Youth Certification (ages 12 to 17) and Youth Lead (ages 14 to 17) are multi-day sessions at various levels. **Rope World** is a seasonal rope obstacle course, sponsored by the St. Vrain Valley School District, 776-6200, in Longmont.

Flatirons Martial Arts, 444-6526, 4770 Pearl Street, and the **American School of**

Martial Arts, 516-1453, Gunbarrel Square, specialize in teaching youngsters the skills and self-discipline of karate and other martial arts. "Karate teaches kids a lot" is the American School's slogan, and Flatirons refers to it as "the art of peaceful confidence."

Northern Colorado Fencers, 3132 Valmont Road, 443-6557, boasts nationally and internationally ranked fencers who give good instruction to children, including respect for the rules and safety. Several places near town offer **horseback-riding** lessons. You can find them by checking the Yellow Pages under "Horse Rentals."

The **Boulder Parks and Recreation Program** offers cooking classes for children ages 6 to 12, such as Lasagna for a Crowd and Snacks for Sleepovers, as well as classes for teens ages 13 to 17. The **Cooking School of the Rockies**, 494-7988, in the Table Mesa Shopping Center, normally schedules Cookies 'n Kids on a Saturday in early December and a parent/child Gingerbread House Baking Class on four Sundays during November and December.

In addition to scores of music teachers specializing in various instruments, the **Suzuki Violin and Cello School**, 499-2807, specialized in string instruction for kids 3 through high school-age. **Dance West**, 545-2252, 1627 Pearl Street, offers ballet, jazz, African, hip-hop, techno tap and family dancing for youngsters of all ages. **The Studio for Performing Arts**, 422-1908, 2010 14th Street, has classes in dance, acting, music, directing and filmmaking. In addition to after-school programs, students put on an annual summer musical performance. In 1996, it was *The Wiz* at the Boulder Theater.

See a Kid Show

Take the kids so you can go. On the last Saturday of the month, October through May, CU-Boulder's own **"CU Wizard"** (actually, there are eight Mr. and Ms. Wizards), 492-5011, gives free morning lectures that pack

INSIDERS' TIP

The local recreation centers, which are open to the public for a fee, have great swimming pools, Lazy Rivers and wading areas.

science lecture halls with laughing, learning kids. The shows are from 9:30 to 10:30 AM. CU's **Science Discovery Program**, 492-7188, also offers a variety of interesting and educational classes for youngsters ages 4 to 14.

Ever heard of the American Girl dolls? Longmont's **Books for the Whole Child**, 772-6326, puts on American Girl Victorian tea parties around Christmas time. Be sure to call ahead, for spaces fill quickly. **Lois Lafond and the Rockadiles**, 444-7095, pack the kids in wherever they play with their funky, high-quality songs with kid lyrics. They appear at such events as various Halloween parades in the metro area, the Taste of Colorado in Denver, Boulder's Out to Lunch series and others. Watch for them! The **Peanut Butter Players**, 786-8727, is a group of theatrical children who perform lunchtime theater for children.

During the warm months, the buskers who perform on the Pearl Street Mall offer great family fun. **Bongo the Balloon-o-matic**, "that balloon guy on the mall," has been voted the Best Kids' Performer by *Daily Camera* readers. The **Longmont Fairgrounds**, 441-3927, has an indoor arena that is the site for horse shows, an exhibition hall that hosts events ranging from dog shows to art shows and spacious grounds that are the venue for the annual Boulder County Fair each August (see our Festivals and Annual Events chapter). The **Central City Opera**, 292-6700, puts on two children's performances (normally in late June and early August), where they explain why those actors have emotions so drenching that they just have to sing.

Other Kinds of Fun

At Longmont's **Roll-O-Rena**, 651-3720, 1201 S. Sunset Street, they still do the hokey-pokey and schedule open skate and family skate sessions. The swooping-walls in the **outdoor skateboard park** at **Scott Carpenter Park** attract hot young skaters when the weather cooperates.

Fun-N-Stuff, 442-4386, in North Boulder at the junction of Broadway and 28th Street,

Photo: Daily Camera/Cliff Grassmick

Collage Children's Museum is open to both members and the public.

has embarked on a complete make-over. They've built a new building for the video arcade and snack bar; restructured the go-cart area, miniature golf courses, batting cages and driving range; and added roller hockey and a human maze. If all goes according to plan, Fun-N-Stuff will reopen in mid-March 1997.

Laser Storm, 499-7756, 635 S. Broadway in Boulder's Table Mesa Shopping Center, and 651-6422, 700 Ken Pratt Boulevard next to the Armadillo in Longmont, offers Laser Tag, video games and other high-tech diversions.

Now for something totally different. . .

For a seasonal diversion, check out farm stands during pumpkin season, generally from September through Halloween. Children often come on school tours. The kids lure parents back on the weekends. Bring your camera!

Dexter's Family Farm's pumpkin display, 665-3969, at 95th Street and Valmont Road, has been so spectacular, Denver-metro area television stations use it to usher in the fall season. The Dexters usually build a jack-o'-lantern totem pole, straw horses and cheery scarecrows. Dexter's includes a small farm area with cows, chickens, horses and pigs.

Munson's Family Farm's Halloween Display, 443-0169, is at 75th Street and Valmont Road. Before frost hits, you and the kids can tromp into the field and twist a pumpkin off the vine. Choose giants and jack-o'-lantern pumpkins, pie pumpkins and winter squash, including Delicata, a sweet, buttery-tasting winter squash that the Munsons say they've made famous.

Summer Camps

A week or more out of the house can go a long way toward relieving the tedium of a bored child's summer. Overnight camps, day camps and camps that provide both options abound in the Boulder. Local child-care experts recommend that you go ahead and ask, "This may sound like a foolish question, but what do you do to make sure kids are safe?" Camps are great for learning about everything from computers to archery, outdoor skills to swimming.

Here is a sampling of summer camps with good reputations, along with a phone contact so you can check exact times and fees. Area newspapers publish special camp issues in spring. Talk with other parents for recommendations. Brochures available at local recreation centers and libraries are also good sources for camp information.

Co-sponsored by CU-Boulder's Science Discovery Program and Experiential Learning Associates, the well-regarded **Science Discovery Summer Camp**, 492-7188, provides five- or six-day environment-oriented experiences to Colorado wonders such as the Great Sand Dunes and Dinosaur National monuments and Cortez Cultural Center. There are local programs and overnight options. Activities include hiking, paleontology, river rafting and mountain biking. The Walker's family-run mountain camp at Gold Hill, called **Colorado Mountain Ranch**, known locally as **Trojan Ranch**, 442-4557, includes both week-long overnight sessions and day sessions with Western riding, swimming in a heated pool, Indian lore, archery, gymnastics, drama and confidence-building outdoor adventures.

Boulder Parks and Recreation, 441-3412, offers many day-camp-type options, from playground programs to a Teen Adventure Program with kayaking and overnight camping plus programs for people with disabilities. The **YMCA of Boulder Valley**, 443-4474, 2850 Mapleton Avenue, offers excursions to Denver-area fun spots, such as Waterworld, plus bike and triathlon training camps. The **Boulder Valley Community School Program**, 447-5252, run by the school district, offers all kinds of classes at various locations around town. In 1996, classes included basketball camps for boys and girls, single-track mountain biking and cartooning. The **Front Range Natural Science School** is the children's environmental education program run by the Ecological Institute, 499-3647, 5398 Manhattan Circle. It gets high marks for offering environmental educational classes that include lots of outdoor exploration. Classes are offered year round, but the summer program is the biggest. **Rainbow Valley Farm**, 651-7222, 10870 N. 49th Street in Longmont, is a low-key farm school where kids can help gather eggs and handle the sheep.

From the mountains to the plains, daytrips from Boulder offer a wealth of activities ranging from culture and history to recreation, shopping, dining and just enjoying the beautiful scenery.

Boulder

Daytrips and Weekend Getaways

From the mountains to the plains, daytrips from Boulder offer a wealth of activities ranging from culture and history to recreation, shopping, dining and just enjoying the beautiful scenery. Among the places we're sending you in this chapter are the Air Force Academy in Colorado Springs, the gambling casinos of Central City and Black Hawk, the ski resorts of Summit County and Winter Park and the museums and other attractions of Denver. We've given some history and vital information for each, along with special events, dining and shopping opportunities. Skiing; Alpine-sliding; sleigh-, hay- and horseback riding are a few popular options in the mountains. Even disabled folks can learn to ski, rock climb and take on other challenges at Winter Park, site of the National Sports Center for the Disabled. For hiking, backpacking, bicycling and cross-country skiing (and other participatory sports) also see our Participatory, Spectator and Professional Sports chapter.

Denver's Zoo, with its recently created Tropical Discovery exhibit, and the Denver Botanic Gardens, will cheer you with lush greenery and tropical creatures even during the cold winter months. Drive up Pikes Peak in the summer and you can say you've been on top of one of Colorado's "Fourteeners" — the 54 highest mountains that reach 14,000 feet or higher. Or take a leisurely sail across scenic Lake Dillon or Grand Lake.

Whatever your inclination, the area offers activities that are fun, challenging, inspirational, educational — or perhaps all of the above.

Denver

Believe it or not, Denver actually has some attractions that Boulder doesn't, though Boulderites hate to admit it. Sprawling Greater Denver can be anywhere from a half-hour to an hour or more drive from Boulder, depending on which part you visit. The attractions listed subsequently are all in the center-city area and an hour's drive or less from Boulder. It's fun to spend a day in the "big city" visiting museums, shops, restaurants or galleries or going to the Colorado Symphony or a show.

Some of Denver's top attractions are the Denver Botanic Gardens, the Denver Zoo, the Museum of Natural History, the elegant Brown Palace hotel (which serves high tea), the Denver Art Museum, Museum of Western Art and the Black American West Museum and Heritage Center. There's also good shopping on Larimer Street, the 16th Street Mall, Cherry Creek at the Tabor Center and the lavish, new Park Meadows Mall — not to mention lots of good restaurants.

If you're a parent, looking for fun activities to do with your children, make sure you see the following "Denver for Kids and the Young at Heart" section. For the complete Insiders' scoop on Denver, check out *The Insiders' Guide® to Greater Denver.*

Getting There

Take U.S. Highway 36 from Boulder to the I-25 exit. The new, improved I-25, with six lanes in some places, can be a bit intimidating for non-city drivers, and it helps to have someone else along for navigation. Once on I-25, stay to the middle/right, because some of the far right lanes are "exit only" to such places such as Denver International Airport or Limon in eastern Colorado. Follow I-25 for a few miles as it nears downtown Denver and watch for the sign for the Speer Boulevard S. exit, which comes up quickly after the sign. Take the exit and head for the tall buildings over Speer Boulevard. There are signs for the Denver Art Museum on Speer past Colfax Avenue.

Or, avoid the hassle of traffic and parking and take the RTD bus, which leaves from the RTD station in Boulder at 14th and Walnut streets (and other stops along Broadway). The bus goes to the Market Street station in downtown Denver, right at the 16th Street Mall. There are numerous trips daily. In Denver, a free shuttle takes riders up and down the 16th Street pedestrian mall. The far end of the mall (and the shuttle stop) is only a few blocks from the State Capitol and art museum. For RTD route and schedule information, call 299-6000. A one-way ticket to Denver is $2.50.

In Denver, RTD runs a **Cultural Connection Trolley** from early May until early September that stops every half-hour at or near Denver's cultural attractions and sights downtown. It runs daily from 9:30 AM to 6:23 PM. A $3 pass allows riders to get on and off as often as they like. Buy tickets and pick up a map at an RTD station (including Boulder's) or the bus itself. Another option is a guided tour on an authentic London Double Decker Bus. The tours last two hours and 15 minutes and cost $8 for adults and $4 for children ages 3 to 11 (children younger than 3 are free). The tours run Wednesdays through Sundays, summer only, and have five different pickup points, including the Oxford Hotel and City Park. Call **Double Decker Tours**, 292-5055, for times and locations.

To get to the Denver Zoo and the Denver Museum of Natural History by car, take I-25 to I-70 eastbound. Follow I-70 to the Colorado Boulevard exit, then proceed south on Colorado Boulevard for 2 miles to 23rd Avenue and turn right. The zoo is on 23rd Avenue

between Colorado Boulevard and York Street (look for signs). The museum is nearby in City Park at Colorado Boulevard and Montview.

To get to the museum from downtown Denver by car, go east on 17th Street (which eventually becomes E. 17th Avenue) and turn left (north) on Colorado Boulevard. Look for signs for the museum and the zoo.

For the Denver Botanic Gardens, from downtown take 14th Street east to York Street, turn right on York (south) and go four blocks; free parking is on the left, and the gardens are on the right.

To reach the Black American West Museum and Heritage Center, go northeast on Stout Street (a block over from California Street) from downtown Denver out to 31st Street.

FYI

Unless otherwise noted, the area code for all phone numbers in this guide is 303.

Attractions

The **Denver Art Museum**, 640-2793, has one of the best and most extensive collections of Native American crafts in the United States plus works of Picasso, Georges Braque, Matisse, Frederic Remington, Winslow Homer, Thomas Hart Benton and many others. You'll find a nice cafeteria and gift shop as well. The museum is at 100 W. 14th Avenue, not too far from the State Capitol. Look for the distinctive castle-like silhouette of cutout geometric shapes. Hours are 10 AM to 5 PM Tuesday through Saturday (10 AM to 8 PM Wednesday) and noon to 5 PM Sunday (closed Monday and major holidays). Admission is $3 for adults; $1.50 for seniors and students; free for museum members and children younger than 6. Admission is free for everyone on Saturday.

The **Denver Museum of Natural History**, 322-7009, at 2001 Colorado Boulevard, is open daily from 9 AM to 5 PM, except Friday when the museum is open until 9 PM. Prehistoric Journey, a new dinosaur exhibit popular with kids, is open to the public (during the school year) from noon until 5 PM Monday through Thursday, from noon to 9 PM on Friday and from 9 AM to 5 PM on weekends. During summer Prehistoric Journey is open to the public during normal operating hours. Besides dino-

They grunt, scream and scratch themselves. No, it's not the NFL.

Primate Panorama

7 lush acres • 9 years in the making • One big hairy place

denver ZOO

OPEN EVERY DAY

saurs, the museum features exhibits of Colorado's birds and animals and a fantastic collection of natural history exhibits and dioramas. From time to time the museum also hosts spectacular world-traveling exhibitions such as "Ramses II" and "Aztec." The **IMAX Theater**, with its four-story-tall screen, shows all types of educational and entertaining movies. Admission to the museum is $4.50 for adults; $2.50 for children ages 4 to 12 and seniors older than 65. IMAX shows cost $5 for adults and $4 children ages 4 through 12 and seniors older than 65. Shows start daily at 11 AM; call for the schedule.

The "Primate Panorama" exhibit is the newest attraction at the **Denver Zoo**, 331-4110 or 331-4100, 23rd and Colorado streets. This $10 million exhibit opened in late 1993 and was designed to re-create a rain forest habitat inside a glass-enclosed pyramid. It contains more than 240 animal species and nearly doubled the zoo's animal population. Zoo hours are 9 AM to 6 PM daily in summer, 10 AM to 5 PM daily in winter. Some exhibits close

earlier. Admission is $6 for adults; $3 for seniors (62 and older) and children ages 4 to 12; free for children 3 and younger. Call for free days for Colorado residents. The zoo's cafeteria serves light meals and snacks.

Enjoy 23 outdoor acres full of beautiful flowers, trees and shrubs, including a Japanese garden and an alpine rock garden, at the **Denver Botanic Gardens**, 331-4000, 1005 York Street, 10 minutes east of downtown Denver. You'll find an indoor conservatory with special tropical and orchid areas plus a library and gift shop. There's increasing focus on Japanese-style designs, native prairie areas and rock gardens. The curator of the Rock Alpine garden, Panayoti Kelaidis, is a Boulder native who has gained a national reputation for his daring eye and superb plant knowledge. For anyone who wants to learn what grows beautifully in this climate, the Botanic Gardens is a required stop. Although most visitors choose the brilliant summer flowers, winter, Colorado's longest season, is a good time to visit — especially to experience the 50-foot-tall tropical forest. For anyone with the winter blues, this lung-full of Hawaii is a sure cure — even if temporary. Hours are 9 AM to 8 PM Saturday through Tuesday; 9 AM to 5 PM Wednesday through Friday. Admission is $4 for adults; $2 for children ages 6 to 15 and for seniors older than 65 (also for students with IDs). Children younger than 6 are free.

The **Museum of Western Art**, 296-1880, 1727 Tremont Place, is downtown right across from the Brown Palace. Housed in the small museum are three stories of works by well-known artists who portrayed the West in various media. Among them are Frederic Remington, Grant Wood, Albert Bierstadt, Thomas Moran, Ernest Blumenschein and Charles Russell. There's a small gift shop that sells jewelry, note cards, prints and postcards and a bookstore with art books on the American West, including rare and new books with editions signed by the authors. Museum hours are 10 AM to 4:30 PM Tuesday through Saturday. Admission is $3 for adults and $2 for students, seniors and children 7 and older (children younger than 7 are free).

Blacks played an important role in the settling of the West, and documentation at the **Black American West Museum and Heritage Center**, 292-2566, 3091 California Street, shows that roughly a third of the West's cowboys were black. There were also many black businessmen, miners, pioneer doctors, politicians, soldiers and teachers — a fact that historians have generally overlooked. At this museum, numerous photos and displays retell the role of blacks as early settlers in Denver and Colorado. Every six months there's a changing exhibit with such subjects as the history of jazz in Denver or black churches in Denver. Summer hours are from 10 AM to 5 PM Monday through Friday and weekends from noon to 5 PM; winter hours are 10 AM to 2 PM Wednesday through Friday and weekends from noon to 5 PM Saturday, and 2 to 5 PM Sunday. Admission is $3 for adults; $2 for seniors; $1 for youths ages 12 to 17; and 50¢

for children ages 3 to 12 (children younger than 3 are free).

Restaurants

On the 1400 block of Larimer Street and along the 16th Street Mall, a potpourri of restaurants offer ethnic foods, sidewalk cafes and lots of ambiance. The **Little Russian Cafe**, 595-8600, in Larimer Square serves such hearty peasant fare as dumplings, stuffed cabbage, borscht and apple strudel. The cafe serves lunch and dinner Monday through Friday; dinner only on Saturday and Sunday. Tucked in the center of Writers Square (across 15th Street from Larimer Square), **La Bonne Soupe**, 595-9169, is a charming stop — either the sidewalk cafe or indoor restaurant — for a simple but well-presented lunch of soup, salad, bread and wine for $7 or an interesting assortment of omelettes, crepes and appetizers such as crab cakes dijonaise and baked brie. The restaurant also serves dinners of filet mignon, seafood and other choices followed by such tempting desserts as chocolate fondue. Around the corner near Starbuck's Coffee, the **Cadillac Ranch**, 820-2288, 1400 Larimer Street, offers such trendy but tasty fare as chipotle-honey-glazed pork chops, a meat-hater's plate with creamy shiitake polenta and applewood grilled vegetables and grilled Portobello mushrooms. Open for lunch and dinner daily, it also serves brunch on weekends. Across the street, **Josephina's**, 623-0166, is a favorite stop for Italian food. **McCormick's Fish House & Bar**, 825-1107, on the corner of 17th and Wazee streets, serves breakfast, lunch and dinner daily, with special weekend brunch on Saturday and Sunday. Both Josephina's and McCormick's are relatively expensive.

Not far from Larimer Square, the **Wynkoop Brewing Co.**, 297-2700, at 1634 18th Street, provides an interesting dining and drinking experience. This was Denver's first brewpub, founded in 1988, and it's housed in an historic

INSIDERS' TIP

Central City's Thomas House is one of the most well-preserved turn-of-the-century buildings you will ever see. Even the spices in the kitchen are authentic.

19th-century building. Though the Wynkoop can be a bit noisy, crowded and smoky, the choice of ales and pub fare at reasonable prices and the lively atmosphere more than compensate. It's open daily for lunch and dinner.

About four or five blocks from the Denver Art Museum (at 13th and Bannock streets) **Racine's**, 595-0418, at 850 Bannock Street, is for desert lovers. Racine's has its own in-house bakery and is known for its great brownies, carrot cake and muffins. Besides sweets, a wide range of meal offerings includes pastas, Mexican entrees and sandwiches. Friendly and inexpensive, Racine's offers something for everyone, serving breakfast, lunch and dinner daily.

You'll have to travel a bit to find restaurants after visiting the Zoo or Botanic Gardens — there are none in walking distance. From the Botanic Gardens go west on 17th Street and west of University Boulevard, to find eateries. (Travel west on 18th Street, however, and backtrack, because 17th Street is one-way east.)

Accommodations

Since Boulder is so close to Denver, most people just visit for the day. But should you decide to have a little Denver holiday, many downtown hotels have special weekend-getaway packages. Call the Colorado Hotel and Lodging Association reservations service line at (800) 777-6880 for information.

The recently renovated **Brown Palace**, 297-3111, at 321 17th Street, is Denver's most famous hotel and is quite elegant and expensive, starting at $185 for a standard room, $195 for a superior and $205 for deluxe per night, single or double occupancy. Suites range from $245 to $725. The hotel has three restaurants: **Elyngton's** and **The Ship Tavern** are casual; **The Palace Arms** is an acclaimed formal dining room. **Churchill's**, a newly opened cigar lounge, serves cocktails, as does The Ship Tavern and the lobby. Lunch and noon and afternoon tea are also served in the beautiful Victorian-style lobby. A favorite bed and breakfast is the **Queen Anne Inn**, 296-6666, 2147 Tremont Place. Just north of downtown in a historic neighborhood, the inn occupies two adjacent Victorian buildings, built in 1879 and

1886 in the Queen Anne-style of architecture. Single rooms are in the $85 to $165 range. The inn is popular with honeymooners and for weddings.

Shopping

Historic **Larimer Square** at Larimer and 15th streets, is packed full of upscale clothing boutiques, art galleries, cafes and other shops. **Writer's Square** is across 15th Street from Larimer Square and has such shops as The Creative Cook, Colorado Peddler, Bennetton, Merle Norman and Avant-Card for unusual greeting cards. Along the **16th Street Mall** are such popular shops as Banana Republic and Anne Taylor. The greenhouse-like **Tabor Center** at the 16th Street Mall's north end houses such fun places as The Kite Store, Tie 1 On (a creative necktie shop), Flag World, African House (arts and handicrafts), It's Your Move (game store) and miscellaneous clothing and other shops.

Denver for Kids and the Young at Heart

Attractions

On the Road to Denver . . .

You could fill several days by picking attractions on the way to Denver. In summer, choose **Water World**, 427-7873, at 88th and Pecos streets. The 60 acres of water rides and 32 attractions make it America's largest family water park. *USA Today* rated its Voyage to the Center of the Earth as one of America's top 10 attractions. To get there, take U.S. Highway 36 to the Pecos exit, close to Denver. Turn north (left) and drive until you see those blue canopies on the hilltop. Water World offers several safe introductions to whitewater rafting. For those missing surf, Water World's big wave pools make plenty. Add an entertaining wading area for tots and grade-schoolers plus many theme rides. Beach Boys music bops from the loudspeakers. A day of splashing costs $16.95 for adults and $15.95 for children ages 4 to 12. Seniors (60 and older) and tots (3 and younger) are free; half-day rates are offered. Water World is open daily from 10 AM to 6 PM, weather permitting, and accepts major credit cards, but no personal checks.

Lakeside Amusement Park, 477-1621, 4601 Sheridan, opened in 1908. The miniature train still circles the lake, powered by a 1903 steam engine. That tortuous, twisty white skeleton marks the 90-foot-tall Cyclone. This ride seems like 3,000 knuckle-white lifetimes, but actually takes only 2½ minutes. The Cyclone's rated one of the top five roller coasters by American Coaster Enthusiasts and is one of only a few wooden roller coasters left in the country. Lakeside opens during the week at 1 PM for kiddie rides and the major rides open at 6 PM, closing at 11 PM. On weekends the whole park is open from noon to 11 PM, from May through Labor Day. Unlimited rides cost $9.75 during the week and $11.25 on weekends, but if you're just riding the bench, it's $1.50 (children 2 and younger are free).

The **Arvada Center for the Arts and Humanities**, 431-3939, 6901 Wadsworth Boulevard, offers participatory fairy tale theater for children many weekday mornings and some Saturdays. Kids are often invited to come on stage to join the acting. Tickets cost around $4 during the week and $5 on Saturdays; summer shows, $3. The evening adult dramas and concerts, which cost from $15 to $24, are excellent, and the free museum has art and cultural displays.

Casa Bonita, 232-5115, 6715 W. Colfax Avenue, is the first, favorite dining experience for many youngsters. Your food generally costs less than $10; children 12 and younger eat for less than $5. The Mexican food is passable, the donut-sweet sopapillas are tasty, but the main draw is entertainment. At the indoor lagoon, a dramatic troupe presents plays that usually end with heavily costumed actors splash-landing in the pool. A dark cave maze is popular for hide-and-seek, and troubadours wander among the tables singing "Happy Birthday" when requested. The experience is hokey beyond belief and adored by children.

Downtown Denver

Any kid who likes money will love the **Denver Mint**, 844-3582, 320 W. Colfax Avenue between Delaware and Cherokee streets (tour entrance on Cherokee). It began when Coloradans made their own money. In those days, real U.S. currency was hard to find this far west, and locals tired of weighing gold dust to exchange for food. Later, this private enterprise became an official U.S. mint. Teeth-rattlingly loud machines stamp coins from sheet metals. People hush as they pass a safe displaying 27.5 pounds of gold in a half-dozen 400 Troy-ounce gold bars. The bars are surprisingly small, like $3 bars of good chocolate in shiny yellow wrappers. They're a fraction of Denver's gold, which is one of three stashes nationwide (West Point and Fort Knox are the other two). Free, 15-minute tours take place weekdays from 8 AM to 2:45 PM on a first-come, first-served basis. Tour slots fill quickly during the summer, so it's best to go get your ticket by mid-morning. The coin sales area operates during the same hours as the tours and is accessible only by taking the tour. The mint is closed on weekends and holidays.

Rent the movie *The Unsinkable Molly Brown*, starring Debbie Reynolds, then tour the **Molly Brown House**, 832-4092, 1340 Pennsylvania Street. It's just a few blocks from Denver's gold-domed Capitol building. Molly Brown was a diamond in the rough whose husband made a gold strike. Denver society snubbed Molly, but she became a heroine when the *Titanic* sank in the freezing North Atlantic. Molly was on board that fateful day, and she saved many by pulling them into her lifeboat. Her mansion is 10,000 square feet of Victoriana. It's open from 10 AM to 4 PM Mondays through Saturdays and from noon to 4 PM Sundays (closed Mondays from September through May). The history-filled 45-minute guided tour is $5 for adults, $3.50 for seniors 65 and older and $1.50 for children ages 6 through 12. (See this chapter's Close-up for more information about Molly Brown.)

Art museums generally aren't for kids (as our description earlier in this chapter might suggest), but the **Denver Art Museum**, 640-2793, 100 W. 14th Avenue, is an exception. From the fantasy fortress facade outside to the hands-on displays, kids' corner and videotape nooks inside, kids may be intrigued enough to look around with you. However, kids are still kids. Count on an hour, maybe 90 minutes, with the kids in tow. The museum is

Photo: Randy Amys

Breckenridge is a former host of the American International Snow Sculpture Championships.

open Tuesday through Saturday (closed Mondays) from 10 AM to 5 PM and Sundays from noon to 5 PM. The entrance fee is $3 for adults; $1.50 for students and seniors; free for kids younger than 6; free for everyone on Saturdays.

West of Downtown, Near I-25

Elitch Gardens Amusement Park, 595-4386, is in such an easy-to-find location, it doesn't have a street address. To get there, take I-25 to Speer Boulevard S. and head for the roller coasters. This is Denver's oldest and grandest amusement park, in a brand-new location near lower downtown Denver. Families can enjoy the live restaurant entertainment and the progression from kiddie rides to hair-raising ones.

The new location lacks the 100-year-old trees and turn-of-the century elegance of the old park, but with 67 acres, it's more than twice the size of the old park. The 1925 carousel with wooden horses is there. Twister, the famous wooden roller coaster, has been rebuilt, which relieves most parents, because although the old roller coaster was safe, sometimes you wanted to take a hammer on the ride and

whack in a few extra nails. Like the old Twister, the new one is listed as one of the top five or six in the country, according to American Coaster Enthusiasts. The famous landscaping is starting fresh, with formal gardens, shade areas and several thousand young trees that someday will grow statuesque. Elitch's is open 10 AM to 10 PM daily in the summer except for Friday and Saturday, when it stays open until 11 PM. Unlimited ride entry fee is $19.95 for ages 8 to adult; $9.95 for ages 5 to 7; $7.75 for 3- to 4-year-olds; and free for kids 2 and younger or adults 70 or older.

Near Elitch's, a square green building seems to wear a burgundy, pyramid cap. This is the **Children's Museum**, 433-7433, 2121 Crescent Drive. The hands-on museum offers changing exhibits such as a science lab and King Soopers grocery store. New this year is an exhibit on water pollution entitled, "We All Live Downstream." The museum is open daily from 10 AM to 5 PM. Entry fee is $4 for ages 2 to 59 and $1.50 for adults 60 and older. Children younger than 2 are free. Admission is free the first Friday of every month. Call for show and schedule information for the Children's Theatre.

The **Forney Transportation Museum**, 433-3643, 1416 Platte Street, is a huge, musty place that once housed the power station for the Denver streetcar system. The 50-foot-high building is full of antique cars, buggies and trains. The largest steam engine in the world, *Big Boy*, is here. The famous woman pilot, Amelia Earhart, drove the Gold Bug Kissel roadster. The basement has a great setup run by the Denver area N-scale model train club. There's also a gift shop. The museum is open 9 AM to 5 PM Monday through Saturday in summer and 11 AM to 5 PM Sundays, and it opens an hour later in the winter. There's a $4 entrance fee for adults; $2 for ages 12 to 18; $1 for ages 5 to 11; and free for kids younger than 5). It's open daily except holidays.

Sports events can make a special occasion, with or without kids. **Mile High Stadium**, 458-4848, 2755 W. 17th Avenue, is where the Broncos battle other National Football League teams, and often practically every seat in the 76,123-seat stadium is occupied. It's very hard to get good tickets to a game. So if someone offers you one, make them a friend for life. **McNichols Sports Arena**, 640-7300, 1635 Bryant Street, is a covered arena where the Denver Nuggets basketball stars play. The National Hockey League's Colorado Avalanche — the 1996 Stanley Cup champions — call Denver home. Thousands of fans watched on a huge TV screen at McNichols as the Colorado Avalanche won its final game in Miami for a four-in-a-row sweep — winning the first-ever major national championship for a Denver team. The International Hockey League team, the Denver Grizzlies, have played here too, winning the 1995 Turner Champions Cup. Mile High and McNichols are easy to reach. They're just off I-25, Exit 210B, near Speer Boulevard, on the west side — the Boulder side — of the highway.

Coors Field, 292-0200, at 20th and Blake streets, is home to the Colorado Rockies. The 50,000-seat stadium is extraordinarily detailed, down to 40 plate-size blue columbines on the exterior. (Columbines are Colorado's state flower.) From I-25, take the Park Avenue W. exit to reach the stadium. A ball game with kids is delightful here. They love the hot dogs, pizza, sodas and snacks. You can find Rocky Mountain Oysters for sale too. Those are fried bull testicles, in case you're munching one right now and wondering what you just ate. Rockies Andres Galarraga, Dante Bichette and Larry Walker often hit home runs, and the mascot, Dinger the Purple Dinosaur, is always performing antics somewhere. Obviously, baseball is not just for kids. We know one guy who takes a first date to the ball game. If the chemistry's dynamite, there's plenty of time for getting acquainted. If things just don't click, suddenly, he can get very, very interested in the game. Naturally, if it's a great game, they grow interested together. You get the idea. The Rockies still have the "Rockpile," where you can come on game day and buy tickets for kids or seniors at $1 each or for adults for $4. Tickets in advance are generally $5 to $16; call (800) 388-7625.

East of Downtown . . .

When you reach Denver, you'll find many child/adult attractions about 10 minutes east of downtown. We've discussed the addresses, hours and fees of these in the previous section on Denver attractions for adults. Here's some detail about them from a kid's point of view.

With 23 lovingly landscaped acres, the **Denver Botanic Gardens** has room for serious gardeners and kids who need to frolic.

At the **Denver Zoo**, the Tropical Discovery and Bird World buildings are full of animals that would need overcoats out in a Colorado December. The polar bears and sea lions make any summer day seem cooler. They're liveliest when you're viewing them from underwater portholes. The old giraffe with his fading spots is fun all year, especially compared to younger long-necks with their crisp brown and white patches.

Next to the zoo is the huge **Museum of Natural History**. No running on the escalators. Just follow the crowd toward the Hall of Life and the wonderful mineral displays. They include twinkling gems, gold-filled boulders and a quirky series of statuettes, all made of different colored stones. We grownups talk the kids into lingering in the Explore Colorado Hall, which has beautiful renditions of Colorado's prairie and alpine forest. Changing exhibits always pack in people.

While at the museum, enjoy the **IMAX Theater**, with 30 speakers to help the sound track thunder into your solar plexus while you watch cliff-hangers about sharks, volcanoes and other wonders.

Shopping and Dining in Denver with Your Kids

We suggest the following plan for happy family shopping: kid store, grown-up store, grown-up store, snack. Grown-up store, kid store, grown-up store, snack.

Denver's premier shopping area is east on Speer Boulevard at Cherry Creek. Here, following our suggested order, you might go to **The Wizard's Chest**, 321-4304, 230 Fillmore Street, then grown-up store, grown-up store, frozen yogurt. Grown-up store, **Warner Bros. Studio Store**, 321-7747, 3000 E. First Avenue, on the second floor of the Cherry Creek Shopping Mall, then grown-up store, **Kazoo and Company**, 322-0973, (there's another, larger store on 2930 E. Second Avenue) then snack. If your kids balk, at any time, substitute the **Tattered Cover Bookstore**, 322-7727, 2955 E. First Avenue. This is Denver's biggest bookstore, and the lower level has a comfortable reading sofa where older kids can peruse books while you browse. If you're double-teaming your kids, one of you can read with them while the other wanders happily away.

Downtown shopping is most fun around the Tabor Center, Larimer Square and LoDo (pronounced low-dough) . . . lower downtown. Here, the kid shopping formula becomes, **Rascals Toys**, 628-7779, 1201 16th Street at the Tabor Center, grown-up store, grown-up store, fresh-baked cookie. Grown-up store, **Union Station Gift Shop**, 534-1012. (It's a chance to look at Union Station and real railroad paraphernalia, and it's open daily from 6 AM until 1

PM and from 6:30 PM until the train comes in, which can be as late as 10:30 PM.) If the kids grow weary, at any time, zip over to Forney's, the Children's Museum or Elitch Gardens. Or substitute shooting pool at one of the new upscale pool halls along Wazee Street. Nothing like a round of snooker, with a stiff cold glass of Shirley Temple at your elbow.

It's not hard to find places to eat with kids. Most shopping areas have casual eateries. Our favorite kid-dining spot (besides **Casa Bonita**, see the previous listing) is **Healthy Habits**, 733-2105, 865 S. Colorado Boulevard. Other top choices are Asian restaurants and pizza parlors. The food court in the Tabor Center, back downtown by Larimer Square, offers pizza, Mexican food, a Vietnamese Kitchen, Burger King, Mrs. Field's cookies, a shop that sells giant cinnamon rolls and many other choices.

As for accommodations, even a rollicking tot might enjoy the turn-of-the-century elegance of the **Brown Palace** (see the previous listing). However, it might not enjoy them back. Head to Boulder and the mountains. If you want to stay overnight in Denver, you're seeking an evening without youngsters. Check the previous section on Denver for ideas.

Colorado Springs

Getting There

Just two hours south of Boulder is Colorado Springs. To get there, take I-25 through Denver, and keep going south through the pretty rolling Foothills until you're at the foot of Pikes Peak mountain and Colorado Springs. Try to avoid Denver rush hour, which can add a half-hour to the trip. If you squeak through Denver on weekends or when the traffic is lightest, some commuters who nudge the speed a bit say you can slip into town in less than two hours.

History

Top attractions in Colorado Springs are the Colorado Air Force Academy, Cave of the Winds, the Cheyenne Mountain Zoo, Garden of the Gods and the Broadmoor Hotel. For quick, up-to-date information on the area, call (719) 635-7506 or (800) DOVISIT. We'll tell you about these many special attractions next. But first, some perspectives from the past.

Way back before 1900, the Denver Rio Grande railroad needed communities near the remote Colorado Foothills in order to profit from buying and selling goods along its train route. In 1871, it backed the Fountain Colony, with 150 buildings and 800 residents. The promoter, Gen. William Jackson Palmer, wanted a genteel, well-bred crowd, so he advertised "villa sites" to wealthy English compatriots. Thus began a community that would grow into Colorado's second-largest city, Colorado Springs, with nearly a half-million people.

One Englander said the brand-new community was a "very high-toned sort of new town" run by a "very tony company on teetotal lines." It was a tourist attraction and resort health spa for wealthy tuberculars, known as lungies.

Colorado Springs has gracefully reached much of its potential. But 100 years ago, early settlers who had been assured they were moving to tree-lined avenues and fenced English farmlands got a big surprise when they saw the windswept plain. One irate Englishman, stepping out of his train in a March snowstorm, huffed in a furious, highbrowed Edwardian "haccent," "And h'is this the H'italian climate of H'america?"

The resort town diversified into many other businesses. Tourism, defense and high-tech are big employers. NORAD is dug deep into hollowed-out Cheyenne Mountain. It stands for **North American Air Defense Command**, (719) 474-2241. Tours of NORAD often fill six months ahead of time, so call early, (719) 474-2238 or 474-2239, for reservations. **Fort Carson**, an active military post, is at (719) 526-5811. The **Winter Olympic Training Center** is at (719) 578-4618. Excellent colleges include the **Air Force Academy**, **Colorado College** and the **University of Colorado at Colorado Springs**.

Colorado Springs and Boulder share similar aspirations of being well-planned, beautiful, wealthy utopian communities. But if you could imagine social values as the pendulum of a great clock, then Boulder's liberal outlook would pull the pendulum left. Swing right, and you have the conservative outlook of Colorado Springs. This typecasting isn't clear-cut. But it's a fair comparison that shows over time. For instance, Boulder opposed Amendment 2, which Boulder residents viewed as a hate vote against homosexuals. A Colorado Springs group called Coloradans for Family Values initiated that amendment. While many of the values they recommend earn praise by focusing attention on family responsibility, this coalition also has raised concerns because of their hostility to homosexuals and a growing demand to include Christian doctrine in public schools.

Attractions

Colorado's leading man-made attraction is the **Air Force Academy** at the base of Rampart Range, just off I-25 north of the city at Exit 156B. The Visitors Center, (719) 472-2555, is open 9 AM to 6 PM daily in the summertime. It closes an hour earlier the rest of the year. More than 4,000 men and women cadets train at the Academy to become astronauts, crack pilots, engineers, scientists and tactical leaders. The campus includes 143 acres of athletic fields, a 2,500-seat ice rink and a 6,000-seat basketball arena. Even though the Air Force Academy is a smaller school than CU-Boulder, the Falcon Football team is stiff competition for opponents. What's more, the setting is memorable. More than 18,000 acres are a wilderness refuge, thick with Colorado's scrubby native oak, Gambel's Oak, pine trees and other native plants.

When the campus was born in 1954, 340 architectural firms competed to design the buildings. Skidmore, Owings and Merrill Architects and Engineers, out of Chicago, won. Their modern ideas stunned Congress. The chapel was described as an "accordion." That seems funny today, when most people consider that chapel a masterpiece. Overall, the buildings are as crisp as their crew-cut era. But their futuristic tone might make them appropriate for *Star Trek's* Star Fleet Academy too.

The Visitors Center displays spacesuits of graduates and shows free 14-minute info-movies every half-hour. Cadets lead a free campus tour. What will catch your eye during this tour depends on your point of view. We were here once with Spanish college women, and it's not clear how much of the botanical scenery and campus history they noticed. They seemed more interested in the human scenery . . . those handsome Air Force men.

The crown jewel is the chapel, with 17 gleaming aluminum spires that rise 99 feet into the clear blue sky. Ribbons of stained glass separate each spire and create a rainbow of color inside. The arrangement inside says something about the '60s world view of American religion. The Protestant chapel on the main floor seats 1,200. The Catholic chapel, seating 500, is on the lower level, and in the back is a 100-seat Jewish worship area with a non-denominational area behind. Generally, chapel hours are 9 AM to 5 PM Monday through Saturday and 1 to 5 PM Sundays (in summer, 8 AM to 6 PM Monday through Saturday and 1 to 6 PM Sundays). You can attend Sunday services at 9 and 11 AM. But it occasionally closes for special services, such as funerals and weddings — and there are a lot of cadet weddings. For an up-to-date schedule, call (719) 472-4515.

Garden of the Gods, (719) 634-6666, off of I-25, is a pleasant stop. Take Exit 146 and continue west until it dead-ends. Then take a left on 30th Street. The park is open 5 AM until 11 PM daily; the visitors center is open 8 AM to 9 PM in the summer, with shorter winter hours. This drive-through garden has 2.5 square miles of eroded red rocks that are remnants of ancient mountain ranges. The highest rock is 350 feet high, and the strange natural "sculptures" include formations known as Kissing Camels and Balancing Rock.

Cave of the Winds, (719) 685-5444, west of the city on U.S. Highway 24 W. in Manitou Springs, offers 45-minute tours. It's open 9 AM to 9 PM daily in summer; otherwise, 10 AM to 5 PM. More than 200,000 people a year choose the standard tour, which costs $10 for adults and $5 for kids older than 6. Or, dress in clothing you won't mind getting muddy, bring a flashlight and join the Explorers Trip, where an experienced guide goes climbing and crawling with you into danker, darker, mysterious places. The Explorers Trip lasts three to four hours, costs $60, requires reservations and depends on a strong confidence that you won't get claustrophobic.

For those who get flutter-nerved just thinking of that Explorers Trip, relax. The regular tour probes caves just deep and narrow enough to feel a little creepy sometimes, but they're perfectly safe. In some areas, tourgoers walk single file, but most corridors open into large cave rooms wondrously lit to show

Children celebrate the holidays during the Lighting of Breckenridge, held every December in Breckenridge, Colorado.

Photo: Carl Scofield

off the stalactites hanging from the ceiling and the stalagmites growing, century by century, from the floor. Hokey lighted areas get dumb names from the guides. In one spot, the crusty gray rock has been rubbed smooth by the oil from millions of human hands, revealing a honeyed glow like alabaster. When you read tales about dwarves, it's easier to imagine that the little folks polished their beloved caves to just such a sheen.

Another home for dwarves . . . and elves . . . and reindeer, is **Santa's Workshop at the North Pole**. If you thought the North Pole was a few thousand miles away, here are new directions. Take U.S. Highway 24 for 10 miles west of Colorado Springs to the workshop, (719) 684-9432. It's open in the summer from 9:30 AM to 6 PM daily. Weather permitting, it's open in the fall from 10 AM to 5 PM, except for Wednesdays and Thursdays. Generally, it stays open through Christmas Eve. This sweet little amusement park has 24 dearly safe rides for little kids, a full-size Ferris wheel (the 7,500-foot altitude makes it the highest wheel in the world), and a colorful cottage in which Santa Claus waits in his rocking chair. Kids can have their picture taken with truly plump Santa, whose curly white beard is real. In summer, he often wears knickers with suspenders and a colorful shirt, or red trousers and boots with a colorful shirt. When it gets cold, Santa dons his red jacket. The cost for unlimited rides here is $8.50 per person; $3.95 for seniors; and free for kids younger than 2.

Cheyenne Mountain Zoo, (719) 475-9555, is west of the Broadmoor Hotel on Cheyenne Mountain Highway. This is one of the largest privately owned zoos in the nation. It started in 1938 as Spencer Penrose's own collection and grew from there (Penrose built the Broadmoor Hotel). From I-25, take Exit 138 west to the Broadmoor, then turn right and follow the signs. More than 145 species are at the 75-acre zoo. Perhaps the 6,800-foot altitude invigorates the animals. Maybe it's the generally spacious pens. Whatever, the zoo is known for babies, including endangered species, such as tiny, beautiful, golden tamarind monkeys, black rhinos, red pandas, snow leop-

FYI

Unless otherwise noted, the area code for all phone numbers in this guide is 303.

ards and Andean condors. The most popular animal is the African elephant, followed by the orangutans in their large climbing area. The zoo's open 9 AM to 5 PM daily in the summer and to 4 PM the rest of the year. Admission is $6.50 for adults; $5.50 for ages 12 to 17 and 64 and older; $3.50 for children ages 3 to 11. The entrance fee also gives you access to the Will Rogers Shrine of the Sun and beautiful vistas.

The **Pikes Peak Highway** starts 12 miles west of Colorado Springs on U.S. Highway 24. Generally it's open May through November, and it's a long, slow way up, with many hairpin turns. A more direct route is the **Pikes Peak Cog Railway**, which starts at 515 Ruxton Avenue in Manitou Springs, (719) 685-5401. To get there, take U.S. Highway 24 to the Manitou exit. Go west on Manitou Avenue to Ruxton Avenue and turn left. In addition to wheels and tracks, a cog train has a center cog gear that pulls the train up the mountain, useful against slipping in steep spots. Since 1891, the bright-red train cars have made the three-hour round trip by following Ruxton Creek through aspen and Englemann spruce forests of Pikes Peak. At 11,578 feet, trees shrink to ground-huggers that might take 100 years to grow an inch. Here, you might spy yellow-bellied marmots. The 14,110-foot Pikes Peak is a boulder-strewn, windswept summit. Take a jacket, even if the temperature in Colorado Springs was more than 90 degrees. And stop at the Summit House, which has been selling delicious donuts and hot chocolate since the turn of the century. Daily trains in summer depart at 8 AM, then every hour and 20 minutes after that, with the last train at 5:20 PM. Tickets cost $21 for adults; $9.50 for children ages 5 to 11 (July 1 to August 15: $22 and $10). Younger children are free if they ride on your lap.

Restaurants

All the prices listed below are the average cost of a lunch or dinner for two, excluding drinks, appetizers, desserts, tax and tip. **The Broadmoor's** many fine restaurants are described under the Broadmoor Hotel, in the next section on accommodations. Other Colorado Springs choices include **The Peppertree**, (719) 471-4888, 888 W. Marino Avenue, which prepares a pepper steak flamed with brandy at your table. The atmosphere is very romantic, on top of a hill with a view of the city. The average price of dinner for two is $36. The **Dale Street Cafe**, (719)578-9898, 115 E. Dale Street, is a former Victorian home. It offers Southern French and Northern Italian cooking, including homemade pizzas, pastas, soups, salads and desserts. Two can dine for around $15. At **Anthony's**, (719)471-3654, 1919 E. Boulder Avenue, the pasta is made fresh on the premises. You'll be tempted by the chicken marsala and seafood pasta. Two meals average around $20. There's also a Sunday champagne brunch from 10 AM to 2 PM. Kids like **Giuseppe's Depot**, (719)635-3111, 10 S. Sierra Madre. Ribs, steak, chicken, spaghetti, pizza and a children's menu are here. This is an old railroad station that has been converted into a restaurant. You can see freight trains go by, and the mountain range too. About $22 covers two diners.

La Casita, 633-9616, is at 1331 S. Nevada Avenue, right next to I-25. This pink stucco restaurant has great personality, down to the black velvet paintings, metalwork frames and murals of tropical birds. Beer-soaked barracho beans, known as drunken beans, are a house specialty. Try chicken or beef fajitas and menudo. Two can easily dine for about $12.

Manitou Springs is a cute community just west of Colorado Springs with lots of good restaurants. The **Briarhurst Manor Inn**, (719)685-1864, at 404 Manitou Avenue, offers rack of lamb, Châteaubriand and trout. The steak tartare and alligator pears (an avocado stuffed with crabmeat and served with a special sauce) are great appetizers. This 115-year-old mansion has eight different dining areas. A couple can dine here for around $50. The **Craftwood Inn**, (719)685-9000, 404 El Paso Boulevard in Manitou Springs, is another mansion, built in 1908. Regional Colorado cuisine includes venison, antelope and wild boar. Each of the seven vegetables served with the meal is cooked separately to perfection then combined in a colorful medley. Entrees usually are served with wild rice or fluffy quinoa. The aver-

age price for two is $38. The **Mission Bell Inn**, (719)685-9089, 178 Crystal Park Road, has good Mexican food. The specialty is green chile with pork. Burritos come stuffed with green chile, and flautas are rolled with beef and onions then baked with red chile. Two dinners, excluding extras, will run about $16.

Accommodations

Colorado Springs accommodations are intertwined with attractions. Read this section, even if you're not planning to stay overnight. If you decide to stay, these places take Visa and MasterCard.

For old-world elegance, check the **Broadmoor Hotel**, (719) 634-7711 or (800) 634-7711, 1 Lake Circle. To get there, take Exit 138 off I-25. This is the Circle Avenue exit. Go right (west). Circle Avenue changes into Lake Avenue, and at the end there's the Broadmoor, with more than 3,000 acres of delights.

The Broadmoor has received Mobil's highest rating longer than any hotel in the country. It was built in 1918 and has 700 rooms in four different buildings. The exterior is Italian Renaissance. Real Chinese lion statues guard the entry. The renovated interiors have rich hunter green and burgundy tones. Although freshly decorated, it feels straight from the Kennedy Camelot era. You might imagine Jackie, in a pink Chanel suit and pillbox hat, pulling on white gloves as she heads toward the Broadmoor's shops. A beautiful new addition is a bridge across the lake that connects the main hotel with the Broadmoor West for the convenience of the guests. "The guests love it," says marketing director Sally Mayo, and the paddleboats can still glide under it, followed by the Broadmoor's famous white and black swans.

Three 18-hole championship golf courses, 12 tennis courts, a 90,000-square-foot golf/tennis clubhouse and spa, bicycle rentals, horseback riding, fly fishing, trap shooting and hot air balloon rides are all here. The children's program is famous, and hiking trails are right out the door.

Nine restaurants make the dining choices exquisitely difficult. Fanciest is the **Penrose Room**, with views of both city and mountains.

This Edwardian salon offers such continental cuisine as Châteaubriand served on silver place settings by tuxedo-clad waiters. The average price of dinner with wine and dessert is at $100 for a couple. **Charles Court** is casual and contemporary, with one of the best wine lists in the country. Dinner for two here is around $60. Some specialties are baked double Colorado lamb chops with goat cheese and mustard seed crust; Prince Edward Sound grilled salmon; seared Colorado native bass; elk with lingonberry compote; and black-diamond rattlesnake quesadillas. Recently remodeled, **The Tavern** offers traditional fresh seafood, prime rib and pasta, an assortment of entrees cooked on the new wood-burning open grill over pine, applewood, mesquite and other flavor-enhancing woods. The average price for two is around $50. Kids prefer **Julie's**. Fare at this sidewalk cafe includes sandwiches, salads and ice cream. Julie's waitresses wear poodle skirts and saddle shoes, the perfect outfit for serving milk shakes near the pool.

Twenty-five specialty shops include **Posh**, for women's sportswear and thousand-dollar evening gowns; **Grandma Grabbers**, for infant and toddler wear; a year-round Christmas store; a lingerie store named **Roses and Ribbons**; **The Goodnight Trail**, for Western wear; and a bookstore, **Broadmoor Bound**. The **Golf Pro Shop** is very popular.

During the summer, the average price for two people staying overnight is $250 for a regular room, with discount rates in the quieter seasons. For $1,800 you can have a night in the Penrose Suite. The sixth floor suite features a parlor, sun porch, 20-seat dining room and three bedrooms. Julie Penrose, wife of the Broadmoor's builder, Spencer Penrose, lived here in her later years. The furnishings include antiques she collected.

At Christmas, a package deal includes a room, dinner and a show called *Colorado Christmas at the Broadmoor*, with carols sung by talent from Nashville's Opryland. There's also a movie theater on the grounds with first-run movies.

For a bed and breakfast experience, go to the **Hearthstone Inn**, (719) 473-4413 or (800) 521-1885, 506 N. Cascade Avenue. Here are two 1885 mansions connected by a carriage-house walkway and containing 25 rooms alto-gether, 23 with private baths. All unoccupied guest rooms are left open so you can peek inside. The Solarium offers an open-air lattice porch with a view of the mountain range, plus a queen-size brass and iron bed and two comfortable rocking chairs. The Fireside is a softly blue room with a king-size iron bed, a big comfortable couch, an oak armoire, a fireplace and latticed private porch. The full gourmet breakfast served to guests might include home-baked banana bread, gingerbread cake, quiche and fresh fruit. The gift shop is open from early morning until 10 PM and includes the *Hearthstone Inn Cookbook*. The inn serves luncheons for groups of 20 or more during the non-summer months. Reservations are required.

The Hearthstone resides in an elegant neighborhood, just south of huge mansions on Cascade and Wood avenues. These rival mansions in Denver, and sometimes win. To reach the Hearthstone, take Exit 143 (Uintah Street). Travel east (away from the mountains) to the third stoplight, turn right for seven blocks, and the inn's at St. Vrain and Cascade streets. Rooms generally cost around $100. It has no TVs or in-room phones, allows no pets or smoking, but children are welcome. A jogging park with swimming and tennis is nearby.

About 50 miles southwest of Colorado Springs is the gaming town of **Cripple Creek**, with gambling, melodrama and more. If you decide to go there, then find you want some peace and quiet to contrast with the hubbub, check out these two places.

Cripple Creek's **Hospitality House Travel Park**, (719) 689-2513 or (800) 500-2513, is at 600 N. B Street in Cripple Creek. Stephen and Bonnie Mackin say you can come and get well — the place used to be a hospital. It has been renovated, then furnished with period furniture and TVs. There's a hot tub, areas for volleyball and horseshoes, and so on. It's very relaxed and has a Victorian feel. There are 50 spots with full hookups for RVs, along with tent spaces. Camping costs around $17; rooms run around $70 with a private bath.

Near Cripple Creek, consider **The Victor Hotel**, (719) 689-3553 or (800) 748-0870, at Fourth and Victor streets in Victor. Take U.S. Highway 24 southwest of Colorado Springs to Colo. Highway 67 and proceed about 18 miles.

This recently renovated Victorian hotel was built in 1899 and, as this book goes to press, is being expanded to include a new wing. It currently has 30 rooms, which generally cost around $95 for two people.

The Gambling Towns: Black Hawk and Central City

Getting There

About an hour southwest of Boulder, on scenic Peak to Peak Highway, you enter tiny Gilpin County. The easiest way there is to take Canyon Boulevard west to Nederland, then head south from Nederland on Colo. Highway 119. Enjoy the aspens and great mountain views. Pretty soon, you'll reach the biggest towns in the county — Black Hawk and Central City. These are Boulder's close-in gambling centers, with colorful extras such as brightly painted buildings, historic cemeteries, nearby ghost towns and one of the finest musical theaters in the west — the Central City Opera.

Those coming from Boulder might want to consider taking the **Boulder Casino Express**, 829-1966 — an especially good way to travel if you're thinking of drinking while you're up in the mountains. Groups or individuals can go anytime at a cost of $22 per person round trip; seniors and groups of 10 or more, $17 each. All round trips also include a casino package for **Colorado Central Station**, which provides a free dinner, $10 in cash, some blackjack money, free drink coupons and other extras.

Love, Hate or Whatever

Depending on your preferences, you'll either love these gambling towns or hate them. If you love them, you'll enjoy the easy entertainment in a beautiful mountain setting, with quaint touches of mining and mountain history.

But if you're after a quaint mountain setting with a bric-a-brac of small mom and pop stores owned by third-generation mountain families, you may hate gambling. This section will describe what the mountain towns offer gamblers. Then it explains what Gilpin County has for those who want something in place of, or in addition to, the one-armed bandits. But first, to understand how legalized gambling has changed the area, consider its history.

History

Placer mining revealed gold south of Boulder, and dozens of mountain towns boomed. Central City and Black Hawk were among them. Up here, the Wild West was not so awfully woolly. Public drunkenness was the biggest crime problem (as it is again today), and miners felt comfortable sleeping in unlocked cabins with their gold dust under their pillows. One Congregational preacher reported that, rather than being rude and wicked, he found a few Central City residents well-educated and cultivated enough to be among the more pleasant families that "demand and appreciate good preaching."

The pros of booming were showing when Central City built the Teller House Hotel in 1872, one of the most lavish hotels west of the Mississippi at that time. It had a luxurious bar and a tall diamond-dust mirror that was carried over precarious mountain roads by an oxen team. The Teller House drew Mae West and Mark Twain. Sarah Bernhardt and Edwin Booth appeared at the opera house in the 1880s. But the mining operations that fueled these fancy places were not so attractive. Mining sluices ruined the countryside. Trees were toppled to build peaked-roof houses on the sloping hills, leaving the mountains barren for decades.

By the end of World War II, the motherlodes were barren and most Gilpin County mining centers were ghost towns. A few, however, experienced a new boom. "We still get the gold," quipped Central City's mayor in the 1950s. "We get it from some 450,000 tourists a year."

Historian Robert G. Anthearn, author of *The Coloradans*, scorned Central City when he wrote in 1976 that it had become a "classical example of fakery in the world of tourist traps." He lamented, "That once charming little town was turned into the Coney Island of the

Rockies, and the onetime Queen of the Little Kingdom became a tired old bawd, painted up beyond recognition, selling her wares for any price to anyone."

Well, it was tawdry, but it didn't have gambling then. Before gambling, the colorful little hillside homes sheltered grizzled miners and third-generation families. The area limped downhill on fading tourism. Buildings were condemned, and many residents commuted to Boulder or Denver for work.

Colorado residents voted for gambling in 1990. The measure passed, with limitations. Bets had to stay low, and gambling would be legal in only three places — Black Hawk, Central City and Cripple Creek. Interestingly, the measure was written so that even if one of the towns hated gambling, the state vote could impose it on them. (Since then, the law has been changed so that a town must want gambling before a state vote can bring it into the gaming community. So far, Coloradans have not voted for any more gambling.)

Gilpin County voters went along with the state's gambling fever in 1990, hoping to save their towns. Many believed gambling would bring renewed tourism to the little shops and help restore the historic buildings. What they've discovered is that maintaining a community alongside a gambling center is an uphill learning process. Businesses that tried to stick a slot machine next to their gift items couldn't compete with national casino chains that put slot machines wall-to-wall. Handling expenses such as buying slot machines and paying gambling taxes required deep pockets for getting started, and many local owners went under. People who owned buildings in easy-to-reach areas made good money by selling. Those who lived out of the way had a harder time selling, even though their regular livelihood was being smothered. So, with some people making fortunes and others losing modest savings, many of the pre-gambling residents left. Meanwhile, residents who stayed discovered that gambling profits did not just stay in their towns. The money went to state taxes and out-of-state investors.

As old-timers left, authentic charm left too. Local services dwindled. In Central City and Black Hawk today, don't count on buying gasoline (you can buy gas at the KOA campground on Colo. Highway 46, about 6 miles north, back toward Nederland). And those buildings that locals hoped would be restored often were gutted, with only the facade, or a copy of the facade, remaining.

People who view gambling more positively point out another set of facts. Many old buildings were beyond repair, and re-creating them has given the town a fresh, glitzy kind of charm. Those gutted interiors had been changed many times in the past already. Streets and utilities are in much better repair, and the towns are much prettier for walking. As for services, there weren't any basic services in Central City at the time that gambling came in. Black Hawk had a little grocery store and two gas stations, which are gone. But a little grocery, **Annie Oakley's**, on Main Street, is now in Central City, and there's a small grocery in the **Wild Card Casino** on Main Street in Black Hawk. Some people who commuted to Denver for jobs at the supermarkets now can earn more in casinos. Some casinos sponsor local athletic teams and provide matching grants to local schools. Some residents who were struggling before now have very nice new homes out of town. New shops can open and close almost weekly, according to Doug Dorsey, chairman of the board of the Black Hawk/Central City Chamber of Commerce, so it's hard to keep track of the businesses in town — so some shops listed in this book at time of publication may no longer exist as you read it now, but new ones will have taken their places.

Without gambling, rural parts of Central City and Black Hawk might have faded into ghost towns. And after the newness of gambling wears off, perhaps diversity will return. Right now, the hunger to build yet another slot palace fuels development. But it's a pretty area, and it has many assets besides one-armed bandits. Thanks to those features, and if the gambling businesses contribute more back into the local economy, a real community might someday grow stronger. Black Hawk has captured 53 percent of all the gaming revenues in the state. Central City and Cripple Creek fight for the remaining revenues. Central City has been blighted with the "extra-mile" syndrome: People either don't realize it's a mile away from Black Hawk or don't want to drive the extra mile to Central City after reaching Black

For better or worse, limited-stakes gambling has changed the mountain towns of Central City and Black Hawk.

Hawk. They see all the casinos in Black Hawk and think they've arrived at both destinations. Central City has a lot more to offer than just casinos — richer history, the opera house and the Gilpin History Museum, 582-5283, 228 E. High Street, that gives visitors a good grasp of the colorful past. New in 1996 is a free valet parking system in Central City that solves the former parking problems. Be sure to visit the museum in Central City, especially if the kids are along, to learn about the area's early mining history — it's only a block from the gaming area.

A Gambler's View of Black Hawk/Central City

Lots, make that "slots," of people have a great time gambling. Colorado's limited stakes tend to keep the focus on fun. Bets are $5 and less. Only poker, blackjack and platoons of one-armed bandits are allowed at the nearly 40 parlors, and the maximum hours are 8 AM to 2 AM.

The common way to have fun is to set aside some dough — anywhere from $1 to $100 — and see how long you can play be-

fore you lose it. One friend sets the limit at $20 for a night. Another goes for $50. They both recall times when they have played into the wee hours and managed to take home more than they brought, then other days when they have lost all their change in the first half-hour.

Slot machines gulp quarters everywhere. Some casinos offer a good deal . . . as in dealt cards . . . with blackjack dealers, restaurants and entertainment. Central City and Black Hawk are less than a mile apart, linked by shuttle buses and plenty of on-the-street attendants. Altogether, the two towns have only six key streets, so it's easy to poke around. In general, Black Hawk gamblers seem more serious, drinking and looking intently at their cards, while Central City is a little more fun. As one gambler puts it, you wander until you find where your luck seems best.

To make your wanderings more efficient, call the **Black Hawk/Central City Chamber of Commerce**, 582-5077, or (800) 331-LUCK and tell them what games you're seeking. Volunteers staff the line from around 10 AM to 2 PM weekdays and there's a 24-hour recording with all types of information including accommodations, casinos, restaurants and a current calendar of events. As you get to town, grab the free shopper, *Colorado Gambler*, which details what games, entertainment and food various casinos offer.

You might want to stop at **Otto's**, 582-0150, 260 Gregory Street, in Black Hawk. Next door is the **Black Forest Inn**, a highly rated German restaurant serving diners for 36 years. Owners Kay and Bill Lorenz have expanded their operations into two gambling houses with Otto's and the **Rohling Inn**, 160 Gregory Street. There's free parking with validation, and blackjack as well as slot machines.

Blackjack tables are in many, but not all, casinos. Table poker is harder to find. Most larger places offer it, including the **Gilpin Hotel**, 582-1133, 111 Main Street, Black Hawk. The eight poker tables play Texas Hold'em, Omaha and occasionally Stud. There's also off-track betting for dog and horse races. A new Colorado-born poker game called Hold'em 88 is now being offered in at least a half-dozen casinos. It's a simpler version of Texas Hold'em, the most popular form of poker played at casinos. In Hold'em 88 in Colorado, where $5 is the maximum amount allowable for any single bet, the player can lose no more than $10 on a single game. In Texas Hold'em, which has four betting rounds and up to five raises per round, a single game can cost a bettor more than $100. The Gilpin Hotel started slot machine tournaments in Colorado, and they still have the biggest. This historic building has the original brickwork facade from 1869. It's a Victorian-styled place, with ornate hardwood everywhere. **The Mineshaft Bar** has been a locals hangout for 100 years. It's full of memorabilia and nightly, live entertainment that sometimes includes karaoke singing. There's also free valet parking right across the street. **Lucille Malone's** restaurant is named after the hotel's resident ghost. After Lucille's fiance died in a wagon accident, the distraught schoolteacher hurled herself off a balcony. Locals say she's been hanging around ever since.

Harrah's, 777-1111, has two casinos, the **Glory Hole** on Main Street in Central City, and **Harrah's**, on Main Street in Black Hawk. The Glory Hole includes a beautiful old bar dating back to 1864. The whole place is 40,000 square feet, but it's in four connected buildings with little nooks and crannies, and it's lavishly restored. Red brick, dark oak woods and tin ceilings are details of the era. The Glory Hole has one of the area's better restaurants, **Emmy's** (details are in the subsequent "Restaurants" section). **The Signature Room** has a wall that famous opera performers have signed, including Mae West, the cast of *Barefoot in the Park* and others. Dining in The Signature Room, however, is mostly for those busy gambling. You order, go back and gamble, get beeped when your food is ready, then go back and eat. The inexpensive fare includes sandwiches, buffalo wings, onion rings, Tex-Mex, popcorn shrimp and fries and, for the more health-conscious, different pastas. There's also pool and a video arcade where kids are welcome. The Black Hawk Harrah's has plenty of slots, poker and blackjack tables too in a building with high ceilings and a big, open feeling, more like Las Vegas. On the third floor is the **Branding Iron**, which serves burgers and quick meals. Both casinos offer live music in the evenings and big-screen TVs.

Colorado Central Station, 582-3000, on Colo. Highway 119 in Black Hawk, is in an authentic railroad depot. The game of Hold'em 88 (explained previously) was recently invented here. It has at least 10 tables of blackjack and seven poker tables, along with 600 slot machines. **Bullwhackers Casinos** are at 101 Gregory Street in Black Hawk and 130 Main Street in Central City. Both can be reached through 271-2500 or (800) GAMBULL. People who play there like how Bullwhackers offers transportation to and from Denver. Patrons describe these casinos as big places with nice carpeting — fancy in a cheesy way.

Look for 24-carat gold on the 105 slot machines at **Papone's Place**, 582-5820, 118 Main Street in Central City. Gaze up at the Austrian crystal chandeliers and beveled mirrors that make it the jewel of Central City. Marble floors and lamb's-wool floral carpets complete the picture. Although the decorations in this little place cost a fortune, spaghetti at **Mamone's Deli** costs only $3, including soup, salad and garlic bread. Children can eat hot dogs and sandwiches here. Papone is a loving nickname for "Grandpa" in Italy, and Mamone means "Grandma." Currently, Papone's is open only from May until October, from noon until 2 PM

Friday and Saturday and noon until 10 PM weekdays.

Last but not least of our recommended casinos is the **Teller House**, 279-3200, 120 Eureka Street in Central City. This began as the Teller Hotel, among the finest hotels west of the Mississippi. The famed **Face on the Barroom Floor** is here plus the **Central City Opera**. We provide a full description of the hotel in the next section, but for now, be assured that they have slots and turn-of-the-century charm.

You can charter buses for large parties heading to the gambling towns, either through **Boulder Casino Express**, 829-1966, or directly with one of the casinos. This is wise when planning a drinking party. High altitude makes liquor more potent, and those are winding — and sometimes icy — roads down.

While we hate to end with a caution, here goes. For most people, gambling's plain fun. But Daniel Minerva, Ph.D., a psychologist at Boulder's **Addiction Exchange**, 442-3110, notes that the tip of the iceberg has grown larger. About six gamblers a year sought his help before 1990. Since legalized gambling, he now works with 30 to 40 people each year who gamble so much they have stopped working, lost their money, started lying. . . . If this ever happens to you, be one of the lucky ones who seeks help. **Gambler's Anonymous**, 754-7119, in Denver is another source.

Black Hawk/Central City When You're Not Gambling

Some gambling friends complain that it gets boring after you've spent all your pocket change and are waiting for your friends to lose theirs. After all, this isn't Vegas. Some slot parlors don't even have a TV ballgame.

Fortunately, many casinos are catching on. Harrah's and the Gilpin Hotel offer live music many nights. Harrah's has a pool hall and video arcade where kids are welcome. Some places offer sports television and good restaurants, and if you step away from the casinos, you'll find other reasons to see these mountain towns.

The **Central City Opera**, 292-6700 or (800) 851-8175, just west of Main and Eureka streets,

graces an historic opera building built in 1878. This summer troupe is one of the oldest opera companies in the country, with a distinguished national reputation. All performances are in English, well-sung and wonderfully acted. Everyone stays in historic Victorian character, including the uniformed ushers, who ring brass hand bells when it's time to take your seat. The theater is beautifully decorated, down to the hand-painted murals of Pegasus and cafe chairs engraved with the names of famous benefactors. Every seat is good. You're close enough that the actors and actresses come across as real people who feel life so strongly, they've just got to sing about it.

It takes more than 200 people to make a production happen. They pick great operas, and these highfalutin classics can be surprisingly engaging. *La Boheme* had a scene in which handsome young men in Victorian vests sang all the way through a pillow fight. Ever heard the aria where a guy sings good-bye to his coat? It might sound hokey, but that coat was his only nice possession, and he pawned it to buy a gift for the dying beauty, Mimi. Sniff, sniff.

Here's practical advice about summer's operas. Evening performances start at 8 PM Tuesday, Friday and Saturday (7:30 PM Thursday) and last around 2½ hours. Weekend matinees begin at 2:30 PM. Tickets range from $22 to $51. Get your tickets as early as possible, since some operas sell out weeks or months in advance (although on some nights, you can buy tickets at the door). When you order tickets, pay $5 for a reserved spot in the opera house's parking lot. Or there's a bus from Denver and Lakewood for every performance and a bus on Fridays from Boulder. Cost is $15 for adults, $13 for seniors 62 and older. New this year are weekend opera dinners at 6 PM at the Teller House in a private banquet room. The dinners were created specifically for opera patrons who prefer to avoid the casino atmosphere. The four-course buffet with dessert, wine and soft music costs $30 per person and is offered on Friday and Saturday evenings; the price of the opera ticket is extra. Remember, it's about an hour from Boulder to the parking lot. Try to reach it at least an hour early. This way, a brief traffic jam won't spell trouble. Be sure you arrive at the opera house at least 10 minutes before the show. If you're late, you'll be allowed to enter only between acts. You can also escape the hassles of driving by taking the bus. See our entry on the Central City Opera in the Boulder Arts chapter for details.

When opera doesn't fit your schedule, sign up for a **Festival Extra**, 292-6700. There are various choices: At **Salon Recitals** on weekends, opera stars do short recitals during a gourmet brunch at the Teller House Hotel, next to the opera house at 11:45 AM. Tickets cost around $20. For **Opera a la Carte**, famous opera scenes are fully staged at 1:15 PM Wednesdays and Fridays and cost $2.50. *Face on the Barroom Floor* is a 30-minute cabaret opera recounting the Teller House's famous legend. These performances are at 1:15 PM Saturday and Sunday at William's Stable, right across the street, and cost $4.

That **Face on the Barroom Floor** is painted in the Teller House Hotel, right next to the opera. When we first saw it, we expected a colossal face. Well, it's not big, but it's pretty. So are the eight Muses of Central City, originally painted in 1883. Five decades later, a restorer added jokes. You might notice a male figure with two left feet, a swan's head twisted backward and Venus's left nipple located on the apple she holds. Take a free tour of the Teller House and, when it's not in use, the opera house, 279-3200. Tours leave every half-hour; the opera house tour costs $2. The tour office is open daily from 8:30 AM to 5 PM.

The **Gilpin History Museum**, 582-5283, 228 E. High Street, is next to the Central Palace casino in Central City. It occupies the first stone schoolhouse west of the Mississippi. During the summer, it's open from 11 AM to 4 PM and costs $2 for adults. About 10,000 artifacts are here, arranged in places such as the Victorian parlor and kitchen. Items from mining-days businesses are here, including the doctor's office, the law office, bank and more. A general store and hand-drawn firefighting equipment are on display plus an early school room from Russell Gulch. A carriage display, doll collection and mining tools are here too.

The **Thomas House**, 582-3435, is at 209

Eureka Street in Central City. It's open 11 AM to 4 PM Thursday through Sunday in summer, with $2 admission for adults. (If you tour the History Museum too, the total cost is only $3 for both.) This is an 1870 Greek Revival Victorian. It's mostly yellow with white trim. However, Marsha Thomas was a free thinker, and on a trip back East she brought back a gallon of salmon paint for the porch. During every world war, the government ordered gold mining to stop, so in World War I Central City took a dive. Ben Thomas, vice president of the local mercantile store, had no business anymore. In 1917, the Thomases locked the house and relocated to Denver. Marsha visited for summer operas, but they never moved back to stay. All the furnishings, from spices to fine art to the 13 different clocks, are intact from 1917. The Playboy-style breast-enhancing corset of 4-foot, 11-inch Marsha hangs beside the long johns of 6-foot-plus-tall Ben. Because Marsha was so short, Ben cut the legs off the kitchen's wood-burning stove so it would match her height.

The **Art Gallery**, 582-5952, 117 Eureka Street in Central City, shows the work of Colorado artists. Jewelry, sculpture, clothing and paintings are all here. It's on the top floor of the oldest public building in Colorado, Washington Hall. Built in 1861, it was Gilpin County's first courtroom. The entrance to the art gallery was once the jail. During summer, the sculpture garden blooms, while an artist-sculpted stream runs inside the building.

Founded in 1859, **St. James Methodist Church**, 582-5882, 123 Eureka Street, is the state's oldest church building. The stone church was erected by Cornish masons in 1871. The stained glass is lovely; the pipe organ was installed in 1899; the church seats 350, and it's active today. It's open for free tours 11 AM to 4 PM daily in the summer.

Just north of Central City, six cemeteries let you glimpse more mining-era history. Was the idea that woodcutters, masons and Catholics would go to separate heavens? Judging from the separated plots, it looks that way. Actually, in those days, not everyone could afford a burial. So people were buried in plots

FYI

Unless otherwise noted, the area code for all phone numbers in this guide is 303.

bought by their fraternity, charity or lodge. A heartache of children's tombstones mark the worldwide flu epidemic of 1919 plus smallpox and other diseases that wiped out whole families. If you're interested in tours, contact the Historic Society at the Gilpin History Museum or the **Central City Chamber of Commerce**, 582-5077.

A mile above Central City is a real live . . . well, maybe not live. . . . **Nevadaville's** a ghost town. In the 1800s, 4,000 people lived here, operating 20 quartz mills, several stores and hotels. Few historic structures still stand. But nothing's left of many other Gilpin County boom towns. Lost cities include Deadwood Diggings, Dogtown, Eureka, Gambell Gulch, Gold Dirt, Glory Hole, Hoosier City, Quincy, Springfield, Trail's End and Wide Awake.

For kids, Black Hawk offers **Daisy's**, a video game arcade. **Coyote Creek Video Arcade** is in Central City along with the **Old Time Candy Shop**, full of ice cream, fudge and old-fashioned candies you weigh by the pound. **The Rock Shop** is a rock and T-shirt shop. There are now nearly 10 gift shops in town, including **Santa Fe Central**, an Indian jewelry shop, and the **Bear Mountain Trading Post** with Indian artifacts and Western art — both in Central City. Locals say these places are all easy to find on the little gambling towns' few main streets. What's more, the towns have wisely hired guides to direct traffic, and those same guides can help you locate stores, restaurants, casinos, etc.

You can still find two funky little places, **Vick's Gold Panning** and **The Old Timer Panning** (across from the Gold Dust Lodge, a 26-room motel), about 2 to 5 miles down from Black Hawk on Colo. Highway 119. They don't have phones, so just drive down to see if they're open.

Restaurants

Many of the casinos offer only fast food — there's a Burger King in Colorado Central Station. For fine dining, it's wise to get a reservation. Consider **The Black Forest Inn**, 279-2333, next to Otto's Casino. It's one of the oldest restaurants in Black Hawk and offers renowned German cuisine. Some casinos offering more relaxed sit-down dining with full menus are the **Teller House**, **Lady Luck** and **Harvey's Wagon Wheel**, which serve seafood, prime rib and other favorites. Both Bullwhackers Casinos have **Bullwhackers Bar & Grill**, with a full menu and on Wednesdays and Fridays there's an all-you-can-eat buffet for $5.99, including a dessert and soft drink. Victorian-style dining takes place at **Emmy's**, 777-1111, in Harrah's Glory Hole in Central City. Emmy's opens at 4 PM Friday through Sunday. Newly remodeled, the historic building's intimate dining parlors were reputedly where Central City's shady ladies once plied their trade. Emmy Wilson owned the original building, where she ran a dining establishment, and today's Emmy's serves such delectables as roast rack of lamb, elk medallions with wild mushroom port wine sauce and black Angus prime rib. Upstairs in the Gilpin Hotel, **Lucille Malone's**, 582-1133, offers everything from burgers and sandwiches to prime rib and seafood plus some Italian choices and a Sunday brunch. The salad bar used to be poor heartbroken Lucille's bedroom. Downstairs, there's **The Mine Shaft**, offering burgers, pizza and a Sunday buffet.

Many places offer plenty to fill you up for less than $10. The **Golden Rose Buffet**, at the Golden Rose Casino, 825-1413 or (800) 929-0255, 102 Main Street in Central City, has deals on good meals along with beveled-glass decorations, red valances over white lace curtains and turn-of-the-century photos. The changing buffet ($6.95 during the day and $7.95 at night) includes eight hot items, such as barbecued ribs, hot fresh vegetables and Oriental food. The salad bar greens are romaine and spinach, and the dessert bar includes mousses, parfaits, pastries and ice cream. Next to the Opera House, the Teller House, 279-3200, has two dining choices, the **Face Bar** and the **Atrium Restaurant**, offering soups, salads and an all-day buffet. The Famous Bonanza has **Ponderosa**, 582-5914, 107 Main Street in Central City, a small, low-priced restaurant with Mexican food, burgers and a $3.99 prime rib dinner for gamblers every day. **Jazz Alley's Restaurant**, 582-1125, has seafood, steaks and pasta. It also offers lots of specials such as $1.99 breakfasts and $3.99 buffets with prime rib, daily from 11 AM to 9 PM. The manager also operates the Gold

Mine Casino's **Sure Shot Restaurant**, 582-0719, with a daily carving cart of prime rib, turkey and other specials from 11 AM to 5 PM. Both restaurants offer weekend specials such as Cajun food and seafood.

Accommodations

The newest casino/hotel, **Harvey's Wagon Wheel**, 582-0800 or (800) 427-8397, 321 Gregory Street in Central City, has 118 rooms that rent for around $85. That gives a big boost to the accommodations in this little county and it's the only casino/hotel in Central City.

One referral number for bed and breakfast inns is **Mountainside Bed and Breakfast**, 582-3171, at 200 Chase Street above Black Hawk. Another is **Gingerbread Estates**, 582-3227 or (800) 582-3226, for little guest cottages.

The **Gold Dust Lodge**, 582-5415, 5312 Colo. Highway 119 in Black Hawk, has 24 nice rooms that rent for around $65. Bed and breakfasts are lovely around these towns. Jan Ward runs the **Primrose Inn** bed and breakfast, 582-5808, 310 E. First High Street. It's right next to the Historic Museum, on the northeast side of Central City. The yellow-and-white Victorian sits high on the hill. Burgundy brocade wallpaper, lace curtains, a brass bed and a 7-foot-tall antique mirror decorate one room. Staying overnight costs around $75, with a continental breakfast. Patty Webb runs the **Winfield Scott Guest Suites**, 582-3433, 210 Hooper Street, Central City, in the historic Hooper House. The house was built in 1878, and the guest suites have been decorated in country Southwest style. Each suite includes a bathroom, kitchen, dining area, fireplace, TV, VCR and phone. The grounds are beautiful. Rates are around $84 for the one-bedrooms and $160 for the two-bedrooms. Three other good bed and breakfasts are **Chateau L'Acadienne**, 582-5209, ($50 to $120 depending upon the season and the room choice); **The Carriage House**, 582-3636, which offers private cottages for $89;

and **The High Street Inn**, 582-0622, around the same price range.

Fun in Ski Country
(Both Summer and Winter)

Winter Park and Summit County offer some of the nation's best skiing and summer recreation. Both are within a two-hour drive of Boulder. The individual ski areas, resorts and towns are listed below with separate contact numbers for each. There are also separate listings for getting there, attractions, restaurants, accommodations, shopping and recreation.

For most of these areas, recreation is the main attraction, though Breckenridge is also of interest as one of Colorado's great mining boomtowns with a large historic district. The nearby towns of Dillon and Frisco have remnants of their old mining days; and the area around Winter Park still maintains something of its ranching flavor.

Remember, if you're not used to the Rocky Mountain altitude, take it easy — especially if you're involved in the physical exertion required for skiing, hiking or bicycling. Just walking around can be tiring! Drink plenty of water and allow yourself time to adjust — a few days if you can. Slow down if you get a headache or feel nauseated, the first signs of altitude sickness.

Winter Park:
The Resort and Area

Winter Park operates on U.S. Forest Service land, as do most Western American ski areas, but it is unique in that the city of Denver owns its assets, which are run by a not-for-profit corporation. It is Colorado's fifth-largest ski area in terms of skier visits. Skiers and snowboarders can move among four interlinked mountains: the original **Winter Park**, **Mary Jane**, **Vasquez Ridge** and **Parsenn Bowl**. Twenty lifts, including seven high-speed express quads, access 1,414 acres

INSIDERS' TIP

The Colorado Air Force Academy and its space-age chapel are the most visited man-made attractions in Colorado.

Breckenridge celebrates "Ullr Fest" every January honoring "Ullr" — the god of snow and winter. The week's festivities include a cross-country ski race, children's concert, parade and fireworks.

of skiable terrain. Children's programs are exemplary, including day care for youngsters ages 2 months to 5 years and ski instruction for 3-year-olds to teens.

Winter Park is also well-known for its handicapped ski program and is the site of the **National Sports Center for the Disabled**, (970) 726-1540. Founded in 1970, it has 38 full-time employees, including instructors and coaches, and 1,000 volunteers who work with people with more than 40 different types of disabilities — cerebral palsy sufferers, amputees, paraplegics and others — and provide nearly 11,000 private, customized lessons each winter. The center has expanded its scope to include snowboarding and snowshoeing lessons as well as a substantial program of adaptive summer sports.

The town of Winter Park, 2 miles north of the ski area, offers numerous restaurants and accommodations. It's set in a beautiful valley surrounded by high peaks. Continuing northwest on U.S. Highway 40 brings you to the small towns of Fraser and Tabernash. Fraser often reports the coldest temperatures in the country, so some Coloradans call it "Freezer." But it's a beautiful area with broad open meadows and spectacular views. If you look up toward the Continental Divide to the east, you might be able to spot the jutting rock formation known as the Devil's Thumb, north of Fraser, for which the nearby cross-country ski resort was named. Continuing north will eventually bring you to the towns of Granby and to the intersection of U.S. Highway 34 to Grand Lake on the western boundary of Rocky Mountain National Park. (See our separate chapters on Grand Lake.)

Getting There

Winter Park is 70 miles west of Denver. From Boulder, drive south on Broadway (Colo. Highway 93) toward Golden and, at the new Golden bypass, follow the signs for I-70 W. or take U.S. Highway 6 up Clear Creek Canyon, which follows the old Colorado Central Railroad bed and deposits you right on I-70 headed west. Follow I-70 and exit onto U.S. Highway 40 W. at Empire and continue over Berthoud Pass, which is well-maintained all winter. There are two entrances to the ski area: Mary Jane offers expert skiing with challenging mogul runs; the main Winter Park base is better for beginners and intermediates. The town of Winter Park is 2 miles farther on U.S. Highway 40. Fraser is 3 miles past Winter Park.

The Ski Train

During winter, the **Ski Train** provides another, more interesting way to get to Winter Park — though it requires going into Denver, making the trip a bit longer than driving directly, but you won't have to deal with traffic or icy mountain roads. The Ski Train departs from Denver's Union Station at 7:15 AM and takes skiers within walking distance of the lifts. It goes through some 30 tunnels, including the 6.2-mile-long Moffat Tunnel, drilled a mile deep below the Continental Divide — a nifty ride and worth experiencing, especially with children. The Ski Train leaves Winter Park at 4:15 PM, just after the lifts close. The trip takes two hours each way. The adult Coach Car fare is $35 for a same-day round trip, $55 in the Club Car including continental breakfast and après-ski refreshments. Discounted lift tickets are available on the train. The Ski Train runs Saturdays and Sundays from mid-December until late March plus additional days during Christmas-New Year's week and on Fridays in March. For information and reservations call 296-I-SKI.

The Ski Bus

Just reinstated, Queen City Transportation's **SkiXpress**, 937-7287, serves five ski areas (Vail, Copper Mountain, Keystone, Loveland and Winter Park) from three RTD Park-n-Ride locations: Foothills in Boulder; the southwest corner of Wadsworth and Hampton in Denver; and the northwest corner of Ward Road and I-70, also in Denver. It operates every Saturday and Sunday from mid-December through March, departing at 7 AM and returning at around 7 PM. Round-trip fare is $15, and discounted lift tickets are available. Call for more information.

Downhill Skiing

In winter, skiing and snowboarding, of course, are the main attractions at Winter Park; call (970) 726-5514 during regular business hours, or from Boulder, 892-0961. The 1996-97 price for a one-day lift ticket was $45 for adults. Tickets discounted to $35 are available at Front Range King Soopers and Albertson's supermarkets, Total gas stations, Gart Sports and Christie Sports. The best deal for frequent skiers is the **Powder Express pass**. Enrollment costs $30 to $40 (renewals or second family member from $15), depending on where and when you purchase it. Benefits are direct lift access, one free early-season day, discounted lift tickets every day and one free day of skiing after every six days.

If you don't know how to ski or snowboard, January is a good month to learn. Winter Park offers a free three-hour beginner lesson with the purchase of an all-day, adult lift ticket. Second- and third-day lessons are just $15, at which point you'll be able to handle a surprising amount of terrain with aplomb. **Discovery Park**, a mid-mountain learning area slope with its own slow-moving chairlift, is like a ski area within a ski area, where novices can practice comfortably. The area is also one of just three in the country to host the annual National Women's Ski Week, with seminars and workshops for levels of skier and snowboarder.

Cross-country Skiing

Devil's Thumb Cross-Country Center, (970) 726-5632, offers 105 kilometers of great groomed trails for beginners to advanced cross-country skiers. There are flat trails for beginners and smooth wide lanes for ski-skaters plus lovely rolling meadows and some steep downhills for thrills. The 1996-97 trail pass remains $10 for adults; $6 for children ages 7 to 12 and seniors 60 and older; free for children younger than 6. **Snow Mountain Ranch**, (970) 726-2152, 867-2152 or 887-2152, has an additional 100 kilometers of groomed trails, including 3 kilometers illuminated for night-skiing.

Backcountry touring skiers like the Jim Creek Trail directly across from the Winter Park ski area or the Fraser Experimental Forest Ranger Station, which offers marked but ungroomed trails. Both are free. Advanced skiers and snowboarders tackle runs from the top of Berthoud Pass to the highway, which requires knowledge of avalanche conditions and procedures. You either need to be in a group with one designated driver per run or hitch a ride back up to the pass.

Other Winter Activities

Besides skiing, there are several winter alternatives. Nonskiers can enjoy the ambiance of the slopes by taking a two-hour mountain tour via snowcat, with frequent departures for the Balcony House at the Winter Park base. The cost is $20 for adults, $15 for children and seniors. **Dog Sled Rides of Winter Park**, (970) 726-8326, takes riders through 2,000 acres of pristine backcountry. Sleds pulled by eight- to 10-dog teams — all purebred Siberian huskies — can attain 30 miles per hour on downhill stretches. The cost for a one-hour ride varies at different times of winter, but figure on more than $100 for two people; reservations are required.

Jim's Sleigh Rides, (970) 726-0944, takes 20 guests in a horse-drawn sleigh past the historic Cozzens Ranch beside the Fraser River. The 70-minute ride includes a bonfire stop with refreshments. The cost — $15 for adults; $12 for ages 3 to 12; free for children 2 and younger — is the same for summer hayrides.

Two dinner sleighrides are also available in the area. **Dinner at the Barn**, (970) 726-4923, combines a ride through the woods and meadows of an 80-acre ranch with a gourmet dinner served by kerosene lantern light, with Western-style entertainment following. In summer, horse-drawn wagons replace sleighs. Advance reservations are required. Cost is $39.50 for adults; $24.50 for ages 4 to 12; and free for ages 3 and younger.

Dashing Through the Snow, (970) 726-5376, has one of Colorado's longest sleigh trails — 3 miles — to a secluded and delightful backcountry cabin, where a six-course gourmet feast with a choice of chicken or rib-eye steak is served, with live entertainment as a bonus. The price is $50 for adults, $39 for children. Bonfire/hot chocolate rides are available as well. (Sleigh rides become carriage rides in summer.)

There's free ice-skating at **Winter Park Ice Skating Rink**, (970) 726-4118. Skate rentals are available at **Ski Broker**, (970) 726-8882, and **SportStalker**, (970) 726-8873. Call the **Winter Park/Fraser Valley Chamber of Commerce**, 422-0666 or (970) 726-4118, for information on snowmobile tours and rentals and other winter diversions.

Summer Attractions

The resort hosts the annual **Winter Park Resort Mountain Bike Race Series**, comprised of five events with different formats, including hill climb, circuit racing and point-to-point racing, held from early June to early August. Two hundred-fifty competitors 8 and older take part in each event. The entry fee is $18 in advance or $20 on race day. For information, call the **Winter Park Competition Center**, (970) 726-1589.

Bicycling is also a popular participant sport. Six hundred miles of marked, mapped and maintained trails and 10 bike shops lace the Fraser Valley, and there are free town rides every Thursday evening and free women-only rides on Wednesdays throughout summer. Area bike trail maps are available at local bike stores or at the Winter Park Chamber of Commerce Visitors' Center on the east side of U.S. Highway 40 in downtown Winter Park. It is open from 8 AM to 5 PM daily.

Another big summer attraction for young and old is the **Alpine Slide**, right at the base of the ski area. There are other activities, including miniature golf, the human maze and chairlift rides to the top of the mountain. Summer hours are 10 AM to 6 PM (5 PM in September, weather permitting). With special bike mounts, Winter Park's **Zephyr Express** chairlift takes mountain bikers to the top where they can ride 45 miles of steep, exciting single-track trails and gentler jeep roads. Rental bikes are available. Each on-mountain summer activity is assigned a point value, ranging from 10 points for the Alpine Slide to six for mini-golf or the human maze. In 1996, prices ranged from $4 for adults ($3 for children ages 6 to 13 and seniors ages 62 to 69) for a six-pointer to $14 (and $13 for kids and seniors) for a 30-point ticket. Full-day park passes for all activities were $30, and morning or afternoon half-day passes were $20. Passes for anyone younger than 6 or older than 70 are free.

Winter Park also hosts the **American Music Festival**, two full days of American music, most recently featuring such popular performers as Colorado's own Big Head Todd and the Monsters as well as regional and local groups. The **Winter Park Jazz Festival**, also in July, hosts nationally known bands.

The **High Country Stampede Rodeo** takes place every Saturday evening from early July to late August at the John Work Arena, a mile west of Fraser. The junior rodeo gets under way at 5:30 PM, followed by the pros. There's bull riding, bronc busting, barrel racing and other popular events. In 1996, admission was $6 for adults and $3 for children, and a low-cost barbecue dinner is also available. Pure gustatory events include the annual **Rocky Mountain Wine, Beer and Food Festival**, in early August, and the **Winter Park**

Famous Flamethrowers High Altitude Cookoff, a month later. For information, call the ski area or the Winter Park Chamber of Commerce, 422-0666 or (970) 726-4118.

The **Pole Creek Golf Club**, (970) 726-8847, offers golfers 18 holes of gorgeous greens and fairways. *Golf Digest* named it the best public course in Colorado. It is 10 miles northwest of Winter Park in the town of Tabernash. In 1996, greens fees were $60 and $45 (for high and low seasons, respectively) Friday through Sunday; Monday through Thursday, rates drop to $55 (high) and $35 (low). Golf carts, which are optional, are $12.50 per rider.

In the **Arapahoe National Forest**, visitors can also enjoy fishing, hiking, horseback riding, jeeping and rafting. Contact the Arapahoe National Forest, Ranger District Office, (970) 887-3331, for activities information. The Winter Park Chamber of Commerce, 422-0666 or (970) 726-4118, has information about outfitters.

Restaurants

The Winter Park ski area has dining options both at the base and on the mountain. The **Coffee and Tea Market** in Winter Park's Balcony House, (970) 726-5095, is open for breakfast and lunch, and the nearby **West Portal Station** day lodge has self-service snack and lunch service as well as the **Derailer Bar**. The Mary Jane Center features a cafeteria as well as a sit-down restaurant called **The Club Car** and **Pepperoni's Pizza and Sports Bar**. The beautiful and monumental Lodge at Sunspot at the top of the Zephyr Express chairlift serves snacks and lunches at **The Provisioner**, a self-service facility, from 10 AM to 3:30 PM in winter and 11 AM to 3 PM in summer. Table service is offered in the **Dining Room**, which is also open for dinner Thursday, Friday and Saturday evenings from 5:30 to 10 PM in winter, with access via gondola. Reservations are recommended; call 780-6446 or (970) 720-1446. Other on-mountain eating facilities include **Snoasis**, mid-mountain at Winter Park; **Lunch Rock** and **Sundance Cafe**, snackbars atop Mary Jane and Vasquez Ridge respectively.

In the town of Winter Park, **Gasthaus Eichler**, (970) 726-5133, is noted for Austrian and German specialties; reservations are suggested. **Hernando's Pizza and Pasta Pub**, (970) 726-5409, is a local favorite for homemade pastas, good pizza and a summer beer garden. **The Shed**, (970) 726-9912, is a longtime Winter Park favorite, now serving hearty breakfasts and Southwestern-style dinners. **Carver's**, (970) 726-8202, tucked into a log cabin behind Cooper Creek Square, offers excellent baked goods and an eclectic, moderately priced breakfast, lunch and dinner menu. In Fraser, the **Crooked Creek Saloon & Eatery**, (970) 726-9250, is a family-style Mexican and American restaurant that is best known for giant burgers and fiery wings. For dinner sleighrides in the area, see the previous "Other Winter Activities" section.

Shopping

The Winter Park area is not known for its shopping opportunities, but a few local shops, mostly centered around Cooper Creek Square, in downtown Winter Park include:

Active Images, (970) 726-8861, U.S. Highway 40, sells all types of T-shirts. The **General Store** in Cooper Creek Square, (970) 726-8697, has mountain mementos, Christmas items and folk-type art. **Simply Scrumptious**, (970) 726-4452, in Cooper Creek Square, specializes in Colorado-made products and gourmet food. **SportStalker**, (970) 726-8873 (retail) and (970) 726-8874 (rentals), also in Cooper Creek Square, rents skis and bikes, and sells a good range of sporting goods and accessories. **The Lonesome Stone**, (970) 726-8554, in Fraser's Safeway Center, sells everything from cards and books to fine gifts and remembrances.

Right at the Winter Park Resort there's **Club T**, (970) 726-9558, for a large selection of nifty T-shirts. The **Winter Park Ski Shop**, (970) 726-5593, is open year round with ski, casual and sports clothing and souvenirs. To take care of a sugar craving, go to **Satisfied Sweet Tooth**, (970) 726-9212, or the **Winter Park Cookie Company**, (970) 726-9667. The **Winter Park Sports Shop**, (970) 726-5554, also sells and rents skis, snowboards and mountain bikes as well as sportswear and gifts.

Accommodations

Reservations are necessary in this popular area for most accommodations. You can make them through **Winter Park Central Reservations**, (800) 729-5839 or (970) 726-5587, or by calling individual properties. (Rates quoted below are for summer 1996 and winter 1996-97):

Located right in town, double rooms at the new **Super 8 Motel**, (970) 726-5294 or (800) 541-6130, run $76 to $125 during winter and $48 to $67 (higher during peak festivals) in summer. Also in downtown Winter Park, **Gasthaus Eichler**, (970) 726-5133 or (800) 543-3899, offers cozy rooms with or without meals from about $60 to $150. The **Iron Horse Retreat**, 573-1545 or (970) 726-8851, between Winter Park and Mary Jane, is the resort's only ski-in, ski-out property. Its attractive condos start around $80 for two during summer and $95 to $225 in winter; ski and golf packages are also available. **The Grand Victorian**, 456-6224, (800) 204-1170 or (970) 726-5881, is the first among equals when it comes to Winter Park's growing selection of charming bed-and-breakfast inns. Secluded in a grove of lodgepole pines, this romantic neo-Victorian offers lodging in three sumptuous fireplace suites for $65 to $95 in summer and $110 to $215 in winter, including gourmet breakfast and afternoon drinks and hors d'oeuvres. On the other end of the spectrum, budget-watchers can bunk in at **Winter Park Hostel**, (970) 726-5356, with dorm space for $10 in summer and $16.50 in winter and private couple rooms for $23 and $36. International Youth Hostel members rates are lower; winter prices might change in 1997.

Slightly farther afield is **Devil's Thumb Ranch Resort**, (970) 726-8231 or (800) 933-4339, a quiet, beautifully located retreat ski lodge open year round and equally nice for cross-country skiing in winter and horseback riding, hiking and fly fishing and access to mountain biking in summer. Cabins rent for $100 to $130 for two people, both summer and winter. Three miles north of Fraser, it's 3.5 miles east (right turn off of U.S. Highway 40) on County Road 83 and down the right fork in the road. **Idlewild Lodge**, (970) 726-8352, 398 Ski Idlewild Road, offers a great downtown Winter Park location and is open year round. A double room at Idlewild costs $120 per night and includes a full buffet breakfast and dinner for two. Summer rates are the same and include three meals plus horseback riding, hayrides, evening entertainment and a children's recreation program. Idlewild is an alcohol- and smoke-free environment (no firearms allowed, either) geared for family vacations. The lodge just underwent a complete gutting and remodeling.

Summit County

The four ski areas of **Breckenridge**, **Keystone**, **Arapahoe Basin** and **Copper Mountain** collectively attract more skiers and snowboarders than any other ski destination in North America. They offer an incredible range of great terrain, and for vacationers and weekenders, the towns of Breckenridge, Dillon and Frisco — and the resort developments of Keystone and Copper Mountain — offer outstanding shopping, restaurants and accommodations — all in proximity to the Greater Denver area and Boulder.

Lift tickets are fully interchangeable among Breck, Keystone and A-Basin (as the locals call them) and are valid for night skiing at Keystone through most of the season until 9 PM nightly. In 1996-97, at-the-window tickets are $45 for adults (one-day passes) with $35 tickets available at King Soopers, Safeway and Albertson's supermarkets, Total and Diamond Shamrock gas stations and Gart Sports. Children's rates are valid through age 14. Front Range skiers and riders can get the Ski 3 ticket free, good for the best daily discounts on lift tickets and ski school lessons plus rental and lodging discounts at all three areas. As this edition of *The Insiders' Guide® to Boulder* was about to go to press, Vail Associates, which operates Vail and Beaver Creek, announced its intention to purchase A-Basin, Breckenridge and Keystone, and Vancouver-based IntraWest planned to buy Copper, so it is also possible that other inter-area deals might be available as early as winter 1996-97.

Copper Mountain, which celebrates its silver anniversary in 1996-97, is treasured for its logical, well-laid-out terrain and congenial ambiance. At-the-window, one-day tickets for '96-97 are $45 for adults and $19 for children ages 6 through 14; kids 5 and younger and seniors 70 and older are free. Discount tickets (prices were not available at press time) are available at King Soopers, Safeway, Albertson's, Diamond Shamrock, Total, Christie Sports and other locations. The **Copper Card**, which costs about $30, enables you to buy up to four lift tickets discounted to the lowest available price every time you visit and offers additional discounts on food at the resort and on goods and services at Copper and elsewhere in Summit County.

During summer, there's hiking and backpacking in the **Arapahoe National Forest**; fishing and boating on Lake Dillon; whitewater rafting on the Blue River; and an excellent network of bike trails and several good golf courses in Summit County, as well as a calendar full of special events and festivals. Forest information is available from the Dillon Ranger District Office, (970) 468-5400.

Getting There From Boulder

Road condition or traffic slowdowns excepted, all Summit County ski areas are less than a two-hour drive from Boulder. Drive south on Broadway (Colo. Highway 93) toward Golden and, at the Golden bypass, follow the signs for I-70 W. or take U.S. Highway 6 up Clear Creek Canyon directly to I-70 W. Follow I-70 to the Eisenhower Tunnel. For Arapahoe Basin, exit at U.S. 6 west over Loveland Pass. For all the other resorts, proceed through the tunnel. Keystone is reached by taking the first exit after the tunnel, which is U.S. Highway 6 east. For Breckenridge, take the Frisco exit and drive south on Colo. Highway 9 for about 9 miles. Copper Mountain is directly off I-70, at Exit 195, just before the highway climbs up to Vail Pass. The aforementioned SkiXpress bus, 937-7287, serves Copper an Keystone.

Breckenridge

Breckenridge, the town, is the oldest and largest of the Summit County communities. It was founded in 1859 when gold was discovered in the area. It remains a picturesque and historic renovated mining town, and the main street is still lined with some of the handsome Victorian homes that housed the first prosperous citizens, and numerous restaurants, cafes, shops and art galleries. Every summer the **National Festival of Music at Breckenridge** mounts a two-month season of classical music.

Alpine Skiing

Breckenridge, the ski area, is huge and wide-ranging. With 126 trails and 16 lifts on four distinct peaks, it is a statistical giant. **Peak 8** is the original ski area, with a complex network of interlaced trails for all ability levels and access to high, above-the-treeline bowls and chutes as well as **Peak 7**, a steep mountain that is patrolled but not groomed and has no lift service — extreme terrain by anyone's standards. **Peak 9** offers the greatest concentration of beginner and novice terrain and access to **Peak 10**, fabled for moguls, steeps and open glades. You can ski from mountain to mountain and back again, crisscrossing Breck's 1,600-acre playground via different routes each time. There are excellent children's facilities at both the Peak 8 and Peak 9 bases. Breckenridge has long welcomed snowboarders with a half-pipe, terrain features and just plain good riding.

Cross-country Skiing

The Breckenridge and Frisco Nordic Centers are under the same management and share an interchangeable trail pass. Both offer instruction and rentals of cross-country skis and snowshoes. The **Breckenridge Nordic Center**, (970) 453-6855, has more than 23 kilometers of groomed track set in the valleys below Peaks 7 and 8. The **Frisco Nordic Center's**, (970) 668-0866, 35 kilometers of trails are groomed daily for classical skiing and skating, with much of the system also offering great views of Lake Dillon and a par-

ticularly congenial log day lodge. Both centers offer a lesson guarantee and free afternoon beginner lessons. **Whateley Ranch**, 2 miles north of town, has an additional 15 kilometers of trails, (970) 453-2600. Miles of marked backcountry trails are found primarily south of Breckenridge.

Restaurants

Breckenridge is noted for its good restaurants, among them **Pierre's Restaurant**, (970) 453-0989, 111 S. Main Street, a fine French restaurant with lovely atmosphere and outdoor dining available in summer. The **St. Bernard Inn**, (970) 453-2572, 103 S. Main Street, specializes in classic Northern Italian food and also offers contemporary cuisine. The **Cafe Alpine**, (970) 453-8218, 106 Adams Street, serves lunch and dinner in a charming Victorian setting. Reservations are suggested at all three. More casual are the **Blue Moose Restaurant**, (970) 453-4859, 540 S. Main Street, or **Mi Casa Mexican Restaurant & Cantina**, (970) 453-2071, 600 S. Park Avenue, for Mexican specialties (no reservations). Most casual is the **Gold Pan**, (970) 453-5499, 105 N. Main Street, which serves huge Tex-Mex breakfasts as well as cheap pizza and bar food at lunch and dinner. The **Breckenridge Brewery & Pub**, (970) 453-1550, 600 S. Main Street, was one of the state's first brewpubs and is still is one of the most popular (there's even a branch near Coors Field in Denver). Avalanche Ale is one of the favorites, and they make their own potent root beer and hearty portions of pub food too.

Accommodations

With lodging for nearly 25,000 visitors, Breckenridge ranks as one of Colorado's major resort towns with all types of overnight options in many price ranges. Call the **Breckenridge Resort Chamber of Commerce Central Reservations**, (970) 453-2918 or (800) 221-1091, for information or reservations at the town's many condominiums, bed and breakfasts and other accommodations. **William's House Bed & Breakfast**, (800) 795-2975 or (970) 453-2975, 303 N. Main Street, is a lovely 19th-century home in classic Victorian style. Some rooms are wheelchair-accessible, and it has a Jacuzzi, fireplace and sitting area. Rates are from $79 to $200, for rooms or the cottage, depending upon the season. **Beaver Run Resort**, (800) 252-2253 and (970) 453-6000, a ski-in/ski-out establishment on Peak 9, is Breckenridge's largest property with lodging ranging from hotel rooms to three-bedroom suites. The fully equipped resort has indoor and outdoor swimming pools, hot tubs, fitness facilities, shops, restaurants and even an indoor miniature golf course. Winter rates begin at $135; summer rates at $95. The nearby **Hilton Resort Breckenridge**, (800) 321-8444 or (970) 453-4500, 550 Village Road, has rooms from $135 to $175 per night in winter (from $95 in summer); children stay free in their parents' room. It has well-appointed rooms, indoor/outdoor swimming pools and full hotel services.

Shopping

It's fun just to walk along Main Street and window-shop among the many clothing shops and galleries that line the colorful Victorian-style downtown area. Gingerbread facades decorate nearly every shop in this charming village, and purveyors of such popular purchases as T-shirts and sports equipment abound. Two excellent galleries are **Hibberd McGrath**, (970) 453-6391, 101 N. Main Street, for fine crafts, and **Kinkopf Gallery**, (970) 453-9095, 320 S. Main Street, for contemporary folk art paintings, sculpture, pottery and fine jewelry. **Amazonia's Sweaters** has two stores: (970) 453-4904, Bell Tower Mall, 555 S. Columbine Road, and (970)453-2554, Pound Square, 100 N. Main Street. Both have interesting hand-knitted sweaters in South American-looking and folk-art influenced styles. The **Twisted Pine Fur & Leather Company** has three locations for Western clothing and home furnishings: (970) 453-6615, 411 S. Main Street, for men's clothing and hats; (970) 453-9588, 100 S. Main Street, for women's wear; and upstairs from the women's shop, (970) 453-8819, for rugs and household furnishings. The **Bay Street Company**, (970) 453-6303, 232 S. Main Street, is a great shop to find unique home furnishings. Look for whimsical children's clothing, skiwear, toys and books at **Two Feet Tall**, (970) 453-0691, 326 S. Main Street.

Summer Activities

Breckenridge really shines in the summer with the recent development of **Riverwalk Center**, an elegant multipurpose facility that is home to the **National Festival of Music at Breckenridge**, (970) 452-2120. This covered, heated facility is mandated by summer nights that are cool at Breckenridge's altitude. Jazz, rock, pop and other groups also perform at the Riverwalk Center, as does the Breckenridge Film Festival, which celebrated its 15th season in 1996. The **Summit County Historical Society**, (970) 453-9200, conducts a variety of walking tours, mainly in summer but also in winter on demand. You can visit a couple of Breckenridge's mines too. Ninety-minute tours of the **Washington Gold Mine** are offered Monday through Saturday at 1 PM and of **Lomax Placer Gulch** at 3 PM. The price for each is $4 for adults, $3 for children. For directions, call the **Breckenridge Guest Services and Activity Center**, (970) 453-5579.

The **Breckenridge Golf Club**, (970) 453-9104, 200 Clubhouse Drive, offers outstanding golf at America's only Jack Nicklaus-designed municipal course. High-season green and cart fees in 1996 were $80 for 18 holes. **Breckenridge Stables**, (970) 453-4438, 1799 Ski Hill Road (above the Super Slide on Peak 8), offers rides over the Tenmile Range and prides itself on its gentle horses. One-hour rides are $18; two hours, $30; children 6 and younger are half-price. Don't forget, there's hiking in the **Arapahoe National Forest** and river rafting on the **Blue River**.

Keystone and Arapahoe Basin

Alpine Skiing

Keystone is a self-contained resort with skiing on three contiguous mountains: **Keystone Mountain**, primarily for novice and intermediate skiers; **North Peak**, with its excellent mogul runs; and **The Outback** and the **Outback Bowl**, with powder-holding glades and steeps. Thanks to a huge and efficient snowmaking system, Keystone is traditionally the first Colorado ski area to open for the season. Mid-October openings are not uncommon, and Halloween skiing is a tradition. For the 1996-97 season, Keystone also welcomes snowboarders to a sensational snowboarding park in **Packsaddle Bowl**. It's the only Summit County area (and one of the few in Colorado) to offer night skiing and snowboarding, nightly until 9 PM during most of the season.

Arapahoe Basin is operated by the same company that runs Keystone, but the two have totally different flavors. Keystone has trails and slopes laced through the trees. A-Basin, 6 miles away, is America's highest ski area, with a base altitude of 10,800 feet and a summit elevation of 12,450 feet. Rugged terrain, fabled steeps, open bowls and high, tree-free snowfields make it paradise for advanced and expert skiers and snowboarders. The lifts can run into summer, as in 1995, when A-Basin finally closed on August 10.

Both areas have child-care facilities. Keystone's nursery, which remains open in the evening during night skiing, takes babies as young as 2 months, and parents may use complimentary pagers to stay in touch with the center. Arapahoe Basin's nursery starts at 18 months. Both offer ski lessons from age 3 and snowboarding lessons from age 8.

Frisco, Dillon and Silverthorne

Frisco and **Dillon** were once mining towns, though the original Dillon is now at the bottom of Lake Dillon, a reservoir, and what you see was either moved before it was filled or rebuilt since then. **Silverthorne** has become known as a major outlet center, with more than 80 manufacturers' outlets (see the subsequent "Shopping" section) as well as lodging near the lake. All three now have numerous stores, restaurants and accommodations (including condos) convenient to all the Summit County ski areas.

Cross-country Skiing

The **Keystone Cross Country Center** is temporarily beside Keystone Lake and will eventually be relocated near the stables on Soda Ridge Road about a mile west of the main lodge. Directed by ebullient former Olympian Jana Hlavaty, it offers outstanding instruction programs and guided ski tours. Nearly 35 kilometers of prepared trails lace through the Snake River Valley and high on the mountain, accessible from North Peak. For information call the **Keystone Resort Activity Desk**, (970) 468-4386.

Several Nordic routes are accessible from the road to Montezuma or directly from this old mining camp. Peru Creek is a good trail for novices, while the routes to the St. John and the Wild Irishman Mine trails are popular with intermediate skiers and snowshoers. All are accessed for free.

Restaurants

The **Alpenglow Stube**, in The Outpost at the top of Keystone's North Peak, serves elegant, Bavarian-influenced contemporary cuisine for lunch and dinner. Dinner reservations are essential. **Der Fondue Chessel**, next door in The Outpost where the mountain-top self-service restaurant operates during the skiing day, serves Swiss specialties to the oompah of live entertainment. For both options at The Outpost, you can ski in during the day, and in the evening, you ride the enclosed gondola from the top of Keystone Mountain to get there. Down in the valley, the elegantly rustic **Keystone Ranch** has garnered accolades for its six-course dinners and an outstanding wine list. **Ski Tip Lodge**, once a stagecoach stop and Summit County's original ski lodge, is reminiscent of an Old New England Inn. Its quaint and charming restaurant serves excellent American and continental cuisine. For reservations at any of them, call **Keystone Resort Activity Desk**, (970) 468-4386.

For a great Margarita — though you'll have to fight the crowds — go to the **Old Dillon Inn**, (970) 468-2791, on Colo. Highway 9 in Silverthorne, north of I-70. The restaurant primarily serves Mexican food and has a 19th-century bar and lively music. **The Mint**, (970) 468-5247, in Silverthorne at 341 Blue River Parkway, is quieter. It's in one of Summit County's oldest buildings (one of those rescued from drowning in the bottom of the lake) and is a good family dining spot where you cook your own steak or chicken on the grill. The **Arapahoe Cafe**, (970) 468-2788, at 626 Lake Dillon Drive in Dillon, is a cozy log cabin serving good breakfasts and moderately priced dinners. The **Snake River Saloon**, (970) 468-2788, 23074 U.S. Highway 6 in Dillon, is popular for après-ski, steak dinners and late-night entertainment.

Accommodations

The original Keystone development centered around Keystone Lake and the surrounding woods. The **Keystone Lodge** offers luxurious mountain- and lake-view rooms for around $160 per night in low season to $220 in winter high season, double occupancy. Keystone also offers nearby condominium and private home rentals of various sizes, styles and prices. As a rule of thumb, figure on paying from $135 nightly in low season for a one-bedroom unit to $285 in high season, and $215 to $415 for a two-bedroom.

Closer to the mountain, the **Chateaux d'Mont** costs $600 to $800 per night for a truly deluxe two- or three-bedroom condo within walking distance of the lifts and featuring a private hot tub on a glass-enclosed balcony. Services include a welcome grocery package, fresh flowers, plush terry-cloth robes, nightly turndown, complimentary newspaper and concierge service. The **Keystone Inn** offers double rooms starting at $130 a night and studio condos starting at $110. A true pedestrian village currently is taking shape at the base of the River Run gondola, offering additional lodging options. For more information or reservations at these lodges contact Keystone Reservations, (970) 468-4242 or (800) 222-0188.

Shopping

If you like outlet shopping, the Silverthorne outlet centers are the place for you. Coloradans and shoppers from far afield come to the famous-name outlet stores such as **Bass Shoes**, **Liz Claiborne**, **Pendleton**, **Nike**, **Royal Doulton** and **Miller Stockman Western Wear**. The stores are open seven days a week and offer a 40 percent average savings over retail. There are three malls just off I-70 at Exit 205. For a complete listing of stores and hours, call (970) 468-9440.

Other Winter Activities

Skiing is the No. 1 activity in winter in Summit County, but other options, snow-related and otherwise, abound. Winter sleigh rides, snowmobiling, dogsled rides and other activities can be arranged through the **Breckenridge Guest Services and Activity Center**, (970) 453-5579 or the **Keystone Resort Activity Desk**, (970) 468-4386. In addition to making reservations, these services can also provide information on prices, hours and availability of off-slope activities.

There's ice skating on **Maggie Pond** in Breckenridge and on **Keystone Lake**, the largest maintained natural ice surface in the country. **Tiger Run**, (800) 318-1FUN or (970) 453-2231, between Frisco and Breckenridge, is one of the nation's top snowmobile tour operators. Breckenridge's outstanding **public recreation center**, (970) 453-1734, at 880 Airport Road, just off Colo. Highway 9, offers indoor lap and recreational pools, a kiddie fountain, tennis and racquetball courts, a running track, fitness facilities, a climbing wall and a variety of other programs. There are also outdoor tennis, basketball and volleyball courts; a skateboard park; and a playground. It is open 6 AM to 10 PM on weekdays, 7 AM to 10 PM Saturdays and 8 AM to 10 PM on Sundays. Nonresident adults pay $6.50; youths ages 13 to 17 and seniors 60 and older, $4; children ages 3 to 12, $3.25; and toddlers are free.

Good Times, (800) 477-0144 or (970) 453-0764, can arrange snowmobile tours, sleigh rides, dogsledding and other activities for Breckenridge-based guests. Special events include the **Lighting of Breckenridge** in December, and the annual **International Snow Sculpture Championships** and **Ullr Fest**, named after the mythical Norse snow god, both in January. Breckenridge is also a frequent stop on the World Cup ski racing, freestyle skiing and snowboarding circuits.

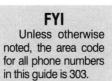

FYI

Unless otherwise noted, the area code for all phone numbers in this guide is 303.

The classic sights of summer in Summit County are often seen on horseback.

Summer Activities

Mountain biking is king all over Colorado, but in Summit County, riding along the paved **Blue River Bikeway** connecting Breckenridge and Frisco is a milder option. The route parallels Colo. Highway 9, winding through meadows and forests. If you can handle the uphill, take the paved **Tenmile Canyon National Recreation Trail** from Frisco up to Copper Mountain, or put your bike on a free Summit Stage bus and coast down. From Copper Mountain, you can also continue on the **Vail Pass Bikeway**, a 20-mile route (one-way) that climbs over 10,600-foot Vail Pass and down into Vail Village. These are beautiful rides anytime, but especially in early fall when the aspen trees are turning gold. For trail maps and information, contact the **Summit County Chamber of Commerce** and **Frisco Visitors' Center** at (970) 668-5800 or (970) 668-0376, or **Dillon Visitors' Center** at (970) 668-3671. Contact the **Dillon District Office of Arapahoe National Forest**, (970) 468-5400, at 680 Colo. Highway 9 in Silverthorne, for mountain biking information. There's a seasonal office at 135 Colo. Highway 9 (a.k.a. Blue River Parkway).

Lake Dillon is a 3,000-acre reservoir offering opportunities and charters for all types of boating, including fishing and sailboats. The **Dillon Marina**, (970) 468-5100 or 468-4355, is open from the end of May through October. Fly fishing in the **Blue River** is popular too.

The **Keystone Golf Course**, designed by Robert Trent Jones Jr., is known for both scenery and challenge. After exiting onto U.S. Highway 6, look for signs to the golf course (take Soda Ridge Road to the end, then go left on Keystone Ranch Road). Greens fees in 1996 were $98 per person including cart; Keystone lodging guests pay less, and golf packages are available. The **Keystone Resort Activity Desk**, (970) 468-4386, takes tee-time reservations. The **Eagles Nest Golf Club**, (970) 468-0681, 305 Golden Eagle Road in Silverthorne, offers a round for $55 until 2 PM and $45 until 4 PM and $30 until 6 PM, all including cart rentals; weekend greens fees are $70, $50 and $30, respectively. This mountainous course was not designed for speed of play; rather, to challenge the intermediate and advanced golfer.

Copper Mountain

Copper Mountain is a self-contained resort that was constructed a quarter of a century ago and has since won kudos for its outstanding trail and slope design as well as for its compact and congenial village. It has the distinction of being the site of Club Med's first and only North American ski village.

Alpine Skiing

Front Range skiers often head into the first parking lot off Interstate-70 and board the nearest lift to snare first tracks in new powder. Resort guests, those who need to check youngsters into Copper's excellent children's programs —or those simply inclined to take a more leisurely approach to the skiing day — start at the village center, where they have the choice of two high-speed express lifts, American Flyer or American Eagle, that respectively shuttle skiers toward **Copper Peak** and **Union Peak**. These two summits, the snow-kissed slopes cascading down on all sides and the valley between them offer a sensational array of ski and snowboard terrain for all ability levels. The **Union Creek** area, with a separate day lodge, is one of Colorado's best novice areas. If you're a new skier who needs practice, you can ride the K and L lifts and ski nearly 1,000 vertical feet of gentle terrain free during part of the ski season.

Copper Mountain is famous for its logical layout. As you are looking at the mountain, with I-70 at your back, most of the easy terrain is on your left, most of the mid-level runs are in the middle, and most of the challenging turf is to the left. Copper Peak, 12,441 feet, is (after A-Basin) Colorado's second-highest liftserved summit. **Spaulding Bowl**, **Union Bowl** and **Resolution Bowl** have long been favorites with powder-loving skiers and snowboarders, but in 1995-96, the area built the first of two lifts in Copper Bowl and catapulted into the top rank of Summit County ski areas. All the bowls are steep snow pockets, treasured by advanced skiers and riders. Copper Mountain now boasts 21 lifts (including three high-speed express chairlifts), 2,601 vertical feet and 2,433 acres of skiable terrain — the most in Summit County.

Belly Button Babies and the Belly Button Bakery, Copper's well-regarded day-care facilities, are in the Mountain Plaza Building. The children's ski school, which offers ski lessons from age 3 as well as snowboarding instruction for older children, is headquartered in its own building, with ski school desk, kids' rentals and food service under one roof.

Cross-country Skiing

Twenty-five kilometers of machine-set tracks and skating lanes start at Union Creek and wind through wooded valleys of the Arapahoe National Forest.

Restaurants

Presce Fresco, (970) 968-2318, Ext. 6505, in the Mountain Plaza Building near the main base area, offers light, contemporary American and continental cuisine at lunch and dinner. O'Shea's, (970) 968-2882, Ext. 6504, at the base of the American Eagle lift, has long been popular for burritos, nachos and other popular choices. Farley's Prime and Chop House, (970) 968-2577, at 104 Wheeler Place, satisfies the urge for steaks, ribs and seafood.

Accommodations

With the exception of Club Med, (800) CLUB-MED, which is geared for week-long ski vacations, all of the overnight lodging at Copper Mountain is in condominiums. Units range from compact studios to luxurious four-bedroom townhomes. Multi-day packages, including excellent family values, are available. All resort guests have free access to the excellent Copper Mountain Racquet & Athletic Club. Copper Mountain Resort, (970) 968-2882 or (800) 458-8386, handles reservations.

Summer Activities

Copper Mountain Resort offers golf, horseback riding, mountain biking, paddleboat rides, tennis and free scenic chairlift rides. Over Labor Day weekend, Michael Martin Murphey's WestFest is held at Copper Mountain, with three days of country-western music, crafts and food. At 9,650 feet, the Copper Creek Golf Course, (970) 968-2339, 104 Wheeler Place, is the highest-altitude 18-hole championship golf course in America. It is said that balls will fly 15 percent to 20 percent farther than at sea level. Golf packages are available. For more information call Copper Mountain Resort, (970) 968-2882 or (800) 458-8386.

The Wheeler-Dillon Pack Trail, which begins across the highway from Copper Mountain and climbs steeply into the rugged Gore Range, offers a challenge for hikers, backpackers and horseback riders. Pack trips can be arranged through Copper Mountain Stables, (970) 968-2232, 355 Beeler Place. The Colorado Trail, a popular hiking and backpacking trail built by volunteers, much like the Appalachian Trail in the East, passes near Copper Mountain too.

Unsinkable Molly Brown and Her Revived House

A visit to the Molly Brown House is more than a trip into Denver's past. Brown was one of the survivors of the *Titanic*, and a small museum on site tells the story. "Typical Brown luck, we're unsinkable," she proclaimed, after rescue. She had traveled to Europe on the *Titanic's* sister ship, *Olympic*, and spent part of the winter in Egypt with the Astors, who encouraged her to book first-class return passage on the *Titanic's* maiden voyage. The *Titanic* was the largest and newest ocean liner of its time and was considered to be unsinkable. Its anchor had 1,050 feet of chain. The ship even had

a gym equipped with stationary weights, a bicycle, rowing machine and an electric camel ride.

On April 14, 1912, at 11:40 PM, the crew of the *Titanic* spotted an iceberg, which the ship could not avoid because it was too big to maneuver quickly. The ship broadsided the iceberg, broke in two and at 2:20 AM sank to the bottom of the freezing North Atlantic, taking most of its 2,228 passengers — only 705 survived, among them Brown. Most of the survivors were women and children because Victorian ethics demanded that they be saved first. Brown assisted in the rescue efforts in the lifeboat and made the women sing so they would stop crying. After they were rescued she raised more than $10,000 for the survivors. She also submitted an insurance claim against the shipping company for more than $27,000, including a necklace valued at $20,000 and three dozen gloves at $50.

Photo: Jeff Black

The name "Molly" was the invention of the 1960s Broadway musical based on the life of Margaret "Maggie" Brown. According to a nine-year guide at the Molly Brown House, the movie version starring Debbie Reynolds — though entertaining — is not very accurate. Brown was born to a Hannibal, Missouri, ditch digger and his wife in 1867. She said Mark Twain inspired her to go west. She went to Leadville, Colorado, and worked as a seamstress at the Daniel and Fisher department store. There, she met her husband-to-be James Joseph Brown (J.J.), who was from Pennsylvania and working for the Ibex Mining Company. After the 1893 silver crash, J.J. found gold in the Little Johnnie mine and became a millionaire. The Browns then moved to Denver, where Molly was considered by Denver society to have three strikes against her: she was Catholic, Irish and nouveau riche. Nevertheless, the Brown home soon became the focus of Denver society.

The Molly Brown House in Denver is a worthwhile stop.
—

She and her husband never got along well, partially due to Molly's unorthodox but charitable behavior. She told impoverished Indians to set up their tents on her front lawn after they were driven off the state Capitol grounds. That was the final straw for her husband, who then moved out. Molly continued to live an extravagant life traveling and circulating in the high society of Denver, Newport and Europe. But she also spent much of her time and money supporting various causes, including women's suffrage, local Catholic charities and the reform of maritime law. She received the French Legion of Honor, with Sarah Bernhardt, for her efforts during World War I. During the 1920s Molly lived at the Brown Palace Hotel, and her lovely home became a boarding house. She died in 1932.

The home fell into ruin, but in 1970 its acquisition and restoration became the first project of Historic Denver, which was created for this purpose. Touring the house is a real treat. Tour guides wear white Victorian dresses and carry white lace parasols. The dark red stone mansion is a late Victorian Queen Anne-style home, with Romanesque touches. The neighborhood was considered to be upper-middle class when the Browns resided there. Nearby Grant Street was millionaire's row, where cattle barons and railroad magnets lived in rambling mansions.

The Molly Brown house is filled with antiques, many of which are the family's original furniture dredged up from various Denver sources, including thrift shops. The beautiful stained-glass windows and golden oak woodwork are original. More than a half-million dollars in private funds have been raised to restore the Molly Brown House, which is well worth a visit. There's a great gift shop in the old carriage house with a room devoted to the *Titanic*. The Molly Brown House Museum and Gift Shop, 832-4092, 1340 Pennsylvania Street, Denver, is open Monday through Saturday from 10 AM to 4 PM and Sunday from noon to 4 PM (closed Mondays from September through May). The last tour is at 3:30 PM. Admission for adults is $5; seniors 65 and older, $3.50; children ages 6 through 12, $1.50. It's three blocks east of the State Capitol and 1½ blocks south of Colfax Avenue.

Boulder offers a big-city selection of arts ranging from local artists with national reputations to the summer Colorado Music Festival with musicians from around the world.

Boulder
Arts

Despite its small-city size, Boulder offers a big-city selection of arts, ranging from local artists with national reputations to the summer Colorado Music Festival with musicians from around the world. The internationally renowned Colorado Dance Festival and the Colorado Shakespeare Festival also attract top talent. The Boulder Museum of Contemporary Art (BMoCA) shows work by both locally and nationally known artists as do the University of Colorado galleries. In addition to exhibitions, BMoCA and Naropa Institute hold innovative arts events.

Proximity to Denver expands the arts horizon with the Denver Art Museum, Colorado Symphony, Denver Center Theatre Company, Fiddler's Green and other venues. Even closer, the Arvada Center for the Arts and Humanities offers theater, music, dance and visual art by Colorado's best and nationally known artists. Other nearby communities of Longmont, Louisville, Lafayette, Lyons, Central City, Golden and Nederland offer their own historical museums, music and theater groups and art exhibitions as well.

In addition to the special film series listed below, Boulder has some 20 commercial movie theaters, among them United Artists and Mann theater complexes, Flatirons Theatre on University Hill and the Basemar Cinema Saver Theatres — the best bargain of all. A new 12-plex of theaters at the Louisville exit of U.S. 36 gives moviegoers an even bigger selection. Note that we have listed museums in our Boulder Attractions chapter. Below are the highlights of the area's arts offerings.

Music

Ars Nova Singers
• 499-3165

This group of 40 singers presents music from the Renaissance and 20th-century periods, including works by Colorado's finest composers. Now beginning its 11th season, Ars Nova is the first and only choir from Colorado funded by the National Endowment for the Arts and one of only 32 such choirs in the country. Ars Nova performs annual Christmas concerts in Boulder and Denver at area churches. The 1996-97 schedule includes an October concert, "Christmas With Ars Nova" in December and another December concert featuring Handel's Messiah in collaboration with the Boulder Philharmonic at the Boulder Theater. Ars Nova will collaborate with the Boulder Phil again in February, and concerts in May close the season. Ticket prices are $10 and $7 (for students and seniors 60 and older).

Artist Series
CU-Boulder Campus, Macky Auditorium or Grusin Music Hall • 492-8008

The University of Colorado-Boulder's Artist Series has been going strong for 60 years with a full season of varied performances. Some 1996-97 highlights include nationally known pianists Emanual Ax and Angela Cheng, who will perform with the Colorado Symphony Orchestra; the Mingus Big Band for jazz lovers; several dance troupes including the Alvin Ailey Repertory Ensemble; and violinist Gil Shaham, who will be accompanied by his brother, pianist Orli Shaham. The Takâcs String Quartet, the Hungarian artists in residence will give three repeat performances of their original shows. The Artist Series is held in the university's Macky Auditorium or Grusin Music Hall and includes performance art, jazz, classics, dance, folk and ethnic performances.

Arvada Center for the Arts and Humanities
6901 Wadsworth Blvd., Arvada • 431-3939

About a 30-minute drive south of Boulder, the Arvada Center is a sophisticated venue for music of all types, from popular to classical, with nationally known groups and performers. During performances, the upper gallery is open for viewing the work of Colorado's best artists and craftspeople. Summer concerts are in an outdoor amphitheater.

Boulder Bach Festival
No central address • 494-3159

It began in 1982 as a one-weekend festival; now the Boulder Bach Festival has evolved into a series of concerts year-round, highlighting the famous composer's work. The annual three-day Bach festival is in January. There are also children's concerts in March and April, a fall concert in the 100-year-old Ryssby Church west of Longmont and a New Year's Eve concert.

Boulder Philharmonic Orchestra
2590 Walnut St., Boulder • 449-1343

The orchestra's full season of performances from September through April includes old and new classics plus special Fireside Concerts at CU-Boulder's Old Main featuring chamber music and other light works. Noted guitarist Pepe Romero opened the Phil's season in September. Another of the year's highlights will be a performance by former Metropolitan Opera soprano Kathleen Battle. A Baroque Festival features five concerts at the Boulder Theater and Arvada Center for the Arts and Humanities with the Four Seasons Chamber Orchestra. The group also holds an annual Fantasy Ball in the spring, sponsored by the volunteer organization, Club Phil, one of the orchestra's greatest assets,

449-0627. The Boulder Philharmonic Academy, 449-9291, with some 200 students, offers group classes and private lessons and has large ensembles. It's rapidly becoming a well-known community arts school in Colorado and is the first and only of its kind in the state. New music director Theodore Kuchar from the Ukraine leads the Boulder Phil into the 1996-97 season.

Boulder Sinfonia
No central address • 442-7539

This 8-year-old volunteer chamber orchestra draws from a pool of 80 professional musicians. The group performs five concerts a year, usually at the First United Methodist Church, on 15th and Spruce streets. Featured works are often from such composers as Mozart, Ravel and Haydn. Tickets are generally $10 and can be ordered by calling the above number. Discounts are available for seniors.

Central City Opera
200 Eureka St., Central City • 292-6700, (800) 851-8175

One of Colorado's favorite outings, the Central City Opera features operatic works sung in English in this old mining town, recently turned gambling haven. This summer troupe is one of the oldest opera companies in the country, with a distinguished national reputation. The CCO also offers daytime cabaret opera and special youth performances. The opera house was built in 1878 to try to bring culture to the formerly rough and rowdy mining town. Performances are frequently sold out, so call ahead for reservations for this summer-only program. Reserved parking is available via a shuttle bus service that takes opera-goers from the parking area (a half-mile away) right to the opera house's front door. The bus leaves about every 10 minutes during the two hours before and after the opera, so there's plenty of time for a meal, gambling or sightseeing in Central City. Evening performances start at 8 PM Tuesday, Friday and Saturday (7:30 PM Thursday) and last around 2½ hours. Weekend matinees begin at 2:30 PM. Tickets range from $22 to $51. (Please see the Close-up for more information.)

Chautauqua Summer Festival Concerts
Main Office, Ninth St. and Baseline Rd.
• 440-7666, 442-3282

Summer in Boulder wouldn't truly be summer without Chautauqua, which features a series of popular-music concerts and performances in addition to the classical Colorado Music Festival (see our subsequent listing and close-up). This historic music venue has been an institution since 1898, when Boulder's Chautauqua first opened as part of a national movement that brought the arts to numerous Chautauqua summer camps around the country. Today, many concert-goers enjoy dinner on the lovely old veranda of the picturesque Chautauqua Dining Hall or bring a picnic to enjoy under the shady trees on the green. The Summer Festival Concerts have featured such groups and performers as Rosanne Cash, Los Lobos, Peter Kater, Michele Shocked, Richard Thompson, Joan Armatrading, Laurie Anderson, A Gospel Extravaganza with the Persuasions, and Leo Kottke. Some folks picnic into the night and enjoy the music (for free) from outside the concert hall. Dance fans can enjoy performances by Cleo Parker Robinson and Danielle Helander. Chautauqua makes it a point to feature quirky concerts such as Corky Siegel's Chamber Blues, a group that uses chamber instruments to play blues; the Reduced Shakespeare Company, "the Bad Boys of Abridgement," this year doing the Bible; and The Barbershoppers, a large barbershop chorus. The Boulder Folk and Blue Grass Festival is held at Chautauqua along with many other performers and performances, such as Carla Bonof, Spaulding Grey and A Tribute to Robert Johnson, with various blues artists performing his work. Tickets range from $8 to $32.

Colorado Symphony
1031 13th St., Denver • 98-MUSIC

Many Boulderites gladly make the trek to Denver to enjoy the Colorado Symphony at Denver's delightful Boettcher Hall. Choices include a regular concert series and special holiday concerts, plus Family, Masterworks and Blue Jeans concert series. The Colorado Christmas concert held in early December features the Colorado Children's Chorale and Colorado Symphony Chorus. A New Years' Eve Celebration features a postconcert dinner dance in Boettcher and the Pavilion of Performing Arts complex. The season ends in May this year (1997) with the Bernstein Mass with the Symphony Chorus, Colorado Children's Chorale and guest vocal soloists and dancers. Tickets prices range from $10 to $38 for regular concerts; ask about senior, student and child discounts. The Masterworks Series from September through May offers different popular classics: The 1996-97 schedule includes *A Night in the West*, *A Night in Space*, (with music from *Star Wars* and *Star Trek*) and music from Gilbert and Sullivan. Family concerts are held in November, December and February with such offerings as *Peter and the Wolf*, *Hands Across the Sea* and *The Fabulous Orchestra*. Performances are on Sundays at 2:30 and 4 PM and last an hour. The entire family series costs $15 for adults or kids or $10 (adults) and $5 (children) for single tickets. At Blue Jeans concerts, casual attire is preferred — in fact, the orchestra members wear blue jeans. The cost for all three Blue Jeans concerts is $25 for adults, $15 for children or $10 and $5 for individual tickets. The symphony also presents three operas with Opera Colorado (call the opera office at the number above or 778-1500 for information).

FYI

Unless otherwise noted, the area code for all phone numbers in this guide is 303.

Colorado Children's Chorale
1031 13th St., Denver • 98-MUSIC

The CCC presents popular and traditional music such as *Beauty and the Beast* and special compositions written for the chorale by resident composers. Children from all over the Denver Metro Area audition to get into one of the five chorales. There are annual U.S. and international choir tours by the group. A December Christmas concert features traditional holiday music, and there's a special spring concert in May. Tickets cost from $7 to $20.

Colorado Music Festival
Year round • 449-1397
Summer tickets • 449-2413

From late June through mid-August each

year, classical musicians from around the country — and world — come to Boulder to participate in the Colorado Music Festival at Boulder's historic Chautauqua. Now in its 20th season, the series includes a well-rounded selection of classics, from all-Bach or Beethoven concerts to Mozart, Gershwin, Tchaikovsky, chamber music and much more. There are several children's and family concerts too. The festival chamber orchestra gives Monday night performances at the historic Stanley Hotel Concert Hall in Estes Park. A Boulder Fourth of July tradition is the Colorado Music Festival's free concert on the Chautauqua lawn, highlighted with foot-thumping John Philip Sousa marches. Some highlights of the 1996 season were pianist Christopher Taylor, violinist Dong-Suk Kang, the Ying Quartet, French horn virtuoso David Jollie and guitarist Eduardo Fernandez. Season tickets are available in advance, or concert-goers can pay at the door. Last-minute tickets are available at the door and range from $6 to $33. (Please see our close-up for additional information.)

University of Colorado's College of Music
CU-Boulder campus • 492-8008

Another popular tradition is CU's College of Music summer lyric theater. In years past it has been a Gilbert and Sullivan Festival. There's usually a light opera or two. The Mile High Jazz Camp is always held in the third week of July. Upcoming fall and winter concerts include *South Pacific*, the *Spanish Hour* and Gianni Schicchi. The internationally renowned Takâcs String Quartet, who are artists in residence, is one of the regular pleasures of the College of Music schedule. The annual sold-out Festival of Christmas is a scholarship benefit for the College of Music. Most concerts are free; tickets are sold only for major productions.

Fiddler's Green
6350 Greenwood Plaza Blvd., Englewood • 220-7000

About an hour's drive from Boulder, Fiddler's Green, a popular outdoor concert hall on Denver's south side, offers nationally known groups that aren't likely to visit Boul-

der. Enjoy these summer-only concerts either with reserved seats or a picnic on the lawn. Tickets are available at the box office or by calling TicketMaster at 830-8497.

Public Library Concert Series
1000 Canyon Blvd. • 441-3100

This free series at the Boulder Public Library Auditorium (Canyon Boulevard entrance) offers music lovers a wealth of listening, from Bach to ragtime. Piano and harp soloists, string quartets, the Boulder Philharmonic and local musicians are among the varied performers.

Red Rocks
Morrison St., Morrison • 640-7334 (recorded information and events)

This spectacular natural-rock amphitheater is the venue for most top performers who come to the Denver area. Red Rocks information and tickets are available through TicketMaster at 830-8497. Check local newspapers for performers appearing at Red Rocks or call the listed number. Tickets range from $15 to $35 and are available with no service charge at McNichols Arena in Denver from 11 AM to 6 PM Monday through Friday and 10 AM to 3 PM Saturday (cash only and in person).

Film

Boulder Public Library Film Program
Main Branch Auditorium • Ninth St. and Canyon Ave. • 441-3197

This ongoing free film series has everything from Laurel and Hardy and Third World Cinema to special series on science-fiction, British classics and other topics not available on video. The library also shows mainstream Hollywood movies. Call for information, or visit the library to pick up the latest schedule. Movies are on Mondays, Thursdays and Fridays at 7:30 PM.

Chautauqua Summer Film Festival
Ninth St. and Baseline Rd. • 440-7666

Moviegoers of all ages will feel like kids at summer camp inside Chautauqua's barn-like auditorium. This summer-only program shows historic silent films such as *Phantom of the*

Photo: Daily Camera/Nico Toutenhoofd

Outreach and children's classes are an important part of each year's Colorado Dance Festival.

Opera and Charlie Chaplin flicks with a live piano player. Prices are $3 for adults and $2 for children (younger than 12) and special prices for film series.

University of Colorado Program Council Film Series
CU-Boulder Campus • Club 156 (in the UMC) and Chem. 140 in Chemistry Building (next building over from UMC), 16th St. and E. Euclid Ave. • 492-2255

These bargain- and student-priced films offer some of the best entertainment around. Catch up on first-run movies you might have missed at the local theater last year. A high-tech Dolby stereo cinema sound processor makes the sound system in the university's Chem. 140 auditorium/classroom one of Boulder's best. Pick up a film schedule at the University Memorial Center (UMC), Boulder Public Libraries, city recreation centers and local supermarkets. The film series does not run during the summer.

International Film Series
Muenzinger Auditorium (CU-Boulder campus) • Muenzinger Plaza, west of Folsom Stadium near the corner of Colorado Ave. and 18th St. • 492-1531

Connected with the CU-based Rocky Mountain Film Center, this series is the West's longest-running continuous forum for international and art film screenings and has entertained university and Boulder audiences for more than 50 years. The First Person Cinema is affiliated with the RMFC and features visiting artists throughout the academic year. It includes avant-garde works by independent and personal filmmakers such as Stan Brakhage, Fred Worden and Caroline Leaf, as well as wonderful, entertaining films from all over the world that aren't available in mall theaters or video stores. Ask about the Stan Brakhage Film Forum, a screening of rare and unusual films each Sunday (at 7:30 PM in Fine Arts Building N141) that's free and open to the public. The series is named for the late, renowned filmmaker and respected CU-Boulder professor. The spacious, steeply sloping Muenzinger Auditorium offers every moviegoer a perfect view for the right price — $3.50. The 24-hour hotline above lists each week's events.

Theater

Actors Ensemble Guild Theatre
4840 Sterling Dr. • 449-3296

Now in its 10th season, the Actors Ensemble strives to present award-winning and provocative contemporary theater. *Landscape of the Body* by John Guare, *The Boys Next Door* by Tom Griffin and *Pterodactyls* have been some featured performances. The ensemble gives three shows per year, with a season running from October through May. Call for a current schedule.

Arvada Center for the Arts and Humanities
6901 Wadsworth Blvd., Arvada • 431-3939

The Arvada Center opened its stage doors in 1976 and has been an equity theater since 1992, bringing professional talent into an intimate setting. The indoor theater seats 500, and the outdoor amphitheater seats 600 with both covered and lawn seating. Some highlights of the 1996-97 season include *Gypsy* in December and the musical *Company* in May. Ticket prices range from $18 to $24 with discounts for seniors and students. Shows run Tuesday through Sunday with matinees. The Arvada Center also has a huge education program offering more than 100 classes for both children and adults in everything from acting, performing arts and music to ceramics and humanities.

Boulder Dinner Theatre
5501 Arapahoe Ave. • 449-6000

From *A Chorus Line* to *Oklahoma*, the Boulder Dinner Theatre is the only local venue for popular musicals. This dinner theater has won a number of awards for its professional performances with excellent sets and staging. The food is quite good too. The theater offers cocktails and a choice of delicious dinners — the prime rib is great! — served by its talented singers and performers. Tickets cost $26 to $36 per person and are discounted for seniors and children on some performances.

The Boulder Repertory Company
Boulder Public Library • 1000 Canyon Blvd. • 449-7258

The Boulder Repertory Company presents three shows a year. Lacking a home of its own, this company has performed in approximately 11 different locations since 1975, including the Guild Theatre and University of Colorado. The Boulder Rep's fine productions are worth seeing. Artistic director Frank Georgianna launched TBRC in 1975, and it has become one of Boulder's most respected companies. Georgianna was a director and actor at the Denver Center Theatre from 1985

to 1994. The performances are usually in the Boulder Public Library auditorium and occasionally in Denver. Call for a current schedule.

Colorado Shakespeare Festival
Mary Rippon Theatre (CU-Boulder campus) • 492-0554

Film actor Val Kilmer took part in these Shakespeare productions one year, and other top performers, such as TV star Jimmy Smits, have likewise been attracted to this highly regarded annual festival. Held at the outdoor Mary Rippon Theatre, this summer festival is another local institution. It includes both traditional and modern renditions of the bard's work. In 1996 the festival presented four shows, *A Midsummer Night's Dream*, *The Merchant of Venice*, *Othello* and the *Miser* by Molière. The theater-goers can order "Falstaff's Fare," a box dinner made by Traditions Catering and dine on the green before the show while Shakespeare himself (actor Chuck Wilcox) strolls about chatting with diners. There are evening and Sunday matinee performances.

University of Colorado Department of Theatre and Dance
CU-Boulder Campus • 492-7355 (box office) • 492-8181

Considered by local critics to present the most consistently good and reliable performances, the CU-Boulder Theatre Department won the 1993 Denver Drama Critics Circle award for Best Season for a Company. Throughout the school year, this university department holds numerous performances at campus theaters. The 1996 schedule includes Shakespeare's *Comedy of Errors* in the fall and *Dancing at Lughnasa*. There's a December Faculty Dance Concert, and other planned performances include *Abingdon Square*, *Machinal* and *You Can't Take It With You* (in April 1997). The department also offers performances by students in the master of fine arts degree program and student dance performances. Call for more information or a complete schedule.

Denver Center Theatre Company
13th and Curtis Sts., Denver • 893-4100

The Denver Center attracts big Broadway shows with national touring companies, but the Denver Center Theatre Company is the local theater company that performs at the Denver Center, featuring a varied menu of entertainment ranging from works by Dickens and Shakespeare to the life of Janis Joplin. Tickets cost $15 to $50.

Opera Colorado
1031 13th St., Denver • 98-MUSIC

Opera Colorado's season consists of three operas presented in March, April and May, plus a student performance in February at Loretto Heights College. In 1997 look for *La Traviata* in March and Mozart's *Don Giovanni* and Gounod's *Faust* in April and May. Tickets cost from $15 to $116, with discounts at selected performances for seniors and students. Some tickets are available at the door if the show is not sold out. Subscriptions and single tickets are available in November.

Peanut Butter Players
2475 Mapleton Ave. • 786-8PBP

Based in the Toadstool Playhouse, one of Boulder's funky landmark buildings, this theater company of local youngsters ages 5 to 18 offers year-round performances. Luncheon theaters are held on weekends in October and November and from February through April, performed by a small troupe of professional child actors (the $7 ticket includes lunch). There are classes during the school year and

a day camp in summer that teach such things as music, puppetry, pantomime, dance, makeup, voice dialects, clowning and theater crafts. Each summer PBP puts on a major production at Boulder High School with about 250 children ($5 for adults, $3 for children). PBP has been in Boulder for five years, after 15 years in Michigan.

Public Theater Boulder Museum of Contemporary Art
1750 13th St. • 443-2122

Held at BMoCA, the theater features the Perforum Music Series the first Saturday of every month, with jazz, avant-garde and experimental music. There are dance and new performances four times a year and traditional performances about three times a year. Call or stop by for a current schedule.

Longmont Theatre Company Performing Arts Center
513 Main St., Longmont • 772-5200

A short drive from Boulder via the Longmont Diagonal Highway (Colo. Highway 119), the Longmont Theatre Company offers some varied and lively performances such as folk singers, serious drama and full-scale musical productions such as *Annie* and *Man of La Mancha*. There's also a Shakespeare Festival. Call for a current schedule of performances.

Photo: University of Colorado

Film actor Val Kilmer is an alumnus of the Colorado Shakespeare Festival, where he starred in *Hamlet*.

Naropa Institute Performing Arts Center
2130 Arapahoe Ave. • 546-3538

Not limited to theater per se, Naropa has speakers, poetry readings and various performances. In 1994 the institute celebrated its 20th anniversary with a special Allen Ginsberg Tribute in honor of the poet who helped found Naropa. The tribute included appearances by well-known "Beat" poets and authors including Ginsberg, Ken Kesey, Gary Snyder and David Amram. Naropa Institute's center offers music, workshops, dance performances and art exhibits. Call for a schedule of events.

Nomad Playhouse
1410 Quince St. • 443-7510

"Just a little off Broadway," is the dual-meaning slogan of the Nomads, housed in North Boulder in a large Quonset hut on Quince just off Broadway. Former Boulderite, now television star, Joan Van Ark says she got her acting start with the Nomads, which hosts some excellent serious and not-so-serious drama. For more than 40 years, the Nomads has entertained audiences with fine local talent and thoughtful performances from fall through spring. Nomads is currently undergoing renovation of the theater and hopes to reopen in January. Call for information.

Upstart Crow Guild Theatre
4840 Sterling Dr. • 442-1415

Now celebrating its 17th season, this low-budget group dresses in period costumes and performs classical plays in their complete and uncut versions. *Hamlet* and *Playboy of the Western World* were some recent performances. The company features "name your price" nights on the first Sunday and second Friday of each run.

Summer in Boulder Means Chautauqua

Black clouds slid down the mountains for the gala opening of the 1996 Colorado Music Festival. As well-dressed attendees sipped wine in white tents on the concert hall lawn, the heavens opened. Soon, drenched waiters in tuxedos were sloshing among the concert patrons offering platters of appetizers. Rivers ran down the nearby sidewalk as people watched in amazement, then suddenly a small river of muddy water rushed through the middle of the tent right under the elegantly set buffet tables, drowning fancy shoes and dampening trouser hems.

The rain stopped long enough for people to move to the concert hall. Giving the season's opening welcome, Boulder Mayor Leslie Durgin, who is also the director of Chautauqua, lauded Boulder's spirit. "Last year at the Asian Children's Concert when the roof started leaking with a downpour like this one, the audience members offered their umbrellas to the performers. But we have a brand-new roof this year," Durgin proudly announced.

The initial soft rain so pleasantly pattering in the background of the all-Beethoven concert soon became a roar of hail that threatened to drown out the orchestra. Through the new roof, rain began to drip on the audience, and one by one umbrellas opened inside the concert hall. Soon it began dripping on the orchestra onstage. In the middle of the featured concerto, pianist Larry Graham leaned back to dodge dripping water, then looked at the audience and laughed, and the entire concert came to a halt. For about 10 minutes the concert became the sounds of nature's fury and the still-leaking new roof. Finally, the rain lessened and the concert resumed, making it a stormy gala night of music to remember.

At the turn of the century there were 12,000 Chautauquas in the United States. Today there are only three. One of them is in Boulder. Chautauqua is a Native American word that means "two moccasins tied together." It's the name of a lake in New York state that was the birthplace of this former national movement of summer camps/retreats

Photo: Daily Camera/Lourie Zipf

Flowers and Flatirons frame Chautauqua Concert Hall.

where people went for cultural or spiritual renewal. Boulder's Chautauqua always focused on arts and entertainment while others around the country focused on religion.

Boulder hosted such famous guests as statesman William Jennings Bryant and musician John Philip Sousa. Boulder's Chautauqua has a lovely park setting on the edge of Boulder's Mountain Park system and is a designated national historic district, jointly run by the National Park Service and the City of Boulder. According to *Inside Performance Magazine*, performing artists voted Boulder's Chautauqua one of the top 10 halls in the United States in which they love to perform — even when the roof leaks.

Visual Arts

Admission to the following galleries and shops is free unless otherwise noted.

ARTcycle
2019 15th St. (between Pearl and Spruce Sts.) • Open (sporadically) daily, call for times • 449-4950

Featuring recycled art at its best, this store offers a high-quality selection of pre-owned art in all media and prices by successful local and nationally known artists. There are paintings, limited-edition prints, sculptures, photographs and more. ARTcycle takes new consignments all the time and also offers custom framing.

Arvada Center for the Arts & Humanities
6901 Wadsworth Blvd., Arvada • Hours: 9 AM to 5 PM Mon. through Sat., 1 to 5 PM Sun. • 431-3080

Nationally known artists and Colorado's best artists and craftspeople show their work in the Arvada Center's excellent gallery. There is also a permanent historical exhibit of the area's early days.

Boulder Museum of Contemporary Art
1750 13th St. • Hours: 11 AM to 5 PM Tues. through Sat., 9 AM to 5 PM Sat.; noon to 5 PM Sun., closed Mon. • Admission: $2; Sun., free on weekends and to members • 443-2122

A nonprofit Boulder institution since 1972,

the museum has hosted most established local and area artists over the years as well as regional, national and international visual and performing artists. BMoCA emphasizes contemporary and multicultural exhibitions. Some well-known artists whose works have been shown include ceramic sculptor Lynda Benglis and silver printmaker Teun Hocks. The nationally acclaimed exhibition *Animals* by photographers James Balog and Joel Peter Witkin showed a few years ago at BMoCA. Photographer Balog lives in the Boulder area. Other notable exhibitions have been *Seven Years in Tibet* by Heinrich Harrer and a 40-year retrospective of works on paper by Dorothy Dehner.

The museum also holds popular annual events including the summertime Sculpture in the Park and Art in the Streets, when local artists paint bus benches that are auctioned off to benefit BMoCA.

BMoCA offers workshops open to the public, including figure-drawing sessions with live models, each Monday from 7 to 10 PM ($4 model fee). The second floor is home to the Public Theater, hosting various performances of dance, music and theater. Admission is free for members.

Boulder Arts & Crafts Cooperative
1421 Pearl St. • Hours: 10 AM to 6 PM Mon. through Sat. (until 9 PM in summer and holidays); 11 AM to 6 PM Sun. • 443-3683

The Co-op has more than 50 members and a total of more than 100 artists, including nationally known artists and participating members and consignees from Colorado and surrounding mountain states. Well-deserved, the Co-op won Westword's Best Craft gallery in the Denver Metro Area for 1996. Nowhere else in the area will you find such a concentrated collection of top-quality pottery, puppets, jewelry, photographs, weavings, stained glass, woodwork and other items. Look for Vivian Jean's lovely, pastel-toned majolica pottery and Harriet Peck Taylor's enchanting Southwestern and rain forest batik images made into cards, T-shirts and framed art. Ruth Ann Maze's pottery, Elaine Jackson's dried wildflowers, Bill Ervin's wildlife photography and other outdoor images are top sellers. The Co-op has an extensive and spectacular jewelry selection with precious metals and contemporary fashion jewelry. Opened in 1971, the member-directed Co-op is currently celebrating its 25th year.

Boulder Public Library
1000 Canyon Blvd. • Hours: 9 AM to 9 PM Mon. through Thurs., 9 AM to 6 PM Fri. and Sat.; noon to 6 PM Sun. • 441-4397

Besides the library's permanent art collection in both wings, there are ongoing exhibitions by contemporary regional artists in various media in an area called The Exhibit Space (entrance on Canyon Boulevard). With a gallery ceiling height of 11 feet, 10 inches and 160 linear feet of exhibition walls, it's one of the largest display spaces in Boulder. Most artists whose work is shown are well-known Colorado painters and sculptors, though some national traveling exhibits are also displayed. Another worthwhile stop is at the display cases on the bridge, where all types of interesting exhibits are shown monthly. The Boulder Public Library Meadows Branch, 4800 Baseline Road, also has a display space, featuring such things as raku pottery and the Hawaiian art of leis and ceremonial capes made of feathers. For historic photographs check out the Carnegie Library, 1125 Pine Street, which has digitized about 7,000 of its best photographs so people can view them on a computer screen without touching them and causing possible damage.

Boulder Stained Glass Studios
1920 Arapahoe Ave. • Hours: 9 AM to 5:30 PM Mon. through Fri. and by appointment • 449-9030

Specializing in glass work in Boulder for 20 years, the studio specializes in custom design and fabrication, whether it be architectural or period work. The studio's general approach is architectural, though there's a selection of beautiful glass items ranging from $10 up, including blown-glass vases, jewelry, clocks and imaginative pieces by various Colorado artists. The studio is known for its high-quality contemporary and period leaded, etched and beveled stained glass. It primarily promotes glass crafts by Colorado artisans.

University of Colorado Art Galleries
Sibell-Wolle Fine Arts Bldg. (east of UMC at Broadway and Euclid), CU-Boulder campus • Hours: 8 AM to 4:30 PM Mon. through Thurs., 8 AM to 8 PM Fri, and 1 to 5 PM Sat (Summer); 8 AM to 5 PM Mon. through Fri. (until 8 PM Tues.), noon to 4 PM Sat. (Winter). Closed Sunday all year. • 492-8300

CU-Boulder's Art Galleries occasionally throw a big opening-night bash when a new exhibit goes up. Large group shows of student and faculty work are especially fun and zany — a little bit of New York in Boulder. The Sibell-Wolle galleries regularly feature impressive and exciting work by students, faculty and international artists. There are also public lectures given by well-known visiting artists.

Denver Art Museum
100 W. 14th Ave., Denver • Hours: 10 AM to 5 PM Tues. through Sat.; noon to 5 PM Sun. • Admission: $3 adults; $1.50 seniors and students; free to members and children younger than 6; free to everyone on Sat. • 640-4433 (hotline)

Whether you like the architectural style or not, the Denver Art Museum has perhaps the most unusual profile of any building in Denver. With its silhouette of see-through geometric shapes, this modern six-story castle of art resembles a giant paper cutout. Inside is one of the best and most extensive collections of Native American crafts in the United States and an internationally acclaimed pre-Colombian art collection. Enjoy the works of Picasso, Georges Braque, Matisse, Frederic Remington, Winslow Homer, Thomas Hart Benton and two beautiful paintings by Monet: *Waterloo Bridge* and *The Water Lily Pond*. You'll find a nice cafeteria and gift shop as well. An entire new lower level is dedicated to educational programs with studios, lecture rooms, classrooms and a reception area. The museum has greatly expanded its public programming with a full schedule of classes in studio art and art history classes year round for adults and children. An underground concourse connects the museum with the public library. Call 640-KIDS for information on family and children's classes and programs; Call 640-ARTS for adult classes. The museum is preparing to reopen its wing of European and American art and is undergoing extensive renovations, including a new entrance, restaurant and permanent gallery devoted to its renowned textile collection — all of which are scheduled to open in the fall of 1997.

Fiske Planetarium
Regent Dr., CU-Boulder campus • Hours: 8 AM to 5 PM Mon. through Fri. • 492-5001 (star shows), 492-5002 (administration and information)

Stargazers and sci-fi fans will enjoy the small gallery outside the planetarium's starshow auditorium, which often displays astronomical or futuristic art work. Take the kids, and take it all in with both art and a star show.

Foothills Art Center
809 15th St., Golden • Hours: 9 AM to 4 PM Mon. through Sat., 1 to 4 PM Sun. • 279-3922

This charming art center is set in an old church in the town of Golden, about a half-hour drive south of Boulder. Two popular and very good national annual shows are the North American Sculpture Exhibition and the Rocky Mountain National Watermedia Exhibitions. The sculpture show is usually April through June, the watermedia in August and September. The art center's church and adjacent buildings are on the National Historic Register. There's a year-round gift gallery too. This spacious art center has five or six galleries all under one roof. Hampton's cafe, housed in the historic Victorian house next door, makes a nice stop before or after viewing the shows.

Handmade in Colorado
1426 Pearl St. • Hours: 10 AM to 6 PM Mon. through Sat. (until 9 PM during summer), 11 AM to 5 PM Sun. • 938-8394

Now in its ninth year, this co-op gallery features the work of 26 Colorado artisans in various media including quilts, photographs, jewelry, stained glass, dried-flower arrangements, wood, glass and pottery. The gallery offers an especially large selection of finely crafted pottery. Owned by eight different artisans, the gallery is now carrying traditional gourd containers and woven grass baskets made by area Native Americans. Some favorite artisans are Jayne Stanley, who won a first place award from the American Indian Art Council for her coiled fiber basketry; stoneware potter Giga Pellouchoud; stained-glass artisans Barbara Marcus and Daniel McKenna; and jeweler Lori Llerandi.

Mackin Katz Gallery of Fine Art
2041 Broadway • Hours: 11 AM to 6 PM Mon. through Sat.; noon to 5 PM Sun. • 786-7887

Described by *Town & Country* magazine as having world-class flair, this gallery features the work of Boulder-based photographer Andy Katz and other internationally shown artists, including painters, photographers, potters, furniture makers and glasswork artists. Katz's black-and-white and color photography captures images from around the world, including vanishing Jewish societies, the scenery and people of France, Costa Rica and Japan and a tour of sunny California wineries. His work is also exhibited in museums and galleries throughout the world.

MacLaren/Markowitz Gallery
1011 Pearl St. • Hours: 10 AM to 5:30 PM Mon. through Wed.; 10 AM to 9 PM Thurs., Fri. and Sat.; noon to 5 PM Sun. (abbreviated winter hours) • 449-6807

Featuring some of the area's most popular fine artists, MacLaren/Markowitz Gallery has a history of top-quality contemporary art in Boulder. Lyrical landscapes by Doug West and the colorful Hispanic-flavored art of Tony Ortega are some of the standard favorites at this attractive downtown gallery. Other popular artists include sculptor Bill Worrell, painters Merrill Mahaffey, Lindsey Leavell, Randy Pijoan, Julia Jordan and Pam Furumo (who also works in pastels).

Middle Fish
1738 Pearl St. 18th and Pearl in the harvest Commons • Hours: 10 AM to 6 PM Mon. through Sat., open daily 11 AM to 5 PM Sun. • 443-0835

This venue tucked in the Harvest Commons near the Harvest Restaurant describes itself as a fine craft and gift gallery. There's a mix of local and national artists' work, including folk art, functional and decorative pottery, blown glass, fused glass, art jewelry, sculpture and unique smaller gifts. Look here for hand-crafted furniture and garden sculpture, including bird baths and bird houses. Spruce up a home or office with fountains, unique functional, lighting, lamps, mirrors and other decorative accessories.

> **FYI**
> Unless otherwise noted, the area code for all phone numbers in this guide is 303.

Ruth Linton-David Haslam
The Boulder Gallery
1217 Spruce St. • Hours: 11 AM to 5 PM Mon. through Sat, (Fri. until 9), 1 to 5 PM Sun., summer hours daily till 9 except Sunday • 444-9116

This gallery features fine art from national and regional artists, including classic Impressionistic and realistic works. There's a good selection of oils, pastels, watercolors and fine bronzes, ceramics, plus jewelry and photography in this attractive gallery a block off the downtown Pearl Street Mall. The gallery also offers workshops and lectures by artists and classes for children. A recent merger with The Montgomery House Frame Shop & Gallery adds nationally recognized artists Ann Herzog Wright, Sandra Bierman, Rich Hilker and Judith Scott and 30 years of combined art business experience. The frame shop staff also provides conservation to museum standards.

Mustard Seed Gallery

1962 13th St. • Hours: 10 AM to 6 PM Mon. through Thurs., 10 AM to 9 PM Fri., 10 AM to 6 PM Sat., noon to 4 PM Sun • 447-8626

Mustard Seed celebrated its 27th anniversary in 1996 and has long been a favorite local source for traditional and contemporary paintings, pottery, prints, art glass, jewelry, photography and fine crafts. This pleasant gallery is just a few steps off the Pearl Street Mall. Mustard Seed participates in First Fridays, a recently begun program promoting downtown Boulder galleries, with about 14 of them open from 6 to 9 PM the first Friday of the month. Fourteen artists operate Mustard Seed, which is a partnership gallery.

Two Hands Bindery

1980 8th St., Ste. E • Hours: 10 AM to 6 PM Mon. through Sat., Sunday 10 AM to 5 PM • 444-0124

This charming shop (look for it behind Lolita's) is a full bindery specializing in restoration and handmade books. It's also stocks a huge selection of handmade paper, cards, photo albums, journals and beautiful waxes, seals, pens and inks. The paper is imported — not made on site. Two Hands recently opened a Denver store.

UMC Fine Art Gallery

Broadway and Euclid, CU-Boulder campus • Hours: 9 AM to 9 PM Mon. through Thurs., 9 AM to 5 PM Fri. (closed weekends and holidays) • 492-7465

National artists exploring contemporary issues are among those exhibiting at this university gallery, which displays work of both individual artists and groups in various media. The gallery also exhibits the work of CU-Boulder graduate students.

Village Custom Framing & Art

The Village • 2525 Arapahoe Ave. • Hours: 10 AM to 7 PM Mon. through Sat., noon to 4 PM Sun. • 413-9110

Village Custom Framing & Art is a small but well-stocked gallery with a unique collection of limited-edition art, etchings and antique art, including prints by such well-known artists as Bateman, Breders, Cole, Larson, Doolittle and Smith. Visitors can browse more than 27,000 works by various artists on the video art-search system and order these works — many of which are no longer available from the publisher. The shop also specializes in quality framing, including conservation framing of all forms of art and memorabilia.

Von Eschen Gallery

2920 Pearl St. • Hours: 9 AM to 5:30 PM Mon. through Fri., Sat. 10 AM to 4 PM • 443-9989

For those who like Western and wildlife art, this is the place to go. There are paintings in all media, bronze sculptures, wood carvings, original work and limited-edition prints. The gallery offers signed and numbered lithographs by such well-known artists as Robert Bateman and Bev Doolittle. Bateman's vivid portrayals of nature have earned national recognition, as have Doolittle's mystifying dual-image watercolors. A new addition is Indian jewelry and pottery.

White Horse Gallery

1218 Pearl St. • Hours: 10 AM to 9 PM Tues. through Sat., 11 AM 6 PM Sun. and Mon. (abbreviated winter hours) • 443-6116

Native American art, including paintings, jewelry, sculpture and other media, are the theme of this well-established gallery right on the Pearl Street Mall. Turn-of-the-century arti-

INSIDERS' TIP

Western architecture buffs will love the Boulder Museum of History, which provides exhibits showing the history of Boulder's neighborhoods and gives detailed information on how to tour Boulder, offering several routes and various recommended walks. Be sure to ask about Boulder's two world-class landmarks: the National Center for Atmospheric Research for its building, and the University of Colorado for its landscaping.

facts, pottery by the Baca family, paintings by Diane Dandeneau, beadwork, basketry and weavings are among this gallery's extensive offerings. Here's where to find jewelry by Colorado Sen. Ben Nighthorse (Campbell) and more jewelry by Ray Tracey and Andy Lee Kirk. The gallery is making an extensive push to reintroduce kachinas and some of the best Navajo weavers' work and has a large selection of traditional native art including Hopi Kachinas and Navajo weavings.

Dance

Boulder Ballet Ensemble
1722 14th St. • 442-6944

Presenting two performances a year, the Boulder Ballet ensemble offers professional training and performance opportunities for students preparing for careers in ballet. The ensemble does an annual *Nutcracker Ballet*, which sells out early, with the Boulder Philharmonic Orchestra and a spring performance. The ensemble has also performed with Opera Colorado. Performances are held in a variety of places, including Denver's Boettcher Hall and Macky Auditorium in Boulder.

Boulder Jazz Dance Workshop
CU-Boulder Campus • 449-0399

Founded in 1978 by Lara Branen, then a graduate student at CU-Boulder, this August workshop with performances returns to Boulder each year, where CU-Boulder's Theatre and Dance Department lends its facilities to this now-independent group. The workshop is open to the public, offering classes for all ages and levels of dancers from beginners to professionals.

Following the workshop (the first two weeks in August), there are performances by students, faculty and the company in residence, Interweave Dance Theatre of Boulder, which is composed of some 30 dancers. Thirty percent to 40 percent of the workshop participants come from out of the state and country, including Mexico, Italy and elsewhere. Participants can receive college credit at CU.

Cleo Parker Robinson Dance
119 Park Ave. W., Denver • 295-1759

Now celebrating its 26th anniversary, this dance company-cum-school and theater holds its fall and holiday performances at the Auditorium Theatre at the Denver Center for the Performing Arts. Jazz and modern-dance aficionados will relish this internationally renowned group with roots mainly in African-American culture. Well-known performers from around the world visit the school and theater, and the ensemble goes on extended tours. A new annual July event is the International Summer Dance Institute that hosts 20 Kenyan dance artists visiting from Africa. The instructors teach all types of African dance, music, theater, storytelling and cultural rituals to children and adults. One of Denver's greatest holiday traditions is the annual December concert, *Granny Dances to a Holiday Drum*. There's also an annual spring performance. Call for information and current schedules for its excellent performances, classes and workshops.

INSIDERS' TIP

The nonprofit Dairy Center for the Arts, 2590 Walnut Street, 444-7826, is struggling to become a full-fledged center for the arts in Boulder promoting visual arts, dance, music and other media. In the old Watts-Hardy Dairy building, it houses the Boulder Philharmonic Orchestra administrative office, Academy and recital hall; the Colorado Dance Festival; the Arts and Humanities Assembly of Boulder, the Naropa Institute class space, a sculpture consortium called FUSE and the Boulder Dance Alliance, which operates Space for Dance. Various performances and arts events take place there. Plans for the future include an auditorium, an art gallery and more.

Photo: Daily Camera

Boulder is home to several dance groups and the Colorado Dance Festival.

Colorado Ballet
1315 Curtis St. (ticket office), 1278 Lincoln St., Denver (administrative office)
• 98-MUSIC (tickets)

In 1993 this Denver-based ensemble debuted nationally at New York's prestigious Brooklyn Center for the Performing Arts. The Colorado Ballet performs such classics as *La Sylphide* and the *Nutcracker Ballet* each Christmas season, but also offers more innovative works such as those of George Balanchine. The 1997 season includes *A Midsummer Night's Dream* and, in spring, a big bash to celebrate artistic director Martin Fredmann's 10th anniversary, including *Wild Bill's Saloon* with music performed by Tim and Molly O'Brien, George Balanchine's *Western Symphony* and Fredmann's *Centennial Suite*. The performance season is from October to May. Series tickets are available.

Colorado Dance Festival
2590 Walnut St. • 442-7666

Now the third-largest dance festival in the nation, the Boulder-based Colorado Dance Festival (CDF) is partially funded by the National Endowment for the Arts. In 1993 the Colorado Council on the Arts/Institutional Partnership Program ranked CDF as the highest of Colorado's top 30 arts institutions. CDF has earned international recognition with its innovative programs and renowned performers, including such top names as Trisha Brown and the late, great tap dancer Honi Coles. The CDF also founded the Boulder-based International Tap Association, 443-7989.

In 1994, CDF began a three-year program on spirituality, the arts and environment called Dances of the Spirit, which includes a multifaceted program of performances, workshops, films, lectures, social dancing and more led by a multicultural team. Call for a current performance schedule.

The Colorado Dance Festival is held in the summer only.

University of Colorado's Department of Theatre and Dance
CU-Boulder Campus • 492-7355, 492-8181 (tickets)

Throughout the year this talent-filled university department presents a number of innovative performances including ballet, modern, African-American and other dance forms. Bachelor of fine arts candidates give an annual October concert, and there's a student dance concert in November. In February the master of fine arts candidates perform, and the dance faculty concert is in April. Call for a current schedule of performances.

The Naropa Institute Performing Arts Series

2130 Arapahoe Ave. • 546-3538

Naropa concentrates mainly on avant-garde and new dance, offering classes, workshops and performances. Call the ticket office above for current events and classes.

Boulder Dance Alliance and Space for Dance

Dairy Center for the Arts • 2590 Walnut St. • 444-1357

With a motto of "Dance is for Every Body," this is your one-stop for dance information.

The Boulder Dance Alliance has been a catalyst for the development of dance in Boulder County, and this organization has information on amateur, experimental and professional dance performances, an annual sock hop, lists for teachers and classes for children and adults, plus weekend performances. Space for Dance, which is part of the Boulder Dance Alliance, offers space available on a first-come, first-served basis for performances. It's in near-daily demand. Some of the dance offerings include method demonstrations; The Rocky Mountain Ragtime Festival; a tango and blues soiree; and skiffle, drag and tea dances .

Central City Opera

Just west of Main and Eureka streets is Central City's historic opera building, built in 1878. The first-rate, sung-in-English performances entertain even lukewarm opera fans. Everyone stays in historic Victorian character, including the uniformed ushers, who form a chorus and sing a tune out in the street about a half-hour before the show. Then they ring brass hand bells every 10 minutes or so announcing that the opera will soon begin.

With hand-painted murals of Pegasus and cafe chairs engraved with the names of famous benefactors, the Victorian theater is a treat. Every seat is good. You're close enough that the actors and actresses come across as real people who feel life so strongly, they've just got to sing about it.

Get your tickets as early as possible, since some operas sell out weeks or months in advance (although on some nights, you can buy tickets at the door). When you order tickets, pay $5 for a reserved spot in the opera house's parking lot. There's a bus from Denver and Lakewood for every performance and a bus on Fridays from Boulder. Cost is $15 for adults $13 for seniors 62 and older. New this year are weekend opera dinners at 6 PM at the Teller House in a private banquet room. The dinners were created specifically for opera patrons who prefer to avoid the casino atmosphere.

The four-course buffet with dessert, wine and soft music, costs $30 per person and is offered on Friday and Saturday evenings; the price of the opera ticket is extra. Or for those on a budget, bring your own picnic dinner, and enjoy it in the little park between the Teller House and the Opera House. It takes about an hour to drive from Boulder to the Opera House

Photo: Central City Opera

Central City Opera House

parking lot. Try to reach it at least an hour early. This way, a brief traffic jam won't spell trouble, and there will be time for a beverage stop or a stroll around town to enjoy the lovely Victorian houses. Be sure you arrive at the opera house at least 10 minutes before the show. If you're late, you'll be allowed to enter only between acts.

For those who'd like just an "opera appetizer" and not the full course, try the Festival Extra. There are various choices: At Salon Recitals on weekends, opera stars do short recitals during a gourmet brunch at the Teller House Hotel, next to the opera house at 11:45 AM. Tickets cost around $20. For Opera a la Carte, famous opera scenes are fully staged at 1:15 PM Wednesdays and Fridays and cost $2.50. *Face on the Barroom Floor* is a 30-minute cabaret opera recounting the Teller House's famous legend. These performances are at 1:15 PM Saturday and Sunday at William's Stable, right across the street, and cost $4.

Certainly the most popular and accessible "park" — and the best way to see Boulder — is the Boulder Creek Path, which cuts through the heart of the city along the creek as it tumbles down Boulder Canyon and flows out to the eastern plains.

Boulder
Parks and
Recreation Centers

From the Boulder Creek Path and mountain parks to the reservoir and recreation centers, Boulder offers a total of 65 parks and facilities. Following is a description of some of Boulder's most popular parks and their special features. Details on outdoor recreational activities can be found in our Boulder Participatory, Spectator and Professional Sports chapter.

Parks

City Parks

Boulder Creek Path
Parallel to Canyon Blvd. and/or Arapahoe Ave. from Four Mile Canyon in Boulder Canyon east to Cherryvale Rd. (approximately 7.5 miles)

Certainly the most popular and accessible "park" — and the best way to see Boulder — is the Boulder Creek Path, which cuts through the heart of the city along the creek as it tumbles down Boulder Canyon and flows out to the eastern plains. The Creek Path hugs Canyon Boulevard down to Broadway then veers off south under Arapahoe and meanders back under Arapahoe after 30th Street.

Bicyclists, walkers and in-line skaters crowd this scenic path, shaded by some of Boulder's oldest cottonwoods and willows. The path branches off into various other routes and is accessible at sidewalk intersections along its length. Many Boulderites use the Creek Path to commute across town, so be sure to stay to the right or you might be run down by those on wheels. Stop and enjoy the scenery, or lunch at one of the many benches.

The Creek Path is described in detail in the Boulder Attractions chapter. Maps of the Creek Path are available for $2.50 from the Boulder Chamber of Commerce, 2440 Pearl Street, 442-1044, and at bicycle shops (see the "Biking" section in our Participatory Sports chapter).

Scott Carpenter Park
Arapahoe Ave. and 30th St., Boulder • 441-3427 (pool)

Named for Boulder's own astronaut, this is a favorite warm-weather spot with its outdoor pool and playground for kids featuring a rocket jungle gym commemorating its namesake. Open swim is from 1 to 5 PM Monday through Friday, 1 to 6 PM Saturday and Sunday. Admission for residents (in 1996) on a per-visit basis was $3.25 for adults, $2 for seniors 60 and older and $1.25 for youth ages 4 through 18; fees for nonresidents on a per-visit basis are $4 for adults, $2.50 for seniors and $1.50 for youth. Rates for 1997 had not been set at press time.

Salberg Shelter
19th and Elder Sts., Boulder • 441-3400

This small park in the north-central part of town has a crafts building, playground and everyone's favorite — a giant, stationary human-propelled barrel. Kids and adults can feel like pet mice in exercise wheels as they run inside the barrel making it spin.

The center can be rented out to private groups by calling the Parks and Recreation Department at the listed number.

Central Park
Broadway and Canyon Blvd., Boulder
• **No phone**

Right in the heart of town, there's always something going on in this pretty park with an old railroad train, waterfalls, a band shell and plentiful green grass for lounging. Right on Boulder Creek Path and across from the Boulder Museum of Contemporary Art, the park is also adjacent to the Saturday and Wednesday Farmers Market along 13th Street.

Spruce Pool
2102 Spruce St., Boulder • 441-3426

This outdoor pool is a favorite of summer swimmers. Open swims are from 1 to 5 PM Monday through Friday and 1 to 6 PM Saturday and Sunday. There are lap lanes, a leisure pool and a slide. Red Cross-certified swim lessons are available. Fees for residents and nonresidents are the same as for the Scott Carpenter Park pool, listed previously.

Eben Fine Park
Third St. and Arapahoe Ave., Boulder
• **No phone**

This sylvan spot is a favorite for picnics and Frisbee throwing. It's right on Boulder Creek and right off the Creek Path. Picnic tables, big shady cottonwood trees and the rippling creek make it a popular summer recreation area.

Mountain Parks

A required experience for all visitors and newcomers to Boulder — and an excellent introduction to the mountain parks — is the drive up **Flagstaff Mountain**. Only a few miles to the top, this hairpin-turn, two-lane drive offers spectacular panoramas along the way as well as pull-offs, trails and picnic spots. To get there, drive south from Broadway and Canyon Boulevard just past the university to Baseline Road and turn right (west). At its west end, Baseline Road curves to the right and continues up Flagstaff. (The elegant Flagstaff House restaurant along the way is open for dinner only.)

Because of the area's great local popularity and use, cars not registered in Boulder County must have a vehicle permit to park on Flagstaff Mountain or in Gregory Canyon (the area below Flagstaff). Annual permits are $15; daily permits are $3; for permit information call City of Boulder Mountain Parks, 441-3408, or stop along the way to Flagstaff at the Chautauqua Rangers' Cottage (address listed subsequently). Self-service stations for the daily permits are available at all the parking areas — and rangers patrol and ticket those without them.

More than 100 miles of hiking trails lace Boulder's scenic mountain backdrop. Popular trailheads begin at Chautauqua Park, Flagstaff Mountain, the National Center for Atmospheric Research and Eldorado Springs and lead up Bear Peak, Green Mountain, Mount Sanitas and to the Devil's Thumb — all of which are popular, substantial hikes taking several hours to most of the day, depending upon your level of fitness. (See some specific locations and suggested hikes listed under "Hiking" in the Participatory Sports chapter.)

Boulder Mountain Parks Trail Maps list the length of trails and degree of difficulty and cost $5 (including county open space) and $4 (mountain parks and trails only). Maps are available from the Boulder Chamber of Commerce, 442-1044, 2440 Pearl Street; the City of Boulder Parks and Recreation Administration Office, 441-3400, 3198 N. Broadway; Boulder Map Gallery, 444-1406, 1708 13th Street; the Chautauqua Rangers' Cottage, 441-3408, 850 Kinnikinnick Road (near Eighth Street and Baseline Road in Chautauqua Park), open daily 8 AM to 4 PM; and at City of Boulder Recreation Centers (addresses listed subsequently). There's another nifty map available at Chautauqua and other locations around town called *Bird's Eye View of Boulder Mountain Parks* ($5.50) by Kent Schulte. It's a hand-drawn, hand-colored, big panoramic picture

FYI

Unless otherwise noted, the area code for all phone numbers in this guide is 303.

Photo: Jeff Stine

The National Sports Center for the Disabled Competition Program trains participants for national and international ski competition.

of the whole area, including the Indian Peaks and various famous local climbers' rocks in the area. On the back is lots of information about local mountain park hikes, climbs and history. Rock climbers will enjoy this map for its rock-climb descriptions, ratings and bouldering information — along with a little history.

Chautauqua Park
Ninth St. and Baseline Rd., Boulder
• 441-3408 (Rangers' Cottage)

At the base of the Flatirons, Boulder's first park opened as a summer camp and retreat for Texas visitors in 1898 and was originally called Texado Park. Perched on a hill overlooking the city, today it's the scene of casual summer sports such as Frisbee throwing and badminton. An auditorium hosts a summer concert series, and a dining room serves meals from Memorial Day through Labor Day. Many concert goers bring their own picnics to enjoy under the shady cottonwoods. The Rangers'

Cottage has information about the numerous hiking trails that begin at Chautauqua, such as the Royal Arch and the Mesa Trail.

State Parks

Eldorado Canyon State Park
Colo. Hwy. 170, Eldorado Springs
• 494-3943

One of the premier rock-climbing areas in the United States, spectacular rock walls line this canyon. It's a great place to watch some world-class rock climbing or do a bit of hiking. The park is open 'til dusk. The entrance fee is $1 for walk-ins, $3 per vehicle and $30 for annual state parks pass ($10 for those 62 and older). Check the new maps at the park entrance and ranger station for length and level of difficulty of the various trails.

On the way to the park you'll pass Eldorado Artesian Springs, 499-1316 Ext. 20, a privately owned historic resort (see our History chapter). The thermal pools and snack bar are open 10 AM to 6 PM daily from Memorial Day through Labor Day; cost per day is $5 for adults, $3 for kids ages 3 through 12 and $3 for seniors 60 and older; children younger than 3 are free.

The park is 8 miles south of Boulder; take Colo. Highway 93 to Colo. Highway 170 and head west.

Recreation Centers

The City of Boulder operates three excellent recreation centers. Nonresident admission for adults is $4 (children ages 4 to 12, $1.50; ages 13 to 18, $1.50) or $79 for a 20-punch pass card ($28 for children's and teens' 20-punch cards). City of Boulder residents may purchase a discount card for $5, which reduces the cost of admission and punch cards to $3.25 per visit and $62 per 20-punch card ($23 for teens and children). One-time admission for resident teens and children is $1.25. The centers are open daily; call for specific hours of operation. Reservations must be made two days in advance for the handball, racquetball and tennis courts, and the cost is $8 per court for an hour. Annual passes to the recreation centers are also available; call for information.

For just about any sport or activity you might want to pursue, the City of Boulder offers courses and instruction. The City of Boulder also offers the EXPAND (Exciting Programs, Activities & New Dimensions) for people with disabilities. For information on available programs, call the Recreation Department at 441-3400.

North Boulder Recreation Center
3170 N. Broadway, Boulder • 441-3444

Facilities at this center include a swimming pool, gymnasium, gymnastics center, dance

and yoga classrooms, a sauna, hot tub, handball/racquetball court, two platform tennis courts, four outdoor tennis courts, two outdoor sand volleyball courts, a weight room, locker rooms and showers.

South Boulder Recreation Center
1360 Gillaspie Dr., Boulder • 441-3448

Here you'll find a swimming pool, hot tub, sauna, locker rooms, showers, classrooms, a gymnasium, weight room, racquetball court, outdoor sand volleyball courts, Viele Lake (canoeing and paddleboating), a fitness course around the lake and four outdoor tennis courts.

East Boulder Recreation Center
5660 Sioux Dr., Boulder • 441-4400

The Senior Center wing, 441-4150, at East Boulder includes a cafeteria, common area and an arts and crafts room.

The recreation facility features a lap pool and leisure pool with water slide and children's play area; gymnasium with adjustable basketball hoops; weight rooms with free and bodymaster weights, rowing machines and stationary cycles; a climbing wall; aerobics room; and dance studio. Outdoors you'll find tennis, basketball and racquetball courts as well as a handicapped-accessible playground.

Boulder Reservoir
51st St., Boulder • 441-3468 (gate), 441-3456 (boathouse)

For those craving a beach, this is the closest thing to it in Boulder County. Swimmers, sailors, windsurfers, canoeists, kayakers and water skiers make this a busy place on summer weekends. Various watercraft are for rent, including sailboats and windsurfers; call the boathouse for rates. Grills and picnic tables provide a nice spot for summer barbecues on the swimming beach. The reservoir hosts sail-

---

INSIDERS' TIP

On a gloomy winter day take yourself and/or the kids to the East Boulder Recreation Center where young and old enjoy the leisure pool, spraying mushroom fountain and water slide. If you feel like climbing the wall there's one here you really can climb, or play basketball or racquetball (advance reservations are required). See address and details in this chapter.

boat races, volleyball tournaments and a national in-line skate series; it's also the scene of the annual Polar Bear Dip on New Year's Day (see our Boulder Festivals and Annual Events chapter). Waterskiing, sailboat and sailboard classes are available. One-day admission for both residents and nonresidents is $3.75 for adults 19 and older; $2.50, youths ages 13 to 18; $1.75, kids ages 4 through 12; $1.75, seniors ages 60 to 64; and free for seniors 65 and older and children younger than 4.

Season passes are available; call the gate for information. Boulder Reservoir is 1.5 miles north of Jay Road via the Diagonal Highway (Colo. 119).

YMCA of Boulder County
2850 Mapleton Ave., Boulder • 442-2778

Boulder's "Y" has a full range of facilities and classes, including racquetball/handball courts; a swimming pool; full gym; indoor running track; Jacuzzi, Cybex, Nautilus and Hydrogym equipment; and single-sex saunas. Admission is $7 for teens and adults; $3.50 for kids younger than 13. Call for membership rates.

University of Colorado Recreation Center
CU-Boulder campus, Boulder • 492-6561

The CU-Boulder Recreation Center is open only to CU-Boulder students, staff, faculty members, alumnae and their spouses. Facilities include four pools; an ice rink; handball/racquetball, squash and tennis courts; a gymnasium; fitness system room; weight room; training room; and saunas. Fees vary widely depending on the season and your affiliation with CU-Boulder.

Boulder has been called "*the* sports town," by *Outside* magazine, and you'll share the trails, routes and roads with some of the nation's and world's best athletes who come here to train.

Boulder
Sports

Many people move to Boulder specifically for what's contained in this chapter: bicycling, hiking, camping, skiing, rock climbing, running and other outdoor sports. As we said in this book's Overview, Boulder has been called "*the* sports town," by *Outside* magazine, and you'll share the trails, routes and roads with some of the nation's and world's best athletes who come here to train. But never mind them; just enjoy yourself and don't try to compete — it's hopeless, even though inspirational.

Non-Olympians abound, and you'll find them poking around in sporting goods shops and in the various clubs and organizations for bicycling, skiing, rock climbing and hiking listed in this chapter.

If you're a spectator rather than a participant, you'll find yourself in the minority, but with plenty of exciting entertainment from CU-Boulder's Buffaloes, who are members of the NCAA Division I Big 12 Conference and former national football champions. There are also CU's men and women basketball Buffaloes, Denver's football Broncos and basketball Nuggets, the Colorado Rockies Major League Baseball team, the Colorado Avalanche National Hockey League team (formerly Quebec's Nordiques, the Avalanche have firmly endeared themselves to Coloradans by winning the 1996 Stanley Cup) and various college sports.

Participatory Sports

Bicycling

Boulder's plentiful bike paths are the obvious place to start pedaling. Cruise right onto the **Boulder Creek Path**, which is most easily accessed at Central Park (Broadway and Canyon), Eben Fine Park (Fourth and Arapahoe), the Regal Harvest House Hotel (1345 28th Street, just south of Arapahoe), or the University of Colorado along Broadway. Most major intersections crossing Arapahoe Avenue have a sidewalk ramp onto the bike path.

Go east or west — both directions offer a great ride and scenery. Going west, the paved section ends after about a half-mile into Boulder Canyon, and a wide packed gravel path continues a little more than 2 miles (from Eben Fine Park) up to Four Mile Canyon where the Creek Path ends. It's not a steep or difficult ride to the end of the path, but those new to Boulder's elevation might be a bit breathless as the trail gradually climbs the canyon, paralleling the highway. It's best ridden on a mountain bike, but skinny tires can make it, too, with care on the gravel and "curbs" at the bridges.

For those who prefer no hills, go east, where the Creek Path sweeps out onto the plains past 30th Street and CU-Boulder's new Research Park for a panoramic view of the Front Range, past duck ponds, cottonwoods and prairie dog towns. See the Boulder Attractions chapter for a detailed description of the path.

South Boulderites can enjoy a beautiful new bike path that heads northeast from Martin Park on the corner of Broadway and Table Mesa Drive. Access the path at the far northeast end of the park. Called the **Bear Creek Greenway**, the path winds along Bear Creek under highways and eventually over Foothills Parkway, where cyclists have the choice of heading farther east on the Centennial bike path or heading north across Arapahoe Avenue and connecting with the Boulder Creek bike path.

Bike paths weave all around and through Boulder, and a map is a good bet if you don't want to get lost. The **Boulder Bicycling Map** ($2.50) is available at the Boulder Chamber of Commerce, 442-1044, 2440 Pearl Street, and also at the bicycle shops listed subsequently.

Bikes can be rented at various shops around town including **Doc's Ski and Sports**, 499-0963, 627 S. Broadway, south Boulder; **University Bicycles**, 444-4196, 839 Pearl Street, downtown; the **Morgul Bismark**, 447-1338, 1221 Pennsylvania Avenue, on University Hill; and **Louisville Cyclery**, 665-6343, 1032 South Boulder Road, Louisville. Average rates are $4 per hour; $14 per half-day; $16 to $21 per full day; and $35 to $50 per weekend.

Other resources for bicycling information are the City's **GO Boulder Bike Program**, 441-3216; **University of Colorado Bike Office**, campus bicycling information, 492-2322; *Colorado Cycling Guide* by Jean and Hartley Alley, two longtime Boulder residents and cyclists.

Paved Roads
(Skinny Tires)

The ride to **Niwot** is flat and pastoral past ponds and pleasant countryside (16 miles from Broadway and Canyon). Go north on Broadway to Nelson Road and turn right (turn right on Neva Road before Nelson for a shorter ride). Follow Nelson Road to Colo. Highway 73, turn right and go to Niwot Road and turn left; proceed into Niwot and enjoy a meal at historic Rev. Taylor's Country Restaurant, 652-2020.

A little hillier are rides to Lyons or Louisville. To reach **Lyons** (16 miles from Broadway and Canyon), ride straight north on Broadway (Colo. Highway 93), which has a wide shoulder, all the way to Lyons, and turn left at the railroad track. Andrea's, 823-5000, is a dandy breakfast or lunch pick (closed Wednesdays).

For **Louisville** (12 miles from Broadway and Canyon), go south on the bike path along the east side of Broadway to Marshall — south of Boulder — through Marshall and over Colo. Highway 170; cross U.S. Highway 36, make a right on Dillon Road, a left on 96th Street, then look for nearby Main Street and Karen's Kitchen, 666-8020.

For a good mountain ride, head for **Jamestown** (17 miles from Broadway and Canyon) on Broadway up Lefthand Canyon (8 miles north of town) and then, after 6 miles, up James Canyon Drive. (Look for mile markers in the canyon.) The picturesque Jamestown Mercantile Cafe, 442-5847, offers breakfast, lunch and snacks.

The truly tough can ride all the way up Left Hand Canyon to **Ward** (23 miles one way from Broadway and Canyon) — all steady climbing from the start of Left Hand Canyon. There are snacks available at Glacier Gateway General Store in Ward. Or if you can make it over the final hill out of Ward to the Peak to Peak (Colo. Highway 72), great meals, homemade pie and local ambiance await you at the Mill Site Inn, 459-3308, just north of Ward.

Macho cyclists can also tackle **Flagstaff Mountain** — a real muscle-buster right in town, due west on Baseline Road. Another strenuous ride is the 17 miles up Boulder Canyon to Nederland, but the curving canyon with its narrow shoulder and speeding cars can be quite hazardous for cyclists. Choose less busy times during midweek and midday.

Lights are required by law for night riding.

Unpaved Roads
(Fat Tires)

Despite all of Boulder's mountain parks, trails and open space, mountain biking on trails is limited to only a few local areas. After the great fat-tire craze began about a decade ago, trails began to erode and hikers began to complain about speeding cyclists running them off trails. As a result, all of the Boulder Mountain Parks trails are closed to mountain bikes.

Nevertheless, there are a few good off-road trails for mountain bikes on the north, south and east ends of town on city and county open space land — and farther afield. The most detailed map available is the **Mountain Bike Map: Boulder County** ($8), available from Boulder County Parks and Open Space (Courthouse Annex), 2045 13th Street, (corner of Spruce and 13th streets). Area bike shops, bookstores and sporting goods shops also sell the map and might charge a bit more for it. A few suggested off-road mountain bike trails follow:

Around Boulder

Greenbelt Plateau Trail

South of Boulder, on the north side of Colo. Hwy. 128, just east of Colo. Hwy. 93
Difficulty — easy; Distance — 1.6 miles on gravel surface road

This gentle trail rolls across a mesa top through open grasslands with beautiful views of the Foothills. At 1.3 miles, bicyclists may choose to take the dirt path to Community Ditch Trail or continue on the service road to Colo. Highway 93.

Community Ditch Trail

South of Boulder, at the Doudy Draw Trailhead on the south side of Colo. Hwy. 170, 1.7 miles west of Colo. Hwy. 93 or at the Marshall Mesa Trailhead, 0.9 mile east of Colo. Hwy. 93 on the south side of Marshall Rd.
Difficulty — moderate; Distance — 4 miles

The Community Ditch Trail is a dirt service road that travels through grasslands, mesas and land with evidence of early farming and mining activity. Taken from the Marshall Mesa Trailhead this ride is a huff and a puff up the mesa, but riders will be rewarded with spectacular views of the mountains and a delightful flat ride along the flower-lined (in spring) mesa and the Community Ditch, which in warm weather invites a swim.

Cross Colo. Highway 93 (Broadway) and continue along the ditch winding back among the cottonwoods. To make a nice loop back to Boulder, head for the Doudy Draw Trailhead at the junction of Community Ditch Bridge. At Doudy Draw Trailhead you can choose between a side trip into Eldorado Springs (turn left on the paved highway) or turn right to return to Colo. 93 to Boulder or the Marshall Mesa Trailhead. Eldorado Springs (about 2 miles) provides a chance to refuel with spring water, swim at Eldorado Artesian Springs ($5), graze at the snack bar or gaze at the daring rock climbers in the state park ($1 to walk in), climbing the impressive Bastille and other rock formations. To return to Boulder or the Marshall Mesa Trailhead, ride back out to Colo. 93 on

the Eldorado Springs road, crossing at the light and continuing straight into the tiny settlement of Marshall. The trailhead is just a little farther east on Marshall Road. If you choose the reverse direction, starting at the Dowdy Draw Trailhead, go left (east) at the junction of Community Ditch bridge and the dirt road you're on. The trail crosses Colo. Highway 93 and goes to the Marshall Reservoir inlet and up a steep hill to the Marshall Mesa Trailhead.

East Boulder Trail

Access Teller Farm S. Trailhead, on Arapahoe Rd., a mile east of 75th St.
Difficulty — moderate; Distance — 7 miles

A 2.2-mile level section goes through a wildlife preserve and past Teller Lake. Then, a 2.7-mile section climbs a mesa on dirt trails and service roads to the Gunbarrel Farm. The Gunbarrel Farm section travels along a dirt service road with moderate grades and turns east at 1.2 miles into the White Rocks area.

FYI
Unless otherwise noted, the area code for all phone numbers in this guide is 303.

In the Mountains

Mountain bikes are allowed only on certain mountain trails, many of which are shared by four-wheel-drive vehicles or cars. Most mountain biking in the local high country requires an outstanding pair of lungs and legs, since it's mostly uphill and at high altitudes.

For a ride right out of town, go west on Mapleton Avenue, which becomes unpaved at Sunshine Canyon and continues to the historic mining town of **Gold Hill**, about 10 miles uphill. From there you can continue to Nederland and return down Boulder Canyon. Or, start the ride at the mouth of Boulder Canyon along the Creek Path, which ends in 2 miles at Four Mile Canyon (County Road 118); proceed up Four Mile Canyon and turn right at the sign for Gold Hill — also about 10 miles uphill from the mouth of Four Mile Canyon.

The historic **Switzerland Trail**, a former single-gauge railroad track, makes for some scenic riding with spectacular mountain views and reasonable climbing grades. Most riders start at the town of Sunset and go south toward Bald and Sugarloaf mountains. To reach Sunset, head up Four Mile Canyon (above), and stay on County Road 118 past Salina and

Wallstreet until you reach Sunset, 17 miles from Boulder. Go right to reach Gold Hill or left to Glacier Lake.

Accessible from the Peak to Peak Highway (Colo. Highway 72) west of Nederland, the **Sourdough Trail** is 17.5 miles long, but has different segments at various trailheads. The trail was constructed with help from the Colorado Mountain Club mainly for ski touring and mountain biking, and features pleasant rolling terrain though the pines. From Camp Dick Campground to Beaver Reservoir is 2.3 miles. From Beaver Reservoir to Brainard Road, it's 7.4 miles, and from Brainard Road to Rainbow Lakes Road, 7.8 miles. All access to the various connections to the Sourdough Trail are made via the Peak to Peak Highway. Camp Dick Campground is on Middle St. Vrain Road, 5.8 miles north of Ward and 0.5 miles west of Peaceful Valley. One Sourdough Trailhead is on the left-hand side of County Road 96 just east of Beaver Reservoir, 2.5 miles north of Ward and 2 miles west on County Road 96. The Red Rock Trailhead is on the right-hand side of County Road 102, just east of Red Rock Lake, 2.5 miles west on Brainard Lake Road. Another Sourdough Trailhead is on the right-hand side of Rainbow Lakes Road (County Road 116), 4.7 miles south of Ward (7 miles north of Nederland) and 0.4 miles west on County Road 116.

For those in really top shape, try **Rollins Pass**, one of Colorado's premier mountain biking (and four-wheel-drive) routes. This former railroad bed crosses the Continental Divide. Cars used to be able to make this exciting drive over rickety railroad trestles perched above thousand-foot drops, until the Needle's Eye tunnel caved in and was never cleared. Today, the tunnel — 1.5 miles from the Divide — is the end of the road for vehicles, but mountain bikers and hikers can bypass the tunnel and continue on the roadbed over the pass and all the way down the other side to Winter Park, if desired. To reach Rollins Pass Road, drive west up Boulder Canyon (Colo. Highway 119) to Nederland, then south on Colo. Highway 72 to Rollinsville. Turn right (west) on the dirt road marked with signs to Tolland and East Portal and drive 8.5 miles to the East Portal and

Moffat Tunnel. The Rollins Pass road begins there, as marked. Bicycling over the pass is an all-day affair requiring another vehicle on the Winter Park side and lodging reservations or plans — not to mention advanced physical fitness.

Camping

Camping beneath the pines in the cool, clear air of the high country — and perhaps near a gleaming mountain lake or stream — is one of the Rockies' greatest joys. The U.S. Forest Service, State of Colorado or City of Boulder maintain many such sites. (For camping in Rocky Mountain National Park, please see that chapter of this book.)

Boulder County

Roosevelt National Forest

The following campgrounds are within the national forest. For information about federal regulations within Roosevelt, call 444-6600.

Kelly Dahl

Three miles south of Nederland on Colo. Highway 119, this campground offers a scenic view of the Continental Divide and limited hiking. There are 46 sites at an elevation of 8,600 feet. The season is from late April or early May through October 31 or the first snow. The fee is $10 with water ($6 without water).

Rainbow Lakes

Set near several small but lovely lakes, this campground is 6.5 miles north of Nederland off Colo. Highway 72. There is no available running water, but good fishing is nearby in the Indian Peaks Wilderness area. There are 18 sites at an altitude of 10,000 feet. The season is late April or early May through October 15 or the first snow. The fee is $5.

Pawnee Campground

Five miles west of Colo. highways 119/72 on County Road 102 (at Brainard Lake), this extremely popular (and heavily used) campground offers beautiful views, fishing and non-motorized boating with access to the wilderness area. The 55 sites are at an elevation of

10,400 feet, and the season is from July 1 through October 15. The fee is $10 ($6 with no water or trash pickup).

Peaceful Valley

Look for this pleasant, pine-shaded campground 15 miles west of Lyons on Colo. Highway 7, then left at the junction with Colo. Highway 72 and 6 miles farther. There are 15 sites and the elevation is 8,500 feet. The season is late April or early May through October 31 or the first snow. The fee is $10 ($6 with no water).

To reach this campground, located a mile west of Peaceful Valley, follow the dirt road to the 34 sites at an elevation of 8,600 feet. The season is from late April or early May through October 31 or the first snow. The fee is $10 ($6 with no water).

Olive Ridge Campground

Nestled close to lush Rocky Mountain National Park, this campground is 15 miles south of Estes Park or 1.5 miles north of Allenspark

on Colo. Highway 7. It offers access to the Park as well as horse rentals at nearby stables. There are 56 sites at an elevation of 8,400 feet. The season is late April or early May through October 31 or the first snow. Reservations are required through **Destinet**, (800) 365-2267, and the fee is $10.

Golden Gate Canyon State Park

Golden Gate, 582-3707, offers many miles of hiking plus backpacking, fishing and camping at 7,900- to 10,500-feet elevation. You'll find 168 sites, including some in the backcountry. Fees are $7 per night for RVs, motor homes or tents (106 sites); $6 per night for tent camping only (35 sites); $2 per night for primitive backcountry tent sites (23 sites); $10 per night for backcountry shelters, wooden lean-tos — no tents necessary (four shelters). Golden Gate is open year round, weather permitting. A day pass costs $3.

The park is 10 miles south of Nederland on Colo. Highway 72 and 2 miles east on Gap Road for the north entrance. For the south entrance drive 3 more miles, then 4 miles east on Colo. Highway 46.

City of Boulder Mountain Parks

Buckingham Campground

The campground, 441-3408, is at an elevation of 10,160 feet and is accessible to Indian Peaks Wilderness. Buckingham's 8 sites, available on a first-come, first-served basis, are very heavily used. Camping is allowed only in the designated sites as the surrounding vegetation is easily damaged. The season runs from early June until snow season. No ground fires or charcoal fires are permitted; only gas grills or camp stoves may be used. No reservations are required, and there's no fee charged for camping, but no water is available.

Buckingham Campground is at the Fourth of July Trailhead, 12 miles northwest of Nederland; take County Road 107 west through Eldora to County Road 130 (a rough road) and proceed to its end.

Climbing

Boulder is internationally known for its great rock-climbing areas, particularly the Flatirons and Eldorado Canyon in the state park (see our Boulder Parks and Recreation Centers chapter for more information on these parks). Those interested in learning to climb have many options. The **Bob Culp Climbing School** at **Naked Edge Mountaineering**, 499-1185, 3330 Eldorado Springs Drive in Eldorado Springs, offers private guiding and semiprivate lessons all year, including ice climbing (winter only) and rock-climbing classes. Founder Bob Culp has mapped and executed first ascents of countless routes in Colorado, Europe, Chamonix and the Dolomites, and is one of the foremost U.S. ice climbers. Naked Edge Mountaineering is a climbing equipment retail shop.

The **Colorado Mountain Club**, 449-1135, holds mountaineering courses in spring and fall. The City of Boulder offers rock-climbing and mountaineering courses as part of its Adventure Program, 441-4401 — with a climbing wall at the East Boulder Community Center. The Boulder Rock Club also has an indoor climbing wall and instructions, 447-2804. Also the **Colorado Mountain School** in Estes Park, 586-5758, is a well-known guide organization.

With proper equipment and training, rock climbing can be a relatively safe sport, and rock jocks dancing up the cliffs at Eldorado Canyon might make it look easy. Tempting as it might be, however, those without proper training and equipment should stay on the ground. Every year there are several fatalities involving inexperienced scramblers without equipment — especially around the Flatirons and Boulder Falls (in the Boulder Canyon).

Another excellent resource for climbing and mountaineering information, books and equipment (though no instruction is offered) is **Neptune Mountaineering**, 633 Unit-A, S. Broadway, Table Mesa Center, 499-8866, owned by Gary Neptune, a prominent U.S. mountaineer who has stood on the top of Mount Everest and many other peaks worldwide. Neptune sometimes teaches and lectures for the Colorado Mountain Club.

About as inexpensive as baby-sitting, **Lizard Tours**, 729 Pearl Street, 938-8030, offers rock climbing for kids (also teens and families). Owner/operator Jerry Greene has worked as an Outward Bound instructor four seasons and observes the utmost safety precautions. He uses top roping, the safest form of climbing, where the climber hangs in a harness by rope from a permanently fixed anchor above (such as a tree). Kids ride their bicycles with

KEEP TRACK! Snowshoers sharing trails with cross-country skiers should make their own tracks, wherever possible, because cross-country skis work best in their own tracks and function poorly in snowshoe tracks. People without skis or snowshoes SHOULD NOT walk in either tracks because it ruins the trail for both skiers and snowshoers, making it frustrating and miserable for both. Please don't ruin someone else's fun.

Greene to one of the local climbing spots, and Greene provides the climbing equipment. "Climbing is a great form of exercise, which builds confidence, grace and poise. Kids take to it naturally," says Greene. Lessons are $4 an hour per student, and parents are welcome to attend classes and observe.

The book *Flatiron Classics* by Gerry Roach — another famous local mountaineer and climber — has detailed route information for experienced climbers who want to climb the Flatirons and other popular routes. *Rock Climbing Colorado* by Stewart M. Green is a very thorough new book that covers the whole state, describing 1,500 routes.

Fishing

Many lakes and streams in the area offer good fishing for both warm- and cold-water species. Some favorite spots in and around Boulder are **Wonderland** and **Thunderbird** lakes, **Walden** (there's a special pond for seniors and the handicapped) and **Sawhill** ponds and **Boulder Reservoir** — good for crappie, catfish and largemouth bass. **Barker Reservoir** in Nederland attracts many anglers at its western end.

Gross Reservoir (up Flagstaff Road) is another favorite of local fishermen and, higher in the mountains, **Brainard** and **Red Rocks** lakes. For those who desire more solitude (which you won't find at Brainard Lake), hike up to beautiful **Diamond Lake**, from the Fourth of July trailhead. To reach Fourth of July trailhead, travel west from Nederland for about 7 miles on County Road 107 — you'll pass through the rustic town of Eldora — then continue up County Road 130 (a rough, dirt road) for about 5 miles. It's about a 2.5-mile hike up to Diamond Lake from the trailhead.

Some easier-to-reach area streams that offer good trout fishing are the Middle and South forks of **St. Vrain Creek**, **Left Hand Creek** between Left Hand Reservoir and Buckingham Park, **North Boulder Creek** between Colo. Highway 72 and Boulder Falls, **Middle Boulder Creek** from its headwaters to 28th Street (special restrictions in city limits) and **South Boulder Creek** from its headwaters to Baseline Road (special restrictions between Walker Ranch and South Boulder

Road). **Golden Gate State Park** is a good place to take kids fishing and also offers camping and numerous hiking trails.

Licenses

Fishing licenses are required, cost $40.25 for nonresidents ($20.25 for residents) and are good for one calendar year. They are available — along with maps — at McGuckin Hardware, 443-1822, 2525 Arapahoe Avenue in Boulder, and at Nederland's Ace Hardware Store, 258-3132, in the shopping center. For more information contact the City of Boulder Open Space Department (local/Boulder fishing, 441-3440), Boulder County Parks and Open Space (local/county, 441-3950), or the Colorado Division of Wildlife, Department of Natural Resources, 297-1192; fishing report: 291-7535, 6060 Broadway in Denver.

Fitness Centers

Boulder has numerous private health clubs and fitness centers, many of which are open to nonmembers.

Flatiron Athletic Club
505 Thunderbird Dr., Boulder • 499-6590

Flatiron offers an enormous array of classes and equipment. For $8 you can enjoy all the facilities for the day, including a lap pool and coed spa, tennis courts, handball, squash and racquetball courts, a "Treadwall" for rock-climbing, volleyball, aerobics classes, an indoor running track and complete weight room.

Pulse Fitness Center
2950 Baseline Rd., Boulder • 443-2639
1375 Walnut St., Boulder • 447-8545

For $10 (both locations) nonmembers can have full run of Nautilus equipment, free weights, STEP classes, low- and high-impact aerobics classes, physical therapy and massage (when accompanied by a member, the charge is $8).

Boulder Rock Club
2952 Baseline Rd., Boulder • 413-1265
2829 Mapleton Ave., Boulder • 447-2804

Boulder Rock Club offers all types of indoor climbing walls for rock climbers (including bouldering, top-roping and lead-climbing) for $14 a day. A full range of lessons and outdoor clinics is available as is rental equipment. The Boulder Rock Club's new 10,000-square-foot Mapleton Avenue facility is more than twice the size of the Baseline one. Both locations are closed during summer.

RallySport
2727 29th St., Boulder • 449-4800
Though it's open to members only, RallySport is open to members of other clubs affiliated with IRSA, the International Recreation Association, for a fee of $10 a day. This club has a full range of facilities including racquetball, squash, handball, tennis, volleyball and wallyball courts plus all types of classes, weight-training equipment and indoor and outdoor pools.

Golf

Golfers have a reasonable choice of public ranges in Boulder and the surrounding area. Most of the courses listed here have driving ranges, equipment rentals, snack bars, pro shops and lessons.

Coal Creek Golf Course
585 W. Dillon Rd., Louisville • 666-7888
Coal Creek has nine and 18 holes, a driving range, snack bar and lounge, golf accessories and rentals. Weekday fees for residents are $10 and $16 ($25 and $15 weekends and holidays) for nine and 18 holes ($14 and $22 for nonresidents weekdays). The pars are 36 and 72 for nine and 18 holes; golf carts are $10 and $20 but generally are not necessary.

Eagle Golf Club
1200 Club House Dr., Broomfield • 466-3322
Eagle has an 18-hole course, driving range, bar, golf accessories and rentals. Greens fees on weekdays are $12 for nine holes and $18 for 18 holes; on weekends (Friday and Saturday), it's $14 for nine holes and $25 for 18 (juniors and seniors pay $7.50 or $15). The par is 35 or 36 (depending upon from what tees you're playing) and 71. Golf carts cost $11 per rider.

Flatirons Golf Course
5706 Arapahoe Ave., Boulder • 442-7851
The City of Boulder operates the Flatirons Golf Course. Nonresident player fees are $13.50 for nine holes and $19.50 for 18 holes. Residents must have a Boulder Parks and Recreation discount card ($5), and the fees are $11 and $16 for nine and 18 holes respectively. Par is 35 and 70.

Golf Haystack
5877 Niwot Rd., Boulder • 530-1400
The choice of "duffers" (according to one self-described local), Haystack is excellent for beginners, and there's no tee time — just show up. The easy nine-hole course is par 32, and fees are $9 on weekdays (Monday through Thursday) and $10 on weekends and holidays. No motorized carts are available, only pull-carts.

Indian Peaks Golf Course
2300 Indian Peaks Tr., Lafayette • 666-4706
Indian Peaks offers nine and 18 holes, a driving range, snack bar and lounge, golf accessories and rentals. Nonresident fees are $15 and $27 every day. Residents pay the same fee on weekends but on weekdays (Monday through Thursday) it's $12 and $17. The par is 36 or 72, and golf carts cost $12 or $20.

Lake Valley Golf Club
County Rd. 34, north of Boulder • 444-2114
Also in Boulder, this is an 18-hole championship course. Par is 70. Fees are $15 for nine holes and $20 for 18 holes on weekdays. Fees after 1 PM on weekends and holidays are $16 and $24; and fees for nine and 18 holes before 1 PM on holidays and weekends are $20 and $27 respectively. Motorized golf carts are available for $12.50 or $20 any time.

Sunset Golf Course
1900 Longs Peak Ave., Longmont • 776-3122
Sunset has both nine and 18 hole rounds, a pro shop, instruction and rentals. Fees for Longmont residents are $9 for nine holes and $13 for 18 (nonresidents pay $10 and $14). Junior and senior weekday rates are $6 and $9 and are the same on weekends after 2 PM.

($11 and $15 for nonresidents). The par is 34 and 68 for nine and 18 holes respectively. Golf carts rent for $10 and $18 but are not usually necessary.

Twin Peaks Golf Course
1200 Cornell Dr., Longmont • 772-1722

Twin Peaks offers nine and 18 holes, a driving range, pro shop, snack bar and restaurant. Instruction and rentals are available. Weekday fees for nonresidents are $10 for nine holes and $13 for 18 holes (juniors and seniors pay $8 and $11. Weekday rates for residents are $10 and $14. Weekend fees (Saturday and Sunday no senior junior rates) are $13 and $17 for nonresidents and $11 and $15 for residents. The par is 35 for each nine holes. Golf carts ($10 and $18) are generally not necessary because it's so flat.

Hiking and Backpacking

If recreation is Boulder's raison d'être, then hiking is, perhaps, the biggest raison. Most people moved to Boulder to be near the mountains, and in Boulder trails are literally out the back door. On the toughest trails and even mountain tops you'll also see anorexic-looking runners in flimsy nylon shorts and singlets, equipped with only water bottles. Don't mind them, they're probably training for the **Leadville Trail 100**, a 100-mile race through the mountains, or some other event for super-humans (or super-masochists — whichever you prefer).

There are so many places to hike it's hard to begin. But in town, the logical place to start is the mountain parks (out the back door). Again, for serious hikers, a map is the best bet for choosing the scenic destination, distance and degree of difficulty accordingly. Maps of the Mountain Parks are available at the many places listed in our Parks and Recreation Centers chapter's "Mountain Parks" section.

In Boulder

For a really short hike, but one with a great view and handicap accessibility, stroll out behind the National Center for Atmospheric Research (NCAR — pronounced "en-car"), at the west end of Table Mesa Drive (see our Boulder Attractions and Boulder Overview chapters for details on the research center). The **Walter Orr Roberts Nature Trail** (0.4 miles round trip), named for NCAR's founder, is perfect for those with limited time or who don't want to walk much. It's also wheelchair-accessible. The drive up the NCAR mesa is beautiful, and you're sure to spot some grazing

Photo: James Kelvorn

This mountain-biker hops down a mountain trail near Boulder.

deer. The nature trail is a pleasant ramble along the mesa top with great views and a fine introduction to the local flora, fauna and terrain.

The NCAR building, known as the Mesa Laboratory, was designed by the internationally acclaimed architect I.M. Pei (who also designed new sections of the Louvre in Paris and National Gallery in Washington, D.C.) and is made of Lyons sandstone mixed with concrete to tint it pink and blend with the flatirons rock formations. The design is reminiscent of Anasazi ruins like those of Mesa Verde.

There are various options for longer hikes at the NCAR Trailhead — including a connection to Bear Canyon and the Mesa Trail (description to follow). For an interesting longer hike (3.2 miles round trip) look for the **Mallory Cave Trail** just south of the NCAR Mesa Trail junction (and north of Bear Canyon). This area has been extensively used and is undergoing restoration to prevent more erosion. Please observe the trail closures, which are allowing revegetation as well as protecting endangered wildlife nesting areas. This trail weaves through a forest of ponderosa pines, leading to a meadow of yucca and low shrubs. Follow the small trail to a huge lichen-covered boulder at the entrance to a stone "staircase" between the rock slabs. Look for a sign at the fork indicating a left turn for the cave, which has been notoriously hard to find for many hikers. The final approach is a shinny up a 50-foot, 40-degree (or so) angle rock chimney with plenty of hand and footholds, but challenging nonetheless. The cave is shallow, but the vista is grand. At the age of 18, E.C. Mallory rediscovered this cave, which was known by locals but never recorded. Mallory later graduated from the University of Colorado and worked as a miner and eventually a chemist for the USGS. For many years he kept the cave a secret.

For a fairly strenuous hike of four to six hours — or more (depending upon your conditioning) — climb **Bear Peak** (8,461 feet). It's 7 miles round trip with an elevation gain of 2,200 feet and many steep sections of trail. But the view from the top is worth it, and if you're there in the early fall, you'll see tens of thousands of ladybugs clinging to the rocks

at the summit, where — amazingly enough — they winter in the rock crevices. Don't disturb them as they prepare for their hibernation. They will emerge in spring to mate and lay eggs. There are several routes up Bear Peak. One good way is from the NCAR Trailhead (described previously) to the Mesa Trail (past the large water tank on the hill and then down the hill). Turn left on the Mesa Trail, which descends and joins Bear Canyon Road below. Turn right on the road and look for the Fern Canyon Trail sign and follow it to the summit of Bear Peak. This is the shortest, but steepest, route. Another alternative is the earlier trail turnoff via Bear Canyon, which affords great views to the west. Just below the summit on the Bear Canyon Trail, a sign points to the Fern Canyon Trail to the northeast. Toward the top, the trail becomes quite steep, and some rock scrambling brings hikers to the summit. A nice loop can be made going up one trail and down the other.

FYI

Unless otherwise noted, the area code for all phone numbers in this guide is 303.

The **Mesa Trail** — also a popular running trail — begins just below the Bluebell Shelter at Chautauqua Park (Ninth Street and Baseline Road) and leads 6 miles south all the way to Eldorado Springs, with close-up views of the Flatirons and Front Range and sweeping vistas of the plains. The steep, strenuous 3-mile (round trip) hike to the **Royal Arch** from Chautauqua is a local favorite. Access it south of Bluebell Shelter at the end of paved Bluebell Road in Chautauqua Park. The trail climbs almost 1,500 feet quickly on the slopes of Green Mountain to this natural sandstone arch that offers superb vistas.

An easier trail and one suited for young children or tired adults is **Enchanted Mesa** and the **McClintock Nature Trail** (2.5 miles round trip). Begin at the picnic shelter next to Chautauqua Auditorium in Chautauqua Park and descend to cross Bluebell Creek and arrive at a fork. Take the right branch that climbs to intersect the Enchanted Mesa Road at an old apple tree. Cross the road and continue uphill along the creek. Look for interesting interpretive signs on the area's natural history. The trail then reaches the Mesa Trail, where you turn left (south) and continue a third of a mile to a large trail intersection. Take the left fork, passing a covered reservoir to reach the Enchanted Mesa Road, which is closed to traffic. Pines and wildflowers invite a picnic on the mesa top, and this gentle trail also makes a nice moonlight hike. Enchanted Mesa Road intersects McClintock Trail at Bluebell Creek, and this makes a return loop to Chautauqua, downhill all the way back.

Several fine hikes start at **Gregory Canyon** at Flagstaff Mountain's base, where Baseline Road becomes Flagstaff Road. Catch the **Flagstaff Mountain Trail** (3 miles round trip, 1,100 feet elevation gain) at the mouth of the dirt road into Gregory Canyon, across from the curving Armstrong Bridge. The trail zigzags back and forth across the paved road to the summit of the mountain. Continue upward, past a fork that leads down to Panorama Point. A small parking lot on the south side of the road from the trail marks a popular bouldering (rock-climbing) area including Monkey Wall, Crown Rock, Alamo Rock, Tree Slab and Pebbles. Though many folks drive up, the hike provides a close-up of rock climbers, wildflowers, native shrubs and wildlife. **Flagstaff Summit Nature Center** is open weekends in summer from 10 AM to 4 PM. Once on top, look for **Boy Scout Trail**, which leads a short distance west to May's Point and Artist's Point with fantastic views of the Continental Divide. Another trail at Flagstaff summit called **Rangeview** leads down from the summit to Realization Point, also with spectacular views of the Divide, North and South Arapaho peaks, Mount Audubon, Mount Meeker and Longs Peak.

Backpacking and overnight camping are not permitted in Boulder's mountain parks, but they are allowed in nearby national forests. See this chapter's "In the Mountains" (to follow) and "Camping" (previous) sections.

Eldorado Springs State Park, south of Boulder (see the Boulder Parks and Recreation Centers chapter) also has spectacular scenery and good hiking trails.

In the Mountains

Called the Snowy Range by the area's first settlers, the spectacular snow-covered mountains just west of Boulder are part of the **In-**dian Peaks Wilderness Area — among them, sky-scraping Mount Audubon, North and South Arapaho Peaks, Mount Toll and others — many above 12,000 feet and several above 13,000 feet. This 73,391-acre area west of Boulder contains some of Colorado's best scenery and highest peaks. The wilderness area was designated in 1978 and encompasses parts of Arapaho and Roosevelt national forests. Indian Peaks shares a boundary with Rocky Mountain National Park to the north and Rollins Pass to the south.

The U.S. Forest Service trails throughout the Indian Peaks Wilderness areas are interchangeable as hiking, backpacking and cross-country skiing trails. Favorites are in the **Brainard Lake Area**, just past Ward on Colo. Highway 72. Drive up Boulder Canyon to Nederland and head north on Highway 72; the turnoff is just past Ward, 200 yards on the left. Or, drive up Left Hand Canyon, north of Boulder past the Greenbriar Inn. Turn left (west) and proceed up the canyon through Ward and on to Colo. Highway 72. Turn right and look immediately to the left for the Brainard turnoff. Brainard Lake is 5 miles up County Road 102.

Two popular hikes at Brainard Lake are **Mount Audubon** (13,223 feet, 8 miles round trip and 2,750 feet of elevation gain), an arduous all-day climb, or much easier **Long Lake**, a 3-mile loop around the lake. Once at Brainard Lake, drive past the lake and look for the Long Lake and Mitchell Lake parking areas for these trailheads. Long Lake is a level stroll around this beautiful lake with spectacular views, colorful wildflowers and handicap accessibility. Hikes from this area to **Mitchell Lake** (1 mile, one way), **Blue Lake** (2.5 miles, one way) and 12,550-foot **Pawnee Pass** via **Lake Isabelle** (4.3 miles, one way) are all spectacular and easy to follow (though not all are easy to ascend) on the well-marked trails. Due to the area's great popularity and heavy use, there is now a $3 per vehicle charge, good for five days, or an annual pass available for $15. The fee goes toward protecting the area.

South of the Brainard Lake area in the Arapaho peaks area are two very popular trailheads: **Hessie** and **Fourth of July**, 8 and 12 miles, respectively, west of Nederland. Follow Colo. Highway 72 or County Road 107 to the town of Eldora. County Road 130 begins at the west end of the Town of Eldora. So popular are these trails — and with good reason — that it's hard to find a parking place on weekends, so weekday hiking is recommended. The left fork leads to the old town site of Hessie, 1.5 miles west of Eldora, now just an old cabin or two. The short road to Hessie (and the trailhead) is usually under water and not "navigable" by ordinary passenger cars. So park, where permitted along the road. Observe the No Parking signs, because they're strictly enforced, and cars are towed.

The 4-mile round-trip hike to **Lost Lake** is especially nice in the fall with the changing aspen leaves. The trail is a gravely road that climbs up through aspen groves. When it sort of levels out for bit, listen for the roar of water, take a short detour to the left (not marked) and look for a gorgeous series of cascades culminating in a thundering waterfalls. Continue on the trail to a junction sign at a bridge. Don't take the Devil's Thumb Bypass Trail; instead, cross the bridge and continue up the left-hand side of the creek past another beautiful falls. The trail leads to **Woodland Flats**, a large, open meadow with fine views of Devil's Thumb and the mountains. Don't miss the sign at this point for Lost Lake to the left, another 0.5 miles up to this pretty, wildflower-lined lake and the site of much early mining activity. Reach the **Fourth of July Trailhead** via the right fork of County Road 130 (left fork described previously leads to Hessie). This trailhead leads to spectacular hikes to Diamond Lake, South Arapaho Peak, Arapaho Pass, Fourth of July Mine and Dorothy Lake.

From the southwest end of Nederland, follow Colo. 72 to the town of Eldora, where County Road 130 begins at the west end of town. Follow this dirt road to the Hessie fork and take the right branch, which is a very rocky and bumpy 5-mile ride to Buckingham Camp-ground (also called Fourth of July Campground). From the campground take the right fork up to the parking lot at the trailhead. From the trailhead (10,121 feet) it's a 3-mile climb to **Arapaho Pass** at 12,061 feet. One mile from the trailhead is a turnoff to **Diamond Lake**, another 1.3 miles away at 10,960 feet. The **Diamond Lake Trail** dips down the valley and crosses the North Fork of Middle Boulder Creek. The trail crosses several small streams and continues upward to a big, wet meadow full of wildflowers. A trail junction sign directs hikers to the left for Devil's Thumb Trail and Jasper Lake, but continue going straight for Diamond Lake, which sparkles like the gem for which it was named. By continuing on the **Fourth of July Trail** (instead of taking the Diamond Lake Trail), hikers reach the **Fourth of July Mine** at 1.5 miles, and a worthwhile destination in itself, with interesting old mining equipment and a great view of Arapaho Pass on the Continental Divide. At the mine, there's the option of turning right and continuing up the Arapaho Glacier Trail to the glacier overlook and on up South Arapaho Peak (13,397 feet and 3.5 miles one way from the start of the trail). North Arapaho Peak (13,502) is another 0.75 miles along a connecting ridge with some exposure. These peaks should be attempted only by strong, experienced climbers with proper equipment and an early start to avoid the regular afternoon lightning storms. (The rule of thumb in summer is to be off a peak and headed back down by noon.) By continuing straight up the trail at Fourth of July Mine, hikers can reach Arapaho Pass in another 1.5 miles along a barren, rocky old wagon road. Listen for the whistles of marmots and pikas along the way, and look for these appealing, high-altitude critters. Marmots are similar to groundhogs, and pikas are guinea pig-size creatures related to rabbits, not rodents. Arapaho Pass is usually extremely

Photo: Daily Camera/Crissy Pascual

The CU-Boulder Buffaloes have played in the Sweet 16 in the NCAA women's basketball tourney.

windy, but the view is sublime — looking over the Continental Divide down the western slope to Caribou Lake and Coyote Park. Another short jaunt of 0.5 miles to the left leads to scenic, snowfield-crowned **Dorothy Lake**, at a chill 12,061 feet with usually an iceberg or two. Take care to avoid trampling the tiny tundra flowers around the lake — rock hopping is best.

Backpacking

Hiking trails are interchangeable as backpacking trails, but backpackers will need permits to stay overnight in the Indian Peaks Wilderness Area, which includes many of the trails described above. Certain trails are also off limits for backpacking, so check with the District Ranger Office (see subsequent information) *before* heading for the hills. Following are various trails there and elsewhere that offer access to good backpacking destinations.

Golden Gate Canyon State Park, 592-1501, south of Nederland on Colo. Highway 72, offers many miles of hiking plus backpacking, fishing and camping at a lower altitude than the Indian Peaks Wilderness Area. It's a lovely spot in the fall with the changing colors.

There are numerous backpacking options in the **Indian Peaks Wilderness Area**. The **Arapaho Pass Area** begins at the Fourth of July Trailhead and offers many choices on both sides of the Continental Divide. The trail climbs 3 miles to the 11,900-foot pass and drops down on the other side to Caribou Lake where it continues southwest over Caribou Pass to Columbine Lake. To reach Fourth of July Trailhead, travel west from Nederland on Colo. 72 to the town of Eldora. County Road 130 begins at the west end of the Town of Eldora. The Fourth of July Trailhead is 5 miles farther (take the right fork at the Hessie intersection). During the summer of 1996 backpacking was extremely limited in this area on the eastern side of the Continental Divide, so be sure to check for approved areas.

The climb to **Pawnee Pass** (12,541 feet) starts at Brainard Lake on the extremely popular Isabelle Glacier Trailhead, on the right side of Long Lake, but the crowds drop off as the going gets rougher and higher. This 4.5-mile hike is quite steep for the last 2 miles. An interesting backpacking loop is over the pass to Monarch Lake and a return to the east side of the Divide over Arapaho Pass — you'll need two cars or a drop-off and pick-up arrangement.

You must have a permit to backpack anywhere in the Indian Peaks Wilderness Area. Permits and detailed maps and routes are available at the **Boulder District Ranger Station** of the U.S. Forest Service, 444-6600 (recorded information line: 444-6003), at 2995 Baseline Road, Room 110, in Boulder. Backpacking group size is limited to 10; permits cost $5 for up to 7 nights. Dogs are allowed in Indian Peaks (but not Rocky Mountain National Park), but must be on a 6-foot (maximum), hand-held leash at all times. (There's a $50 fine for those that are not.) It's important to observe this regulation because the great number of hikers with dogs has caused considerable disturbance to wildlife and other hikers, particularly in recent years. Backpacking permits for Indian Peaks are available on weekends (when the Boulder District Ranger Station is closed) at Nederland's Ace Hardware, 20 Lakeview Drive (in the shopping center). National forest maps of Indian Peaks cost $3 ($6 for waterproof) and are also sold at area climbing, hardware and sporting goods stores.

Many books have been written on area hiking and backpacking trails with detailed descriptions and interesting historical notes; look for them at local mountain sporting goods shops. An especially good, newer book is *Boulder Hiking Trails* by Ruth Carol Cushman and Glenn Cushman. Another good one is *50 Front Range Hiking Trails* (including Rocky Mountain National Park and the Indian Peaks Wilderness Area) by Richard DuMais. Hikes in Rocky Mountain National Park are described in that chapter of this book.

Horseback Riding

What could be more Western than riding a horse? Most stables are out of town a bit, on the plains or in the mountains.

American Wilderness Experience
2820-A Wilderness Pl., Boulder • 444-2622

American Wilderness Experience (AWE) is the central reservations service of an adventure-travel company of the same name that offers a variety of eco-activities, including horse pack trips, sea kayaking in Mexico, dog sledding, hiking, biking and rafting.

Old West Dude Ranch Vacations, (800) 444-DUDE (to request catalog), a division of AWE, offers dude ranch vacations throughout the West.

Bradley Stables
1375 N. 111th Ave., Lafayette • 665-4637

Bradley Stables offers guided rides, lessons and birthday parties year round at your place or theirs. The hourly rate is $14 per person. Rides are in the Lafayette and Boulder areas. Trail rides in the flatlands east of Lafayette are $19 each. Lessons cost $18 for an 90-minute group lesson, $21 for a semiprivate lesson (two people) and $25 for a private lesson.

Gold Lake Mountain Resort
Peak to Peak Hwy. (Colo. Hwy. 72), just north of Ward • 459-0225

This resort offers hourly trail rides, wagon rides and customized rides. The hourly rate is $25; for customized rides prices vary. It's 15.5 miles north of Nederland (a half-mile north of Ward). The superb view of Longs Peak and a delightful gourmet restaurant make for a great getaway for a day or longer.

The Lazy H Guest Ranch
Colo. Hwy. 7, about a mile south of Allenspark • 447-1388

Lazy H offers a full dude-ranch program in June, July and August and hourly rides in May, September and October. The cost is $975 for a week (including horseback riding, meals and children's program), and hourly rides are $15 an hour per person (children and adults).

Peaceful Valley Lodge and Guest Ranch
Peak to Peak Hwy. (Colo. Hwy. 72), 8 miles north of Ward • 440-9632

Peaceful Valley offers non-guests pack trips, breakfast rides and guided trail rides mid-May through mid-October — based on availability. Hourly rides cost $20 per person. All-inclusive weekly packages (see our Boulder Accommodations chapter) cost $1,135 to $1,390 per adult, double occupancy.

Hunting

Hunting in Boulder County is tricky business since public land is so fragmented by private land, where permission to hunt is required. Locations, seasons and regulations for particular animals are complicated (too much so to outline here), so it's necessary to get the appropriate information for elk, deer, bear, mountain lion, grouse, rabbit, squirrel, etc. Pamphlets and information are available wherever hunting licenses are sold, such as **Gart Bros. Sporting Goods**, 449-9021, 3320 28th Street; **McGuckin Hardware**, 443-1822, 2525 Arapahoe Avenue; **Kmart**, 443-7850, 3325 28th Street; and, of course, the **Colorado Division of Wildlife**, 291-7227, 6060 Broadway in Denver; call 291-7530 for hunter education and 291-7529 for big-game information.

Licenses for Colorado residents cost $20.25 for deer and $30.25 for elk; for nonresidents, licenses cost $150.25 for deer and $250.25 for elk. License costs vary according to the animal being hunted. (25¢ per license sold goes to search-and-rescue services, if necessary, provided by the state.)

In-line Skating

The **Boulder Creek Path** is the most popular spot for this popular sport, but any of the city's bike paths are good (check previous "Bicycling" section). Rent in-line skating equipment at **The Bikesmith**, 443-1132, 2432 Arapahoe Avenue (Arapahoe Village Shopping Center); **Boulder Ski Deals**, 938-8799, 2404 Pearl Street; and **Doc's Ski and Sports**, 499-0963, 627 S. Broadway (Table Mesa Center). Rates are around $5 an hour and $15 to $20 a day.

Kayaking, Canoeing and Rafting

The City of Boulder's **Adventure Program**, 441-4401 or 441-3412 (class registration), offers a variety of river trips plus kayaking and canoeing instruction. So does the **Boulder Outdoor Center**, 444-8420, 2510 N. 47th Street — an excellent, professional operation dedicated to river preservation — which also sells and rents all of the necessary equipment. Boulder Outdoor Center offers raft trips and resort package trips that include kayaking and canoeing instruction. Boulder kayakers practice on Boulder Creek and the Reservoir and head to the Arkansas River, near Buena Vista (a few hours' drive from Boulder) or to Utah and other states for extended river trips.

Acquired Tastes Inc., 443-4120 or (800) 888-8582, is another reputable Boulder guide service specializing in whitewater excursions on the Arkansas River, with one-, two- and three-day trips available from mid-May through August.

Rugby

Rugby aficionados can contact the **Boulder Rugby Club** (which currently has no telephone number) through Dave Brown at 443-5171.

Running

Anywhere you look in Boulder, you'll see people running. If you're lucky it might be Olympian Frank Shorter, three-time Boston Marathon women's winner Uta Pippig or former world 10K record holder Arturo Barrios. Runners choose just about any location: the Boulder Creek Path, quiet streets through town, the Mesa Trail, various open space trails and even mountains. The **Boulder Road Runners** (mailing address: P.O. Box 1866, Boulder, Colorado 80306) has organized runs and programs for runners of all ages and abilities. For serious runners there are training and running groups and speed workouts; for information, call Connie Harmon, 499-2061, or Rich Castro, 492-8776. Other good sources of information are the staff and bulletin board at the **Runner's Roost**, 443-9868, at 1129 Pearl Street; **Runners Choice**, 499-7974, at 4800 Baseline Road (Meadows Shopping Center) and 2460 Canyon Boulevard (Village Center near McGuckin's) 449-8551; and Boulder's newest running store, **Boulder Running Company**, 2775 Pearl Street (28th and Pearl streets), 786-9255.

Sailing, Sailboarding and Powerboating

With Boulder's capricious Chinooks and occasional gale-force winds, sailing and windsurfing can be exciting experiences. Sailboats and sailboards can be rented at **Boulder Reservoir** through the City of Boulder-operated boathouse there, 441-3456, 51st

Street, 1.5 miles north of Jay Road via the Diagonal Highway (Colo. Highway 119). The City of Boulder offers instruction at Boulder Reservoir. Classes are offered in sailing as well as windsurfing. Daily admission with a sailboard or sailboat (weekdays only) is $15 for city residents, $25 for county residents and $40 for out-of-country residents. For weekends, a season pass is required; cost is $105 for city residents, $175 for county residents and $290 for out-of-county residents. McGuckin Hardware sponsors a wind-conditions hotline at 581-WIND.

Powerboats are permitted at Boulder Reservoir, 441-3468. Admission, weekdays only (Monday through Friday), is $30 for residents and $50 for nonresidents (it's necessary to have $300,000 watercraft liability insurance). For boats with 49 horsepower or less, admission is $15 for residents and $25 for nonresidents (the same insurance coverage is necessary). For weekends there are no daily passes; it's necessary to purchase a (seven-day) season permit. These cost $165 for city residents $250 for county residents and $575 for out-of-county residents (for boats with more than 49 horsepower). For boats with less than 49 horsepower, the pass costs $65 for city residents and $100 for both county and out-of-county residents.

Another popular sailing spot (no powerboats) is **Union Reservoir** in Longmont, 772-1265, 461 Weld County Road 26. From Boulder, take the Diagonal Highway (Colo. Highway 119) east to Weld Country Road 1, and follow the signs. Or, from Longmont take Ninth Avenue east to County Line Road, turn right and follow the signs. The gate fee is $5 on weekends and $4 on weekdays.

Skiing

Since skiing, in all its variations, is so popular with Colorado residents and visitors, we've presented information on the sport in several places in this book. For a brief review, see the subsequent sections. For more information — prices, related activities, lodging — on Ski Country, see our Boulder Attractions and Daytrips chapters.

Downhill

It's not Vail or Aspen, but it's only 21 miles from Boulder and there are no mountain passes or giant ski-traffic jams to contend with. **Eldora Mountain Resort**, 440-8700, is a great little ski area right in Boulder County with nine lifts: three surface, five double chair and one triple chair. With a top elevation of 10,600 feet,

Mountain Safety and Environment

Colorado's Rocky Mountains can take the unwary and unprepared by surprise. Remember: Going above or near timberline is the same as visiting the Arctic regions of the world. Mountain weather can change from a warm, sunny day to hail, snow, thunder and lightning in minutes. It can snow at any time of the year. Summer

daytime temperatures in Rocky Mountain National Park on Trail Ridge, Fall River and West Slope roads average in the 50s (10 C). The record high temperature in the alpine tundra is 63 (17 C). Wind chill can make these temperatures much lower — and it's usually windy in the mountains.

Visiting the high mountains can be a safe and extremely rewarding experience, as long as people are prepared and aware of the following dangers. As usual, prevention is the best way to make your trip safe and enjoyable.

1. **Hypothermia**. More of a threat to backpackers, dayhikers and skiers, hypothermia occurs from prolonged exposure to the cold and a resulting drop in body

temperature. It's more common among elderly people. Symptoms include a slowed heart rate, puffiness, pale skin, lethargy and confusion. In severe cases, breathing slows and intravenous liquids are required. Hypothermia is a killer and has claimed many victims in the mountains. ALWAYS bring a hat, rain and wind gear and extra warm clothing (layers are best) when going into the mountains. Staying well-hydrated by drinking liquids frequently also helps to prevent hypothermia. Keep a hat on if it's chilly — most body heat is lost from the head.

2. **Dehydration**. Colorado's dry climate, combined with exertion at high altitudes, can cause dehydration: a drop in the body's water level and often a drop in the body's level of salt. Symptoms include severe thirst, dry lips, increased heart and breathing rate, dizziness and confusion. The skin is dry and stiff. There's little urination, and what is passed is dark. Salt loss causes headaches, cramps (often in the legs), lethargy and pallor. Drink liquids frequently in the mountains. If you're feeling thirsty, your body's telling you that you're already about a quart low on liquids. Take salty snacks such as pretzels, chips and crackers. Rehydration drinks, such as Gatorade, are also good aids to take along.

3. **Lightning**. Lightning is much more dangerous above timberline. Every year lightning claims a number of lives in Colorado's high country. If a storm develops, stay off ridges and peaks. Keep away from trees, boulders, isolated buildings and metal objects. The safest place is in your car. A tingling sensation at the base of the neck or scalp and hair standing on end with static electricity are both signs that lightning is about to strike near you. Move rapidly to your car. Do not stand still, no matter what. If you are unable to return to your car, squat and wrap your arms around your knees, keeping your head low. Do not lie or sit on the ground (because if lightning strikes you or the ground and travels through your body, you want it to have a way out — an open circuit).

To estimate your distance from a lightning strike, count the seconds between the flash and the accompanying thunder and divide by five to get the distance in miles. It takes five seconds for the sound to travel a mile.

4. **Altitude sickness**. Symptoms include headache, dizziness, nausea, shortness of breath and impaired mental abilities. Breathing into a paper or plastic bag for five minutes reduces these symptoms. In severe cases, fluid can build up in the lungs, causing breathlessness, heavy coughing and heavy phlegm. If untreated, these symptoms can lead to seizures, hallucinations, coma, brain damage and death. There is 40 percent less oxygen in the air above 8,000 feet (2,438 meters) than at sea level. To avoid altitude sickness, refrain from strenuous activity for the first few days at high altitude. Move slowly above timberline, eat lightly and drink fluids frequently. Alcoholic beverages may aggravate the symptoms. Move to a lower elevation if symptoms persist. People with respiratory or heart problems should check with a physician before going to high elevations.

5. **Sunburn**. Sunburn is much more severe at high altitudes because the reduced atmosphere is less able to filter out the sun's harmful ultraviolet radiation. With 5 percent more ultraviolet (light) per 1,000 feet, Colorado has 25 percent more damaging sun rays than Florida's beaches. Skiers and other winter sports enthusiasts need to be especially careful, because reflection from snow can cause severe sunburn. Skiers have been known to get sunburned inside their nostrils. In summer, to avoid burning, wear a long-sleeved shirt and a brimmed hat, and use sunscreen with at least a 15 SPF (sun protection factor) rating.

6. **Dangerous currents and floods**. Though they look shallow and serene, mountain streams have strong currents, slippery rocks and cold temperatures that have been contributing factors in many drownings. Be especially careful when fishing or when children are playing near streams. Sudden rains can raise stream levels rapidly and even cause flash floods. If rain continues, move to higher ground.

7. **Giardia**. Don't drink water from streams and lakes. Tempting though it might be, many mountain streams and lakes contain bacteria and a microscopic organism called *Giardia lamblia*, which can cause long-term intestinal problems. The organism is transmitted into water by cysts in human, domestic animal and wildlife feces. Dogs and cats can catch and transmit Giardia. Symptoms of Giardia include violent diarrhea, gas, cramps, loss of appetite and nausea. Carry your own water bottle filled with tap water. Campers and hikers should boil all stream or lake water for 10 or more minutes, use water-purification kits or the now-popular (and expensive) microfilters (portable pumps that filter water). A microfilter must filter down to four microns to filter out Giardia.

8. **Ticks**. Not usually a problem in the higher mountains, wood ticks appear in the spring after vegetation begins to leaf in the Lower and Upper Montane zones — the areas below 9,500 feet (2,896 meters). They can appear as early as February in forested and shrubby areas and remain active into late summer. They are rare in the subalpine zone and above the tree line (above 9,500 feet). Wood ticks can transmit Colorado tick fever and the more serious (but fairly uncommon) Rocky Mountain fever. Applying insect repellent and wearing long pants and long-sleeved shirts helps prevent tick bites. The best precaution is to check frequently for ticks on your clothing, hair and body, because it takes several hours for a tick to attach. After being outdoors, undress in a shower or tub or on a ground cloth OUTSIDE your tent. Inspect clothing carefully before putting it back on. Destroy ticks, but do not crunch them with your fingers.

To remove an attached tick, disinfect the area. Grasp the tick firmly with tweezers close to its head. Gently remove it by pulling it upward and out from the skin. Never twist or jerk on it. Putting nail polish, cooking oil or petroleum jelly on the tick can make it release its grip more easily. Consult a physician if you have localized swelling, a rash, enlarged lymph glands or a fever in the days or weeks after a tick bite. Lyme disease is uncommon in Colorado, but it does occur — from non-native ticks that somehow hitch a ride into the state.

Eldora has 1,400 feet of vertical gain — and beautiful views from the top. You'll probably get more skiing in at Eldora and less standing in lift lines than at the bigger resorts. There's a ski school, rentals, a lodge, races, leagues and even an RTD bus from Boulder that makes numerous daily trips right to the resort.

Other ski areas, such as Keystone, Loveland, Arapahoe Basin, Breckenridge, Copper Mountain and Winter Park are within a two-hour drive of Boulder (see the "Ski Country" section of our Daytrips and Weekend Getaways chapter). For information on these and other Colorado ski areas, call Colorado Ski Country USA Monday through Friday, 825-SNOW (recorded information) or 837-0793 (ad-

ministrative office). Discount lift tickets to the aforementioned areas are available at King Soopers and Safeway, among other places.

Rocky Mountain Skiing by Claire Walter, this book's co-author and Western editor for *Skiing Magazine*, is a great resource book for the entire Rocky Mountain region and is available at local bookstores.

Cross-country

Before you head to the mountains, you can warm up and practice right in Boulder. The **Boulder Nordic Club**, which is cooperative with the Boulder Parks and Recreation Department, sets a nice track around North

Boulder Park (Ninth and Dellwood), whenever there's enough snow on the ground. Skiing at the park is free. The Boulder Nordic Club is full of very serious skiers, most of whom compete in the various citizens' races throughout Colorado and beyond. For information about the club, call 530-1253.

Eldora Mountain Resort's Nordic Center, 440-8700, is one of Colorado's largest and most popular cross-country centers with 45 kilometers of marked and groomed trails. There's a cozy log cabin lodge with refreshments, rentals and lessons.

At Eldora Mountain Resort, there's also access to the free national forest **Jenny Creek Trail**. Climb up the Ho-Hum downhill run next to the Little Hawk lift, turn right and look for the trail signs. The trail weaves up and down through the woods and then descends on a narrow trail (bad when icy) to the Jenny Creek Road. You can turn around here or follow the creek bed, eventually leading up to Yankee Doodle Lake (9 miles round-trip from the Eldora parking lot). Or at the Jenny Creek Road, another trail to the right, the **Guinn Mountain Trail**, leads up a steep, difficult climb to the distant Guinn Mountain cabin (10.5 miles round trip), operated by the **Colorado Mountain Club**. Skiers can bring camping gear to spend the night; call the subsequently listed CMC number for information.

Many national forest hiking trails in the summer become cross-country ski trails in winter. The favorite spots are in the **Brainard Lake Area**, **East Portal** from Rollinsville (see directions to Rollins Pass Road in this chapter's "Mountain Biking" section), the **Hessie and Fourth of July roads** at the west end of the town of Eldora and **Peaceful Valley** (north of Nederland and Ward on Colo. Highway 72). (See the previous "Hiking" section for more directions to these areas.)

For absolute beginners who want no hills or spills, the **Brainard Lake Road** offers nearly level terrain to the lake with no surprises and great scenery. Just follow the road up past the closure — 2.2 miles to the lake.

Left Hand Reservoir at Brainard Lake is more challenging, but the wide trail offers plenty of margin for error. Begin on the south side of the Brainard Road below the gate closure and follow the trail signs up a roadbed about 2 miles to the reservoir. There are thrilling downhill runs back on the wide trail.

The **Colorado Mountain Club South Trail** begins on the south side of Brainard Road 50 yards west of the closure gate and is a bit longer and narrower through wooded areas. Climb a short hill and ski the rolling 2.5 miles to Brainard Lake.

For intermediate to advanced skiers comfortable on narrow, steep hills and turns, there's the **Waldrop North Trail**, about 5.5 miles round-trip, accessible just north of the closure.

Buchanan Pass Trail begins at the curve on Colo. Highway 72 (5.8 miles north of Ward) at Peaceful Valley. Follow the trail on the north side of the creek west of Camp Dick campground. An 11-mile loop can be made by returning on the Middle St. Vrain four-wheel-drive road (some snowmobiles), but you can ski whatever distance you like.

The **Sourdough Trail** is 17.5 miles long, but has different segments at various trailheads. From Camp Dick Campground to Beaver Reservoir, it's 2.3 miles. From Beaver Reservoir to Brainard Road, it's 7.4 miles, and from Brainard Road to Rainbow Lakes Road, 7.8 miles. The trail was built mainly for ski touring and mountain biking, and is pleasant rolling terrain though the pines. All access to the various connections to the Sourdough Trail are on the Peak to Peak Highway (Colo. 72), west of Nederland. Camp Dick Campground is on Middle St. Vrain Road, 5.8 miles north of Ward and 0.5 miles west of Peaceful Valley. One Sourdough Trailhead is on the left-hand side of County Road 96 just east of Beaver Reservoir, 2.5 miles north of Ward and 2 miles west on County Road 96. The **Red Rock Trailhead** is on the right-hand side of County Road 102, just east of Red Rock Lake, 2.5 miles west on Brainard Lake Road. Another Sourdough Trailhead is on the right-hand side of Rainbow Lakes Road (County Road 116), 4.7 miles south of Ward (7 miles north of Nederland) and 0.4 miles west on County Road 116.

The **Colorado Mountain Club**, 449-1135, and **Flatirons Ski Club**, P.O. Box 6120, Boulder 80306 (no official phone number), have weekly scheduled trips open to the public (membership is eventually expected). They both provide a great way to meet other skiers and explore area ski trails for those new to the area.

Ski rentals, books, maps and trail information are available at **Mountain Sports**, 443-6770; **Eastern Mountain Sports**, 442-7566; **Neptune Mountaineering**, 499-8866; **Doc's Ski and Sports**, 499-0963; **Breeze Ski Rentals**, 443-9188; and **Crystal**, 449-7669.

Excellent sources for local cross-country skiing are *Peak to Peak Ski Trails of the Colorado Front Range* by Harlan N. Barton and *Backcountry Skiing* by Brian Litz.

For information on snow and avalanche conditions call the U.S. Forest Service hotline, 275-5360.

Snowboarding

All of Colorado's ski areas, except Aspen Mountain, allow snowboarding, rent the equipment and offer lessons. Snowboards are now generally available for rent at skiing and mountaineering equipment shops, and a whole new raft of snowboard (and skateboard) specialty shops have sprung up to accommodate the popularity of this growing sport. Some shops that rent snowboards include **Max**, 447-8822, 2428 Arapahoe Avenue (Arapahoe Village Shopping Center); **Brothers Boards**, 473-0266, 3330 Arapahoe Avenue; **University Bicycles**, 444-4196, 839 Pearl Street; the **Boulder Outdoor Center**, 444-8420, 2510 N. 47th Street; **Kind Groovy Boards**, 545-6324, 1437 Arapahoe Avenue; and **Twist Snowboard Shop**, 440-6581, 1700 Pearl Street (high-performance equipment). One-day snowboard rentals cost around $20 for the board and $8 for the boots.

Snowshoeing

The growing popularity of snowshoeing is also evident on all the local trails in winter. One needs no real lessons for this simple sport. Simply strap on the snowshoes and start walking. Snowshoes provide the easy ability to leave the crowds on the trails and make your own route — and the cross-country skiers would appreciate it if you did. Snowshoes can be rented at most local mountaineering and ski rental shops (listed in the previous "Skiing" section), and cost about $12 a day to rent.

Please note: Snowshoers sharing forest trails with cross-country skiers should make their own tracks, wherever possible, and avoid walking in existing ski tracks. This is because cross-country skis work best in ski tracks and don't work well on snowshoe paths. People without skis or snowshoes should not walk in either tracks — it ruins them both, making it frustrating and miserable for skiers and snowshoers.

Soaring and Paragliding

A silent glider ride over the Front Range is an experience of a lifetime. The **Cloud Base** at Boulder's Municipal Airport, 530-2208, 5534 Independence Road, offers such rides plus instruction and other scenic glider flights.

For those who want nothing to stand between them and the great blue sky — other than a chute of sheer nylon — there's paragliding. **Alpine World Adventures**, 449-5620, is co-operated by Freddie Snalam of Freddie's Hot Dogs, on the Pearl Street Mall. Besides being a noted hot dog vendor, Snalam is a expert mountaineer, having done exten-

---

INSIDERS' TIP

Even people who have no intention of ever hanging from a rope themselves might enjoy watching others do so. A short drive or walk up Boulder Canyon (on foot up the Creek Path from Eben Fine Park, it's less than a mile) takes you to the Elephant Buttresses and the Dome (just past where the Creek Path goes under Canyon Boulevard), two of Boulder's most popular rock-climbing spots. On the Dome, watch climbers tackle a route called the "Disappearing Crack" — you'll see why. A bench along the creek invites spectators.

sive climbing (and some paragliding) in the Himalayas.

Parasoft Inc. Paragliding School, 494-2820, 4445 Hastings Drive, also teaches paragliding. Parasoft offers towing — from an airplane, paragliders are launched like a kite and can fly as much as 25 miles across country out on the plains. Instruction takes place at the north and south ends of Boulder. The school also gives instruction on motorized paragliders (paramotors).

Another choice is **Fly Away**, based in Golden, Colorado, 642-0849. Owner Bill Lawrence, who has competed in two national championships, is the only tandem-rated instructor in the Boulder area and has been flying for seven years. He originally trained in Switzerland. He runs trips out of state but mostly works out of Boulder. His company specializes in pilot training and small classes.

Swimming

Until the really big one hits California and the Pacific Ocean laps the foot of the Rockies, pools and reservoirs are the main swimming options around Boulder. The three City of Boulder-operated Recreation Centers (see "Recreation Facilities" in our Boulder Parks and Recreation Centers chapter) all have indoor pools. **East Boulder Community Center** has a water slide and Lazy River with innertubes for kids plus a mushroom waterfall. Outdoor pools are open during summer months only at **Scott Carpenter Park** and **Spruce Pool** (also in the Parks chapter). **Boulder Reservoir's** sandy swimming beach helps relieve ocean homesickness a bit (no sharks, only carp), and historic **Eldorado Artesian Springs**, 499-1316, in Eldorado Springs, offers warm, therapeutic mineral waters in a scenic canyon setting. The thermal pools and snack bar are open from Memorial Day through Labor Day from 10 AM to 6 PM daily. Rates are $5 for adults, $3 for kids and seniors.

Tennis

Free, public tennis courts are usually in great demand and short supply in Boulder. Courts can be reserved for $7.50 for 90 min-

utes through the city-operated **North**, **South** and **East Recreation centers**, 441-3444, 441-3448 and 441-4400, and the city offers instruction at various levels. There's a smattering of free courts around town at various parks and schools including: **Arapahoe Ridge**, 1280 43rd Street (two courts); **Baseline Middle School**, 700 20th Street (two courts), **Burbank Middle School**, 290 Manhattan Drive (four courts); **Centennial Middle School**, 2005 Norwood Avenue (eight courts); **Fairview High**, 1515 Greenbriar Boulevard (eight courts); **Boulder High**, 1604 Arapahoe (three courts); **Martin Park**, 36th Street and Dartmouth Avenue (two courts); **Chautauqua Park**, Ninth Street and Baseline Road (one court).

The **Boulder Tennis Association**, 449-5984, has tennis ladders and formal and informal tournaments.

Spectator Sports

Football

College

University of Colorado
Athletic Ticket Office • Folsom Field, Colorado Ave., Boulder • 492-8337

The Golden Buffaloes belong to the Big 12 Conference in NCAA Division I and play home games at Folsom Field, seating capacity 51,748. The regular season runs from September into November. For season ticket information call the Athletic Ticket Office, Stadium room 126, 492-8337.

In 1996, the previous Big Eight expanded to become the Big 12, adding teams from the Southwest Conference (the University of Texas, Texas A&M, Baylor and Texas Tech). It's a kind of super conference like the Southeastern (with 12 teams) and the Western Athletic (with 16 teams) conferences. These larger conferences are the current trend in college athletics — primarily to attract a broader-based TV viewing audience (read as a money-making venture). Instead of the Big Eight, where every team played each other every year, there

Quarterback John Elway leads
the Denver Broncos.

Photo: Daily Camera/Cliff Grassmick

Division and play home games at Mile High Stadium, seating capacity 75,103, at 19th and Eliot streets in Denver. As this book goes to press, quarterback John Elway, although hobbled by a hamstring injury, is having a banner season, and the team is on-track to contend for the conference championship and a Super Bowl berth.

The regular season runs from September into December. For ticket information call the listed number; season tickets are sold out for the foreseeable future, with a waiting list of more than 5,000 names. Single game tickets, if available, are offered the week prior to each game at the Broncos Ticket Office.

are two divisions in the Big 12 — a north (with the universities of Colorado, Nebraska, Missouri and Kansas plus Iowa and Kansas states) and a south (with the four Texas teams plus the University of Oklahoma and Oklahoma State). The teams play all five opponents in their division plus three from the other division for two years in a row (one year at home and one away). Then, during the next two years, the other three teams in the other division are played. There are eight conference games instead of the old schedule of seven games (one less non-conference game and three non-conference games out of the total 11 games). The two division winners, Nebraska and Texas, played for the conference championship in a 12th game (in St. Louis on December 7 in 1996) to determine the Big 12 Conference Champion; Texas surprised the Cornhuskers with a hard-fought victory, quashing Nebraska's bid to repeat as national champions.

Professional

Denver Broncos
Denver Broncos Ticket Office • 1900 Eliot St., Denver • 433-7466
The Broncos belong to the National Football League's American Conference Western

Basketball

College

University of Colorado
Athletic Ticket Office • Folsom Field, Colorado Ave., Boulder • 492-8337
The men's and women's teams belong to the Big 12 Conference and play home games at the CU Coors Events/Conference Center, Regent Drive in Boulder on the CU campus, capacity 11,198. The regular season runs from December to March. Call to order tickets, or for season tickets write to the Athletic Ticket Office, Box 372, Boulder 80309.

Professional

Colorado Xplosion
800 Grant St., Ste. 410, Denver • 832-2229, 830-8497 (TicketMaster)
This women's pro basketball team plays home games at the Denver Coliseum, 4600 Humboldt Street, 295-4444, and McNichols Arena, 1635 Clay Street, 893-6700, both in Denver. They play in the eight-team American Basketball League. Tickets are available at the game site's box office 1½ hours before each game and at all TicketMaster outlets. Single-game ticket prices range from $9 to $36; seven- and 11-game ticket packages and group tickets also are available.

Denver Nuggets
McNichols Sports Arena • 1635 Clay St., Denver • 893-6700

The Nuggets belong to the National Basketball Association's Western Conference and play home games at McNichols Sports Arena, 1635 Clay Street in Denver, capacity of 17,171. The regular season runs from November into April. For season tickets call the listed number or write to 1635 Clay Street, Denver 80204. Some discounts are available.

Ice Hockey

Professional

Colorado Avalanche
McNichols Sports Arena • 1635 Clay St., Denver • 893-6700, 575-1900

Yes, Coloradans are nuts about their 1996 Stanley Cup Champions — and rightly so. The Colorado Avalanche (formerly the Quebec Nordiques) belong to the National Hockey League and play home games at McNichols Sports Arena, 1635 Clay Street in Denver, capacity of 17,171. The regular season runs from October through June. Call for ticket prices and game schedules.

Baseball

Professional

Colorado Rockies
Coors Field • 2001 Blake St., Denver • 292-0200

The Rockies belong to Major League Baseball's National League West Division and play their home games at the snazzy Coors Field in Denver, capacity 50,249. The season runs from April through October. Tickets are available by calling (800) 388-ROCK; for group tickets (25 people or more), and general customer service, call ROCKIES, or write to Colo-

---

Wilderness Ethics for Hiking, Camping and Backcountry Travel

Various wilderness areas and national forests have their own sets of use regulations, but the following general guidelines apply to all areas. Remember: Even when we are careful, our presence and actions have an impact on the natural world. As our human population grows, negative impacts become more and more severe.

Backcountry Travel

•Travel quietly and in small groups. Avoid disturbing others.

•Spread out impact by exploring less heavily visited areas.

•Leave your pets at home to keep from bothering wildlife and other visitors.

•Stay on maintained trails whenever possible. Do not take shortcuts; doing so destroys vegetation and causes erosion.

•Be especially careful when trails are muddy, and minimize horse use when trails are wet.

•On narrow trails, walk single file rather than several abreast, and try to avoid congregating large groups in sensitive areas.

•Don't pick wildflowers or dig up plants; it's illegal in all parks, and permission is needed on private land. Be judicious in picking fruit so that you leave enough for wildlife.

•Comply with signs regarding vehicles and mountain bikes, which are prohibited on many trails because of erosion problems. Refrain from using bikes on muddy slopes, where deep ruts develop quickly, and yield to other trail users.

•If you are photographing or observing wild animals and they become nervous, you are too close. Back away.

•Give right of way to horses, keeping to the downhill side. The same rule applies to all large mammals, who will become stressed if you remain above them.

•Avoid disturbing nesting birds, and comply with closures designed to protect plants and animals.

•Leave gates as you find them unless signs instruct otherwise.

Campsite Selection

•In heavily visited areas, use existing campsites to confine impact to a small area.

•In less-visited areas, choose a site well away from streams and lakes and out of sight of other users. Eliminate all traces of your camp.

•Carry out all trash. DO NOT bury it. If you must use soap for washing or bathing, do so at least 150 feet from any water sources, and pour the water into absorbent ground.

Stoves and Fires

•Use a gas stove for all cooking. Wood is scarce in the high country and an essential part of the ecosystem. Gas is quicker, cleaner and won't leave a scar of charred and sterilized soil.

•Campfires are becoming controversial. If you absolutely must build a fire, use only dead and down wood. Use existing fire rings and keep the fire very small. Use only as much wood as will burn completely.

•Never leave fires unattended, even for a moment. When you leave, make certain that the fire is dead and cold. Clean out fire rings so they will be ready for the next visitor.

Sanitation

•Bury human waste in a small cat-hole about 6 inches deep and dug in organic soil (not just leaves or rocks) away from heavy-use areas and at least 150 feet from any water.

•Soiled toilet paper, diapers and sanitary napkins should be carried out.

•Place all trash in trash cans. In Colorado's climate, organic wastes such as orange peels, egg shells and paper can take more than 100 years to decompose if left outside.

•If you feel like doing a good deed, carry out litter left by others.

This safety and environmental information comes from the American Medical Association's *Encyclopedia of Medicine*, *A Roadside Guide to Rocky Mountain National Park* by Beatrice Elizabeth Willard and Susan Quimby Foster, *A Climbing Guide to Colorado's Fourteeners* by Walter Borneman and Lyndon Lampert and the *Boulder County Nature Almanac* by Ruth Carol Cushman, Stephen Jones and Jim Knopf. The latter three are excellent resources for detailed information on these areas of Colorado.

---

rado Rockies Baseball Club, P.O. Box 120, Denver 80201.

The Silver Bullets

Various home sites • (800) 642-6116, (800) 388-7625 (Denver games)

A traveling women's baseball team, The Silver Bullets compete against men's teams of varying levels and ages. In 1996 the team played three home games during summer in Denver, Colorado Springs and Pueblo. Call for ticket information.

Roller Hockey

Professional

Denver DareDevils

McNichols Sports Arena • 1635 Clay St., Denver • 893-6401

The DareDevils belong to the Roller Hockey International League and play home games at McNichols Arena. Single-game tickets are

$14 for adults, $8 for youths 16 and younger and seniors, and $36 for a family of four (two adults and two youths or one adult and three youths). Season tickets are available at adult, family, youth and senior-citizen rates.

games at Mile High Stadium in Denver, with a seating capacity of 25,000 for soccer. The regular season runs from April to October. Ticket prices range from $8 to $19. Call for discount and special group rates.

Soccer

Professional

Colorado Foxes
Mile High Greyhound Park • 62nd Ave., Commerce City • 893-6937

The Foxes, who belong to the A-League, play home games at Mile High Greyhound Park, with a seating capacity of 10,000. The regular season runs from May to September. Ticket prices range from $6 to $15 with special season club and group rates available.

To reach the park, take I-270 to N. Vasquez Boulevard to Colo. Highway 2, then proceed to 62nd Avenue.

Colorado Rapids
Mile High Stadium • 19th and Eliot Sts., Denver • 299-1599

Members of the new and burgeoning Major League Soccer, the Rapids play home

Volleyball

College

University of Colorado
Athletic Ticket Office • Folsom Field, Colorado Ave., Boulder • 492-8337

The Buffs belong to the Big 12 Conference and play home games at the CU Coors Events/Conference Center on the CU-Boulder campus. The season runs from September into November. Call for ticket information.

Other College Sports

University of Colorado
Other varsity sports teams at CU-Boulder include golf, cross-country, track and field, tennis and skiing as well as numerous club sports. For information about schedules call 492-7931. For non-varsity club sports call 492-5471.

NIWOT

The Town That Time Forgot

Boulder
Neighborhoods and Nearby Communities

As long as you aren't set on oceanfront, you might fall in love with a Boulder home. This chapter is for looky-lous who enjoy residential areas. It highlights neighborhoods in Boulder and around the county. Boulder's older neighborhoods get the spotlight first. Next is a description of mountain places, then cities of the Plains. If you want more practical information on settling down, check our Real Estate chapter, especially if you become smitten with Chief Niwot's curse, which has been interpreted that anyone who sees Boulder Valley will always long to return.

Historic Boulder Neighborhoods

If you like historic homes, call **Historic Boulder**, 444-5192. The organization itself is headquartered in a fanciful turreted Victorian at 646 Pearl Street, just a few blocks west of the Pearl Street Mall. From mid-May through September, volunteers lead walking tours of historic areas. The downtown tour starts at 10 AM every Friday. The Mapleton Hill tour starts at 1 PM every Sunday. Both meet in the Hotel Boulderado lobby. The Chautauqua tour meets at the Dining Hall at 10 AM every Sunday. The University Hill tour takes place on the first and third Monday of each month, meeting at Columbia (Pioneer) Cemetery and Ninth and Pleasant Streets at 10 AM. For a tour of the cemetery itself, meet at the corner at 10 AM on the second Saturday of each month. The tour of the Whittier neighborhood meets at 10 AM every second and fourth Monday in the Hotel Boulderado. Tours cost $4, including a 22-page historic guidebook.

You can take a more informal sidewalk amble of your own. Our version starts at the **Whittier Historic District** east of the Pearl Street Mall. Many buildings here are as crisp as a Busby Berkeley girl, while others are zanier than a television sitcom. "Mork & Mindy's" house, the turreted, mauve Victorian at 1619 Pine Street, is a private residence, but you can enjoy it from the sidewalk. At 12th and Spruce streets, a giant owl guards the home of artist Bob Bellows, who creates sculptures from old farm tools. The "feathers" around the owl's beak are spoons. Some homes are painstakingly authentic; others have been altered with abandon. Good and bad in-fill is frequent, where homes added behind existing structures allow more density near the city core.

Step inside the Boulder Victoria Bed and Breakfast Inn, then the Hotel Boulderado, catty-corner from each other at 13th and Pine streets, if you like historic interiors. Another to check is the whimsical Gothic revival at 646 Pearl Street that is now Historic Boulder's home. When you visit the gift shop, notice the spiral stairs and other 19th century features.

The **Mapleton Hill Historic District**, northwest of Broadway and Pearl Street, has both grand old homes and more modest ones. The simple stone house at 1019 Spruce Street is Boulder's oldest house. Mapleton Avenue at the crest of the hill has a distinctive landscaped median, flagstone sidewalks and a canopy of silver maples. Those 100-year-old maples are dear, for this city started as a windblown prairie, and as they age, the city is replacing them to maintain the distinctive character of the neighborhood. Behind Mapleton Hill's handsome front doors might be a scatter of children's toys. Some homes have marvelous decorations and superb art. In others, the stereo sits on an orange crate. The area is frequently on Historic Boulder tours, and homeowners selected work hard to shine things up. As one dad once blurted, entering his "tour-decorated" Mapleton home, "There's even a Christmas wreath on my bike!"

University Hill and **Chautauqua Park** are two more historic areas. Before you start up there, keep in mind you're going to put in some distance. Head south on Ninth Street and cross over Boulder Creek, where you'll see two interesting buildings. The recently renovated and expanded main Boulder Public Library is on your left, and Highland Office Park, a beautiful renovation of an old school, is on your right. It's OK to go inside. Farther up Ninth Street, as you cross Euclid Avenue, see that red brick home with the castle look? Legend has it two Boulder brothers fell in love with the same woman. They held a house-building contest. The woman chose this octagonal house — and the guy who came with it.

Turn left (east) on Euclid. At 1206 Euclid Avenue, you'll find the Boulder Museum of History set in a beautifully landscaped park. The museum was began in 1899 as a summer "cottage" for a New York stock broker. If this is a cottage, that New Yorker's regular home must have filled three blocks. It now features a Tiffany window, fascinating snippets of Boulder history and a gift shop. When you leave the museum, proceed north again until it deadends at Baseline Road. At 12th Street and Baseline Road, the northwest corner, is a Glenn Huntington home. This local architect's stately brick buildings set the tone for 1930s University Hill. Continue west (right), passing an interesting art deco-era home on 15th Street.

Chautauqua Park fills the triangle between Baseline Road, the Flatirons and a hilly neighborhood of contemporary homes. You can still rent a little old wooden summer cabin at Chautauqua, but many people live now there full-time. Street names honor mountain flowers, such as the daisy-shaped gaillardia and the nodding blue lupine. Northeast of the big Chautauqua barn, it's a short hike up Enchanted Mesa. With the purchase of this meadow of grasses and strong-limbed Ponderosa pines in the 1960s, Boulder became the first town in the nation to buy open space through a sales-tax bond. Enchanted Mesa is one reason Boulderites can gaze out their windows and see pine forests, rather than houses, in the Foothills. Also check the Chautauqua Rangers' Station on Kinnikinik Road, where you can get information on the Boulder Mountain Park system. Displays depict drought-tolerant native plants that thrive in Boulder yards.

Contemporary Boulder Neighborhoods

While you can hoof through Boulder's oldest neighborhoods, you'll probably want to drive to see the newer ones. Some of Boulder's most futuristic homes were designed by the late Boulder architect Charles Haertling. The easiest to spot are just up **Flagstaff Road**. To get there, follow Baseline Road up Flagstaff Mountain. A tenth-mile past the fire danger sign is a home of round white towers beside one with sand-colored, pyramidal roofs. These are two of Haertling's 52 creations. If you haven't driven up Flagstaff Road before, by all means, do it now. The panorama of Boulder Valley is gorgeous, and if you've got a map, you can spot most landmarks from up there. If you don't have a Boulder County license plate on your car, you'll have to pay a modest use fee at the overlook parking area and elsewhere in the Mountain Parks system. If you continue up Flagstaff Road past the park boundary, you'll pass widely scattered homes in diverse styles, from one that resembles a French château to monumental log houses.

Return down the mountain to Baseline and turn left on Sixth Street. Then turn left again at Willowbrook Road, then left once more at the fork. Willowbrook ends at a white building some call a spaceship. It's the Volsky house, a 1960s-era Haertling design that earned him a feature in *Life* magazine. Haertling, considered one of America's finest architects, often used drama and fluid forms. If you are ever invited inside a Haertling home, go gladly, for he designed with reverence for Boulder's vistas.

If you've had your fill of fancy homes, check out **Martin Acres**, Boulder's first tract-home neighborhood, north of Baseline Road, south of Table Mesa Drive and east of Broadway. In 1955, when these 200 little ranch houses of similar shoebox style were built, a new three-bedroom model cost $13,000. They now sell for about 15 times that price. A few droop with neglect, whimpering for someone to fix them up . . . maybe you? Others are so pristine, you can imagine Donna Reed stepping out, finger on chin, to ponder her day's good deeds. The trees are now 40 years old. Some renovations are, well, sort of like a kid's party hat on a businessman. But more and more are enthralling transformations. Martin Acres proves that homes from a plain area, filled with interesting people, add character to a neighborhood. Having said that, there is hope — four decades hence — for some of Boulder's more sterile new subdivisions.

More '70s-vintage, and generally pricier, is **Table Mesa**, an area of split-levels and raised ranches below the National Center for Atmospheric Research. It lies west of Broadway and south of Table Mesa Drive. The Table Mesa Shopping Center is convenient for Table Mesa residents. Follow Broadway south to the stoplight at Greenbriar Boulevard. Turn right, and head west past Fairview High School into a neighborhood of brown homes called **Shannahan Ridge**. Townhomes, condominiums and single-family homes pack the street's north side. The south is open space — a whole valley-full. Residents awaken to meadowlark songs. Open space near residential areas has been one of Boulder's finest achievements. People pay a premium to live near open, natural areas. Dominating South Boulder is the I.M. Pei-designed National Center for Atmospheric Research. This is one of America's finest public buildings, and in typical Boulder fashion, it is also the gateway to easy and popular nature trails. To reach it, drive west on Table Mesa Drive and up to the mesa.

Backtrack to Baseline Road, continue west to **Sixth Street** and turn north again. You're driving by some of Boulder's most prestigious homes. This is not a neighborhood filled with mansions (though some homes are grand), but rather of modest ranch-styles and innovative serendipitous designs. When you reach Sixth Street and Arapahoe Avenue, look at the cute green Victorian behind the hedge that is one of the few creekside buildings that survived the 1894 flood. We're due for another big flood, although no one can say exactly when. Flash floods are why creek-loving home builders must observe strict building codes. You need to do a little zigzagging to reach Fourth Street and Mapleton Avenue. Turn left (west) on Mapleton, left again and drive south on posh **Knollwood Drive**. The long building embracing the boulder is another Haertling home.

Return again via Mapleton Avenue, driving east past some of Boulder's loveliest homes, to Ninth Street. Turn left (north) past low-income public housing that you might not notice. Approximately 2,000 subsidized-housing units are sprinkled around Boulder, in small, unobtrusive pockets. Subsidized housing is often close to Boulder's trendiest areas. In this case, it's the neighborhood around **North Boulder Park**. This is another area worth an amble. Note the bungalows, some original and others spectacular renovations and "scrape-offs," where an owner demolishes the old house and builds a bigger one on the site. When you're ready, you can reach Broadway most easily by driving east on any one of the streets and turn left (north) on Broadway.

Follow north past Iris Avenue and turn left (west, toward the mountains) on Linden Avenue, to enter posh **Pine Brook Hills**, with grandiose designer homes perched on hillsides with commanding views. Up Linden Avenue is S. Cedar Brook Road, and at its very top are the last two homes Haertling designed before he succumbed to cancer in his 50s. You can probably find these homes yourself, but here's a clue. One is round and white. The other's roof mimics an aspen leaf, gently curling upward in the wind.

Return to Broadway, going north again, to Poplar Avenue and **Wonderland Hills**,

FYI

Unless otherwise noted, the area code for all phone numbers in this guide is 303.

Boulder's first planned multiunit development. Several bike paths wind through the neighborhood. In landscaped areas, weeping crab apples, native red-twig dogwood and evergreens make homes seem more secluded than in many areas with much larger yards. Office complexes are tucked next to townhomes. Within a two-minute walk of the smallest condo are Boulder-style mansions. Did you spot the white "barnacle" house featured in Woody Allen's futuristic film, *Sleeper*? It's another Haertling home.

Go anywhere you want now, and you'll find a new neighborhood. This "point of interest" tour has focused on the older side of Boulder. The far northern reaches of Boulder reflect a mix of fancy homes, townhomes, cottages and the adobe brick house with the blue metal roof say "quintessentially Boulder." East of Broadway are many more homes, generally less than 20 years old and more affordable. These new areas are ripe for homeowners eager to add their style to a highly creative town. West of Broadway, off Lee Hill Road, is a brand new subdivision called **Dakota Ridge**. Some people think this area would have been better dedicated as an addition to Boulder Open Space land than to yet more homes.

Mountain Towns

To get an overview of mountain living, take Canyon Boulevard west out of town and head up Boulder Canyon. Turnoffs to Fourmile Canyon, Magnolia Road and Sugarloaf Road lead to more areas of mountain homes of various styles, but if you continue 17 miles up the canyon, you will reach Nederland and the Peak to Peak Highway (Colo. Highway 72), which leads to other mountain communities. Most of them are along this scenic highway, comprised of Colo. Highways 119, 72 and 7. These paved roads are beautiful all year, from the sparkling skies of summer to the golden aspen trees of fall to crisp winter days with snow. Not all mountain towns are listed here, so keep your eyes open to discover one on your own.

Allenspark

Population: 800 in winter; 3,000 in summer • Elevation: 8,520 feet

Founded by Alonzo N. Allen as a mining town, and once a stagecoach stop between Ward and Estes Park, Allenspark is now a peaceful retirement and vacation community nestled in pine forest on the eastern edge of Rocky Mountain Park. The style tends to rustic cabins and barns full of trail horses. It has a volunteer fire department, a post office, is near the Wild Basin hiking area and offers lodges, cabins and restaurants. The Fawn Brook Inn, 747-2556, is a fine dining spot, worth the 32-mile drive from Boulder. To reach Allenspark, go to Ward and Nederland and head north on the Peak to Peak Highway (Colo. 72). From Lyons, take Colo. Highway 7.

Eldorado Springs

Population: 650 • Elevation: 5,760 feet

This is the closest "mountain" community to Boulder. The gold in these hills comes from the orange and yellow lichens that color the walls of Eldorado Canyon State Park, one of the nation's premier rock-climbing areas. The springs area was winter home for a Ute Indian tribe. In the early 1900s, these same springs sustained a 40-room resort. Trombone player Glenn Miller used to leave studies at CU to play with the Eldorado Springs resort band. Mary Pickford, the sweet-faced movie star, and soon-to-be-president Eisenhower were vacationers here. A quarry once yielded Eldorado Canyon's beautiful red rock. It has closed, but that mining scar remains, a reminder of the trade-offs between promoting industry and natural grandeur.

To see Eldorado Springs, drive south on Broadway. Three miles past Table Mesa, turn west on Colo. Highway 170. After 3 more miles,

The West Pearl Street neighborhood mixes new homes next door to historic structures.

you'll meet a riffraff of cabins, precariously balanced along a steep mountain stream. Welcome to bumpy dirt roads. Adds character, some residents say with a smile, and discourages the tourists. Welcome to a town like Li'l Abner's Dogpatch, Colorado, yuppie-style, of course.

Most Eldorado Springs residents are romance-smitten commuters. You can see their influence in the flowers that wink in rock gardens, in the misty wash of rainbow colors on a potter's garage, the blue cow bells cascading near a shake-shingle entry. Drive past the pool and head over the rutted wooden trestles of that one-way bridge. Near a handsome stone lodge called, "The House the Jack Built," do you see the pink trailer home? You took the wrong fork. Go back to the caramel-colored chalet called "L'il Abner," past the '50s-style, minty green place named "Jitterbug" and by that upscale cottage called "Chelsea Morning." The owner of "Chelsea Morning" recalls how, when she first saw the cabin, she thought, "If my soul could speak, this is where it would want to live." Now she, her husband and young kids love sitting out on their deck, listening to rustling tree leaves and the babbling mountain stream.

Jamestown
Population: 352 • Elevation: 7,000 feet

Gold, silver and flourspar once brought 10,000 miners to "Jimtown." The name was later "upgraded." Douglas Fairbanks Sr. was born in this shady town with equal quantities of mountain cottonwood trees and nearby forest. The Jamestown Mercantile Building is a classic false-front store from the mining-town days. The town hall, 449-1806, is open Monday mornings and all day Tuesday. There's a public elementary school and plenty of family values in town, including a desire to keep the children safe. So watch for the speed bumps as you enter and leave. Jamestown is 18 miles northwest of Boulder via U.S. Highway 36 to Left Hand Canyon, turning into the mountains and, at the big fork, jogging right.

Lyons
Population: 1,350 • Elevation: 5,375 feet

The red sandstone around Lyons has been the source of much quarry rock, often locally called flagstone. Fifteen sandstone buildings, including the Old Stone Congregational Church, are in Lyons's historical district. This dark brown flagstone church, kind of square with a short steeple, is just north of Main Street, on High Street. The quarries that provided the stone for these buildings still operate around Lyons and are excellent choices if you want flagstone for your patio, classic Colorado stones for your home or beautiful boulders for your garden. Lyons itself has a small-town atmosphere, with cottonwood trees shading the sparkling St. Vrain River, towering blue spruce trees standing beside turn-of-the-century bungalows and plenty of pretty contemporary homes. Vacation cabins and high-tech companies are here plus many good restaurants and antique shops, some decorated to give a Germanic/Slavic feel to the shopping areas.

The prettiest way to reach Lyons is to take 28th Street or Broadway north from Boulder, which become U.S. 36. The route winds beside the Foothills and less than 20 miles from Boulder, at the junction with Colo. Highway 66, you'll see Merlino's cider stand. Turn left here, pass roadside shops and eating places and you're in Lyons. The Town Hall, 823-6622 or 443-3956, is at 432 Fifth Avenue.

Nederland
Population: 1,541 • Elevation: 8,236 feet

Nineteen miles up Canyon Boulevard, just past the big blue lake formed by Barker Dam, is Nederland, the largest mountain town near Boulder. Here, the aspen trees shimmer next to pretty plots of colorful mountain flowers during the summer, with mountainsides of pine trees and aspen in every direction. Nederland has a good mix of shopping, tourist-oriented businesses and basic services. In fact, you can stretch that "basic services" to include a Laundromat, a video shop, doctors, dentists and vets in a friendly, easygoing community that includes mountain people who wanted to be close to high alpine fields, hippies who came here decades ago to found communes, New Age yuppies and Boulder intellectuals who retreated from the city below. All this makes for an eclectic, worldly, remote but close-enough-to-it-all mountain town. If you want some fun reading about Nederland history, find a copy of local author Margaret Milhauser's *The Mirror*. This fantasy novel describes a Boulder woman who trades places in time with her Nederland grandmother, then discovers the rigors of being a miner's wife, the challenges of driving a wagon team up a treacherous dirt canyon road, and the red light district that even tiny Nederland supported.

Near Nederland is the Eldora Mountain Resort, with its downhill and cross-country skiing and the Indian Peaks Wilderness. Kids love Nederland's local rock store, Nature's Own of Nederland, and the picture of the fierce predatory rabbit at Renee's Bakery. The shops are comfortably close together, picturesque and easy to amble through. It's worth the trip just to hang out at the Acoustic Coffee Shop (see our Nightlife chapter), and Annie's is a good neighborhood restaurant (see Restaurants). All this means that Nederland has settled, by fits and bounds, into the intriguing community its beginnings hinted. Originally a gold-, silver- and tungsten-mining area, Nederland had more than 3,500 residents at the height of the mining boom in 1874. Today, gambling in Blackhawk and Central City, south on Peak to Peak Highway, plus Boulder's spillover prosperity, have fueled Nederland's latest boom. Many residents work in Boulder or elsewhere in the "lowlands" to the east.

Summer events usually include a Kinetic Wind Festival (see our Festivals and Annual Events chapter), a Native American Pow Wow, and a replay of the pioneer days. Check in at the Visitors' Center, on West First Street, where the RTD bus stops. Across from the Visitors' Center is Town Hall, 258-3266 or 444-3588.

Pinecliffe
Population: 475 year round; 525 in summer • Elevation: 7,960 feet

Retired miners and nature lovers live in this enclave southeast of Nederland on Colo. Highway 72. Some are upscale commuters, and some people live "off the grid." That means they're in homes without power, water or sewage hookups. "Off the grid" can mean rough-hewn cabins or a high-tech home complete with photovoltaic cells to provide solar electricity and heat.

Ward
Population: 180 • Elevation: 9,253 feet

An 1890s gold strike brought 4,000 people to this greatest gold camp of northern Colorado. Ward merits a footnote to Colorado history, for this is where silver baron (and briefly U.S. Senator) Horace Tabor served as a postmaster toward the end of his life, which he passed in unaccustomed poverty. By 1930, the mines died out, and only three residents stayed behind. Hippies arrived in the 1960s, and many of them have never left. It's still a place of shaggy hair and beards to match, fringed vests and love beads. On weekends, intrepid Lycra-clad bicyclists, with great pride, perch outside the general store, suck up cold mineral water and swap stories about their 23-mile ride to reach the hilly streets of Ward from Boulder. Tourists gaze at the rustic buildings, their colors as faded as sand-washed jeans, within the thick mountain forests. The old Ward School, now the town hall and post office, is typical of wood-framed rural schoolhouses. Ward has an honor-system public library and a general store. There are some restaurants up on the Peak to Peak Highway (Colo. Highway 72), about 8 miles north of Nederland. The beautiful alpine hiking area around Brainard Lake is just west of Ward.

Towns of the Plains

All the towns around Boulder have modern 'burbs, for most of Boulder's building boom — most dramatically the current one — have occurred since the 1960s. Here you'll find Boulder County's more affordable housing. Although these towns are more development-friendly and growth-oriented than Boulder, they are beginning to pay more attention to such quality-of-life enhancements as open space. The prosperity of these Plains towns is evident in their golf-course competitions and swimming-pool wars. Actually, these aren't wars, but they reflect a trend toward family-oriented community centers. New or remodeled recreation centers have opened in Louisville, Lafayette and Broomfield, and Longmont is planning to enhance its. The water slides and Lazy River pools for kids are great attractions. Residents want cherished natural areas preserved. To keep seeing eagles flying overhead, even as these communities grow, their citizens are beginning to raise more open

space purchase funds. It might not happen in time to save all the favorite local nature walks, but sentiment is growing to preserve more.

These communities offer many personalities. Rock Creek is nothing but brand-new homes. Other towns are as old as Boulder, complete with traditional downtowns and beautiful Victorian neighborhoods. Lafayette, Louisville and Longmont offer the contrast between modern developments and older parts of town, known for their quaint atmosphere and lovely trees.

Broomfield
Population: 33,250 • Elevation: 5,200 feet

When the Pony Express needed to get overland mail from Julesburg, Scottsbluff or Fort Laramie to Denver, Colorado's Territorial Capital, carriers changed horses at Broomfield. Travel gave the farming town fame again in 1952, when Broomfield became the site of a toll station on the new Boulder/Denver Turnpike (now known as U.S. Highway 36). The road was especially popular during Saturday CU-Boulder football games. In 1967, it became the nation's first toll road to pay for itself, approximately 13 years ahead of schedule. The Broomfield tollbooth operators had a special friend, a black-and-white dog they named Shep. For more than a dozen years, Shep watched each driver pay 10¢ to stop at Broomfield and 25¢ for the 8-mile drive on to Boulder. His tombstone, near U.S. Highway 36, reads, "Shep. Part Shepherd, Mostly Affection."

Today, residential construction is phenomenal and more businesses are settling in Broomfield around the renovated and expanding central retail center. Southeast of Broomfield is the campus-like Interlocken office park, which plans to provide tenants with an IDSN-compatible fiber-optic network. You need geek genes to understand exactly what an Integrated Digital System Network does, but techies say it might help all of us, someday, get more information into our homes. Interlocken is zoned for at least 25 percent open space including wetlands and natural grasses plus a golf course next to a hotel, which have yet to be built.

Many of Broomfield's workers are commuters — the RTD Park-n-Ride facility south of town is the biggest in the Denver/Boulder area. As Boomfield, oops Broomfield, grows it is developing a plan that many hope will preserve open space within the city. A popular bumper sticker reads, "Keep the Field in Broomfield." Additional open space should connect to existing parks and a community center. The Bay, Broomfield's outdoor aquatic park, is very popular. For more information on this growing community, contact the Broomfield Chamber of Commerce, 466-1775, at 741 Burbank Street.

Erie

Population: 1,500 • Elevation: 5,020 feet

The town was first settled around 1867 by a Methodist pastor who named it after his hometown of Erie, Pennsylvania. Like its namesake, Colorado's Erie is a former coal town. Located 8 miles east of Boulder, it is an area of tilled farm fields and new subdivisions and is the site of the 119-acre Tri-County Airport. Some homes near the airport have hangars and taxiways to the airport in their back yards, mirroring the garages and driveways they have in the front. Its current major industries are landfills and junk yards near town. Sound boring? This is Boulder County, remember! Blake's Small Car Salvage has been on national television for being one of the prettiest

Photo: Daily Camera

Louisville's main street preserves its small-town charm.

junk yards around. And a nearby business, Construction Recycling, recycles over 80 percent of the building scraps it receives; see our Boulder Shopping chapter for more details on these two spots. What a great idea for the environment.

You can reach Erie by taking Arapahoe Road east out of Boulder past U.S. Highway 287. You'll be on a dirt road for a while, which dead-ends. Turn left (north). Go about 1.5 miles and you're in Erie. See the woodworking factory? It welcomes visitors. The Town Hall, 828-3843, is at Lincoln School, 645 Holbrook Street.

Gunbarrel
Population: 12,000 • Elevation: 5,145 feet

Great mountain views and fancy homes around a golf course/country club are hallmarks of this large neighborhood of subdivisions, about 7 miles northeast of downtown Boulder. It was first developed in 1963 as a 558-acre subdivision not far from IBM. The commercial part of Gunbarrel, which includes Celestial Seasonings, IBM and Valleylab, is part of the city of Boulder. Much of the residential area is in unincorporated Boulder County. Even though the City of Boulder has offered to annex twice, residents prefer the autonomy of being in the county.

Take the Diagonal Highway (Colo. Highway 119) north toward Longmont. Just out of Boulder, turn right on Jay Road. Keep going, and to see the fancy houses, turn left on a street such as Carter Road. To get deeper into Gunbarrel, continue on the Diagonal to 63rd Street and turn right (south). The homes and enterprises of Gunbarrel are both to your right and left.

Hygiene
Population: 250 • Elevation: 5,100 feet

In the 1880s, farmers battled grasshopper plagues and other woes to settle this fertile area. The town earned its name when people suffering from tuberculosis moved to a local sanitarium called Hygiene House. Fresh air and sunshine revived many, as the elements still do today. Hygiene is about a mile northwest of Longmont in an area full of towering old cottonwoods, Siberian elms, ancient lilac hedges and farm homes with horses mowing the grasses in the back. It's at the intersection of N. 75th Street and Hygiene Road. A local hangout is Clark's Food Store, the little shop with a rickety, tilting porch awning that hangs like half-closed eyelashes above the front door. Here's a town where the neighbors all know each other, so if you decide to hang out for a while, you can be sure they'll talk about you.

Lafayette
Population: 19,500 • Elevation: 5,260

Lafayette Miller ran a farm, a stagecoach and a hotel. After he died, Mary Miller discovered coal on their homestead. In 1890, she named a new town after her husband. Coal and farming were the main industries for 50 years. Today, the town is a burgeoning residential community for the high-tech industry and brand-new home tracts, green patches of lawn and hopeful baby trees. To reach Lafayette, head 11 miles east, on either Baseline Road or South Boulder Road through Louisville.

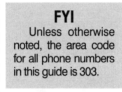

FYI

Unless otherwise noted, the area code for all phone numbers in this guide is 303.

"Old Town" Lafayette has its tidy little bungalows and big street trees. Efrain's is a good Mexican restaurant (see our Restaurants chapter). The city offices, 665-5588, are at 1290 S. Public Road, the northeast corner of "Four Corners," a new business district at the intersection of U.S. Highway 287 and South Boulder Road. The Lafayette Chamber of Commerce, 666-9555, is in the old historic district at 309 S. Public Road.

Local sentiment favors keeping small-town charm even as affordable and upscale subdivisions boom. There's a move to protect favorite open areas such as Waneka Lake, where people can paddle rented canoes to a blue heron's marshy shallows. You can find a map of these places at the beautiful new recreation center on 111 W. Baseline Road, 665-0469, and in 1996, a proposal was put forth to build a 45,000-square-foot complex including an ice skating rink, fitness center, teen center gym and other facilities on Arapahoe Road and 95th Street. Some residents would like Lafayette to grow no larger than 25,000 people. The Indian Peaks Golf Course is within city limits.

Several festivals occur in Lafayette each year, including a Loyalty Parade in May and Lafayette Days in the fall; see our Festivals and Annual Events chapter for details.

Lafayette is home to a community of Hmong families, refugees from Laos. It also has one of the nation's few co-housing communities, the Nyland Community Association, 494-2778. It features 42 passive-solar homes built around a common area and the "community house" with guest rooms, activity rooms, a child-care center and dining hall open to residents who don't want to cook evening meals in their homes or else want company for dinner. Cars are parked outside the community. Only pedestrians are allowed inside.

Longmont
Population: 57,200 • Elevation: 4,979

Longmont, named after Longs Peak, which in turn was named after Maj. Stephen Long, started as a 30,000-acre farming community and sugar beet center. The city celebrated its 125th anniversary in 1996. It is the county's second-largest town and is sometimes called Boulder's twin. Sure enough, it offers many services similar to Boulder's, including a hospital, school district, daily newspaper, branch of the County Clerk's Office, state Motor Vehicle Division office and other services. But these twins are not identical. For one thing, Longmont's kind of modest about how pretty it is, and publicity for local events is often low-key.

From the old Main Street shopping district to the Boulder County Fairgrounds at 9595 Nelson Road, which hosts dog shows, antique shows and the Boulder County Fair in August (see our Festivals and Annual Events chapter), Longmont retains a farming-town hospitality even as it grows and grows. With the exception of far larger Boulder, more homes were sold in Longmont during the first half of 1996 than in any other town in the county, and sometimes it seems that the fields surrounding the town have been planted with house

seeds instead of grain. This house crop is sprouting overnight, with townhouses here, single-family homes there and a naked, surprised look to many of these late 20th-century homesteads, as they wait for the saplings in their front yards to catch up and shade their peaked roofs.

To reach Longmont from Boulder, head northeast on Colo. Highway 119 (also called the Diagonal Highway or just the Diagonal for short). Except during the rush hour, it's about a 20-minute drive. To get a feeling for the Victorian houses and tree-canopied streets near Main and Third, check the Callahan House. New houses are in developments all around town. Municipal offices, 775-6050, are at the Civic Center, at Third Avenue and Kimbark Street. The Longmont Chamber of Commerce, 776-5295, is at 528 Main Street.

Louisville
Population: 18,250 • Elevation: 5,350 feet

Louis Nawatny founded this town in 1878, after discovering coal 200 feet below a settler's farm. Twelve mines eventually thrived in Louisville, providing high wages for sometimes dangerous work. In the early 1900s, labor organizer Mother Jones spoke to coal miners in the town. In the same period, European miners came to town, occasionally as strikebreakers. Today, the town takes pride in ethnic, family-style restaurants. Italian eateries include The Blue Parrot and Colacci's, in the Main Street area of Old Town Louisville. The downtown area also has Asian restaurants, Karen's Country Kitchen, The Old Louisville Inn and a host of little shops.

Like Lafayette, Louisville is a coal-mining town that has transformed itself into the epitome of a modern suburb. Two of Boulder County's largest employers, StorageTek and Neodata, are based here. So is the new PorterCare Hospital-Avista, along with future plans for a senior citizen's residential area and nursing home. The Coal Creek Golf Course was listed by *Golf Digest* magazine

INSIDERS' TIP

Can you believe that Boulder once was a windswept prairie? All those lovely trees have been planted by people who decided to stay.

as one of the top 25 new golf courses in 1990. When the golf course first went in, next to U.S. Highway 36, there was concern that errant golf balls would hit cars, but it has been no problem. The highway interchange is booming, with Louisville's first modern hotels, shopping center, 12-plex theater and outlets for practically every chain restaurant that you can imagine.

Louisville's population has more than tripled since the 1970s, making it Colorado's fastest-growing community, but the goal is now to stabilize the population around 25,000 and put some effort into preserving open spaces. Newcomers here are legion, and the East Boulder County Newcomers Club, 665-9011, meets monthly at Karen's in the Country, 666-8503. Most of the population growth has come from young families, with young kids galore. Still, Louisville strives to maintain small-town charm with events such as a Fourth of July Community Picnic and a Labor Day food celebration (see our Festivals and Annual Events chapter).

Louisville's city offices, 666-6565, are at 749 Main Street. The Louisville Chamber of Commerce, 666-5747, is at 901 Main Street.

Niwot
Population: 3,700 • Elevation: 5,095 feet

The town is named after Chief Niwot, whose name means "left hand" in the Arapaho language. The original downtown comprises supply shops and a school for local farmers. The original downtown core is filled with antiques shops, now surrounded by brand-new housing developments. The old town center also boasts the Niwot Auction, a big bimonthly mecca for antique hounds and an annual auction festival in the summer. Rev. Taylor's Country Restaurant, 652-2020, is a popular hangout. Niwotians like their left-handed town, leading to Left-Hand Turn, a store for lefties and creative types; Lefty's Pizza Parlor; and the Left Hand Grange. Sometimes Pete Wernick and his Live 5 band rent the Grange Hall for bluegrass concerts. Well, maybe retro-Dixieland is a better description of their music, played on a banjo, bass guitar, drums, clarinet and vibraphone. It's an informal affair on folding chairs, with kids selling cookies during intermission. But the music is excellent — many band members have performed with world-famous Doc Watson.

To reach Niwot, take the Diagonal Highway (Colo. Highway 119) north toward Longmont. One mile after IBM is the Niwot road. Hang a right, and you're there. It's about a 10- to 15-minute drive from Boulder.

Superior
Population: 3,000 • Elevation: 5,400 feet

The coal mine closed in 1945 and Superior languished with a rural and remote flavor

Multiuse on the Boulder Creek path.

Photo: Daily Camera

Photo: Daily Camera

Some folks relocate to the Boulder area just because of the outdoor winter lifestyle the Flatirons and surrounding mountains afford.

that belied its location between Denver and Boulder. But it languishes no more. Superior is in a new boom now because of Rock Creek, a massive development on land annexed by Superior in 1987 and given water rights in 1990. Rock Creek sprawls across more than 3 square miles of rolling grassland. By 2010, it could eventually include up to 8,000 homes and 15 million square feet of commercial space, extending east along U.S. Highway 36 all the way to the Interlocken Office Park at Broomfield and south to Colo. Highway 128. Some large homes stand beside the meticulously landscaped, new wide boulevards, decorated by statuary and leading to a tennis courts and a swimming pool. There are also townhomes and an abundance of smaller single-family homes on more modest lots.

Despite the town's fast growth, the Colorado Department of Highways forgot to show it on their 1994 map. Maybe that's because in the 1990 census, only 208 people lived in Superior. The town is still catching up with much of this growth. The Superior Elementary School opened in the fall of 1996, and until then, children were bused to schools in neighboring communities — and secondary-school students still are.

The town hall, 499-3675, at 24 E. Coal Creek Drive, is a good information place, as are Rock Creek's real estate offices and show houses. Superior is just south of the Superior/Louisville interchange on U.S. Highway 36.

at least
financing
your
new home
is easy.

Packing boxes, sending out change-of-address notices, finding a new school for your children. And what about finding a mortgage lender who can simplify the home-buying process. There's no question, moving is never simple.

But it can be easier - with **Greenco Financial.**

**G GREENCO FINANCIAL, INC.
MORTGAGE BANKERS**

Colorado's Own Premiere Mortgage Lender

Main Office: 3005 Center Green Dr., Suite 200
Boulder, CO 80301 • **(303)444-8900** • FAX (303)444-8979

Boulder
Real Estate

Colorado generally and Boulder specifically have been among the hottest housing markets in the nation. How hot? In 1993, Karen Bernardi, a Realtor with RE/MAX Realty Consultants of Boulder, ranked as one of the most productive residential agents in the world. In a survey of 90,000 real estate offices, *REALTrends*, an independent real estate newsletter, rated another office, RE/MAX of Boulder, No. 1 in the nation in volume sold per agent and No. 2 based on volume per office. That's a lot of fame for such a little county! In 1996, superstar Bernardi sent shockwaves through the real estate community by affiliating with Century 21, the nation's largest chain.

For a while, the housing market was so hot that Boulder home buyers had a half-hour to run through a home, then sign up before the next buyers beat them to it. Since the fall of 1994, the sizzle has cooled to a normal simmer. People were calling the summer of 1995 "a buyer's market," though that was probably just a relative term, and the new, slightly slower sales pace continued through the first half of 1996. Prices have leveled off in Boulder, but they have increased dramatically in other county towns — notably Lafayette, Longmont and the mountain towns. While prices continue to rise in surrounding communities, home buyers have a better inventory from which to select the home of their dreams.

This chapter provides a glimpse of home prices in Boulder County, rental prices and bargain-hunting tips. It gives ideas about what to look for in a Boulder home and neighborhood, and it ends with real estate resources. If you're looking for a Boulder home, happy hunting!

The Homebuyer's Market

In late spring 1996, many Realtors said prices had leveled off and even eroded slightly from the previous two years. The bad news for buyers (and the good news for sellers) is that the average single-family home in the city of Boulder cost nearly $269,000. The good news for buyers (and the bad news for sellers) is that a year earlier, the average sales price was $272,900. At the same period in 1994, it had been $257,800.

In mid-'96, about $270,000 would have bought a 3-year-old, 2,280-square-foot home with an 890-foot unfinished basement and a three-car garage in Gunbarrel or a 10-year-old, 2,475-square-foot two-story house in North Boulder with three bedrooms, 2½ baths and one-car garage. "Anything with history or charm or in certain neighborhoods will be higher," says Rich Alpers of Fowler Better Homes Real Estate. If you're looking for such qualities plus remodel potential, that sum would have bought a 70-year-old, 1,000-square-foot, two-bedroom bungalow, splendidly near Chautauqua.

Boulder encompasses a wide range of houses and housing styles, from historic cottages, between-the-World-Wars Tudor mansions, postwar ranch houses and new subdivisions with contemporary homes.

In mid-1996, the most expensive house for sale in the city of Boulder was a 2,160-square-foot, five-bedroom, two-bath home that was built in 1968. The great location in West Boulder, on the edge of University Hill, and the panoramic views of the Flatirons in one direction and the city lights in the other help explain the $2 million asking price for a home that could not be described as a mansion.

The cheapest house for sale in Boulder in mid-1996, excluding condos, townhomes and patio homes, was an 841-square-foot cottage in North Boulder, built in 1951, that listed for $145,000.

Quality of life, the cachet of a Boulder address and the Danish Plan are what have driven local house prices into the stratosphere. Boulder was one of the first cities in the nation to adopt a residential growth-control ordinance (called the Danish Plan after City Councilman Paul Danish), which limits the number of permits for new construction that are issued annually. The law of supply and demand is in effect in Boulder, and with limited new construction coupled with a strong economy, property values have soared, and the issue of "affordable housing" has become a community hot button.

Housing costs considerably less in Boulder County's other communities. During the first half of 1996, the average single-family home prices were roughly $195,000 in Louisville, $199,000 in Lafayette, $145,000 in Longmont and $245,000 in the mountains. In the Plains, where sales prices often reflected properties set on more acreage, the average price was nearly $308,000. Generally, rural lots in both the mountains and Plains offer good deals, but price swings are enormous. And if you're thinking about building, you need to take into consideration zoning and the cost of water and utilities. When rural sellers put high price tags on agricultural land, most likely, they expect a city to annex the land, and when county land does get annexed, the annexing city can change its zoning to allow much greater density.

As of summer 1996, the inventory of Boulder homes for sale was greater than in the previous two years, and homes were on the market an average of four months, compared to five minutes in 1994. (All right, that's an exaggeration. In all honesty, it was 30 days, which seems like 2 milliseconds when you're trying to find your dream home.) The market price depends, as always, on location, maintenance and (this being Boulder) the way your horoscope is interacting with current mortgage rates. The Boulder market is softest on the upper end and hottest for condominiums, but no matter what the price, special homes on special lots still sell fast.

Two-thirds of Boulder's residential real estate buyers are locals who are trading up, which is one reason that the for-sale inventory is up, since these people sell their old homes even as they buy new ones. Even with leveling off of prices and greater inventory of available houses, finding the right place at the right price isn't always easy. Locals, whether tire-kickers or serious buyers, and newcomers alike flock to the open houses (or open homes, as they are pretentiously called these days) held year round, rain or shine, on Sunday afternoons. Check the Saturday and Sunday newspapers, or be alert for "open house" signs if you are out for an afternoon drive to scout neighborhoods. A real estate agent will be on hand to answer questions, often pass out leaflets on the property and perhaps give a very soft sell on the home you're looking at. It's an easy way to comparison shop without the commitment of being taken around by an agent to look at homes by appointment.

Real Estate Resources

So you're sure you want to move to Boulder County, but where do you start? You can get information on buying or renting in Boulder County from the local Chambers of Commerce and from the Board of Realtors. The Boulder Chamber of Commerce, for instance, issues a useful relocation packet, as do many real estate agencies. City halls, listed in our Boulder Neighborhoods chapter, can provide general local information. Recreation centers and most grocery stores display free publica-

tions about places to live. *Homes & Land of Boulder County* and *Where to Live in Boulder County* are the two biggest and slickest. You can also call one or more of these groups: **Boulder Chamber of Commerce**, 2440 Pearl Street, Boulder, 442-1044; **Boulder Area Board of Realtors**, 4885 Riverbend Road, Suite A, Boulder, 442-3585; **Office of Human Rights Department of Housing and Human Services**, 1101 Arapahoe Avenue, Second Floor, Boulder, 441-3157.

Real Estate Firms

With the booming real estate market, it seems as if there's an agency on every corner. Most of the bigger agencies serving Boulder County provide newcomer relocation services and as well as matching you with a place to live. The Boulder Area Board of Realtors can provide you with a list of real estate agencies, and you'll find others in the phone book, the local newspaper and such free periodicals as *Where to Live in Boulder County*.

Century 21 – The Bernardi Group
3301 30th St., Boulder • 402-6000, (800) 421-2174

This new agency burst on the Boulder real estate scene in 1996 with the dazzle and flair of a Roman candle when Karen Bernardi left RE/MAX Realty Consultants of Boulder and started her own agency, affiliated with Century 21. The agency has 15 brokers and specializes in single-family homes, condominiums and vacant land in Boulder County.

Fowler Real Estate/Better Homes and Gardens
2970 Wilderness Pl., Boulder • 443-6050, (800) 443-6050

Eighty agents work here at Boulder's oldest real estate agency. Fowler has grown to be the third-largest Realtor group, in terms of sales volume, in the county, with branch offices in Louisville, (665-6300 or (800) 598-6300, 1021 South Boulder Road) and Nederland (258-7020 or (800) 866-9981, 286 N. Bridge Street), and a home information center next to JCPenney's at Crossroads Mall.

RE/MAX of Boulder
2425 Canyon Blvd., Ste. 200, Boulder
• 449-7000, (800) 825-7000

In 1995, RE/MAX of Boulder ranked No. 1 among RE/MAX Mountain States agencies in terms of volume per agent, which amounts to a lot of sales since more than 60 agents work out of this office. The agency is particular strong in relocation services and has a website with relo information.

RE/MAX Realty Consultants of Boulder
4770 Baseline Rd., Boulder • 499-9880, (800) 499-9880 (Relocation Hotline)

Founded in 1931, this is the county's second-largest realty office, based on volume of sales. This company has more than 50 agents in its own mortgage brokerage services.

Moore and Company Realtors
4875 Pearl E. Cr., Boulder • 444-7800, (800) 444-8927

This 60-plus-year-old, Denver-based business has 21 branches and 600 agents throughout the state. The Boulder County office has nearly 40 real estate agents handling residential and commercial properties.

Walnut Realty
1911 11th St., Ste. 107, Boulder • 442-3180

Broker Tom Kahn describes Walnut Realty as "Boulder's downtown Realtors," and indeed, the office is in a historic building a block from the Pearl Street Mall. However, the firm specializes in a variety of types of property, from ordinary residential to vacant land, farms, rural and mountain homes and downtown commercial buildings. This company staffs about 25 agents.

Wright-Kingdom Realtors Inc.
1844 Folsom Ave., Boulder • 443-3215

Lew Kingdom and Stuart Wright started this real estate company in 1976, when Boulder was a town of around 60,000 people and

the average home cost $85,000. This is one of the longer-established agencies in town. It has 29 associates and includes an all-points relocation service.

Buyer Brokers

Traditional real estate agencies work for the seller, who pays the commission on an eventual sale. The buyer's broker is a fairly new concept in real estate. He or she works for the buyer and therefore has no financial stake in selling a particular home. The buyer pays a small fee; charges vary. Two such companies in Boulder include **Buyer's Resource of Boulder**, 4141 Arapahoe Avenue, 444-6660 or (800) 424-3355; and **Colorado Buyer Brokers**, 4450 Arapahoe Avenue, 442-0552.

Lone Eagles

Boulder County also includes more than 100 single-person realty offices, and some are outstanding. You can check these and other agencies through the Boulder Board of Realtors, although keep in mind that the Board doesn't handle Longmont or Lyons.

Do It Yourself

Some people also try to sell their own homes to avoid paying a commission to a Realtor. **For Sale By Owner**, 938-8701, puts out a $150 video and manual, and issues a free magazine on available properties. For additional fees, the company also offers various other optional services, including multiple listing, marketing checklists, advertising and representation at closing.

About Home Builders

With boom times come large, California-style subdivisions put up by major developers and builders. Boom times also bring the need for more schools, more utilities, more roads

To Make a House Your Home... Trust Eric Jacobson

Let's talk about what's really important!

Eric has made a specialty of understanding what families really need! He knows about neighborhoods, floorplans, schools, parks and areas great for kids.

Son Alex and daughter Cecelia keep Eric in touch with the growing needs of today's family.

Let Erics' 24 years in Boulder real estate make buying or selling your next home a pleasant experience!

CeCe, Alex and Eric Jacobson

ERIC JACOBSON
The Realtor who says: "Bring the Kids!"

303-441-5619
1-800-825-7000

2425 Canyon Blvd., Suite 200
Boulder, CO 80302
ericjacobson@boulderco.com

303 **449-7000.**
RE/MAX of Boulder inc.

and more services. Communities are leveling "impact fees" at builders, and these fees are built into the price of new construction. **Home Builders Association of Metropolitan Denver**, 778-1400, can supply a list of its members, including some large firms building in Boulder County.

Fixer-uppers

If you've bought a house that needs work, or if you are renovating your current home and are having problems finding suitable contractors, **Home Improvement Referral Inc.**, P.O. Box 26012, Colorado Springs 80936, 449-5093 (in Boulder area), provides free information and a referral service that lists 300 Colorado contractors and subcontractors who handle everything from maintenance and repair to custom-built homes.

House-hunting Tips

Whether you plan to be a yuppie commoner living in a simple condominium or the royal owner of a grand mansionette, count on a few rules. Spend time looking, and keep location in mind. The closer to a city center, the more you pay, for it puts you closer to the activities and services that make Boulder and other cities so inviting. The lot itself matters — a good mountain view, a babbling creek, adjacent city open space, a golf course, good entertainment or a public park all add value. So does beautiful, mature landscaping. That's why a tiny Boulder condominium with all these location features might cost more than a spacious single-family home in outlying areas.

On the other hand, Boulder doesn't have many "wrong side of the track" homes, or acres and acres of homogenized housing — although vast housing tracts are blanketing former farmland surrounding outlying communities. One great feature of this city is how mansions can exist right next to apartment buildings, quirky little bungalows and subsidized public housing. This magical mixture happens because many Boulder neighborhoods add diversity in neighbor-friendly ways. Drive with a real estate agent through sought-after Mapleton Hill, Whittier, University Hill or North Boulder neighborhoods. Look closely,

and you'll see how diversity can help a neighborhood thrive. Even in developments where every house seems to have been cloned from the one next door, a mix of high and moderately priced housing often develops as the trees have grown and people have renovated their properties, whether in modest areas like Martin Acres or more prepossessing ones like Table Mesa. You can find exclusive "mono-communities" in and around Boulder, but if the only thing stopping you from choosing a more eclectic mix is a fear that it would lower your house value, relax. Diverse neighborhoods that are well-loved in Boulder do just fine.

However, an eclectic neighborhood might not be your cup of tea. Perhaps you prefer a brand-new house in a brand-new neighborhood, where you are no more of a newcomer than anyone else. Area developers and Realtors showcase their offerings in the annual Boulder County Tour of New Homes, generally held the first two weekends in May and again in October. In 1996, featured homes ranged from a modest 1,500-square-footer with three bedrooms and two baths in Longmont to a grandiose 6,300-square-foot hillside mansion overlooking Boulder for just less than a cool $1.4 million.

What to Look for in a Boulder House

Boulder has a cold semi-arid climate, which means most energy goes into heating, not cooling. Insulation matters. Because it's so sunny, passive solar can do wonders. This doesn't mean you must settle for a '70s-style solar home, with a long wall of south-facing glass and the sun blasting black-painted oil drums. Energy-efficient homes can blend into any style and still keep January gas bills low. One regular-looking Boulder home earned a national energy efficiency award. Its owner, Craig Cristensen, has no heater at all. He relies on passive solar, super insulation and a 1,000-gallon hot water storage tank, so that even if a rugby team burst in, asking for showers during a cloudy February week, enough solar-heated water would be on hand to douse them all.

Photo: McStain

McStain's Meadowview development is in Longmont.

Some homes are energy-efficient, but not all. Check winter utility bills before buying. A few summer days get awfully hot (witness the heat wave during the summer of 1995 when temperatures rose to the high 90s), but heat spells tend to be short, and summer nights cool. As long as a home is positioned to keep out the fiercest summer rays, either with deep eaves or shade trees, most residents don't miss air-conditioning.

Keeping the garden green is a problem in the dry heat of summer. A sprinkler system is a plus, and a modern, water-saving drip system is a super-plus. While some of Boulder's older, most desirable neighborhoods boast the mixed blessing of large, non-indigenous shade trees that provide atmosphere and character but are not really suitable for the region's climate, xeriscaping is a plus in contemporary homes. Xeriscaping is the art and science of landscaping with indigenous drought-tolerant plants that is increasingly popular in the Southwest and Mountain States. See our Shopping chapter's Close-up on xeriscaping.

Want to Live in the Mountains?

One of Boulder's most distinctive characteristics is that it is a true city with remote mountain living close by. Is a mountain house your dream? Mountain living is not for the faint-hearted. Residents keep their snow chains handy. One winter day, the snow on Magnolia Road hid a steeply tilted skating rink. One woman's sporty truck skidded off near the top and plummeted nearly 100 feet. The truck's bed hit first and collapsed like an accordion. Maybe NASA should study the event to improve their hard-landing techniques, for the lucky lady walked out of that truck alive.

Notice a rocky mountainside covered with charred black sticks marking the 1989 Black Tiger Gulch wildfire. As smoke billowed miles away, one mountain couple packed favorite Navajo rugs in the station wagon. They joked that the scare would end in a few hours, and they'd be unpacking. Suddenly they heard a train-like roar and felt blistering heat. The fire had leapt up their ridge. If they had to do it over again, they would have packed the family photo album instead of those rugs. They raced down their bumpy mountain road and will never forget how it felt to breathe searing, hollow air, the oxygen sucked out by the firestorm. That fire caused $10 million in damage and destroyed 39 homes. Another fire in 1990 burned 2,200 acres and 10 homes. Such fires are a natural part of mountain ecosystems. On dry, windy summer days, even the big bomber planes, dropping payloads of slurry, cannot slow the flames.

Icy roads and forest fires are nothing compared to your love of nature? Suppose one dusky evening, a mountain lion eats your dog. The kids are horrified. You're just glad it was the dog. So you build a fence. A mountain lion can jump most fences. And you've blocked land that was open to migrating deer, mountain lions and everything natural up there. Endangered wildlife is one reason Boulder County has decided to slow mountain developments. A mountain home can be wonderful, but unless you're committed to the mountain lifestyle, you can always visit.

On the other hand, if you realize the trade-offs you're making and the negative impacts you might create, you can do plenty to minimize the problems. Before you build a home, ask your architect about low-impact choices. For instance, architect Dave Barrett of Barrett-Steele, 449-1141, has been written up nationally for his environmentally sensitive homes. If you move into an existing home, you can remodel with attention to fire-fighting materials. Consider replacing cedar shingles with tile, slate, metal or asphalt (if you build new, you won't be permitted to use cedar shakes). Stucco, brick and stone siding do not burn and will protect the interior better than a wood exterior. Be sure dead brush is kept away from your home. Such changes minimize flammability.

Pop into an eco-shop, such as **Planetary Solutions**, 442-6228, 2030 17th Street, which offers materials and consulting services for environmentally sound building. **Jade Mountain**, 449-6601, 717 Poplar Avenue, is an appropriate-technology company with solar electric systems and composting toilets. Just being at such a store will give you ideas. Take a course in environmentalism from the University of Colorado, 492-6309, or the Naropa Institute, 444-0202. Check with the Colorado Division of Wildlife, 291-7327, to see how to live with animals. The **Thorne Ecological Institute**, 499-3647, 5398 Manhattan Circle, is another resource. Train your children about mountain safety, and keep your pets — especially cats — indoors. Mountain lions consider cats tasty tidbits, and cats themselves are miniature mountain lions whose hunting has led to the decline of many rare birds.

A Few, Few Words About Crime

Some Boulder County residents leave their doors unlocked. Others have security systems on everything except their running shoes. Most people take care walking at night, especially when in deserted areas of CU-Boulder, downtown or the Creek Path. Others head into the dark at 5 AM all by themselves and have a grand time listening to the morning birds. Boulder County's biggest enforcement concerns involve speeding cars and loud parties. Yes, the county has crimes, including murder and abduction. But there are some, well, endearing criminals too.

Take the fleet-footed Gunbarrel burglar. Under cover of night, he slipped into homes along golf course greens. He stole silver; he stole jewels. Fifty officers and a helicopter tried an ambush. The SWAT team's fastest sprinter cornered him, but that burglar leapt the fence like a deer. Finally, in 1992, they nabbed him with a backpack full of jewels. Turns out he was a marathon runner. He had girlfriends around the world. They didn't know about each other but had enjoyed his dazzling gifts. Over seven years, the bold, handsome runner had burglarized 244 homes. Golf course communities sleep better, now that he runs his laps at the jail.

The Renter's Market

Of Boulder's 96,000 residents, 25,000 are CU-Boulder students, and a good majority rent off-campus. They're not the only ones. In the nonstudent population, almost 50 percent of Boulder city residents rent. That's higher than the United States overall, where less than 35 percent of all households live in rented dwellings. Many people moving here rent while searching for something to buy. Others can't afford to buy and remain renters for years. Many who move from Boulder hang onto their homes while they look elsewhere or contemplate returning. Others move up in the market, then use their former digs as an investment.

So brace yourself. Between 1980 and 1990, city rents here went up 40 percent, compared to 20 percent in the United States overall. Much of this was fueled by an extraordinarily low vacancy rate that squeaked down to 1.2 percent in 1992. By the mid-'90s, vacancies hovered around 4 to 5 percent, so rent increases have been easing. Rents tend to be higher near CU and lower in the county. As of summer 1996, prices had stayed near recent levels — meaning you could get a studio or efficiency for about $520 in the city, a one-bedroom apartment for $575, a two-bedroom apartment for about $820, or a five-bedroom house for around $2,000 a month. Reduced rents are available through CU married-student housing and Boulder family assistance programs, but waits for such spaces can run years, so apply early.

Although the real estate market has settled from a sprint to a trot, popping into town and finding a place right away is not a sure thing — except in spring or early summer, when relatively few students are in residence and there are more apartment vacancies. Many rental agencies prefer at least 45 days advance notice, and they can match you with a place best if you visit for a few days so they can show you around.

The city of Boulder has adopted landlord/tenant laws, including such things as handling of security deposits, when a lease is required, when the landlord can raise the rent and so on. Check these laws before you rent, for your own protection. The **Community Mediation Service**, 2160 Spruce Street, 441-4364, issues a Tenant Information Handbook that covers these subjects and also can help resolve disputes including landlord/tenant relations. As for the county, Colorado doesn't have many renter-protection laws, so your lease is where you'll find most of your rights and responsibilities. Read it while wearing your fine-print glasses. Also, some areas allow only three unrelated people per dwelling, and if you're caught cheating, you can be fined until the situation is corrected, so check your tenant responsibilities.

Questions of Affordability

Another dilemma in Boulder is affordability. The effort to preserve open space limits new homes, and people's sentimental attachment to the present character of their block often leads to strong opposition to increased density. Managing these issues is like squeezing a balloon — squeeze new housing away from open space and fearful neighborhoods, and housing prices balloon. That's why more and more people with moderate incomes either choose much smaller places than they originally envisioned or buy homes a long drive from their jobs. Some people say, "Big deal. Things always cost more in a city, but it's worth it." Or they say, "Big deal. Commutes of nearly an hour are common near urban centers." Other people fear that our very success will destroy what's best about Boulder. If the topic of affordability interests you, attend one of the frequent city meetings at which planning experts from around the nation share ideas. In 1995, the City also started round-table discussions that meet in residential homes. Such meetings

can educate you about how each community in Boulder County deals with the trade-offs between affordability, open space and density.

Rental Resources

Housing Helpers
4800 Baseline Rd., Boulder • 499-4499

This company offers a number of services, including a free Renter's Line, 499-4497; a Roommate Line, 499-4494, which can match you with potential housemates for a modest fee; and a Sublease Line, 499-4495, which is free to the renter. The free Realtor referral service, 499-4499, helps you select a Realtor, based on the requirements you outline.

University of Colorado Off-Campus Housing
University Memorial Center, Rm. 336 (CU-Boulder campus), Boulder • 492-7053

This referral service helps students find rooms, apartments, houses and roommate requests. It also provides free copies of Boulder's tenants rights and responsibilities, free model leases and subleases and general information about renting in Boulder.

City of Boulder Housing Authority
3120 Broadway, Boulder • 441-3150

Subsidized housing in the city is available by application to the housing authority. There's a one-year wait for a one-bedroom apartment to a two- to four-year wait for a four-bedroom place.

Boulder County Housing Authority
2040 14th St., Boulder • 441-3929

In the county, the waiting list for subsidized housing is two to four years, depending on the house size.

Retiring for some Boulderites means their first backpack trip to Nepal, and for others, that longed-for second career.

Boulder
Retirement

In many ways, Boulder so epitomizes the youth culture that many people don't realize it is a splendid place to retire as well. Excellent community services, an increasing commitment to public transportation and a benign four-season climate make it congenial for retirees. But "retirement" doesn't automatically equate to "inactivity," and many so-called "retirees" put working folks to shame when it comes to a range of interests. Retiring for some Boulderites means their first backpack trip to Nepal, and for others, that longed-for second career. For others, doing as they please means working at a new job, and the **50+ Employment Opportunities Program**, 441-3985, connects people with job-retraining programs and employment possibilities.

A "retired" engineer studies ethics at CU-Boulder and works summers at a greenhouse. When his children were young, this high-level manager left escalating salaries and a thirst for fancier things. He and his wife spend more time with their sons now. The dad loves both his scholarly pursuit and plants. "Retirees" include the fiftysomething former satellite communications expert who retired early and started hiking, backpacking and knocking off fourteeners, Colorado's 54 peaks that are 14,000 or more feet above sea level, when he moved to Boulder in the early '90s; and the eightysomething famous Boulder author who writes less these days because she's so busy managing her very successful stock portfolio. The "Chronologically Gifted" who hike or bike miles might seem intimidating to seniors who plan to age more conventionally. Keep in mind these super seniors impress people a third their age. When we grow up, can we do it too? What's their secret?

About 8 percent of Boulder residents are 65 and older, compared with 12 percent nationwide. (Boulder's large student and early post-grad population explains much of the difference.) "Although Boulder offers nine retirement complexes aimed at the senior market, most older residents opt for more individuality. Two city-sponsored senior centers and even a community Internet link provide a sense of connection with the most recreational opportunities and services," writes Diana Somerville, editor of the *Daily Camera's* monthly "Prime Times" page for seniors. "Prime Times" features seniors' accomplishments and activities and discusses issues local seniors consider important.

Fans of the *Camera's* other seniors-issues columnist, Dave Jackson, have shared ideas for improving Boulder. The saltier ones say "confine the cats" or "send joggers to South America." They are still nostalgic for 19¢-per-gallon gasoline, passenger trains and manners. But many say the good old days are now, and 78 percent of the seniors who responded to Jackson's survey said they're happy. In many cases, especially in Boulder's more traditional neighborhoods, seniors mix with other age groups.

Job and Volunteer Opportunities

Most Boulder seniors consider retirement a chance to do as they please. No golf courses are reserved only for retirees, but plenty of golf courses are easy to use during weekday working hours. Many public swimming pools reserve senior swim times, and in other ways public facilities gear themselves to seniors.

Volunteering is another avenue to freedom and contribution. It might be with the Audubon Society, 499-0219. It might be through Boulder Rotary, 444-2407, or other service organizations. It might be helping out in the schools, such as the retired IBMer who teaches advanced math and electronics to grade-school kids. A few phone calls quickly create connections. The major clearinghouse is **Volunteer Connection**, 444-4904. Another is the **Retired and Senior Volunteer Program** (R.S.V.P.), 443-1933, which has more than 2,000 registered volunteers in the county. This means one out of every 10 people 60 and older volunteers each year through R.S.V.P., which celebrated its 24th anniversary in October 1996. People join because they want to roll up their sleeves and keep active and productive. The Handyman Program, which does fix-it-up jobs for other seniors, attracts seniors as volunteers too. The **Service Exchange**, 678-3228, matches volunteers with each other to earn service credits for work, which they can draw on when they want or need assistance.

Senior Centers

These are the best one-stop shops for senior-related offerings. The county has six urban centers with comprehensive resources and four rural centers open for limited hours and with limited on-site staffing. Boulder's centers are just west of the downtown library and at the East Boulder Recreation Center. Both are on an RTD bus line. Senior Centers are social, informative places. They can connect you with reduced-cost medical, tax and legal aid. For instance, by paying $20 to enroll at the 55+ Health Clinic, 441-0444, Boulder County residents can receive 12 months of preventative healthcare, including routine blood-pressure checks, review of prescription medicine, individual wellness counseling and skin-cancer screenings. The centers also offer up-to-date information on places to live, classes and assisted-care help. Services are offered to people 55 or older and their families (age limits vary with the center).

> ### FYI
> Unless otherwise noted, the area code for all phone numbers in this guide is 303.

People who equate senior centers with "old" tend to avoid them, but the centers provide useful services and opportunities for seniors to connect with their peers. When asked why they use the more serene centers, women report that they're interested in learning and improving their lives. Men more often list the challenge of staying active. The most popular Boulder Senior Center services are affordable dinners on Tuesday nights and weekday lunches, medical screenings, classes, trips and, significantly, resource specialists' guidance.

Gossip, the useful kind, is free — and is perhaps the greatest benefit of all, especially for live-alone seniors who need to keep connecting with other people. Habitués of the centers discuss the trivial and the serious. They might swap opinions about favorite eating places, such as the Red Lion, a short ride away in Boulder Canyon, Longmont's Country Buffet and trendy salad bars such as Healthy Habits and the Boulder Salad Company. They might exchange information on such controversial and important issues as how to connect with the Boulder Hemlock Society, which discusses the ethics and practical side of how rational, thoughtful people who are faced with a terminal illness can make end-of-life decisions for themselves.

The following senior centers are in Boulder County; call for hours and services: **Boulder West Senior Center**, 909 Arapahoe Avenue, Boulder, 441-3148; **Boulder East Senior Center**, 5660 Sioux Drive, Boulder, 441-4150; **Broomfield Senior Center**, 300 Community Park Drive, Broomfield, 469-0536; **Lafayette Senior Center**, 103 S. Iowa Street, Lafayette, 665-9052; **Longmont Senior Center**, 910 Longs Peak Avenue, Longmont, 651-8411; **Louisville Senior Center**, 900 W. Via Appia, Louisville, 666-7400.

INSIDERS' TIP

CareLink, 441-3905, is an "adult day-care" program at the West Boulder Senior Center that provides companionship, structured activities and medication assistance for Alzheimer's patients and others who are ambulatory but benefit from getting out of the house in a safe, controlled environment.

Additional services and resource clearinghouses for seniors in Boulder County include: **Allenspark Aging Services for Boulder County**, at Allenspark Nursing Clinic, Colo. Highway 7, Allenspark, 747-2592; **Lyons Aging Services Resources**, Bloomfield Community Room, 722 Fifth Avenue, Lyons, 823-9016; and **Niwot Senior Resources** (branch of Boulder County Office of the Aging), Left Hand Grange Hall, corner of Second Avenue and Franklin Street, Niwot, 652-3850.

Senior Classes

Many Boulder agencies and private groups offer discounted or age-geared classes to seniors. At **CU-Boulder**, 492-8484, with a professor's permission, a senior may audit virtually any class tuition-free (with a small processing charge). Boulder Parks and Recreation offers senior yoga, swimming and tennis. The Senior Centers (listed previously) have offerings too. People write in with endorsements of popular activities, such as senior cross-country skiing at Eldora Mountain Resort:

Like to ski without the fuss?
Ride the Tuesday senior bus!
Fast and fleet, or slow as snails,
You'll love the user-friendly trails:
Wide and smooth and worry free
Eldora is the place for me.
— from "Ode to Eldora," by G.S. Ball

Classes include t'ai chi for seniors, tennis tournaments and a Boulder Creek walking group. There are book discussions of Ibsen's plays. Very popular is the **55/Alive Driving Class** — a way to brush up on driving skills, learn new driving laws and, often, get a break on insurance.

Getting Around

The Senior Centers have offered trips to Yellowstone and Australia. Daytrips have included chauffeured excursions to the Denver Center Theatre, gambling towns and Denver's Cherry Creek Mall.

RTD charges only 15¢ for seniors who ride buses during off-peak hours (not 6 to 9 AM or 4 to 6 PM). An RTD shopping bus goes from the senior housing sites to grocery stores. Many buses accommodate wheelchairs.

Don't live near RTD routes and can't afford a taxi? Consider **Special Transit**, 447-9636, which provides accessible, door-to-door service, including for wheelchair users. This nonprofit group charges $1 each way within the city; $2 between various cities in the county. It's quite a discount — the real cost of this subsidized service is closer to $10 per person. Call several days to a week ahead to schedule your ride.

Another Boulder service is **The Hop**, which takes people between major shopping areas and CU-Boulder for 25¢.

See our Boulder Getting Around chapter for more transportation information.

Meal Services

Meals on Wheels is Boulder's most frequently requested senior service. It enables people of all ages to eat regular, nutritious meals, even when they're short on money or are unable to handle food preparation and cleanup. More than 17,000 Boulder County seniors might live below the poverty level. The county is part of a nationwide issue in this regard: Between 2.5 million and 4.9 million elderly Americans struggle to purchase affordable meals. Another Boulder program, **ElderShare**, delivers basic groceries twice a month to nearly 500 seniors throughout the county.

Housing

The No. 1 worry among Boulder seniors is the physical degeneration of aging and the resulting cost of healthcare. For this reason, Boulder works to help seniors receive care at home or in a special facility.

Often Boulder seniors live in single-family homes. Neighborhoods benefit when seniors live near. It helps the streets be safer when people are in and out during the day, and it can make for great intergenerational interactions. A child's first job might be watering an older neighbor's lawn or shoveling snow, and seniors may be unofficial substitute grandparents when the real ones live far away. When a

Photo: Daily Camera/Jay Quadracci

Volunteers help maintain historic buildings and the homes of local seniors.

favorite local retiree broke her hip, kids came by with flowers. Did she flinch at their worried faces? "Guess what!" she said with a grin. "I have metal parts now. That means I'm a bionic woman!" Her humor delighted them, as does seeing her back on morning walks. As one Dave Jackson fan quips, "The snap, crackle and pop you hear isn't always your cereal." And another, asked what's worst about growing old, replied, "Where did I put it?"

When they tire of yard work or keeping up a big house, many seniors do the Boulder yuppie thing and move to a townhome or condominium. Most housing inquiries at the Senior Centers regard finding independent-living quarters, often with no stairs, affordable and near bus routes and shopping.

Multilevel Facilities

While various specialized levels of senior housing, including independent and assisted living, respite care and nursing homes, are available in Boulder, several multilevel facilities provide the range of options and give people the opportunity to move to increasing levels of care if and as needed.

Boulder Good Samaritan
2525 Taft Dr., Boulder • 449-6150
Boulder Good Samaritan offers independent- and assisted-living options as well as a nursing home. Taft Towers is Good Samaritan's lowest level of care, with 75 independent-living units as big as two-bedroom, two-bathroom apartments that rent for $890 to $1,525 per month; at this writing, there is a three-month waiting period. Thirteen assisted-living residents pay $1,425 to $1,924 per month; the current waiting period is three to six months. The nursing home accommodates 60 residents at $110 to $120 per day. Good Samaritan has a dining room, transportation services, a full activities program (participants were out touring the Denver Mint and lightheartedly requesting samples on the day we checked), a swimming pool and housekeeping services. The Older Boulder Wellness Center, a Nautilus-equipped workout facility, is at Good Samaritan, which makes it (as far as we know) the only nursing home in the nation with a Nautilus facility. How Boulder! Nonresidents also may use the center for $48 per month for three visits a week.

Golden West
1055 Adams Cir., Boulder • 499-4888
Golden West was established by the First Christian Church and has been around for more than 30 years. There are currently 255 apartments for independent living and 56 assisted-living units in three adjacent, interconnected elevator-equipped buildings. There is a six- to 12-month waiting period for efficiency

apartments, which cost $338 per month, and an 18- to 36-month waiting for one-bedroom apartments, which are $456 per month. An optional meal plan for either the noon or evening meal is an additional $137 per month. The assisted-living units are 307 square feet and rent for $1,300 to $1,700 per month, based on a resident's income and the availability of the desired rent slot (the lowest rates are for Medicaid recipients). The maximum wait, as of this writing, is about three months, and the monthly fee includes 14-hour staffing, three meals a day, snacks, medical monitoring, laundry, housekeeping and minimal daily living assistance. On site are a library, recreation room, beauty salon, sitting and guest rooms, a gift shop and coin laundry facilities. Recreational activities for all residents include exercise classes, educational programs, musical programs (the Golden West Choral Group and Kitchen Band are popular), crafts classes, slide presentations and the Residents' Council, which is sort of like a Student Council for seniors living at Golden West.

Independent Living

Some retirees simplify their lives so they can travel and pursue more hobbies while increasing the availability of medical care. Take the woman who moved to one of Boulder County's independent-housing facilities with assisted-care and nursing facilities on the grounds. When she announced that she was renting out the old family home, her children were aghast. She replied, "Well, it's about time. After all, I am going to be 90 this year." She now hosts her women's group in the meeting room of her living center.

Heed this — the independent-living housing market is tight. Although you can get into some places quickly, the waiting list for others is four years long.

The Atrium
3350 30th St., Boulder • 444-0200

The 80 apartments here range from studios to two-bedrooms. Amenities include a craft room, exercise room, beauty parlor and barber shop, underground parking, ice cream parlor, dining room (serving three meals a day) and free laundry facilities. The Atrium frequently schedules special events such as fashion shows, barbecues, a St. Patrick's Day corned beef and cabbage dinner and a New Year's Eve dance (it typically ends at 10 PM), open to residents and nonresidents (for a fee). Rates at The Atrium are $1,195 to $2,615 a month, including weekly housekeeping, linens and linen service.

Presbyterian Manor
1050 Arapahoe Ave., Boulder • 444-0642

Presbyterian Manor is a not-for-profit, independent-living facility with modest costs and a four-year waiting list. The 80 units all have small kitchenettes. The monthly costs are: buffet unit, $225; studio, $250; one-bedroom, $300; and two-bedroom, $350. The Boulder West Senior Center and the main branch of the Boulder Public Library are practically across the street, and the YMCA will pick up groups of three or more participating in Y programs, so residents don't have problems keeping busy, even though the activity schedule is sparse. The manor puts on an annual Christmas dinner and monthly birthday parties, which are held as picnics from June to September and indoors the rest of the year.

Assisted Living

As with independent-living facilities, the waiting list for assisted-living options can be long — six to 12, even 18, months. If you want affordable housing with any assisted-living options, start checking as soon as you can.

The Beatrice Hover Assisted-living Residence
1380 Charles Dr., Longmont • 772-8102

This facility accommodates 55 residents — eight in double suites and the rest in private rooms, all with private baths. The 6-year-old facility provides three meals per day, housekeeping and laundry services, medication assistance and a van to take residents to doctors' appointments and outside activities. The rate structure is complex, based on three levels of service (the third being daily assistance with bathing and dressing, considered the last step before skilled-nursing care is needed) as well as the size and location of the accommodation; costs range from $1,900 to $2,700 per month. Nearby is a 121-unit independent-living facility called Hover Manor. All but 10 percent of these 580-square-foot, one-bedroom apartments are HUD-subsidized and therefore carry strict income guidelines; the 12 free-market units currently rent for $442 per month.

The Mary Sandoe House
1244 Gillaspie Dr., Boulder • 494-7317

The Mary Sandoe House has 24 assisted-living rooms that residents furnish with their own belongings. The fee, which for private-pay residents is $1,850 per month, includes three meals per day, housekeeping, medication management, laundry service and what is called "minimal assistance" bathing and dressing. The Mary Sandoe House has an activity staff too. Currently the waiting list for private-pay residents is six months; for Medicaid recipients, 1½ years.

Respite Care

Friends or families who care for loved ones with chronic illnesses can find the task emotionally and physically demanding. Resource specialists can discuss options that give relief to caregivers, who themselves are often elderly spouses — or perhaps adult children of aging parents. These options include Volunteer Respite Care, adult day care, home health aids and other possibilities. Senior Centers hold programs each spring, summer and fall to guide adult children of aging parents, 441-3148.

Nursing Homes

For people who need 24-hour care, Boulder County offers a broad range of nursing homes and nursing home services. If you need to select one, check homes carefully, personally or by having someone visit them for you.

Some services provide in-home care similar to that offered in a nursing home. For instance, **HomeCare**, offered through PorterCare Hospital-Avista (see our Boulder Healthcare and Wellness chapter), 665-3228, provides home visits from nurse aides, nurses, physical therapists and other medical professionals and are designed as an alternative to nursing-home care.

Boulder Manor
4685 Baseline Rd., Boulder • 494-0535

This nursing home has 167 beds, including 27 in a rehabilitation unit that is used by clients of Kaiser-Permanente and other HMOs. In addition to all meals, nursing care and activities, Boulder Manor offers full therapy services for rehab patients and anyone else who can use it. The rates are $108 to $135 per day, including prescription medication — reportedly the only nursing home in Boulder whose rates include prescribed drugs. Boulder Manor also accommodates Medicaid patients.

Manor Care
2800 Palo Pkwy., Boulder • 440-9100

Manor Care is licensed to provide 24-hour nursing-home care to 150 residents and patients. It provides short-term rehabilitation, long-term care and, increasingly, short-term respite stays to provide relief for care recipients' families who are going on vacation or otherwise are unable to care for a loved one for a time. In addition, Manor Care has a specialized Alzheimer's unit. Inpatient and outpatient physical, speech and occupational therapies are available. There is currently a two- to three-month wait for private rooms. Fees are $102 to $138 per day, depending on the unit, including all meals (selective menu and special therapeutic diet needs are met) and activities. Manor Care accepts Medicaid patients.

Terrace Heights Care Center
2121 Mesa Dr., Boulder • 442-4037

This facility has 162 beds, including up to 34 in the Alzheimer's unit. This unit has its own courtyard, balcony and activities coordinator, but it is secured. Activities include accompanied visits to the on-site ice cream shop and occasional excursions in Terrace Heights' van. In addition, there is a full rehabilitation unit, staffed six days a week by a team of physical, occupational and speech therapists from Theratx, an organization that provides such services. Lower levels of therapy are provided under the facility's own restorative nursing program, and 24-hour, seven-day respiratory therapy is also available. Long-term care and respite care are available at $105 to $130 per day, including all meals, laundry services and housekeeping as well as any necessary nursing and other assistance.

OUR DIVERSE PROGRAMS INCLUDE

▶ **Boulder Evening Credit Program** - University credit courses offered at a convenient time for everyone

▶ **Noncredit Program** - courses that allow you to explore new areas, such as foreign languages, fine arts, test preparation, and more, without the pressure of grades or tests

▶ **Management Development** - business courses in supervision, marketing, etc. to hone individual skills or earn a certificate

▶ **Computer Applications** - hands-on courses ranging from the basics, word processing, graphics, and programming on Windows and Macintosh platforms

▶ **Real Estate and Appraisal** - courses for broker or appraiser licensing and license renewal

▶ **High School Summer Scholars Program** - credit and noncredit courses for students who want a friendly introduction to university life

▶ **SAVE** - available Fall and Spring for those people not currently seeking degree status but who would like to take Boulder campus courses

▶ **Independent Study** - credit and noncredit correspondence courses including select offerings available on the world wide web

Call our catalog request line at **492-5146**, toll free 800-331-2801, and specify which program you would like more information about, or visit our offices at:

1221 University Avenue
University of Colorado at Boulder

Offered as part of the Statewide Extended Studies Program.
The University of Colorado is an equal opportunity/affirmative action institution.
Continuing Education receives no state tax support to administer its programs and services.

Boulder
Child Care and Education

Boulder offers many good options for child care and schools. This chapter starts with the main child-care information centers and reviews how to screen child-care options. It explains how to find a sitter fast then goes to checking out nannies, day care and preschools. The chapter ends with both public and private schools, including universities. For fun with children and summer camps, see the Boulder Kidstuff chapter.

Choosing Child Care

Information Centers

Head to Boulder's **Children's Services**, 441-3180, at the Crossroads Mall, 30th and Walnut streets. It offers the county's most comprehensive lists of everything: more than 500 family child-care homes, nannies, day care centers, preschools, babysitting co-ops, public and private school information, financial assistance for housing and food, parenting classes and more. It also has a library of helpful books and videos. This city-run agency is open 8 AM to 5 PM, Monday through Friday.

If money's a problem, Children's Services now also runs the reduced-rate child-care program and can also tell you which centers/preschools offer a sliding fee or tuition reduction.

There are also other resources for families with young children. The Colorado Preschool Program subsidizes the tuition for kids who qualify; placement is made through **Child Find**, 530-1664. **Head Start**, 441-3980, operates at two locations in Boulder and two in Lafayette with preschool enrichment for qualifying 3- to 5-year-olds. The **Parenting Place** in Boulder, 449-0177, and Lafayette, 666-4598, are low-cost centers with support groups, education and play groups. You can bring children as old as 5 with you. The **Boulder County Parents of Twins and More Club**, 494-4168, is a support group for parents with multiple-birth siblings. In 1996, there were 98 families with twins and six with triplets in the group.

Finding a Sitter

You need a sitter, and Children's Services is closed. If the play starts in five minutes, good luck. Boulder might be a spontaneous kind of town, but good sitters get booked fast. Let's hope for the best . . . you're calling at least a week ahead. Some services advertise that they can even provide a sitter with at least 24 hours' notice, but don't bank on it.

Before you call sitters, it's good to prepare a list of screening questions. Do you have them now (see our Close-up in this chapter)? Good. **Children's Alley**, 449-1951, is a YWCA short-term care facility for infants through 12-year-olds. Rates are $1.35 to around $3.50 per hour per child, depending on your income. It's open on weekdays, generally between 7:30 AM and 9:45 PM (it closes at 5:45 PM on Fridays). Call at 7 PM the evening before for reservations. College students interested in sitting are listed through CU-Boulder's **Student Employment**

Office, 492-7349, which takes calls 9 AM to 5 PM Monday through Friday during the school year and until 4:30 PM in the summer.

The Boulder County Employment and Training Center's **Older Workers Program**, 441-3985, makes referrals for pre-screened senior sitters, primarily retirees looking for jobs. **Rent-a-Mom**, 322-1399, has a nanny program. Their pre-screened employees can drive and generally are hired for an evening or up to two weeks. The **YMCA**, 442-2778, offers a list of teenagers who have passed a Red Cross babysitting course. If your child is sick but you still need to go to work, call PorterCare at Home II's **Child At Heart**, 665-3022; **Heart of Colorado Caregivers**, 440-0384; **International Nursing Services**, 393-1515; and **Take-A-Break**, 665-9741. Rates are generally $8 to $10 an hour. Your employer might even cover part of the cost. PorterCare at Home II's Child At Heart also provides postpartum care, rents breast pumps and provides other services for new parents.

If you are visiting Boulder and need a sitter, the hotel's front desk or concierge can probably help. If you've just moved to town and need to find reliable sitters or child care, ask the mom you see on Pearl Street Mall, call neighborhood churches and schools and talk with workmates. Ask, ask, ask. It's just like home (or your last home). Sometimes, you find a good sitter fast. Sometimes, you've got to keep trying.

Nannies and Au Pairs

A "nanny" can be anyone from a local college student to a grandmother who regularly cares for your child, either live-in or coming to work in your home every day. An "au pair" is a live-in caretaker, often from Europe. Generally between 18 and 25 years old, the au pair lives with you for a year in exchange for child care for with modest pay, room and board. One service that has worked successfully for the families enrolled is **AuPairCare**, out of San Francisco, (800) 4AUPAIR. The Yellow Pages and Children's Services both list local referral services.

> **FYI**
>
> Unless otherwise noted, the area code for all phone numbers in this guide is 303.

Day-care Homes and Centers

Every parent who wants the best possible place for their children is being wise. Poor-quality child care can harm a child's self-esteem, ability to learn and ability to thrive later in life. *Working Mother* magazine generally lists Colorado in the top 10 states for the quality of child care, but many experts believe we must set higher standards nationwide. A report by local early childhood expert Mary Culkin recently highlighted infant/toddler care as an area of special concern. She found wide variation in the nurturing and interpersonal interaction at child-care centers, vital indicators of care quality. What's more, just because a center was more expensive did not always correlate with the caregivers being kind to the children. That's why visiting, to check center quality for yourself, is an excellent idea. We've listed questions to ask yourself under the heading, "Check It Out! Visit!" Look there for ideas of how to evaluate a child-care program.

Full-time child care in the Boulder area averages more than $150 per week, but cost depends on where you live. Longmont is less; Boulder is more. Smaller caregiver/child ratios, better caregiver training, more nutritious snacks and age-appropriate play materials all add up. Check with Children's Services if you need information about sliding scale fees. And keep your screening questions handy to help narrow your search.

We're going to name some accredited day-care centers. Before we do, remember that many excellent, nonaccredited day-care homes provide a warm, safe environment with just a few children. Many top-notch day-care centers and preschools have not gone through the fees, paperwork and visits required for official accreditation. For these reasons, check other places too, and use our short list to compare.

The 13 centers and preschools that follow are accredited as of 1995 by the National Association for the Education of Young Children or the National Association of Family Childcare

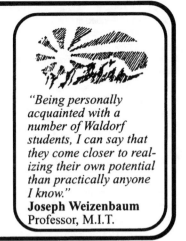
Providers. These are the only national, volun-tary, professionally sponsored accreditation system for preschools, kindergartens and child-care centers. They base their decisions on interaction among staff and children, staff and parents, location, staff qualifications, health, safety and physical environment. They are **Mary Lou Schaefer**, 666-8080; **Sue Stevens**, 666-8774; **Messiah Lutheran Pre-school**, 776-2573; **Sunflower Preschool**, 494-2012; **Boulder Day Nursery**, 442-7605; **Boulder Day Infant Center**, 444-0290; **Mountain View Preschool**, 494-3557; **Peter Pan Cooperative Preschool**, 499-5231; **Children's World** on Wedgewood in Longmont, 776-6118; **Children's World** in Broomfield, 465-2053; **Commerce Children's Center**, 497-5063, and **Children's World South**, 494-3694. The **CU-Boulder Family Housing Children's Center**, 492-6185, also has national accreditation, but it is only avail-able to University of Colorado student, staff and faculty families. Another option is avail-able at **Town & Country School**, 938-1314, which begins with preschool for kids 2½ and older and continues through kindergarten and elementary school through age 8. The school sits on a big, open play yard on an acre lot,

and each preschool class includes a group-certified teacher.

The **Colorado Preschool Program**, 447-5075, conducts development screening and subsidizes the placement of nearly 100, spe-cial-needs preschool students in existing, high-quality, community-based preschools, includ-ing **Alicia Sanchez Elementary School's** bi-lingual preschool in Lafayette, 665-2044; the **Child Language Center** at CU-Boulder's Communications Disorders Clinic, 492-5375; **Children's House Preschool**, 444-6432; **Friends'N'Fun Children's Center** in Lafayette, 666-5111; Kohl Elementary School's **Cottage Preschool** in Broomfield, 466-5885; **Mountain View Preschool**, 494-3557; Nederland Elementary School's **Caribou Mountain Preschool**, 258-7092; **New Hori-zons Cooperative Preschool**, 442-7434; **The Family Learning Center's** bilingual preschool, 442-8979; and **Our School Preschool Teacher-Parent Cooperative**, 494-4112.

Marcello Games, a volunteer at Our School, has produced a film depicting chil-dren during a typical school day. He also cap-tured a touching scene of how the children prepared a burial ceremony for an unexpected occurrence, the death of the school's pet

INSIDERS' TIP

Boulder's public schools include magnet schools designed for children with special interests or needs.

guinea pig. You can call Our School to borrow or purchase the video (it sells for around $20), which is an excellent example of top-quality, respectful interactions between two director-certified preschool teachers and their young students.

Extended Care for Older Kids and Other Family Issues

Latchkey children are a problem in Boulder County, as are adolescents who are old enough to stay alone but still need structure and time with a caring adult.

If you can't be there when your kids come home, you can help them by connecting them with employment or volunteer opportunities. If they're looking for Friday night entertainment, keep in mind that many local music clubs and pool halls bar anyone under age, even if they aren't planning to drink. On the dark side, that explains brawling and drinking parties that have happened on the Hill during weekends (a problem the community as a whole is working to reduce), and on a brighter note, the popularity of places such as Red Robin or Crossroads Mall for younger teens and coffeehouses for older teens. Youngsters often plug into programs and facilities available at the **YMCA** and **North, South and East Boulder recreation centers** (see our Parks and Recreation Centers chapter), which have excellent swimming programs, gyms and other attractions.

Church groups, **Boulder Youth Services**, 441-4357, and your local school are other places that can help you get ideas. In 1996, **City on the Hill Ministries**, 440-3873, at 7483 Arapahoe Avenue, built a skateboard park outside the church and welcomes youngsters to use it free.

Jobs for youngsters, especially those younger than 16, are hard to come by — and vacation periods can stretch interminably for teens with little to do. In 1996, the three Boulder Recreation Centers began offering free access to weight rooms for teens every weekday afternoon. One of the finest recreation programs, begun in 1966, is the **Boulder Junior**

Rangers. Since then, some 3,000 teens ages 14 to 17 have undertaken a variety of construction and maintenance projects in the Boulder Mountain Park System. Digging, hauling, planting, and cleaning have not only provided teens with a modest summer income and tired them out, but also have given them insight into conservation and ecology. At age 18, Junior Rangers may graduate to assistant Senior Rangers and at 21 to Senior Rangers, supervising teams of 10 to 12 Juniors. The YMCA's **Youth Employment Center**, 442-2778 Ext. 218) operates as a clearinghouse for jobs from lawn-mowing and babysitting to tutoring younger children. They've helped find work for teens as young as 13.

If a family is in real trouble, Children's Services is a source for information about other organizations, classes, counseling and further options to help resolve ongoing family conflicts and even abuse issues that can be damaging. Boulder County's **Family Preservation Program**, funded by the Boulder County Department of Social Services, Medicaid and the state's juvenile justice system, draws on the expertise of several agencies to offer intensive short-term intervention techniques to stabilize families in crisis.

Schools

Public Schools

Two school districts serve Boulder County — Boulder Valley and St. Vrain.

The **Boulder Valley District**, 447-1010, includes Boulder, Broomfield, Gold Hill, Jamestown, Lafayette, Louisville and Nederland. Nearly 25,000 students attend 32 elementary schools, nine middle schools, one middle/senior high school, six high schools and one technical education center. Average class size is 25. Most teachers have more than 10 years of teaching experience and hold master's degrees. Some schools offer before- and after-school meals and care, enrichment programs and summer sessions. The annual budgeted operating expenditure per pupil is $5,541.

The **St. Vrain District**, 776-6200, serves Dacono, Erie, Firestone, Federick, Hygiene,

Longmont, Lyons, Mead, Niwot, Peaceful Valley and Raymond. It has around 16,500 students in 28 different schools, including 17 elementary schools, five middle schools, three middle/high schools, three traditional high schools, two alternative high schools and one career development center. It employs 980 teachers. Average child/teacher ratio is 22-to-1, and the annual expenditure per pupil is $4,374. Some schools offer before- and after-school meals and care and enrichment programs.

Even though Boulder public schools place quite high in national and statewide rankings (and were rated by *Money* magazine as one of the top 100 school districts in the nation in 1996), controversies have stirred the system in recent years. Such issues as middle school versus junior high school, individualized learning versus back-to-basics, phonics versus whole language for beginner readers, a disquieting pattern of threatened and rescinded teacher layoffs and other thorny problems have taken an inordinate amount of community energy. On top of what appears to be chronic district-wide dissension, the Boulder Valley Schools' "site-based management" approach means that each school sets its own policies within the framework of district goals. This in turn means more wrangling among policy-setting parents with different ideas about education and goals for their children. Boulder's Open Enrollment policy means that you have a choice between sending your child to your neighborhood school, a different neighborhood's school or one of the focus or alternative schools popping up around Boulder. So check around to see which suits you and your youngster.

Boulder students do much better than those in the rest of Colorado — also not surprising considering that Boulder parents are among the most well-educated in the nation. Boulder's college-bound students had an average SAT verbal score 58 points higher than college-bound students nationwide and an average SAT math score 72 points higher than college-bound students from other areas. St. Vrain's ACT scores are on par with the rest of the state, as are their SAT verbal scores. SAT math scores in St. Vrain are somewhat higher than the rest of the state, but not as high as in Boulder Valley.

But what do those scores mean? Back-to-basics proponents mean that they test firm knowledge and are necessary to get into a good college. Others believe that worshiping the Dow Kid Instructional Average can skew education into nothing but a testing drill. When choosing a school, here are other important matters. What's the school's curriculum? How many children will be in your child's class? What's the ratio of adults to kids? Are parents encouraged to help in the classroom? What's the school's teaching style? Do the desks face forward and the teachers fill the walls with chemical element charts, or do kids study in a reading nook with old sofas and decorate the walls with their own creations? Testing scores won't tell you which schools are as homogenous as Wonder Bread and which have a richer cultural diversity. Test scores won't tell you what it's like to be at the school. Visits and talks are crucial, for your school is a community, where you and your children can make friends, build memories and learn about life.

Here's one warning: Boulder County has grown fast. That can mean overcrowding. This was a winning theme in a student editorial cartoon contest. In the cartoon, one adult says, "I feel sorry for those goof-offs at our school. They're not getting the education they need." The other adult replies, "I agree. But it's a good thing they ditch class, or we'd have to hold class on the football field." Since 1990, more than 3,000 students have been added to classrooms. The average enrollment has increased more than 4 percent a year. Budget constraints mean facilities and staff haven't kept up with increased enrollment, and some new communities are catching up on building schools nearby, forcing children from those communities to face busing to more distant schools or overcrowding. So ask about this "growing" issue.

Public Magnet Schools

Some children thrive in any situation, like hardy garden plants. Others need a special environment before they bloom. If you've got a unique bloomer, check the focus and alternative schools, often called "magnet" schools. Some provide more structure than a traditional classroom. Others offer more open-ended explorations. There are programs with specially trained staff for bilingual children or children with unusual developmental needs. A few include **Family Resource Schools**, outreach programs as good as having a wonderful aunt or uncle around, ready to help plan after-school activities and improve the school's community.

You'll get the best information about magnet schools if you visit. Here are some teasers: See the beautiful rain forest mural kids designed at **University Hill Elementary**, 442-6735. Also check out Uni Hill's **Rainbow Press**, where kids edit and publish real books, in languages including English, Spanish and Asian dialects. **Horizons Alternative Elementary School**, 447-5580, keeps class sizes small and parental involvement high. **Washington Bilingual School**, 449-6618, has a goal of 50 percent English-dominant and 50 percent Spanish-dominant children. Platt Middle School's **Choice Program**, 499-6800, boasts one of the most interesting science rooms around. Even in politically correct Boulder, **Casey Middle School**, 442-5235, stands out with its emphasis on multiculturalism and a motto of "Pride in Diversity."

Fairview High School, 499-7600, has added an **International Baccalaureate** program for juniors and seniors. It is designed with more rigorous, internationally academic regarded standards. Of the 446 students enrolled in IB in 1996-97, nearly half took at least four of these challenging courses and less than a quarter took just one. **New Vista High School**, 494-8037, includes interdisciplinary cross-fertilization, a strong emphasis on the arts and community volunteering. It graduated its first class in 1996, sending 50 percent of its

students on to college and boasting one National Merit Scholar. **Project Hold**, 447-5573, is a dropout prevention program for high school students.

A strong move is afoot to create a new middle school program with more focus on rigorous academic testing and ability grouping, to be called the Summit School. Call Boulder Valley School District for more information, and when you do, perhaps you'll learn about even more new focus schools (schools that offer a special, nontypical way of teaching, operated by the school district) or charter schools (schools that offer a special, nontypical way of teaching, funded by the school district but managed by the citizens forming the school) in the works. On the one hand, diversity such schools offer gives people more choices and helps teachers learn from a rich variety of styles. However, there are fears that too much diversity could spread resources thin and create factions that turn attention toward bitter arguments on style rather than letting teaching occur in a nonpolitical, caring environment. Your input is needed here.

The **Boulder Valley Area Vocational Technical Education Center** (nicknamed VoTec), 447-5220, offers both high school and adult education in trade skill programs. This one isn't such a fun teaser, but it's worth knowing: **Halcyon**, 499-1121, is a day-treatment program for troubled adolescents. It includes around 30 staff people working with 20 students.

St. Vrain has dropout prevention programs with smaller class sizes and more individualized instruction at **Main Street Middle School**, 682-9377, and **Olde Columbine High School**, 772-6363. The **Career Development Center**, 772-3333, is a vocational school for adults and for high-school students who take electives in the CDC building. Courses include welding, automotive and building trades, health and dental, agriculture, horticulture, accounting, office systems and other specialties.

Private Schools

You can find private schools run by religious organizations and schools as nondenominational as a pin-striped suit. At some, kids aren't expected to read until they're past

3rd grade. At others, the academic drills start in preschool. Boulder's Children's Services lists private schools in Boulder County. In addition to the local schools below, some students commute to Denver:

Jarrow Montessori
3900 Orange Ct., Boulder • 443-0511

Class sizes are generally small (between 16 and 20) in this school on 3 acres in a pretty, quiet part of North Boulder. There's a toddler program for kids 18 months to 3 years, a primary program for 3- to 6-year-olds, then an elementary program through 6th grade. Different age groups are blended in each classroom. This is a certified American Montessori Society school, with child-guided education. Teachers gather the interest of the student, and with the teacher's help, children guide their own learning. Education goes from concrete, hands-on experiences to abstract associations.

Friends School
5465 Pennsylvania Ave., Boulder
• 499-1999

About 125 kids attend, ranging from 2 years 9 months through 11 years old (preschool through 5th grade). The average class size for preschool is 14 and for elementary about 20, with two teachers per classroom. Lots of hands-on materials, a custom curriculum for each student, and a caring atmosphere characterize Friends School.

Boulder Country Day School
3800 Kalmia Ave., Boulder • 444-3603

Preschool through 6th grade are taught at a very traditional, academically oriented program for 250 students. French and Latin are part of the curriculum. Computers, art, music and drama are taught here too. Class sizes are no bigger than 10 in the preschool and no larger than 15 in the elementary grades. Students wear uniforms and the principal greets them by name as they arrive each morning, holding an umbrella for them if it's raining. The 4th- and 5th-grade teachers send home biweekly progress reports about how each child is doing. In late 1996, Boulder Country Day bought a large tract of land in Gunbarrel on which it plans to relocate, eventually add-

ing middle and high schools. The most optimistic estimates slate the move for sometime in 1998.

Shining Mountain Waldorf School
987 Locust Ave., Boulder • 444-7697

From preschool through high school, this school offers a rich blend of arts, music and drama interwoven with academic curriculum. There are 385 students and 50 faculty. For a chemistry experiment, students might draw what they observe as well as describe it in words. Primary class lessons can include lore about traditional fairy tales, folk stories and weaving. People who are not familiar with a Waldorf School should give it a visit, for the warm, comfortable pace at which children learn and the richness of materials are marvelous. The philosophy behind Waldorf is more than 75 years old, and in addition to regular accreditation, teachers receive two years of training in Waldorf methods.

Shepherd Valley Waldorf School & Garden
6545 Gunpark Dr., Boulder • 530-2644

This is Boulder's second Waldorf School. It was opened because there is such a demand for Waldorf education in this area. This Gunbarrel-area school has preschool through 6th grade. Class sizes are 15 to 20 students. And if you're not familiar with Waldorf schools, check the previous entry.

Sacred Heart of Jesus School
1317 Mapleton Ave., Boulder • 447-2362

This Catholic school has a preschool child-care program then a school from kindergarten through 8th grade. It's well-regarded for its traditional academic program and religious coursework. Lots of parents volunteer here, helping to add to the community atmosphere. Nearly 400 children attend.

September School
1902 Walnut Ave., Boulder • 443-9933

Hands-on learning and creativity distinguish this grade 9 through 12 high school of about 100 students. Class size averages 8 to 10 students. The teaching staff is dedicated and excellent, including professional scientists and musicians with a knack for communicating with students as peers. It's an informal atmosphere with freedom to be an individual, which is a successful formula for youngsters who find it hard to fit in and be productive in other schools. The four-building campus includes a small, former church at Canyon and 19th streets. Students painted fantastic murals on it many years ago, and it has become a Boulder landmark, right up there with some of the highly respectable, designer-decorated Victorian homes. This is not to imply that the two styles are similar. To give you an idea of their flavors, the fancy Victorians would be hot-fudge sundaes with whipped cream. The September School mural is salsa.

Alexander Dawson School
4801 N. 107th St., Lafayette • 665-6679

Alexander Dawson is a college preparatory, full middle/senior high school for more than 220 students. For the 1997-98 school year, Dawson will add 5th grade. The following academic year, the school is eliminating its boarding program and adding a full elementary school with 120 students. When this expansion is complete, Dawson will accommodate a total of 420 students in grades K through 12. First comes an expansion of the middle school building to house the 5th grade, then a new K through 4th-grade building. The sprawling campus east of Boulder includes tennis courts, art rooms, a pottery studio, horseback riding and a theater. The buildings look as clean as new pennies, and the staff takes a rigorous, academic approach — the traditional tried-and-true basics, from Latin through Advanced Placement Biology plus interscholastic sports and a creative-writing magazine.

Bridge School
2305 Canyon Blvd., Boulder • 494-7551

Boulder's newest private secondary school for grades 6 through 12 is the Bridge School, designed for motivated, intellectually curious learners. The school also seeks youngsters with good character and a willingness to take risks and challenge themselves. High school includes computer competency, an interdisciplinary approach to science, senior seminars in English (including one on literature written before 1914), foreign languages, art and physical education are part of the mix. Community service is also part of the graduation requirement. Founded with just a handful of students, the student body is now well into double digits and growing annually.

The Final Decision

If only Boulder had just one little red schoolhouse, you wouldn't have to agonize about what will be best for your child. Here's a comforting story: One teacher, substituting throughout Boulder County, wore jeans to a school where the children called her by her first name and she read story books to them from a rocking chair. She loved the friendly environment but worried that its open-ended structure let some kids slide. At another school, she wore a business suit, the kids called her "Mrs." and she lectured from a desk. While academic performance was more easily measured here, she worried that creativity was stifled. Which school was better? She rated them equally good. But at the more casual school, she wove in more structure. At the more traditional school, she slipped in creative moments. If you know a school's program and your child's needs, the fit doesn't have to be exactly, always perfect. You're a parent. You're a wonderful part of your child's life. You can help provide balance, just as this excellent teacher does.

Extra Help

Boulder also has resources for children who need assistance in boosting study skills. **fLearn**, 499-4386, 4800 Baseline Road, No. B-102, offers tutoring and sells educational materials to classroom teachers, home-schoolers and parents. A certified teacher oversees the program. Other options include **Sylvan Leaning Center**, 1600 38th Street, 449-1700, and **Huntington Learning Center**, 545-2100, 1722 14th Street, both offering help with general study skills, reading, writing and math, motivation and other issues designed to lead to better grades and the enhanced self-esteem deemed so important to Boulder students.

School officials also can refer you to private tutors for you child. Some tutors advertise in the local classifieds, and the university is also a reservoir of older students, both education majors and specialists in other disciplines.

Colleges and Universities

Boulder students can choose from a wealth of higher education opportunities. Before discussing the colleges and university in Boulder, consider others, near enough that a Boulder student could commute to Denver, site of the **University of Denver**, 871-2000; the **University of Colorado at Denver**, 556-3287; and **Metropolitan State College**, 556-2953. **Colorado State University**, (970) 491-1101, is in Fort Collins, roughly an hour north of Boulder. The **Colorado School of Mines**, 273-3000, and **Red Rocks Community College**, 988-6160, are in Golden, about a half-hour's drive south of Boulder.

Higher education centers in Boulder itself include:

University of Colorado at Boulder
Office of Admissions • Regent Administrative Center 125, Campus Box 6, Boulder • 492-6301

With all those red-roofed buildings, CU-Boulder is known as one of the nation's prettiest campuses. It's also close to recreational activities that make attending CU-Boulder lots of fun, including watching top teams such as the CU Buffs football team and CU women's basketball. But for serious students, it offers excellent opportunities too.

CU-Boulder is most renowned for its science programs. Psychology, biology and English are among the most popular undergraduate majors. More CU undergraduate and gradschool alumni have become astronauts than graduates of any other school, including the service academies. Classics and dance are among the smallest. Ten faculty are members of the American Academy of Arts and Sciences. Fourteen belong to the National Acad-

emy of Sciences, and CU-Boulder professor Thomas Cech won the 1989 Nobel Prize in chemistry. In 1995, history professor Patricia Nelson Limerick was awarded a prestigious McArthur Foundation grant, given for intellectual creativity. With such high-powered brains, it's no surprise that CU-Boulder got more than $150 million in outside research funds in 1995.

Approximately 25,000 students attend CU-Boulder, with 20,000 undergraduates and 5,000 graduates. As a state school, it gives tuition breaks to in-state residents, who make up nearly 70 percent of the students. About 1,000 foreign students attend from more than 80 countries. Non-degree candidates may pay to attend university classes as part of the university's continuing education program. People older than 55 can audit classes for a nominal fee, 492-8484, with the professor's permission. CU-Boulder also offers many classes to the community as part of the city's Lifelong Learning program, 492-5148.

Naropa Institute
2130 Arapahoe Ave., Boulder • 444-0202

Naropa is the only accredited college in the United States offering contemplative education based on Buddhist philosophy. This small but nationally recognized college is known for outstanding programs and plenty of unique offerings, such as its Jack Kerouac School of Disembodied Poetry, a public meditation hall and those solo Chinese dances called t'ai chi ch'uan. Naropa enrolls around 700 students in bachelor's and master's degree programs.

To get a feel for Naropa's classes, consider its fast-growing environmental studies program. This includes coursework in anthropology, ecology, horticulture and Native American studies. Students read Aldo Leopold's *A Sand County Almanac* and writing by Arne Naess, who coined the phrase, "Deep Ecology." A Sustainable Communities course, according to Naropa's catalog, emphasizes "ef-

---

INSIDERS' TIP

Thirteen astronauts are alumni of the University of Colorado at Boulder. Other graduates include retired Supreme Court Justice Byron White, 1958's Miss America Marilyn Van Derber-Atler, film actor/director Robert Redford and *M*A*S*H* actor Larry Linville.

fective action projects in the Boulder bioregion including landscape restoration, wilderness protection, environmental legislation, energy-efficient homes, cultural diversity and environmental arts." Naropa, in addition to full-time, degree-seeking students, has a widely expanding continuing-education program open to the community at large.

Boulder School of Massage Therapy
3285 30th St., Boulder • 443-5131

Day and evening classes help students earn federally accredited, massage therapy certification. Approximately 200 students attend, ranging from 19-year-olds to senior citizens. The year-long program requires nearly 900 hours of in-class, hands-on training plus study of anatomy and physiology. Students must undergo 55 hours of internships at places such as Boulder Community Hospital, a hospice or with an athletic team. Discounted rates ($25 for one full hour) are offered for community members at the supervised massage clinic, 443-REST, where students spend an additional 57 hours refining their art before graduation.

Front Range Community College
5490 Spine Rd., Gunbarrel • 447-5220
6600 E. Arapahoe Rd., Boulder • 786-7018

Two-year degree and certificate programs are available at both locations of this metro-area community college. Many students use the lower tuition at Front Range to prepare them for a four-year college or university. The Boulder campus works closely with CU to provide preparatory and transfer courses.

Continuing Education

One of the most valuable lessons an educated person can learn is to keep on learning. If you have that attitude, you're going to love Boulder. Young and old, dabblers and those intent on gaining a specific new skill and, well, everybody, if they're lucky, take courses from time to time. To get one of the enticing catalogs for these offerings, call or write the phone numbers below. Or, if you're already in Boulder, head to the library, a recreation center or a major grocery store, where these catalogs are usually available for free.

Boulder Parks and Recreation, 441-3412, 3170 Broadway, offers skill-building courses. Gymnastics for kids and pottery for adults are very popular. The dance classes for both are very popular. Then there's yoga, martial arts, guitar, cooking, sign language, investing and whitewater kayaking. Most of these classes take place at the recreation centers. When the Parks and Recreation offerings first get published each season, the registration phones can be busy a long time. Then, it's quicker to come to any of Boulder's three recreation centers and register in person.

CU-Boulder Continuing Education, 492-5148 or (800) 331-2801 (out-of-state), (800) 332-5839 (in-state), 1221 University Avenue, offers 300 courses each semester — everything from full-credit, college-level courses taught by CU-Boulder professors to noncredit pursuits such as Beginning Excel for the Macintosh and art/poetry workshops. Noncredit classes often are taught by professionals — some just starting out in their fields and willing to share boundless enthusiasm, others nationally famous who will always love teaching. Classes usually take place right on the CU-Boulder campus, in the evenings and on weekends.

Lifelong Learning, 447-5252, 4545 Sioux Drive, operated by the Boulder Valley School District, offers classes for both children and adults. Kids' classes range from two-session etiquette lessons to rock-climbing and horseback lessons. Photography, dancing, Spanish, writing and floral design are just a few of the offerings for adults. Lauren Springer, author of *The Undaunted Garden*, has taught classes about bulbs and perennials. There are even driver's education courses and classes for your dog (and you) in obedience training. Classes take place in various schools around town.

The **Naropa Institute**, 546-3568, 2130 Arapahoe Avenue, is very popular for classes that people take either for credit or not, depending on their goals. Classes include the disciplines of early childhood education, Buddhist studies, dance and writing, gerontology management, art therapy and contemplation, to name a few. Most classes take place in the pretty red schoolhouse that has been expanded to be the institute's main building. Study-abroad programs in Bali and Nepal are offered too.

The **Cooking School of the Rockies**, 494-7988, 637 S. Broadway, Suite H, has a big kitchen area and store that's open 10 AM to 5 PM Monday through Saturday. In the cooking school, students can refine their wine-tasting skills, watch famous chefs from around the world demonstrate their favorite techniques, or learn hands-on everything, from professional French cooking to sushi rolling and gingerbread house baking. A professional chef's course is the newest addition to the curriculum.

Other intriguing courses abound. The **School of Natural Cookery**, 444-8068, focuses on just that. Many churches offer classes in spirituality, Bible study and building better relationships. The **Shoshoni Yoga Retreat**, 642-0116, offers restful days where you can learn yoga techniques in a beautiful mountain setting.

Poke around for a class in something you enjoy or want to do better. In the process, you'll meet some great people and have a great time.

Check It Out! Visit!

Don't you wish someone could hand-hold you into the child care of your dreams? Boulder's Children's Services would get in big trouble if it tried. As a government agency, it can't show favoritism. Besides, your child is so important, you shouldn't trust his or her welfare to a recommendation alone. You need firsthand knowledge. That's

why you should ask questions and evaluate child care by visiting. An Insider's tip — get started early on this. Good child care is in hot demand in Boulder, and the waiting lists can be long.

Children's Services provides brochures about how to evaluate child care on your own. When interviewing a caregiver, ask for experience and references. Observe whether he or she is relaxed with children. When visiting a center (and if parents aren't encouraged to visit or help, consider that a red flag), be sure the children look happy. Are there enough adults? What are the qualifications of the people actually in the room with the children? What's the turnover rate of the staff? Do kids put cotton-ball bellybuttons on identical paper snowmen, or is creativity flourishing in beautiful, kid-generated art and play projects? As a final check, ask the **State Department's Office of Child Care Services**, 866-5958, in Denver to share their licensing files, which will reveal complaints and reviews about the center. To see a file, make an appointment, or order copies of file information at 50¢ per page.

Boulder has been a mecca for people seeking better health in unconventional ways — and the word "wellness" is used as much as "healthcare" or "medicine."

Boulder
Healthcare and Wellness

Many people come to Boulder for the inherently healthful and congenial lifestyle, but even happy people sometimes get sick, have babies or are injured. This section describes major medical facilities. Then, following, we give you an Insider's look at how to choose from Boulder's large selection of alternative care providers — in case you're in Boulder County partly because you want to get even healthier.

Emergency

Call 911 if you are any place in Boulder County and need help fast. Not only can you get help, but our 911 is designed so that it automatically locates you unless you're calling from a party line.

Hospitals

Boulder Community Hospital
1100 Balsam St., Boulder • 440-2273 (general), 440-2037 (emergency)

With 265 beds, Community is the largest full-service hospital in Boulder County. It takes pride in its emergency, maternity, cancer (full radiation service) and open-heart surgery centers, among other specialties. It emphasizes high-quality and family-centered care. For inpatient care, the Colorado Hospital Association's data indicates Community is one of the state's best hospitals for success rate, short length of stay and low-cost service.

The care is first-rate here, and the atmosphere tends toward the friendly and relaxed. Labor and delivery rooms might include old-fashioned rocking chairs and other homey touches, with lots of encouragement for family and new baby to happily bond. A friend who's had surgery in the cancer care center reports that her room's stereo system was top-notch. She's a professional hospital worker from out of state, and she gives the cancer unit an A+ for the personal attention she received. With advance notice, pet visitation is allowed (be sure the pet's with a trained handler and you have a recent copy of vaccinations). While there are sort of official visiting hours, staff tend to be pretty relaxed about visitors if you would like them more often.

A satellite clinic in Lafayette is Community Medical Center, 666-4345, at 2000 South Boulder Road. The hospital also operates senior medical care centers in Boulder, 442-1616, and Louisville, 604-1616, to provide outpatient services to Medicare recipients.

Mapleton Center
311 Mapleton Ave., Boulder • 443-0230

The Seventh-Day Adventists built their tuberculosis sanitarium here nearly a century ago. The location is beautiful, near Mount Sanitas Trail and the peace of the Foothills. Today the hospital is a division of Boulder Community, offering rehabilitation services for victims of strokes, accidents, brain injury, developmental disabilities and more, and behavioral health services for people suffering from psychiatric disorders, chemical dependency, alcoholism, depression, drug abuse, eating disorders and teen behavior problems.

"Easy Street," a special part of the rehabilitation facilities, has stores, curbs, cars and restaurants so patients can practice real-world situations again. For patients working on balance, there is equestrian therapy and a low-ropes course. Therapy for head-injury patients might include whitewater rafting. A warm-water, non-chlorinated therapy pool is open to anyone. Call for hours and fees. A new satellite facility, 530-4675, at 6685 Gunpark Drive, Suite 130, in Gunbarrel, offers physical therapy, speed and occupational therapy and pediatric rehabilitation.

Behavioral-health services at Mapleton include inpatient psychiatric care and day-treatment programs for adults and adolescents. The hotline for emergency evaluation is 440-5656.

PorterCare Hospital-Avista
100 Health Park Dr., Louisville • 673-1000 (general), 673-1111 (emergency)

This hospital, commonly referred to simply as Avista Hospital, was built in 1990 in booming Louisville and has beds for 58 patients. This well-regarded, full-service hospital offers 24-hour emergency service, single-room family-centered maternity, nursery, pediatric unit, cardiac unit, inpatient and outpatient rehabilitation services and diagnostic services including whole-body MRI and CAT scan . . . the works. Ask-A-Nurse is a 24-hour phone line for physician referral, healthcare information and community information, 777-6877.

Charter Centennial Peaks Behavioral Systems
2255 S. 88th St., Louisville • 673-9990, (800) 242-7837

Centennial has facilities and programs for children, adolescents, adults and seniors. There are 72 beds for inpatient care and day-treatment and outpatient programs for anyone with emotional, behavioral or substance-abuse problems. The Counseling and Assessment Center, a free consultation service, can help determine whether someone needs

therapy and counsel where to get it, for instance, from counselors, social workers, support groups or psychiatrists.

Longmont United Hospital
1950 Mountain View Ave., Longmont
• 651-5111 (general), 651-5000 (emergency)

This 142-bed hospital has a full range of services, from a whole-body CAT scanner to emergency services, home healthcare, a therapy pool, maternity, psychiatric services and an adult day-care program. In 1996, the hospital built a medical office building next door and leases space to physicians and other medical providers.

The Spaulding North Rehabilitation Center is on the hospital grounds. This way, instead of having to go to Denver or Boulder, locals can get rehabilitation services here. In addition, patients who need minimal rehabilitation as they head home can get transitional care. Longmont United added a cancer care unit in 1995, with full chemo- and radiation-therapy services.

Hospice

Hospice of Boulder County, Inc.
2825 Marine St., Boulder • 449-7740

This hospice, one of the first in the nation, offers an interdisciplinary program of home care, counseling, educational services and bereavement support to meet the needs of terminally ill patients and their family members. Services are provided in patients' homes and in nursing homes; there is no inpatient facility, and care for the terminally ill is provided regardless of a person's ability to pay. The hospice also has a volunteer training program.

County Health Department Clinics

Boulder County residents come to clinics for low-cost immunizations, well-child care, confidential HIV testing, senior clinics, environmental health screening and more. There's

> **FYI**
> Unless otherwise noted, the area code for all phone numbers in this guide is 303.

a free directory of services available through the Boulder County Health Department. Call 441-1100 for the guide. Clinics are in Boulder, 441-1160, at 3305 N. Broadway; Longmont, 678-6166, at 529 Coffman Street, Suite 200; and Lafayette/Louisville/Superior, 666-0515, at 1345 Plaza Court, Lafayette. The Ark is the county's Addiction Recovery Center, 441-1275, at 3470 N. Broadway, offering detox and treating substance abuse and co-dependency. The center also operates an impaired-driver prevention program, 441-1279.

The Boulder County AIDS Project, 444-6121, at 2118 14th Street in Boulder, offers information about prevention and treatment along with a food bank, counseling and buddy systems for clients with HIV. The Mental Health Center of Boulder County, 1333 Iris Avenue, Boulder, has a crisis line, 447-1665, and a general line, 443-8500. The Rape Crisis Team's 24-hour crisis line is 443-7300.

The Boulder Heart Institute, 440-3222, at 2750 Broadway in Boulder, offers services ranging from a basic cardiac risk-factor screening to various types of cardiac wellness programs and state-of-the-art exercise testing to assess athletes' fitness levels.

How to Find a Doctor or a Dentist

Ask friends or coworkers, check the Yellow Pages under "Physicians" or "Dentists" or call one of the area's referral services. The **Boulder County Medical Society**, 545-6178, lists around 370 doctors; and (800) DOCTORS operated by Community Health has a local phone number, 443-2584, which provides referrals to about 300 Boulder-area doctors, dentists, counselors, chiropractors, midwives and other licensed healthcare professionals. Three of the larger medical clinics also offer referrals. The **Boulder Medical Center's Patient Services**, 440-3000, lists more than 50 physicians and has satellite clinics in Louisville and Avista Hospital in Louisville. **Longmont Clinic**, 776-1234, lists around 40 local physicians and operates two satellite clinics in Longmont and one in Niwot. **Kaiser Permanente**, 440-0884, is a large health maintenance organization, which can also refer its own patients to more than 450 of their associated physicians in the Denver/Boulder area.

Cutting-edge Research

As a center for biotechnology businesses, Boulder has many experts in the latest medical breakthroughs. These businesses are described in the chapter on Boulder Business. See the "High-Tech, Biotech and The Information Highway" section.

How to Find Holistic Healthcare

At the turn of the century, tubercular patients came to Boulder to die then discovered that fresh air, mountain hikes and happy thoughts helped many live. Ever since, Boulder has been a mecca for people seeking better health in unconventional ways — and the word "wellness" is used as much as "healthcare" or "medicine." Counselors might help you strengthen the three foundations of health: nutrition, exercise and peace of mind. They go by many names: Pilates trainers, massage therapists, Chinese doctors, acupuncturists, chiropractors, naturopathic physicians, registered dietitians or herbalists . . . the list goes on.

In Boulder, the line between conventional medicine and alternative approaches is blurred. Many Boulder medical doctors appreciate how alternative practitioners can complement standard medical care. After all, it makes sense to prevent potential maladies rather than waiting for an emergency that must be treated with surgery and/or medications. Some M.D.s even point out that Western medicine earns its best stars in emergency, life-threatening situations or diseases with a clear cause. They add that with lifestyle issues, many alternative healers know a bunch more than the average medical doctor. At the excellent CU School of Medicine in Denver, for instance, basic nutrition lectures still account for only 30 hours of classroom training. Compare that to alternative healers in Boulder with hundreds, sometimes thousands, of federally accredited lecture hours focused on nutrition and nutritional counseling.

Still, even in Boulder, some traditional M.D.s mistrust alternative practitioners. It's like the mallard calling the ruddy duck "quack." A U.S. Office of Technology Assessment study found only 20 percent of all procedures used in conventional U.S. medical practice have been subjected to scientifically controlled trials. This is not to say that the other 80 percent are awful, but to point out that we're complex humans, so the issues of being, staying or getting well aren't always just black and white decisions.

If you still feel like an odd-ball for considering alternative health experts, consider this: In 1993, The New England Journal of Medicine reported that a third of all Americans used alternative medicine during 1990, making nearly a half-billion visits — more than to family physicians, pediatricians and internists combined. These consumers tended to be well-educated and between 25 and 49 years old. They spent $13.7 billion on alternative care, with around 75 percent of that money paid out-of-pocket, since many insurance plans don't cover alternative healthcare.

If you decide it's worth your money to seek alternative healthcare, you're not alone, but it will take some research. Finding the right practitioner is complicated by Colorado's vague licensing requirements, which might someday change. For the uninitiated, it's easy to confuse a certified dietitian with one who has one or two years of non-federally certified training with a registered dietician who has several years of university training. The same is true with naturopathic physicians. Some have attended federally accredited, four-year programs that have the same basics as medical school then specialize in the science and counseling skills that can help a person stick with a good diet, exercise and reduce stress. Others who call themselves naturopathic physicians have taken a correspondence course for six months through the mail. Depending on what you need, the less-qualified caregiver might be fine or a disaster.

If you are seeking an expert in wellness counseling, choose carefully. Listen for word-of-mouth recommendations. The Daily Camera's Monday FIT magazine includes a regular weekly column featuring three healers (usually an M.D. and two alternative professionals) discussing a health question from different perspectives. It's a great way to compare treatment philosophies and glean names of reputable professionals. Read the local holistic journals such as Nexus and The Light Pages, which are available at many grocery stores, especially the health-food ones. You're bound to notice possibilities that seem reasonable and appropriate for you, as well as some that are totally off-the-wall. Those aren't what you need. Look for an offering that makes sense to you. Then ask the healthcare provider about qualifications. Which program did he or she attend? What was its accreditation — for instance, federal or state? How many years of study did he or she undertake, and what is he or she qualified to do? Can he or she provide references?

Here's the most important decision regarding alternative care. Be ready to work hard yourself, whether choosing your foods more sensibly, exercising more or learning not to beat yourself up with too-high expectations. Don't expect a magical quick fix, for improving your health through lifestyle changes requires your faithful participation. But that's exactly why it can do wonders.

Interdisciplinary groups and practitioners, as well as specialists, abound. For instance, naturopathic physician Charley Cropley, 499-7574, has developed a system called Health Coach in which professionals conduct seminars to teach regular folks how to care for their health. Chiropractor Jay Wilson, 449-7414, also is knowledgeable about nutrition issues. Nancy Rao, 545-2021, and JoHanna Reilly, 541-9600, are among Boulder's half-dozen naturopathic physicians with excellent reputations in the alternative health community.

INSIDERS' TIP

Boulder Medical Equipment, 530-9640, is Boulder's most complete purveyor of wheelchairs and home medical equipment. It also services such apparatus.

Medical doctor Bob Rountree of the **Helios Health Center**, 499-9224, coauthored an excellent reference book, *Smart Medicine for a Healthier Child*, for those wanting to compare conventional and alternative therapies. Coauthor Rachel Walton is a Boulder pediatric nurse who teaches classes to new mothers on using natural medicine to care for babies and young children. Helios is an example of physicians and health professionals teaming up because they appreciate the way conventional and alternative healthcare can complement each other. In fact, one of Helios' doctors is a board-certified acupuncturist and homeopath, as well as an M.D.

Similarly, **Wellspring for Women**, 443-0321, is a group of women nurse practitioners, acupuncturists and homeopaths who have designed a practice focusing on the health needs of women. Check out these professionals and clinics, and ask them about referrals to other qualified professionals. Naturopathic physician Todd Nelson, 449-1330, and chiropractor Darryl Hobson, 449-4498, don't work out of the same office but have teamed up on Vital Health Through Wellness seminars, which include fasting and cleansing.

Wellness for Pets

So that cat isn't frisky, the dog just ate your socks, or your parrot has a cold in its beak. If you need help fast, you'll be glad to know that Boulder has many excellent vets. **Allpets Clinic**, 499-5335, at 5290 Manhattan Circle, stands out because it offers 24-hour veterinary care. This pet clinic has a welcoming fire hydrant out front for the dogs and separate entrances and waiting areas for clients with dogs and cats. In 1992, Allpets received the veterinary economics hospital design award, and in 1993 they were chosen as Boulder's small business of the year. Other vets specialize. The **Boulder Valley Cat Clinic**, 444-MEOW, at 2825 Wilderness Place, deals with feline medical and behavioral problems, offers a low-cost vaccination clinic and boasts of "no barking dogs." **Centennial Valley Animal Hospital**, 666-9363, at 360 S. McCaslin Boulevard in Louisville, handles cats, dogs and exotics. **Dr. Nancy Loving**, 444-9494, at 2160 James Canyon Drive, specializes in performance and sport horse care.

Businesses appreciate
Boulder's superb
work force, drawn by
good homes, good
education, good
services and the area's
natural grandeur.

Boulder
Business

Boulder may seem to be a laid-back tourist valley and college town. But the backbone of this county is business, and an impressive amount is clean, professional and homegrown. Manufacturing generates more than 20 percent of all jobs, making it the largest economic sector, and most manufacturing is high-tech. **StorageTek**, currently ranked number 589 on the Fortune 1,000 list, is famous for its data storage devices, employs 3,400 and has revenues around $1.9 billion each year. What's a data storage device? Imagine a box the size of a small room. This StorageTek product contains 6,000 tape cartridges that could store 5,000 years of *Wall Street Journals*. A robot inside retrieves whichever tape you need. It's not as cute as R2D2, but it always puts things back where they belong.

A StorageTek spin-off, **Exabyte**, is among the top seven companies in Boulder County, with more than 1,000 employees and nearly $380 million in gross earnings annually. And Exabyte is just a baby — not yet a dozen years old. Altogether, high-tech computer companies supply about 12,000 county jobs. Medical equipment, biotechnical products and doctor referral services provide another 4,000. Magazine subscriptions are a big deal here, for it takes high-powered databases to manage customer lists, and it takes lots of experience to promote magazine sales. **Neodata**, which provides direct marketing services for magazines, is the second-largest private employer in the county, with more than 2,500 Boulder County employees and yearly revenues of $244 million.

But high-tech isn't the only industry. The county's diversity gobbles along in **Longmont Foods'** turkey products, barrels by in **Bestop** sporty car tops, shines behind **Hunter Douglas Duette** brand window coverings, brews nicely with **Celestial Seasonings'** herb teas and grows healthily with **White Wave** tofu products. The county also emphasizes education. Public schools employ more than 5,000. Another 4,000 work at the **University of Colorado** in Boulder. The appetite for retail goods, services and entertainment supports around 300 restaurants, 40 bookstores, 1,100 lawyers and a dozen stage theater companies. Sure, thriving tourism is an asset. But even in Boulder's tourist mecca, the Pearl Street Mall, most of the shoppers and diners are Boulder residents.

This chapter describes how Boulder business developed and notes today's key industries. You'll find job statistics here and ideas on landing a Boulder career. Even if you're not a job-hunter, read on. Just as learning about wildflowers can enhance a hike, a little business lore can enrich your appreciation of Boulder. So enjoy!

Area Chambers of Commerce

Boulder	442-1044
Broomfield	466-1775
Lafayette	666-9555
Longmont	776-5295
Louisville	666-5747
Nederland	258-3926

Gritty Booms and Beautiful Dreams

Boulder County business began with transients and a single gritty industry. Virtually every mountain town above Boulder was born with gold or silver linings. Ward boomed to life in 1859 with one of the biggest gold strikes in the nation. Guess how Gold Hill got its name.

Boulder's first entrepreneurs ran a base camp for miners, supplying hay, blacksmiths, lodging and groceries. Those mother lodes didn't last, but then farmers in east Boulder County plowed up black rocks, leading to coal mining in Louisville, Lafayette, Erie and Superior.

Mining created dirty work, but it brought railroads and roads. Mining lured unscrupulous speculators, but it attracted settlers who fell in love with the valley. In 1874, before Colorado earned statehood, farmers donated 45 acres on a windswept hilltop to become a university. In 1897, the city of Boulder's well-tended residential areas, emphasis on education and beautiful natural setting attracted a summer **Chautauqua** site, bringing Texas tourists. Tourism also led to the **Hotel Boulderado** in 1909.

After World War II, the G.I. Bill brought more students to CU-Boulder and new energy for the sleepy town. Meanwhile, coal mining declined. The city of Boulder, population 20,000, decided to woo research groups such as the **National Institute of Standard Technologies**, which settled on donated land in 1950 and now employs nearly 400. In 1957, **Ball Aerospace** erected battleship-gray buildings in the town's first industrial park and won government projects so secret, windows were once boarded up. Around 1,600 work at Ball today, often assisting the space shuttle program. The giant "contact lenses" for the blurry-visioned Hubble space telescope are a Ball product. We're talking fancy eyepieces. They cost $30 million, but they have provided our most clear pictures of distant galaxies.

The honeymoon between Boulder and the **National Center for Atmospheric Research** started in 1960 and has never ended. Today NCAR employs nearly 1,000 people. Scientists from all over the world use NCAR's climate modeling center, studying topics from radar to global warming. Their enviable workplace is a stunning architectural landmark designed by I.M. Pei, set against Boulder's signature Flatirons formation.

Big Blue has been a prize catch. In 1965, **IBM** bought 604 acres of alfalfa fields and built a campus-like facility known for men in pin-striped suits, the kind who might sing Ivy League fight songs. Things are more informal now. After downsizing from 5,000-plus and

"up-sizing" from 2,000, it is currently the county's second-largest private employer, with a work force of nearly 3,000. Like other research groups, IBM offers top-notch professional jobs. It and other research anchors generate spin-off businesses that grow, thrive and lead to spin-offs of their own. Many of these operate at the Big Blue facility north of town, so the halls still buzz.

New business parks as well as new and renovated commercial buildings in downtown cores and industrial neighborhoods are attractive to companies and their workers. Businesses appreciate Boulder's superb work force, drawn by good homes, good education, good services and the area's natural grandeur. Open space purchases, bike trails and tree-lined boulevards are among our finest assets. And the mother lodes that brought the first settlers have proved less of a gold mine than the beautiful mountains themselves.

Business Today

Boulder is a leader in research and development. More than 140,000 people work in the county. In the city of Boulder, 43 percent of the labor force works in executive, managerial or professional occupations. That's nearly twice the white collar employment rate of the United States overall. Business diversity has given the economy so much resiliency, it has grown even as traditional county leaders, such as IBM and Ball Brothers, downsize. Remember when "structural unemployment," that is, the time between posting a want ad and filling it, meant unemployment could not go below 4 percent? Boulder's unemployment rate has been below that for the last few years. In March 1996, county unemployment was 3.5 percent, up slightly from the previous year.

High-tech, Biotech and The Information Highway

While computer-related businesses provide most of the county's high-tech jobs, information highway companies are growing too. Through phone lines, power lines, fiber-optic cables and more, they're designing better ways to stay informed. Boulder's biggest information think-tank is **US West Technologies**, with nearly 700 employees, the county's 12th-largest private employer.

Up-and-comers are everywhere. You know that annoying squeal you hear when you dial a fax line? **Radish Communications** provides ways to talk on the phone while your computer silently sends faxes and other data on the same line. Suppose a friend has a heart attack, and you're so scared, you forget your address. **SCC** specializes in software for emergency-response groups. Its enhanced 911 service identifies your location automatically. **Information+Graphic Systems** designs mapping software for phone companies and other utilities.

High-tech wouldn't be high-tech without new ways of communicating, and the Internet and World Wide Web are the most high-profile means among new ways. Among the Boulder companies that can design websites and/or provide Internet services are **The Internet Connection**, 442-3909 (e-mail: corkill@boulder.net) and **Lucrative Links**, 440-4950 (e-mail: goffinet@bcbr.com). To learn more about area providers, put the annual **High Country NEXPO**, held annually in Denver in mid- to late September, on your calendar or check it out on the Web (http://www.press-1.com/nexpo/).

Boulder is also into biotechnology. **Valleylab's** laparoscopic equipment allows surgeons to make tiny incisions, then use miniature video cameras to display the operating site. For a patient, this means less trauma and faster recovery time. Valleylab employs some 900, making it the county's eighth-largest private employer. **Ohmeda** made its name with a monitor that nurses clip on a patient's finger to show whether he or she needs extra oxygen. **Somatogen** is developing a blood substitute that someday might guarantee disease-free transfusions. **Hauser** extracts special products from natural sources, ranging from exquisitely aromatic vanilla to cancer-fighting drugs. **Colorado Medtech** specializes in products related to respiratory diagnosis and therapy. **NeXstar Pharmaceuticals** is on the cutting edge of AIDS research and received FDA approval for a drug that treats Karposi's sarcoma, an AIDS-related form of cancer.

Lifestyle and "Vision" Companies

Personal passions have built great businesses. Ex-ski racer Dave Jacobs designed the super-sleek, spider-logo suits worn by members of the U.S. Ski Team, made by Boulder's **Spyder Active Sports**. Cycling champion Davis Phinney not only runs a local bike shop but is a principal in cyclewear-maker **Pearl Izumi**, which is moving to Broomfield in 1997. Broomfield-based **Lowe Alpine**, which makes climbing gear, packs and climbing equipment, was started by passionate climbers and mountaineers. A world-class wine expert runs the **Boulder Wine Merchant**. The founder of Boulder-based **Soldier of Fortune** magazine is also the director of the National Rifle Association. The owner of the greeting card company **Leanin' Tree** loves, collects and displays Western art at the company's Gunbarrel headquarters.

Not all labor-of-love enterprises started in Boulder. Scwhinn bicycles were manufactured in Chicago for a century before the venerable company was rescued from bankruptcy and re-created in Boulder as **Schwinn Cycling and Fitness**. The company still makes its trademark chrome-trimmed, whitewall-adorned classics for nostalgic buyers, but it is now also a leading supplier of thoroughly modern mountain, racing, freestyle, BMX and children's bikes as well as stationary bikes for health and fitness centers.

Some of Boulder's finest mainstream successes are the actualization of New Age, hippie dreams. Hand-gathered mountain herbs, sold in muslin bags, led to **Celestial Seasonings**. Owners of **The Peppercorn**, the posh kitchen store, still consider themselves flower children. **Alfalfa's** and **Wild Oats** mirror their founders' faith that cooks want fresh, natural and organic foods. Each of these health-food/gourmet groceries, which are now part of the same corporation, has grown well beyond the county, with two dozen stores in five different states.

Environmentalism is a vision too. **E Source** is a research group that helps power companies think in "negawatts" by giving them the latest information about energy-saving equipment. **Environmental Communication Specialists**, or ECOS, is a communications firm that educates people about the environment. **Planetary Solutions** sells energy-saving light bulbs and carpet made of recycled soda bottles. **Communication Arts** finds ways to enhance the city environment. It helped plan Boulder's Pearl Street Mall, renovated Madison Square Garden and is designing projects for Disney.

Sometimes the environmental job is grim. At the now-closed, formerly top-secret **Rocky Flats** nuclear weapons plant south of Boulder, engineers are trying to undo the mess left by plutonium trigger manufacturing. Their goal is to make the area stable and safe, and possibly so clean that a child would be safe eating a "mud pie" made from Rocky Flats dirt. It will be a pricey mud pie — the cleanup cost is estimated at $10 billion, with the EPA footing the bill.

More upbeat are people selling optimism. When Jimmy Calano told his college professor he wanted to help people have great careers, the professor called it a dead-end idea. True to his motivation seminars, Calano persevered. **ETC w/ CareerTrack**, which he co-founded in 1982, employs more than 400, grossing nearly $80 million a year, and is now owned by the cable TV giant TCI and New Networks Inc., an electronic media development company.

In 1996, the University of Colorado created **University Technology Corp.** to handle licensing and royalty agreements, invention disclosures, patent filings and other forms of technology transfer on behalf of CU's fertile-minded faculty. Revenues from commercially viable projects undertaken by faculty members and researchers are shared between the university and the faculty members, and well-marketed, successful inventions, discoveries and developments also add cachet both to the university and to the Boulder community.

And, of course, Boulder is full of dance, music, arts and crafts because creative people make it their home.

Real Estate

The Boulder real estate market got so hot, many brokers were saying, "Hey, don't get too jealous of us. We've been in some lean years before." The market cooled in 1995 and rebounded again in 1996. Still, price increases have left affordable housing as a key concern among city of Boulder residents. Which begs an important question: If you decide you love it here, how do you afford to live here?

Working in Boulder

Statistically, a Boulder worker is likely to be 25 to 44 years old, as likely to be single as married, in a household of roughly two people. He or she (46 percent of Boulder's workers are women) has lived in Boulder about seven years, with a professional job that earns roughly $33,000. That's well above the national average. More than 20 percent of Boulder's families have a total income of more than $75,000, compared with 11 percent in the United States overall. The typical Boulder worker is white — in case you hadn't noticed, 92 percent of Boulderites are white. Age, sex, race and disability discrimination in Boulder are not considered major obstacles. Since diversity has given the Boulder business economy strength, more ethnic and cultural diversity within the working population would be great.

Finding a Job

Boulder's job market is strong but competitive. About 60 percent of Boulder's adults have a bachelor's degree or higher, making

Photo: Daily Camera

The National Center for Atmospheric Research was the first federal research facility built in Boulder.

them among the very best educated work forces in the United States. But many move to Boulder because they love it and then start looking for jobs. Also, professional jobs go through their own kinds of booms and busts. Computer types reeled from the blow dealt by StorageTek's 1987 bankruptcy (from which it successfully emerged). Real estate and mortgage bankers flocked to Boulder a few years ago, but the flock has thinned since the real estate boom flattened. Counselors and therapists discovered Boulder is a mecca for those who can guide people in how to be healthier and happier. Other specialists including massage therapists, exercise physiologists, personal trainers and assorted counselors have found Boulder's health-, lifestyle- and fitness-oriented populations so congenial that the city has one of the highest ratios of such professionals in the nation. But so many have moved to town that some eventually left to find less competition and greener pastures, and others have joined the ranks of the underemployed. You might find that the supermarket checkout clerk, the doctor's receptionist, waiter or the painter touching up your cabinets has a Ph.D. — or at least is a doctoral candidate.

For newcomers, the specter of similar underemployment and the rising cost of living in the city of Boulder, primarily due to the high cost of housing, are issues that must be considered. Unless you land a well-paying job, you may have to live outside the city.

A common, fast job route is using temporary employment agencies such as **Express Personnel Services**, **Olsten Staffing Services**, **Boulder Temporaries** and **COREStaff**. For some people, temporary work is a stop-gap until they find a permanent position. Others enjoy the variety and flexible schedules of temp work. For still others, a good working day leads to a month-long contract, then a full-time job.

Finding a Career

Landing the job that leads to the career you've wanted takes longer. Many employers who place help-wanted ads get deluged with hundreds of applications. And in a fast-moving, entrepreneurial environment, people tend to hire someone they know, making a resume hire a more remote possibility. Getting involved in the business community and volunteering can acquaint you with potential businesses — and vice versa. Or if you take an entry-level job in a promising company, then do a fantastic job, you may get promoted. There is always the option of living in Boulder or one of the surrounding communities and commuting to Denver and its close-in suburbs.

Starting Your Own Business

According to the Small Business Association, 75 percent of all businesses fail in the first five years. Boulder's failure rate is similar, but success, when it happens, seems sweeter here. The market gets more competitive every year as major companies and national chains move in. But opportunities remain. More than 4,000 small businesses make Boulder their home. The **Boulder Chamber of Commerce** runs many programs to help such small business people, including a CEO exchange, where business leaders meet regularly and take turns role-playing as executives and board members to help each other sort out key decisions facing entrepreneurs.

The Crystal Ball

The biggest challenge to Boulder's dynamic community is its own success. Classic growth/success models require more people and more activity for an economy to remain vital. But growth for growth's sake could consume the remaining open space, smother the air, continue to increase traffic congestion and destroy the quality people cherish. An alternative would be to "Aspen-ize" or "Santa Barbara-ize" Boulder. That is, let the population become a haven for rich retirees or free-spending vacationers. The stereotypical Aspen lifestyle raises eyebrows in Boulder because its job opportunities have shifted to low-paying service jobs such as operating ski lifts, waiting on tables and cleaning rooms. Mean-

while, Aspen's rents and living costs have skyrocketed, meaning many who work there must make their homes in more affordable communities miles away. Boulderites are facing a similar trend.

Private-sector employees as well as municipal employees from street maintenance workers to teachers who once could live within the Boulder neighborhood where they worked now often buy in Lafayette, Broomfield or Longmont, where homes are more affordable, and then commute into Boulder. Such demographic shifts have caused the dreaded traffic-congestion monster to rear its head. Different options are considered and debated all the time by citizens and municipal officials alike.

In September 1995, the City Council passed a growth-management ordinance, whose feature was limiting commercial, industrial and retail building permits. With the mid-'90s boom in full swing, it wasn't long before this controversial descendant of long-standing residential construction limits resulted in a huge backlog of applications. By April 1996, after strong protests from some of the city's most respected and best established businesses, the Council began rethinking the ordinance, but there still remains strong commitment both to slowing business growth within the city of Boulder and mitigating traffic that such growth brings. Other concepts including "downzoning," raising commercial development fees and encouraging businesses to consider some of the booming "bedroom" communities surrounding Boulder. Indeed, some businesses that found they could not expand in Boulder — Pearl Izumi and Rockbottom Brewery among them — have begun moving to Longmont, Louisville and Broomfield.

Boulder struggles to steer a steady course

to keep high-quality jobs, high education and a high quality of life balanced with open space and density, affordable housing and prosperity, and careful planning with a zaniness that fosters both genius and serendipity.

No other area represents what most Boulderites hope our county can be. But in Boulder, the very air can sparkle with those inventive, "Eureka!" ideas. This place is blessed with people who pluck inspiration from the sky, wrestle it to the ground and create real services, real products and a real quality life.

So, if you love it here, you've got a chance. You may be just what this area needs. If you have the guts, the talent and, dare we say — karma — then give Boulder your very best.

Celebrating its 16th anniversary, *Nexus* describes itself as a holistic health and natural lifestyles directory and magazine for Boulder, Denver and the whole of Colorado.

Boulder
Media

Boulder has its own fairly comprehensive media system through newspapers and magazines but relies on Denver for much of its television and radio information — though local radio stations (see this chapter's Close-up) are the favorites and provide National Public Radio news and information, BBC news and other sources. Surrounding communities provide some excellent radio stations as well.

Newspapers and Magazines

Boulder has one complete daily newspaper, the *Daily Camera*, which is a Knight-Ridder Inc. newspaper. Knight-Ridder is one of the nation's largest newspaper companies. The *Colorado Daily* focuses more on University of Colorado news and readers. The 3-year-old *Boulder Weekly* is an alternative paper. Of course, the large Denver papers, the *Denver Post* and *Rocky Mountain News*, and Denver's arts and entertainment weekly, *Westword*, are also available locally and cover Boulder County news to a much lesser degree. Following are the most popular local publications.

Boulder County Business Report
4865 Sterling Dr., Ste. 200, Boulder
• 440-4950

This monthly newspaper is a leading information source on trends in real estate, high technology, finance, tourism and business. A subscription is $20 per year, or the paper is free at 250 local drop sites.

Boulder County Guide
P.O. Box 1075, Boulder 80306 • 442-3909

Published annually, this free guide has numerous local restaurant menus completely re-produced plus shopping, services and recreation and a professional directory. Look for it in local shops, bookstores, supermarkets and other drop sites.

Boulder Magazine
1919 14th St., Ste. 709, Boulder • 443-0600

Published three times a year, summer, fall and winter/spring, this handy guide has all kinds of local information and interesting articles on local people, places and things to do. Subscriptions are $15 per year, or people can request a specific issue for $5. The magazine is free at numerous local drop sites.

Boulder Weekly
690 S. Lashley Ln., Boulder • 494-5511

Specializing in news, arts and entertainment, this 3-year-old, weekly paper was possibly the first, nationally, to break the news of the militia connection to the Oklahoma City bombing. A local Branch Davidian member had telephoned the office on the day of the bombing with word of the connection. It has columns, investigative articles and interviews with local people plus entertainment, a classified section and other special sections. The paper is free at numerous local drop sites.

Broomfield Enterprise
1006 Depot Hill Rd, Ste. G, Broomfield
• 466-3636

This free weekly community paper covers all the news from and is the local source of information for the nearby city of Broomfield, including sports, schools, editorials, a quarterly special section on business, classified ads and features. Special sections cover such topics as homes, gardens, car care and holiday shopping. The *Enterprise* is the only paper that is delivered to every household and business in Broomfield.

Colorado Daily
5505 Central Ave., Boulder • 443-6272

Published since 1897, this free and informative independent paper serves the university community and Boulder. It's published five days a week — Friday is an extra-large weekend edition. In summer, it cuts back to two days a week. The paper covers local, regional and national news plus sports and entertainment, and has a very vocal editorial and letters to the editor section. There are also classified advertisements.

Daily Camera
1048 Pearl St., Boulder
• 442-1202

The *Camera*, Boulder's only complete daily newspaper, covers the people, issues and events of Boulder, CU-Boulder, neighboring towns and Boulder County. Regular daily sections and pages present local, national and international news, business news and entertainment news. The *Camera's* award-winning sports section is competitive with Denver dailies and covers local preps, CU and Denver's professional teams and features special sections on skiing and the Bolder Boulder 10k race.

The larger Sunday *Camera* includes separate sections for business, lifestyles, entertainment, a TV guide, color comics, news-focus stories, local guest opinions and *The New York Times'* Crossword Puzzle. Among the weekday special-interest sections are *FIT*, a weekly health and fitness tabloid; *Business Plus*; a food section; *Discovery*, a science and technology section; *Outdoors* for local recreation; and *Friday Magazine* for entertainment in Boulder, Denver and along the Front Range. *Neighbors* is a weekly tabloid that covers and is circulated in other Boulder County cities and towns, including Lafayette, Louisville, Superior, Erie and Broomfield.

Special sections throughout the year include the *Boulder County Almanac*, *Best of Boulder*, back to school and college sections, a *Holiday Guide* and *Memories*, a monthly tab-

> ## FYI
> Unless otherwise noted, the area code for all phone numbers in this guide is 303.

loid of engagement, wedding and anniversary announcements.

Camera writers, photographers, ads, sections and the whole paper have won awards from various state and national organizations.

The *Camera* has just started putting its information on the Internet through BoulderNews (http://www.bouldernews.com).

Nexus: Colorado's Holistic Journal
1680 Sixth St., Ste. 6, Boulder • 442-6662

Celebrating its 16th anniversary, Nexus describes itself as a holistic health and natural lifestyles directory and magazine for Boulder, Denver and the whole of Colorado. Readers will be amazed at the variety of therapies available locally. Subscriptions are $18 per year (six issues), or the paper is free at health-food stores, bookstores, restaurants, shops and universities around Boulder and the state.

Radio Stations

The numerous Denver radio stations that broadcast in Boulder are listed here along with the more popular local stations. See this chapter's Close-up for details on Boulder's local radio favorites.

Adult Contemporary
KOSI 101.1 FM
KHHT 107.5 FM

Big Band
KEZW 1430 AM (Nostalgia, Big Band and easy listening)

Christian
KRKS 990 AM and **94.7 FM** (Christian/talk)

Classical
KCFR 90.1 FM (Colorado Public Radio, classical, National Public Radio and local news)
KVOD 92.5 FM (Classical, public radio news)

Community

KGNU 88.5 FM (in Boulder/Denver); **93.7** (in Ward and the mountain regions)

Country

KYGO 98.5 FM
KLMO 1060 AM (Country, Paul Harvey and ABC News)

Jazz

KHIH 95.7 FM (Jazz, other music, news)

News/Talk

KHOW 630 AM (News, talk and popular morning show)
KTLK 760 AM
KOA 850 AM (News, talk, sports)
KHOW2 1190 AM (Simulcast and satellite talk shows)
KBVI 1490 AM (Boulder Valley news and music)

Oldies

KXKL (KOOL) 105.1 FM

Public Radio

KUNC 91.5 FM (Classical, jazz, oldies, new and alternative)

Rock

KTCL 93.3 FM (Modern rock and new music)
KXPK 96.5 FM (Alternative and retro)
KBCO 97.3 FM Boulder (Adult album alternative)
KKHK 99.5 FM (Classic rock)
KIMN 100.3 FM (Classic rock)
KRFX 103.5 (Classic rock)
KBPI 106.7 FM (Classic and progressive rock)

Sports

KKFN 950 AM (Sports/talk)

Top-40

KALC 105.9 FM

Television Stations

Depending on the location in Boulder, TV reception can be a bit fuzzy to completely nonexistent because of the mountains. Reception without cable is even worse in mountain towns, such as Nederland. For this reason many area residents have cable.

Besides the broadcast stations listed subsequently, there are more than 30 cable stations, including Channel 8, the City of Boulder station, which is available only on Boulder Cable. The city channel has all types of programs on local issues, such as the environment, seniors, arts, city council meetings, sports and leisure and information programs on science, travel and much more. TCI cable Channel 54 is Community Access TV of Boulder and sort of local public television with talk shows and community interest programs. It also provides the audio for Radio Reading Services of the Rockies, a program for the blind with reading of the *Daily Camera*, *Rocky Mountain News*, *Denver Post* and *Colorado Daily* newspapers plus BBC News and local weather.

Broadcast Television Stations

KWGN Channel 2 (Independent/WB)
KCNC Channel 4 (CBS)
KRMA Channel 6 (PBS)
KMGH Channel 7 (ABC)
KUSA Channel 9 (NBC)
KBDI Channel 11/12 (Community/PBS)

INSIDERS' TIP

Through BoulderNews (http://www.bouldernews.com), online users can browse the daily *Camera*, access special sections and dining and entertainment listings, and keep up with the CU-Boulder Golden Buffaloes teams. BoulderNews also offers a link to the *Camera's* news library. Plans call for *The Insiders' Guide®* to *Boulder and Rocky Mountain National Park* and *The Insiders' Guide®* to *Greater Denver* to also have links from BoulderNews.

KTVD Channel 20 (Independent/UPN)
KVDR Channel 31 (Independent Fox)

Cable Television

There are only two cable suppliers for Boulder: **Jones Intercable Inc.**, 978-9771, and **Boulder Cable** (owned by TCI Cablevision of Colorado Inc.), 930-2000. Residents don't have a choice and must use the company that supplies cable for their particular address. For Nederland, in the mountains, the cable company **Pagosa Vision**, 258-0304 or (800) 222-1332, is the only choice other than satellite dish.

Boulder's Local Radio Favorites

From Boulder Community Broadcast Asso. Inc., **KGNU 88.5 FM** has been going strong in Boulder for 18 years. This community radio station is as varied as any station you'd hope to find, even in a big city. It features interviews with all types of people and plays all types of music, including folk, rock, rap, punk and thrash, bluegrass, country, honky-tonk, jazz, rhythm and blues, ragtime, reggae and world beat (music

from foreign countries), gospel, classical, international folk and cultural music. You'll also enjoy local music, spoken word, radio drama, news and public affairs, including the BBC news hour every afternoon, Pacifica Network News, Christian Science Monitor News, Hemispheres, Latin American News, Latino USA and La Lucha Sigue. There are talk shows, including "Connections" on Friday from 8:30 to 9:30 AM and a Thursday evening call-in show from 6 to 7 PM. Environment and science programs include "Living on Earth," 4 to 4:30 PM Monday and Boulder-produced "E-Town," Saturday from noon to 1 PM. "New Dimensions" features philosophical conversations on Sundays from 11 AM to noon, and "Love of Wisdom" by Alan Watts is a show on spirituality every Tuesday from 9 to 9:30 AM. *Counterspin* is an alternative news magazine from *FAIR* (Fairness and Accuracy in Reporting) magazine that airs at 5:30 and 9 AM Mondays. "Naturally" with Brigitte Mars, a local herbalist, airs weekly at 10:30 AM on Monday and 8:25 AM Wednesday. Tune into the "Grateful Dead Hour" at 8 PM Saturdays — and much more. For those interested in helping out, KGNU has a large volunteer contingency. Call 449-4885 for a complete program.

Also the favorite of many Boulderites, **KUNC 91.5 FM**, (800) 321-5862, broadcasts from the University of Northern Colorado in Greeley and plays classical, jazz, oldies, new music and an eclectic variety of other sounds. KUNC has regular NPR news in the morning and evening and such commentary favorites as "Morning Edition" from 4 to 9 AM on weekday mornings and 6 to 10 AM Saturday and Sunday. "All Things Considered" runs 4 to 5:30 PM and 6 to 6:30 PM Monday through Friday; 6 to 7 PM Saturday and Sunday. "Marketplace" is on Monday through Friday from 5:30 to 6 PM. Other popular shows include "Music From the Hearts of Space" from 9 to 10 PM on Tuesday and "Echos" from 10 PM to 2 AM Sunday through Thursday.

Excellent locally produced shows are "New Dimensions," philosophical conversations from 7 to 8 PM Saturday, and "Air Currents," new music selected by announcer Julie Amacher from 1 to 2 PM Sunday and 9 to 10 PM Monday. Garrison Keillor's "A Prairie Home Companion" is on from 4 to 6 PM every Saturday and from 10 AM to noon Sunday. For jazz lovers, Saturday evening features "Jazz Profiles" at 8 PM and "Jazz from the Lincoln Center" at 9 PM, followed by "Jazz After Hours" from 10 PM to 4 AM (same time on Fridays too). The Boulder-produced music and environmental news radio show "E-Town" is on from 3 to 4 PM Saturdays. The national favorite "Car Talk" is on from 10 to 11 AM Saturday mornings. "Thistle and Shamrock," on from noon to 1 PM Sunday, features Celtic music. KUNC is partially funded by education grants from the university and by membership donations.

The vista from the
Flagstaff Mountain
Amphitheater
makes it a favored
wedding site.

Boulder
Worship

In the studio of her Boulder home, an iconographer creates beautiful icons for her Antiochian Orthodox Church and for other orthodox churches in the Denver area. Across the street, a couple holds Jehovah's Witness meetings in their living room. Next door, a Protestant family has taken in another church member's kids for the day to give the parents some respite. Down the street, a conservative Jewish family leaves the car behind on Saturdays and strolls, dropping by to visit neighbors. Their friends include a family where the mom's agnostic, the dad's atheist and the kids have classmates ranging from Episcopalians to Unitarians to Buddhists.

How people worship is one of the best aspects of Boulder. Many Boulderites gain deep meaning from their religious focus but feel that, just as many phone companies can help a person make a long-distance call, many fine creeds can help a person connect with spirituality.

This chapter provides some history and current events involving Boulder's religious community. It then describes worship centers located downtown — easy for both tourists and newcomers to reach. It ends by describing other groups that are part of the rich texture of Boulder worship.

From Pioneer Churches to the Gay-rights Debates

In 1859 a Methodist circuit preacher delivered Boulder's first sermon to 50 people. Churches of other denominations followed, their spires leading pioneers across the prairie. The First Congregational Church, now site of the Carnegie Library on Pine Street, had Boulder's first full-time pastor, building and church bell. A few churches of historical sig-

nificance still stand. Longmont's **St. Stephen's Episcopal Church**, 776-1072, 470 Main Street, was built in 1881. The building now houses an art gallery, and worship is held at 1303 S. Bross Lane. That same year, Colorado's first Swedish community built the **Swedish Evangelical Lutheran Church of Ryssby**, 776-2704, on 63rd Street south of Nelson Road. They styled it after Swedish churches but built with local sandstone. Members hold special midsummer and Christmas ceremonies with sermons in Swedish. For the winter service, they decorate the simple chapel with evergreen boughs and candles that make halos on winter-frosted panes. The church is very popular for weddings, and brides and grooms often leave in horse-drawn buggies. Another church still standing is the **Lafayette Congregational Church**, 665-4206, where wives and mothers prayed for peace during a 1910 coal-miners' strike. The plain, white church at 300 E. Simpson Street is currently the public library's theater.

For many people, worship includes a loving connection with the past. That's one reason the **Columbia Cemetery**, between Pleasant and Ninth streets in Boulder, is so special. It was started by the Columbia Masonic Lodge No. 14 in Ward. The mining lodge wanted town plots because plots in the mountains were frozen in the winter. Columbia became a more general cemetery later. Town fathers and mothers buried under the grand trees include Mary Rippon, the first female CU professor and the woman for whom the Mary Rippon Theatre was named, and Andrew Macky, for whom CU's Macky Auditorium was named. Perhaps the most poignant memorial is a child's tombstone, shaped like a lollipop.

If you enjoy religious history, check with **Historic Boulder**, 444-5192, at 646 Pearl Street. This nonprofit group occasionally conducts tours of sacred places and has a self-guided tour for sale (see our Attractions chapter for details). They also keep lists of historic buildings in which people may hold weddings. The vista from the **Flagstaff Mountain Amphitheater** makes it a favored wedding site. Many such special places around Boulder exude much greater spirituality than anything man-made, and feeling closer to a higher power is one reason many walk Boulder's nature trails.

But worship is about more than creating, or finding, special places. The **First Congregational Church** was Boulder's first church. It helped raise funds to bring CU to town, and for many years, its ministers taught philosophy at the new university. Grandma Dartt was a Seventh-Day Adventist who trudged through young Boulder's saloons, offering temperance and religious information. In 1895, the Seventh-Day Adventists began building a tuberculosis sanatorium where Mapleton Avenue heads up Sunshine Canyon. A popular hiking trail, Mount Sanitas Trail, is named after the health center, and the Mapleton Rehabilitation Clinic stands there today. (The **Seventh-Day Adventist Church**, 442-1522, is nearby at 345 Mapleton Avenue.)

In addition to contributing to a community's social welfare, religion helps define its point of view. The Seventh-Day Adventists made education headlines in 1897 when they asked that references to God be deleted from the Pledge of Allegiance. While they believed in God, the Adventists objected to any union of church and state. Many other churches, and legal experts, agreed, pointing out that state law prohibited "religious tests" in the classroom. European Catholics and Jews arriving during the 1920s, when the Ku Klux Klan was strong in Colorado, sometimes encountered burning crosses. It took time for the largely Protestant community to welcome these foreigners and their religious outlooks.

Separation of church and state crops up periodically as an issue. During the 1960s the State Board of Education backed religious and civic groups that asked that schools refrain from Christmas pageants. These days, school kids may sing songs from many religions at "winter festivals." "The Bible as Literature" is taught in high school, but the focus is on informing people about various religions rather than requiring a religious choice. Still, seemingly small events create a large furor where issues of separation of church and state are concerned. Before Christmas 1995, a big fuss developed after people started hanging little angel ornaments from a tree on public land, and the following spring, law enforcement officials were taken to task for marking sites of fatal vehicular accidents with white crosses as part of a safety awareness campaign.

The **Interfaith Council**, 443-2291, embodies Boulder's egalitarianism. Its members represent many of the world's major religions. The group includes approximately 40 of Boulder's hundreds of religious communities — mainstream Protestant and Catholic churches, synagogues, Buddhists, Baha'i, Islam and some evangelical churches. The Interfaith Council has helped establish the **Boulder Shelter for the Homeless**, **Share-a-Gift** and the **Counseling Center**. The council also grapples with social issues. Giving women more choices in church leadership and alleviating hunger are topics the council tackles. Various members share religious perspectives. The Muslims have given talks about Islam. Michael Medved, a nationally known movie reviewer who is Jewish, talked before the council on violence in the media.

Although no longer in Boulder, another group with a prolific history is the **Promise Keepers**, 421-2800 in Wheat Ridge and 964-7500 in Denver, founded in 1990 by former CU-Boulder Football Coach Bill McCartney. With friends, he organized the Promise Keepers as a "Christ-centered ministry, dedicated to uniting men through vital relationships to become Godly influences in their world." Members follow conservative evangelical and Catholic teachings. Promise Keepers' gatherings held nationwide generally draw 50,000 men at a time to hear speeches and participate in one-on-one, personal conversations. Common topics are how to be a better husband and father, how to manage money and

FYI

Unless otherwise noted, the area code for all phone numbers in this guide is 303.

The Scandinavian midsummer festival is celebrated at historic Ryssby Church.

how to pray. Initially held on the CU-Boulder campus — creating controversy — the local gathering has now moved to Denver.

Worship Centers

The *Daily Camera* newspaper's weekly religion calendar lists groups, sites and congregations ranging from the Ability Development for Christian Scouts to the Zen Practice Center. And with such variety, Boulder offers something to meet everyone's spiritual needs or desire for spiritual exploration.

Near the Pearl Street Mall

It's no surprise that most of Boulder's oldest — and many of the biggest — houses of worship are downtown, within walking distance of the Pearl Street Mall, which has been the civic center of town for a long time.

First Presbyterian, 442-3523, at 1820 15th Street, has an estimated 2,400 members, with 2,000 attending Sunday services. The building celebrated its 100th year in 1995. Members describe it as a reformed, evangelical church with a big, warm congregation. It has large teen, singles and college groups plus other smaller groups so people can become affiliated. The church provides space for performances by local music groups, such as the Boulder Bach Festival, and for recitals by stu-

dent groups. It offers summer camps, snow camps and weekly school programs in everything from crafts and cooking to family conflict resolution.

Sacred Heart of Jesus, 442-6158, at 2312 Mapleton Avenue, is a Roman Catholic church with more than 1,200 registered households and lots of people who drop in. Sacred Heart School, across the street, is affiliated with the parish. The large community outreach program includes a lunch program for transients and distribution of food baskets. The church offers daily masses in English and a weekly Spanish mass.

Karma Dzong Shambhala Center, 444-0190, at 1345 Spruce Street, is a center for Tibetan Buddhism called "Vajrayana," which translates as "diamond vehicle." The center includes 600 adult members, making it one of the largest communities of practicing Tibetan Buddhists in the West. The top floor, a shrine room, is full of traditional Tibetan red and gold. People are welcome to drop by in the afternoon. Every Sunday, there's a 10:30 AM open house that includes a talk on Buddhism, meditation and a question-and-answer session. Members say although Buddhism may sound exotic, it's very ordinary; it's about living your life well, with compassion and wisdom.

St. John's, 442-5246, at 1419 Pine Street, is a traditional Episcopal Church with very contemporary sensibilities. Among Boulder Episcopalian churches, it's the only "AIDS-aware faith community" — and is one of the few such of any denomination. The congregation, which now numbers about 800, was founded in 1873 and is one of the oldest in town. The present church, where the big *Messiah* Sing-along happens each December (see our Festivals and Annual Events chapter), dates back to 1902.

The **First Baptist Church**, 442-6530, at 1237 Pine Street, was founded in 1872, making it one of the oldest churches in town. Their Chancel Choir and the Handbell Choir are well-known for concerts and cantatas. A group called The Creation is a gathering for celebrating diversity and community through theater, music, dance and art.

First United Methodist Church, 442-3770, is at 1401 Spruce Street, and **Grace Lutheran Church**, 442-1883, is at 1001 13th Street. The **Christian Science Reading Room**, 442-0335, is at 1434 Pearl Street, on the Pearl Street Mall. It is an extension of the **Church of Christ Science**, 442-0335, nearby at 2243 Mapleton Avenue. The **First Congregational Church**, 442-1787, at 1128 Pine Street, across from the original Congregational church site, is a medium-size, liberal church with about 800 members.

That's just a sampling of the worship centers near downtown.

Around the County

The **Unitarian Universalist Church**, 494-0195, at 5001 Pennsylvania Avenue, mirrors Boulder's liberalism. The church welcomes diversity of race, age, abilities, sexual orientation, culture and religious backgrounds to its adults' services and children's classes.

Boulder Vineyard Christian Fellowship, 449-3330, at 7845 Lookout Road in Niwot, is a nondenominational/evangelical/charismatic church, started in 1982. Close to 2,000 people attend Sunday services, which often include contemporary Christian music, lively sermons and homey, inspirational stories. Pastor James Ryle calls the last 20 years of his life God's gift to him of undoing the first 20 years of his life, which included time in a bleak orphanage and a stint in prison. Teaching biblical insights and positive family-raising skills are important parts of his ministry, and the church prides itself on its active and involved children's and youth ministry as well.

Unity of Boulder, 442-1411, at 2855 Folsom Avenue, is a New Age, Christian church. It has grown considerably since 1975, when minister Jack Groverland came to town. He's a dynamic speaker, and sermons are full of both laughter and seriousness. The Unity newsletter goes out to 2,600 people, and 1,000 people come to two different Sunday services. Nearly 3,000 people have taken the church's Course in Miracles, a year-long course that starts each quarter. Unity puts on a professional-quality Christmas play that ends up being both entertaining and enlightening, thanks to the great singing, music, philosophical religious themes and humor. The church offers both Sunday school and a summer day camp called Angel Camp.

Camp St. Malo, 444-5177, a Catholic conference facility at 10758 Colo. Highway 7, near Allenspark, is where Pope John Paul II rested on his 1993 trip through Colorado. **St. Catherine's**, better known as the "Chapel on the Rock," is at the same location. During the summer, it is open to the public, with Sunday masses occasionally held from Memorial Day to Labor Day.

Just east of Boulder is the **Benedictine Catholic Abbey of St. Walburga**, 494-5733, at 6717 South Boulder Road. The Abbey is a monastic working community, right down to the farm. The nuns also run a retreat house and a gift shop, where they sell home-baked cookies and arts and crafts. It is open Saturday afternoons and by appointment. The lovely chapel and retreat house are generally open to the public, but some areas are closed. The novel *Lilies of the Field* supposedly was inspired by the Abbey, but not in any way by its history. Due to growing development and traffic in this once-tranquil area, the Abbey plans

---

INSIDERS' TIP

Karma Dzong Shambhala Center is one of the largest communities of practicing Tibetan Buddhists in the West.

to move to a quieter location outside Boulder. At this writing, the projected moving date is September 1997.

Next door is the **Sacred Heart of Mary**, 494-7572, at 6739 South Boulder Road, which was built in 1873 and is the oldest Catholic church in Boulder County. It started as a Prairie Church and still has an old cemetery in the back. Its priest describes it as a progressive, medium-size congregation with lots of families, meeting in a beautiful church. The church offers classes in adult education and centering prayer. Drop-ins are welcome at daily mass.

Around 8 percent of the Boulder population is Jewish, according to Allied Jewish Federation surveys. The Jewish community is very active in civic and local affairs. Area synagogues include **Bonai Shalom**, 442-6605, 1527 Cherryvale Road, a conservative synagogue of nearly 150 households, nestled near a pretty stream, and **Har Hashem**, 499-7077, 3950 Baseline Road, a reform congregation. Both offer programs for youths, singles and families, and Hebrew school education.

The **Second Baptist Church of Boulder**, 499-4668, 5300 Baseline Road, has 300 members and a great musical presence. The Community Choir is open to any church member who likes to sing; the Men's Chorus, to males who like to do so; and Angels Without Wings, a chorus for children ages 3 to 13. The Shekinah Glory Choir is a young adult choir of superb voices and has performed all around the Denver area. **Boulder Meeting of Friends**, 447-2168, Quaker group, meets at 1825 Upland Avenue for Sunday morning worship. The **Boulder Mennonite Church**, 443-3889, at 1520 Euclid Avenue, has a strong emphasis on family, service and faithful daily living. It founded the **Victim-Offender Reconciliation Program**, in which volunteers are trained to mediate in the community court system in property-related teen offenses. The **Islamic Center of Boulder**,

444-6345, is at 1530 Culver Court. The **Jesusonian Foundation**, 581-0456, at 4699 Nautilus Court S., #304, sells Urantia Books and secondary works. Urantia study groups have approximately 100 members. Mo Siegel, president of Celestial Seasonings, is a proponent of the Urantia Books, which use lots of the lessons in the Bible but add accounts of times such as the childhood of Jesus.

The **Shoshoni Yoga Retreat**, 642-0116, 21614 Colo. Highway 119, has log cabins, massage and health therapy rooms and hiking trails. Many come to practice yoga or meditation or for spiritual renewal. Shoshoni members who founded Rudi's Restaurant, a well-regarded natural-food restaurant, have published a vegetarian cookbook, *The Shoshoni Cookbook*. It has become one of the bestselling cookbooks at local bookstores. **Dances of Universal Peace**, 440-5714, offers attendees a chance to learn key phrases and gestures from many different religions through participatory song and dance.

The **Church of Gaia**, 443-1096, 8563 Flagstaff Road, is an Earth-centered church offering training in such Native American ceremonies as sweat lodges, pipe circles, vision quests and other ceremonies. Those interested in learning more about Native American worship also find programs at the 20-year-old **Naropa Institute**, 444-0202, 2130 Arapahoe Avenue. The institute has an environmental studies program, and some classes are taught by Native Americans. Naropa is the only accredited, Buddhist-inspired institute of higher learning in North America. Its department on religious studies includes coursework in Christianity, Hinduism, Buddhism and Native American perspectives. For more information on the Institute, see our Child Care and Education chapter.

CU-Boulder also has a department of religious studies, 492-8041, and ethics classes through the Philosophy Department, 492-6132.

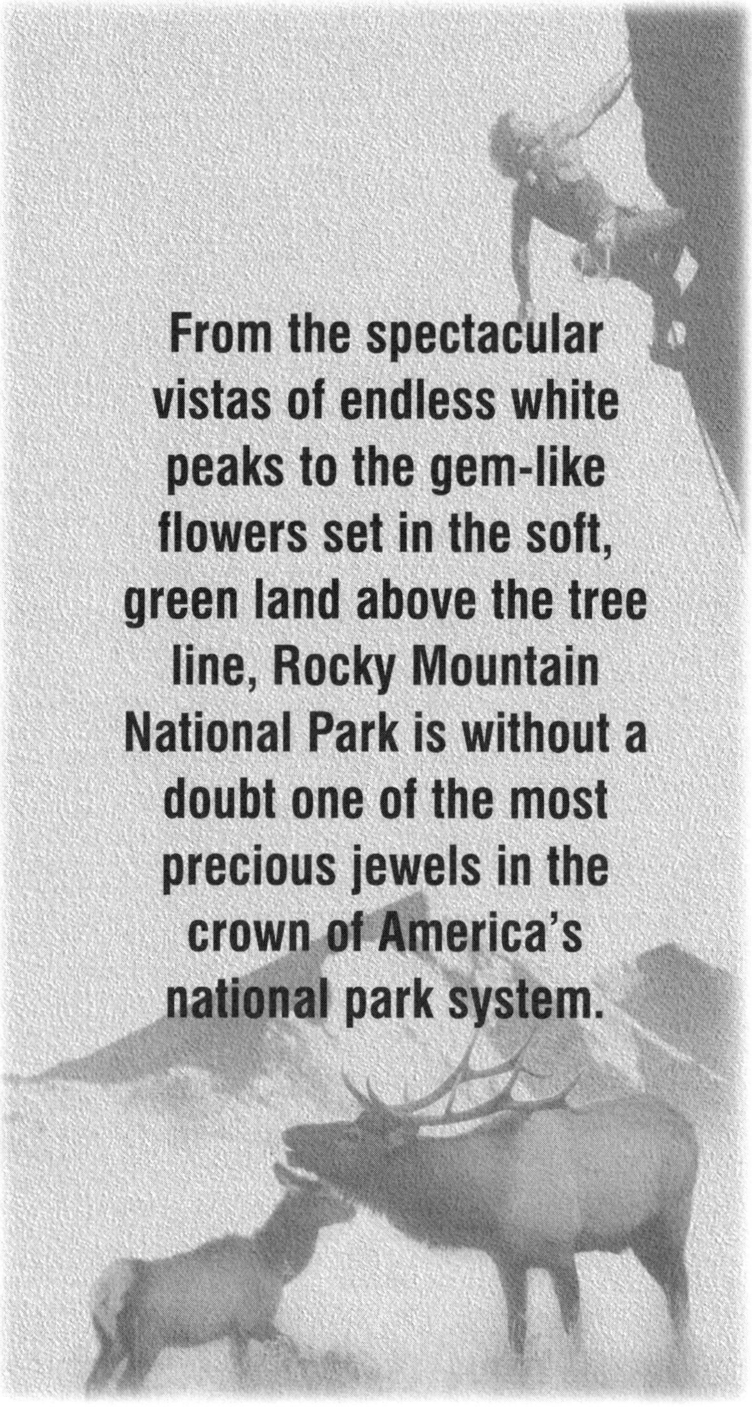

From the spectacular
vistas of endless white
peaks to the gem-like
flowers set in the soft,
green land above the tree
line, Rocky Mountain
National Park is without a
doubt one of the most
precious jewels in the
crown of America's
national park system.

Rocky Mountain National Park

A trip over Trail Ridge Road in Rocky Mountain National Park is a peak experience, literally. Spectacular mountains — the nation's highest — sparkling lakes and mountain streams, radiant wildflowers and fascinating wildlife make this a five-star natural scenic attraction that will leave visitors breathless from the beauty as well as the altitude.

Trail Ridge Road transports visitors to another world. It's a world of different life zones, climates and vegetation that would take thousands of "horizontal" miles to reach — a trip comparable to driving more than 2,500 miles from Denver to Fairbanks, Alaska. But this world is compressed "vertically" in just a 50-mile drive over Trail Ridge Road. Each 300 feet of elevation equals one degree of latitude or 70 statute miles north.

From the spectacular vistas of endless white peaks to the gem-like flowers set in the soft, green land above the tree line (one-third of the Park's 415 square miles is above this level), Rocky Mountain National Park is without a doubt one of the most precious jewels in the crown of America's national park system.

You're almost sure to see grazing deer and elk and, if you're lucky, maybe some Rocky Mountain bighorn sheep, the Park's symbol. Above timberline by boulder fields, listen for the whistle of the pikas, cute, furry animals that look like rodents but are related to rabbits. You may spot a yellow-bellied marmot, a large rodent similar to a groundhog, sunning on a rock. Gray jays or spiffy black-trimmed Clark's nutcracker birds will swoop down looking for handouts (but don't feed them, it's illegal and unnatural for them). Bears and mountain lions are rare to encounter, being very wary of humans.

Leave the crowded roadsides, walk a mile or two along one of the park's 355 miles of trails, and you'll begin to feel like one of the first humans ever to set eyes on this beautiful wilderness area.

Area History

As with the rest of Colorado, the first humans wandered through the area that is now Rocky Mountain National Park approximately 10,000 to 12,000 years ago. Part of what is now the Park's Trail Ridge Road was once part of the Ute Trail, a major route across the mountains for Native Americans.

The first Europeans to visit the area were French fur traders, collecting valuable pelts. The area became U.S. territory in 1803 as part of the Louisiana Purchase. Mineral deposits in the area proved unproductive, so there was never great mining activity.

Because of its astounding beauty, the area was destined to be a tourist attraction from its earliest days. For centuries, Native Americans had visited the area and considered it sacred. Braves visited the area west of present-day Estes Park for vision quests and supposedly climbed Longs Peak to trap bald eagles for their feathers. When the settlers arrived, the Utes occupied the area, after driving out the Arapaho.

After chasing the California Gold Rush in 1849, Joel Estes heard about Colorado gold and came looking in 1859. Estes and his family homesteaded a beautiful parklike valley in 1860. Other settlers arrived slowly to try ranching and farming at elevations below 9,000 feet. Indian agent and soldier Kit Carson built a cabin on the eastern edge of the Park in Tahosa Valley.

More visitors began arriving in 1864, challenged by climbing Longs Peak, northern Colorado's highest mountain. Among them was William Byers, who was editor of the *Rocky Mountain News* in Denver. He and two friends stayed with the Estes family when they made their attempt at the climb. Though they were unsuccessful, Byers went back to Denver and wrote glowingly about the area, dubbing it Estes Park after his host. In 1868 Byers returned with Maj. John Wesley Powell (the renowned one-armed explorer of the Colorado River and Grand Canyon), and the two made the first recorded summit of Longs Peak. Byers wrote another story about Longs Peak and Estes Park, attracting more tourists, hunters and adventure seekers. Settlers were finding it profitable to house the increasing number of tourists in their cabins and later began building rustic lodges. These lodges became dude ranches, which were very popular in the early 20th century.

If Joel Estes had only stayed, he might have become one of the richest men in the area, but the long, snowy winter of 1866 was too much for Estes, and later that year he sold off his claim and cattle for a yoke of oxen and headed south. Griffith Evans bought the Estes homestead, which he operated as a makeshift hostel until he added some cabins and opened a full-scale dude ranch in 1871.

By the 1870s the area was becoming known around the world for its spectacular scenery. British writer and world traveler Isabella Bird visited the area in 1873 and stayed at Evans' ranch. Her adventures and travels in the area were published in 1879 in the extremely popular book, *A Lady's Life in the Rocky Mountains*, and by 1882 the book was in its seventh edition.

Another guest at Evans ranch was Lord Dunraven (the Fourth Earl of Dunraven, Viscount of Mount Earl and Adare). At the time, it was common for European gentry to visit the United States, and this Irish nobleman and avid hunter was so taken with Estes Park that

he decided he must have it for his very own. Although foreigners were forbidden to homestead, Dunraven managed to acquire more than 15,000 acres through third-party purchases and other under-the-table deals and created a private hunting sanctuary for himself and his European hunting cronies. The earl even announced in the *Rocky Mountain News* that "admission to Estes Park, his game preserve, was by invitation only." But he was eventually defeated by the area's sheer beauty, which attracted so many others disputing the legality of his claims.

Meanwhile, in 1876, Lord Dunraven invited Western landscape painter Albert Bierstadt to Estes Park to capture its beauty on canvas and help the earl select a spot for his English Hotel. A lake and moraine in the park are named for the painter, whose exhibited works attracted even more attention — and tourists — to the area.

At his English Hotel near Lake Estes, Dunraven entertained such guests as Buffalo Bill Cody, Kit Carson, Gen. William Tecumseh Sherman and other notables in the early 1880s. Initially it catered mainly to foreign clientele — the earl's hunting buddies. Its name was later changed to the Estes Park Hotel, which operated until it burned to the ground in 1911.

Settlers continued to homestead and began contesting the earl's land claims. Dunraven eventually leased the land to ranchers and left. Failing to establish exclusive rights to the preserve and challenged about the legality of his claim, Dunraven stopped visiting Estes Park in 1881. He leased his land and hotel to Theodore Whyte, his property manager, and in 1904 the land was purchased by well-known inventor Freelan O. Stanley (inventor of the Stanley Steamer). Diagnosed with tuberculosis, Stanley, like many of his time, came to be cured in the dry mountain air (and eventually was cured).

In 1905 the town of Estes Park was platted at the confluence of the Fall and Big Thompson rivers on land sold by John Cleave. Like many locals, Cleave said he "couldn't stand to see the danged place overrun by tenderfeet tourists," so he moved away.

FYI

Unless otherwise noted, the area code for all phone numbers in this guide is 970.

Photo: Daily Camera

At 14,246 feet, Longs Peak towers over Bear Lake in Rocky Mountain National Park.

Construction in Estes Park came from logging operations in Hidden Valley, Hollowell Park and Wild Basin. On the western side of the park, the Kawuneeche Valley, other logging operations provided materials to build dude ranches and the developing Grand Lake village, west of the Continental Divide from Estes Park.

Designation of Rocky Mountain National Park

With the ever-growing tourism prevalent by the early 1900s and use of the area by individuals and businesses, local residents became concerned about preserving the area's pristine beauty.

In 1905 President Theodore Roosevelt had added the area as part of the new national forest system, but many felt that greater protection and preservation were needed, among them H.M. Wheeler, who had opened a national forest office in Estes Park in 1907. Wheeler suggested creating a "wildlife reserve" in the nearby mountains. Further promoting this idea was Enos A. Mills, a 20-year resident of Estes Park and a naturalist, writer, conservationist and innkeeper. Around 1909 Mills began campaigning to preserve the area.

Other citizens joined Mills, among them the well-known Stanley. The group formed the Estes Park Protective and Improvement Association to protect and preserve the area's scenery and wildlife.

So eloquent was Mills that President Roosevelt commissioned him to tour the country promoting the preservation of wild lands. The national park concept had begun with an act of Congress in 1872 designating Yellowstone as the first national park. The stated objectives of national parks were first to preserve natural and historical objects including wildlife, scenery and ecosystems, and second to promote the enjoyment of these resources by the public.

After years of debate on the size and boundaries of the Park, President Woodrow Wilson signed a bill passed by Congress in 1915 designating Rocky Mountain National Park as the nation's and world's 10th national park. Soon after, the first Park superintendent was installed, and rangers were hired to enforce the new restrictions on hunting and cattle grazing.

Over the next decades, evidence of human settlement in the Park, such as the briefly booming silver mining town called Lulu City in the late 1870s, was removed, and natural vegetation was painstakingly restored.

Sixty years later, in 1975, Rocky Mountain National Park was named the 21st biosphere reserve in the world. The biosphere reserve system was established by the United Nations Man and Biosphere Programme to observe and monitor changes in natural ecosystems, especially those resulting from human activities. There are more than 220 biosphere reserves worldwide in 63 countries.

Visitors' Centers

Back in the early part of the 20th century, Enos Mills and others probably never imagined that more than 3 million visitors would come to Rocky Mountain National Park every year — or perhaps they did. Today, five Visitors' Centers at the Park accommodate this yearly crush of humanity.

The main **Visitors' Center/Headquarters** is located 2.5 miles west of Estes Park on U.S. Highway 36 and is open daily year round. Call the staff at 586-1206 for weather, camping and other specific information, 586-1333 for a recorded message and 586-1319 for the hearing-impaired.

On the west entrance to the Park the **Kawuneeche Visitors' Center**, 627-3471, is 1.3 miles north of Grand Lake on U.S. Highway 34, also open daily year round.

The **Moraine Park Museum** lies 5 miles west of Estes Park on Bear Lake Road and is open daily from May to mid-October.

Most spectacularly situated of all, the **Alpine Visitors' Center** at 11,796 feet atop Trail Ridge Road, is 25 miles west of Estes Park and is open daily from June to September, weather permitting. Next door, a park concessionaire operates Trail Ridge Store and a snack bar, where diners can enjoy a simple meal along with a panoramic view. Call the main park number, 586-1206, for information about the Alpine Visitors' Center.

Lily Lake Visitors' Center, 6 miles south of Estes Park on Colo. Highway 7, is open daily from May to October, depending upon snow conditions.

Besides providing education about the Park's different ecosystems, plus maps and directions, the centers remind visitors of the park's regulations:

1. No pets are allowed on trails or away from roadways. Pets must be on a leash at all times.

2. Feeding or touching wild animals is prohibited, along with hunting or harassment of wildlife. This includes stalking wild animals for photographs, which frightens them and makes them less viewable for other visitors.

3. Picking wildflowers or plants is prohibited. Removing, disturbing, damaging or destroying natural features, including rocks and pine cones, is illegal.

4. Fishing requires a valid Colorado state fishing license. Only artificial lures may be used (but children 12 years of age and younger may use bait, in open waters only).

5. Camping is restricted to designated areas.

6. A permit is required for all overnight stays in the backcountry. There are restrictions on the use of pack animals.

7. Gathering firewood is prohibited. Fires may be built only in picnic areas and campsites with grates. Either bring your own wood or ask at the ranger stations or park headquarters about purchasing some.

8. Vehicles must remain on roads or in parking areas. Parking any vehicle or leaving property unattended for more than 24 hours without prior permission is prohibited.

9. Hitchhiking is permitted from road shoulders only.

10. Trail bikes, snowmobiles and all other vehicles are restricted to roads.

11. Firearms are to be kept unloaded.

12. All your own trash must be removed from picnic areas and campsites and disposed of in trash cans and recycling receptacles.

13. Having open alcoholic beverages in a vehicle on Park roads and in parking areas is illegal.

Recreation and Participatory Sports

Bicycling

Bicycling in the Park is allowed only on roads, and these are heavily used by cars. Since the roads climb from about 9,000 feet to more than 12,000 feet, riding is quite strenuous throughout. No off-road or mountain biking is allowed on any trails.

But for a challenging ride on a dirt road, follow **Old Fall River Road**, the first auto route over the Continental Divide, which is described by Park officials as a "motor nature trail." You'll be sharing the road with vehicles as it climbs 9.4 miles before joining Trail Ridge Road at the summit of 11,796-foot Old Fall River Pass (see more information under the section on Driving, below). Old Fall River Road is one-way uphill — for cans and bicycles. Plan to ride down Trail Ridge Road.

Bicycling over 50-mile-long **Trail Ridge Road** is only for the hardiest of the hardy, and even they will want to spend the night on the other side at Grand Lake before returning. Trail Ridge Road crosses the Continental Divide, and at its highest point is 12,183 feet, making it one of the world's most spectacular bike rides. But this road, too, is heavily traveled by cars.

Bear Lake Road is a strenuous 10-mile climb of 1,500 feet from the Beaver Meadows Entrance Station to Bear Lake at 9,475 feet.

Camping

NOTE: Camping reservations can be made no earlier than five months in advance for individuals and groups. The maximum stay in the Park is seven days during summer and 14 days during winter. At Longs Peak Campground, the limit is three days, and only tents are allowed. Permits are required for all backcountry camping; call the Backcountry Office at 586-1242.

Five campgrounds and some group camping areas listed below offer a great way to enjoy the Park at close range. There are no electrical, water or sewer connections in any of the campgrounds. Sewer dumping stations are located at Moraine Park, Glacier Basin and Timber Creek campgrounds. Public telephones are located at Moraine Park, Glacier

Basin, Timber Creek and Aspen Glen. For general information about the Park and specific information on recreation, rentals, campgrounds or even ticks, call the public information office at 586-1206. For emergencies, call 586-1399 or 911.

Glacier Basin: Located 9 miles from Park Headquarters off U.S. 36 on Bear Lake Road, this campground has 150 sites. Reservations are required May through September. The site accommodates recreational vehicles (it has dump stations, but like all the Park's campgrounds, no hookups). The season is from early June through Labor Day. The fee is $12 per night, and reservations are made through Destinet at (800) 365-2267.

Moraine Park: The Park's largest campground, Moraine Park has 247 sites and is located 7 miles west of Estes Park off Bear Lake Road. It's open all year and accommodates recreational vehicles and tents. Water is turned on mid-May and turned off mid-September. The fee is $12 per night, and reservations are required Memorial Day through Labor Day. Make reservations through Destinet at (800) 365-2267.

Longs Peak: This smaller campground is 11 miles south of Estes Park and a mile west on Colo. Highway 7. It offers 26 tent campsites (no RVs or motor homes) on a first-come basis. The fee is $10 per night. It's open all year with water turned on mid-May and turned off mid-September.

Timber Creek: Also open all year, Timber Creek is 9 miles from the Grand Lake entrance to the Park and has 100 sites accommodating tents and recreational vehicles. The fee is $10 per night, and water is turned on in early June and off in mid-September. The campground operates on a first-come basis with no reservations.

Aspen Glen: Aspen Glen is open mid-May through late September on a first-come basis. It is located immediately inside the Fall River entrance of the Park and has 54 sites for tents,

---

INSIDERS' TIP

Although the little chipmunks and birds are so appealing, don't feed them or other wildlife. For one thing, it's against the law. For another it's better for them in the long run. When wild animals learn to expect an easy handout in summer, they starve in winter.

motor homes or recreational vehicles. The water is turned on mid-May and turned off in late September. The fee is $10.

Group Sites: The Park has 15 group sites in Glacier Basin (see previous entry for location) that accommodate groups of 10 to 50 people. They are open mid-May through Labor Day with water turned on and off the same times. The fees range from $30 to $60, depending upon the size of the group. Reservations are needed from May 28 through September 6 through Destinet at (800) 365-2267. All other times, sites are available on a first-come basis at Moraine Park Campground.

The **Sprague Lake Handicamp** offers backcountry camping for a maximum of 10 people/five wheelchairs. The camp is a half-mile from the parking lot at Sprague Lake. Park in the lot and haul your equipment along the path around the lake.

Climbing

Whether you want to do a technical rock climb of the famous east face of Longs Peak, known as the Diamond, or hike to the top of Longs Peak, the Park's climbing challenges are renowned and unlimited. Technical climbers should familiarize themselves with the Park's climbing regulations at Park Headquarters. A Park concessionaire offers mountaineering and technical climbing instruction and a guide service for those who'd like to learn; information is available at the Park Headquarters.

Registration is not required for technical climbers, but be sure to tell a reliable friend or relative of your climbing plans, should you be overdue. Registration is required for overnight bivouacs, and $10 permits are available at Park Headquarters, the West Unit Office and at most Rangers' Stations. To obtain a permit, call the Backcountry Office at 586-1242. A permit cannot be obtained in advance, although a reservation can be made in advance by phone until May, then by letter during summer months.

Driving

Trail Ridge Road, the main drive through the Park, is the highest continuous highway in the United States. It runs 50 miles from Estes Park to Grand Lake over the Continental Divide and was built in 1932. It's the most spectacular trip through the Park and should be taken by anyone who visits. The road climbs through the evergreen forests amidst the eerie, gnarled krummholz — wind-sculpted trees

Source: Daily Camera

Elk and other wild game are common sights in Rocky Mountain National Park.

— and up to the alpine tundra above the tree line, comparable to being in the Arctic Circle. Krummholz means "crooked wood" in German.

Depending upon weather conditions, the road is generally open from Memorial Day until mid-October. Allow three or four hours for this scenic drive, with stops at the numerous overlooks for stupendous vistas of glacier-carved peaks, snowfields and cirques, and perhaps a snack at the **Alpine Visitors' Center** on top. Take the short half-hour round-trip **Tundra Walk** to see the tiny delicate flowers that have adapted to this harsh environment. Be sure to stay on paths because the alpine tundra is fragile.

Another scenic drive is up the **Bear Lake Road**, leading to a beautiful high mountain basin. Traffic during summer months through the Park is very heavy. In some areas, shuttle buses take visitors to certain trailheads, such as Bear Lake, where there's a choice of trails. A shuttle runs from Glacier Basin to Bear Lake. Parking lots at Bear Lake and Glacier Gorge Junction will be full between 10 AM and 3 PM on summer days, so plan accordingly.

Old Fall River Road runs from Horseshoe Park Junction to Fall River Pass. It is one-way uphill west of Endovalley Picnic Area. A gravel road with many switchbacks, it gives visitors an idea of early travel across the mountains since it was the first road over the Divide in northern Colorado. A guide booklet is available at the Visitors' Centers describing interesting sights along the way. You can make a loop up Old Fall River Road and return on Trail Ridge Road. Old Fall River Road is west of Estes Park on U.S. 34 at the Fall River Entrance Station. The road is paved for the first 2 miles from the entrance. Take note of the Alluvial Fan along the way, caused by a flood in 1982. RVs and trailers are not allowed on Fall River Road because of the narrow switchbacks. The road opens July 4th and is closed in winter.

Fishing

Four species of trout are found in the mountain streams and lakes of the Park: German brown, rainbow, brook and cutthroat. Valid Colorado fishing licenses are required for all fishing in the Park; use of live bait is prohibited except for children 12 and younger. See the fishing regulations at Park Headquarters or one of the Rangers' Stations or the "Fishing" section in our Boulder Sports chapter. No fishing is allowed in Bear Lake, and some lakes and streams on the east side of the Park are closed to protect the greenback cutthroat trout, which is being reintroduced to its native habitat.

Sprague Lake at the east edge of the Park is good for catching pan-sized brook trout; however, it's right next to the road and is heavily used. From Estes Park, drive west on U.S. 36 to the Beaver Meadows Entrance Station. Turn left (south) at the first intersection after the entrance, and continue on the Bear Lake Road for about 6 miles.

For a day's outing — a combination hiking and fishing trip — go to **Peacock Pool**. Begin at the East Longs Peak Trailhead and hike about 4 miles up the trail to a spur that leads to Peacock Pool, 11,360 feet high. This is a hard hike but offers spectacular views. Another 1.5 miles from Peacock Pool is **Chasm Lake** with deep water, but according to latest reports, no fish, though it's a scenic spot right under the spectacular diamond east face of Longs Peak. The Longs Peak Trailhead is 9.2 miles south of Estes Park on Colo. 7; turn right at the sign.

Hiking and Backpacking

Rocky Mountain National Park has 355 miles of trails, and there's something for everyone from the wheelchair-bound to backpackers. Below are some day hikes, rated accordingly. It's best to get a map at one of the Visitors' Centers for detailed descriptions, including distance, elevation and type of terrain.

Very Easy

Many hikers enjoy the Bear Lake Nature Trail. This is a half-mile paved path circling Bear Lake. Elevation is 9,475 feet. Leave from the Bear Lake parking area.

Try the Sprague Lake Nature Trail. Known as the Five Senses Trail, this half-mile trail around Sprague Lake is wheelchair-accessible. Take the road to Bear Lake, and turn off where marked for Sprague Lake.

Easy

Take the trail from Bear Lake to Nymph, Dream or Emerald lakes.

Gem Lake, round-trip, makes for a pleasant walk. This hike starts outside the Park on Devil's Gulch Road.

Moderate

Bear Lake to the top of Flattop Mountain is a little more difficult.

Bear Lake or Glacier Gorge to Mills Pond or Black Lake is a good hike that takes a few hours, as does Bear Lake or Glacier Gorge to Sky Pond.

Chasm Lake is a bit more strenuous at 4.2 miles one-way but well worth the gorgeous view of the Diamond on Longs Peak and the beautiful lake. Start at the Longs Peak Trailhead, off Colo. 7, north of Meeker.

Long or Difficult

The hike to Thunder Lake starts at Wild Basin off Colo. 7 between Allenspark and Meeker, and you should plan on it taking most of the day.

For Ypsilon Lake, start at the Lawn Lake Trailhead at Horseshoe Park on Fall River Road. Don't forget your lunch or rain gear.

A Classic

Long considered America's Matterhorn, Longs Peak, 14,255 feet high, is the highest peak in the Park and the northernmost "fourteener" in the Rockies (these are the highest peaks, of at least 14,000 feet). It has captured the imagination of writers, artists, climbers and explorers since the first recorded American sighting of the peak in 1820 by

Stephen Long. The Arapaho are believed to have climbed Longs to obtain eagles feathers on its summit, but the first whites to make the top were famed, one-armed Colorado River explorer John Wesley Powell and Denver newspaperman William Byers in 1868.

Climbing Longs is still an exciting accomplishment today and an all-day affair — usually taking about 14 hours round-trip. It should be attempted only by strong hikers who are already acclimated to the altitude and should not be attempted by novices. It's crucial to be off the peak and on the way back down by noon to avoid the daily summer thunderstorms and dangerous lightning, which has claimed a number of hikers' lives.

The most popular (and only nontechnical) route is the East Longs Peak Trail, usually called the Keyhole Route, which starts at the Longs Peak Trailhead and climbs 8 miles and 4,850 vertical feet to the top. The first 6 miles are the easiest and follow an ever-climbing trail through beautiful forests of pine and aspen up to timberline with fantastic views. Those who want to bail out before this point can take the well-marked turnoff to Chasm Lake, at around 4 miles, to a gorgeous lake right beneath the 1,000-foot vertical diamond on Longs' sheer, spectacular 1,675-foot east face (a popular world-class technical climbing route). Chasm Lake is 4.2 miles from the trailhead.

But, continuing on the Keyhole Route, at mile 6 you reach the Boulderfield and hop from boulder to boulder for one mile up to the Keyhole, a prominent rock formation. To the left of the Keyhole is the chilly-looking Agnes Vaille Shelter Cabin. Vaille made the first successful winter ascent of the east face with Walter Kiener in 1925 but collapsed from exhaustion on her way back and froze to death while Kiener went for help.

After passing through the Keyhole, at 13,100 feet, the hard part begins. The route is marked by red and yellow paint circles over

Longs Peak in Rocky Mountain National Park is the northernmost of the fourteeners — Colorado's highest peaks, 14,000 feet or more. Longs Peak has an elevation of 14,255 feet and is the 15th highest peak in the state.

A 1915 *Denver Post* cartoon honored Enos Mills, the main force behind the creation of Rocky Mountain National Park.

the rocky Ledges, which have intimidating drop-offs. The Ledges lead to a 600-foot steep couloir of loose gravel and running rivulets called the Trough. After climbing the Trough and negotiating the huge boulder at the top, you pass through the notch and cross the Narrows — more rock ledges with even more dizzying exposure. The Narrows lead to the Homestretch, a short, steep couloir to the top, not really difficult, but at this point in the game a bit much. The Homestretch requires some hand-holds but has solid footing. At the top of Homestretch, you have reached the huge summit of Longs, which encompasses four acres. Enjoy the view, do a few push-ups to show how really tough you are and take a look down the diamond, but don't stay too long if noon is approaching. If there is any snow — possible well into July — ice axes are necessary for safely climbing the Ledges, Trough, Narrows and Homestretch.

The Longs Peak Trailhead is 9.2 miles south of Estes Park on Colo. 7; turn right at the sign. From the Ranger Station at the trailhead to the summit the distance is 6.9 miles with an elevation gain of 5,000 feet.

A Final Note About Backpacking

It's possible to backpack part of the way up Longs and camp in the Boulderfield, a spectacular but rather inhospitable campground — cold and windy and around 12,000 feet in elevation — among the boulders. But you'll need to reserve your permit well in advance by writing the Backcountry Office, Rocky Mountain National Park, Estes Park, 80517.

There are numerous backcountry sites and zones for individuals and groups throughout the Park. For more information, maps or reservations, either call the Backcountry Office at 586-1242, write to the address above, or show up in person.

Horseback Riding

Hi Country Stables has two locations inside the Park at Moraine Park and Glacier Basin. Reservations are suggested, 586-2327 or 586-3244 (open only in summer months).

Snow Skiing

Though most visitors to the Park come in summer, winter offers great cross-country skiing opportunities. Bear Lake and Wild Basin are the Park's two most popular cross-country areas. The Visitors' Center on U.S. 36, 2.5 miles west of Estes Park, is staffed daily from 8 AM to 5 PM except Christmas Day. Rangers can answer questions and provide trail maps for skiers detailing 40 miles of marked trails around Bear Lake and 88 miles of mainly unmarked trails around Wild Basin. There's a $3 entrance fee for skiers, walkers or cyclists and a $5 car fee on weekends and holidays. For more information call the Park at 586-1206.

Cross-country ski equipment can be rented in Estes Park (see cross-country rentals under the Estes Park Participatory Sports chapter of this book).

Here are a few of our favorite ski sites:

Glacier Basin Campground: (Easy) Drive 5 miles up Bear Lake Road. Park on the west side of the road at the large parking area (which is the shuttle bus parking area during summer months) and walk across to the east side to begin skiing on the main trail from the campground, which heads southwest for a mile on level terrain to Sprague Lake. There are many trails in and around the campground as well.

Black Lake: (Intermediate to Difficult) Begin at the Glacier Gorge Junction parking lot, which is about 11 miles up Bear Lake Road. Follow the signs southwest toward Alberta Falls and The Loch. After the intersection of Icy Brook and Glacier Creek, turn south and follow Glacier Creek to Mills Lake. Continue past Mills and Jewel lakes along the creek. When you leave the trees, continue up the open slope to Black Lake and enjoy the spectacular view of Longs Peak to the east, McHenrys to the west and Chief's Head Peak to the south.

Wild Basin Trailhead: (Difficult) Drive 13 miles south from Estes Park on Colo. 7 (past the Longs Peak trail at 9.2 miles) to the Sandbeach Lake Trailhead. Turn right and drive another mile to the National Park Service parking lot. The Sandbeach Lake Trail starts at the large sign in the parking area and climbs northeast through the pines 4.2 miles to Sandbeach Lake.

Tours

The park offers **elk-bugling tours** in the fall. Stop by or call the Visitors' Center/Headquarters, 586-1206, for a reservation.

Charles Tour & Travel Services in Estes Park offers scenic tours of Trail Ridge Road, Fall Foliage/Elk Bugling tours and arranges horseback riding trips in the Park and Bear Lake hikes: (800) 586-5009 (metro Denver area only) or 586-5151.

Auto Tape Tours are cassette tapes that narrate the drive over Trail Ridge Road. The tapes give highlights of history, facts, legends and nature and cost $12.95 at all of the park visitors' centers. The tapes are available starting from either the Estes Park or Grand Lake side of Trail Ridge Road.

> ## FYI
> Unless otherwise noted, the area code for all phone numbers in this guide is 970.

Driving Tips

1. Since there are no service stations in the Park, enter with a full tank of gas.

2. Observe posted speed limits — roads are narrow, winding and heavily used.

3. Travel in early morning or late afternoon. Wildlife is more active at these times, and the light is more beautiful. During midday, traffic can be bumper to bumper.

4. Downshift to lower gears when going up or down steep grades. This will reduce engine stress and save your brakes from burning out. Manually downshift automatic transmissions. Go down hills in a lower gear than you use to go up.

5. Tap brakes gently and repeatedly on downhills to reduce brake wear and possible overheating (or failure).

6. Be sure to look first and signal at turnouts and parking areas. Watch for oncoming traffic. Sound the horn on blind corners to alert oncoming drivers, if necessary.

7. When you stop, always set the emergency brake, and park in gear (for manual transmissions).

8. Lock your car when unattended and place valuables out of sight, or take them with you.

9. Stay in your own lane. Don't drive in the middle to avoid being near the edge. The roads were designed with plenty of room, and you'll only cause an accident by driving down the center.

10. Don't be surprised if your car doesn't perform normally at high altitudes. Cars tuned for lower elevations may overheat or act as though they're not getting enough gas. Drive in a lower-than-usual gear to keep RPMs up and to avoid overheating. Don't pump the accelerator, as it will cause flooding and make matters worse.

On warm days some cars may get vapor lock in the fuel line. If this occurs, try to get the car off the road at the nearest pullout. Stop the engine and allow it to cool. If there is snow or cold water nearby, put it on the fuel pump and the line leading to the carburetor. Let the car cool for 15 minutes before trying to start it again.

The histories of Estes Park and Rocky Mountain National Park are so deeply intertwined that one would probably not exist without the other.

Estes Park

Estes Park (elevation 7,522 feet) lies 70 miles northwest of Denver at the eastern entrance to Rocky Mountain National Park and is home to almost 4,000 permanent residents. It exists primarily as a base camp and service area for visitors to the Park, offering hotels, restaurants, shopping, equipment rentals, tours and other diversions for tourists — with a nearly endless choice during the summer months. Since almost three million visitors come to Rocky Mountain National Park every year — and most of them during summer — things can get a bit hectic along Estes Park's main drag.

In winter, some of the shops close, with their owners heading south, but many shops stay open — particularly the art galleries. Some restaurants have abbreviated hours during winter. But winter and other "low-season" months may be the best time to get the flavor of this small town beautifully situated at the base of spectacular Longs Peak and Rocky Mountain National Park, with quite an interesting history all its own.

Victorian traveler and writer Isabella Bird wrote extensively and lovingly about the scenic beauty of Estes Park in the fall of 1873. For those interested in the area's history and a fascinating glimpse of life for the first settlers, *A Lady's Life in the Rocky Mountains* by Bird is required — and entertaining — reading. Ms. Bird might not approve of some of today's additions to her beloved mountain retreat, however.

The history of Estes Park and Rocky Mountain National Park are so deeply intertwined that one would probably not exist without the other. Even the Estes Park Chamber of Commerce brochure begins with "The Park." Estes' main employers are the school district, medical center, Town of Estes Park, Holiday Inn, Estes Park Center/YMCA of the Rockies, Harmony Foundation (a drug and alcohol rehabilitation center), Rocky Mountain National Park, Michael Ricker Pewter Casting Studio and the Estes Valley Recreation and Park District. The town receives all Denver TV stations through a TV translator or cable and has one radio station, KRKI 1470 AM. The *Trail Gazette* newspaper is published twice weekly.

Visitor Information

For information about almost anything in the area, call the Estes Park Chamber of Commerce at (800) 443-7837 or (800) 44-ESTES.

For reservations and other businesses in the area call 762-5968 or (800) ROCKY MT.

Community Information

Some tourists enjoy connecting with the quieter, community side of an area. Others suddenly need a community service. These days, many visitors stand transfixed by the beautiful surroundings and decide to make Estes Park their permanent home. This chapter provides information for all three, starting with medical care and worship, moving on to real estate and retirement, then ending with schools and child care.

For general information, start with the Estes Park Chamber of Commerce, (800) 443-7837. Their Relocation Package is free. It has an area overview plus demographics and real estate information. They'll also mail out the Estes Park phone book for $5. The Community Development Department also may have helpful information. It's at 586-5331.

Medical and Dental Care
. . . Even Pet Care

The **Estes Park Medical Center**, 586-2317, at 555 Prospect Avenue, has a staff of 10 full-time doctors, plus 20 specialists who

Photo: Daily Camera/Lourie Zipf

Lake Estes lies adjacent to Estes Park.

visit weekly or monthly. The center includes 24-hour emergency care, radiology and 16 in-patient rooms. Emergency helicopter service can transport patients to specialized hospitals. Via helicopter from Estes Park, it takes no more time to reach the Fort Collins hospital than it does to transport a Denver heart-attack victim via ambulance, during rush hour, to a Denver hospital. Check the Yellow Pages under "Medical Clinics" for more information. Hospitals and clinics in Longmont, Boulder and Fort Collins are less than an hour away. Also see the Boulder chapter on Healthcare and Wellness.

For a nasty toothache, **Estes Park Dental**, 586-9330, at 343 S. St. Vrain, has Saturday and evening hours plus same-day emergency care. Other possibilities appear in the Yellow Pages under "Dentists."

What if your dog, Duke, kisses a porcupine? It's unlikely — porcupines are shy and rare, even in the Rocky Mountains. How about if he's just not his regular, bouncy self? The **Estes Park Animal Clinic**, 586-4231, is at 851 Dry Gulch Road. Normal office hours are 8 AM to 5 PM Monday through Friday (closed 1 to 2 PM) and 8 AM to noon on Saturdays. They offer 24-hour emergency service too. Next door is the **Boarding House for Dogs and Cats**, 586-6606. They're a good place if you're thinking of leaving dear Duke shut in the car while

you wander the lovely local shops (don't!). Colorado's intense sun can turn a car into an oven within minutes. This can happen even on a cool day, even with a window rolled down. Much kinder is to board your pets while you spend time without them. Weekends, the Boarding House books fast, but generally a few days' notice works for short-term boarding. Reservations a few weeks in advance work best.

Worship

Estes Park has more than a dozen churches, with an average church membership around 300. Many offer Bible schools, evening programs and summer camps. Churches include **Our Lady of the Mountains Catholic Church**, 586-8111. The moss rock and log church, opened in 1949, replaced tiny wooden St. Walter's, which now serves as an apartment building. During summer tourist months, Our Lady of the Mountains offers four masses on weekends. The **Presbyterian Community Church of the Rockies**, 586-4404, has nearly 600 members, a good adult education program and Sunday School plus strong youth groups. Members of the **First Baptist Church**, 586-3395, enjoy the warm, caring congregation. It's affiliated with the Baptist General Convention. Check the Yellow Pages under "Churches" for details. Every Friday, the local newspaper, the *Trail Gazette*, lists services and church news. Then there's the **Estes Park Center/YMCA of the Rockies**, 586-3341, with a full-time pastor on staff plus programs and facilities for church-related events.

It's less than an hour's trip to Boulder as the angel flies. Some Boulder County churches actually are closer to Estes Park than to the City of Boulder. So, you can broaden your choices by also checking the Boulder Worship chapter.

Real Estate

Estes Park is becoming a more year-round community. While it has always drawn retirees, lately a new breed of resident has grown. If you've envisioned linking to the world via your computer in a beautiful setting like Estes Park, you're not alone. People who can work out of their home are more common in Estes Valley these days. As the Front Range booms, highly skilled industries move closer to Estes Park, increasing its draw as a bedroom community to Boulder. All this means Estes Park is getting younger, drawing families and a wider range of business skills.

FYI

Unless otherwise noted, the area code for all phone numbers in this guide is 970.

In the good old days, you could find a rental when everyone left for the summer, but people aren't leaving so often anymore. For a summer rental, start checking six months in advance. For a longer-term rental, get your name in six months early, then check in monthly. Homes to purchase are more available than homes for rent. Something for less than $100,000 is unusual; the average price of a three-bedroom home in 1996 was $215,044 — up from $141,000 in 1994 — so the real estate market has been booming. The pop of air-gun hammers is more common around town these days, but it's usually for the construction of luxury-style homes. There's a little more time before a house sells on the luxury end, but anything good goes mighty fast. Builders are booked a year in advance. Investors are holding their income properties, and just a few timeshare opportunities are available. All this is not to discourage. But it should remind you to start looking.

The Estes Park Chamber of Commerce provides a list of local Realtors, including **Coldwell Banker**, 586-4425; **Range Realty**, 586-2345; and **Ponderosa Realty**, 586-3331.

Retirement

Some locals estimate that more than half the full-time residents of the Estes Valley are retired. That doesn't mean nonworking or seniors — many people have jobs because they enjoy keeping busy, and many others have taken early retirement from big companies. The 1990 census indicated that around 1,100 of the town's 3,700 full-time residents were 55 and older. That's not quite a third and certainly not half! And no census figures are available to identify the age groupings of the more than 9,000 people in the valley. Whatever age they are and whatever "work" residents do, it's true that many people look all over the nation then choose to retire in Estes Valley. If you're among them, visit the **Estes Park Senior Center**, 586-2996, at 220 Fourth Street. It's open 9 AM to 3 PM Monday through Friday. The Senior Center serves meals five days a week. In the summertime, approximately 40 people enjoy dining here every day. During the winter, the number is in the low 30s. About 25 meals a day are transported to seniors' homes. There's a blood pressure clinic once a month. Exercise classes happen three times a week.

The Senior Center is a good place to connect with town activities, including book groups, lectures, art classes, pinochle and bridge clubs. It hosts card games twice a week and a weekly oil-painting class. For the **Retired and Senior Volunteer Program** (R.S.V.P.), call 586-9486. The local quilt guild and the rock and mineral club hold meetings here too.

Most seniors live in homes, townhomes and apartments that cater to everyone. Those on a limited income might consider two subsidized apartments. At **Pine Knoll Apartments**, 586-8407, for seniors 62 and older the basic rent is $270 for all 48 one-bedroom units. The rental rate goes up if your income exceeds roughly $12,000. If you're on rental assistance,

10 units are available at less than $270 per month. **Trail Ridge Apartments**, 586-0216, offer one-bedrooms where the rent is 30 percent of your adjusted annual income. **Prospect Park Nursing Home**, 586-8103, is a 60-bed facility with a staff numbering around 50.

Regarding transportation, one local senior warns that you shouldn't come up here without your own, since there is no public bus system. Unless you have your own transportation, use a tour service or rely on your own friends, you're stuck. Maybe it's time to ride a mountain bike! Plenty of places rent them. There are plenty of horses in the valley too. Or, maybe you're one of these Front Range engineers who is tinkering with a solar-powered runabout that can zoom down highways at 200 miles per hour and climb mountains in second gear.

Education and Child Care

Public Schools

The Park School District R-3, 586-2361, includes almost 450 square miles and the towns of Estes Park, Allenspark, Glen Haven, Pinewood Springs and the eastern slope of the Rocky Mountain National Park. The district employs around 180 people, serving the more than 700 school-age children in the valley.

Though small, Park School District R-3 includes art, music, gifted and talented programs, special education, reading and sports programs. Volunteers contribute nearly 150 hours each month. The district runs an Aquatic Center, open to the community during non-school periods. Computer and industrial technologies are part of many classrooms. Around 40 percent of teachers have master's degrees. The pupil/teacher ratio is 16.5-to-1. Nearly 95 percent of Park District children graduate from high school, and 80 percent of these go on to higher education.

Here are places to visit or write for more information:

• **Park School District R-3** (administrative office), 1501 Brodie Avenue, 586-2361

• **Estes Park High School**, 1600 Manford Avenue, 586-5321

• **Estes Park Middle School**, 1500 Manford Avenue, 586-4439

• **Park Elementary School**, 650 Community Drive, 586-9529

Private Schools

Eagle Rock School and Professional Development Center
2750 Notaiah Rd., Estes Park
• **(303) 442-7655**

This is a year-round, tuition-free, ungraded residential high school. It has been developed and funded by the American Honda Corporation as a public service. A beautiful setting, excellent staff and facilities for science, arts and physical education are here. It focuses on young people who are not experiencing success in their current school settings and are willing to commit to growth and change. Individualized learning opportunities are offered to 100 students, who are accepted through a careful application process.

Preschools and Child-care Centers

During the winter, it's easier to find child care. But as summer brings wildflowers to the mountains, it brings visitors into Estes Park Valley. If you might need summer child care, even for a week or a few days, day-care centers recommend you start looking at least by midwinter.

INSIDERS' TIP

Those who would like to rub shoulders with the daring rock jocks who climb the "Diamond" face of Longs Peak (a world-renowned climb), should try an early breakfast at either The Mountaineer or Molly B's. Climbers reputedly have their pre-climb (and hopefully not their last) breakfasts at these cafes.

To connect with child-related programs in the valley, visit the **Estes Park Public Library**, 586-8116, 335 E. Elkhorn Avenue. Parents can check out stuffed animals for their children there, and it also offers a list of babysitters who can come to your home or hotel room. Most are teenagers who have gone through a Red Cross Training Program for first aid and CPR. Summer reading programs for children also are there. The **Larimer Country Social Services Program** in Estes Park, 577-2150, has a list of licensed day-care centers and homes plus applications for reduced fee services. Some larger centers include **Meadowbrook Preschool and Childcare Center**, 586-8726, and **Mountain Top Preschool**, 586-6489. Here is a description of a few other special places.

Kreative Kids
650 Community Dr., Estes Park • 586-6727

This is a private, nonprofit kindergarten/day-care learning center for children ages 5 to 12, located next to the elementary school. It leases space from the school district and has a good relationship with the schools. It's $2 per hour for each child. Drop-ins are considered if there is still space after the regularly enrolled children get there.

House on Pooh Corner
404 Stanley Ave., Estes Park • 586-9481

Known for its caring environment, this low-key center takes 12 toddlers and preschoolers in a more homelike setting. This place is so popular, there's a long waiting list.

Circle of Friends Montessori Preschool
2515 Tunnel Rd., Estes Park • 586-3341 Ext. 1137

In the Estes Park Center/YMCA of the Rockies, the school has 20 to 25 children with about 20 full-time. There's a parent-toddler program offered in spring for children ages 18 months to 3 years. New for 1996 is a kindergarten program.

Restaurants

Estes Park has a large number of restaurants and casual cafes to choose from, ranging from doughnut shops and pizzerias to fine French restaurants and gourmet Italian inns. Italian and Mexican food seem to predominate, but steaks, burgers and trout are ubiquitous as well. Watch out for "Rocky Mountain Oysters," they come from a part of the bull that you might not want to consume.

Even if you can't afford a meal at the historic Stanley Hotel, it's worth a visit for its landmark status, lovely setting and to see the shiny green Stanley Steamer automobile parked in the lobby. Those on a budget can still enjoy coffee or afternoon tea at the Stanley on the front veranda or a snack from the Dunraven Grill's bar menu. The Stanley also hosts free classical concerts on Sunday afternoons.

Reservations are not required at most Estes Park restaurants but are accepted and recommended at some of the more popular spots, particularly for groups during the crowded summer season. Almost all restaurants of any size beyond a hole in the wall accept MasterCard and Visa credit cards, and many additionally accept American Express, Carte Blanche, Diners and Discover cards. The chart below shows the price range for an average dinner for two (no fancy wine or desserts factored in).

Price-code Key	
Less than $25	$
$26 to $50	$$
$51 to $75	$$$
$76 and more	$$$$

The Baldpate Inn
$-$$ • 4900 Colo. Hwy. 7 S., south of Estes Park • 586-6151
(Open Memorial Day until Oct. 1)

You'll get a lot more than lunch or dinner if you visit the Baldpate Inn. This classic mountain inn and historic local landmark was placed on the National Register of Historic Places in 1996. The inn is 7 miles south of Estes Park across from the Rocky Mountain National Park Visitors' Center at Lily Lake and serves lunch and dinner daily during summer. There's a unique salad bar set in an old claw-foot bathtub plus delectable homemade soups, breads and pastries. Dinner is equally charming and delicious and reservations are a must. Mae

West, Jack Dempsey and Rin Tin Tin stayed here, and you'll see their photos — along with opera singer Tetrazinni and world leaders — in the amazing collection in the dining room assembled by the two original owners. The inn has the world's largest key collection (please see our Close-up in the Estes Park Accommodations chapter), which is open to the public.

Bruce's Dark Horse Restaurant & Lounge

$-$$ • Fawn Valley Inn • 2760 Fall River Rd., Estes Park • 586-5654

Specializing in relaxed family dining with special attention to service, this large restaurant and lounge is connected to the Fawn Valley Inn a few miles out of town. Sometimes there's live entertainment, including piano players, at the full bar. The restaurant serves breakfast, lunch and dinner throughout the year.

Donut Haus

$ • 342 Moraine Ave., Estes Park • 586-2988

If it's just a doughnut you're craving, line up at the Donut Haus — there usually is a line stretching out the door of this tiny doughnut bakery that also has a large variety of other fresh-baked items. It's right beside the multi-colored giant slides.

Estes Park Brewery

$-$$ • 470 Prospect Village Dr., Estes Park • 586-5421

The brewery has a pub, family restaurant and outdoor deck, serving pizza, sandwiches, burgers and salads. During summer it's open from 11 AM to midnight daily. (Check for winter hours, which may vary.) There are free brewery tours with free samples of the nine microbrews sold on tap and by the bottle. The Renegade Red has won a gold medal at the Great American Beer Festival.

Safeway

$ • Stanley Village • North of the intersection of U.S. Hwys. 34 and 36, Estes Park • 586-4447

For picnic or camping supplies on the way to Rocky Mountain National Park, look for the big Safeway supermarket up on the hill above the downtown area. There's also a salad bar and deli in the store.

Ed's Cantina and Grill

$ • 362 E. Elkhorn Ave., Estes Park • 586-2919

In addition to all the Mexican favorites plus barbecued ribs and sandwiches for lunch and dinner, this comfortable South-of-the-Border spot serves the local microbrew from Estes Park Brewery. Ed's is open for breakfast too.

Mountain Home Cafe

$ • Stanley Village • At the intersection of U.S. Hwys. 34 and 36, Estes Park • 586-6624

Formerly known as Johnson's and right in the shopping center, this little cafe isn't glamorous. But the food is quite good, especially the Swedish potato pancakes with sour cream and apple sauce. It's a favorite of area residents for breakfast before a ski or hike. You can also get lunch here Monday through Saturday, and the cafe is open Sundays for breakfast from 8 AM until 1 PM (closed afterward).

Laura's Fudge Shop

$ • 129 E. Elkhorn Ave., Estes Park • 586-4004

Though it's not exactly a meal, for some it's considered daily bread. Of all the cotton candy and caramel apple stores, Laura's Fudge Shop really stands out. There are 16 flavors of this delicious fudge that's made with whipping cream. Locals have braved the summer weekend crowds packed on Elkhorn Avenue just for a piece of this stuff. Laura's also has homemade cookies, soft pretzels and ice cream.

Notchtop Baked Goods & Natural Foods Cafe and Pub

$ • Upper Stanley Village • At intersection of U.S. Hwys. 34 and 36 • 586-0272

This local favorite has now added a pub with its own microbrew — Notchtop, of course. Stop here for delicious pastries or an inexpensive lunch. Very casual, with newspapers and magazines to read (such as *Mother Earth News*), this little cafe is a nice break from the tourist scene and serves nutritious food and natural beverages, plus great locally roasted

Silver Canyon coffees. The cafe is open daily from breakfast through dinner.

The Other Side
$ • 900 Moraine Ave., Estes Park • 586-2171

Specializing in an "all-American" menu, this restaurant at the entrance to Rocky Mountain National Park at Mary's Lake Road has a pleasant view of a little duck pond. The menu offers seafood, steaks, prime rib, burgers and a Sunday champagne brunch. Breakfast, lunch and dinner are served daily.

The Mountaineer
$ • 540 S. St. Vrain Rd., Estes Park • 586-9001

Fast and friendly service is the hallmark of this unpretentious little cafe, with lots of granny-type knickknacks and corny paintings on the wall. But it's quite cozy and out of the hustle-bustle of downtown Estes Park. It's about a half-mile south on Colo. Highway 7 across the street from the Diamond Shamrock gas station and Estes Park Rehabilitation Center. Open daily for an early breakfast (at 6 AM), the restaurant features lots of morning food choices, including homemade biscuits and gravy and cinnamon rolls, and is quite inexpensive. Local climbers and mountaineers (and tourists) like to stop here for a tasty and inexpensive breakfast, lunch or dinner.

Molly B Restaurant
$ • 200 Moraine Ave., Estes Park • 586-2766

For coffee, a light breakfast or a big meal, try this casual cafe that's open year round. Along with the usual breakfast foods, you'll also find great choices for lunch or dinner, including seafood, vegetarian dishes and burgers. It's another favorite stop of local mountaineers for an early breakfast or a late snack. Note that the restaurant takes a brief break daily between 3 and 5 PM.

Nicky's Restaurant and Resort
$-$$ • 1350 Fall River Rd., Estes Park • 586-5376

Nicky's claim to fame is the delicious prime rib roasted in rock salt. Out a few miles on Fall River Road, a pleasant drive, this large, attrac-tive restaurant has a huge menu with lots of variety, including Italian and Greek specialties, steaks and a salad bar. It's open year round: summer for breakfast, lunch and dinner daily; during winter for lunch and dinner, with breakfasts on weekends only.

Poppy's Pizza & Grill
$ • 342 E. Elkhorn Ave., Estes Park • 586-8282

In the spiffy Barlow Plaza, this pleasant pizzeria has all types of pizza — pesto, Polynesian, Mexican, to name a few — for reasonable prices. Some of the individual pizzas are less than $3. There are also homemade soups, salads and sandwiches. When the weather cooperates, you can sit outside on the nice patio overlooking the river. Poppy's is open for lunch and dinner year round.

Mama Rose's
$ • Barlow Plaza • 338 E. Elkhorn Ave., Estes Park • 586-3330

This tidy Italian restaurant in a pretty reproduction of an old Victorian home has a large selection of dishes. It offers a very pleasant veranda overlooking the river for dining. Choose from chicken Parmesan in wine sauce, seafood fettuccine, fresh basil pesto, baked pasta and other Italian dishes. The restaurant serves lunch and dinner daily and Sunday breakfast buffets during the summer and weekends during spring and fall. The restaurant closes from January through March.

Wild Basin Lodge & Smorgasbord
$ • Off Colo. Hwy. 7, 13 mi. south of Estes Park • 747-2545

Casual, come-as-you-are dining with lots of food and a great view of a rushing river are the highlights of this landmark lodge. The all-you-can-eat smorgasbord costs $10.50 for adults, $9.50 for seniors, and the charge for children is 85¢ per year of their age. The smorgasbord is a daily dinner occurrence during summer Monday through Saturday, and for lunch and dinner on Sunday. After summer the restaurant is open weekends until November 1 and reopens weekends on Palm Sunday. During July and early August, the lodge is sometimes the scene of the Allenspark Melodrama performances (see the Estes Park

Tours, Attractions and Festivals chapter). Wild Basin is at the south entrance to Rocky Mountain National Park.

Black Canyon Inn
$$-$$$ • 800 MacGregor Ave. (Devil's Gulch Rd.), Estes Park • 586-9344

This historic mountain lodge offers a romantic fireside atmosphere to complement the fine dining. Seafood specials with pasta include salmon fettuccine or tomato fettuccine with fresh sea scallops. The restaurant also offers some wild game selections, including elk, plus duck and prawns. Black Canyon serves dinner only every day, and reservations are required.

Dunraven Inn
$-$$ • 2470 Colo. Hwy. 66, Estes Park • 586-6409

Probably not quite what Lord Dunraven had in mind, the Dunraven Inn calls itself the "Rome of the Rockies" and specializes in Italian food. (Lord Dunraven was the Irish nobleman who bought all of Estes Park in the 19th century to create his own private hunting reserve, but was eventually ousted by locals.) The Dunraven Inn has long been a favorite stop for steak and Italian dishes including shrimp scampi, lasagna, eggplant Parmesan and chicken cacciatore plus a large selection of Italian wines. Be sure to notice the Mona Lisa wallpaper, and be sure to make reservations during the summer months, when the restaurant is packed. Dinner is served daily.

The Stanley Hotel
$$-$$$ • 333 Wonderview Ave., Estes Park • 586-3371, (800) 976-1377

For a special treat, try the Stanley's Sunday champagne brunch, served year round from 10 AM to 2 PM in the hotel's MacGregor ballroom. Unlimited champagne or mimosas accompany an unbelievable spread — every pastry you can imagine and every breakfast dish plus seafood, prime rib and much, much more. Charles, one of the MacGregor room's chefs, works hard to make this buffet unforgettable — and he succeeds. For those with time and a hearty appetite, it's a real bargain for the $16.95-per-person price. Dinners at the Stanley are served in the Dunraven Grille, which was just completely renovated and has a brand-new bar. Choices include teriyaki ahi, chorizo-smoked chili rellenos, prime rib and elk with such side dishes as ahi or duck salad and spicy red bean or beer-cheese soup. The Dunraven Grille also offers a bar menu from 11:30 AM until 3 PM Mondays through Saturdays. During summer there's usually a long waiting list for tables on the hotel's lovely front veranda with its spectacular mountain view, and where breakfast, lunch and dinner are also served. The Stanley serves breakfast, lunch and dinner daily year round.

La Casa and La Casa Grande
$ • El Centro Mall • 222 E. Elkhorn Ave., Estes Park • 586-2807

La Casa's a Mexican restaurant with some extra spice — Cajun. If there's a difference of opinion on what spicy cuisine to have, La Casa restaurant offers the perfect alternative with its traditional Mexican and Cajun favorites, including blackened redfish, burritos and fizzy Margaritas. There are also choices on La Casa's international menu for those who don't like it hot. La Casa Grande on the riverside is used for receptions and special parties. It's open for lunch and dinner daily.

La Chaumiere
$$-$$$ • U.S. Hwy. 36, Pinewood Springs • 823-6521

Those with sophisticated palates who savor sauteed sweetbreads say La Chaumiere offers the best around. Another popular item is the duck liver pate. Classic French dining in a serene setting with its own deer park is what La Chaumiere has used for years to draw its faithful patrons. Though a bit out of the way (12 miles southeast of Estes Park), French food lovers don't mind the extra drive for the diverse changing menu, including specialty game meats, lamb, beef and seafood. The restaurant has its own smokehouse and organic garden and makes its own ice cream. A six-course, $15 dinner special is served Sunday. The restaurant is open for dinner daily, but is closed Mondays.

Some Estes Park restaurants offer al fresco dining.

Nightlife

Estes Park isn't big on nightlife, but there are a few choices for not-too-weary travelers or residents.

The Old Gaslight Pub
246 Moraine Ave., Estes Park • 586-0994

Live music is featured here on weekends, usually country-western or oldies. There are dinner specials such as fish and chips, Italian dishes and other favorites. The bar has some British beers on tap and local microbrews.

Park Village Playhouse
900 Moraine Ave., Estes Park • 586-2885

Visit this playhouse to enjoy good, old-fashioned melodrama. The curtain goes up at 8 PM, doors open at 7 PM; reservations are suggested.

Park Theatre
Corner of Moraine Ave. and Rockwell St., Estes Park • 586-8904

Enjoy first-run movies every night from May through September here. The cafe is open until 6 or 7 PM during summer.

Wheel Bar
132 E. Elkhorn Ave., Estes Park • 586-9381

Now celebrating 51 years of operation, this local landmark has been owned and operated by the same family since 1945. This comfort-able neighborhood bar offers beers, microbrews on tap and cocktails at happy-hour prices. Upstairs there's Orlando's steakhouse for a full meal.

The Stanley Hotel
333 Wonderview Ave., Estes Park • 586-3371, (800) 976-1377

The Stanley presents theater and fine arts performances and claims to put on more performances than any other private property in the West. The Stanley also hosts free concerts on Sundays, Big Band dancing during the summer and holiday galas like "The Shining" Halloween Ball and a popular New Year's Eve party. There's a year-round jazz series and a Friday-night dance program. Call for the current schedule of events and ask about special honeymoon and "romance" packages.

Estes Park Brewery
470 Prospect Village Dr., Estes Park • 586-5421

The brewery has a pub, family restaurant and outdoor deck, serving pizza, sandwiches, burgers and salads. During summer it's open from 11 AM to midnight daily. (Check for winter hours, which may vary.) There are free brewery tours with free samples of the nine microbrews sold on tap and by the bottle. The Renegade Red has won a gold medal at the Great American Beer Festival.

Accommodations

Estes Park has so many motels, bed and breakfast inns, lodges and cabins, visitors will have a large choice and range in quality and atmosphere. But reservations are a good idea during the crowded summer months and a must over holiday weekends. Choose a modern, shiny motel, a rustic lodge or cabin or a place right out of history.

For your convenience, we provide a code (see subsequent gray box) showing what you'll pay on average for a double room. All of these accommodations accept major credit cards, with the exception of the cabins at Estes Park Center/YMCA of the Rockies. Pets are not allowed at any of these properties except for the cabins at Estes Park Center/YMCA of the Rockies.

Price-code Key	
Less than $30	$
$31 to $50	$$
$51 to $75	$$$
$76 to $90	$$$$
$91 and more	$$$$$

Alpine Trail Ridge Inn
$$$-$$$$ • 927 Moraine Ave., Estes Park • 586-4585

This tidy blue-trimmed white motel is right on the highway, but its clean and pleasant rooms are a good value. There's a heated swimming pool, and family and kitchen units are available. Smoking and nonsmoking rooms are available. The Sundeck Restaurant right on the property serves good meals.

Aspen Lodge at Estes Park
$$$$$ • 6120 Colo. Hwy. 7, Estes Park • 586-8133, (800) 332-6867

South of Estes Park 7.5 miles, this beautiful 3,000-acre ranch is a full resort offering hayrides, swimming, fishing, tennis, racquetball, horseback riding, hikes and a great children's program. It's the largest log lodge in the state, according to the owners. There are cozy cabins, a hot tub, saunas and winter sleigh rides. Three-, four- and seven-day packages make this all-inclusive resort quite affordable, with all meals and activities (except horseback riding) included. Smoking is prohibited at this property.

The Baldpate Inn
$$$$ • 4900 Colo. Hwy. 7 S., Estes Park • 586-6151

In January 1996, the Baldpate was placed on the National Register of Historic Places. Family-owned and operated as a bed and breakfast, this classic mountain inn and historic local landmark is unsurpassed in charm and history. Built from local wood and stone in 1917, it's the quintessential rustic mountain getaway. The inn is 7 miles south of Estes Park across from the Rocky Mountain National Park Visitors' Center at Lily Lake. Guests can stay in the Mae West and Jack Dempsey rooms, where these and many other stars stayed. The Baldpate Inn has 12 rustic rooms and three cabins with colorful homemade quilts, calicos, gingham and alluring log-cabin decor. One cabin is a newly redecorated honeymoon suite. There are five massive stone fireplaces and a library. The inn has the world's largest key collection and an amazing photograph collection (see this chapter's Close-up). Breakfast is included in the room rate and the dining room serves delicious meals with homemade pies, pastries, breads and soups and full dinners (reservations required). Smoking is not allowed. The Baldpate Inn is open Memorial Day until October, weather permitting.

Estes Park Center/YMCA of the Rockies
$$$, no credit cards • 2515 Tunnel Rd., Estes Park • 586-3341

There's something for almost everyone (except maybe honeymooners) at the Y. This enormous facility, just outside Estes Park, can accommodate 3,469 and runs numerous camps and programs. The Y is the place for families or other groups and offers everything from rustic two-bedroom cabins for four to six, vacation homes that sleep seven, lodges that sleep three to six and cabins for up to 12 people. There's a miniature golf course, tennis courts, livery, craft shop, library, museum, post office and theater. Concerts are given regularly. It's open year round. Pets and smok-

ing are allowed in the cabins but not in the rooms.

Romantic River Song Bed & Breakfast Inn
$$$$$ • Lower Broadview Rd. (off Mary's Lake Rd.), Estes Park • 586-4666

Reservations are a good idea at this lovely, secluded bed and breakfast set on 27 acres right along the Big Thompson River. Guests like it so much they return from year to year, often booking a year in advance. During the high season reservations need to be made about 15 weeks in advance. During the rest of the year it's not nearly as busy. Each of the rooms is custom-decorated either with lovely antiques or whimsical handmade furniture. One room has the beautiful 200-year-old bed of the owner's grandmother; another has a delightful bed made of gracefully arching willow twigs complete with (decorative) nesting birds. There's a river stone-faced Jacuzzi in one room and fireplaces in most rooms. The list of amenities goes on and on at this lovely

old home. Gourmet breakfast comes with the price of the room. This is a no-smoking inn.

Fawn Valley Inn
$$$$-$$$$$ • 2760 Fall River Rd., Estes Park • 586-2388, (800) 525-2961

Only a half-mile from Rocky Mountain National Park, these year-round condominiums are set on more than 8 acres along the Fall River. They feature complete kitchens and fireplaces, and there's a heated outdoor pool. Bruce's Dark Horse Restaurant & Lounge offers fine and casual dining and is popular for its weekend dining specials. There are facilities for reunions and conferences. Smoking is allowed in some of the units.

Streamside Cabins
$$$$ • 1260 Fall River Rd., Estes Park • 586-6464, (800) 321-3303

Describing itself as a "Village of Cabin Suites," these cabins are for those who want to "rough it" in luxury. They have skylights, fireplaces, wall-to-wall carpeting, private decks, gas grills, steam rooms and jetted tubs. The cabins are on a wooded hillside on Fall River about a mile from Estes Park. The 16-acre site offers fishing and solitude. The cabins are listed among the 19 "Best of Estes," by an Estes Park *Trail Gazette* survey. Special honeymoon and other packages are available. Smoking is permitted.

Wild Basin Lodge
$$ • Off Colo. Hwy. 7, Allenspark
• 747-2545

Three modern rooms with private baths and balconies overlook the North St. Vrain River in this community near some beautiful hiking trails. The lodge is often the location for popular summer melodramas. The smorgasbord restaurant, open spring through fall, has a soup and salad bar plus home-cooked roast chicken, mashed potatoes and gravy, green beans and home-style comfort. The lodge also has a horseback-riding stable and banquet room. It's 45 minutes from Boulder and 20 minutes from Estes Park. Full breakfast is free. Children are welcome.

Misty Mountain Lodge
$$$ • 232 E. Riverside Dr., Estes Park
• 586-4100

This attractive and very reasonably priced lodge is a great value right in town. It's set against a hillside, away from the crowd across the river. There are multi-room suites, kitchens and fireplaces, a hot tub and great off-season rates. Smoking is allowed.

The Stanley Hotel & Conference Center: A Grand Heritage Hotel
$$$$-$$$$$ • 333 Wonderview Ave., Estes Park • 586-3371, (800) 976-1377

The stately queen of the area's hotels, the Stanley is truly a classic — and on the National Register of Historic Places. The inspiration for Stephen King's book, *The Shining*, the Stanley was also the scene for shooting the new TV miniseries of the same name. King

returned in 1996 as screenwriter and executive producer and stayed six months for the shooting. During the filming for the new version, the hotel lobby and MacGregor room were restored to a more authentic turn-of-the-century look by the film directors and Grand Heritage (the company that owns the Stanley), going from white walls back to natural woods and patterned wallpapers.

Ghosts aside, the Stanley stands on its own as a show stopper and has hosted the rich and famous since its construction in 1906 by F.O. Stanley, inventor of the Stanley Steamer automobile. Diagnosed with tuberculosis and given little time to live, Stanley came to Colorado for the curative value of the pure mountain air and lived another 30 years. During those years he built his classic hotel and helped promote the establishment of Rocky Mountain National Park.

Among the Stanley's treasures are a 1909 Steinway piano in the music room and a shiny, green Stanley Steamer with brass trim and wooden fenders in the hotel lobby. Stanley proclaimed it was an excellent mountain car because it didn't stall, and to prove his point he once drove the car up the steps of the U.S. Capitol.

The hotel was purchased recently by Grand Heritage, which owns and operates castles and historic buildings around the world. Grand Heritage is financing a $3.6 million restoration of the Stanley set for completion by May 1, 1997. Grand Heritage will maintain the hotel's turn-of-the-century decor. Rooms have canopy beds, Victorian wallpaper and other period details. Smoking is allowed at the Stanley. Those feeling extravagant should ask for the Stephen King suite. Though there are no skeletons in the closet, it's where the Emperor and Empress of Japan stayed during their visit a few years ago as well as author King and other VIPs over the years.

Historic tours of the hotel are offered year round five times a day, and there's a small museum on the ground level. Tours cost $5 per adult; $3 per adult with groups of 12 or more, and children 12 and younger are free. The tours go through all of the public rooms and down into the tunnel underneath the hotel, which is built on solid rock. Visitors will see fool's gold glittering in the rock that supports the original hotel beams. The Stanley also hosts free concerts every Sunday, "fairy tale weddings," dinner theater, holiday galas, Big Band dancing, the Colorado Music Festival during summer and the famous "The Shining" Halloween Ball.

Arts

Estes Park offers the full range of choices for quality art. Shops, galleries and boutiques dot the main streets with a plethora of Native American art and representations of Rocky Mountain National Park in every medium. Besides visual arts, performing arts include theater and classical concerts, jazz and contemporary music. Larger performing-arts events and festivals generally take place during the summer.

Visual Arts

The **Charles Eagle Plume Gallery and Museum of Native American Arts** has been a local landmark since 1917 and is a favorite stop. Located 10 miles south of Estes Park on Colo. Highway 7, it has a huge collection of art and artifacts, including rugs, jewelry, pottery, baskets and beautiful beadwork of the Plains Indians. Active in the Native American rights movement, owner Charles Eagle Plume graduated from the University of Colorado in 1932 and was later awarded an honorary Doctorate of Humanities from CU-Boulder. The gallery is open mid-May through mid-September 9 AM to 5 PM, 586-4710.

Sundance Center for the Arts on 150 E. Riverside Drive is a complex of galleries and

The Keys to Baldpate's Allure:
Hollywood, History, World-Famous Collections

Listed in the *Guinness Book of World Records*, the Baldpate Inn has the largest key collection in the world — some 16,000 keys. For more than 75 years, guests have been charmed by the inn and have gone to the ends of the earth to find special keys to donate to the collection. There are keys from Mozart's wine cellar; Jack Benny's Paramount Studios dressing room; cake-mix magnate Duncan Hines' golden Cadillac; Hitler's desk; Fort Knox; the El Paso, Texas, public library; Westminster Abbey; the Pentagon; and thousands more. Why the key collection?

The Baldpate Inn gets its name from Earl Derr Biggers's 1913 mystery novel, *Seven Keys to Baldpate*, which was a runaway national favorite. George M. Cohan — "Mr. Yankee Doodle," one of America's best-known musical composers — wrote the stage-play version, which ran on Broadway the same year. Jack Benny later starred in the radio-play version.

Story has it that author Biggers stayed at the inn before it officially opened. Because it was so similar to the one in his story, Biggers mutually agreed with the Maces, the owners, that their lodge could become the "real" Baldpate Inn, which officially opened in 1917.

With its Hollywood connections, the inn attracted such stars as Mae West, Jack Dempsey, Gregory Peck and Rin Tin Tin (the dog). Several films were made at the inn, including part of the TV series *Centennial*.

The land was originally homesteaded by the Mace family, who built the lodge by hand. It's now the only Western stick construction still used as a tourist accommodation in the Estes Park area. Two of the Mace brothers were professional photographers, one for the *Denver Post*, who also won a national Eastman Kodak photo contest and was Gen. John J. Pershing's personal photographer during World War I. Together the brothers photographed U.S. presidents, Hollywood stars and other celebrities and amassed a prodigious photo collection of well-known people from all over the world, which now bedecks the walls of the dining room. This collection includes opera stars (if you thought Tetrazinni was only an Italian chicken dish, you can see his photo here), musicians and many signed photos of U.S. presidents. It's worth a tour all to itself. Even if you don't stay at the Baldpate, it's also worth a visit for its historic interest and a tasty meal (see Estes Park Restaurants).

Both the key and photo collections are open to the public at no charge.

---

frame shops specializing in Western and nature art. **Impressions Ltd.**, 586-6353, and **Colorado Essence**, 586-0832, in the complex, are the biggest galleries in town with regular programs of shows and openings. Look for animals and other woodcarvings at the **Mountain Wood Carvers**, 586-8678.

Creativity in Wood at the Old Church Shops, 157 W. Elkhorn Avenue, 586-6866, has a huge array of work by 50 different woodcarvers. Owner Hugh Bekham, a woodcarver himself, gives regular woodcarving demonstrations. The **Glassworks Studio and Gallery**, 323 W. Elkhorn Avenue, 586-8619, is the only hot glass studio and gallery in the area. There are free public glass-blowing demonstrations daily, year round, by owner Garth Mudge, who displays the delicate art. The **Politically Incorrect Art House**, 170 Moraine Avenue, 586-3141, houses the Jose Perez collection of satirical art, poking fun at political and social issues. The museum features more than 150 paintings and drawings by Perez, who combines a kind of Norman Rockwell style with a Will Rogers attitude.

The **Art Center** in the lower level of Stanley Village has a wide range of quality art with changing monthly exhibits. **Artisans of Colorado**, 157 W. Elkhorn Avenue, 586-2151, displays the work of more than 75 of the state's best artists and artisans. The **Michael Ricker Pewter Museum, Gallery and Casting Studio**, 586-2030, is 2 miles east of town on U.S. Highway 34 and is the world's largest pewter-casting studio. It also houses the world's largest pewter sculpture (10 feet by 30 feet). Ricker's presentations and commissions include The White House, the U.S. Olympic Committee, Disney World and the Pope (John Paul II). Several of Ricker's works are on display in the Smithsonian Institution. Children will enjoy the re-creation of a turn-of-the-century American town. There's also a new **Ricker Pewter** retail shop in town at 167 E. Elkhorn Avenue.

The *Estes Park Gallery Guide* is published by the **Galleries of Estes Park Association** and lists the town's shops and galleries. For information write to the association at P. O. Box 987, Estes Park 80517, or call the **Cultural Arts Council of Estes Park** at 586-9203. For other information try the **Chamber of Commerce** at 586-4431 or (800) 44-ESTES.

> **FYI**
> Unless otherwise noted, the area code for all phone numbers in this guide is 970.

Performing Arts

Chamber Music Society of Estes Park
P.O. Box 1331, Estes Park 80517
• 586-9203

This society of some 100 chamber-music-loving members sponsors concerts all year in the Estes Park area, inviting different musicians from around the state and nation. The society also sponsors an annual Chamber Music Festival, held over a weekend in fall. The 1996 festival featured the American Chamber Players and The Mendelssohn Trio. Information is available on concert locations, dates and prices from the Cultural Arts Council at the listed number listed or from artistic director Louise Dickey in Boulder (303) 494-8934.

The Estes Park Music Festival
Stanley Concert Hall, Stanley Hotel, Estes Park • 586-9203

Boulder's nationally acclaimed Colorado Music Festival Orchestra comes to Estes Park on Monday evenings during the summer from late June through early August. For more about this better-than-the-best orchestra, see our Boulder Arts chapter. Ticket prices vary.

Music in the Mountains
Rocky Ridge Music Center • Colo. Hwy. 7 • 12 miles south of Estes Park • 586-4031, (402) 486-4363 (in winter)

Rocky Ridge offers chamber music and opera. Student and faculty recitals take place here on Fridays and Sundays around 3 PM from late June until the end of August. Call for current ticket prices.

The Stanley Hotel
333 Wonderview Ave., Estes Park • 586-3371, (800) 976-1377

For year-round entertainment check the Stanley Hotel, which presents theater and fine arts performances and claims to put on more performances than any other private property in the West. The Stanley also hosts free concerts on Sundays. There's a year-round jazz series and a Friday-night dance program. Call for the current schedule of events.

Shopping

Estes Park's shopping area is an attractive but bewildering sort of gingerbread glitz with a theme and style somewhere between Switzerland and Coney Island. Saltwater taffy in the Rocky Mountains? Unfortunately, some of the clothing, jewelry, knickknacks, "art" and other items found in the shops have nothing to do with Estes Park, Colorado or the Rocky Mountains. Other offerings are more Southwestern and related to Native American tribes nowhere near the area.

Despite this, a really nice feature of the Estes Park shopping area is the riverside walkway called Confluence Park behind the main street shops and right on the Big Thompson River. Lots of little wooden bridges provide access across the river to free parking lots all around. Almost all of the shops along the south side of Elkhorn Avenue go through to this very pleasant and relaxing walkway beside the tumbling river, with shade trees, flowers and lots of benches to rest on.

MacDonald Book Shop
152 E. Elkhorn Ave., Estes Park • 586-3450

Established in 1928, this large bookstore in an old log cabin was originally the home of turn-of-the-century residents. The owners of the bookstore and adjacent coffee shop (below) have had the shops for four generations. Out-of-town newspapers, including *The New York Times*, are available along with a wide selection of hardbacks, paperback children's books, books on cassette, magazines and calendars. Be sure to read the history plaque out front explaining how the first bookstore on the site was opened in the owners' living room. Wonderful plaid carpet and exposed log beams set the interior mood.

MacDonald Paper & Coffee House
150 E. Elkhorn Ave., Estes Park • 586-3451

Right behind the bookstore of the same name, this cozy coffeehouse has a casual relaxing atmosphere that invites visitors to stay for a while. The shop has a great selection of stationery, greeting cards, gift wrap and posters and also offers espresso, cappuccino, a wide variety of teas, tempting pastries, fresh-squeezed orange juice, Italian fruit drinks and other beverages. Tables are sprinkled around upstairs and down among the cards. It's light, bright and pleasant, decorated throughout in blond wood. Sit down with a cappuccino and write a card or letter. The coffeehouse opens daily at 7:30 AM.

Here's a roundup of our other favorite places:

Outdoor World, at 156 E. Elkhorn Avenue, offers a great selection of high-quality boots, backpacks, jackets, water bottles and everything you need for the outdoors.

Those who would like a blown-glass hummingbird can find one of the best selections in the area at **Glass Blowers**, 126 E. Elkhorn Avenue. Most of the blown glass is made at the shop's other studio in Manitou Springs, Colorado. You'll find hummingbirds in every color of the rainbow here, from red and green ruby throats to copper rufous hummers.

The **Hiking Hut**, at 110 E. Elkhorn Avenue, offers a nice selection of backpacks, jackets, sunglasses and other accessories for hiking and camping in the mountains.

The **Talking Teddy**, 521 Lone Pine Drive, has a mind-boggling assortment of teddy bears in all sizes and styles, teddy bear-related items such as Smokey Bear hats, teddy bear-decorated T-shirts and individual bears made by various "teddy bear artists." The shop also sells various plush animals and other collectibles.

If it's a hat you need, stop at **Western Brands**, 141 E. Elkhorn Avenue. There's a great selection of cowboy hats plus wonderful felt bowlers, top hats and more. Western Brands also carries lots of Levi's, T-shirts, jackets, blankets, "cattle drover" coats and other items to make you feel right at home on the range.

Up on the corner of Moraine Avenue and Rockwell Street is the historic **Park Theatre**, built in 1913, with its impressive white tower that is Estes Park's tallest structure. The tower was added to the building by a former owner as a monument to a woman who left him at the altar. The Park Theatre's cafe and snack shops are a good place to stop in summer, open from 8 AM until 9 PM daily. Down the

INSIDERS' TIP
In fall, elk make an eerie but beautiful mating call that's one of the area's top evening attractions. (The elk bugle at dawn and dusk.) Rocky Mountain National Park offers bus trips for the public to listen to these impressive animals bugle to discourage individual drivers and traffic jams at Horseshoe Park and other popular listening spots. Contact the Estes Park Chamber of Commerce, (800) 443-7837, or the national park's headquarters, 586-1206.

The Longs Peak Scottish Festival is held each year in early September.

lane next to a little shopping mall is **Ye Old Tin Shop**, at No. 134, with a charming collection of reproductions of antique metal tins, including Morton Salt, Lipton Tea and Hershey's Kisses tins, and many more unusual antique signs and metal plaques — all quite inexpensive.

Stanley Village is the shopping center directly below the imposing, white Stanley Hotel, which is perched on a hillside above town — you can't miss it. Slightly to the east is a **Safeway** and a shopping area that offers visitors lots of necessary services. To the east of Safeway is a **Coast to Coast Hardware** store and a **Ben Franklin** for those little gadgets one always ends up needing on a trip. There's also the **Notchtop Baked Goods & Natural Foods Cafe and Pub** and **Mountain Home Cafe** (see the Estes Park Restaurants chapter for details on each) as well as many other shops.

Winona Knits, 344 E. Elkhorn Avenue, in Barlow Plaza, offers an attractive and affordable selection of sportswear with golf, fishing and tennis themes and other nice casual clothing.

Stamps-N-Stuff, 586-1029, in the Sundance Center for the Arts, 150 E. Riverside Drive, has an amazing collection of hundreds of rubber stamps with designs covering everything from animals to entire landscape scenes. Stamps have become a new, anyone-can-do-it art form in which people combine several stamps to make colorful scenes that take only minutes to create. **Canyonlands Indian Arts**, 146 W. Elkhorn Avenue, is a new shop featuring top-quality Indian and Southwest jewelry, authentic pottery, kachinas, carvings and Navajo rugs.

Tours, Attractions and Festivals

All those beautiful mountains could keep you happy for years. But even the most dedicated nature lover sometimes needs a change. And, after all, there's a lot to see in Estes Park, since much of the early Colorado history was made here by settlers such as Alexander MacGregor and F.O. Stanley — not to mention 19th-century writer Isabella Bird and Enos

Photo: Longs Peak Scottish Festival

Mills, the "Father of Rocky Mountain National Park."

This chapter begins with tours that are fun to take, followed by the main year-round attractions you'll want to be sure to see. Then there's information on festivals, both big and homespun — Estes Park diversions that happen around the same time each year. Estes is such a family-oriented place, you'll notice many of these diversions are perfect for kids. Summer camp programs follow — definitely kidstuff. The chapter ends with Events Central, including event addresses and how to find them. Most of these events can use volunteers. It's a great way to get acquainted, so don't be shy about lending a hand.

By the way, Boulder County is just a stone's throw from the Estes Valley. Some Boulder County attractions are closer to Estes than they are to the city of Boulder. Even events smack on Boulder's Pearl Street Mall are less than an hour away, making them fair game for your fun. See the Boulder Festivals and Annual Events and Attractions chapters.

Tours

Charles Tour & Travel Services offers tours over Trail Ridge Road, a Grand Lake Tour, horseback riding trips in the park, Bear Lake hikes and Fall Foliage/Elk Bugling tours. Call 586-5151 for current rates.

American Wilderness Tours, 586-1626, has six-wheeled vehicles to take you off the beaten path and into the back country. Some tours include steak dinners and sing-alongs. Tours for private groups are available.

Aerial Tramway, right in town, offers a short (three- to five-minute) ride overlooking the town with great views of Longs Peak and the Continental Divide. Price is $8 adults, $4 kids 6 to 11 (free, younger than 6). The office is at 420 E. Riverside Drive, 586-3675.

Colorado Bicycling Adventures: Want to ride a bicycle through the mountains but not uphill? This company, 586-4241, offers downhill bike tours in Rocky Mountain National Park and other scenic spots. See details in the Estes Park Participatory Sports chapter under "Bicycling."

Attractions

Estes Park Area Historical Museum
200 Fourth St., Estes Park • 586-6256

This interesting museum shows the history and heritage of the area's first settlers, including an 1859 photograph of just-arrived first settler Joel Estes and six of his 13 children. Look for the original National Park Headquarters building out back next to an old homestead cabin. The museum includes a Stanley Steamer, pioneer artifacts, historical photos and documentation of the founding of Rocky Mountain National Park. Open May through October from 10 AM to 5 PM Monday through Saturday and from 1 to 5 PM Sunday. Open in March and December from 10 AM to 5 PM Tuesday to Saturday and from 1 to 5 PM Sunday. Open by appointment only during the rest of the year. Admission is $2.50 for adults, $2 for seniors (60 and older) and $1 for children ages 5 to 12. The museum is being renovated in 1997 and will be closed from January through March.

MacGregor Ranch Museum and Education Center
180 MacGregor Ln., 0.5-mile north of Estes Park • 586-3749

The MacGregor Ranch Museum and Education Center is a working ranch commemorating the Alexander Q. MacGregor family, one of the valley's largest and most influential ranching families. MacGregor battled the infamous Lord Dunraven over an illegal land claim at Estes Park — Dunraven had bought up all the land for his private hunting reserve. The museum displays domestic items, furniture,

---

INSIDERS' TIP

For a change of pace, why not take a bicycle tour of the area? Colorado Bicycling Adventures, 586-4241, in Estes Park, offers tours for all levels and abilities. See details under "Bicycling" in this chapter.

silver mining and ranching equipment plus photos of life in the area in the 1870s through the mid-20th century. Historical photos and documents of MacGregor's battle with Dunraven are on display. Admission is free, but donations are encouraged. Open Tuesday through Friday from June through August (closed weekends). The facility is open to school groups year round. It's a half-mile north of Estes Park off Devil's Gulch Road.

Enos Mills Cabin
At the base of Twin Sisters Mountain, Estes Park • 586-4706

The Enos Mills Cabin operates as a nature center and museum today, but it was the home of the well-known "Father of Rocky Mountain National Park." Mills campaigned nationally for the establishment of the national parks in general and specifically for Rocky Mountain National Park. A naturalist, writer and inn owner in Estes Park, his cabin is at the base of Twin Sisters Mountain and has several nature trails on the property. His daughter, Enda Mills Kiley (yes, it's Enda, not Edna), and others offer tours of the house, which also has on display Mills' books, photos and other memorabilia. Copies of his books are for sale. Admission is free. The cabin is open from 11 AM to 4 PM Tuesday through Sunday, Memorial Day through Labor Day, and other times by appointment only.

Estes Park Brewery
470 Prospect Village Dr., Estes Park • 586-5421

Open summers from 11 AM until 10 PM daily, the brewery with its pub and restaurant offers free tours and samples of the six microbrews. See the Estes Park Nightlife chapter for details.

Estes Park Public Library
335 E. Elkhorn Ave., Estes Park • 586-8116

Looking for Internet access? The library has it plus CD-ROMs that can be checked out. This library is also kid-friendly. It loans toys as well as books and has a parent-child center with educational activities that change monthly. Librarian Kerry Aiken is a local puppeteer and performer. She does a children's story hour on Thursdays and Saturdays and also works with the parent-child center. The library is open 9 AM to 9 PM summer weekdays, 9 AM to 5 PM Fridays and Saturdays, and 1 to 5 PM Sundays. During winter the library opens at 10 AM Monday through Saturday.

Ferncliff Grocery Store
23 Main St., Ferncliff • (303) 747-2531

On your way up Colo. Highway 7 to Estes Park, on the Allenspark Business Loop, is this little combo bakery and deli/full-service grocery store. Maybe in a big town it would be less of a landmark, but here, in the virtual wilderness, it's something of an all-purpose entertainment center and mini-resort complete with a liquor store, laundromat, ice cream and pizza parlor, fishing lake and cabins, video rentals, gasoline and camping supplies.

Miniature Golf

Miniature golf may be little, but in Estes it's big. Courses are all mini-amusement parks, where it's easy to spend money on silly activities. The cost is usually fairly reasonable. You might pay as little as $1.50 for a game, but you're likely to want to stay and spend more if your party is having fun. During the summer, these places often stay open from early morning until 10 at night. **Estes Park Ride-A-Kart**, 586-6495, 2250 Big Thompson Avenue, has 36 holes of miniature golf, go-karts, bumper boats and a miniature train. **Fun City**, 586-2070, 375 Moraine Avenue, has a 36-hole golf course, bumper cars, video arcade and two slides. Then there's a 19-hole course at **Tiny Town Miniature Golf**, 586-6333, 840 Moraine Avenue.

Stanley Hotel
333 Wonderview Ave., Estes Park • 586-3371, (800) 976-1377

On the top of a hill east of Estes Park, with a perfect view of Longs Peak, is a wedding-cake-white hotel with a history that has always blessed the town. It started in June 1903, when a frail tuberculosis patient weighing little more than 100 pounds chugged up the rugged road to Estes Park. His transportation was unusual — a steam-powered automobile he and his brother had invented. An East Coast doctor had given this sickly man just a few more years to live, but Freelan O. Stanley had some sparks left. After all, the Stanley Steamer car wasn't the only invention he had ever made. He and his brother had figured out a dry-coating process for photographic paper, and they had made a fortune selling the patent to Kodak.

When F.O. Stanley found his health improving in Estes Park, he decided the place was worthy of a fine hotel. The grand one he erected had modern conveniences, including an all-electric kitchen. There wasn't much electricity in Estes Park then, but it was no problem for Stanley. He provided the obvious solution, a hydroelectric plant, so his hotel could have power. It happened to supply more power than the hotel needed, so he sold the remainder to the town. Now, it always helps a hotel if a good road leads up to it. Estes Park didn't have a great road, but it had Stanley. He helped finance a real road through the North St. Vrain Canyon, connecting Estes Park with the railhead at Lyons and, thus, with the rest of the growing Front Range.

The Stanley continues to be a testament to a grand era. Tourists are welcome to visit, and historic tours are offered year round five times daily ($5 per adult; $3 per adult with groups of 12 or more, and children 12 and younger are free). The tours go through all of the public rooms and down into the tunnel underneath the hotel, which is built on solid rock. Visitors will see fool's gold glittering in the rock that supports the original hotel beams. There's a small museum on the ground level. Many community events take place at the Stanley. You can also stay as a guest. See the Estes Park Accommodations chapter for more information.

Sunday Concerts
Stanley Hotel • 333 Wonderview Ave., Estes Park • 586-3371, (800) 976-1377

Jazz, folk, opera and chamber groups all play at the Stanley. The Stanley Hotel Music Room is a charming space. This historic room is fully restored, including the piano stage. It's white and pale green with big windows looking out toward Longs Peak. Smaller concerts take place here, while larger ones are held in Stanley Concert Hall, a separate building designed to hold 200 attendees. Musicians who

have played there say the hall has among the best and liveliest acoustics in the state. The concerts generally start around 2 PM Sunday afternoons — but call to check — and most are free.

Estes Park Center/YMCA of the Rockies
2515 Tunnel Rd., Estes Park • 586-3341

The YMCA of the Rockies is a huge facility with log cabins, lodges and a leisurely pace that makes you automatically switch to strolling gear. It offers loads of family-oriented activities. During the winter, when the town is quieter, you can purchase a day pass for $3 to use the YMCA's facilities. The pass lets you have fun at the indoor gym and roller rink. There's an indoor swimming pool plus outdoor volleyball, basketball and tennis. Using the Nautilus training room costs another $2.

There's also a library and museum.

During the summer, more than 4,000 people stay at the YMCA of the Rockies. (If you'd like to be one or stay during the winter, check the chapter on Estes Park Accommodations.) To use the facilities in this busy season, the Y personnel asks that you either be staying there as a guest or that you have proof of membership in a hometown YMCA. Once you've shown that proof, a number of programs are open for your enjoyment.

In addition to winter offerings, there's an outdoor mini-golf course here. Complimentary family programs usually give you six options each day, ranging from survival classes and Indian lore to games of water balloon volleyball and campfire songs. For a fee, YMCA registered guests and hometown YMCA members can also enjoy Y-organized horseback riding, mountain bike rentals (including kids' sizes) and whitewater rafting.

Summer Camps

Many accommodations around Estes Park offer special programs for children. Check the chapter on Estes Park Accommodations for possibilities. Summer camps around Estes Park also get organized by church groups, so check the Worship section of the Estes Park

FYI

Unless otherwise noted, the area code for all phone numbers in this guide is 970.

Community chapter for some phone numbers you can call for more information. For instance, **Covenant Heights**, 586-2900, is a conference center with facilities for up to 200 people that is used for a number of children's programs. The programs must be church-related, educational or nonprofit.

Glacier View Ranch, 459-3244, is also near Estes Park. It's operated by the Seventh-Day Adventists and has many church-related programs. When space is available, they sometimes will rent to families too. We've been up there in the summertime for birthday overnighters, and it's very pretty, with a little lake for canoeing, an indoor pool where some kids learn to kayak and comfortable hotel-type rooms in the lodges. Another family we know went up there during the winter and had a great time cross-country skiing.

Presbyterian Highlands Camp, south of Allenspark, (303) 747-2888, is yet another big facility, often used by elementary grade classes on overnight adventures. It's a favorite choice for field trip excursions by our sons' public school. The kids love the volleyball area, the bluebirds and the big, noisy mess hall. Be sure to ask about the huge boulder group with a secret room in the middle. At Highlands, the meeting hall gets used as a chapel by church groups and as a meeting area by school groups. There are week-long camps for children, often with church-related themes. Big youth groups, both local and from out of state, also rent the place. When there's space, individual families can rent a cabin. It's a very pretty setting, with a choice of rustic old-fashioned cabins or new places with vaulted ceilings. Here are two other possibilities:

Cheley Camp
(In winter) P.O. Box 6525, Denver 80206 • (800) 226-7386
(In summer) 3960 Fish Creek Rd., Estes Park • 586-4244

Cheley's summer camp program has been featured in national magazines such as Country Living. It's probably the largest privately owned camp west of the Mississippi and has been around since 1921. Nearly 500 kids enjoy the fun, in camps of 60 each, grouped by age and sex. The camps are four weeks or eight weeks. Mountaineering, with fabulous vistas everywhere, and horseback riding on nearly 150 camp-owned horses are especially popular. And with hiking right out the back door, it's easy to guess that the children get to know the Rocky Mountains. Cheley starts filling up by January, so apply early. Cost for one session is $2,500, including room, board and all programs.

Estes Park Center/YMCA of the Rockies
2515 Tunnel Rd., Estes Park • 586-3341

The YMCA has a summer day-camp program for potty-trained 2½-year-olds through high-schoolers. It's from 8:30 AM to 3:30 PM and costs $17 a day. Programs are geared by age. The older kids can be in leadership programs and adventure hikes. The youngest kids are more likely to stay close by. Preregistration is required and parents must either be staying at the Y or be Y members.

Festivals and Annual Events

Winter

December

Round the Table Sing-Along
Stanley Concert Hall • Stanley Hotel, 333 Wonderview Ave., Estes Park • 586-3371, (800) 976-1377

Generally during the first weekend in December, the Estes Park Chorale sings traditional and contemporary songs of the season, and the audience is invited to join in. The sing-along starts around 7 PM. Contributions are welcomed.

Holiday Home Tour
Throughout Estes Park Valley • 586-4644

Proud owners of six fine Estes Park homes decorate for Christmas, then open their doors on a Saturday in mid-December so you can wander inside. The Quota Club, a local businesswomen's group, sponsors the event, and profits go to local health and social needs.

Usually the tour is from 11 AM to 4 PM. The fee is generally less than $10.

A Christmas Memory
Stanley Hotel Theatre • Stanley Hotel, 333 Wonderview Ave., Estes Park • 586-3371, (800) 976-1377

A Stanley tradition, this dinner-theater production is a funny, tear-jerker, family classic about Truman Capote's boyhood with a wise but dotty aunt who makes holiday fruit cakes. The play usually begins the day after Thanksgiving and continues on weekdays and weekends until just before Christmas. Check with the hotel for show times and ticket prices, which are generally $10 for the evening show and around $30 for dinner and the show. Also making a visit to the Stanley a treat is an annual Christmas tree show sponsored by the Estes Park Women's Club with about 50 dazzling, decorated tabletop trees in the main lobby contributed by different local groups. Visitors can buy a $1 chance and perhaps win a tree. The trees are displayed the Monday after Thanksgiving until December 21.

January

Frost Giant 5K or 10K Race
Municipal Building • 170 MacGregor Ave., Estes Park • 586-8191

You might be a mild-mannered human, but you'll become an Estes Park frost giant if there's a little humidity and freezing weather, for your breath will add lacy frozen filigrees to your eyebrows and hair. The 200 or so runners and walkers who compete in this event have rosy cheeks and smiles, so they're cute frost giants. If you join the throng, you'll puff up a scenic road to MacGregor Ranch and circle back for a total of either 5 or 10 kilometers (roughly 3 to 6 miles). The 5K race starts around 11 AM; the 10K starts at noon. Entrance fees to this late-month event are roughly $18 and include a Frost Giant T-shirt. It costs less without the T-shirt, more if you register late.

February

Romance of the Rockies
Downtown Estes Park • 586-6641

Simple pleasures bless the 100 or so sweethearts who arrive this weekend to tie the knot. You have two chances to marry or renew wedding vows on Valentine's Saturday or Sunday. The group ceremonies generally are at a nice restaurant or the municipal building. Saying "I do," the sheet wedding cake and glass of punch are free. Pay extra for champagne and photographs. Then tour the town in antique Stanley Steamer cars, limousines or hay-rack rides for a small price. Some years a Valentine's Dance is featured too. Local hotels and motels offer special sweetheart packages. Call ahead.

Imagine This!
Estes Park High School • 1600 Manford Ave., Estes Park • 586-9203

The rest of this event's title is See It! Hear It! Do It! Be It! This is the single biggest arts event of the year sponsored by the Cultural Arts Council of Estes Park, which represents all the arts in the area. Artists, musicians, jugglers and actors give youngsters and adults a chance to create art at more than 26 hands-on activities areas. The event, held the third weekend in February, generally goes from 11 AM until 4 PM. There's also a silent auction of original art work, gift certificates and merchandise. In the evening a benefit performance of

---

INSIDERS' TIP

Stephen King hated the movie version of his book, *The Shining*, which he felt departed too much from his original story. The 1997 TV miniseries of *The Shining*, filmed at the Stanley Hotel in Estes Park — the original Inspiration for his book — is "King's Revenge," according to informed sources. King stayed at the Stanley for six months as screenwriter and executive producer during the filming of the TV version, which reflects King's original story. During that time Hollywood revamped parts of the hotel to better suit its starring role.

dancers, musicians and other artists from the Estes Valley keeps the entertainment going. Dubbed as the main "friend-" and fund-raiser of the year for the nonprofit Arts Council, a small donation is requested at the door.

Dog Weight Pull
Estes Valley • (800) 44-ESTES

In Jack London's *Call of the Wild*, Buck pulls a 1,000-pound sled over a wager of gold. This isn't quite as dramatic, but it's more the real thing — a four-state, regional dog-pull contest held the last weekend in February. Dogs wear special harnesses to prevent injury, and weights are added incrementally. The winner pulls the most weight for 16 feet within a minute in a sled on snow and a cart on wheels. Small challengers have included a 10-pound poodle mix. A 200-pound Irish Wolfhound was among the largest. The little guy and the bruiser don't face off; they're in different classes and compete against dogs their own size.

Fine Arts Guild of the Rockies Annual Musical
Stanley Concert Hall and various locations, Estes Park • 586-9203

Generally during two weekends in late February or early March, a guest director works with the community to present a favorite musical, such as *Mame*, *Brigadoon* or *The King and I*. Local guild members star in this community-theater event. Tickets are around $8 for adults, $4 for children. The curtain rises at 7 PM for the Thursday through Saturday performances, and there's also a 2 PM Sunday matinee. Call for exact dates and location.

March

Estes Park Oratorio and Chamber Concert
Stanley Concert Hall • Stanley Hotel, 333 Wonderview Ave., Estes Park • 586-9203

This free Sunday concert offers a special

way to celebrate Easter with music for the season. Call for the exact date (generally the last Sunday in March).

Spring

May

Annual Duck Race
Downtown Estes Park • 586-4431, (800) 443-7837

On the first Saturday in May, thousands of floating yellow ducks, each tagged with a sponsor and charity choice, raise more than $20,000 at this annual event. To help you remember the date, the Rotary Club sponsors it on Kentucky Derby Day. But ducks aren't as quick as a thoroughbred. They start at Nicky's Restaurant, 1350 Fall River Road, and depending on the runoff, bobble downtown on the Fall, then, nearly two hours later, reach the Wheel Bar, 132 E. Elkhorn Avenue. The mayor and police chief pull out the winning duck and distribute great prizes, such as trips to Disneyland and Hawaii. Sponsoring a duck costs around $20. Watching is free. Proceeds go to local nonprofit charities.

Art Walk and Jazz Festival
Downtown Estes Park • 586-9203

More than 20 galleries feature special exhibits and artists' demonstrations Friday through Sunday. Children's art activities are offered, and from 1 to 5 PM, live jazz concerts put an extra spring in the step of revelers in downtown Estes Park. This festival usually happens the second weekend in May.

Kite-Flying Contest
Stanley Park Ballfields, across from Estes Park Fairground • Community Dr., Estes Park • 586-6104

Register at 9:30 AM, and you, too, can add a homemade creation or a store-bought fancy to the sky. Participating in this pretty, mid-May event is the main reason grandparents and other folks bring kids . . . much more fun than just watching. You might even win a prize, such as dinner or movie theater passes. The event is free.

Parade of the Years
Old-time Car Rally
Estes Park Historical Museum • 200 Fourth St., Estes Park • 586-6256

Estes Park is a center for old-time cars, partly because Stanley Steamer Mountain Wagons were invented by Freelan Oscar Stanley, who built that big white hotel. This rally is sponsored by the Estes Park Historical Museum, where around 25 cars in the Estes Park Historical Automobile and Touring Society are displayed Saturday and Sunday. Meanwhile, around 40 or 50 old-time cars drive up from Loveland, re-enacting Stanley's historic arrival in his Stanley Steamer. You'll see them around town all weekend. Stanley Steamers, by the way, are huge touring cars with steam engines, similar to the engines in steam locomotives but smaller. Other wonderful cars you may see during the weekend include Ford Model A's, 1930 Ford Roadsters and Pierce Arrows plus '60s vintage Jaguars, Mustangs and Corvettes. A fee of $2.50 ($1 for children and $2 for seniors) lets you into the museum and car show. The rally is held in late May, usually during Memorial Day weekend.

Summer

Throughout the Summer

Allenspark Melodrama
Wild Basin Lodge • County Rd. 84 W., 2 miles north of Allenspark • 747-2545

Performed by the Allenspark Community Theatre, these summertime-only shows (every Monday in July and the first Monday in August) have a special Old West flavor in this beautiful setting. Melodramas are outrageously exaggerated Wild West plays. The villain may sneer and twist his handlebar mustache, the sweet heroine might bat long eyelashes, and a Handsome Dudley Do-Right type will save her, although, since women's liberation, sometimes she saves herself. Shows in this community theater begin around 8 PM. Keeping young audiences in mind, the price includes popcorn to eat or throw at the villain. Cheering, hissing and booing are required. Reservations are strongly recommended. Tickets are $5 for adults and $2 for children younger than 12.

Bruiser the Dog and
Bob Aiken the Puppeteer
Various locations in Estes Park • 586-6365

If you're lucky, you may spot Bruiser while you're in Estes Park. Bruiser is the cutest, clumsiest, biggest-pawed puppy you'll ever see. He's really Bob Aiken, a local puppeteer and performer who regularly charms the crowds. He often performs at Barlow Plaza. That's on Elkhorn Avenue near Poppy's Pizza and Mama Rose's Restaurant. Dick Barlow often hires performers to entertain at his plaza during the summer. Bob Aiken and his performance group, Four Hands and a Cloud of Dust, also enchant crowds at the YMCA on Thursday nights during the summer. And you can hire his troupe for private performances.

Music in the Mountains
Rocky Ridge Music Center • Colo. Hwy. 7, 12 miles south of Estes Park • 586-4031

Locals call Rocky Ridge a real educated, into-classical-music group that does chamber music and opera. Student and faculty recitals take place here on Sundays around 3 PM from late June until the end of August. Call for current ticket prices.

The Estes Park Music Festival
Stanley Concert Hall • Stanley Hotel, 333 Wonderview Ave., Estes Park • 586-9203

Boulder's nationally acclaimed Colorado Music Festival Orchestra comes to Estes Park on Monday evenings during the summer from late June through early August. For more about this better-than-the-best orchestra, see the Boulder chapter on Arts. Ticket prices vary.

June

Lake Estes Fishing Derby
Lake Estes Marina • U.S. Hwy. 36, near Lake Estes • 586-2011

Every three weeks during summer, the Division of Wildlife drops 400 fish at many points along the Estes Valley river system, making trout plentiful. They double-stock the rivers and lake for this event, and the town buys some extra-big fish to tempt anglers. What's more, the Cline Trout Farm in Boulder donates some fish for the weekend (the first one in June). All this means contestants in the 8 AM to noon fishing derby are likely to pull in fine catches. Entrance fees are around $3. Proceeds go to the fire department and local youth programs.

Wool Market
Estes Park Fairground • Community Dr., Estes Park • 586-6104

Tourists are welcome to enjoy this working wool market. Around 10,000 wander among the market's animal shows, demonstrations and fiber items. Events start the Thursday prior to the second weekend in June with workshops and seminars on spinning, weaving, dying, raising animals, tax laws, shearing and grading wool. Throughout the weekend, enjoy spinning and weaving contests and a children's tent. See llamas, angora rabbits, alpacas and sheep, or consider buying one of the beautiful sweaters, yarns or other wool-related items. Admission is free.

Teddy Bear Picnic
YMCA of the Rockies • 2515 Tunnel Rd., Estes Park • 586-6483

Why don't you and your family introduce your teddy bears to Estes' other teddy bear families? About 800 people did just that in 1995. The Talking Teddy Store has sponsored this picnic since 1983. Cute silly events may include a dentist who talks to children about care of their bear's teeth (and children's teeth). Celebear-ties, such as Smokey Bear and Celestial Seasoning's Sleepytime Bear, have appeared. There are prizes for the largest bear family, biggest bear and cutest bear costume. Sandwiches, cake and beverages might be on hand for nibbling. The picnic starts mid-morning and lasts until the teddies get tired. Admission is free to this Father's Day weekend event.

Scandinavian Midsummer Festival
Bond Park, Downtown Estes Park • 586-9203

The local Scandinavian Club's festival honors traditional celebrations for the year's long-

est day in late June. Friday, they erect a maypole ("May" is a Swedish word for dressing in green), and onlookers decorate it with greens and live flowers. Norwegians, Danes and Finns used to start a bonfire in a Viking longboat to scare away the evil spirits on this long, long day. The Scandinavian Club hasn't found any people in Estes willing to burn up boats. So enterprising club members hammer one together and launch it near the Lake Estes Marina. The fire reflects on the water, reminding celebrants of Norwegian fiords brooding under tall mountains. Revelers then dance into the evening. All weekend, professional dancers in bright-colored folk costumes invite onlookers to learn new steps. You also can attend workshops, where sages share Scandinavian history. Food booths offer Swedish pancakes with bright red lingonberries. Or nibble potatas korv — a beef, pork and potato sausage. Crafts for sale include wheat weaving items, painted-wood folk paintings and rosemaling items, which are paintings of traditional flower designs. Proceeds go to pay the dancers, who sometimes come from around the world.

July

Estes Park Fireworks Display
Lake Estes, Estes Park • 586-6104

Locals arrive around 8 PM on the Fourth of July, generally gathering in the Stanley Village Shopping Center or near Lake Estes. Outdoor bands entertain the crowds. Around 9:15 PM, the fireworks shoot up at the edge of the lake, so the reflections bloom in the water below. If you position yourself well, you get to see all this drama with the mountains as a backdrop. The event is free.

Western and Wildlife Art Show
Call for location • 586-9203

Sponsored by the Fine Arts Guild of the Rockies, this annual late July favorite features more than 30 participating artists from Colorado and the West with work in a variety of media including painting, sculpture, prints and more. Western landscapes and characters from the Old West are the main subject matter There's a "quick draw" and auction of original works.

Rooftop Rodeo
Estes Park Fairground • Community Dr., Estes Park • 586-6104

The rodeo started in 1923 as the Estes Park Stampede, stopped during WWII, but revived right afterward and has been galloping ever since. Team roping, bulldogging, broncos and steer wrestling are part of the week's events, sanctioned by the Professional Rodeo Cowboys Association. A carnival offers plenty of rides. Cowboy poets read on a stage with a campfire scene. Sometimes, the poet brings his harmonica or strums a guitar. Then there's country-western music, with the likes of Sweethearts of the Rodeo and the Darn Thirsty Cowboys.

Generally, these mid-July events cost less than $10 for adults and less than $5 for children, but prices vary depending on who's in the main corral. By the way, it's not called "Rooftop Rodeo" because you have to watch from a roof. The name is to remind people of the 7,200-foot elevation and the United States' highest paved highway, Trail Ridge Road.

Fall

Throughout the Fall

Bull Elk Bugling
Rocky Mountain National Park • 586-1206

Anyone who expects the bull elk's mating call to sound like a royal French horn is in for a surprise. These huge animals belt out a whistling squeal. It might strike you as wimpy, but, boy, does it ever carry! The haunting call can cross valleys and reach high mountain meadows. Forest rangers say the best time to witness (and hear) elk bugling is throughout the fall in the morning, from sunrise to an hour after, and then at dusk, starting about an hour before sunset. Three areas tend to provide good viewing: Moraine Park, Horseshoe Park and Upper Beaver Meadows. To view wildlife, don't leave the designated trails and roadways. While bull elks rarely charge tourists, there are incidents of rangers charging visitors . . . and the fine they charge for harassing wildlife can be stiff. The Bighorn Brigade will be around to answer questions and remind you to stay out of the meadows. If you prefer smaller crowds, come on a weekday.

Quaking Aspen
Rocky Mountain National Park • 586-1206

Mother Nature gives us hot dry years when the leaves turn gold early, and she also bestows cool, moist summers when the green leaves never quite believe it's time to change. Because the golden aspen season varies, call the Park's information office to learn the best time (generally mid-September through mid-October) and places, which tend to be around Bear Lake Road and Moraine Park. Park officials say aspen stands outside the Park can be even more spectacular. The highway to Allenspark is designated a scenic byway, with huge aspen stands. Colo. highways 119 and 72, heading south to Nederland and Central City, are good too. Wherever you drive, find a chance to step out on a trail and walk. Get the aspens between you and the sunlight to take in their luminescence and brilliant color. Listen to the fluttering leaves. Smell the tannin. While strolling, you may notice elk coming down from the high country to beat the winter snows. Rangers request that you don't pick any aspen leaves, since our thin mountain soil needs their nutrients. To preserve the Park's beauty for the future, remember to leave with only your memories and photographs.

September

Labor Day Crafts Show
Bond Park, Estes Park • 586-9203

On Labor Day weekend, craftspeople from all over the state set up about 100 booths with pottery, bronze and wood sculpture, sewing, jewelry, photography and oil painting. One lady sells bean soup mixes. The local volunteer fire department puts on this event, and it benefits the Muscular Dystrophy Association and the fire department.

Longs Peak Scottish Festival
Estes Park Fairground • Community Dr., Estes Park • 586-6308

This four-day festival in early September is a 10-ring circus. It's so grand, *USA Today* has listed it as one of the nation's top 10 things to do. At least two and sometimes three top ceremonial bands come to play in the tattoo concerts, which include drums, bugles and bagpipes. The White House Drum and Bugle

Corps has performed here, as have the Governor General's Foot Guard from Canada and the Royal Highlands Scot Guards. Celtic folk musicians arrive for competitions. Irish stepdancers display their dazzling footwork. Evening concerts thrill Celtic hearts all over town. There's always at least one chance to sing "Auld Lang Syne."

Music isn't the only drawing card at this festival. Highland games include tossing a stone the size of a shot put, throwing a caber, which is the size of a telephone pole, and other heavy athletics. Highlanders demonstrate how to shoot antique cannon and how to fly fish with lures. Dr. James Durward, founder of this festival, points out that lure fishing had to start in Scotland. After all, a thrifty Scot isn't going to dig up a new worm every time he casts his line!

Altogether, about 3,000 performers come to this event, and approximately 30,000 people come to see it. Those wanting products can buy quilts, sweaters and other crafts related to these island peoples. Hungry revelers can buy scones, which are slightly sweet biscuits; Scotch eggs, hard-boiled then rolled in bacon crumbs; sausages; hot dogs; and pastie, sort of a non-flaking turnover with hamburger inside. Don't forget the shortbread. When you're full, you can quaff it down with Scotch or Irish libations. There's plenty of soda on hand for the lads and lassies.

Ticket prices in 1996 were $13 for a one-day field pass and $22 for a two-day pass. Children younger than 15 could get in one day for $5, and the wee bairns who had not yet reached the tender age of 5 were free. All the money earned by the festival goes back into the festival and other local nonprofits.

Fine Arts and Crafts Show
Bond Park, Estes Park • 586-9203

Sponsored by the Fine Arts Guild of the Rockies, this mid-September event is a juried, national art show. More than 80 booths display everything from pottery and small items to paintings and photography. Estes Park is working to become more of an art community, for instance bringing in national traveling art shows. This show has been going on for more than 19 years and is a pleasant way to pass the afternoon.

Kids and Folks March
Stanley Park Ballfields • 380 Community Dr., Estes Park • 586-8191

This 10K (6.2 miles) walk goes through downtown Estes along the Fall River's pedestrian walks to the Donut Haus, 342 Moraine Avenue, and back. Check-in is 8 AM, but you can start as late as noon. Some people stop and shop or eat along the way. It's free, but many locals march with pledges to support community projects. The march takes place in mid-September.

Chamber Music Festival
Call for location • 586-9203

Sponsored by the Chamber Music Society of Estes Park, here's a special weekend (in late September or early October) for Chamber music aficionados. There's a variety of concerts with local and Colorado performers presenting an entertaining program. Call for ticket prices.

October

"The Shining" Costume Ball
Stanley Hotel • 333 Wonderview Ave., Estes Park • 586-3371, (800) 976-1377

Stephen King wrote his horror classic, *The Shining*, after being inspired by a stay at the Stanley Hotel. Once you see what a lovely, elegant place the Stanley is, you'll be even more impressed by how creepily King remade it in his pull-up-the-covers-and-keep-the-lights-on story. You can make a similar transformation by dressing up for the Stanley's annual costume ball, held Halloween night. You don't have to be horrible and ghoulish. After all, being a fairy tale princess is a transformation too (for some of us). Just be sure whatever you wear is good dancing clothes and easy to sit in for dinner. Dinner and the dance are around $30.

Halloween Night
Downtown Estes Park

Here's an informal, grassroots event. Halloween night, many locals go downtown in costumes, often with kids in tow. It's a low-key celebration, fun because it's so easy and unpressured. What's more, many stores hand out candy to the kids.

November

A Christmas Memory
The Stanley Hotel• 333 Wonderview Ave., Estes Park • 586-3371, (800) 976-1377

This annual dinner theater production is a family-oriented, funny account for the holidays. Tickets to the play alone are around $10, and for the play and dinner, they're closer to $30. Performances are generally Friday and Saturday from the weekend following Thanksgiving until Christmas.

Christmas Parade
Estes Park Fairground • Community Dr., Estes Park

When the downtown Christmas lights come on, the parade begins. It starts on the west side of town around 5:30 PM the Friday after Thanksgiving, heads through the main shopping district and ends at the chamber of commerce on the east side of town around 7 PM. In 1994, there were nearly 50 float entrants. One recent favorite was the Sugar Plum, all white and plum colors with 5,000 twinkle lights and girls dressed in white angel costumes. Bruiser, a wonderfully dog-like puppeteer, sits atop his dog house performing tricks. Santa's sleigh is always the last float in line. Onlookers dress in winter woolens, parkas and blankets. On a mild evening, a jacket will do. If it's cold, some people wear everything they've got. No matter what the thermometer says, the sight is heartwarming — and free. Stores downtown stay open to sell Christmas goods and warm refreshments.

Oratorio Concert
Community Church of the Rockies • 1700 Brodie Ave., Estes Park • 586-4404

Portions of the Messiah are performed by the Oratorio Society and Estes Park Chamber Orchestra. It's a concert where the performers have practiced and practiced. If you show up for all the rehearsals, you might be part of the oratorio. When you just come for the performance, you can hum along with "The Hallelujah Chorus" if you must, but do it softly — this is a performance, not a sing-along. The concert usually starts around 7 PM the Sunday after Thanksgiving. Call for exact time. Donations are appreciated.

Events Central

Here are the names, phones and locations of the main event centers in town.

Estes Park Chamber of Commerce and Visitor Information Center
500 Big Thompson Ave., Estes Park • 586-4431, (800) 44-ESTES

This center has more information about Estes Park than there are petals in a clump of columbine flowers. To reach the center, coming from Boulder on U.S. Highway 36, go to the second stoplight and make a right. The center is right across from the Taco Bell on U.S. Highway 34. They're open from 8 AM to 8 PM Monday through Saturday, then from 9 AM to 6 PM on Sunday.

FYI

Unless otherwise noted, the area code for all phone numbers in this guide is 970.

Cultural Arts Council
P.O. Box 4135, 160 Moraine Ave., Estes Park 80517 • 586-9203

The CAC represents all the arts in the area with the broad goal of enhancing the quality and accessibility of the arts in the Estes Valley. Call or write to these folks for music, art or theater events and programs.

Estes Park Fairground
Community Dr., Estes Park • 586-6104

The fairground is near Lake Estes. To get there, you take either U.S Highway 34 or 36 to the east side of town. The fairground is on U.S Highway 36. Right after you pass Lake Estes, turn south onto Community Drive. You'll see arenas, the stables, the covered building for special events and ballfields. You're at the fairground now!

Stanley Hotel
333 Wonderview Ave., Estes Park • 586-3371, (800) 976-1377

Once you're in downtown, you'll see the big white Stanley Hotel on a hill northeast of town. The Stanley Concert Hall is up there too. You can't miss it; but if you do, just pull over anywhere and ask for directions. Everybody knows the Stanley. Call to check on the schedule of events.

Estes Park Center/YMCA of the Rockies
2515 Tunnel Rd., Estes Park • 586-3341

To reach the YMCA, take U.S. Highway 36 to the second stoplight. Take a left at Elkhorn Avenue. At the second stoplight, turn left on Moraine Avenue. Follow the signs to the YMCA. The tree-lined road winds through a lot of countryside, but you'll soon be there.

Even if you're not staying at the YMCA, it can be a good place to call. They don't publicize their events very much, because they've got a built-in audience. But they often welcome others who aren't staying at the center. For instance, the public is welcome to attend the Christian Artists Music Seminar Concerts held from June through August with all types of music.

Participatory Sports

Most people visit Estes Park to see Rocky Mountain National Park and go camping, hiking or fishing. But, Estes Park has just about every outdoor activity you'd like, from windsurfing on Lake Estes to golf and tennis. Horseback riding is a popular activity in the area, with trails leading into the Park or the surrounding national forest. Several rafting companies take thrill-seekers to such frothy rivers outside the immediate area as the Poudre and Arkansas. The following are some of the town's many options.

Bicycling

For information about where to bicycle or to rent a bike, go to **Colorado Bicycling Adventures**, 586-4241, the only bike shop in town. It's a full-service bike shop offering sales and shipping. This shop not only rents brand-new mountain bikes in different models, but also offers several different guided bicycle tours, including a downhill ride from the top of Trail Ridge Road in Rocky Mountain National Park. Cost is $65 per person and includes bike,

helmet and souvenir water bottle plus a continental breakfast.

There's also a downhill tour in the North Fork Canyon ($45 per person), better-suited to younger and older riders — they've taken bicyclists ages 4 to 90. Another tour is Johnny Park, in Roosevelt National Forest, for more aggressive riders who don't mind a few hills ($45 per person). Bicycle rentals are $5 per hour; $9 for two hours; $15 per half-day; and $20 for a full day. Performance models with shock absorbers cost slightly more.

The shop also rents all types of bike accessories, including trailers to pull children, locks, packs and car racks. The shop sells a guidebook of all off-road areas in Roosevelt National Forest for $3.50 and has free maps that show cyclists where to ride right from the store on their own.

Camping

(See the Rocky Mountain National Park Overview chapter for information on camping in the national park.) Two campgrounds are run by the Estes Valley Recreation and Park District: **Mary's Lake Campground** and Estes Park Campground. Though not exactly remote or secluded Mary's Lake, 586-4411, has great views by a pleasant lake plus a heated swimming pool, hot showers, 30- or 50-amp service, a playground, store and laundry. Drive south of town on U.S. Highway 36 and turn left on Mary's Lake Road. The campground is 3 miles from town and the national park; open mid-May through September. Prices to camp range from $18 to $22 per night depending upon services chosen. For more than two people there's a $2 charge per person.

More peaceful and secluded is the **Estes Park Campground**, 586-4188, which has 65 tent sites and 12 RV sites (no hookups). Head west on U.S. Highway 36 and then left for 3 miles on Colo. Highway 66 (becomes Tunnel Road) a mile past the Estes Park Center/YMCA of the Rockies at the end of a paved road and adjacent to the Park. The campground is open late May through early September. Cost is $18 per tent and $20 to $22 for RVs.

Olive Ridge Campground in Roosevelt National Forest has 56 wooded campsites and is open year round. It's 15 miles south of Estes Park on Colo. Highway 7. Reservations must be made at least 10 days in advance. Camping is $10 per night. Call Destinet at (800) 365-2267.

Right at the Park's Fall River entrance, **National Park Resort Campground**, 586-4563, is AAA-approved and adjacent to the national park at 3501 Fall River Road. It has hot showers, hookups, cable TV, a livery and secluded, terraced sites. In addition to tent, camper and RV sites, **Park Place Camping Resort**, 586-4230 or (800) 722-2928, offers housekeeping and camping cabins; it's 5 miles southeast of Estes Park at 5495 U.S. Highway 36. Another option is **Paradise RV & Travel Park**, 586-5513, near the YMCA along the Big Thompson River, 1836 Colo. Highway 66. All three are open May through September and charge

from $18 to $22 per night for two people and $2 for each extra person. Pets and children are welcome.

Climbing

Learn rock climbing or mountaineering at the highly regarded **Colorado Mountain School**. One-day introductory classes prepare people to begin climbing with guides. The school offers guided hikes, climbs (including technical routes of Longs Peak) and equipment rentals. Open year round; reservations are requested. The school's address is P.O. Box 2062, 351 Moraine Avenue, Estes Park 80517, or call 586-5758 or (800) 444-0730 (outside Colorado). **Colorado Wilderness Sports**, 358 E. Elkhorn Avenue, 586-6548 or (800) 369-4165 offers instruction and guiding both in-

Summertime Horse Shows

This n-e-e-e-i-i-i-g-h-borly valley is full of summer horse shows. Each event brings around 250 sleek beauties to the Estes Park Fairground, 586-6104, on the east side of town near Lake Estes. Admission is free for all shows except the Westernaires. Here's a general calendar:

Around the third week in June, the quarter horses show off their spin-on-a-dime and quarter-mile sprinting skills in barrel racing, roping, pole bending and riding displays.

The fourth week in June features miniature horses. Some baby miniatures stand only a foot tall, and even adults are less than three feet. These knee-high ponies dance to music and can pull a little surrey. Hitch six to a buckboard wagon, and you've got a team. Sometimes, a contestant brings a miniature stagecoach with a team of eight. While miniatures may seem just right for tucking in with a child's toy animals, experts say they act like regular horses. Only cuter.

As June ends and July begins, in thunder the Arabians. The International Arabian Show started here more than 40 years ago then outgrew little Estes Valley. But many of the nation's best Arabians still come here. Two days feature Arabian cattle-cutting championships. It's the second-largest such event in the United States. We promised not to print this but couldn't help ourselves — some local experts say Arabians can be as good or better at cutting cattle as quarter horses. The costume class is the favorite spectator event. Watch for Arabian sheiks and princesses and even horses in flowing capes.

When July ends and August begins, as many as 500 horses leap to the Hunter-Jumper events. They keep three show rings hopping, we mean, jumping.

Westernaires normally take on the town during the second weekend in August. The precision riders are dazzling, dedicated, Denver-area teens. In past years, they've done some routines in black lights so their costumes glow, and their lively, Old West skits are always popular. The fee is usually $5 per person for the Friday and Saturday shows, which start around 7:30 PM.

doors and out. The company has an indoor rock-climbing wall.

Fishing

Stop by **Scot's Sporting Goods**, 586-2877, 870 Moraine Avenue, and ask owner Scot Richie — the local fishing authority — where to catch the big ones. He can also suggest — and sell you — the best things to catch them with. **Estes Angler**, 586-2110, (which is also a nationwide 800 number), 338 W. Riverside Drive, is another good outfitter. Some local spots include the Big Thompson River, Lake Estes and Mary's Lake.

The best spot on the **Big Thompson River** is said to be the stretch 8 miles downstream from Lake Estes called Grandpa's Retreat (flies and lures only), where the Colorado Division of Wildlife and the National Forest Service have created several deep holes. The Big Thompson runs along U.S. Highway 34; there are small parking areas along the shoulder. You'll also find several handicapped-accessible fishing ramps along this stretch.

Lake Estes, on the east side of town between U.S. highways 34 and 36, is stocked by the Colorado Division of Wildlife with rainbow trout and also has a few German brown trout. Mary's Lake inlet is another good spot to try. Follow U.S. Highway 36 to the east end of town to Mary's Lake Road at the traffic light, turn left and drive 1.5 miles.

Then, of course, for the less serious angler who doesn't want a wilderness experience but wants a guaranteed catch, there's **Trout Haven**, 810 Moraine Avenue, 586-5525 — no license required, everything provided and pay 48¢ an inch — a little more than a mile west of downtown on U.S. Highway 36 behind Kentucky Fried Chicken. They'll cook your catch on the spot (Trout Haven, that is), or you can trade it in for smoked trout and take it with you or have it packed and frozen to go.

Golf

There are two challenging golf courses run by the Estes Valley Recreation and Park District: the nine-hole **Lake Estes Executive Course**, 586-8176, at 690 Big Thompson Avenue, along the banks of the Big Thompson River ($11 daily; $7 after 3 PM), and the 18-hole **Estes Park Golf Club**, 586-8146, at 1080 S. St. Vrain Road ($30 daily; $18 after 2 PM) one of the oldest golf courses in the state, dating from 1912. In early fall elk wander onto the course — watch out for their divots.

Hiking and Backpacking

Most hikers head to **Rocky Mountain National Park**, but the nearby **Roosevelt National Forest** also offers excellent backcountry trails. Stop at the Estes Park Office of Roosevelt National Forest for maps and information about hiking trails: 586-3440, 161 Second Street, P.O. Box 2747, Estes Park, 80517. See "Hiking" under the Rocky Mountain National Park chapter for other hiking opportunities. A few local trails include:

Lily Mountain Trail, an easy 1.5-mile hike begins near Estes Park and climbs to 8,800 feet with fantastic summit views of Estes Park, Longs Peak to the south and the Continental Divide to the west. The trailhead is 6 miles south of Estes Park on Colo. Highway 7. Just before the 6-mile marker look for a small turnoff on the right and a parking area and trailhead sign.

Crosier Mountain Trail is a harder 8-mile round trip that climbs to the top of Crosier Mountain (elevation 9,250 feet), through lush meadows and aspen groves past ruins of old homesteads. You'll have superb views from the summit. The trailhead is about 8 miles northeast of Estes Park on Devil's Gulch Road, a mile past Glen Haven. Look for a large gravel cut on the south side of the road to the right.

Lion Gulch is another pleasant trail of moderate difficulty. It leads to an area of old homesteads about 3 miles one way. The trailhead is at mile marker 8 from Estes Park on U.S. Highway 36.

Horseback Riding

Estes Park has numerous stables and outfitters offering everything from kids' pony rids to trail rides and pack trips into the mountains. Most rides head into Rocky Mountain National Park. The following are a few stables.

Elkhorn Stables, 586-5225, at 600 W. Elkhorn Avenue, has breakfast rides, steak rides, hourly rides and ponies for children. Open year round, it offers trips into the national park for around $18 an hour. Offering rides into the national forest (not the park) is **Sombrero Ranch**, 586-4577, on the Dam on Lake Estes, U.S. Highway 34 E. Rides cost $17 an hour or $28 for two hours.

Aspen Lodge, 586-8133, is a 3,000-acre ranch resort that offers rides into both the national park and Roosevelt National Forest. It's south of Estes Park on Colo. Highway 7.

Rides cost $18 an hour or $35 for a longer "ranch ride" or meadow ride or steak dinner ride. A two-hour breakfast ride costs $28.

Miscellaneous Sports – Stanley Park

Run by the Estes Valley Recreation and Park District, **Stanley Park** has a playground, basketball, volleyball and tennis courts, baseball/softball and soccer fields, shelters and a picnic area. It's at 380 Community Drive, 586-8189 (Youth Center); for the administrative office, call 586-8191.

Rafting

There's no rafting to speak of right in the Estes Park area, but there are numerous outfitters that will take you on full- or half-day trips on the Poudre or Arkansas rivers and rather far afield to the Dolores and Colorado rivers — among them **Colorado Wilderness Sports**, 586-6548 or (800) 369-4165. The company, which also has an indoor rock-climbing wall, is at 358 E. Elkhorn Avenue in Estes Park. Similar trips are also available through **Rocky Mountain Adventures**, 586-6191 or (800) 858-6808, and **Rapid Transit**

Rafting, 586-8852 or (800) 367-8523. Reservations are required.

Cross-country Skiing

(See the Rocky Mountain National Park Overview chapter for ski trails in the national park.) Rental equipment is available at many of the outdoor shops in Estes Park, including **Estes Park Ski Shop**, 586-4241, 184 E. Elkhorn Avenue, and **Colorado Wilderness Sports**, 586-6548 or (800) 369-4165, 358 E. Elkhorn Avenue. The **Colorado Mountain School**, 351 Moraine Avenue, also has rental ski equipment, 586-5758 or (800) 444-0730 (outside Colorado). Rental cross-country ski packages (skis, boots, poles) average about $10 (downhill skis $14; snowshoes $10, snowboards $14).

Swimming

Just south of Lake Estes, the **Estes Park Aquatic Center**, 586-2340, has an indoor/outdoor pool at 660 Community Drive.

The waters of Lake Estes are too chilly for swimming unless you like wearing a wet suit, which can be rented at the **Lake Estes Marina**, 586-2011, along with windsurfing equipment and other small craft. The marina, which has beaches and picnic areas, is east of town on U.S. Highway 34 at 1770 Big Thompson Avenue.

Tennis

There are six courts in **Stanley Park**, operated by the Estes Valley Recreation and Park District — free, unless you want a reservation. They are at 380 Community Drive just south of Lake Estes, 586-8191.

Grand Lake's main attraction is the area's beauty, and it prides itself on being a family town.

Grand Lake

For those who want to visit Rocky Mountain National Park but also want to avoid the crush and hustle of Estes Park, Grand Lake is an alternative for a base camp. A little more than a mile from the western entrance to the Park and on Colorado's largest natural lake, Grand Lake offers a quieter experience. One of the oldest communities on the Western Slope, this six-block town is a rustic community of some 350 permanent residents, with picturesque false-front buildings, wooden boardwalks and a bar with a hitching post where local cowboys sometimes ride up on horses to have a cold one.

Grand Lake's main attraction is the area's beauty, and it prides itself on being a family town. There's no nightlife to speak of, other than a few bars with music in summer and on weekends in spring and fall. There's no movie theater, but in summer there's professional theater and a good children's recreation program. The town has two tennis courts, a town park and a beautiful beach on the lake. The Grand Lake Golf Course is one of the best in the state.

The area offers access to some of the state's best hiking, fishing and other outdoor activities. The trio of large lakes — Grand Lake, Lake Granby and Shadow Mountain Reservoir — offer a variety of water sports, including boating, water skiing, windsurfing and fishing. Routt and Arapahoe national forests offer great hiking and backpacking, as does the western side of the Indian Peaks Wilderness Area.

In summer, Grand Lake's population swells to about 4,000, with many tourists coming through daily on their way to Rocky Mountain National Park or for various outdoor pursuits. In winter, there's excellent cross-country skiing at Grand Lake Ski Touring Center and national forest trails and downhill skiing nearby at Winter Park and Silver Creek.

Because of its more isolated location — literally at the end of the road — Grand Lake never experienced the development of Estes Park, and residents consider this a blessing. Nevertheless, the town and area offer the necessary amenities for visitors, including guest ranches, cabins, motels and lodges along with gift shops, galleries, cafes and fine-dining establishments. Abundant camping, fishing, hiking and natural beauty lure nature lovers to the area.

History

Grand Lake's name comes from the early name for the Colorado River, the "Grand," with headwaters beginning on the Continental Divide just north of the lake. Ute Indians frequented the area for hunting expeditions over the Continental Divide, following trails along Grand Lake's North Inlet and Tonahutu Creek up into the mountains. Arapaho and Cheyenne also visited the area to hunt the plentiful game and fish in the large lake, but relations were not peaceful.

Grand Lake was known as Spirit Lake by the Utes after a particularly tragic incident. During an attack by the Cheyenne and Arapaho, the Utes put their women and children on a makeshift raft and sent them out to the middle of the lake to escape harm. But a storm came up and the raft capsized in the deepest part of the lake, drowning all aboard. Back on land, most of the Ute warriors died in the battle. After this, the Utes never camped near the lake again and believed that the early morning mists and fogs rising from the lake were the spirits of their dead.

The area was settled in 1867 by homesteader Joseph "Judge" Westcott, who supported himself by trapping and fishing, selling the live, boxed fish to hotel restaurants around

Grand Lake lies on the western side of Rocky Mountain National Park.

the region. In the next decade, other families began arriving, and there was a short-lived gold boom.

But it was the area's natural beauty and abundant fishing and hunting that brought other settlers. Wealthy families built summer homes on the beautiful lake in the late 1800s. In 1905, the Grand Lake Yacht Club was registered as the world's highest at 8,369 feet.

The biggest tourist boom started in 1952 when the Colorado-Big Thompson Project was completed, bringing irrigation to the eastern slope through a series of dams, reservoirs, channels and a 13-mile tunnel under the Continental Divide. The project created Shadow Mountain Lake and Lake Granby, greatly enlarging the area's water recreation opportunities.

Getting Around

Grand Lake is 85 miles northwest of Denver, via Interstate 70 west to U.S. Highway 40 (Exit 232). Follow U.S. 40 over Berthoud Pass (11,315 feet, well-maintained year round) and through Winter Park, Fraser and Granby. Grand Lake is 40 miles north of Winter Park. Just past Granby, follow U.S. Highway 34 (and signs to Rocky Mountain National Park) 16 miles north.

If coming from Boulder or Estes Park during the summer, just cross Trail Ridge Road (closed in winter, 44 miles from east to west) through Rocky Mountain National Park to the other side. Grand Lake is 1.3 miles south of the Kawuneeche Visitors Center at the west entrance of Rocky Mountain National Park.

Tourist Information

For information about everything in the Grand Lake area, call the **Grand Lake Chamber of Commerce** at 627-3402. For a vacation-planner packet call (800) 531-1019. The chamber is open daily from 9 AM to 5 PM from May 15 to October 15.

Participatory Sports

Bicycling

There is no organized mapping of the mountain biking trails in the area. But **Rocky Mountain Sports**, 627-8327, 1137 Grand Avenue, Grand Lake, is open year round and offers information for local mountain biking. The folks here also rent bikes and other equipment, along with sleds and show shoes in winter.

Camping

There's abundant camping in the area in the National Park, forest and recreation area. The **Kawuneeche Visitors Center** of Rocky Mountain National Park is 1.3 miles north of Grand Lake and is open daily year round. For information, call 627-3471.

Sites in Rocky Mountain National Park

A $10 permit is required for all overnight camping in the park. The permits are limited in number and are available year round at the West Unit Office at the western entrance of the park on U.S. 34. Permits are available on a first-come basis but may also be obtained in advance by writing (see the Rocky Mountain National Park Overview chapter).

Timber Creek Campground is 7 miles north on U.S. 34 into the Park. One hundred sites are available, and a fee of $10 per night is charged.

Sites in Arapahoe National Recreation Area

Fees are charged at the 350 campsites in four different campgrounds. About 3 miles south on U.S. Highway 34, turn left on County Road 66 and go a mile to **Green Ridge Campground** on Shadow Mountain Lake (80 sites).

Six miles south of Grand Lake on U.S. 34 is **Stillwater Campground** on Lake Granby (145 sites).

To reach **Arapahoe Bay Campground** continue a mile south of Stillwater Lake Campground, turn left on County Road 66, and go 10 miles (77 sites).

For **Willow Creek Campground** go south 8 miles on U.S. Highway 34, turn right on U.S. 40 and go 3 miles to this campground on Willow Creek Reservoir (35 sites).

Fees are $10 per night for campgrounds on lakes; $8 for inland campgrounds. For more information, call the Arapaho National Forest, Sulphur Ranger District Office, 887-4100.

Sites in Arapaho National Forest

To reach **Sawmill Gulch Campground** go 3 miles northwest of Granby on U.S. 40, turn right on Colo. Highway 125 and go 10 miles (five sites). A fee of $8 per night is charged. **Denver Creek Campground** is 2 more miles up Colo. Highway 125 (25 sites) and charges no fee.

A combination campground, bed and breakfast and recreation park, privately owned **Winding River Resort Village**, 627-3215, has more than 160 campsites adjacent to Rocky Mountain National Park with hot showers, RV hookups, a store and laundry — plus luxurious bed and breakfast rooms. Continental breakfast is included. There's a huge list of activities, including hayrides, horseback riding, a Frisbee golf course, mountain biking and much more. Drive a mile north of Grand Lake on U.S. 34 and turn left across from the National Park Visitors' Center. Follow the signs for 1.5 miles. Tents cost $17 per night for two and $3 for each additional person. RV sites cost $9 to $22 per night for two people and $3 for each additional person.

Fishing

Test your luck in Grand Lake, Lake Granby, Shadow Mountain Reservoir, the Colorado River, Willow Creek and Monarch Lake. **Budget Tackle** shop owner Bill Leach, 887-9344, is a good local source of information and has a shop about 3 miles from Grand Lake on U.S. Highway 34 and another in Granby. Check the *Daily Tribune* or the weekly *The Prospectus* for his weekly fishing report. Colorado fishing licenses are required for anyone 15 or older.

Golf and Tennis

Grand Lake Golf Course, 627-8008, is one of Colorado's toughest and most beautiful, set among the aspen and pines with gorgeous views of the Continental Divide. If your ball goes astray on a narrow fairway, it's likely to winter over in the forest — you'll never find it. At an altitude of 8,420 feet, it can be chilly, and afternoon showers are common, so bring a jacket and rain gear. To reach the course go a quarter-mile north of town on U.S. 34, turn left on County Road 48, and drive another mile. **Pole Creek Golf Club**, 726-8847, in Winter Park, is another award-winning public course. This picturesque 18-hole, par 72 layout features varied and challenging terrain.

There are public tennis courts at Grand Lake Golf Course (small fee) and in town (free).

Hiking and Backpacking

It's best to pay a visit to the local forest service office or the National Park for detailed maps and information about local trails. Maps are available at the **Sulphur Ranger District Office**, 887-4100, 62429 U.S. Highway 40, Granby 80446. Grand County also publishes an excellent recreation guide, which is available from the chamber of commerce, visitors centers or the forest service office. Another good source of information for both hiking and backpacking is **Never Summer Mountain Products**, 627-3642, 919 Grand Avenue, Grand Lake.

Sites in Rocky Mountain National Park

Just a few miles into the park are numerous trailheads, including Green Mountain, Onahu Creek, Timber Lake and the Colorado River Trail. The first two can be short dayhikes of a mile or so to the intersection with the **Tonahutu Creek Trail**, which ventures ever farther into more remote areas of the park.

The latter two are more challenging. The **Colorado River Trail** — the easier of the two — goes a scenic 2 miles to Shipler Park and 4 miles to Lulu City, an early mining town site, where all vestiges of civilization were removed when the park was created. The more difficult **Timber Lake Trail** winds 5.5 miles up to a lovely, high, tree-lined lake surrounded by wildflowers with a view of 12,000-foot Mount Ida on the Continental Divide.

From Grand Lake are two nearby trails: the 27-mile, three-day Tonahutu Creek/North Inlet Loop and the easier, shorter **East Inlet Trail**, better for dayhikes. The former is a spectacular trip that crosses Andrews Pass and penetrates the heart of the national park — for experienced backpackers only. The latter offers several alternatives with a short trip to beautiful Adams Falls (0.75 miles each way) or a bit farther to a lovely high meadow perfect for lunch. Lone Pine Lake and Lake Verna are another 4.5 and 5.25 miles respectively.

To reach the East Inlet Trailhead, follow W. Portal Road 1.5 miles from Grand Avenue to the end. The **Tonahutu Creek/North Inlet Loop** begins at the north end of the town at the Park boundary.

Sites in Indian Peaks Wilderness Area

Permits are required for overnight camping in the wilderness area and are available at the **Sulphur Ranger District Office**, 62429 U.S. Highway 40, Granby 80446. Call 887-4100 for more information. Permits cost $5 for a limit of seven nights. Group size is limited to 12 (including pack animals). Advance reservations are required for Crater, Jasper, Diamond and Caribou lakes.

Arapaho Pass Trail follows Arapaho Creek 10 miles to the top of the pass at 11,900 feet. The first 8 miles are an easy, gradual climb; the last two are tougher and steeper. The trail begins at Monarch Lake, as does the **Buchanan Creek Trail**, a more difficult hike along Buchanan and Cascade creeks to Crater Lake, a good spot for camping and fishing. For an alternative and longer trip that climbs the divide, follow the **Pawnee Pass Trail** east instead of turning south to Crater Lake. It's a difficult 3-mile climb to the top of the 12,541-foot pass. (Also see Pawnee Pass Trail in the Boulder Participatory Sports' hiking and backpacking sections.)

To reach Monarch Lake and the trailhead for these routes, take U.S. 34 south to County Road 6, turn left and go 10 miles to Monarch Lake.

Horseback Riding

Sombrero Stables, 627-3514, 304 W. Portal Road, offers everything from pony rides for kids to breakfast and steak-fry rides for Mom and Dad to pack trips into the Park for several days for the more adventurous. Rides are $17 an hour and $28 for two hours. Prices vary for rides with meals. Call for reservations.

Winding River Resort Village, 627-3215, U.S. Highway 34, also offers hourly guided rides for around $18 an hour.

FYI

Unless otherwise noted, the area code for all phone numbers in this guide is 970.

Snowmobiling and Skiing

Snowmobiling

Grand Lake is the "Official Snowmobiling Capitol of Colorado," according to *Snow West* magazine, with more than 300 miles of groomed and ungroomed trails. It's also one of the few places where you can snowmobile right into town. Many local shops rent snowmobiles, among them **Grand Lake Snowmobile Rental**, 627-8304, 801 Grand Avenue, and **Catride**, 627-8866, 724 Grand Avenue — both in town, or **Grand Lake Motor Sports**, 627-3806, 6 miles out of town at 10438 U.S. Highway 34.

Cross-country Skiing

Green Mountain Trail, a one-way trail in the national park, makes a nice tour if you have two cars: Leave one car at Green Mountain Trailhead and the other at the Tonahutu Creek/North Inlet Trailhead. Starting at Green Mountain Trail, 3 miles north of Grand Lake on U.S. Highway 34, the trail goes uphill for 2 miles then turns right on Tonahutu Creek Trail. It's a pleasant 4-mile downhill run to your waiting second car.

During ski season, the Grand Lake Golf Course becomes the **Grand Lake Touring Center**, 627-8008, with 25 kilometers of groomed ski trails around the course and a connecting trail to Soda Springs Ranch and other trails. (Directions are given under Golf.)

At Tabernash, 12 miles north of Winter Park, the **YMCA Snow Mountain Ranch Nordic Center**, (303) 887-2152, offers many kilometers of groomed trails, lighted night skiing and a whole range of facilities including lodging, pools and a roller-skating rink.

Farther down the road toward Winter Park in Fraser is **Devil's Thumb Ranch**, 726-8231, which offers more than 100 kilometers of trails including some nice meadows and rolling terrain as well as more challenging tracks.

All the touring centers above rent ski equipment as well as Grand Lake's **Never Summer Mountain Products**, 627-3642, 919 Grand Avenue, which also sells ski and other outdoor equipment.

Downhill Skiing

Winter Park Ski Resort is 40 miles from Grand Lake (central reservations: 726-5514 or (800) 453-2525) and offers some of the state's best skiing. Smaller and quieter, **Silver Creek**, (303) 629-1020, (970) 887-3384 or 800-448-9458, is 15 miles from Grand Lake and a great family resort for beginning to intermediate skiers (17 miles north of Winter Park on U.S. Highway 40).

Watersports

All around the area are numerous watersport rental shops — especially along the shores of Lake Granby and Shadow Mountain Lake. **Spirit Lake Marina**, 627-8158, 1030 Lake Avenue, offers boat rentals and lake tours from mid-May 'til mid-October. Bumper boats (like bumper cars) are also available to rent.

Boater's Choice, 627-9273, 11246 Lake Avenue, rents a variety of watercraft, including motorboats, fishing boats, canoes and paddleboats.

Annual Events

(See the Estes Park Festivals and Annual Events chapter for additional events.)

Western Week Buffalo BBQ, 627-3402, takes place in mid-July and is an old-time celebration. Included in the week of events is the Spirit Lake Mountain Men Rendezvous, a parade down Grand Avenue and, of course, a grand barbecue with all the fixin's.

The annual **Lipton Cup Regatta** in early August is named for English tea baron Sir Thomas Lipton, who was wined and dined by early members of Grand Lake's Yacht Club. Though the race is not open to the public, spectators can watch the yacht club sailors compete for the prestigious sterling silver Lipton Cup.

Grand Lake is alive and well in the winter months as well with ice fishing derbies, snowmobile drag races, an ice golf tournament, ice/snow sculpture competition, concerts, sled-dog races and other events.

Restaurants

Grand Lake's six-block main street, Grand Avenue, is lined with numerous small eateries with a variety of offerings, from beer and burgers to cappuccino and pastries. There are also a few fine dining establishments tucked away at both ends of town and a little ways out of town. For a tasty treat, stop in at the Rocky Mountain Chocolate Factory about midway down Grand Avenue.

The price chart below is based on dinner for two people, excluding cocktails, beer or wine, appetizer, dessert, tax and tip. Most restaurants have sections for smokers and non-smokers, and the ones we've noted here accept major credit cards.

Price-code Key	
Less than $25	$
$26 to $50	$$
$51 to $75	$$$
$76 and more	$$$$

Boardwalk Deli
$ • 826 Grand Ave., #B, Grand Lake
• 627-5029

For soups, salads, sandwiches or snacks, this new eatery is a winner. There's a seating area upstairs. It's open daily year-round for breakfast and lunch.

$ • 1131 Grand Ave., Grand Lake
• 627-3509

Searching for a hearty breakfast? Try the Chuckhole, which features a full breakfast menu, plus lunch and snack choices of burgers, chili, sandwiches, salads, homemade pies and cappuccino. The Chuckhole serves breakfast and lunch daily.

Motel Waconda
$ • 725 Grand Ave., Grand Lake • 627-8312

Another good choice for breakfast — the only meal served here — is the motel's cafe, serving big portions of pancakes and omelettes. Open daily for breakfast, with brunch offered on weekends.

Grand Pizza
$ • 717 Grand Ave., Grand Lake • 627-8390

Locals recommend the pizza here, along with the subs and pasta. Enjoy beer and wine with your pizza or wash it all down with a cappuccino. Grand Pizza is open daily for lunch and dinner with outside seating available during summer.

Pancho & Lefty's
$ • 1101 Grand Ave., Grand Lake
• 627-8773

No town in Colorado is complete without a Mexican restaurant. Here, the Pancho & Lefty combo means both Mexican and American dishes. Have a tasty taco, burrito, burger or steak, and there's a full bar too. The cafe is open daily for lunch and dinner.

Caroline's Cuisine
$$ • 9921 U.S. Hwy. 34 (Soda Springs Ranch), Grand Lake • 627-9404

For quite a reasonable price, enjoy French-

INSIDERS' TIP

The efforts of local environmental activists have preserved the area called Bowen Gulch, adjacent to Rocky Mountain National Park at the Bowen/Baker Trailhead just past Never Summer Ranch on the western side of Trail Ridge Road (U.S. Highway 34). Bowen Gulch was slated to be logged several years ago by a major lumber company. There were demonstrations at the site, and construction firms in Boulder boycotted the lumber company to protest the cutting. This stand of virgin timber contains "grandfather trees" that have been standing since the discovery of America.

American cuisine and an extensive wine list at this attractive restaurant. There's a children's menu and a full bar. Caroline's is open for dinner daily except Mondays. There's Sunday brunch from 10 AM to 2 PM.

Back-Street Steakhouse at Daven Haven Lodge
$-$$ • 604 Marina Dr., Grand Lake • 627-8144

Steaks, seafood and pasta are the favorites at the lodge's excellent restaurant, which won't disappoint diners in search of a delicious meal. Try an appetizer of baked brie with a splash of butterscotch schnapps or the Jack Daniels pork chops with a touch of cream. Teetotalers might try teriyaki ribeye or top sirloin. The restaurant serves dinner daily.

E.G.'s Garden Grill
$-$$ • 1000 Grand Ave., Grand Lake • 627-8404

A potpourri of creative cuisine is the specialty at this casual dining establishment. Pizza, ribs and gourmet burgers and sandwiches are served, but try something more exotic like mustard catfish with jalapeño tartar sauce and jicama slaw (jicama is a potato-like Mexican vegetable). The blackened ribeye, seafood fettuccine and grilled salmon also sound appetizing. The grill serves lunch and dinner daily year round with outdoor seating in summer.

Grand Bayou
$-$$ • 1120 Grand Ave., Grand Lake • 627-8992

If it's Cajun you're cravin' this is the place for you. Featuring Louisiana cuisine with fresh seafood, steaks and homemade pie, this restaurant offers a lake view, outside seating in summer and a full bar. There are also sandwiches, pastas and a children's menu. The restaurant serves lunch and dinner daily except Tuesdays.

The Mountain Inn
$ • 612 Grand Ave., Grand Lake • 627-3385

Judging from the crowded parking lot and the full tables inside, this cozy restaurant, specializing in "Grandma's cooking," is a local favorite. The catch of the day complements the menu, which features homemade chicken pot pie, old-fashioned stews, real mashed potatoes (which seem to be a big item in Grand Lake) and Mexican food. The restaurant is open year round.

The Rapids Lodge and Restaurant
$-$$ • East end of town; turn left at the end of Grand Ave., Grand Lake • 627-3707

Ask for a table by the window here to enjoy the beautiful, rushing Tonahutu River. And why not celebrate with a $200 bottle of 1979 Chateau Haut Brion Graves (first growth) or a slightly less expensive Dom Perignon in an atmosphere worthy of such grand libation. Those on a budget needn't be dissuaded; there are less expensive drink and food offerings, including pasta dishes for less than $10 and children's dinners. The meal includes an extensive hors d'oeuvres tray with shrimp, two delicious pates and sorbet. Dinner offerings include Alaska king crab legs, trout stuffed with crab, filet mignon and other delectable choices. Steamy espresso or cappuccino can accompany the dessert of the evening. The serene dining room offers a rustically elegant Victorian atmosphere. Rapids is open year round for dinner only.

Red Fox
$$ • 441 W. Portal Rd., Grand Lake • 627-3418

Perched on a hilltop at the end of town, this restaurant serves American and Continental cuisine and continues to win the praise of locals and visitors. Try any of the steaks, pasta, poultry or seafood dishes for a delicious meal in a pleasant atmosphere with a nice lake view. Red Fox is open for lunch and dinner daily.

Grand Lake Lodge Restaurant
$$ • 0.25-mile north of Grand Lake off U.S. Hwy. 34, Grand Lake • 627-3967

Enjoy an evening cocktail or full meal on the lodge's open porch, or enjoy the same grand view inside the comfortably rustic dining room. Either way, you'll have a glorious view of the lake and surrounding area. The restaurant specializes in Continental cuisine with open grill. There are full breakfasts and a spectacular Sunday champagne brunch. There's weekly entertainment in the bar. The dining room serves breakfast, lunch and dinner and is open daily from Memorial Day through the week after Labor Day.

Accommodations

Grand Lake has a large selection of lodges, motels and cabins. Many are right on the lake; others along scenic creeks tumbling down from the mountains. It's always a good idea to ask to see a room before you put your money down, should you decide to strike out on your own, but below are some recommended places to stay.

The chart below is based on the average cost of double occupancy. All the accommodations listed except Shadowcliff accept major credit cards, but leave Spot or Fluffy behind — no pets are allowed in any of these properties.

Price-code Key	
Less than $30	$
$31 to $50	$$
$51 to $75	$$$
$76 to $90	$$$$
$91 and more	$$$$$

Columbine Creek Ranch
$$$ • 14814 U.S. Hwy. 34, Grand Lake • 627-2429

This early 20th-century lodge with its own trout ponds once hosted Lucille Ball and Desi Arnaz. There are seven unique rooms and four cabins. The ranch specializes in family reunions, and for groups of 30 or more, a pig roast is included. There's a fireplace and big-screen TV in the family living area and a hot tub nearby. Fishing equipment is furnished free, but there's a fee for each fish caught. Gas grills are available for guests wishing to cook their own trout. Smoking is not allowed.

Daven Haven Lodge
$ • 604 Marina Dr., Grand Lake • 627-8144

Between the highway and the lake and only a block or so from the swimming beach, Boulder families say Daven Haven is a good place to stay with kids. The convenient restaurant for the lodge serves delicious dinners. The lodge's rooms are simple but comfortable.

The Rapids Lodge
$$$-$$$$ • East end of town; turn left at end of Grand Ave., Grand Lake • 627-3707

The oldest lodge in Grand Lake, built in the early 1900s, the Rapids Lodge looks quite rustic from the outside. But inside, guests will be charmed by the lovely restored Victorian decor and antiques. The dining room looks out on the rushing Tonahutu River — a feast for the eyes with its frothy water spraying over large boulders. Carpeted and comfortable, the rooms in the lodge are a nostalgic combination with lace curtains and hearts-and-flowers wallpaper. Each room has a big brass bed or a four-poster wooden one, mounded with fluffy quilts. You can easily imagine yourself back at the turn of the century in this delightful retreat. Those who relish the sight and sound of the rushing water should ask for a room on the creek side. Nonsmoking rooms are available in the adjacent Rapids Chalet; there are also individual cabins and bright, modern condominiums along the creek that sleep up to 12 people. The lodge is open year round.

Lemmon Lodge
$$$-$$$$ • East end of town behind yacht club; turn right at the end of Grand Ave., Grand Lake • 627-3314 (summer), 725-3511 (winter)

Situated right on Grand Lake's lapping edge, Lemmon Lodge offers a variety of small and large (up to 12 persons) cabins in a pleasant, wooded area of five private acres. There

---

INSIDERS' TIP

Grand Lake is considered to be on the "western slope." Estes Park and Boulder are on the "eastern slope" (almost always referred to as the Front Range). The Continental Divide that runs along the spine of the Rocky Mountains in Colorado is the dividing line between east and west as far as slopes and river drainages go.

are barbecue grills and picnic tables on the grounds and a children's playground right on the beach. The lodge's location on the North Inlet of the lake offers great fishing and a private boat slip, so bring your rod and boat. Cabins are often reserved a year in advance, and there's a four-day minimum stay required from late June to early September (three-day minimum over Memorial and Labor Day weekends). Smoking is allowed in some of the cabins.

Grand Lake Lodge

$$$$ • 0.25 miles north of Grand Lake; look for the sign, and turn on U.S. Hwy. 34, Grand Lake • 627-3967 (in-season), 759-5848 (off-season)

Without a doubt, Grand Lake Lodge occupies a spectacular spot overlooking the lake. The historic, log-beamed main lodge sits atop a woodsy knoll on the boundary of Rocky Mountain National Park with an inviting heated swimming pool right in front. The lodge's window-lined dining room sprawls out onto a front porch affording a grand view for an alfresco meal. In the evenings, guests gather in the lodge's friendly, relaxed atmosphere to watch a movie, play cards or warm their toes around the big circular freestanding fireplace. A 14-person hot tub has been added. The cabins, tucked away in a lodgepole pine forest up the hillside, don't share the lodge's grand view. The comfortable, austere cabins range from two-person modern duplexes to the Ford Cabin (where Henry Ford stayed in 1927), which sleeps 10 people. The lodge opens the first weekend in June and stays open through the second weekend in September (minimum stays of two and three days are required on weekends and holidays, respectively). Smoking is allowed.

The Inn at Grand Lake

$$ • 1103 Grand Ave., Grand Lake • (800) 722-2585

Built on top of the old courthouse and jail, here's an authentic Old West setting, newly refurbished and upgraded. Rooms can accommodate one to five persons and have cable TV, ceiling fans, phones and heat controls.

Right in the heart of town, this inn's location alone can make guests feel like Insiders. Smoking and nonsmoking rooms are available.

Shadowcliff

$$$, no credit cards • Off W. Portal Rd., Grand Lake • 627-9220

Shadowcliff is a combination lodge, American Youth Hostel (AYH) and retreat for religious and other groups such as Elderhostel. Its location is spectacular and breathtaking, with the main lodge perched on a precipitous cliff overlooking the roaring North Inlet Stream and the entire lake area. Guests can bunk with others in separate men's and women's dorm rooms for around $10 a night, with especially low rates for AYH members, or rent a private room or whole cabin. The cozy, comfortable lodge lounge overlooks the lakes and has a library, lots of easy chairs and an inviting fireplace. Trails on the property go directly into Rocky Mountain National Park. Shadowcliff is open from late May to October 1. Inquire about minimum stays in the cabins. Smoking is not allowed.

> **FYI**
> Unless otherwise noted, the area code for all phone numbers in this guide is 970.

Spirit Mountain Ranch

$$$$$ • Country Rd. 41 (off U.S. Hwy. 34), 6 miles south of Grand Lake • 887-3551, (800) 887-3551

Located on 72 private acres, this bed and breakfast occupies an aspen grove frequented by elk, deer, fox, coyote and other wildlife. Hand-built by the owners "to soothe body and soul" it's recommended for those seeking solitude and beauty. Each of the four extra-large rooms has a private bathroom. The whole house can also be reserved for meetings, getaways, workshops, weddings and family reunions. A two-day minimum stay is required. Smoking is not allowed.

Snow Mountain Ranch/YMCA of the Rockies

$$$ • U.S. Hwy. 40 (10 miles north of Winter Park; 25 miles south of Grand Lake) • 887-2152, (800) 777-YMCA

In a beautiful setting on 4,900 acres, this YMCA-owned and operated facility is a great place to stay or visit. There's an indoor pool, roller-skating rink and indoor basketball and volleyball courts. Outside, there's miniature golf, mountain biking, horseback riding, snowshoeing, cross-country skiing (with lighted trails for night skiing), sleigh rides and ice skating. There are all types of accommodations from very inexpensive dormitories to motel-type rooms and private cabins. A restaurant serves three meals a day, reasonably priced. In winter, it's the scene of cross-country ski races. Membership isn't required and child care is available. Children are welcome; pets and smoking are allowed in cabins but not in rooms. Group reservations are available for parties of 15 or more.

Trail Mountain Bed & Breakfast

$$$$$ • 4850 County Rd. 41 (6 miles south of Grand Lake or 8.4 miles north of Granby on U.S. 34) • 887-3944

Ideal for adult couples or small groups looking for privacy in a pristine setting with a taste of luxury, this bed and breakfast inn is nearby lots of area activities such as golf and skiing. Each of the three large guest rooms has a private bath, shower, gas fireplace and two-person Jacuzzi tub. Each room has a deck, and two rooms have private entrances. There's a big fireplace in the great room, near the dining area, plus a wet bar. Smoking is not allowed.

Index of Advertisers

Index

C

E

E Source 302
E-Town 68
E.G.'s Garden Grill 371
Ead's News & Smoke Shop 104
Ead's News and Smoke Shop 92
Eagle Golf Club 228
Eagle Rock School and Professional
    Development Center 334
Eagles Nest Golf Club 192
Earl House Historic Inn 77
East Boulder Recreation Center 218
East Boulder Trail 223
East Inlet Trail 368
East Longs Peak Trail 326
Eastern Mountain Sports 92, 119
Eben Fine Park 139, 216
Eco-Cycle 147
ECO-Passes 33
Econo-Lodge 84
Eddie Bauer 92
Ed's Cantina and Grill 336
Education 281
Education, Estes Park 334
Efrain's 61, 99
Egghead Software 92
El Chapultepec 68
El Mercado 113
ElderShare 275
Eldora Mountain Resort 152, 236
Eldora Mountain Resort's Nordic Center 239
Eldorado Artesian Springs 241
Eldorado Canyon State Park 217
Eldorado Springs, Colorado 250
Eldorado Springs State Park 231
Electronics Boutique and Software Etc. 91
Elegante Limousine 36
Elfriede's Fine Fabrics 92
Elfriede's Fine Fabrics Studio Bernina 109
Elitch Gardens Amusement Park 165
Elk-bugling Tours 328
Elkhorn Stables 362
Ellen's Bed & Breakfast in a Victorian House 81
Elyngton's 163
Emerson Green 92
Emmy's 176, 179
Enchanted Mesa 230
Enos Mills Cabin 350
Environmental Communication Specialists 302
Erie, Colorado 254
Espresso Roma 98
Estes Angler 362
Estes, Joel 319
Estes Park Animal Clinic 332
Estes Park Aquatic Center 363
Estes Park Area Historical Museum 349
Estes Park Brewery 336, 340, 350
Estes Park Campground 360
Estes Park Center 333, 341, 351, 352, 360
Estes Park Chamber of Commerce
    and Visitor Information 359
Estes Park, CO 320
Estes Park, Colorado 331

Estes Park Dental 332
Estes Park Fairground 359
Estes Park Fireworks Display 356
Estes Park Golf Club 362
Estes Park Hotel 320
Estes Park Medical Center 331
Estes Park Music Festival 346, 355
Estes Park Oratorio and Chamber Concert 354
Estes Park Public Library 335, 350
Estes Park Ride-A-Kart 350
Estes Park Senior Center 333
Estes Park Ski Shop 363
ETC w/ CareerTrack 302
European Cafe 51, 92
Evans, Griffith 320
Exabyte 299
Express 109
Express Personnel Services 303

F

Face Bar 179
Face on the Barroom Floor 177, 178
Falafel Man 59, 92
Fall Foliage/Elk Bugling Tours 328
Farley's Prime and Chop House 193
Farmers Markets 110
Fashion Bar 99
Fawn Brook Inn 52
Fawn Valley Inn 342
Federal Aviation Administration Tours 148
Feet First 107
Feet First and Rocky Mountain Kids 92
Ferncliff Grocery Store 350
Festival Extra 178
Festivals 125
Festivals, Estes Park 348
Fiddler's Green 69, 200
Film 200
Fine Arts and Crafts Show 358
Fine Arts Guild of the Rockies
    Annual Musical 354
First Baptist Church 316, 332
First Congregational Church 314, 316
First Presbyterian 315
First United Methodist Church 316
Fish Observatory 140
Fishing 227, 325
Fishing, Grand Lake 367
Fishing Licenses 227
Fiske Planetarium 143, 207
Fitness Centers 227
Five Senses Trail 325
Flagstaff House 52, 69
Flagstaff Mountain 216
Flagstaff Mountain Amphitheater 314
Flagstaff Mountain Trail 231
Flagstaff Nature Center 146
Flagstaff Summit Nature Center 231
Flatiron Athletic Club 227
Flatirons Aviation 34
Flatirons Golf Course 228
Flatirons Martial Arts 154
Flatirons Ski Club 239

Q

R

S